Effective Project Management

Traditional, Agile, Extreme

Sixth Edition

Robert K. Wysocki, Ph.D.

WILEY
Wiley Publishing, Inc.

Effective Project Management: Traditional, Agile, Extreme, Sixth Edition

Published by
John Wiley & Sons, Inc.
10475 Crosspoint Boulevard
Indianapolis, IN 46256
www.wiley.com

Copyright © 2012 by John Wiley & Sons, Inc., Indianapolis, Indiana
Published simultaneously in Canada

ISBN: 978-1-118-01619-0
ISBN: 978-1-118-17973-4 (ebk)
ISBN: 978-1-118-17974-1 (ebk)
ISBN: 978-1-118-17975-8 (ebk)

Manufactured in the United States of America

10 9 8 7 6 5 4 3 2

About the Author

Robert K. Wysocki, Ph.D., has over 40 years' experience as a project management consultant and trainer, information systems manager, systems and management consultant, author, training developer, and provider. He has written 20 books on project management, business analysis, and information systems management. One of his books, *Effective Project Management, 5th Edition*, has been a best-seller and is recommended by the Project Management Institute for the library of every project manager. He has over 30 publications and presentations in professional and trade journals and has made more than 100 presentations at professional and trade conferences and meetings. He has developed more than 20 project management courses and trained over 10,000 project managers.

In 1990 he founded Enterprise Information Insights, Inc. (EII), a project management consulting and training practice specializing in project management methodology design and integration, Project Support Office establishment, the development of training curriculum, and the development of a portfolio of assessment tools focused on organizations, project teams, and individuals. His clients include AT&T, Aetna, Babbage Simmel, British Computer Society, Boston University Corporate Education Center, Computerworld, Converse Shoes, the Czechoslovakian government, Data General, Digital, Eli Lilly, Harvard Community Health Plan, IBM, J. Walter Thompson, Novartis, Peoples Bank, Sapient, The Limited, the State of Ohio, Travelers Insurance, Walmart, Wells Fargo, ZTE, and several others.

He is a member of the ProjectWorld Executive Advisory Board, the Project Management Institute, the American Society of Training and Development, the International Institute of Business Analysts, and the Society of Human Resource

Management. He is past Association Vice President of AITP (formerly DPMA). He earned a B.A. in mathematics from the University of Dallas, and an M.S. and Ph.D. in mathematical statistics from Southern Methodist University.

About the Technical Editor

Brenda K. Gillingham is a principal program manager and business analyst who specializes in enterprise-level business transformation projects within high-tech industry PMO structures. She also teaches a wide range of project management and business strategy courses in university and corporate professional learning environments. Brenda's diverse program management career includes three Fortune 100 companies and an Ivy-Plus university. One of her many successful business process restructuring projects was a front-page feature in various U.S.-based national technical publications.

An active member of the Project Management Institute since 1996, Brenda served 9 years on the Board of Directors of the 2,500+ member Mass Bay Chapter and is a certified Project Management Professional (PMP) since 1999. Brenda earned her MBA in Management of Technology with high distinction from Bentley University and is a member of the Beta Gamma Sigma Honor Society. She also holds certifications in Organizational Change Management, Process Reengineering, Six Sigma, and Prince2 project management methodology.

Credits

Executive Editor
Bob Elliott

Senior Project Editor
Kevin Kent

Technical Editor
Brenda K. Gillingham

Production Editor
Kathleen Wisor

Copy Editor
Kim Cofer

Editorial Manager
Mary Beth Wakefield

Freelancer Editorial Manager
Rosemarie Graham

Associate Director of Marketing
David Mayhew

Marketing Manager
Ashley Zurcher

Business Manager
Amy Knies

Production Manager
Tim Tate

Vice President and Executive Group Publisher
Richard Swadley

Vice President and Executive Publisher
Neil Edde

Associate Publisher
Jim Minatel

Project Coordinator, Cover
Katie Crocker

Proofreader
Jen Larsen, Word One

Indexer
Robert Swanson

Cover Designer
Ryan Sneed

Acknowledgments

This acknowledgment is really my special thanks to the teaching faculty of at least 250 universities and colleges all over the globe who have adopted previous editions. Many of them have offered feedback that I find most useful. Many of their suggestions have been incorporated in this sixth edition. I also owe a debt of gratitude to the many consultants and companies across the globe that have used APF and taken the time to comment on their experiences. I am aware of APF being adopted in several industries including banking, insurance, film production, retailing, drug research, distribution, professional services, supply chain management, and logistics. To them I offer my heartfelt thanks.

Contents at a Glance

Preface		**xxiii**
Introduction		**xxv**
Part I	**Defining and Using Project Management Process Groups**	**1**
Chapter 1	**What Is a Project?**	**5**
Chapter 2	**What Is Project Management?**	**23**
Chapter 3	**Understanding the Project Management Process Groups**	**63**
Chapter 4	**How to Scope a TPM Project**	**103**
Chapter 5	**How to Plan a TPM Project**	**149**
Chapter 6	**How to Launch a TPM Project**	**225**
Chapter 7	**How to Monitor and Control a TPM Project**	**279**
Chapter 8	**How to Close a TPM Project**	**311**
Part II	**Establishing Project Management Life Cycles and Strategies**	**321**
Chapter 9	**Complexity and Uncertainty in the Project Management Landscape**	**323**
Chapter 10	**Traditional Project Management**	**339**
Chapter 11	**Agile Project Management**	**377**
Chapter 12	**Extreme Project Management**	**453**

Part III   **Building an Effective Project
                Management Infrastructure**   479

Chapter 13   **Establishing and Maturing a
                Project Support Office**   481

Chapter 14   **Establishing and Managing
                a Project Portfolio Management Process**   527

Chapter 15   **Establishing and Managing a Continuous
                Process Improvement Program**   583

Part IV   **Managing the Realities
                of Projects**   625

Chapter 16   **Prevention and Intervention
                Strategies for Distressed Projects**   627

Chapter 17   **Organizing Multiple Team Projects**   657

Chapter 18   **Managing the Professional
                Development of Project Teams**   689

Appendix A   **Glossary of Acronyms**   711

Appendix B   **What's on the Website?**   717

Appendix C   **Bibliography**   719

Index   729

Contents

Preface   **xxiii**

Introduction   **xxv**

Part I   **Defining and Using Project Management Process Groups**   **1**

Chapter 1   **What Is a Project?**   **5**

Defining a Project   6
   Sequence of Activities   6
   Unique Activities   6
   Complex Activities   7
   Connected Activities   7
   One Goal   7
   Specified Time   7
   Within Budget   8
   According to Specification   8
   A Business-focused Definition of a Project   8
Defining a Program   9
   Establishing Temporary Program Offices   9
   Establishing Permanent Program Offices   9
Defining a Portfolio   10
Understanding the Scope Triangle   10
   Scope   11
   Quality   11
   Cost   12
   Time   12
   Resources   13
   Envisioning the Scope Triangle as a System in Balance   13
   Prioritizing the Scope Triangle Variables for
    Improved Change Management   14
   Applying the Scope Triangle   15

Ix

Managing the Creeps   16
  Scope Creep   16
  Hope Creep   17
  Effort Creep   17
  Feature Creep   17
The Importance of Classifying Projects   18
  Establishing a Rule for Classifying Projects   19
  Classification by Project Characteristics   19
  Classification by Project Application   21
Putting It All Together   22
Discussion Questions   22

Chapter 2   What Is Project Management?   23
Understanding the Fundamentals
  of Project Management   24
  What Business Situation Is Being
    Addressed by This Project?   25
  What Do You Need to Do?   25
  What Will You Do?   26
  How Will You Do It?   26
  How Will You Know You Did It?   26
  How Well Did You Do?   26
What Are Requirements — Really?   28
Introducing Project Management Life Cycles   33
  Goal and Solution Clarity   34
  Traditional Project Management Approaches   39
  Agile Project Management Approaches   44
  Extreme Project Management Approach   50
  Emertxe Project Management Life Cycle Model   53
  Recap of PMLC Models   55
Choosing the Best-Fit PMLC Model   56
  Total Cost   57
  Duration   58
  Market Stability   58
  Technology   58
  Business Climate   58
  Number of Departments Affected   58
  Organizational Environment   59
  Team Skills and Competencies   59
Putting It All Together   60
Discussion Questions   60

**Chapter 3   Understanding the Project
               Management Process Groups   63**
Defining the Five Process Groups   64
  The Scoping Process Group   64
  The Planning Process Group   65

The Launching Process Group   65
The Monitoring and Controlling Process Group   66
The Closing Process Group   67
Defining the Nine Knowledge Areas   67
Integration Management   67
Scope Management   67
Time Management   68
Cost Management   68
Quality Management   68
Human Resource Management   69
Communications Management   74
Risk Management   75
Procurement Management   85
Mapping Knowledge Areas to Process Groups   99
What the Mapping Means   99
How to Use the Mapping   100
Using Process Groups to Define PMLCs   100
A Look Ahead: Mapping Process Groups to
Form Complex PMLCs   100
Putting It All Together   101
Discussion Questions   101

Chapter 4   How to Scope a TPM Project   103
Using Tools, Templates, and
Processes to Scope a Project   104
Managing Client Expectations   105
Wants versus Needs   106
Project Scoping Process   106
The Project Scoping Meeting   110
Project Scoping Meeting Deliverables   112
Putting It All Together   147
Discussion Questions   147

Chapter 5   How to Plan a TPM Project   149
Using Tools, Templates, and Processes to
Plan a Project   151
The Importance of Planning   152
Using Application Software Packages to
Plan a Project   153
Determining the Need for a
Software Package   154
Project Planning Tools   154
How Much Time Should Planning Take?   156
Running the Planning Session   157
Planning and Conducting Joint Project
Planning Sessions   157
Planning the JPPS   158
Conducting the JPPS   164

Building the WBS   164
  Using the RBS to Build the WBS   165
  Uses for the WBS   167
  Generating the WBS   168
  Using the WBS for Large Projects   171
  Iterative Development of the WBS   171
  Six Criteria to Test for Completeness in the WBS   172
  Approaches to Building the WBS   176
  Representing the WBS   180
Estimating   183
  Estimating Duration   184
  Resource Loading versus Task Duration   185
  Variation in Task Duration   187
  Six Methods for Estimating Task Duration   188
  Estimation Life Cycles   191
  Estimating Resource Requirements   192
  Resource Planning   195
  Estimating Cost   196
Constructing the Project Network Diagram   199
  Envisioning a Complex Project Network Diagram   200
  Benefits to Network-Based Scheduling   200
  Building the Network Diagram Using the
    Precedence Diagramming Method   202
  Dependencies   204
  Constraints   205
  Using the Lag Variable   209
  Creating an Initial Project Network Schedule   210
  Analyzing the Initial Project Network Diagram   214
  Compressing the Schedule   215
  Management Reserve   217
Writing an Effective Project Proposal   218
  Contents of the Project Proposal   219
  Format of the Project Proposal   221
Gaining Approval to Launch the Project   221
Putting It All Together   221
Discussion Questions   222

Chapter 6   How to Launch a TPM Project   225
Using Tools, Templates, and
  Processes to Launch a Project   226
Recruiting the Project Team   227
  Core Team Members   227
  Client Team   231
  Contract Team Members   231
  Balancing a Team   233
  Developing a Team Deployment Strategy   235
  Developing a Team Development Plan   235

Conducting the Project Kick-Off Meeting   236
  Sponsor-Led Part   236
  Project Manager–Led Part   237
  Purpose of the Project Kick-Off Meeting   237
Establishing Team Operating Rules   241
  Situations that Require Team Operating Rules   241
  Team War Room   252
Managing Scope Changes   254
  The Scope Change Management Process   254
  Management Reserve   257
  Scope Bank   258
Managing Team Communications   258
  Establishing a Communications Model   259
  Managing Communication beyond the Team   262
Assigning Resources   264
  Leveling Resources   265
  Acceptably Leveled Schedule   267
Resource-Leveling Strategies   268
  Utilizing Available Slack   268
  Shifting the Project Finish Date   268
  Smoothing   269
  Alternative Methods of Scheduling Tasks   269
  Cost Impact of Resource Leveling   271
Finalizing the Project Schedule   271
Writing Work Packages   273
  Purpose of a Work Package   274
  Format of a Work Package   275
Putting It All Together   276
Discussion Questions   278

Chapter 7   How to Monitor and Control a TPM Project   279
Using Tools, Templates, and Processes to
  Monitor and Control a Project   280
Establishing Your Progress Reporting System   281
  Types of Project Status Reports   281
  How and What Information to Update   285
  Frequency of Gathering and Reporting
    Project Progress   286
  Variances   286
Applying Graphical Reporting Tools   288
  Gantt Charts   288
  Stoplight Reports   290
  Burn Charts   290
  Milestone Trend Charts   290
  Earned Value Analysis   293
  Integrating Milestone Trend Charts and
    Earned Value Analysis   298

Managing the Scope Bank   301
Building and Maintaining the Issues Log   302
Managing Project Status Meetings   302
    Who Should Attend Status Meetings?   302
    When Are Status Meetings Held?   303
    What Is the Purpose of a Status Meeting?   303
    What Is the Status Meeting Format?   304
    The 15-Minute Daily Status Meeting   305
    Problem Management Meetings   305
Defining a Problem Escalation Strategy   306
    Project Manager–Based Strategies   306
    Resource Manager–Based Strategies   306
    Client-Based Strategies   307
    The Escalation Strategy Hierarchy   307
Gaining Approval to Close the Project   308
Putting It All Together   309
Discussion Questions   309

Chapter 8   How to Close a TPM Project   311
Using Tools, Templates, and Processes
    to Close a Project   312
Writing and Maintaining Client Acceptance Procedures   312
Closing a Project   312
Getting Client Acceptance   313
    Ceremonial Acceptance   313
    Formal Acceptance   313
Installing Project Deliverables   314
    Phased Approach   314
    Cut-Over Approach   314
    Parallel Approach   314
    By-Business-Unit Approach   315
Documenting the Project   315
    Reference for Future Changes in Deliverables   315
    Historical Record for Estimating Duration and
        Cost on Future Projects, Activities, and Tasks   315
    Training Resource for New Project Managers   315
    Input for Further Training and
        Development of the Project Team   316
    Input for Performance Evaluation by the
        Functional Managers of the Project
        Team Members   316
Conducting the Post-Implementation Audit   317
Writing the Final Report   319
Celebrating Success   319
Putting It All Together   320
Discussion Questions   320

Part II **Establishing Project Management Life Cycles and Strategies** **321**

Chapter 9 **Complexity and Uncertainty in the Project Management Landscape** **323**

Understanding the Complexity/Uncertainty Domain of Projects 324
    Requirements 326
    Flexibility 327
    Adaptability 328
    Risk vs. the Complexity/Uncertainty Domain 328
    Team Cohesiveness vs. the Complexity/Uncertainty Domain 329
    Communications vs. the Complexity/Uncertainty Domain 330
    Client Involvement vs. the Complexity/Uncertainty Domain 331
    Specification vs. the Complexity/Uncertainty Domain 333
    Change vs. the Complexity/Uncertainty Domain 335
    Business Value vs. the Complexity/Uncertainty Domain 336
Putting It All Together 337
Discussion Questions 338

Chapter 10 **Traditional Project Management** **339**

What Is Traditional Project Management? 340
Linear Project Management Life Cycle 341
    Definition 341
    Characteristics 342
    Strengths 347
    Weaknesses 348
    When to Use a Linear PMLC Model 351
    Variations to the Linear PMLC Model 351
    Adapting and Integrating the Tools, Templates, and Processes for Maximum Effectiveness in Linear PMLCs 354
Incremental Project Management Life Cycle 355
    Definition 356
    Characteristics 356
    Strengths 356
    Weaknesses 358
    When to Use an Incremental PMLC 361
    Adapting and Integrating the Tools, Templates, and Processes for Maximum Effectiveness in Incremental PMLCs 361
Using Critical Chain Project Management 362
    What Is the Critical Chain? 363
    Variation in Duration: Common Cause versus Special Cause 363

Statistical Validation of the Critical Chain Approach 364
The Critical Chain Project Management Approach 366
Establishing Buffers 368
Managing Buffers 370
Track Record of Critical Chain Project Management 372
Putting It All Together 373
Discussion Questions 376

Chapter 11 **Agile Project Management** **377**
What Is Agile Project Management? 379
Implementing APM Projects 380
Co-Located APM Project Teams 382
Iterative Project Management Life Cycle 384
Definition of the Iterative PMLC Model 384
Characteristics 389
Strengths 389
Weaknesses 390
Types of Iterative PMLC Models 391
When to Use an Iterative PMLC Model 397
Adaptive Project Management Life Cycle 398
Definition 398
Characteristics 403
Strengths 403
Weaknesses of the Adaptive PMLC Model 405
Types of Adaptive PMLC Models 406
When to Use an Adaptive PMLC Model 443
Adapting and Integrating the APM Toolkit 445
Scoping the Next Iteration/Cycle 445
Planning the Next Iteration/Cycle 446
Launching the Next Iteration/Cycle 446
Monitoring and Controlling the Next Iteration/Cycle 447
Closing the Next Iteration/Cycle 447
Deciding to Conduct the Next Iteration/Cycle 447
Closing the Project 448
Putting It All Together 448
Discussion Questions 449

Chapter 12 **Extreme Project Management** **453**
What Is Extreme Project Management? 454
Extreme Project Management Life Cycle 454
Definition 454
Characteristics 455
Strengths 456
Weaknesses 457
INSPIRE Extreme PMLC Model 457
What Is Emertxe Project Management? 471
The Emertxe Project Management Life Cycle 471

When to Use an Emertxe PMLC Model   471
Using the Tools, Templates, and Processes for
  Maximum xPM Effectiveness   472
   Scoping the Next Phase   472
   Planning the Next Phase   473
   Launching the Next Phase   474
   Monitoring and Controlling the Next Phase   474
   Closing the Phase   475
   Deciding to Conduct the Next Phase   475
   Closing the Project   475
Putting It All Together   475
Discussion Questions   475

Part III **Building an Effective Project
Management Infrastructure**   **479**

Chapter 13 **Establishing and Maturing a
Project Support Office**   **481**
Background of the Project Support Office   482
Defining a Project Support Office   484
  Temporary or Permanent Organizational Unit   484
  Portfolio of Services   485
  Specific Portfolio of Projects   487
Naming the Project Support Office   487
Establishing Your PSO's Mission   489
Framing PSO Objectives   489
Exploring PSO Support Functions   490
  Project Support   490
  Consulting and Mentoring   491
  Methods and Standards   492
  Software Tools   493
  Training   494
  Staffing and Development   495
Selecting PSO Organizational Structures   497
  Virtual versus Real   497
  Proactive versus Reactive   498
  Temporary versus Permanent   498
  Program versus Projects   498
  Enterprise versus Functional   499
  Hub-and-Spoke   499
Understanding the Organizational
  Placement of the PSO   499
Determining When You Need
  a Project Support Office   501
  The Standish Group Report   501
  Spotting Symptoms That You Need a PSO   505
Establishing a PSO   507

PSO Stages of Maturity Growth   508
Planning a PSO   509
Facing the Challenges of Implementing a PSO   519
Speed and Patience   520
Leadership from the Bottom Up   520
A Systems Thinking Perspective   520
Enterprise-Wide Systems   520
Knowledge Management   521
Learning and Learned Project Organizations   521
Open Communications   521
The PSO of the Future   521
Hub-and-Spoke BP⁴SO   522
Staffing the BP⁴SO   523
Other Considerations   524
Putting It All Together   525
Discussion Questions   525

**Chapter 14   Establishing and Managing
a Project Portfolio Management Process   527**
Introduction to Project Portfolio Management   528
What Is a Portfolio Project?   528
What Is a Project Portfolio?   529
What Is Project Portfolio Management?   530
The Project Portfolio Management Life Cycle   530
ESTABLISH a Portfolio Strategy   532
EVALUATE Project Alignment to the Portfolio Strategy   539
PRIORITIZE Projects and Hold Pending
  Funding Authorization   540
SELECT a Balanced Portfolio Using the Prioritized List   546
MANAGE the Active Projects   556
Roles and Responsibilities of the PSO in
Portfolio Management   564
Project Sponsor   564
Portfolio Manager   564
Preparing Your Project for Submission to the
Portfolio Management Process   566
A Revised Project Overview Statement   566
A Two-Step Submission Process   569
A New Submission Process   570
Agile Project Portfolio Management   572
Integrating a PMLC Model into the Agile Project Portfolio
  Management Process   574
Challenges of Managing Agile Portfolios   576
SELECT a Balanced Portfolio   577
MANAGE Active Projects   580
Putting It All Together   581
Discussion Questions   581

Chapter 15 **Establishing and Managing a Continuous Process Improvement Program** **583**

Understanding Project Management Processes and Practices 584
  The Project Management Process 584
  The Practice of the Project Management Process 586
Defining Process and Practice Maturity 589
  Level 1: Ad Hoc or Informal 589
  Level 2: Documented Processes 589
  Level 3: Documented Processes That Everyone Uses 589
  Level 4: Integrated into Business Processes 590
  Level 5: Continuous Improvement 590
Measuring Project Management Process and Practice Maturity 591
  The Process Quality Matrix and Zone Map 591
  What Process Has Been Defined So Far? 596
Using the Continuous Process Improvement Model 598
  Phase 1: Foundation 599
  Phase 2: Assessment and Analysis 600
  Phase 3: Improvement Initiatives 602
  Phase 4: Check Results 603
Defining Roles and Responsibilities of the PSO 603
Realizing the Benefits of Implementing a CPIM 604
Applying CPIM to Business Processes 604
  Characteristics of Business Processes 605
  Watching Indicators of Needed Improvement 609
  Documenting the "As Is" Business Process 610
  Envisioning the "To Be" State 610
  Defining the Gap between "As Is" and "To Be" 610
  Defining a Business Process Improvement Project 611
Using Process Improvement Tools, Templates, and Processes 612
  Fishbone Diagrams and Root Cause Analysis 612
  Control Charts 615
  Flowcharting 615
  Histograms 617
  Pareto Analysis 617
  Run Charts 619
  Scatter Diagrams 619
  Force Field Analysis 620
  Trigger Values 622
Putting It All Together 623
Discussion Questions 623

Part IV	**Managing the Realities of Projects**	**625**
Chapter 16	**Prevention and Intervention Strategies for Distressed Projects**	**627**
	What Is a Distressed Project?	628
	Why Projects Become Distressed or Fail	629
	Managing Distressed Projects	632
	Prevention Management Strategies	632
	Using Tools, Templates, and Processes to Prevent Distressed Projects	633
	Intervention Management Strategies	639
	An Intervention Process Template	651
	Roles and Responsibilities of the PSO with Respect to Distressed Projects	653
	Analyzing the Current Situation	654
	Revising the Desired Goal	655
	Evaluating the Options	655
	Generating the Revised Plan	655
	Putting It All Together	655
	Discussion Questions	656
Chapter 17	**Organizing Multiple Team Projects**	**657**
	What Is a Multiple Team Project?	657
	Challenges to Managing a Multiple Team Project	659
	Working with Teams from Different Companies	660
	Working with Fiercely Independent Team Cultures	660
	Working with Different Team Processes	661
	Accommodating Competing Priorities	661
	Communicating within the Team Structure	661
	Establishing a Project Management Structure	661
	Establishing One Project Management Life Cycle	661
	Building an Integrated Project Plan and Schedule	662
	Defining a Requirements Gathering Approach	663
	Establishing a Scope Change Management Process	663
	Defining the Team Meeting Structure	663
	Establishing Manageable Reporting Levels	664
	Sharing Resources across Teams	664
	Staffing across the PMLC	665
	Searching Out Your Second	665
	Classifying Multiple Team Projects	665
	Two Teams	666
	Multiple Teams	666
	Project Office Structure	667
	Project Office Characteristics	668
	Project Office Strengths	670
	Project Office Weaknesses	672

When to Use a PO 672
Core Team Structure 673
 Core Team Characteristics 673
 Core Team Strengths 676
 Core Team Weaknesses 678
 When to Use a CT 679
Super Team Structure 680
 Super Team Characteristics 681
 Super Team Strengths 684
 Super Team Weaknesses 685
 When to Use an ST 685
Putting It All Together 686
Discussion Questions 687

**Chapter 18 Managing the Professional
Development of Project Teams** **689**
What Career and Professional Development
 Situation Is Being Addressed? 690
What Do You Need To Do? 690
 Experience Acquisition 691
 On-the-job Training 691
 Off-the-job Training 691
 Professional Activities 692
What Will You Do? 692
How Will You Do It? 692
How Will You Know You Did It? 692
How Well Did You Do? 693
Where Do You Go from Here? — A New Idea to Consider 693
 The PM/BA Position Family 693
 Using the PM/BA Landscape for
  Professional Development 701
 What Might a Professional
  Development Program Look Like? 702
 Career Planning Using the BA/PM Landscape 706
An Even Newer Idea to Consider 707
Putting It All Together 709
Discussion Questions 710

Appendix A Glossary of Acronyms **711**

Appendix B What's on the Website? **717**

Appendix C Bibliography **719**

Index **729**

Preface

All five of the previous editions of *Effective Project Management* (*EPM*) have been successful and have grown in value from the feedback I have received from them. I owe that to faculty worldwide who are using my books. With the help and support of John Wiley & Sons we have branded Effective Project Management. I'm seeing others play off that name recognition, and I am encouraged. I am aware of over 250 colleges and universities worldwide that have adopted my materials. Their feedback and that of the professional market has been overwhelmingly supportive of my practical and easy to read format. *Effective Project Management, Sixth Edition* (*EPM6e*) will continue to meet the needs of higher education and the professional markets. Even after this sixth edition goes to press I still view *EPM* as a work in process. One of my biggest problems is that I have so much I want to include, but we have made a decision to limit the book to about 800 pages. As I and my readers gain further experience with its use and as I hear about the experiences of clients, trainers, faculty and project management professionals, the work will undoubtedly improve. You might say that the development of *EPM6e* and its successor editions is an agile project. The goal is to produce a perfectly intuitive and common sense approach to project management. The solution, however, continues to be elusive. But we are converging on that solution with every edition of *EPM*!

I would like to think that this edition offers you a complete view of effective project management as it is now practiced and how I believe it should be practiced in the very near future.

The training and higher education market has been a strong market for *EPM*. In response to numerous requests from trainers and teaching faculty for a slide presentation, I have continued that offering on the web site (accessible at www .wiley.com/go/epm6e). That slide presentation is a cradle to grave mirror image of the text. These are the very same slides that I use when teaching or training using *EPM6e*. You can use it right out of the box to teach EPM, or you might want to modify it to fit your specific needs.

The professional reference market has been equally strong. In response to numerous requests from practicing professionals I have expanded the coverage of contemporary approaches to project management.

My clients have been a constant source of input. Their guidance has been invaluable to me. From them I have learned about implementation experiences and ways to improve my presentation of the processes and practices of contemporary project management.

Thank you again for adding my book to your project management library. If you have any questions or would just like to comment, please let me hear from you at `rkw@eiicorp.com`. You have my promise that I will quickly respond personally to each and every communiqué.

Enjoy!

Robert K. Wysocki, Ph.D.

Introduction

Effective Project Management: *Traditional, Agile, Extreme, Sixth Edition* (*EPM6e*) represents a significant change from the Fifth Edition. All of the pedagogical and organizational strengths of *EPM5e* are retained and expanded in *EPM6e*. *EPM6e* offers five different project management life cycle (PMLC) models (Linear, Incremental, Iterative, Adaptive, and Extreme) to managing a project. The choice of the best-fit PMLC is based on the characteristics of the project and the business and organizational environment in which the project will be undertaken. These approaches recognize that major differences exist among projects and that those differences require different management approaches if the project is to be managed and successfully completed. Those differences become obvious through an analysis of the Requirements Breakdown Structure (RBS).

We commonly define a project as a unique experience that has never happened before and will never happen again under the same set of circumstances. So, then, why don't we define the management of such projects the same way? There are a number of factors affecting the choice of PMLC and the adaptation of those models as the project unfolds and conditions change. This is the approach I have taken for years and have been successful beyond the statistics on failure that we are all familiar with. I hope to convince you of the benefits of that view in this book. Forty years of experience managing projects of all types has led me to this conclusion. I want to share my thinking with you and convince you to follow my lead.

The Contemporary Project Environment

The contemporary project environment is characterized by high speed, high change, lower costs, complexity, uncertainty, and a host of other factors. This presents a daunting challenge to the project manager as is described in the sections that follow.

High Speed

The faster products and services get to market the greater will be the resulting value to the business. Current competitors are watching and responding to unmet opportunities, and new competition is waiting and watching to seize upon any opportunity that might give them a foothold or expansion in the market. Any weakness or delay in responding may just give them that advantage. This need to be fast translates into a need for the project management approach to not waste time — to rid itself, as much as possible, of spending time on non-value-added work. Many of the approaches you will study are built on that premise.

The window of opportunity is narrowing and constantly moving. Organizations that can quickly respond to those opportunities are organizations that have found a way to reduce cycle times and eliminate non-value-added work as much as possible. Taking too long to roll out a new or revamped product can result in a missed business opportunity. Project managers must know how and when to introduce multiple release strategies and compress project schedules to help meet these requirements. Even more importantly, the project management approach must support these aggressive schedules. That means that these processes must protect the schedule by eliminating all non-value-added work. You simply cannot afford to burden your project management processes with a lot of overhead activities that do not add value to the final deliverables or that may compromise your effectiveness in the markets you serve.

Effective project management is not the product of a rigid or fixed set of steps and processes to be followed on every project. Rather the choice of project management approach is based on having done due diligence on the project specifics and defined an approach that makes sense. I spend considerable time on these strategies in later chapters.

High Change

Clients are often making up their minds or changing their minds about what they want. The environment is more the cause of high change than is any ignorance on the part of the client. The business world is dynamic. It doesn't stand still just because you are managing a project. The best-fit project management approach must recognize the realities of frequent change, accommodate it, and embrace it. The extent to which change is expected will affect the choice of a best-fit PMLC model.

Change is constant! I hope that does not come as a surprise to you. Change is always with you and seems to be happening at an increasing rate. Every day you face new challenges and the need to improve yesterday's practices. As John Naisbitt says in *The Third Wave*, "Change or die." For experienced project managers as well as "wannabe" project managers, the road to breakthrough performance is paved with uncertainty and with the need to be courageous, creative, and flexible. If you simply rely on a routine application of someone else's methodology, you are sure to fall short of the mark. As you will see in the pages that follow, I have not been afraid to step outside the box and outside my comfort zone. Nowhere is there more of a need for change and adaptation than in the approaches we take to managing projects.

Lower Cost

With the reduction in management layers (a common practice in many organizations) the professional staff needs to find ways to work smarter, not harder. Project management includes a number of tools and techniques that help the professional manage increased workloads. Your staffs need to have more room to do their work in the most productive ways possible. Burdening them with overhead activities for which they see little value is a sure way to failure.

In a landmark paper "The Coming of the New Organization" (*Harvard Business Review*, January/February 1988), written over 20 years ago but still relevant, Peter Drucker depicts middle managers as either ones who receive information from above, reinterpret it, and pass it down or ones who receive information from below, reinterpret it, and pass it up the line. Not only is quality suspect because of personal biases and political overtones, but also the computer is perfectly capable of delivering that information to the desk of any manager who has a need to know. Given these factors, plus the politics and power struggles at play, Drucker asks why employ middle managers? As technology advances and acceptance of these ideas grows, we have seen the thinning of the layers of middle management. Do not expect them to come back; they are gone forever. The effect on project managers is predictable and significant. Hierarchical structures are being replaced by organizations that have a greater dependence on projects and project teams, resulting in more demands on project managers.

Increasing Levels of Complexity

All of the simple problems have been solved. Those that remain are getting more complex with each passing day. At the same time that problems are getting more complex, they are getting more critical to the enterprise. They must be solved. We don't have a choice. Not having a simple recipe for managing such projects is no excuse. They must be managed, and we must have an effective way of managing them. This book shows you how to create common sense project management approaches adapting a common set of tools, templates, and processes to even the most complex of projects.

More Uncertainty

With increasing levels of complexity comes increasing levels of uncertainty. The two are inseparable. Adapting project management approaches to handle uncertainty means that the approaches must not only accommodate change but also embrace it and become more effective as a result of it. Change is what will lead the team and the client to a state of certainty with respect to a viable solution to its complex problems. In other words we must have project management approaches that expect change and benefit from it.

Challenges to Effective Project Management

As discussed earlier in this introduction the contemporary project environment presents the project manager and the client with a number of challenges to managing such projects effectively. The use of the best-fit PMLC model will rise to these challenges and adapt as necessary.

Flexibility and Adaptability

Traditional Project Management (TPM) practices were defined and matured in the world of the engineer and construction professional where the team expected (and got, or so it thought) a clear statement from clients as to what they wanted, when they wanted it, and how much they were willing to pay for it. All of this was delivered to the project manager wrapped in a neat package. The "i"s were all dotted, and the "t"s were all crossed. All the correct forms were filed, and all the boxes were filled with the information requested. Everyone was satisfied that the request was well documented and that the deliverables were sure to be delivered as requested. The project team clearly understood the solution they would be expected to provide, and they could clearly plan for its delivery. That describes the naive world of the embryonic project manager until the 1950s. By the mid-1950s the computer was well on its way to becoming a viable commercial resource, but it was still the province of the engineer. Project management continued as it had under the management of the engineers.

The first sign that change was in the wind for the project manager arose in the early 1960s. The use of computers to run businesses was now a reality, and we began to see position titles like programmer, programmer/analyst, systems analyst, and primitive types of database architects emerging. These professionals were really engineers in disguise, and somehow, they were expected to interact with the business and management professionals (who were totally mystified by the computer and the mystics that could communicate with it) to design and implement business applications systems to replace manual processes. This change represented a total metamorphosis of the business world and the project world, and we would never look back.

In the face of this transformation into an information society, TPM wasn't showing any signs of change. To the engineers, every IT project management problem looked like a nail, and they had the hammer. In other words, they had one solution, and it was supposed to fit every problem. One of the major problems that TPM faced, and still faces, is the difference between *wants* and *needs*. If you remember anything from this introduction, remember that what the client wants is probably not what the client needs. If the project manager blindly accepts what the clients say they want and proceeds with the project on that basis, the project manager is in for a rude awakening. Often in the process of building the solution, the client learns that what they need is not the same as what they requested. Here you have the basis for rolling deadlines, scope creep, and an endless trail of changes and reworks. It's no wonder that 70-plus percent of projects fail. That cycle has to stop. You need an approach that is built around change — one that embraces learning and discovery throughout the project life cycle. It must have built-in processes to accommodate the changes that result from this learning and discovery.

I have talked with numerous project managers over the past several years about the problem of a lack of clarity and what they do about it. Most would say that they deliver according to the original requirements and then iterate to improve the solution one or more times before they satisfy the client's current requirements. I asked them, "If you know you are going to iterate, why don't you use an approach that has that feature built in?" Until recently with the emergence of Agile Project Management approaches the silence in response to that question has been deafening. All of the agile and extreme approaches to project management emerging in practice are built on the assumption that there will be changing requirements as the client gains better focus on what they actually need. Sometimes those needs can be very different than their original wants.

Obviously, this is no longer your father's project management. The Internet and an ever-changing array of new and dazzling technologies have made a permanent mark on the business landscape. Technology has put most businesses in a state of confusion. How should a company proceed to utilize the Internet and extract the greatest business value? Businesses are asking even the more basic questions — "What business are we in?" "How do we reach and service our customers?" "What do our customers expect?" The dot.com era began quickly with a great deal of hyperbole and faded just as quickly. A lot of companies came into existence on the shoulders of highly speculative venture capital in the 1990s and went belly up by the end of the century. Only a few remain, and even their existence is tenuous. The current buzzwords *e-commerce*, *e-business*, and *knowledge management* have replaced *B2B* and *B2C*, and businesses seem to be settling down. But we are still a long way from recovery.

The question on the table is this: "What impact should this have on your approach to project management?" The major impact should be that project management approaches must align with the business of the enterprise. Project management needs to find its seat at the organization's strategy table. Project managers must first align to the needs of the organization rather than their own home department. That is today's critical success factor. The appearance of the business analyst has added new challenges, as discussed in the next section.

Deep Understanding of the Business and Its Systems

The best project managers understand the business context in which project deliverables must be defined, produced, and function. This means not only an understanding of the internal systems and their interaction but also the external systems environment of suppliers and customers in whose environments the deliverables must function. The systems analyst and business analyst are key components in that understanding. There is a good argument that can be offered for the morphing of the project manager and the business analyst into one professional having the requisite skills and competencies of both. That discussion is out of scope for this book but it is a discussion that needs to take place. For a series of articles that I wrote on this morphing of the project manager and the business analyst, a series that others have since commented on, see the *Business Analyst Times*.

Take Charge of the Project and Its Management

I like simplicity, and I believe my definition of the project landscape using only two variables — goal and solution — with two values each — clear and not clear — is simple yet all inclusive of all projects. The result is four categories of projects.

- When the goal and solution are clear, it generates the **Traditional Project Management (TPM)** category.
- When the goal is clear but the solution is not, it generates the **Agile Project Management (APM)** category.

- When neither the goal nor the solution is clear, it generates the **Extreme Project Management (xPM)** category.
- And finally when the goal is not clear but the solution is, it generates the **Emertxe Project Management (MPx)** category (though this may seem nonsensical, it is not — more on this one later).

Every project that has ever existed or will exist falls into one and only one of these four categories. Each category gives rise to a PMLC, and each PMLC has at least one specific project management approach in it. This four-category classification gives rise to five PMLC models. It is these models — their recognition and use — that is the subject of this book.

Project Management Is Organized Common Sense

The PMBOK definition of project management is crisp, clean, and clearly stated. It has provided a solid foundation on which to define the process groups and processes that underlie all project management. But I think there is another definition that transcends the PMBOK definition and is far more comprehensive of what project management entails. I offer that definition as nothing more than organized common sense. Projects are unique, and each one is different than all others that have preceded it. That uniqueness requires a unique approach that continually adapts as new characteristics of the project emerge. These characteristics can and do emerge anywhere along the project life cycle. Being ready for them and adjusting as needed means that we must be always attentive to doing what makes the most sense given the circumstances. Hence, project management is nothing more than organized common sense.

We are not in Kansas anymore! The discipline of project management has morphed to a new state, and as this book is being written, that state is not yet a steady one. It may never be. What does all of this mean to the struggling project manager?

To me the answer is obvious. You must open your minds to the basic principles on which project management is based so as to accommodate change and avoid wasted dollars and wasted time. For as long as I can remember, I and my colleagues have been preaching that one size does not fit all. The characteristics of the project suggest what subset of the traditional approach should be used on the project. This concept has to be extended to also encompass choosing the best-fit PMLC model based on the characteristics of the project at hand. For the interested reader you can learn more about this mindset in my book *Effective Software Project Management* (Wiley, 2006). In that book I define a discipline that fully integrates PMLCs and systems development life cycles (SDLCs) into a strategy that I have called a Software Development Project Methodology (SDPM). The result is an approach that aligns with the needs of the client, the enterprise, and the project.

Why I Wrote This Book

I believe a number of professionals and practitioners are looking for some help. I am trying to fill their needs with this book. When scheduled training is not available or practical, my book can help. It is written to be studied. It is written to guide you as you learn about and practice effective project management. It is written to be a self-paced resource, one that will immerse you in managing a project for a simulated company. Let it work with you through the entire project life cycle.

On a more altruistic level, I have four reasons for writing this sixth edition:

- **I've learned a lot about contemporary project management since the publication of *EPM5e* in August of 2009**. Experience with my clients has made me rethink how we should explain the ever-changing discipline of project management and how we should approach the education and training of project managers. *EPM5e* did a good job of that. However, there is much more to be said, and *EPM6e* fills that gap.

- **To come to the rescue of the discipline of project management**. I believe that it is seriously out of alignment with the needs of our businesses. Project managers are trapped and need some alternatives and a working knowledge of their use. The high failure rates of projects are evidence of that misalignment. The problem is that project management is the hammer, and all projects are seen as nails. This is a one-size-fits-all approach to project management, and it simply doesn't work. The nature and characteristics of the project must dictate the type of management approach to be taken. Anything short of that will fail. As I have already shown, projects have fundamentally changed, but our approach to managing them has not changed much. We need a more robust approach to project management — one that recognizes the project environment and adapts accordingly.

- **To further document Adaptive Project Framework (APF)**. APF is really a hybrid that takes the best from TPM and xPM. It is an agile approach that works for all types of projects rather than just for software development projects as do most other agile approaches. It breaches the gap between projects with a clearly defined goal and solution and projects where the goal and the solution are not clearly defined. The work that I report here is a work in progress. APF has been adopted as the de facto agile model for several large and small companies. By putting it before my colleagues, I expect that others will contribute to its further maturation and application.

- **My continual challenge to offer a practical how-to guide for project managers in the management of all of their projects**. My style is applications-oriented. While the book is based on sound concepts and principles of project management, it is by no means a theoretical treatise. It is written from the perspective of the practicing project manager — me. I offer it to you to be your companion and to be used.

EPM6e, like all of its previous editions, was written for three distinct markets: the education market, the training market, and the professional reference market. It has been successful in all three. In this respect it occupies a unique position in the literature of project management.

Education Market

Nearly 100 educators from colleges and universities all over the world have requested the *EPM5e* Discussion Question Answer File, so I know that at least that many educational organizations have adopted *EPM5e*. In fact, I have maintained a database of all those faculty and institutions that have adopted the EPM materials. That database numbers more than 250 adopters. A number of educators have shared their experiences with me. To them I owe a debt of gratitude. I've tried to incorporate their suggestions as best I can. The resulting book is much better for their inputs. On the *EPM6e* website (www.wiley.com/go/epm6e) are files containing a set of slides for each chapter and a collection of class, team, and individual exercises I have used and recommend to you. These are comprehensive and may be modified to meet your specific needs. I encourage you to use them and adapt them to your training and education environment. If you have a need for other training materials to support your project management or business analyst curriculum, please contact me at rkw@eiicorp.com.

Training Market

In addition to many adoptions in the higher education market, *EPM5e* is also used in many training programs and corporate universities. *EPM6e* will continue to serve that market. All of the instructional materials available to the educator apply equally well to the trainer. I have successfully offered a number of variations of the *EPM6e* content in training programs of all lengths and configurations. I would be happy to share my experiences with any interested parties. You may reach me at rkw@eiicorp.com.

Professional Market

Originally the *EPM* series was written for the practicing professional. I have tried to maintain my allegiance to those professionals in the trenches who are trying to master a complex and ever-changing world of projects. They need answers, and I believe *EPM6e* provides those answers. If I can be of any help or give you any advice on your particular project management challenges, please contact me at rkw@eiicorp.com.

How This Book Is Organized

EPM6e is organized into 4 parts containing a total of 18 chapters.

Part I: Defining and Using Project Management Process Groups

The purpose of Part I is to introduce you to the tools, templates, and processes that comprise the effective project manager's toolkit. Because many of my readers will be familiar with the PMI PMBOK standards document, I have decided to group the toolkits around the five process groups, which I call Scoping, Planning, Launching, Monitoring and Controlling, and Closing. The nine Knowledge Areas defined in PMBOK are also introduced and briefly described. Each process group has a chapter devoted to it in which I provide working knowledge material for the tools, templates, and processes in that process group.

All of the subject matter content of *EPM5e* is contained in *EPM6e*. The case used in *EPM5e*, Pizza Delivered Quickly (PDQ), is continued and expanded in *EPM6e*.

For the college and university faculty who are using my book in their courses, I have revised many of the discussion questions at the end of each chapter. These are designed to actively engage the class in a sharing of ideas about how they would handle the situations presented.

Part II: Establishing Project Management Life Cycles and Strategies

Part II begins with Chapter 9, "Project Management Landscape," which is defined by the goal and solution that are either clear or not clear. This two-by-two grid defines four types of project management categories: Traditional Project Management (TPM), Agile Project Management (APM), Extreme Project Management (xPM), and a fourth category called Emertxe Project Management (MPx). On the surface the MPx category looks like a solution out looking for a problem. That is one interpretation, but there is another far more serious interpretation. I discuss that in Chapter 9. The TPM, APM, and xPM categories give rise to a landscape of five PMLC models: Linear, Incremental, Iterative,

Adaptive, and Extreme. Each of these models presents different challenges to the project manager. Chapters 10–12 discuss each approach in detail, focusing on their characteristics, strengths, weaknesses, when to use them, and how to adapt the toolkits to them.

Part III: Building an Effective Project Management Infrastructure

In Parts I and II I developed the PMLC models that I feel span the entire landscape of project types. In this part I develop the Project Support Office, Project Portfolio Management, and Continuous Process Improvement Programs. These are the organizational infrastructures to support project management. Their presence is necessary for any environment in which effective project management takes place. These might be considered advanced topics by some, but they are included to round out your understanding of the project management environment.

Part IV: Managing the Realities of Projects

Part IV discusses two topics. I have encountered both of these situations more than once in my consulting career. Very little is written about distressed projects and managing multiple team projects. I hope to at least make some contribution.

Chapter 16, "Prevention and Intervention Strategies for Distressed Projects," continues with the discussion introduced in *EPM5e*. Given the high failure rate of projects I felt it was important for the practitioner to know how to prevent projects from becoming distressed and, if distressed, how to create effective intervention strategies. The practitioner should find good value here. New to this edition is the intervention template that I use when starting an intervention effort.

Chapter 17, "Organizing Multiple Team Projects," was introduced in *EPM5e* and is continued in *EPM6e*. In larger organizations it is not uncommon that projects will involve teams from different parts of the organization. Each of these teams comes with their own tools, templates, and processes and somehow must be integrated into a single team with a common set of tools, templates, and processes. Three models for accomplishing this integration are discussed.

Chapter 18, "Managing the Professional Development of Project Teams," has been elevated from an epilogue to a chapter in this edition. The challenges to staffing and managing complex projects have taken on a strategic importance. Organizations need to design and implement a comprehensive program of career and professional development and this chapter is designed to kick-start that effort.

The Rationale for Using This Book Organization

This book does not advocate following recipes and stepwise procedures lists for managing projects. Rather it is based on constructing a best-fit project management approach based on the characteristics of the project, its environment, the business climate, the team skills profile, and other descriptors.

A Bottom-Up Learning Experience

To begin your study I introduce six questions that form an architecture for any effective project management approach. As long as your chosen approach provides answers to these six questions, you will have defined an effective approach.

Learning about Process Groups

The Project Management Institute (PMI) has provided a comprehensive definition of the basic building blocks from which every project management methodology can be defined. You first learn these and then apply them later in the book to specific project management methodologies and models.

Learning about How Process Groups Form Life Cycle Processes

PMI defines the five basic process groups that can be used to form project management life cycle processes. Every effective project management life cycle will contain these five process groups. In some life cycles the process groups will appear once, in others several times.

Learning about Forming Strategies for Effective Life Cycle Management

In this book the profile of the project and the degree to which requirements are specified and documented form the strategies for defining the best-fit project management life cycle. As the project work commences, the profile of the project and the requirements definition may change, prompting a change of strategy. Always keeping the project management approach aligned with the changing profile of the project is the unique feature of my approach to project management.

Learning How the Organization Can Support Effective Project Management

The organization itself can be a supporter of or a hindrance to effective project management. I explore this in the three chapters Part III comprises.

Learning How to Adapt to the Realities of Projects

In Part IV you learn about two project situations that arise frequently and that are not discussed earlier in the book. Despite all of your planning and strategizing to choose best-fit project management approaches, the project can still fall into a distressed state. Knowing how to prevent this from happening through early warning metrics is of primary importance, and how to recover from a distressed state is also important. One chapter focuses on that topic. Another chapter focuses on the increasingly common multiple team project situation.

The final chapter in Part IV discusses a serious problem that most organizations have done very little to address — the career and professional development of their cadre of project managers. We are in the midst of an evolution of projects from defined efforts to very complex and uncertain efforts. The preparation of project managers to manage these challenges effectively won't happen by accident. It has to be planned, and it has to match the foreseeable future demands of these types of projects.

How to Use This Book

As I noted earlier in this introduction, *EPM6e* simultaneously accommodates the education, training, and professional reference markets.

Introductory (Chapters 1–8)

A good introductory 3-credit undergraduate course or 3-day training course would consist of Chapters 1–8. Chapters 1–8 introduce the tools, templates, and processes used by the contemporary project manager. These chapters are structured around the five process groups defined by the PMBOK.

Intermediate (Chapters 1–12)

A good upper division undergraduate or introductory graduate course or 3-day intermediate training course would consist of Chapters 1–12. The prerequisite would be an introductory course in project management. However, my experience with training programs is not to have a prerequisite. I would recommend a 5-day training course that covers Chapters 1–12.

Chapter 9 defines the project management landscape in terms of Traditional Project Management (Linear and Incremental), Agile Project Management (Iterative and Adaptive), and Extreme Project Management (Extreme). Chapters 10–12 provide a detailed discussion of each of these project situations.

Advanced (Chapters 9–18)

A good graduate level course would consist of Chapters 9–17. For scheduling or topic interests, some subset from Chapters 9–17 could be chosen. This would open the opportunity for more in-depth coverage with supplemental readings and for course projects drawn from those chapters.

Chapter 18 can be included in almost any application of *EPM6e*. It is a chapter that helps novices through experts understand the opportunities that they can take advantage of through personal planning of their own career development.

Who Should Use This Book

The original target audience for *EPM* was the practicing project manager. However, as I discovered, many of the second and third edition sales were to university and college faculty. I certainly want to encourage their use of my book, so with each edition I further expanded the target market to include both practicing project managers and faculty. I added discussion questions to each chapter, and to assist in lecture preparation, I put copies of all figures and tables on the website. *EPM6e* takes it to the next level with much more collateral content for the instructor.

Practicing Professionals

This book adapts very well to whatever your current knowledge of or experience with project management might be:

- If you are unfamiliar with project management, you can learn the basics by simply reading and reflecting.
- If you wish to advance to the next level, I offer a wealth of practice opportunities through the case exercises.
- If you are more experienced, I offer several advanced topics, including TPM, APM, and xPM in Part II and a number of advanced topics in Parts III and IV.

In all cases, the best way to read the book is front to back. If you are an experienced project manager, feel free to skip around and read the sections as a refresher course.

The seasoned professional project manager will find value in the book as well. I have gathered a number of tools and techniques that appeared in the first edition of this book. The Joint Project Planning session, the use of sticky notes and whiteboards for building the project network, the completeness criteria for generating the Work Breakdown Structure, the use of work packages for professional staff development, and milestone trend charts are a few of the more noteworthy and original contributions.

Undergraduate, Graduate, and Adjunct Faculty

A significant adopter of *EPM1e* through *EPM5e* has been the education market. *EPM6e* offers even more to that market than all previous editions. The addition of complete PowerPoint slide files for each chapter was added in *EPM5e* and is further expanded in *EPM6e*. The slides contain all of the content that should be in the class lectures. Faculty can add to, delete, or modify these files to suit their specific purpose and style for each lecture. I have also included a PowerPoint file of exercises. These are designed as individual, team, or class exercises.

> **NOTE** The PowerPoint slide files and exercise file are available for download on the book's website at www.wiley.com/go/epm6e.

Corporate Trainers

EPM6e also has the corporate trainer's needs in mind. In addition to the materials available to the faculty for their credit courses, I will make available several venues for offering *EPM6e*. These range from 3-day programs to 13- and 24-session programs. Contact me at rkw@eiicorp.com with a statement of your specific needs.

Introducing the Case Study: Pizza Delivered Quickly (PDQ)

Pizza Delivered Quickly (PDQ) is a local chain (40 stores) of eat-in and home delivery pizza stores. Recently PDQ has lost 30 percent of sales revenue due mostly to a drop in their home delivery business. They attribute this solely to their major competitor who recently promoted a program that guarantees 45-minute delivery service from order entry to home delivery. PDQ advertises one-hour delivery. PDQ currently uses computers for in-store operations and the usual business functions, but otherwise is not heavily dependent upon software systems to help them receive, process, and home deliver their customers' orders. Pepe Ronee, their Supervisor of Computer Operations, has been charged with developing a software application to identify "pizza factory" locations and create the software system needed to operate them. In commissioning this project, Dee Livery, their president, said to pull out all the stops. She further stated that the future of PDQ depends on this project. She wants the team to investigate an option to deliver the pizza unbaked and "ready for the oven" in 30 minutes or less or deliver it pre-baked in 45 minutes or less.

These pizza factories would not have any retail space. Their only function will be to receive orders, prepare, and deliver the pizzas. The factory location nearest the customer's location will receive the order from a central ordering facility, process, and deliver the order within 30 or 45 minutes of order entry depending on whether the customer orders their pizza ready for the oven or already baked.

Pepe has identified six software applications for the solution.

Pizza Factory Locator Subsystem

The first is a software subsystem to find pizza factory locations. It is not known how many such factories will be needed nor where they should be located. The software subsystem will have to determine that. Clearly this subsystem is a very complex application. The goal can be clearly defined, but even at that the solution will not be at all obvious. This subsystem will have to use a very sophisticated modeling tool. The requirements, functionality, and features are not at all obvious. Some of the solution can probably be envisioned, but clearly the whole solution is elusive at this early stage. Exactly how to model it is not known at the outset. It will have to be discovered as the development project is underway.

Order Entry Subsystem

The second is an order entry subsystem to support store and factory operations. Telephone orders will come to a single location, be taken there, and then be routed to the appropriate store or factory electronically. This system focuses on routine business functions and should be easily defined. Off the shelf commercial software may be a big part of the final solution to support store and factory operations. This subsystem can utilize COTS (commercial off the shelf) order entry software.

Order Submit Subsystem

This subsystem will direct the order to a store, factory, or pizza van. The logistics for making this assignment are not at all clear, and subsystem design will be complex.

Logistics Subsystem

This subsystem is the most complex of the six subsystems. It will require a holistic view of the entire PDQ system. Its complexity arises from the fact that the pizza vans are a mobile production and delivery facility. So the assignment of an order to a pizza van must take into account where the van is likely to be when it is time for order delivery.

Routing Subsystem

This software application will be a routing subsystem for the delivery trucks. This application is straightforward and will probably involve having GPS systems installed in all the delivery trucks.

Inventory Management Subsystem

The final application will be an inventory control system to manage inventories at all stores and factories and automatically reorder from the single vendor that PDQ has been using since it first started in the business. PDQ has been informed by their vendor that they can earn discounts by using the automatic reordering feature. This application should also be a COTS application.

These applications are obviously very different software development projects requiring very different approaches. The Pizza Factory Locator subsystem will be a very sophisticated modeling tool. The requirements, functionality, and features are not at all obvious. Some of the solution can probably be envisioned, but clearly the whole solution is elusive at this early stage. Exactly how it will do modeling is not known at the outset. It will have to be discovered as the development project is underway. The Order Entry subsystem can utilize COTS order entry software that will have to be enhanced at the front end to direct the order to the closest factory and provide driving directions for delivery and other fulfillment tasks on the back end. The requirements, functionality, and features of this subsystem may be problematic.

The six subsystems that make up the PDQ solution may each require a different project management approach. There will be a number of case-related exercises incorporated in many chapters that require strategy formation and other decisions in order to find and maintain a best-fit project management approach.

What's on the Website

EPM6e offers more support to the educator and trainer than *EPM5e* did. Both of the slide files explained in this section were introduced in *EPM5e* and expanded in *EPM6e*. I owe a great debt to those adopters who commented on the contents and offered improvement suggestions.

> **NOTE** You can find *EPM6e's* website at www.wiley.com/go/epm6e.

Slide Presentation

There is a PowerPoint file for each chapter available for download. Each file includes a complete set of slides for delivery of the content of the chapter. Instructors may add, delete, or modify to suit their interests and purposes.

Individual, Team, and Class Exercises

EPM6e also offers at the website another PowerPoint file containing several exercises that have been used successfully in both education and training offerings.

In addition to these downloads, *EPM5e* included a question-and-answer file (based on the discussion questions at the end of each chapter) that could be obtained by certified faculty and instructors by writing me at rkw@eiicorp.com and requesting the file. *EPM6e* continues that offer.

Putting It All Together

EPM6e is a valuable addition to the library of every professional with an interest in being an effective project manager. It is my intention to help project managers learn to think like effective project managers. To me an effective project manager is like a master chef. They know how to create recipes rather than just blindly follow existing recipes. As I've said already in this introduction, project management is nothing more than organized common sense, and this book will help you wake up the common sense you already possess and channel it into effective project management.

Defining and Using Project Management Process Groups

The purpose of Part I is to provide you with a working knowledge of the five Process Groups and nine Knowledge Areas that make up the Project Management Body of Knowledge (PMBOK). For each Process Group, the tools, templates, and processes aligned with that Process Group are explained in detail. This is very much an application orientation. Part II discusses how to use the Process Groups (and the tools, templates, and processes aligned with them) in specific situations, when to use them, and how to adapt them to meet your project needs. This is consistent with the bottom-up learning model used in this book.

Upon completing Part I, you will have a working knowledge of all the contemporary tools, templates, and processes used to scope, plan, launch, monitor, control, and close projects.

Overview of Part I

The following chapters comprise Part I and should be read and studied in the order presented.

Chapter 1: What Is a Project?

To be called a *project*, an undertaking must meet a specific set of conditions. If an undertaking meets those conditions, then it must follow the prescribed project management methodology defined by the organization. A formal definition is put forth and the characteristics of the project are explored. Project management methodologies are often defined for specific types of projects. Project classification rules are explored.

Chapter 2: What Is Project Management?

In the last 10 years project management has undergone significant change. Chapter 2 introduces contemporary project management at a high level. Rather than having just one approach, you now have a variety of approaches, all based on the characteristics of the project. So in effect the uniqueness of the project translates into the uniqueness of the best-fit approach for managing it. The purpose of this chapter is to establish a landscape that categorizes projects and then define project management life cycle (PMLC) models that align with each type of project. The taxonomy I use allows all known project management approaches to be classified in this landscape.

Chapter 3: Understanding the Project Management Process Groups

This chapter aligns with the PMBOK defined by the Project Management Institute (PMI). PMBOK is the standard by which project management methodologies are gauged. PMBOK defines five Process Groups and nine Knowledge Areas, which are discussed in this chapter. The tools, templates, and processes used in each Process Group are presented. A common misconception is that the five Process Groups define a project management methodology. They do not. The discussion of methodologies is taken up in Part II.

Chapter 4: How to Scope a TPM Project

Unless you know where you are going, how will you know if you ever get there? Completely and clearly documenting the client's requirements is difficult and many would say impossible. The degree to which that exercise is satisfactorily done will be the major factor in deciding how the project should be managed.

Chapter 5: How to Plan a TPM Project

For some projects, a complete plan can be generated before any work begins. For others, planning is done just in time. The specific approach for your project depends on the completeness of the requirements specification.

Chapter 6: How to Launch a TPM Project

Assembling the team, establishing how it will function, and finalizing the project schedule are the major topics of this chapter.

Chapter 7: How to Monitor and Control a TPM Project

If you can't measure it, you can't manage it. Status reporting and other control tools are discussed in this chapter.

Chapter 8: How to Close a TPM Project

The project is done when the client says it is done. The acceptance criteria should have been defined during the planning phase and maintained throughout the project. The steps to closing the project are discussed in this chapter.

What Is a Project?

Things are not always what they seem.
—Phaedrus, Roman writer and fabulist

CHAPTER LEARNING OBJECTIVES

After reading this chapter, you will be able to:

- **Define a project, program, and portfolio**
- **Understand the scope triangle**
- **Envision the scope triangle as a system in balance**
- **Prioritize the scope triangle for improved change management**
- **Apply the scope triangle**
- **Manage the creeps**
- **Know the importance of classifying projects**

To put projects into perspective, you need a definition — a common starting point. All too often, people call any work they have to do a "project." Projects actually have a very specific definition. If a set of tasks or work to be done does not meet the strict definition, then it cannot be called a project. To use the project management techniques presented in this book, you must first have a project.

Defining a Project

DEFINITION: PROJECT A project is a sequence of unique, complex, and connected activities that have one goal or purpose and that must be completed by a specific time, within budget, and according to specification.

This is the commonly accepted definition of a project and tells you quite a bit about it. This is a good place to start this discussion but I will improve upon it later with a more business-focused definition. To appreciate just what constitutes a project, take a look at each part of the definition.

Sequence of Activities

A project comprises a number of activities that must be completed in some specified order, or *sequence*. An *activity* is a defined chunk of work.

CROSS-REFERENCE Chapter 5 expands on this informal definition of an activity.

The sequence of the activities is based on technical requirements, not on management prerogatives. To determine the sequence, it is helpful to think in terms of the following inputs and outputs:

- What is needed as input in order to begin working on this activity?
- What activities produce those deliverables as output?

The output of one activity or set of activities becomes the input to another activity or set of activities.

Specifying a sequence based on resource constraints or statements such as "Pete will work on activity B as soon as he finishes working on activity A" should be avoided because this establishes an artificial relationship between activities. What if Pete wasn't available at all? Resource constraints aren't ignored when you actually schedule activities. The decision of what resources to use and when to use them comes later in the project planning process.

Unique Activities

The activities in a project must be *unique*. A project has never happened exactly in the same way before, and it will never happen again under the same conditions. Something is always different each time the activities of a project are repeated. Usually the variations are random in nature — for example, a part is delayed, someone is sick, or a power failure occurs. These are random events that can happen, but you never are sure of when or how, and what impact they will have on the schedule. These random variations are the challenge for the project manager and what contributes to the uniqueness of the project.

Complex Activities

The activities that make up the project are not simple, repetitive acts, such as mowing the lawn, painting the house, washing the car, or loading the delivery truck. Instead they are *complex*. For example, designing an intuitive user interface to an application system is a complex activity.

Connected Activities

Connectedness implies that there is a logical or technical relationship between pairs of activities. There is an order to the sequence in which the activities that make up the project must be completed. They are considered connected because the output from one activity is the input to another. For example, you must design the computer program before you can program it.

You could have a list of unconnected activities that must all be complete in order to complete the project. For example, consider painting the interior rooms of a house. With some exceptions, the rooms can be painted in any order. The interior of a house is not completely painted until all its rooms have been painted, but they may be painted in any order. Painting the house is a collection of activities, but it is not considered a project according to the definition.

One Goal

Projects must have a single *goal* — for example, to design an inner-city playground for AFDC (Aid to Families with Dependent Children) families. However, very large or complex projects may be divided into several *subprojects*, each of which is a project in its own right. This division makes for better management control. For example, subprojects can be defined at the department, division, or geographic level. This artificial decomposition of a complex project into subprojects often simplifies the scheduling of resources and reduces the need for interdepartmental communications while a specific activity is worked on. The downside is that the projects are now interdependent. Even though interdependency adds another layer of complexity and communication, it can be handled.

Specified Time

Projects have a specified *completion date*. This date can be self-imposed by management or externally specified by a client or government agency. The deadline is beyond the control of anyone working on the project. The project is over on the specified completion date whether or not the project work has been completed.

Within Budget

Projects also have *resource limits,* such as a limited amount of people, money, or machines that are dedicated to the project. These resources can be adjusted up or down by management, but they are considered *fixed resources* by the project manager. For example, suppose a company has only one web designer at the moment. That is the fixed resource that is available to project managers. Senior management can change the number of resources, but that luxury is not available to the project manager. If the one web designer is fully scheduled, the project manager has a resource conflict that he or she cannot resolve.

CROSS-REFERENCE   Chapter 6 covers resource limits and scheduling in more detail.

According to Specification

The client, or the recipient of the project's deliverables, expects a certain level of functionality and quality from the project. These expectations can be self-imposed, such as the specification of the project completion date, or client-specified, such as producing the sales report on a weekly basis.

Although the project manager treats the specification as fixed, the reality of the situation is that any number of factors can cause the specification to change. For example, the client may not have defined the requirements completely, or the business situation may have changed (which often happens in projects with long durations). It is unrealistic to expect the specification to remain fixed through the life of the project. Systems specification can and will change, thereby presenting special challenges to the project manager.

CROSS-REFERENCE   Chapters 4, 9, and 11 describe how to effectively handle client requirements.

A Business-focused Definition of a Project

The major shortcoming of the definition of a project I have been discussing thus far is that it isn't focused on the purpose of a project, which is to deliver business value to the client and to the organization. So lots of examples exist of projects that meet all of the constraints and conditions specified in the definition, but the client is not satisfied with the results. The many reasons for this dissatisfaction are discussed throughout the book. So I offer a better definition for your consideration.

DEFINITION: PROJECT A project is a sequence of finite dependent activities whose successful completion results in the delivery of the expected business value that validated doing the project.

Defining a Program

A *program* is a collection of related projects. The projects must be completed in a specific order for the program to be considered complete. Because programs comprise multiple projects, they are larger in scope than a single project. For example, the United States government had a space program that included several projects such as the Challenger Project. A construction company contracts a program to build an industrial technology park with several separate projects.

Unlike projects, programs can have many goals. For example, every launch of a new mission in the NASA space program included several dozen projects in the form of scientific experiments. Except for the fact that they were all aboard the same spacecraft, the experiments were independent of one another and together defined a program.

Establishing Temporary Program Offices

As the size of the project increases, it becomes unwieldy from a management standpoint. A common practice is to establish a temporary program office to manage these large projects. One of my clients uses a team size of 30 as the cutoff point. Whenever the team size is greater than 30, a program office is established. That program office consists of nothing more than the management structure needed for the project. There will be a program director and one or more program administrators as support. The program administrators support the program manager as well as the teams. Even for teams of 30, there will often be a subteam organization put in place to simplify the management of the team. Each subteam will be led by a project manager. When the program is completed, the program office disbands.

Establishing Permanent Program Offices

A permanent program office is established to manage an ongoing and changing portfolio of projects. The portfolio consists of projects that have something in common — for example, all might be funded from the same budget, might be linked to the same goal statement, or might use the same resource pool. The permanent program office, unlike the temporary program office, manages a continuously changing collection of projects.

CROSS-REFERENCE Chapter 13 discusses the details.

Defining a Portfolio

A simple definition of a *project portfolio* is that it is a collection of projects that share some common link to one another. The operative phrase in this definition is "share some common link to one another." That link could take many forms. At the enterprise level, the link might be nothing more than the fact that all the projects belong to the same company. While that will always be true, it is not too likely the kind of link you are looking for. It is too general to be of any management use. Some more useful and specific common links might be any one of the following:

- The projects may all originate from the same business unit — for example, information technology.
- The projects may all be new product development projects.
- The projects may all be research and development projects.
- The projects may all be infrastructure maintenance projects from the same business unit.
- The projects may all be process improvement projects from the same business unit.
- The projects may all be staffed from the same human resource pool.
- The projects may request financial support from the same budget.

Each portfolio will have an allocation of resources (time, dollars, and staff) to accomplish whatever projects are approved for that portfolio. Larger allocations usually reflect the higher importance of the portfolio and stronger alignment to the strategic plan. One thing is almost certain: whatever resources you have available for the projects aligned to the portfolio, the resources will not be enough to meet all requests. Not all projects proposed for the portfolio will be funded and not all projects that are funded will necessarily be funded 100 percent. Hard choices have to be made, and this is where an equitable decision model is needed.

Your organization will probably have several portfolios. Based on the strategic plan, resources will be allocated to each portfolio based on its priority in the strategic plan, and it is those resources that will be used as a constraint on the projects that can be supported by the specific portfolio. Chapter 14 discusses the details.

Understanding the Scope Triangle

You may have heard of the term "Iron Triangle." It refers to the relationship between Time, Cost, and Scope. These three variables form the sides of a triangle and are an interdependent set. If any one of them changes at least one other variable must also change to restore balance to the project. That is all well and good, but there is more to this triangle.

The following five constraints operate on every project:

- Scope
- Quality
- Cost
- Time
- Resources

These constraints form an interdependent set — a change in one constraint can require a change in one or more of the other constraints in order to restore the equilibrium of the project. In this context, the set of five parameters form a system that must remain in balance for the project to be in balance. Because they are so important to the success or failure of the project, each parameter is discussed individually in this section.

Scope

Scope is a statement that defines the boundaries of the project. It tells not only what will be done but also what will not be done. In the information systems industry, scope is often referred to as a *functional specification*. In the engineering profession, it is generally called a *statement of work*. Scope may also be referred to as a document of understanding, a scoping statement, a project initiation document, or a project request form. Whatever its name, this document is the foundation for all project work to follow. It is critical that the scope be correct. Chapter 3 describes exactly how this should happen in its coverage of Conditions of Satisfaction (COS).

Beginning a project on the right foot is important, and so is staying on the right foot. It is no secret that a project's scope can change. You do not know how or when, but it will change. Detecting that change and deciding how to accommodate it in the project plan are major challenges for the project manager.

CROSS-REFERENCE Chapter 4 is devoted to defining project scope, and scope management is discussed in Chapter 7.

Quality

The following two types of quality are part of every project:

- **Product quality** — The quality of the deliverable from the project. As used here *product* includes tangible artifacts like hardware and software as well as business processes. The traditional tools of quality control, discussed in Chapter 3, are used to ensure product quality.

▪ **Process quality** — The quality of the project management process itself. The focus is on how well the project management process works and how it can be improved. Continuous quality improvement and process quality management are the tools used to measure process quality. These are discussed in Chapter 15.

A sound quality management program with processes in place that monitor the work in a project is a good investment. Not only does it contribute to client satisfaction, but it helps organizations use their resources more effectively and efficiently by reducing waste and revisions. Quality management is one area that should not be compromised. The payoff is a higher probability of successfully completing the project and satisfying the client.

Cost

The dollar cost of doing the project is another variable that defines the project. It is best thought of as the budget that has been established for the project. This is particularly important for projects that create deliverables that are sold either commercially or to an external customer.

Cost is a major consideration throughout the project management life cycle. The first consideration occurs at an early and informal stage in the life of a project. The client can simply offer a figure about equal to what he or she had in mind for the project. Depending on how much thought the client put into it, the number could be fairly close to or wide of the actual cost for the project. Consultants often encounter situations in which the client is willing to spend only a certain amount for the work. In these situations, you do what you can with what you have. In more formal situations, the project manager prepares a proposal for the projected work. That proposal includes an estimate (perhaps even a quote) of the total cost of the project. Even if a preliminary figure has been supplied by the project manager, the proposal allows the client to base his or her go/no-go decision on better estimates.

Time

The client specifies a time frame or deadline date within which the project must be completed. To a certain extent, cost and time are inversely related to one another. The time a project takes to be completed can be reduced, but costs increase as a result.

Time is an interesting resource. It can't be inventoried. It is consumed whether you use it or not. The objective for the project manager is to use the future time allotted to the project in the most effective and productive ways possible. Future time (time that has not yet occurred) can be a resource to be traded within a project or across projects. Once a project has begun, the prime resource available to the project manager to keep the project on schedule or get it back on schedule is time. A good project manager realizes this and protects the future time resource jealously.

CROSS-REFERENCE Chapters 5, 6, and 7, which discuss scheduling project activities, cover this topic in more detail.

Resources

Resources are assets such as people, equipment, physical facilities, or inventory that have limited availabilities, can be scheduled, or can be leased from an outside party. Some are fixed; others are variable only in the long term. In any case, they are central to the scheduling of project activities and the orderly completion of the project.

For systems development projects, people are the major resource. Another valuable resource for systems projects is the availability of computer processing time (mostly for testing purposes), which can present significant problems to the project manager with regard to project scheduling.

Envisioning the Scope Triangle as a System in Balance

The major benefit of using the scope triangle shown in Figure 1-1 instead of the three-variable Iron Triangle can now be discussed. Projects are dynamic systems that must be kept in equilibrium. Not an easy task, as you shall see! Figure 1-1 illustrates the dynamics of the situation.

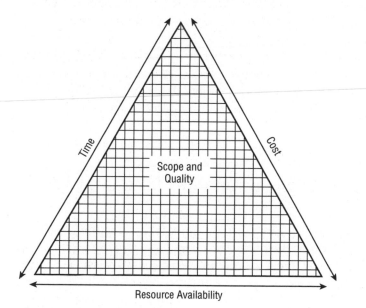

Figure 1-1: The scope triangle

The geographic area inside the triangle represents the scope and quality of the project. Lines representing time, cost, and resource availability bound scope and quality. Time is the window of time within which the project must be completed. Cost is the dollar budget available to complete the project. Resources are any consumables used on the project. People, equipment availability, and facilities are examples.

NOTE While the accountants will tell you that everything can be reduced to dollars, and they are right, you will separate resources as defined here. They are controllable by the project manager and need to be separately identified for that reason.

The project plan will have identified the time, cost, and resource availability needed to deliver the scope and quality of a project. In other words, the project is in equilibrium at the completion of the project planning session and approval of the commitment of resources and dollars to the project. That will not last too long, however. Change is waiting around the corner.

The scope triangle offers a number of insights into the changes that can occur in the life of the project. For example, the triangle represents a system in balance before any project work has been done. The sides are long enough to encompass the area generated by the scope and quality statements. Not long after work begins, something is sure to change. Perhaps the client calls with an additional requirement for a feature that was not envisioned during the planning sessions. Perhaps the market opportunities have changed, and it is necessary to reschedule the deliverables to an earlier date, or a key team member leaves the company and is difficult to replace. Any one of these changes throws the system out of balance.

The project manager controls resource utilization and work schedules. Management controls cost and resource level. The client controls scope, quality, and delivery dates. Scope, quality, and delivery dates suggest a hierarchy for the project manager as solutions to accommodate the changes are sought.

CROSS-REFERENCE Chapters 6 and 7 discuss this topic in greater detail.

Prioritizing the Scope Triangle Variables for Improved Change Management

The critical component of an effective project management methodology is the scope management process. The five variables that define the scope triangle must be prioritized so that the suggested project plan revisions can be prioritized. Figure 1-2 gives an example.

Variable \ Priority	Critical (1)	(2)	(3)	(4)	Flexible (5)
Scope				X	
Quality			X		
Time	X				
Cost					X
Resource Availability		X			

Figure 1-2: Prioritized scope triangle variables

A common application of the prioritized scope triangle variables occurs whenever a scope change request is made. The analysis of the change request is documented in a Project Impact Statement (PIS). If the change is to be approved, there will be several alternatives as to how that change can be accommodated. Those alternatives are prioritized using the data in Figure 1-2.

Applying the Scope Triangle

There are only a few graphics that I want you to burn into your brain because of their value throughout the entire project life cycle. The scope triangle is one such graphic. It will have at least two major applications for you: as a problem escalation strategy and as a reference for the Project Impact Statement, which is created as part of the scope change process.

Problem Resolution

The scope triangle enables you to ask the question, "Who owns what?" The answer will give you an escalation pathway from project team to resource manager to client. The client and senior management own time, budget, and resources. The project team owns how time, budget, and resources are used. Within the policies and practices of the enterprise, any of these may be moved within the project to resolve problems that have arisen. In solving a problem, the project manager should try to find a solution within the constraints of how the time, budget, and resources are used. They do not need to go outside of their sphere of control.

The next step in the escalation strategy would be for the project manager to appeal to the resource managers for problem resolution. The resource manager owns who gets assigned to a project as well as any changes to that assignment that may arise.

The final step in the problem escalation strategy is to appeal to the client. They control the amount of time that has been allocated to the project. They control the amount of money that has been allocated. Finally, they control the scope of the project. Whenever the project manager appeals to the client, it will be to get an increase in time or budget and some relief from the scope by way of scope reduction or scope release.

Scope Change Impact Analysis

The second major application of the scope triangle is as an aid in the preparation of the Project Impact Statement. This is a statement of the alternative ways of accommodating a particular scope change request of the client. The alternatives are identified by reviewing the scope triangle and proceeding in much the same way as discussed in the previous paragraph. Chapter 6 includes a detailed discussion of the scope change process and the use of the Project Impact Statement.

Managing the Creeps

While some of your team members may occasionally seem like creeps to you, that is not creep management I am talking about. *Creeps* here refer to minute changes in the project due to the obscure, and for awhile unnoticeable, actions of team members. Many of these go undetected until their cumulative effect creates a problem that raises its ugly head. You need to be aware of four types of creeps so you can take the appropriate management action. They are described in the sections that follow.

Scope Creep

Scope creep is the term that has come to mean any change in the project that was not in the original plan. Change is constant. To expect otherwise is simply unrealistic. Changes occur for several reasons that have nothing to do with the ability or foresight of the client, the project manager, or a project team member. Market conditions are dynamic. The competition can introduce or announce an upcoming new version of its product. Your management might decide that getting the product to market before the competition is necessary. Scope creep isn't necessarily anyone's fault. It is just a reality that has to be dealt with. It doesn't matter how good and thorough a job you and the client did in planning the project, scope creep is still going to happen. Deal with it!

Your job as project manager is to figure out how these changes can be accommodated — tough job, but somebody has to do it. Regardless of how the scope creep occurs, it is your job as project manager to figure out how, or even if, you can accommodate the impact.

Hope Creep

Hope creep happens when a project team member falls behind schedule but reports that he or she is on schedule, hoping to get back on schedule by the next report date. Hope creep is a real problem for the project manager. There will be several activity managers within your project team who manage a hunk of work. They do not want to give you bad news, so they are prone to tell you that their work is proceeding according to schedule when, in fact, it is not. It is their hope that they will catch up by the next report period, so they mislead you into thinking that they are on schedule. The activity managers hope that they will catch up by completing some work ahead of schedule to make up for the slippage. The project manager must be able to verify the accuracy of the status reports received from the team members. This does not mean that the project manager has to check into the details of every status report. Random checks can be used effectively.

Effort Creep

Effort creep is the result of the team member working but not making progress proportionate to the work expended. Every one of us has worked on a project that always seems to be 95-percent complete no matter how much effort is expended to complete it. Each week the status report records progress, but the amount of work remaining doesn't seem to decrease proportionately. Other than random checks, the only effective thing that the project manager can do is to increase the frequency of status reporting by those team members who seem to suffer from effort creep.

Feature Creep

Closely related to scope creep is *feature creep*. Feature creep results when team members arbitrarily add features and functions to the deliverable that they think the client would want to have. The problem is that the client didn't specify the feature, probably for good reason. If the team member has strong feelings about the need for this new feature, formal change management procedures can be employed.

CROSS-REFERENCE The change management process is discussed in Chapter 6.

Here's an example of how feature creep can occur. The programmer is busy coding a particular module in the system. He or she gets an idea that the client might appreciate having another option included. The systems requirements document does not mention this option. It seems so trivial that the programmer decides to include it rather than go through the lengthy change process. If this feature is not documented, it will go unnoticed until it's too late, and trouble will result. (Trust me, I have seen it happen on several occasions.)

Here's another example, which I personally experienced. This time it was induced by the client, and I was the project manager. The project involved the collection, storage, editing, retrieval, and reporting of an extensive database of teacher education data. The client called ahead and told me that she had just come up with a major design breakthrough with the raw input data and wanted to come over and show me. A few minutes later, she arrived at my office door. She proceeded to go through a lengthy demonstration of the color coding scheme she developed and used for the most recent data set. She was so proud of what she had done and it really was a stroke of genius, but not for me, because I had to read and interpret the data sheets. It broke my heart to have to tell her that I was profoundly color blind and couldn't read her data sheets.

Even when adding a feature or function seems rather insignificant, you need to look at the possible consequences. First of all, if the feature is not in the system requirements document, it is also not in the acceptance test procedure, the systems documentation, the user documentation, and the user training program. What will happen if something goes wrong with the new option? How will another programmer know what to do? What will happen when the user discovers the option and asks for some modification of it? You can see the consequences of such an innocent attempt to please. The message here is that a formal change request must be filed, and if it is approved, the project plan and all related activities will be appropriately modified.

The Importance of Classifying Projects

There are many ways to classify a project such as:

- By size (cost, duration, team, business value, number of departments affected, and so on)
- By type (new, maintenance, upgrade, strategic, tactical, operational)
- By application (software development, new product development, equipment installation, and so on)
- By complexity and uncertainty (see Chapter 2)

Projects are unique and to some extent so is the best-fit model to manage them. Part II of the book is devoted to exploring five best-fit models and when to use them. For now it is sufficient to understand that a one-size-fits-all approach to project management doesn't work and has never worked. It is far more effective to group projects based on their similarities and to use a project management approach designed specifically for each project type. That is the topic of this section.

Establishing a Rule for Classifying Projects

For the purposes of this chapter, two different rules are defined here. The first is based on the characteristics of the project, and the second is based on the type of project. Chapter 2 defines a third rule, which is based on the clarity and completeness of the goal and the solution.

Classification by Project Characteristics

Many organizations choose to define a classification of projects based on such project characteristics as the following:

- **Risk** — Establish levels of risk (high, medium, and low).
- **Business value** — Establish levels (high, medium, and low).
- **Length** — Establish several categories (such as 3 months, 3 to 6 months, 6 to 12 months, and so on).
- **Complexity** — Establish categories (high, medium, and low).
- **Technology used** — Establish several categories (well-established, used occasionally, used rarely, never used).
- **Number of departments affected** — Establish some categories (such as one, a few, several, and all).
- **Cost**

The project profile determines the classification of the project. The classification defines the extent to which a particular project management methodology is to be used. In Part II, you will use these and other factors to adjust the best-fit project management approach.

I strongly advocate this approach because it adapts the methodology to the project. "One size fits all" does not work in project management. In the final analysis, I defer to the judgment of the project manager. In addition to the parts required by the organization, the project manager should adopt whatever parts of the methodology he or she feels improves his or her ability to help successfully manage the project. Period.

Project characteristics can be used to build a classification rule as follows:

- **Type A projects** — These are high-business-value, high-complexity projects. They are the most challenging projects the organization undertakes.

Type A projects use the latest technology, which, when coupled with high complexity, causes risk to be high also. To maximize the probability of success, the organization requires that these projects utilize all the methods and tools available in their project management methodology. An example of a Type A project is the introduction of a new technology into an existing product that has been very profitable for the company.

- **Type B projects** — These projects are shorter in length, but they are still significant projects for the organization. All of the methods and tools in the project management process are probably required. Type B projects generally have good business value and are technologically challenging. Many product development projects fall in this category.

- **Type C projects** — These are the projects that occur most frequently in an organization. They are short by comparison and use established technology. Many are projects that deal with the infrastructure of the organization. A typical project team consists of five people, the project lasts 6 months, and the project is based on a less-than-adequate scope statement. Many of the methods and tools are not required for these projects. The project manager uses those optional tools only if he or she sees value in their use.

- **Type D projects** — These just meet the definition of a project and may require only a scope statement and a few scheduling pieces of information. A typical Type D project involves making a minor change in an existing process or procedure or revising a course in the training curriculum.

Table 1-1 gives a hypothetical example of a classification rule.

Table 1-1: Example of Project Classes and Definitions

CLASS	DURATION	RISK	COMPLEXITY	TECHNOLOGY	LIKELIHOOD OF PROBLEMS
Type A	> 18 months	High	High	Breakthrough	Certain
Type B	9–18 months	Medium	Medium	Current	Likely
Type C	3–9 months	Low	Low	Best of breed	Some
Type D	< 3 months	Very low	Very low	Practical	Few

These four types of projects might use the parts of the methodology shown in Figure 1-3. The figure lists the methods and tools that are either required or optional, given the type of project.

Project Management Process	Project Classification			
	A	B	C	D
Define				
Conditions of Satisfaction	R	R	O	O
Project Overview Statement	R	R	R	R
Approval of Request	R	R	R	R
Plan				
Conduct Planning Session	R	R	O	O
Prepare Project Proposal	R	R	R	R
Approval of Proposal	R	R	R	R
Launch				
Kick-off Meeting	R	R	O	O
Activity Schedule	R	R	R	R
Resource Assignments	R	R	R	O
Statements of Work	R	O	O	O
Monitor/Control				
Status Reporting	R	R	R	R
Project Team Meetings	R	R	O	O
Approval of Deliverables	R	R	R	R
Close				
Post-Implementation Audit	R	R	R	R
Project Notebook	R	R	O	O
	R = Required O = Optional			

Figure 1-3: The use of required and optional parts of the methodology by type of project

Classification by Project Application

Many situations exist in which an organization repeats projects that are of the same type. Following are some examples of project types:

- Installing software
- Recruiting and hiring
- Setting up hardware in a field office
- Soliciting, evaluating, and selecting vendors
- Updating a corporate procedure
- Developing application systems

These projects may be repeated several times each year and probably will follow a similar set of steps each time they are done.

CROSS-REFERENCE You look at the ramifications of that repetition in Chapter 5 when Work Breakdown Structure (WBS) templates are discussed.

The value of classifying projects by type is that each type of project utilizes a specific subset of the entire project management methodology. For example, projects that involve updating a corporate procedure are far less risky than application systems development projects. Therefore, the risk management aspects of each are very different. Risk management processes will be less important in the corporate procedure project; conversely, they will be very important in the applications development project.

Putting It All Together

It should be clear to you by now that I advocate a very specific definition of a project. If a collection of work is to be called a project, it must meet the definition. Once you know that you have a project, it will be subjected to a specific set of requirements regarding its management.

Discussion Questions

1. Compare and contrast the two definitions of a project.

2. Suppose the scope triangle were modified as follows: Resource Availability occupies the center, and the three sides are Scope, Cost, and Schedule. Interpret this triangle as if it were a system in balance. What is likely to happen when a specific resource on your project is concurrently allocated to more and more projects? As project manager, how would you deal with these situations? Be specific.

3. Where would you be able to bring about cost savings as a program manager for a company? Discuss these using the standard project constraints.

4. Discuss ways in which scope creep occurred on projects with which you have been associated. Was the project manager able to reverse scope creep? Is it possible to reverse scope creep? Defend your yes or no answer.

CHAPTER 2

What Is Project Management?

The design, adaptation, and deployment of project management life cycles and models are based on the changing characteristics of the project and are the guiding principles behind practicing effective project management.

Don't impose process and procedure that stifles team and individual creativity! Rather create and support an environment that encourages that behavior.

—Robert K. Wysocki, Ph.D., President, EII Publications

CHAPTER LEARNING OBJECTIVES

After reading this chapter, you will be able to:

- **Understand and apply a working description of project management**
- **Apply a business value definition of requirements**
- **Use goal and solution clarity to define the project landscape**
- **Understand and explain the four quadrants of the project landscape**
- **Know the characteristics of Traditional Project Management (TPM), Agile Project Management (APM), Extreme Project Management (xPM), and Emertxe Project Management (MPx)**
- **Know how complexity and uncertainty affect the project landscape**
- **Understand the similarities and differences between Linear, Incremental, Iterative, Adaptive, and Extreme PMLC models**

I suspect that for many of you this chapter will be your first exposure to just how broad and deep the world of managing projects can be. It never ceases to amaze me that even after more than 40 years of practicing project management I am still encountering new challenges and learning wondrous things about this amazing discipline. You should realize that project management is not just a matter of routinely filling in forms and submitting reports, but rather it is a challenging world where you will be called upon to be an effective leader, to function at the limits of your creativity, and to be courageous at all times. It is a world in which you will continually face situations you have never faced before and will have to look inside your toolkit and concoct workable approaches.

For those of you who are practitioners, it's no secret to you that your project management landscape has changed and continues to change. With the change comes a constant challenge to assess project conditions and adjust your approach to managing the project. We live in a world where the characteristics of the project and the environment within which the project takes place are constantly changing, and those changes should inform you as to the tools, templates, and processes that will be most effective. As you closely examine those characteristics, you will gain an appreciation of just how challenging the task of effective project management can be.

You're not in Kansas anymore! The discipline of project management has morphed to a new state; as this book is being written, that state has not yet reached a steady state. In fact, the practice of effective project management may never reach a steady state. The business world is in a constant state of flux and change, and it will always be that way. That continues to influence how you need to approach managing projects. And your approach itself is going to be in a constant state of flux and change. What does this mean to the struggling project manager? Take courage: It's not as grim as it may seem. In the chapters that make up Part II later in this book, I am going to clearly point the way for you. If you really understand what I am presenting in the chapters that make up Part I, you will have acquired a robust tool kit and an enduring strategy for delivering effective project management.

So let's get started on your journey to becoming an effective project manager.

Understanding the Fundamentals of Project Management

The Project Management Institute (PMI) formally defines project management as follows: "The application of knowledge, skills, tools, and techniques to project activities to meet the project requirements."[1]

Even though that definition is open to broad interpretation I have no problem with it because I prefer to keep things simple and intuitive and that is what PMI has done. For our purposes here I'm going to add a little more content than the PMI definition offers. The definition that I offer shortly in this chapter is designed to be a working definition.

---

[1] Project Management Institute, (2008). *A Guide to the Project Management Body of Knowledge. 4th Edition* (Newtown Square, PA: Project Management Institute, ISBN 978-1-933890-51-7).

NOTE Project management is a set of tools, templates, and processes designed to answer the following six questions:

- What business situation is being addressed by this project?
- What do you need to do?
- What will you do?
- How will you do it?
- How will you know you did it?
- How well did you do?

Let's quickly look at the answers to these questions.

What Business Situation Is Being Addressed by This Project?

The business situation is either a problem that needs a solution or an untapped opportunity. If it is a problem, the solution may be clearly defined and the delivery of that solution will be rather straightforward. If the solution is not completely known, then the project-management approach must iteratively embrace the learning and discovery of that solution. Obviously, these will be higher-risk projects simply because the deliverables are not clearly defined and may not be discovered despite the best efforts of the client and the project team.

Keep in mind that your project is usually competing for resources with other projects that are addressing the same business situation but from a completely different perspective. For example, your project may be attacking one part of the problem while another project is considering a different part of the problem. It would be good if you knew this, because integrating the two projects into a single program may be cost beneficial and more likely to come to a successful conclusion. At least you would have more points of view to consider. The importance to senior managers of finding that solution or taking advantage of that untapped opportunity will also compete with the importance of other project proposals.

What Do You Need to Do?

The obvious answer is to solve the problem or take advantage of the untapped opportunity. That's all well and good; but given the business circumstances under which the project will be undertaken, it may not be possible. Even in those rare cases where the solution is clearly known, you might not have the skilled resources to do the project; and if you do have them, they may not be available when you need them. When the solution is not known or only partially known, you might not be successful in finding that heretofore-unknown solution. In any case, you need to document what needs to be done. If the solution is known, that document will be easy to develop. If that solution is unknown or only partially known what you need to do will emerge over time rather than being developed at the outset.

What Will You Do?

The answer to this question will be framed in your project goal and objectives statements. Maybe you and others will propose partial solutions to the problem or ways to take advantage of the untapped opportunity. In any case, your goal and objective statements given as part of a Project Overview Statement (POS) will clearly state your intentions.

How Will You Do It?

This answer will document your approach to the project and your detailed plan for meeting the goal and objective statements discussed in the POS. That approach might be fully documented at the outset or only developed iteratively but it will be developed.

How Will You Know You Did It?

Your solution to the problem or approach to the untapped opportunity will deliver some business value to the organization. That is your success criteria. It will have been used as the basis for approving your doing the project in the first place. That success criterion may be expressed in the form of Increased Revenue or Avoided Costs or Improved Services. IRACIS is the acronym that represents these three areas of business value. Whatever form that success criteria takes, it must be expressed in quantitative terms so that there is no argument as to whether or not you achieved the expected business results. As part of the post-implementation audit, you will compare the actual business value realized to the estimated business value stated in the project plan that justified doing the project in the first place.

How Well Did You Do?

The answer to this question can be determined by the answers to the following four questions:

> **How well did your deliverables meet the stated success criteria?** The project was sold to management based on the incremental business value that would be returned to the organization if the project were successful. Did the project deliver those results and to what extent?

How well did the project team perform? The project team was following some project management life cycle (PMLC) model. There should be some assessment of how well they followed that model.

How well did the project-management approach work for this project? In addition to doing things right the team needed to do the right thing. Given that several approaches could have been used, the team should have used the best fit model.

What lessons were learned that can be applied to future projects? This question is answered through the post-implementation audit.

The answers to these six questions discussed in the preceding sections reduce project management to nothing more than organized common sense. In my world to be "organized" means that the process(es) used are continuously adapted to the meet the changing needs of the project. To be "common sense" means the management process did not require that non-value added work be done. If it weren't organized common sense, you need to question why you are doing it at all. So a good test of whether or not your project-management approach makes sense lies in how you answered the preceding six questions. With all of that as background our working definition of project management can be succinctly stated as follows:

DEFINITION: PROJECT MANAGEMENT Project management is an organized common-sense approach that utilizes the appropriate client involvement in order to deliver client requirements that meet expected incremental business value.

This definition is a marked change from any you may have seen before. First, it is the only definition that I know of that explicitly refers to business value. Business value is the responsibility of the client through their requirements statements. The project manager is responsible for meeting those requirements. Meeting requirements is the cause and incremental business value is the effect. What this boils down to is the meaningful involvement of the client in the project. In effect the client plays the role of another team member. Oftentimes their role will be as co-project manager. I'll have more to say on that throughout the book.

Second, and equally important in the definition through the common-sense term is that effective project management is not a "one size fits all" approach. Because it is a "common sense approach" it must adapt to the changing project conditions. What I will develop in this book are the rules of the engagement for effectively managing projects. The definition of the PMLC models given in the section "Introducing Project Management Life Cycles" is the beginning of your journey to become a complex project manager. You will learn in this book that the effective complex project manager is a leader who at the same time is creative, adaptive, and courageous. In effect I will define the contents of the pantry from which you will build the recipes you will need for managing your projects. It will be up to you to be the chef.

Third, you need to clearly understand requirements. Requirements and their documentation will establish the project characteristics and be your guide to choosing and adapting the project management approach you will use. I am going to take a rather unconventional approach based on my own definition of requirements.

What Are Requirements — Really?

Requirements define things that a product or service is supposed to do to satisfy the needs of the client and deliver expected business value. A more formal definition is given by the International Institute of Business Analysis (IIBA) in "A Guide to the Business Analysis Body of Knowledge":

"A requirement is:

(1) A condition or capability needed by a stakeholder to solve a problem or achieve an objective.

(2) A condition or capability that must be met or possessed by a solution or solution component to satisfy a contract, standard, specification, or other formally imposed documents.

A documented representation of a condition or capability as in (1) or (2)."

That is all well and good and I'm not going to challenge the definition. I assume it does what it is supposed to do. But let me offer a different perspective for your consideration and practical application. I believe we execute a complex project to solve a critical problem heretofore unsolved or take advantage of an untapped business opportunity. Two things link the deliverables:

- **The need to deliver business value** — The more the better
- **Complexity and uncertainty** — All of the simple projects have been done

Generating business value is really the only measure of project success. I've long felt that the criterion for defining project success as meeting a specification within the constraints of time and cost is misdirected. It really ignores the business, the client, and organizational satisfaction. My criterion is that project success is measured by delivering expected business value. Nothing more. After all isn't it expected business value that justified the need to do the project in the first place? There are of course some exceptions in the case of mandated and otherwise required projects regardless of whether or not they deliver business value.

DEFINITION: REQUIREMENT A requirement is a desired end-state whose successful integration into the solution delivers specific, measurable, and incremental business value to the organization.

Furthermore the set of requirements forms a necessary and sufficient set for the attainment of incremental business value.

The necessary and sufficient conditions statement means that all requirements are needed in order to achieve the success criteria and none of the requirements are superfluous. This is important because the project was justified based on the expected business value as described through the success criteria. Linking requirements to the success criteria provides a basis on which to prioritize not only the requirements based on their contribution to expected business value but also to the prioritization of the functions, sub-functions, processes, activities, and features that define requirements decomposition.

This definition of a requirement is quite different than the IIBA definition but in its simplicity and uniqueness it puts the connection between requirements and the project in a much more intuitive light. I have no particular concern with the IIBA definition but I believe that a working definition linked to business value is a better choice. I will use my definition throughout this book.

Requirements will be the causal factors that drive the attainment of the success criteria as stated in the POS. Every requirement must be directly related to a project success statement. This definition results in a small number (8–12) of requirements at the beginning of the project, whereas the IIBA definition generates hundreds and even thousands of requirements which can never be considered complete at the beginning of the project. The human mind cannot possibly absorb and understand that many requirements. To expect that a decision as to completeness can be made is highly unlikely. Subject to the learning and discovery that may uncover other requirements, the list generated using my requirements definition can be considered complete at the beginning of the project. The decomposition of those requirements is not fully known at the beginning of the project however. My requirement is a more business-value-oriented definition than the IIBA definition. The learning and discovery derived from completed project cycles will clarify the requirements through decomposition to the function, sub-function, process, activity, and feature levels. The first-level decomposition of a requirement is to the functional level and can be considered equivalent to IIBA requirements. So while you can identify all requirements at the beginning of the project you cannot describe the details of the requirements at the functional, sub-functional, process, activity, and feature levels. This detail is learned and discovered in the context of the cycles that make up the project.

I believe that this definition of requirements should be preferred to the IIBA definition because it ties requirements directly to the project success criteria, which is not the case with the IIBA definition. That makes it possible to prioritize

requirements where no similar case can be made for prioritizing IIBA requirements. I'll have much more to say about requirements elicitation, gathering,
decomposition, and completeness in Chapter 4 and in Part II where you will learn
how requirements completeness relates to the choice of best-fit PMLC model.

WARNING   Linking requirements to measurable business value can be difficult because the entire set of requirements is necessary and sufficient to attain
expected business value. They form a dependent set and it may not be possible
to ascribe a certain business value to a single requirement. In that case a prioritization of requirements will be sufficient.

So you are probably wondering if my definition is better than the IIBA definition and whether using it in your organization makes business sense. Here
are six reasons that I put forth for you to think and talk about with your team.

- **Reduces the number of requirements from dozens to six or eight.** I think
  of requirements at a higher level than most professionals. Using the IIBA
  definition it is unlikely that requirements can be complete at the beginning of a project. In fact, most professionals would agree that a complete
  and documented set of requirements cannot possibly be generated at the
  beginning of a project. They can only be learned or discovered as part
  of project execution. That is the approach I take in my Adaptive Project
  Framework (APF). On the other hand, using my higher order definition
  I expect to generate a complete set of requirements at the beginning of a
  project. Through experience I have found that my higher order definition
  gives the client and the project team a more holistic view of the project
  and enables much better business decisions that impact the solution.

- **Identifying the complete definition of most requirements happens only
  through iteration.** The requirements list will be complete using my higher
  order definition. The challenge arises in identifying the component parts
  of each requirement — the Requirements Breakdown Structure (RBS):

Requirement

    Functions

        Sub-functions

            Processes

                Activities

                    Features

These details can only be documented as part of project execution. The
criterion for inclusion in the solution is that the component part must
either directly contribute business value or support a higher order component part that does contribute business value. This tends to eliminate

frivolous additions to the solution that have no obvious business value. Chapter 4 discusses the RBS in more detail. Chapter 5 establishes the link between the RBS and the Work Breakdown Structure (WBS). Basically the RBS documents what must be done to deliver a complete solution and the WBS documents how it will be done, so that using my definition of requirements we establish a strong connection between the work of the project and the delivery of business value.

■ **Simplifies the search for a solution with acceptable business value.** If you are emotionally attached to some component part of the solution and cannot demonstrate that it contributes to business value, don't expect to see it in the solution. That eliminates the expenditure of time, money, and resources on something that adds no business value to the solution.

■ **Choosing among alternative solution directions is simplified.** Business value is the great tie breaker when faced with competing alternatives from which choices must be made. I have had experiences where a component part didn't seem to generate business value early on and so wasn't included but at some later iteration the team or client learned that it did and so was included. So "when in doubt, leave it out" is a good practice as you build out the details of a solution. If a component part can contribute business value it will be discovered later in the project.

■ **Provides for better use of scarce resources (money, time, and people).** Using this higher order definition of a requirement there is a return on investment from every part of the solution. The complex project is filled with uncertainty and risk and knowing that your approach uses available resources effectively and efficiently is reassuring to the client and your management.

■ **It is a working definition.** It is directly related to the expected business value that will result from a successful project. These requirements can be prioritized with respect to that business value, which is not possible with the IIBA definition.

I have always strived for simplicity and intuitiveness in all the tools, templates, and processes that I use. I find that my higher order definition of a requirement meets that goal for me and makes sense too.

The RBS is the key input to choosing the best-fit PMLC model. This decision-making process is really quite simple. By working through the process of generating the RBS, you and the client will be able to assess the completeness and confidence you have in the resulting RBS. If the project is one that you have done several times, you should have a high degree of confidence that the RBS is complete. This might be the case with repetitive infrastructure projects.

However, don't be lulled to sleep thinking that the RBS can't change. Remember, the world doesn't stand still just because you are managing a project. Change is inevitable during any project. That change can be internal to the organization and come from the client or even from the team, and it is unpredictable except for the fact that it can happen and you must be able to respond appropriately. Change can also come from some external source such as the market, the competition, or the arrival of some new technological breakthrough. These changes could have no effect, a minimal effect, or a major effect on your project. Again, you must be able to respond appropriately.

Traditional practices require client requirements to be clearly and completely defined before any planning can take place. Most contemporary thinkers on the topic would suggest that it is impossible to completely and clearly document requirements at the beginning of any project. Whether you agree or not, that condition is likely to exist in most contemporary projects, and there are many reasons for that:

- Changing market conditions
- Actions of competitors
- Technology advances
- Client discovery
- Changing priorities

That is the motivation that resulted in my defining requirements as given earlier. In Part II you will consider these situations as well as how the scope change process is handled and its impact on project management processes. In doing that, you will learn alternative project-management approaches to handle these difficult situations while maintaining a client focus throughout the entire project life cycle.

The market is different today than it was 30 years ago. The PC is about 30 years old, and look at the impact it has had. Social networking is very new and its impact yet to be defined. Technology has been the prime mover to these market changes. Leveraging technology to get to market as fast as possible must now be the strategy. Leveraging technology to get the most innovative product or service to market before the competition gets there must also be the strategy. Leveraging technology to create barriers to entry is critical to every successful strategy. Project management is the only enabler of those strategies. It must provide approaches that support high change, speed, and increasing complexity. The old ways had to strain to keep up with the realities of projects such as these. It's no wonder that a reported 70+ percent of projects fail. That has to stop. Project managers need approaches that are built around the expectation of change — ones that embrace learning and discovery throughout all of the project life cycle. These approaches must have built-in processes to integrate the changes that result from this learning and discovery.

WARNING You can never know for sure that the RBS is complete. When in doubt, err on the side of concluding that it is not complete. In any case, suppose that a TPM approach seems to be the best-fit approach initially. If at some point in the project you come to the conclusion that your original choice was not correct and that parts of the solution are indeed not represented in the RBS, you should consider changing your choice to one of the Iterative or Adaptive approaches. Finally, when not even the goal is clearly specified, an Extreme approach will be appropriate. In Part II, I explore how these decisions are made in much more detail.

Introducing Project Management Life Cycles

To plan your journey you need a project landscape that is simple and intuitive and will remain valid despite the volatility of the business environment. It will be your unchanging roadmap for further analysis and action. For several years now, project management professionals have proclaimed, "One size does not fit all." If it did, the life of a project manager would be boring and this book would be less than 100 pages in length. Unfortunately (or fortunately for those with an adventuresome spirit) being an effective project manager is exhilarating and demanding of all your creative energies. A "one size fits all" mentality doesn't work and probably never worked. I am of course talking about how the characteristics of the project should inform the project manager as to the tools, templates, and processes that should be used on a given project. To help you build a decision making model for choosing a project management model, I will first define a very general project landscape and then a strategy for drilling down in that landscape to a specific project management life cycle (PMLC) model, and then I will discuss the tools, templates, and processes and their adaptation to the specific characteristics of the project. You need to understand at the outset that there are no silver bullets. Project management is not a matter of following a recipe. Rather it is the ability to create and use recipes. I want you to be a chef not just a cook. A cook only has the ability to follow the recipes of others. A chef, on the other hand, has the ability to create recipes. You are going to have to work hard to reach a point where you can create recipes.

DEFINITION: PROJECT MANAGEMENT LIFE CYCLE MODEL
A project management life cycle (PMLC) model is a sequence made up of the five process groups (Scoping, Planning, Launching, Monitoring and Controlling, and Closing) to accomplish the goal of the project. All of the process groups must be included at least once in the sequence, and any or all process groups may be repeated as required.

Goal and Solution Clarity

I like simple and intuitive models, so I have built my project landscape around two variables: goal and solution. These two variables can each take on two values: clear and complete or not clear and complete. Those two values for each variable generate the four-quadrant matrix shown in Figure 2-1.

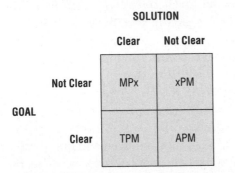

Figure 2-1: The four quadrants of the project landscape

Traditional Project Management (TPM) defines Quadrant 1; Agile Project Management (APM) defines Quadrant 2; Extreme Project Management (xPM) defines Quadrant 3; and Emertxe Project Management (MPx) defines Quadrant 4. I don't know where the dividing line is between clear and not clear, but that is not important to this landscape. These values are conceptual not quantifiable. A given project can exhibit various degrees of clarity. The message in this landscape is that the transition from quadrant to quadrant is continuous and fluid.

As an example, say that the project goal is to cure the common cold. Is this goal statement clear and complete? Not really. The word *cure* is the culprit. Cure could mean any one of the following:

- Prior to birth, the fetus is injected with a DNA-altering drug that prevents the person from ever getting a cold.

- As part of everyone's diet, they take a daily dose of the juice from a tree that grows only in certain altitudes in the Himalayas. This juice acts as a barrier and prevents the onset of the common cold.

- Once a person has contracted a cold, they take a massive dose of tea made from a rare tree root found only in central China, and the cold will be cured within 12 hours.

So what does *cure* really mean? As another example, consider this paraphrasing of a statement made by President John F. Kennedy in his 1961 State of the Union Address: By the end of the decade, we will have put a man on the moon and returned him safely to earth. Is there any doubt in your mind that this goal statement is clear and complete? When the project is finished, will there be any doubt in your mind that this goal has or has not been achieved?

Every project that ever existed or will exist falls into one of these four quadrants at any point in time. This landscape is not affected by change of any kind. It is a landscape that will remain in place regardless. The quadrant in which the project lies will be an initial guide to choosing a best-fit PMLC model and adapting its tools, templates, and processes to the specific project. As the project work commences and the goal and solution become clearer, the project's quadrant can change, and perhaps the PMLC will then change as well; however, the project is always in one quadrant. The decision to change the PMLC for a project already underway may be a big change and needs to be seriously considered. Costs, benefits, advantages, and disadvantages are associated with a mid-project change of PMLC. Part II will aid you in making this decision.

Beyond clarity and completeness of the goal and solution, you have several other factors to consider in choosing the best-fit PMLC and perhaps modifying it to better accommodate these other factors. By way of example, one of those factors is the extent to which the client has committed to be meaningfully involved. If the best-fit PMLC model requires client involvement that is heavy and meaningful, as many Quadrant 2 and 3 projects do, and you don't expect to have that involvement, you may have to fall back to an approach that doesn't require as much client involvement. Alternatively you may want to put a program in place to encourage the desired client involvement. This is a common situation, and you will learn strategies for effectively dealing with it in Part II.

I have practiced project management since 1963, which pre-dates the Project Management Institute (PMI) by a few years. Across the 45+ years, I have seen project management mature from a simple approach based mostly on Gantt Charts to a multi-disciplined array of tools, templates, and processes tailored to fit all types of situations. Project management is no longer just another tool in the toolkit of an engineer. It is now a way of life as many businesses have morphed themselves into some form of project-based organization. Although there will continue to be applications for which the old ways are still appropriate, there is a whole new set of applications for which the old ways are totally inappropriate. The paradigm must shift and is shifting. Take agile project management, for example, which formally came on the scene in 2001.[2] It represented a marked formal departure from the then-current practices. Any company that hasn't embraced that shift is sure to risk losing project management as a strategic asset. "Change or die" was never a truer statement than it is today. From that humble introduction in 2001 has emerged an entire portfolio of project management approaches. These are mentioned later in this section and covered in detail in Part II.

Why do we need yet another way of managing projects? Don't we have enough options already? Yes, there certainly are plenty of options, but projects still fail

---

[2] Fowler, Martin and Jim Highsmith. "The Agile Manifesto." *Software Development* 9, No. 8, August 2001: pgs 28-32.

at an unacceptably high rate. In the past, the efforts of project managers have not been too fruitful. There are lots of reasons for that failure. I believe that part of the reason is because we haven't yet completely defined, at a practical and effective level, how to adjust our management approaches to embrace the types of projects that we are being asked to manage in today's business environment. Too many project managers are trying in vain to put square pegs in round holes because all they have are square pegs. We need to approach project management as the art and science that it truly is. That means basing it on irrefutable principles and concepts and building on those to produce a scientifically defined discipline. This chapter and Part II are my attempt to do just that.

> **NOTE**   **Observation: The discipline of project management is morphing to a new state and that state is not yet a steady state. It may never reach a steady state.**

To me the answer to our project management difficulties is obvious. Project managers must open their minds to the basic principles on which project management is based so as to accommodate change, avoid wasted dollars, avoid wasted time, and protect market positions. For as long as I can remember, I have been preaching that one size does not fit all. The characteristics of the project must be the basis on which project management approaches are defined. This concept has to be embedded in your approach to project management. Your thinking must embrace a project management approach that begins by choosing the best-fit PMLC model based on the characteristics of the project at hand. The RBS is the artifact that will allow you to do that. Then you can choose how that model should be adapted to effectively manage the project.

Traditional practices require client requirements to be clearly and completely defined before any planning can take place. Most contemporary thinkers on the topic would suggest that it is impossible to completely and clearly document requirements at the beginning of any project. Whether you agree or not, that condition is likely to exist in most contemporary projects, and there are many reasons for that. In the chapters of Part II you will consider these situations as well as the inevitable scope change requests and their impact on project management processes. In doing that, you will learn alternative project management approaches to handle these difficult situations while maintaining a client focus throughout the entire project life cycle.

As presented in the introduction to this book, the old ways of project management were defined and matured in the world of engineer and construction professionals. These professionals provided what they thought was a complete and accurate description of what the client wanted. It was assumed that the project team clearly understood the solution they were to provide and that they could clearly plan for its delivery. Unfortunately that was not the case, and the result was a project failure rate exceeding 70 percent. Adjustments were implemented in an attempt to appease the client, but it was too late. The project had failed. That describes the world of the project manager until the mid-1950s, when the computer became a viable commercial resource. Using computers to run businesses was now a reality, and position titles such as programmer, programmer analyst, systems analyst, and primitive types of database architects started emerging. The business world and the project world had changed, and we would never look back.

In the face of that change, the old ways still weren't showing any signs of change. To engineers, every project management problem looked like a nail, and they had the hammer. It seemed to be working, or at least no one was complaining or knew how to complain when it wasn't.

Fast forward to the 1970s. Buried beneath the mysticism that surrounded the computer was another problem that would soon surface — that is, the inability of the businessperson to tell the difference between wants and needs. The confusion arose from the glamour surrounding the computer. It was touted as the silver bullet: All users needed to do was push a button and the rest would be automatic. The conduct of business was going to become simple. The wants got in the way of seeing the real needs.

Here we are more than 40 years later, and that problem still persists. If you remember anything from this discussion, remember that what the client wants is probably not what the client needs. Wants are associated with a solution envisioned by the client, whereas needs are associated with an underlying and unstated problem. If the project manager blindly accepts what the client says they want and proceeds with the project on that basis, that project manager is in for a rude awakening. Often in the process of building the solution, the client will begin to see that what they need is not the same as what they requested, which leads to rolling deadlines, scope creep, and an endless trail of changes and reworks.

The market is different today than it was 30 years ago. The PC is less than 30 years old, and look at the impact it has had. Technology has been the prime mover to those market differences. Leveraging technology to get to market as fast as possible must now be the strategy. Leveraging technology to get the most innovative product or service to market before the competition gets there must also be the strategy. Project management is the only enabler of those strategies. It must provide approaches that support high change, speed, and increasing complexity. The old ways had to strain to keep up with the realities of projects such as these. It's no wonder that 70+ percent of projects fail. That has to stop. Project managers need approaches that are built around the expectation of change — ones that embrace learning and discovery throughout all of the project life cycle. These approaches must have built-in processes to integrate the changes that result from this learning and discovery.

A *project management life cycle* (*PMLC*) is a sequence of processes that includes:

- scoping
- planning
- launching
- monitoring and controlling
- closing

the projects to which it applies. A valid PMLC always starts with a scoping process and ends with a closing process. All five of the processes must each be done at least once and may be repeated any number of times in some logical order. These process groups are defined in Chapter 3. The logical ordering of these processes is a function of the characteristics of the project. This book defines five different PMLC models. Each is constructed to meet the specific needs of a project type to which it is aligned.

In previous editions of this book, I introduced a way to organize and manage complex projects in the face of uncertainty. To that end I defined the following five models across the four quadrants:

- **TPM** — Linear and Incremental models
- **APM** — Iterative and Adaptive models
- **xPM** — Extreme model
- **MPx** — Extreme model

These five models form a continuum that ranges from certainty about the solution (both the goal and solution are clearly defined) to some uncertainty about the solution (the goal is clearly defined, but the solution is not clearly defined) to major uncertainty about the solution (neither the goal nor solution are clearly defined).

In Figure 2-2, certainty is measured with respect to requirements and solution. The less certain you are that you have clearly defined requirements and a solution to match, the more you should choose an approach at the high uncertainty end of the continuum. Once you understand the nature of the project to be undertaken, you can confidently choose the model that offers the best chance of a successful completion.

Figure 2-2 shows how the five PMLC models are distributed across the four quadrants that were defined in Chapter 1. Note that there is some overlap. It would seem that as the project solution and its requirements becomes less clear, the best-fit PMLC could be chosen from among Linear, Incremental, Iterative, Adaptive, or Extreme. That, in fact, is the case. The decision as to which of these five PMLCs is best for the project is based on factors that include solution clarity. For projects that are near the boundaries of TPM and APM, you will always have a judgment call to make as to which PMLC model is the best-fit model. In Part II the ramifications of that subjective decision are described.

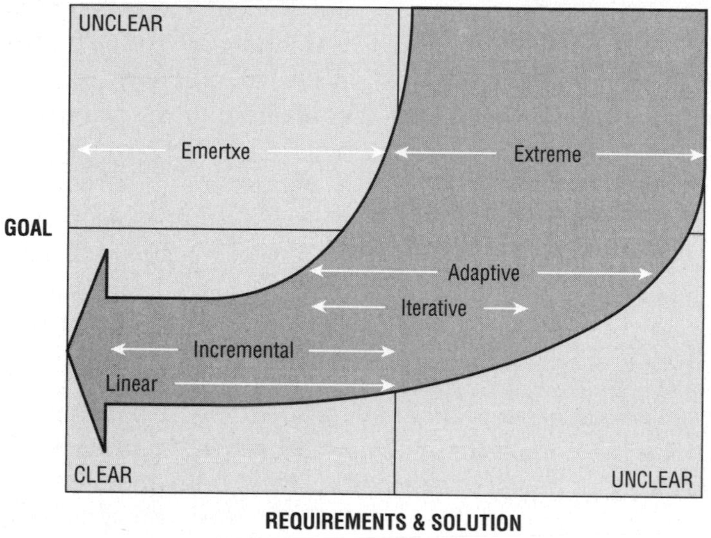

Figure 2-2: PMLC approaches

Traditional Project Management Approaches

How could it be any better than to clearly know the goal and the solution? This is the simplest of all possible project situations, but it is also the least likely to occur in today's fast-paced, continuously changing business world. Testimonial data that I have gathered from all over the world suggests that about 20 percent of all projects legitimately fall in the TPM quadrant. Projects that fall into the TPM quadrant are familiar to the organization. Many infrastructure projects will fall in the TPM quadrant. Perhaps they are similar to projects that have been done several times before. There are no surprises. The client has clearly specified the goal, and the project team has defined how they will reach that goal. Little change is expected. There are different approaches that are in use for such projects, and you will learn how to choose from among them the approach that best fits your project. Such projects also put the team on familiar technology grounds. The hardware, software, and telecommunications environments are familiar to the team. They have used them repeatedly and have developed a skilled and competent developer bench to handle such projects.

The limiting factor in the TPM plan-driven approaches is that they are change-intolerant. They are focused on delivering according to time and budget constraints, and rely more on compliance to plan than on delivering business value.

The plan is sacred, and conformance to it is the hallmark of the successful project team.

Because of the times we live in, the frequency of projects legitimately delivered via the TPM quadrant is diminishing rapidly. The simple projects have all been done. The projects that remain in the TPM quadrant are those which have been done many times before and well-established templates are probably in place. As TPM approaches are becoming less frequent, they are giving way to a whole new collection of approaches that are more client-focused and deliver business value rather than strict adherence to a schedule and budget.

In addition to a clearly defined goal and solution, projects that correctly fall into the TPM quadrant have several identifying characteristics as briefly identified in the following sections.

Low Complexity

Other than the fact that a low-complexity project really is simple, this characteristic will often be attributable to the fact that the project rings of familiarity. It may be a straightforward application of established business rules and therefore take advantage of existing designs and coding. Because these projects have been done many times, they will often depend on a relatively complete set of templates for their execution. To the developer, it may look like a cut-and-paste exercise. In such cases, integration and testing will be the most challenging phases of the project.

There will be situations where the project is complex but still well defined. These are rare.

Few Scope Change Requests

This is where TPM approaches get into trouble. The assumption is that the RBS and WBS are relatively complete, and there will be few, if any, scope change requests. Every scope change request requires that the following actions be taken:

- Someone needs to decide if the request warrants an analysis by a project team member.
- The project manager must assign the request to the appropriate team member.
- The assigned team member conducts the analysis and writes the Project Impact Statement.
- The project manager informs the client of the recommendations.
- The project manager and client must make a decision as to whether the change will be approved and if so how it will be accomplished.
- If the scope change request is approved, the project scope, cost, schedule, resource requirements, and client acceptance criteria are updated.

All of this takes time away from the team member's schedule commitments. Too many scope change requests and you see the effect they will have on the project schedule. Furthermore, much of the time spent planning the project before the request was made becomes non-value-added time.

So the answer to too-frequent scope change requests is some form of management monitoring and control. Those management controls can be built into every TPM, APM, xPM, and MPx approach but are different for each type of project.

Well-Understood Technology Infrastructure

A well-understood technology infrastructure is stable and will have been the foundation for many projects in the past. That means the accompanying skills and competencies to work with the technology infrastructure are well grounded in the development teams. If the technology is new or not well understood by the project team, there are alternative strategies for approaching the project. These strategies are discussed throughout Part II.

Low Risk

The requirement for TPM projects is that their environment is known and predictable. There are no surprises. All that could happen to put the project at risk has occurred in the past, and there are well-tested and well-used mitigation strategies that can be used. Experience has rooted out all of the mistakes that could be made. The client is confident that they have done a great job identifying requirements, functions, and features, and they are not likely to change. The project manager has anticipated and prepared for likely events (not including acts of nature and other unavoidable occurrences). There will be few unanticipated risks in TPM projects. That doesn't mean you can skip the risk management process in these projects. That will never be the case, regardless of the quadrant the project occupies. However, the intensity, analysis, monitoring, and mitigation strategies will be different in each quadrant.

Experienced and Skilled Project Teams

Past projects can be good training grounds for project teams. Team members will have had opportunities to learn or to enhance their skills and competencies through project assignments. These skills and competencies are a critical success factor in all projects. As the characteristics of the deliverables change, so does the profile of the team that can be most effective in developing the deliverables. TPM project teams can include less experienced team members and project managers. They can be geographically dispersed and still be effective.

Plan-driven TPM Projects

Because all of the information that could be known about the project is known and considered stable, the appropriate PMLC model would be the one that gets to the end as quickly as possible. Based on the requirements, desired functionality, and specific features, a complete project plan can be developed. It specifies all of the work that is needed to meet the requirements, the scheduling of that work, and the staff resources needed to deliver the planned work. TPM projects are clearly plan-driven projects. Their success is measured by compliance and delivery to that plan.

Knowing this, you can use a TPM approach to managing such projects. For example, you can build a complete Work Breakdown Structure (WBS) and from that estimate duration, estimate resource requirements, construct the project schedule, and write the project proposal. This is a nice neat package and seemingly quite straightforward and simple. Oh, that the life of a project manager were that simple. But it isn't, and that's where the real challenge comes in. You'll see that later as I show how to adjust this quadrant for more complex project situations discussed in Chapters 11 and 12.

Testimonial data that I have gathered from more than 10,000 project managers worldwide suggests that not more than 20 percent of all projects require some form of TPM approach. The two models discussed in the subsections that follow are special cases of the TPM approach.

Linear Project Management Life Cycle Model

I start with the simplest TPM approach — the Linear PMLC model — as a foundation for the variations presented in this section. Figure 2-3 illustrates a Linear model approach to project management.

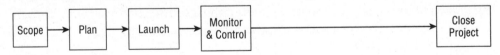

Figure 2-3: Linear PMLC model

Note that the five process groups are each executed once in the order shown in the figure. There is no looping back to repeat a process group based on learning from a later process group. This is a major weakness of all Linear PMLC models in that knowledge gained from one process group, such as Launching, cannot be used to revise and improve the deliverables from a previously completed process group, such as Scoping. There is no going back to improve deliverables. For example, suppose the project involves the development of a software application.

The Monitoring and Controlling Phase includes a systems development life cycle, which might simply consist of Design, Build, Test, and Implement. That, too, is done without going back to an earlier part of the systems development life cycle, so an improved solution discovered during Build cannot be reflected in a revised and improved Design. There is no going back.

So you might argue that going back and improving the solution is in the best interest of the client. It probably is, but if that is the possibility you are willing to accept, why not make the decision at the beginning of the project and choose a PMLC model that includes repeating process groups? And you have several to choose from.

A scope change request from the client upsets the balance in the Linear PMLC model schedule and perhaps the resource schedule as well. One or more of the team members must analyze the request and issue a Project Impact Statement. (The Project Impact Statement is discussed in Chapter 6.) This takes one or more team members away from their scheduled project work, potentially putting the project behind schedule.

You can always choose to use a Linear PMLC, but if a better choice was another PMLC, you are in for a rough ride.

WARNING   The Linear PMLC model is change intolerant.

Incremental Project Management Life Cycle Model

On the surface, the only difference between the Linear and Incremental approaches is that the deliverables in the Incremental approach are released according to a schedule. That is, a partial solution is initially released, and then at some later point in time, additional parts of the solution are added to the initial release to form a more complete solution. Subsequent releases add to the solution until the final increment releases the complete solution. The decision to use an Incremental PMLC model over the Linear PMLC model is a market-driven decision. In both models, the complete solution is known at the outset. Getting a partial solution into the market is viewed as a way to get an early entry position and therefore create some leverage for generating increased market share. I'll have more to say about the advantages and disadvantages of this model in Chapter 10.

All of this incremental release happens in a linear fashion, as shown in Figure 2-4, so that in the end, the solution is the same as if a Linear PMLC model had been followed. Ideally, the project ends with the same deliverables and at approximately the same time. There is some additional management overhead associated with the Incremental PMLC model, so those projects will finish later than the Linear PMLC model.

The sequences of Launch Increment through Next Increment decision boxes are strung out in series over time.

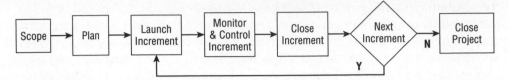

Figure 2-4: Incremental PMLC model

A more in-depth investigation would show that significant differences exist between the Incremental PMLC model and the Linear PMLC model. The following two are worth mentioning:

- The first difference has to do with scope change requests. In the Linear PMLC model, these are not expected or encouraged. As a hedge against the time they require, management reserve is often added to the end of the schedule. (See Chapter 5 for a discussion of management reserve.) Because of the structure of the Incremental PMLC model change is actually encouraged. It happens in a subtle and unsuspecting way. The initial release of a partial solution gives the client and the end user an opportunity to experiment with the partial solution in a production scenario and find areas that could be improved. That encourages change requests. A smart project manager will build schedule contingencies into the plan in the event of these scope change requests. There is more detail on this in Chapter 10.

- The second difference is related to how the full solution is decomposed into partial solutions whose development would then be planned in a sequential fashion and released in that same order. The release schedule needs to be consistent with the dependencies that exist between each partial solution. To be clear, what if a particular release depended upon the features and functions scheduled for development in a later release? There goes the integrity of the release schedule. Extensive re-planning often follows, significantly changing the release schedule.

WARNING   The Incremental PMLC model encourages unwanted scope change.

Agile Project Management Approaches

What about cases where what is needed is clearly defined but how to produce it isn't at all that obvious? These types of projects occupy a space in the landscape somewhere between traditional and extreme projects. Many managers have observed that the vast majority of their projects are a closer fit with APM approaches than either TPM or xPM approaches. Clearly TPM won't work when the solution is not known. For TPM to work, you need a detailed plan. But if you don't know how you will get what is needed, how can you generate a detailed plan? What about the extreme approach? I'm guessing that the "agilists" would argue that any one of the extreme approaches would do just fine. I agree that you could use an extreme approach and probably do quite well. Unfortunately, you would be ignoring the fact that you know what is needed. It's a given. Why not use an approach that incorporates the fact that you know what's needed?

Projects that correctly use an APM approach have several defining characteristics as briefly identified in the sections that follow.

A Critical Problem without a Known Solution

These are projects that must be done. You have no choice. Because there is no known solution, a TPM approach, which requires a complete RBS and WBS, will not work. Despite the realities, it amuses me how many project managers try to use a hammer when a screwdriver is needed (maybe some of them only have hammers). The only approaches that make sense are those that enable you to discover an acceptable solution by doing the project. These projects fly in the face of all of the traditional practices of project management. Executives are uncomfortable with this situation because all of the valid approaches have variable scope. Resources are being requested without knowing what final product will be delivered. Some of the functions and features of the solution may be known, but there is not enough business value in the known partial solution for it to be implemented.

A Previously Untapped Business Opportunity

In these types of projects, the company is losing out on a business opportunity and must find a way to take advantage of it through a new or revamped product or service offering. The question is what is that business opportunity and how can you take advantage of it? Here very little of the solution is known.

APM Projects Are Critical to the Organization

You should have guessed by now that an APM project can be very high risk. If previous attempts to solve the problem have failed, it means the problem is complex and there may not be an acceptable solution to the problem. The organization will just have to live with that reality and make the best of it. Projects to find that elusive solution might work better if they are focused on parts of the problem or if approached as process-improvement projects. See Chapter 15 for a discussion of how to design and implement a continuous process and practice improvement program.

Meaningful Client Involvement Is Essential

The solution will be discovered only if the client and the development team meaningfully collaborate in an open and honest environment. For the client this means fully participating with the project team and a willingness to learn how to be a client in an agile world. For the development team this means a willingness to learn about the client's business and how to communicate in their language. For the project manager this means preparing both the client team and the development team to work together in an open and collaborative environment. It also means that the project manager will have to share responsibility and leadership with a client manager.

My project governance model is a co-project manager model. I share project management with the client representative. This could be the client manager or a senior business analyst assigned to the business unit. I have found that this fosters ownership on the part of the client and that is important to implementation success.

APM Projects Use Small Co-located Teams

If the project requires a team of more than 30 professionals, you probably should partition the project into several smaller projects with more limited scopes. As a rule, APM approaches do not scale well. To manage a 30+ project team, partition it into smaller teams, with each of these teams being responsible for part of the scope. Set up a temporary program office to manage and coordinate the work of the smaller project teams.

Two model types fall into the APM quadrant. The first is the Iterative PMLC model. It is appropriate to use with projects for which some of the features are missing or not clearly defined. When the solution is less clearly specified — functions as well as features are missing or not clearly defined — then the best-fit choice favors using the other model type: the Adaptive PMLC model.

There are various Iterative and Adaptive approaches to managing APM projects that can be used when the goal is clearly defined but how to reach the goal — the solution — is not. Imagine a continuum of projects that range from situations where almost all of the solution is clearly and completely defined to situations where very little of the solution is clearly and completely defined. This is the range of projects that occupy the APM quadrant. As you give some thought to where your projects fall in this quadrant, consider the possibility that many, if not most, of your projects are really APM projects. If that is the case, shouldn't you also be considering using an approach to managing these projects that accommodates the goal and solution characteristics of the project rather than trying to force-fit some other approach that was designed for projects with much different characteristics?

I contend that the Adaptive and Iterative class of APM projects is continuously growing. I make it a practice at all "rubber chicken" dinner presentations to ask about the frequency with which the attendees encounter APM projects. With very small variances in their responses, they say that at least 70 percent of all their projects are APM projects, 20 percent are TPM projects, and the remaining 10 percent is split between xPM and MPx projects. Unfortunately, many project managers try to apply TPM approaches (maybe because that is all they have in their project management arsenal) to APM projects and meet with very little success. The results have ranged from mediocre success to outright failure. APM projects present a different set of challenges and need a different approach. TPM approaches simply will not work with APM projects. For years I have advocated that the approach to the project must be driven by the characteristics of the project. To reverse the order is to court disaster. I find it puzzling that we define a project as a unique experience that has never happened before and will never happen again under the same set of circumstances, but we make no assertion that the appropriate project management approach for these unique projects will also be unique. I would say that the project management approach is unique up to a point. Its uniqueness is constrained to using a set of validated and certified tools, templates, and processes. To not establish such a boundary on how you can manage a project would be chaotic. Plus the organization could never be a learning organization when it comes to project management processes and practices.

NOTE It bears repeating: We define a project as a unique experience that has never happened before and will never happen again under the same set of circumstances, but we make no assertion that the appropriate project management approach for these unique projects will also be unique. I find that truly puzzling.

As the solution moves from those that are clearly specified towards those that are not clearly specified, you move through a number of situations that require different handling. For example, suppose only some minor aspects of the solution are not known, say the background and font color for the login screens. How would you proceed? An approach that includes as much of the solution as is known at the time should work quite well. That approach would allow the client to examine, in the sense of a production prototype, what is in the solution in an attempt to discover what is not in the solution but should be. At the other end of the APM Quadrant, when very little is known about the solution, projects have higher risk than those where a larger part of the solution is known. A solution is needed, and it is important that a solution be found. How would you proceed? What is needed is an approach that is designed to learn and discover most of the solution. Somehow that approach must start with what is known and reach out to what is not known. In Chapter 11, I will share a process that I developed called Adaptive Project Framework (APF). APF is the only APM PMLC model I know of that includes work streams designed specifically to discover rather than implement aspects of the solution. I call these work streams "Probative Swim Lanes." They are defined and fully discussed in Chapter 11.

There are several approaches to APM projects. These approaches all have one thing in common — you cannot build a complete WBS without guessing. Because guessing is unacceptable in good project planning, you have to choose an approach designed to work in the absence of the complete WBS. All APM approaches are structured so that you will be able to learn and discover the missing parts of the solution. As these missing parts are discovered, they are integrated into the solution. There are two distinct PMLC models for use in APM projects: Iterative PMLC models and Adaptive PMLC models. The choice of which model to use depends somewhat on the initial degree of uncertainty you have about the solution. You'll see this in Chapter 11 as you adjust the APM PMLC models to accommodate more complex situations.

Iterative Project Management Life Cycle Model

As soon as any of the details of a solution are not clearly defined or perhaps are even missing, you should favor some form of Iterative PMLC model. For software development projects, the most popular models are Evolutionary Development Waterfall, Scrum, Rational Unified Process (RUP), and Dynamic Systems Development Method (DSDM). See the bibliography in Appendix C for references to all four models. The Iterative PMLC model is shown in Figure 2-5.

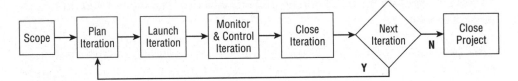

Figure 2-5: Iterative PMLC model

You might notice that this is quite similar to production prototyping. That is, a working solution is delivered from every iteration. The objective is to show the client an intermediate and perhaps incomplete solution and ask them for feedback on changes or additions they would like to see. Those changes are integrated into the prototype, and another incomplete solution is produced. This process repeats itself until either the client is satisfied and has no further changes to recommend or the budget and/or time runs out. The Iterative PMLC model differs from the Incremental PMLC model in that change is expected. In fact, change is a necessary part of this model.

Iterative PMLCs definitely fit the class of projects that provide opportunity to learn and discover. In Figure 2-5, the learning and discovering experience takes place as part of each feedback loop. With each iteration, more and more of the breadth and depth of the solution is produced. That follows from the client having an opportunity to work with the current solution and give feedback to the project team. The assumption is that the client learns and discovers more details about the solution from the current iteration. In the prototyping mode, the development team usually takes client input and presents alternatives in the next version of the prototype. As you can see, there is a strong collaborative environment in APM approaches that is usually not present and not required in TPM approaches.

Adaptive Project Management Life Cycle Model

The next step away from a complete solution is the Adaptive PMLC model. Here the missing pieces of the solution extend to functionality that is missing or not clearly defined. At the extreme end of the APM, part of the landscape would be projects where almost nothing about the solution is known. In other words, the less you know about the solution, the more likely you will choose an Adaptive PMLC model over an Iterative PMLC model. Unfortunately, all of the current Adaptive PMLC models were designed for software development projects. Because not all projects are software development projects, that left a giant gap in the PMLC model continuum. In my consulting practice, this was a serious shortcoming in the agile space and led me to develop the Adaptive Project Framework (APF) for application to any type of project. APF is an APM approach that spans the gap between TPM and xPM approaches for all types of projects. I have successfully used APF on product development, business process design, and process improvement projects. Chapter 11 discusses APF in detail.

Figure 2-6 is a graphic portrayal of how the Adaptive PMLC is structured. At the process group level, it is identical to the Iterative PMLC model. Within each process group, the differences will become obvious. Chapter 11 covers the Adaptive PMLC model in considerable detail.

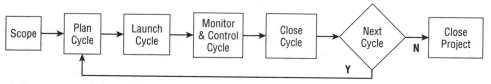

Figure 2-6: Adaptive PMLC model

WARNING   Scope is variable for all agile PMLC models.

Extreme Project Management Approach

The third model type arises in those projects whose solution and goal are not known or not clearly defined. Here you are in the world of pure R & D, new product development, and process improvement projects. These are high-risk, high-change projects. In many cases, they are also high-speed projects. Failure rates are often very high.

When so little is known about the goal and solution, you might be concerned about how to approach such projects. What tools, templates, and processes will work in these cases? Will any of them work? This can be a high-anxiety time for all but the most courageous, risk-taking, flexible, and creative project teams. Very heavy client involvement is essential. When you are venturing into the great unknown, you won't get very far unless an expert is standing at your side.

What do you do if what is needed is not clearly defined? What if it isn't defined at all? Many have tried to force-fit the traditional approach into these situations, and it flat-out doesn't work. xPM is designed to handle projects whose goal can only be fuzzily defined or really not defined at all. Building a business-to-business (B2B) web site with no further specification is an excellent example. Much like the early stages of an R & D project, building the B2B web site starts out with a guess, or maybe several guesses. As the project commences, the client reflects upon the alternatives chosen and gives some direction to the development team. This process repeats itself. Either the partial solution converges on a satisfactory solution, or it is killed along the way. In most cases, there is no fixed budget or timeline. Obviously, the client wants it completed ASAP for as little as possible. Furthermore, the lack of a clear goal and solution exposes the project to a lot of change. Unfortunately, the nature of this project does not lend itself to fixed time and cost constraints.

Chapter 12 defines the xPM project and provides a detailed view of the phases that constitute the xPM PMLC model.

The xPM Project Is a Research and Development Project

The goal of an R & D project may be little more than a guess at a desired end state. Whether it is achievable and to what specificity are questions to be answered by doing the project. In this type of xPM project, you are trying to establish some future state through some enabling solution. Because you don't know what the final solution will be, you cannot possibly know what the goal will be. The hope is that the goal can be achieved with a solution and that the two together deliver acceptable business value.

The xPM Project Is Very High Risk

Any journey into the great unknown is fraught with risk. In the case of an xPM project, it is the risk of project failure and that is very high. Even if the goal is achieved, the cost of the solution may be prohibitive. The direction chosen to find the solution may be the wrong direction entirely and can only result in failure. If the project management process can detect that early, it will save money and time.

Failure is difficult to define in an xPM project. For example, the project may not solve the original problem, but it may deliver a product that has uses elsewhere. The 3M Post-It Note Project is one such example. Nearly 7 years after the project to develop an adhesive with certain temporary sticking properties failed (that was an xPM project), an engineer discovered an application that resulted in the Post-It Note product (that was an MPx project).

xPM extends to the remotest boundaries of the project landscape. xPM projects are those projects whose goal and solution cannot be clearly defined. For example, R & D projects are xPM projects. What little planning is done is done just in time, and the project proceeds through several phases until it converges on an acceptable goal and solution. Clearly the PMLC for an xPM project requires maximum flexibility for the project team, in contrast to the PMLC for a TPM project, which requires adherence to a defined process. If instead, there isn't any prospect of goal and solution convergence, the client may pull the plug and cancel the project at any time and save the remaining resources for alternative approaches.

If goal clarity is not possible at the beginning of the project, the situation is much like a pure R & D project. Now how would you proceed? In this case, you use an approach that clarifies the goal and contributes to the solution at the same time. The approach must embrace a number of concurrent Probative Swim Lanes. Concurrent Probative Swim Lanes might be the most likely ones that can accomplish goal clarification and the solution set at the same time. Depending on time, budget, and staff resources, these probes might be pursued sequentially or concurrently. Alternatively, the probes might eliminate and narrow the domain of feasible goal/solution pairs. Clearly, xPM projects are an entirely different class of projects and require a different approach to be successful.

The goal is often not much more than a guess at a desired end state with the hope that a solution to achieve it can be found. In most cases, some modified version of the goal statement is achieved. In other words, the goal and the solution converge on something that hopefully has business value. Chapter 12 provides much more detail.

In addition to a goal and solution where neither one are clearly defined, projects that correctly fall into xPM have several identifying characteristics as briefly identified in the sections that follow.

The Extreme Model

The Extreme PMLC model is shown in Figure 2-7. By its very nature, xPM is unstructured. It is designed to handle projects with "fuzzy goals" or goals that cannot be defined because of the exploratory nature of the extreme project. The theme here is that the learning and discovery take place between the client and the development team in each phase, thus moving the project forward. Note that the major difference between APM and xPM PMLC models is the use of the Scope Process Group. In an APM project, scope is done once at the beginning of the project. That flows mostly from the fact that the goal is clearly defined. In the xPM project, scope is adjusted at each phase. That follows from the fact that the goal can change.

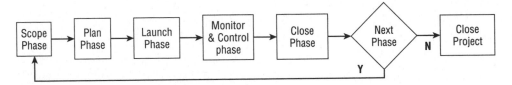

Figure 2-7: Extreme PMLC model

Similar to APM PMLC models, the Extreme PMLC model is iterative. It iterates in an unspecified number of short phases (1- to 4-week phase lengths are typical) in search of the solution (and the goal). It may find an acceptable solution, or it may be cancelled before any solution is reached. It is distinguished from APM in that the goal is unknown, or, at most, someone has a vague but unspecified notion of what the goal consists of. Such a client might say, "I'll know it when I see it." That isn't a new revelation to experienced project managers — they have heard this many times before. Nevertheless, it is their job to find the solution (with the client's help, of course).

xPM is further distinguished from APM in that xPM requires the client to be more involved within and between phases. In many xPM projects, the client takes a leadership position instead of the collaborative position they took in APM projects. Drug research provides a good example. Suppose, for example, that the goal is to find a natural food additive that will eliminate the common cold. This is a wide-open project. Constraining the project to a fixed budget or fixed timeline makes no sense whatsoever. More than likely, the project team will begin by choosing some investigative direction or directions and hope that intermediate findings and results will accomplish the following two things:

- The just-finished phase will point to a more informed and productive direction for the next and future phases. In other words, xPM includes learning and discovery experiences just as APM does.

- Most important of all is that the funding agent will see this learning and discovery as potentially rewarding and will decide to continue the funding support.

There is no constraining scope triangle in xPM as there is in TPM and APM projects. Recall that TPM and APM projects have time and funding constraints that were meaningful. "Put a man on the moon and return him safely by the end of the decade" is pretty specific. It has a built-in stopping rule. When the money or the time runs out, the project is over. xPM does have stopping rules, but they are very different. An xPM project stops when one of the following occurs:

- The project is over when a solution and the goal it supports are found and they both make business sense. Success!

- The project is over when the sponsor is not willing to continue the funding. The sponsor might withdraw the funding because the project is not making any meaningful progress or is not converging on an acceptable solution. In other words, the project is killed. Failure! But all is not over. It is common to restart such projects but to search for a solution in a different direction.

WARNING Extreme PMLC models may all be looking for solutions in all the wrong places.

Emertxe Project Management Life Cycle Model

The solution is known, but the goal is not. Don't be tempted to dismiss this as the ranting of professional service firms who have the answer to your problem. They are out there, and you probably know who they are. All you have to do is state your problem, and they will come to your rescue armed with their solution! That is not where I am going with this discussion.

MPx projects are a type of R & D project but in reverse. When you think of an R & D project, you think of some desired end state and the project has to figure out if and how that end state might be reached. In so doing, it might be necessary to modify the end state. So for the MPx project, you reverse the R & D situation. You have some type of solution, but you have not yet discovered an application for that solution (unknown goal). You hope to find an application that can be achieved through some modification of the solution. You are successful if the application has business value.

Figure 2-7 works for both the xPM and MPx project.

Note here that each phase is a complete project in its own right. Scoping starts each phase, and the decision to begin another phase ends the current phase. In an MPx project, phase and project are basically identical.

WARNING Emertxe PMLC models will usually find a goal, but most often that goal will not deliver acceptable business value. Don't be lured in by the technology and lose sight of making good business decisions.

These approaches are for MPx projects whose solution is completely and clearly defined but whose goal is not. This sounds like nonsense, but actually it isn't. (Just trust me for now — I'll return to this approach in Chapter 12.) I find it easiest to think of these projects as a backwards version of an extreme project, hence the name "Emertxe" (pronounced a-mert-see). The solution or a variant of it is used to help converge on a goal that it can support and that hopefully delivers acceptable business value. So rather than looking for a solution as in the xPM project, you are looking for a goal. The PMLCs for both xPM and MPx projects have a lot in common, so they are discussed together in Chapter 12.

You have the solution; now all you need is to find the problem it solves. This is the stuff that academic articles are often made of, but that's okay. It's a type of R & D project but in reverse. Post your solution and hope somebody responds with a problem that fits it. It has happened. Take the 3M Post-It Note saga, for example. The product sat on the shelf for several years before someone stumbled onto an application. The rest is history. Major drug research firms encounter these projects often.

In addition to a goal that is not clearly defined and solution that is clearly defined, projects that correctly fall into the MPx category have several identifying characteristics as briefly identified in the sections that follow.

A New Technology without a Known Application

I'm reminded of the Radio Frequency Identification (RFID) technology for reading coded information embedded in an object as it moved down a conveyor belt and routing the object to a destination based on the encoded information found. When RFID was first announced, several warehouse applications came to mind. One of the largest retailers in the world commissioned a project team to find applications for RFID in their logistics and supply chain management systems. The technology was only about 70 percent accurate at the time, and the team concluded that it would have good business value if only the accuracy could be significantly improved. That has since happened, and RFID is now commonly used in warehousing and distribution operations.

A Solution out Looking for a Problem to Solve

Commercial off-the-shelf application software provides several examples of these situations. For example, say a new human resource management system (HRMS) has just been introduced to the commercial software market by a major software manufacturer. Your project is to evaluate it for possible fit in the new HRMS design that has just been approved by your senior management team. Among all MPx projects, this example is the simplest case. You already know the application area. What you need to find out is the degree of fit and business value. At the other extreme would be to have something whose application is not known. A juice taken from the root of some strange Amazon tree would be an example of a more complex situation. The project is to find an application for the juice that has sufficient business value.

Recap of PMLC Models

The five PMLC models bear a closer look and comparison. If you have been counting, you expected to see six PMLC models. Because the xPM PMLC and MPx PMLC models are identical, there are really only five distinct PMLC models. Figure 2-8 gives you that view.

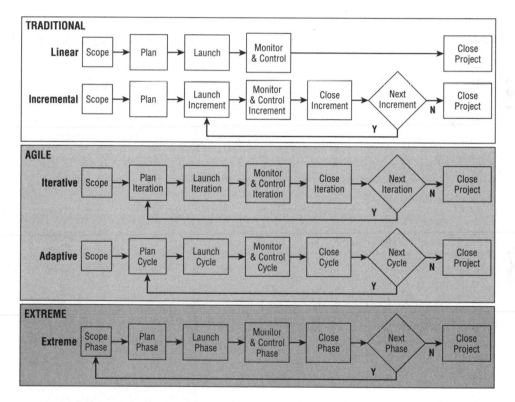

Figure 2-8: The five PMLC models

There is a very simple and intuitive pattern across the life cycle when viewed at the process group level. A note on terminology before I proceed. In the APM and xPM approaches, I use the terms *iteration*, *cycle*, and *phase* to distinguish between the Iterative, Adaptive, and Extreme model types, respectively. I'll need that later on in the discussion to clarify what I am referring to. To reinforce your understanding of the PMLC models, I want to point out their similarities and differences.

Similarities between the PMLC Models

Their similarities are as follows:

- All five process groups are used in each PMLC model.
- Each PMLC model begins with a Scope Process Group.
- Each PMLC model ends with a Close Process Group.

Differences between the PMLC Models

Their differences are evident when viewed from the degree of solution uncertainty, as follows:

- The models form a natural ordering (Linear, Incremental, Iterative, Adaptive, Extreme) by degree of solution uncertainty.
- The processes that form repetitive groups recognize the effect of increasing uncertainty as you traverse the natural ordering. Those groups move more towards the beginning of the life cycle as uncertainty increases.
- Complete project planning is replaced by just-in-time project planning as the degree of uncertainty increases.
- Risk management becomes more significant as the degree of solution uncertainty increases.
- The need for meaningful client involvement increases as the degree of solution uncertainty increases.

Choosing the Best-Fit PMLC Model

Choosing and adapting the best-fit PMLC model is a subjective decision based on several variables. Figure 2-9 is a display of the decision process.

Part II discusses the details further. It is sufficient at this point to be aware of the fact that having chosen a specific project approach you are not yet prepared to begin the project. Specific internal and external factors will have to be taken into account and final adjustments to that approach made. These are discussed throughout Part II.

Although you may have easily arrived at a best-fit approach and best-fit PMLC model based on the confidence you have with the RBS and the degree of completeness of the WBS, there is more work to be done before you can proceed with the project. First you have to assess the impact, if any, of a number of other factors. These are discussed below. Second, you have to make the necessary adjustments to the chosen PMLC model to account for that impact. These are discussed in Chapters 10, 11, and 12. The factors that I'm talking about here are those that might affect, and even change, your choice of the best-fit PMLC model. For example, if the PMLC model requires meaningful client involvement, and you have never been able to get that, what would you do? You'll examine the options in the chapters of Part II. For now I want to take a look at those other factors and how they might impact the PMLC model.

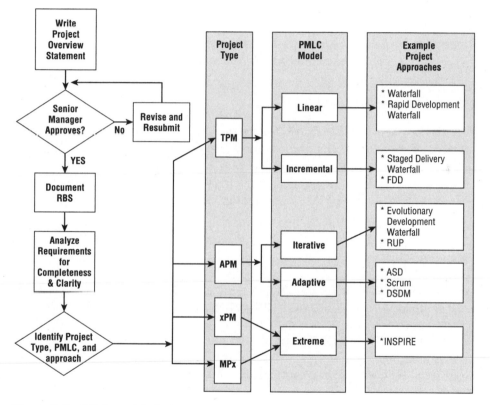

Figure 2-9: PMLC model choice process

Total Cost

As the total cost of the project increases, so does its business value and so does its risk. Whatever PMLC model you have chosen, you might want to place more emphasis on the risk management plan than is called for in the chosen model. If one of the team members isn't already responsible for managing risk, appoint someone. Losses are positively correlated with the total cost, so you should be able to justify spending more on your mitigation efforts than you would for a project of lesser cost.

Duration

A longer duration project brings with it a higher likelihood of change, staff turnover, and project priority adjustments. None of these are for the good of the project. Pay more attention to your scope change management plan and the Scope Bank. Recall that the Scope Bank contains all of the suggested ideas for change that have not been acted upon and the total labor time available for their integration into the solution. Make sure the client understands the implications of the Scope Bank and how to manage their own scope change requests. Staff turnover can be very problematic. Put more emphasis on the mitigation plans for dealing with staff turnover. Project priority changes are beyond your control. The only thing you control is the deliverables schedule. That needs to be on an aggressive schedule to the extent possible.

Market Stability

Any venture into a volatile market is going to be risky. You could postpone the project until the market stabilizes, or you could go forward but with some caution. One way to protect the project would be to implement deliverables incrementally. A timebox comprising shorter increments than originally planned might make sense, too. As each increment is implemented, revisit the decision to continue or postpone the project.

Technology

We all know that technology is changing at an increasing rate. It is not only difficult to keep up with it, but it is difficult to leverage it to your best advantage. If the current technology works, stick with it. If the new technology will leverage you in the market, you might want to wait but make sure you can integrate it when it is available. Don't forget that the competition will be doing the same, so rapid response is to your advantage.

Business Climate

The more volatile the business climate, the shorter the total project duration should be. For APM projects, the cycle timeboxes could also be shorter than typically planned. Partial solution releases will have a higher priority than they would in business climates that are more stable.

Number of Departments Affected

As the number of departments that affect or are affected by the project increases, the dynamics of the project change. That change begins with requirements gathering. The needs of several departments will have to be taken into account. Here are three possible outcomes you need to consider:

- The first possible outcome is scope creep during the project scoping process. Each department will have its list of "must haves" and "wouldn't it be nice to haves." Not all of these will be compatible across departments, but one thing is for certain: these differences will cause scope creep. You may have to think about versioning the project — that is, decomposing it into several versions or releases.

- The second possible outcome is a higher incidence of "needs contention," which means the needs from two or more departments may contradict one another. You will have to resolve the conflicts as part of validating requirements.

- The third possible outcome impacts the PMLC Model. As the project becomes more of an enterprise-wide project, the likelihood of the project becoming a multiple team project increases. There are several implications if this should occur. Chapter 17 takes up this important topic.

Organizational Environment

If your company announces reorganizations and changes in senior-management responsibilities quite frequently (such as once a week), you have a problem. The single most-frequent reason for project failures as reported in the past several Standish Group surveys is lack of executive level support. That includes loss of support resulting from company reorganization. For example, say a sponsor who was very enthusiastic about your project, and a strong and visible champion for you, has been replaced. Does your new sponsor feel the same? If so, you dodged a bullet. If not, you have a very serious problem to contend with, and you will need to amend the risk list and provide suggested mitigation strategies.

Team Skills and Competencies

The types of skilled professionals you ask for in your plan are often not what you eventually get. It's almost like availability is treated as a skill! One of the principles I follow in proposing resource requirements is to ask for the "B" player and build my plan on the assumption that that is what I will get. Requesting the "A" player can only lead to disappointment when a "B" or even a "C" player shows up. In general, TPM projects can handle a team of "B" players, and they don't even have to be co-located. APM projects are different. APM projects use two different PMLCs. When you are missing some of the features of the solution, "B" players, with supervision, will often suffice. When you are missing some of the functions of the solution, you would prefer "A" players, but you may be able to work with a few "B" players under supervision. The less you know about the solution, the more you are going to have to staff your project with "A" players or at least with team members who can work independent of supervision.

Putting It All Together

The definition of the project landscape is mine and mine alone. I like simplicity and intuitiveness, and my definition provides exactly that. It is also a definition that encompasses every project that ever existed and ever will exist, so there is no reason to ever change it! That means it can be used as a foundation for all further discussion about PMLC models. There is a certain academic soundness and theoretical base to that approach. In fact, it is the beginnings of a project management discipline. At the same time, the definition has a very simple and practical application. That base will be the foundation on which all best-fit project management approach decisions can be made. As you will see in the chapters that follow, I will be able to exploit that base from both a conceptual and applications perspective.

Using the project landscape as the foundation for managing projects, I have defined five PMLC models at the Process Group level of detail. The definitions give a clear and intuitive picture of how project management approaches can vary as the degree of uncertainty changes. Within each PMLC model, there will be a number of specific instantiations of the model. You explore each of these in Chapters 10, 11, and 12.

Discussion Questions

1. Consider a project management methodology that specifies only the six questions stated in the "Understanding the Fundamentals of Project Management" section of this chapter. All that is required of the project manager and client is to provide answers to those six questions. Could this approach be made to work? If yes, how? If not, why not?

2. Compare and contrast the PMI and business value definitions of project management. Include a list of advantages and disadvantages of each.

3. For each of the five PMLC models, identify the specific points where client involvement is needed. What specific actions would you take as project manager to ensure that involvement?

4. Where in each of the five PMLC models would you expect the most failures occur? Defend your answer.

5. Where in each of the five PMLC models would you expect the greatest risk? What mitigation strategies would you consider? Defend your choices.

6. For each of the five PMLC models, identify a project from your experience that would seem to have been a good fit. Would using that PMLC for that project have improved the outcome? Why?

CASE STUDY – PIZZA DELIVERED QUICKLY (PDQ)

7. Referring to the PDQ case study, what PMLC model would you use for each of the six subsystems (Order Entry, Order Submit, Logistics, Routing, Inventory Management, and Pizza Factory Locator)? Defend your choices.

CHAPTER 3

Understanding the Project Management Process Groups

The PMI PMBOK Process Groups are not a project management life cycle;
they are the building blocks of every project management life cycle.
—Robert K. Wysocki, Ph.D. President, EII Publications

CHAPTER LEARNING OBJECTIVES

After reading this chapter, you will be able to:

- **Define the five Process Groups**
- **Define the nine Knowledge Areas**
- **Explain the relationship between the five Process Groups and nine Knowledge Areas**

All of the project management life cycles (PMLCs) presented in Part II are constructed from the five Process Groups introduced in this chapter. The five Process Groups were originally defined by the Project Management Institute (PMI) in their standards guidelines called the Project Management Body of Knowledge (PMBOK). The PMBOK Guide has become the de facto standard for the practice of project management worldwide. This book is compatible with the five Process Groups and the related nine Knowledge Areas of the PMBOK Guide. It is important that you understand the traditional processes and Knowledge Areas in detail because they are the basis of the project management models that you will learn about in Part II. This book extends its treatment beyond those traditional practices into the contemporary world of project management.

Defining the Five Process Groups

In addition to answering the six questions posed in Chapter 2 that a valid project management methodology must answer, whatever project management life cycle model that is used must contain all of the following Process Groups:

- Scoping Process Group (which PMI calls the Initiating Process Group)
- Planning Process Group
- Launching Process Group (which PMI calls the Executing Process Group)
- Monitoring and Controlling Process Group
- Closing Process Group

These five Process Groups are the building blocks of every PMLC. In the simplest of cases, the Process Groups will each be completed once and in the sequence listed here. In more complex situations, some or all of them might be repeated a number of times.

These five Process Groups are defined in the PMBOK Guide. What follows is my adaptation of these Process Groups for use in this book and to prepare you to adapt them for your own use. I have added other processes to conform to the PMLC requirements in Part II. None of these adaptations contradict any of the principles underlying the PMBOK Guide.

The Scoping Process Group

The PMBOK Guide calls this the Initiating Process Group. However, the term *initiating* can be confusing if you are new to project management. I find the term *scoping* to be clearer. This Process Group includes all processes related to answering two questions: "What business situation is being addressed?" and "What do you need to do?" It does not include any processes related to doing any project work. That project work is defined in the Planning Process Group to be done later in the project life cycle. The Scoping Process Group also includes establishing the business success criteria that will be the metrics used to answer the question "How will you know you did it?"

The Scoping Process Group includes the following processes:

- Recruiting the project manager
- Eliciting the true needs of the client
- Documenting the client's needs
- Negotiating with the client about how those needs will be met
- Writing a one-page description of the project
- Gaining senior management approval to plan the project

As you can see, the successful completion of the Scoping Process Group is to gain the approval of senior management to move to the next phase of the project. Be advised, however, that not all projects are approved to go to the Planning Phase. In every PMLC, the next phase will be defined by the Planning Process Group. For some models that planning will encompass the entire project, and for others it will encompass only the first cycle or iteration of the project. This direct linkage of the Scoping and Planning Process Groups is present in every PMLC you will study in Part II.

The Planning Process Group

The Planning Process Group includes all processes related to answering two questions: "What will you do?" and "How will you do it?" These processes are as follows:

- Defining all of the work of the project
- Estimating how long it will take to complete the work
- Estimating the resources required to complete the work
- Estimating the total cost of the work
- Sequencing the work
- Building the initial project schedule
- Analyzing and adjusting the project schedule
- Writing a risk management plan
- Documenting the project plan
- Gaining senior management approval to launch the project

Each of the processes in the Planning Process Group can be done in a number of ways. The way that they are done may be a function of the PMLC model being used or any of several other factors. I'll offer my experiences in executing each process and in many cases offer several alternative ways of conducting the process. Choosing which to use in a given situation is where organized common sense again takes its stance.

The Launching Process Group

The PMBOK Guide calls this the Executing Process Group. It is that and more. The Launching Process Group includes all processes related to recruiting and organizing the team and establishing the team operating rules. These processes are preparatory to executing the project. The Launching Process Group also includes all of the processes related to getting the project work started. These would be the executing processes.

The Launching Process Group includes the following processes:

- Recruiting the project team
- Writing a project description document
- Establishing team operating rules
- Establishing the scope change management process
- Managing team communications
- Finalizing the project schedule
- Writing work packages

All of these processes relate more to the art of project management than to the science of project management. During the execution of this Process Group, the entire team may be coming together for the first time. There will be client members and your delivery team members present. Perhaps they are mostly strangers to one another. At this point, they are nothing more than a group. They are not yet a team but must become one in very short order. Thinking back over my early experiences as a project manager when meeting my team members for the first time, I think of my task to create a team as something akin to herding cats. You can't herd cats. There will be confusion and anxiety as they stare across the table at each other wondering why they are there, what they will be doing on the project, and what is happening on the project they should be working on in their home department. Being fully aware of this, the project manager will conduct that first team meeting with care, giving team members an opportunity to introduce themselves to each other and explain what they bring to the project.

The Monitoring and Controlling Process Group

The Monitoring and Controlling Process Group includes all processes related to answering the question "How will you know you did it?" The Monitoring and Controlling Process Group includes all processes related to the ongoing work of the project. These processes are as follows:

- Establishing the project performance and reporting system
- Monitoring project performance
- Monitoring risk
- Reporting project status
- Processing scope change requests
- Discovering and solving problems

Here is where the real work of the project takes place. It is a Process Group that consists of both the art and science of project management. It occupies the project manager with activities internal to the project team itself (mostly science but a dose of art as well) and with activities external to the project team and dealing with the client, the sponsor, and your senior management (mostly art but a dose of science as well). As problems and change requests arise, the strength of your relationship with your client will in large measure contribute to the success or failure of the project.

The Closing Process Group

The Closing Process Group includes all processes related to the completion of the project, including answers to the question "How well did you do?" These processes are as follows:

- Gaining client approval of having met project requirements
- Planning and installing deliverables
- Writing the final project report
- Conducting the post-implementation audit

The end is finally coming into sight. The client is satisfied that you have met the acceptance criteria. It's time to install the deliverables and complete the administrative closedown of the project.

Defining the Nine Knowledge Areas

The nine Knowledge Areas are part of the PMBOK and are all present in every project management life cycle. They define the processes within each Process Group and often are part of more than one Process Group. This section covers all nine Knowledge Areas. The names of the Knowledge Areas used here are the same as the names used by PMI.

Integration Management

This Knowledge Area addresses the glue that links all of the deliverables from the Process Groups into a unified whole. This linkage begins with the project description document and extends to the project plan and its execution, including monitoring progress against the project plan and the integration of changes, and finally through to project closure.

Scope Management

The major focus of the Scope Management Knowledge Area is the identification and documentation of client requirements. Many ways exist to approach requirements gathering and documentation. The choice of which approach or approaches to use depends on several factors. Following requirements gathering and documentation, you choose the best-fit project management life cycle and develop the Work Breakdown Structure (WBS) that defines the work to be done to deliver those requirements. That prepares the team and the client with the information they need to estimate time, cost, and resource requirements. The Scope Management Knowledge Area overlaps the Scoping and the Planning Process Groups.

Time Management

Time management includes both a planning component and a control component. The planning component provides time estimates for both the duration of a project task (that is, how long will it take in terms of clock time to complete the task) and the actual effort or labor time required to complete the task. The duration is used to estimate the total time needed to complete the project. The labor time is used to estimate the total labor cost of the project. The control component is part of the Monitoring and Controlling Process Group and involves comparing estimated times to actual times as well as managing the schedule and cost variances.

Cost Management

Cost management includes both a planning component and a control component. The planning component includes building the project budget and mapping those costs into the project schedule. This provides a means of controlling the consumption of budget dollars across time. Variance reports and earned value reports are used in the Monitoring and Controlling Process Group.

Quality Management

Good quality management is probably one of the Knowledge Areas that gets a rather casual treatment by the project manager and the team. A good quality management program contains the following three processes:

- Quality planning process
- Quality assurance process
- Quality control process

The focus on quality is usually on the product or deliverable that is produced. If it meets specific physical and performance characteristics, it will be validated as fit for use and can be released to the client. Validation that a product is fit for use is the result of the product passing certain tests at various points in the product development life cycle. Passing these tests allows the product to pass to the next stage of development. Failure to pass a test leads to reworking the product until it passes or to outright rejection if reworking the product to remove whatever defects were discovered does not make good business sense.

Quality in this context means the product meets the following criteria:

- It's fit for use.
- It meets all client requirements.
- It delivers on time, within budget, and according to specification.

Note that this says nothing about exceeding requirements. Many project managers are ingrained with the idea that they have to "delight the client." For example, if you promised product delivery on Friday, you try to get the product to the client on Thursday. Or if you estimated that the product would cost $2.00, you try to get the cost down to $1.95. These are all well and good and are part of excellent client service, but they have nothing to do with quality. Quality refers to meeting agreed requirements, not exceeding them. Your quality management program should focus on meeting product and process requirements.

Quality Planning Process

There will be standards that the product and the process will have to meet. These may be external to the organization (federal or agency quality requirements) or internal (company policies and guidelines). In addition, there will be project-specific requirements that must be met. Quality planning must integrate all of these into a cohesive program.

Quality Assurance Process

Quality assurance includes activities that ensure compliance to the plan. The specific tools, templates, and processes that you use to do this are discussed in Chapter 15.

Quality Control Process

This process involves the actual monitoring of the project using the quality tools, templates, and processes discussed in Chapter 15 as well as other project management monitoring and reporting tools.

Human Resource Management

Some would suggest that the job of the project manager is to manage the work of the project. They would add that it is not the job of the project manager to manage the members of the team. Management of the team members is the province of their line manager. In a utopian world, this might be acceptable management practice, but in the contemporary project world, the situation is quite different. More than likely your request for a certain profile of skills and experiences among your team members will not be met by those who are assigned to work on your project. Skill shortages, unavailability of a specifically skilled person, and other factors will result in a less-than-adequate team. What you get is what you get, and you will have to make the best of it. Therefore, I don't think it is that simple, and both the line manager and the project manager share the people management responsibilities. Because the skills and/or competency of the team you have to work with may not be ideal, staff development will be one area where you and the line manager share responsibility. The line manager is responsible for assigning people to projects in accordance with each person's skill and competency profile as well as his or her career and professional development plans. Once a person is assigned to a project, it is then the project manager's responsibility to make assignments in accordance with the person's skill and competency profile and their professional development plans. Obviously this will be a collaborative effort between you and the line manager.

Having motivated team members is in the best interest of the project, the project manager, and the organization. It is my opinion that when you align people's interests and professional development needs to their project assignments, you gain a stronger commitment from the team members. Again, the line manager and the project manager share the responsibility for making this happen.

Not everyone can be motivated. To assume otherwise is risky. In fact, in most cases all that the manager can do is create an environment in which the subordinate might be motivated and then hope that he or she is. It's really like farming. All the farmer can do is pick the crop to plant, the acreage to plant it on, and the fertilizer to use, and then hope that nature supplies the right amounts of rain, wind, and sunshine. The same scenario applies to the project manager. He or she must create a working environment that is conducive to and encourages the development of the team members, leaving it up to them to respond positively.

Fortunately, you do have some information on what professional staffs perceive as *motivators* and *hygiene factors* on the job. Motivators are behaviors or situations that have a positive impact on the worker — they motivate the worker to better performance. Hygiene factors, on the other hand, are things that, by their absence, have a negative impact on performance, but don't necessarily motivate the worker if they are present. To put it another way, workers have certain expectations, and to not fulfill them is to demotivate them. These are hygiene factors. For example, workers expect a reasonable vacation policy; to not have one acts as a demotivator. Conversely, having a good vacation policy does not necessarily motivate the worker. The following list of motivators was created as a result of a 1959 survey of professionals by Frederick Herzberg,[1] a professor known for his research in motivational theory. Although the survey was conducted 50 years ago, it has become a classic study and still applies today.

Motivators

Herzberg identified the following motivators:

- Achievement
- Recognition
- Advancement and growth
- Responsibility
- Work itself

Hygiene Factors

Herzberg identified the following hygiene factors:

- Company policy
- Administrative practices
- Working conditions
- Technical supervision
- Interpersonal relations
- Job security
- Salary

Note that motivators are related to the job, specifically to its intrinsic characteristics, whereas hygiene factors are related to the environment in which the job is performed. The good news is that the manager has some amount of control over the motivators relating to the job. The bad news is that the hygiene factors, being environmental, are usually beyond the control of the project manager. As a project manager, you can bring hygiene factors to the attention of your senior management, but you're otherwise powerless to change them.

Motivating Factors

J. Daniel Couger, a professor of Computer Science at the University of Colorado, conducted a similar survey in 1988. Here the respondents were analysts and

---

[1]Both Herzberg and Daniel Couger studies are reported in "Another Look at Motivating Data Processing Professionals" by Ramon A. Mata Toledo and Elizabeth A. Unger. Department of Computer Science, Kansas State University, Manhattan, KS: p. 4, 1985.

programmers. The responses were grouped by areas that the respondents considered motivators and areas that they considered demotivators. The following is a combined list of these areas, ordered from highest motivator to lowest motivator:

- The work itself
- Opportunity for achievement
- Opportunity for advancement
- Pay and benefits
- Recognition
- Increased responsibility
- Technical supervision
- Interpersonal relations
- Job security
- Working conditions
- Company policy

The motivators that are high on the list tend to be intrinsic to the job, such as providing opportunities for advancement and recognition, whereas the demotivators, which are lower on the list, tend to be environmental factors such as working conditions (for example, parking areas) and company policy (for example, sick leave and vacation time).

Several of the motivators are directly controlled or influenced by actions and behaviors of the project manager regarding the work that the team member will be asked to do. They are as follows.

Challenge

Professionals respond to a challenge. In general, if you tell a professional that something cannot be done, his or her creative juices begin to flow. Some may even view such a statement as an insult to their intelligence and creativity. The result is a solution. Professionals dread nothing more than practicing skills, long since mastered, over and over again. Boredom sets in quickly and can lead to daydreaming and lack of attention to detail, which results in errors. Challenging the professional does not mean that every moment of every day should be spent solving previously unsolved problems. Usually, an hour or two on a new and challenging task per day is sufficient to keep a professional motivated throughout the day.

Recognition

Professionals want to know that they are progressing toward a professional goal. Publicly and personally recognizing achievements and following with additional challenges tells the professional that his or her contribution is valued. Recognition, therefore, does not necessarily mean dollars, promotions, or titles.

Job Design

Because the job itself is such an important part of motivation, take a look at job design for just a moment. The following five dimensions define a job.

Skill Variety

Jobs that do not offer much task variety or the opportunity to learn and practice new skills become boring for most people. In designing jobs, it is important to consider building in some task variety. This variety, at the very least, can provide a diversion from what otherwise would be a tedious and boring workday. It can also provide a break during which the person can learn a new skill. With a little bit of forethought, the project manager can find opportunities for cross-training by introducing some task variety for new skills development.

WARNING You, as the project manager, must consider the risk involved in such actions. The person may not rise to the challenge of the new task or might not have the native ability to master the skills needed to perform the new task.

Task Identity

People need to know what they are working on. This idea is especially true for contracted team members. The project manager should help them understand their work in relation to the entire project. Knowing that their task is on the critical path will affect their attitude and the quality of their work.

Task Significance

In assessing a task's significance, workers ask themselves questions such as these: Does it make any difference if I am successful? If I am late, will anybody notice? Just how important is my work to the overall success of the project? Am I just doing busywork to pass the time? Team members need to know whether their effort and success make any difference to the success of the project.

Autonomy

Professionals want to know what is expected from them — what are the deliverables? They don't want to hear every detail of how they will accomplish their work. That is blatant micro-management and must be avoided at all costs. It's okay to tell team members what they need to deliver, but not how they should go about delivering it. They want to make that decision themselves. Professionals tend to be rugged individualists. They want to exercise their creativity. They want freedom, independence, and discretion in scheduling their work and determining the procedures they will follow to carry it out.

Feedback

Good, bad, or indifferent, professionals want to know how effective they are in their work. Paying attention to what a team member is doing is motivating in itself. Having something good to say is even better. When a person's performance is below expectations, tell them. If you can convince them that they own the problem, ask them for an action plan to correct their marginal performance. Then help them do it.

Communications Management

At the heart of many of the top ten reasons why projects fail is poor communications. As many as 70 percent of the IS/IT project failures can be traced back to poor communications. It is not difficult to plan an effective communications management process, but it seems to be very difficult to execute that plan. A good communications management process will have provisions in the process that answer the following questions:

- Who are the project stakeholders?
- What do they need to know about the project?
- How should their needs be met?

Who Are the Project Stakeholders?

Any person or group that has a vested interest in the project is a stakeholder. Those who are required to provide some input to the project affect the project and are therefore stakeholders. They may not be willing stakeholders, but they are stakeholders nevertheless. Those who are affected by the project are stakeholders. Often they are the same group requesting the project, in which case they will be willing stakeholders. There will also be unwilling stakeholders who are affected by the project but had little or no say in how the project actually delivered against stated requirements. The project manager needs to be aware of all these stakeholder groups and communicate appropriately to them.

What Do They Need to Know about the Project?

There will be a range of concerns and questions coming from every stakeholder group. Some of the more commonly occurring are as follows:

- What input will I be required to provide the project team?
- How can I make my needs known?
- When will the project be done?

- How will it affect me?
- Will I be replaced?
- How will I learn how to use the deliverables?

Your communications management plan will be effective only if it accounts for each group and their individual needs.

How Should Their Needs Be Met?

This depends on the purpose of the communication. If it's to inform, there will be many alternatives to choose from. If it's to get feedback, you have fewer alternatives from which to choose. Chapter 6 provides all of the details on building an effective communications management plan.

Risk Management

In project management, a risk is some future event that happens with some probability and results in a change, either positive or negative, to the project. For the most part, risk is associated with loss, at least in the traditional sense. But there might be a gain if the event happens. For example, suppose you know that a software vendor is working on a language translator, and if it is available by a certain date, you will be able to use it to save programming time.

More commonly, though, a risk event is associated with a loss of some type. The result might be a cost increase, a schedule slippage, or some other catastrophic change. The cost of loss can be estimated. The estimate is the mathematical product of the probability that the event will occur and the severity of the loss if it does. This estimate will force the project manager to make a choice about what to do, if anything, to mitigate the risk and reduce the loss that will occur.

This estimate is the basis of a series of choices that the project manager has to make. First of all, should any action be taken? If the cost of the action exceeds the estimated loss, no action should be taken. Simply hope that the event doesn't occur. The second choice deals with the action to be taken. If action is called for, what form should it take? Some actions may simply reduce the probability that the event will occur. Other actions will reduce the loss that results from the occurrence of the event. It is usually not possible to reduce either the probability or the loss to zero. Whatever actions are taken will only tend to reduce the loss in the final analysis.

The business decision is to assess how the expected loss compares to the cost of defraying all or some of the loss and then taking the appropriate action. With project management, the risks that need to be managed are those that will hurt the project itself. Although the project may affect the total business, the total business isn't the domain of the project manager.

NOTE As I alluded to earlier, newer risk theories deal with entrepreneurial risk for which there is not only a probability of loss, but also a possibility of gain. This is common in businesses where capital is put at risk in order to fund a new business venture. For the most part, this book deals with risk in the traditional sense, where risk is the possibility of loss.

Risk management is a broad and deep topic, and I am only able to brush the surface in this book. A number of reference books on the topic are available. The bibliography in Appendix C lists some specific titles you can use as a reference. The risk analysis and management process that I briefly describe answers the following questions:

- What are the risks?
- What is the probability of loss that results from them?
- How much are the losses likely to cost?
- What might the losses be if the worst happens?
- What are the alternatives?
- How can the losses be reduced or eliminated?
- Will the alternatives produce other risks?

To answer these questions, the following sections define risk management in four phases: identification of risk, assessment of risk, risk response planning, and monitoring and controlling.

Every project is subject to risks. Some can be identified and plans can be put in place if they occur; others cannot and must be dealt with as they occur. The events that this section focuses on are those that could compromise the successful completion of the project. No one knows when they will occur, but they will occur with some likelihood and cause some damage to the project. For example, the loss of a team member who has a critical or scarce skill is one such event. The longer the project lasts, the more likely this will happen. The history of some organizations might suggest that this is a certainty. Knowing this, what would you do? That is the question answered this section. The answer lies in understanding what the risk management life cycle is and how to construct a risk management plan.

Unfortunately, many project managers view risk as something they pay attention to at the beginning of the project by building some type of risk management plan and then file it away so they can get on with the real work of the project. How shortsighted. Effective project managers treat risk management as a dynamic part of every project. Their plan has the following four parts:

- Risk identification
- Risk assessment

- Risk mitigation
- Risk monitoring

Risk Identification

In order to establish a risk management program for the project, the project manager and project team must go through several processes. The first is risk identification, and it generally occurs as part of project planning activities. In this part of the process, the entire planning team is brought together to discuss and identify the risks that are specific to the current project.

Developing a risk management plan is a significant part of the project planning process. The more complex and uncertain the project, the more important it is to have a dynamic and maintained risk management plan. Some have said that the project manager does nothing more than manage risk on the project. That is too restrictive, but it does speak to the importance of a good risk management plan for every project. Although the experienced project manager will certainly know what general types of risks there are on each project, the professional project manager takes nothing for granted and always engages the project planning team in identifying risks for the project. The list of risks can be cumulatively developed in parallel with other project planning activities. After that list is built, the team can move to the second step in the risk management process.

There are four risk categories. Each category is listed here with its potential risks. Use these as suggestions only. Your specific project will probably suggest these or other risks within each of these categories. The planning team should review each list and modify it as needed.

Technical Risks

These may include the following:

- Quality and performance goals generally relating to the technology of the project
- The suitability, reliability, and quality or performance standards surrounding the technology
- Technology availability and complexity issues

Project Management Risks

These may include the following:

- Poor allocation of the project's resources
- Inadequate project management structure — proper planning processes to define critical deliverables for each project phase

- Inadequate planning, resource inexperience, or poor use of management disciplines
- Cost and schedule risks due to the aforementioned project management risks

Organizational Risks

These may include the following:

- Supportability risks or inadequate prioritization of projects
- Inadequacy of or interrupted funding and/or resource assignments
- Conflicts with other competing projects
- Policies that do not support efficient management and could potentially introduce supportability risks
- Politics and agendas that impede the development of the project's executing objectives

External Risks

These may include the following:

- Shifting legal or regulatory requirements
- Supplier and contractor risks and/or contract issues
- Economic collapse or work stoppages (strikes)
- Programmatic or supportability risks caused by external parties
- Deliverables from teams that are external to your own (IT or client)

Risk Assessment Template

Figure 3-1 shows a template that you can use for defining risks in each of these categories and making a preliminary assessment of how they might impact the scope matrix.

The first step in the Risk Management Process is to identify the risk drivers that may be operative on a given project. These are the conditions or situations that may unfavorably affect project success. As an example, Figure 3-2 shows a candidate list from which the list of risk drivers appropriate for a given project can be chosen.

To establish the risk management for the project, the project manager and project team must go through several processes. The first is identifying risk.

In this part of the process, the entire team is brought together to discuss and identify the risks that are specific to the current project. I recommend that the meeting focus solely on risk. A meeting with such a single focus enables the entire project team to understand the importance of risk management, and it gets everyone thinking about the various risks involved in the project.

RISK CATEGORIES AND RISKS	SCOPE TRIANGLE ELEMENTS				
	Scope	Time	Cost	Quality	Resources
Technical					
Project Management					
Organizational					
External					

Figure 3-1: Risk identification template

Risk Assessment

When the team puts together the risk identification list, nothing should be ruled out at first. Let the team brainstorm risk without being judgmental. Some risks are so small that you will eventually ignore them. For instance, the risk that a meteor will destroy the building in which you work is miniscule. If you're worrying about things like this, you won't be much of a project manager. You need to manage the risks that actually might occur.

There are two major factors in assessing risk. The first one is the probability that the risk event will occur. For instance, when a project involves migrating legacy systems to new systems, the interface points between the two are often where problems occur. The professional project manager will have a good sense of these types of risks and the chances that they will occur.

NOTE If you are certain that an event will occur, it's not a risk; it's a certainty. This type of event isn't handled by risk management. Because you are sure that it will occur, no probability is involved. No probability, no risk.

Candidate Risk Driver Worksheet

P/I LEGEND: Very high   VH   MITIGATION LEGEND: Yes   Y
            High   H   Monitor   M
            Medium   M   No   N
            Low   L
            Very Low   VL

Risk Category	Scope Triangle	Event #	Event	Y/N	Prob.	Impact	Priority	Mitigate Y/M/N
Tech	Scope	TS01	Available HW/SW technology limits scope					
		TS02	New technology does not integrate with old					
Tech	Time	TT01	Integrating technologies impacts schedule					
Tech	Cost	TC01	Unexpected need to acquire hardware					
Tech	Cost	TC02	Unexpected need to acquire software					
Tech	Quality	TQ01	Technology limits solution performance					
Tech	Res	TR01	New/unfamiliar technology					
Tech	Res	TR02	Inadequate software sizing					
Tech	Res	TR03	Inadequate hardware sizing					
Proj Mgt	Scope	PS01	Senior scope change request too significant					
Proj Mgt	Time	PT01	Schedule too aggressive					
Proj Mgt	Time	PT02	Interproject dependencies compromise schedule					
Proj Mgt	Time	PT03	Task duration estimates too optimistic					
Proj Mgt	Time	PT04	Difficulty scheduling meetings					
Proj Mgt	Quality	PQ01	Inaccurate assumption					
Proj Mgt	Res	PR01	Loss of critical team member					
Proj Mgt	Res	PR02	Unexpected resource conflict					
Org	Scope	OS01	Unrealistic expectations					
Org	Scope	OS02	Poorly defined requirements					
Org	Scope	OS03	Continuous requirement changes					
Org	Scope	OS04	Too frequent scope change requests					
Org	Scope	OS05	Competing priorities arise					
Org	Time	OT01	Changing priorities					

Figure 3-2: Candidate risk driver template and assessment worksheet *(Continues)*

Org	Cost	OC01	Volatile budget conditions					
Org	Cost	OC02	Budget not adequate					
Org	Cost	OC03	Unexpected staffing cost increases					
Org	Quality	OQ01	Inconsistent client involvement					
Org	Res	OR01	Unexpected organizational changes					
Org	Res	OR02	Inadequately skilled personnel					
Org	Res	OR03	Lack of political support for the project					
Org	Res	OR04	Skilled personnel not available when needed					
Org	Res	OR05	Lack of organizational support					
Org	Res	OR06	Unable to hire personnel when needed					
Org	Res	OR07	Unexpected loss of personnel					
Org	Res	OR08	Unexpected change of leadership					
Ext	Scope	ES01	Changing competition					
Ext	Scope	ES02	Unexpected changes in policy, stds, regs					
Ext	Time	ET01	Competing priorities with vendors					
Ext	Cost	EC01	Unexpected price increases from vendor					
Ext	Res	ER01	Misunderstood contract terms					
Ext	Res	ER02	Unavailable vendor resources					
Ext	Res	ER03	Unexpected state budget cuts					
Ext	Res	ER04	Unexpected county budget cuts					
Uncl	Uncl	UU01	Intellectual property & copyright obstacles					
Uncl	Uncl	UU02	Problem/Project details not available					
Uncl	Uncl	UU03	Aversion to divulging sensitive information					
Uncl	Uncl	UU04	Access to information					
Uncl	Uncl	UU05	Demand for space exceeds available space					

Figure 3-2: Candidate risk driver template and assessment worksheet *(Continued)*

The second part of risk assessment is the expected loss the risk will have on the project. If the probability is high and the impact is low, you may be able to ignore the risk. If the probability is low but the impact is high, you might also be able to ignore the risk. The decision is based on the product of the probability of the event happening and the impact it will have. For example, if the probability of losing a critical skill is 0.8 (probability is a number between 0 and 1.0) and the impact is $50,000, the expected loss is $40,000 (0.8 × $50,000). As a further example, suppose the probability of the Bull on Wall Street being stolen is $1 \times 10{-10}$ and the impact is $75,000,000; then the expected loss is $750.

You should ignore the risk if the cost of avoiding the risk is greater than the expected loss. In other words, don't solve a $100 problem with a $1,000 solution. In the two examples, you would most likely not ignore the risk of losing the critical skill, but you would ignore the risk of the Bull on Wall Street being stolen.

Static Risk Assessment

If you don't want to get hung up on numeric risk assessments, you might want to try using the risk matrix shown in Figure 3-3. There is nothing magic about using a 3 × 3 matrix. A 5 × 5 matrix works just as well.

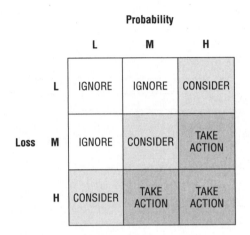

Figure 3-3: Risk matrix

For each risk, evaluate the probability that it will occur on a Low, Medium, High scale and the impact on a Low, Medium, High scale. The combination of these two assessments identifies a specific cell in the risk matrix with the recommended action, if any. The situation regarding this risk may change later in the project. So, my advice is to monitor the risk, but don't act unless reason dictates that you do so.

Dynamic Risk Assessment

The preceding risk assessment is basically static. By that I mean an analysis is done during planning, and a risk management plan is put in place for the entire project. It does not change as the project progresses. That is the simplest approach and probably less effective than the dynamic risk assessment discussed in this section. I have used the following dynamic risk assessment approach with great success. In this approach, risk is continuously reassessed at each phase of the project. An example will help explain how this approach is used.

After the risk drivers have been identified, they must be ranked from most likely to have an impact on the project to least likely to have an impact on the project. Label them A (most likely) through J (least likely) and array the data as shown in Figure 3-4. The column entries are 1 = low risk, 2 = medium risk, and 3 = high risk. Actually, any metric can be used as long as the lower numbers are at the low-risk end and the higher numbers are at the high-risk end. Sometimes a "0" might be used to indicate no risk. Other modifications I have seen and used are changing the impact scale to 1–5 or even 1–10.

Project Activity	A	B	C	D	E	F	G	H	I	J	Score
Rqmnts Analysis	2	3	3	2	3	3	2	2	1	1	22
Specifications	2	1	3	2	2	2	1	2	2	3	20
Preliminary Design	1	1	2	2	2	2	1	2	2	2	17
Design	2	1	2	2	2	3	1	2	2	1	18
Implement	1	2	2	3	3	2	1	2	2	1	19
Test	2	2	2	2	2	3	2	2	2	2	21
Integration	3	2	3	3	3	3	2	3	3	2	27
Checkout	1	2	2	3	3	3	2	3	2	2	23
Operation	2	2	3	3	3	3	3	3	1	1	24
Score	16	16	22	22	23	24	15	21	17	15	191

Maximum score is 270. Risk level for this project is 191/270 = 71%.

Figure 3-4: Risk assessment worksheet

The data given in the worksheet is from a hypothetical project. The columns are the top risk drivers that were identified from the candidate list, and the rows are steps in a process. For the sake of an example, I chose steps from a hypothetical systems-development life cycle. Any collection of process steps may be used, so the tool has broad application for a variety of contexts. A score of 1 is given to risk drivers that will not impact the process step if they should occur, 2 is for a medium impact, and 3 is for a strong impact. Actually, any numeric scale may be used. The row and column totals are evaluated relative to one another and to scores from similar projects. These totals tell the story. High column totals suggest a risk driver that is operative across a number of steps in the process. High row totals suggest a process step that is affected by several risk drivers. Finally, the total for the whole worksheet gives you a percentage that can be used to compare this project against similar completed projects. The percentage is relative, but it may suggest a rule that provides an early warning of projects that are high risk overall.

To analyze the resulting scores, first examine column totals that are large relative to other column totals. In the example, you should focus on the risk drivers associated with columns C, D, E, and F. Because their column totals are high, they can potentially affect several process steps. The project team should identify strategies for either reducing the probability of the risk occurring or mitigating its impact, or both, should the event associated with that risk occur. The row totals can be analyzed in the same fashion. In the example, integration has the highest row total (27). This indicates that several risk drivers can impact integration. The project team should pay attention to the work associated with integration and look for ways to improve or better manage it. For example, the team might choose to have more skilled personnel work on integration than they might otherwise choose.

In the example, the risk factor is 71 percent. This value can be interpreted only in comparison to the risk factor of completed projects. There will be a pattern of project failures for projects whose risk factor is above a certain number. If 71 percent is above that number, the example project is a high risk for failure. The decision to do this project will have to be offset by the business value the project expects to contribute.

Risk Mitigation

The next step in risk management is to plan, as much as possible, the responses that will be used if the identified risks occur. For instance, you may want to include a clause in your hardware contract with the vendor that if the servers don't get to you by a certain date, then the vendor will pay a penalty. This penalty gives the vendor an incentive to analyze and mitigate the risks involved in late delivery of key equipment. For all the risks listed in the risk identification that you choose to act upon, you should have some type of action in mind. It's not enough to simply list the risks; you need to plan to do something about the risk events should they occur.

Another example of risk planning is planning for key personnel. What will you do if one of the key developers leaves the company before finishing the coding? This risk will impact the project severely if it occurs. Having someone capture code as it is written and debriefing with the developer each day are two ways of dealing with the risk of key personnel loss. How many others can you come up with? Coming up with contingency plans such as these is risk response planning.

There are five different risk responses. They are briefly defined in the following list:

- **Accept** — There is nothing that can be done to mitigate the risk. You just have to accept it and hope it does not occur.

- **Avoid** — The project plan can be modified so as to avoid the situation that creates the risk.

- **Contingency Planning** — If the risk event occurs, what will you do?

- **Mitigate** — What will you do to minimize the impact should the risk event occur?
- **Transfer** — Pass the impact should the risk event occur (that is, buy an insurance policy).

Risk Monitoring

Once you've identified the risk, assessed the probability and impact of the risks, and planned what to do if the risk event occurs, you need to monitor and control the project risks. The process of writing down the risks, assessing them, and posting them in the Team War Room makes everyone on the project team aware of their existence and is a good place to start. Start by creating a risk log. This document lists all risks that you want to manage, identifies who is supposed to manage the risk, and specifies what should be done to manage the risk event. A risk log is a simple template that can be created in a text document or spreadsheet package.

A risk log is a simple template that you can create in Microsoft Word. A typical risk log will contain the following five fields:

- **ID number** — This always remains the same, even if the risk event has occurred and been managed. If you take the risk off the list and file it elsewhere, don't assign the old number to a new risk. Keep the original number with the discarded risk and never use it again, or there will be a great deal of confusion.
- **Risk description** — This is a short statement of the risk event.
- **Risk owner** — This is the person who has the responsibility of monitoring the status of the listed risk.
- **Action to be taken** — Lists what the risk owner is going to do to deal with the risk event.
- **Outcome** — Describes what happened as a result of your mitigation strategy.

Use the risk log to keep track of risk in the project, and you'll have control over it. When you go to status meetings, you should always talk about risks and their management by the team. Keep the risks in front of the team so that each member will be aware of what risks are coming up and what is to be done about the risk event. Continuously paying attention to the risks is a good insurance policy against project failure.

Procurement Management

The Procurement Management Knowledge Area consists of processes that span the Planning, Launching, Monitoring and Controlling, and Closing Process

Groups. An effective procurement management life cycle consists of the following five phases:

- Vendor solicitation
- Vendor evaluation
- Vendor selection
- Vendor contracting
- Vendor management

As a project manager, you will always have projects for which you must obtain hardware, software, or services from outside sources. This process is known as *procurement*, and the professional project manager must have a basic understanding of the acquisition procedure so that he or she can ensure that the organization is getting the right materials at the best cost or the best services at the best cost. To manage procurement, you need to go through a few processes, which are summarized in the next few sections.

Vendor Solicitation

After you've done your requirements gathering and have made the decision that you need an outside vendor, you can begin to prepare procurement documents for solicitation. These documents, called Requests for Proposals (RFPs), are what vendors use to determine if and how they should respond to your needs. The clearer the RFP, the better off you and the vendor are, because you will be providing basic information about what you want (don't forget about the earlier discussion of needs versus wants). The more specific you are, the better the chance that the vendor will be able to respond to you quickly and efficiently.

Many organizations have a procurement office. In this case, you need to give them a document with your requirements and let them do their work. If you don't have a procurement office, you need to prepare a document to send to the vendors. You'll want to have a lead writer (preferably not you) and someone from the legal department to ensure that what you've asked for in the document is clear and forms the basis for a contract between you and the vendor.

You have several ways to build a list of potential vendors, as outlined in the following sections.

Publishing a Request for Information

The Request for Information (RFI) is frequently used when you have little knowledge of exactly what is available on the commercial market or you can't identify vendors who have the specific capability you are looking for. The RFI is a broad net designed to find possible vendors who have some product or service to offer that may meet your needs. The RFI is a letter, and the response usually comes in the form of a letter or brochure. Based on the response to your RFI, you will decide the following:

- Who should be invited to respond to your Request for Proposal (RFP)
- Specific content to include in your RFP
- If one of the vendors should be invited to write the RFP

Advertising

Pick any medium that a potential vendor would likely read and advertise your project there. Many vendors will belong to professional associations. If such associations exist, get their mailing lists or advertise in their trade publications.

Renting a Targeted List

Many sources are available for such mailing lists. The reputable ones will have exhaustive profiling capabilities so that you can narrow the list as much as you wish.

Asking Previous Vendors

Vendors who have worked with you in the past may be good sources for your current project, or they may be able to recommend other vendors who can meet the specific needs of this project.

Attending Trade Shows

Attend trade shows where potential vendors are likely to have a booth. This is a non-threatening approach and may even gain you some references to other vendors.

Preparing and Distributing a Request for Proposal

After you've created the RBS, you can begin to prepare procurement documents for solicitation. These documents, called Requests for Proposals (RFPs), are what vendors use to determine how they should respond to your needs. The clearer the RFP, the better off you and the vendor are, because you will be providing basic information about what you want. The more specific you are, the better the chance that the vendor will be able to respond to you quickly and efficiently.

NOTE Remember that a contract always implies some type of adversarial relationship. Both parties to the contract want to get the best possible terms for their side. When you're creating an RFP, keep in mind that although you definitely want to get the best possible terms for your side, you must make sure the terms aren't so difficult that they prohibit many people from responding. You must encourage as much participation in your RFP as possible. Don't get into a draconian mode whereby the RFP almost punishes the people who are responding to it.

You need to state the time conditions for response, which means that you state how many days you will give people to respond, as well as how long you will need to review the responses before making a choice. By putting a time line on both the vendor and your organization, the process goes faster, and expectations are clear at the beginning of the process.

The RFP is the heart of the procurement process and provides the basis for the contract and the work to be completed. It clearly explains all of the deliverables expected of the vendor.

I recommend that your RFP contain the following:

- Introduction
- Business profile
- Problem or opportunity
- POS (optional)
- RBS (optional)
- Vendor responsibility
- Contract administration
- Instructions to vendors
- Vendor point of contact
- Time and cost estimates
- Pricing
- Evaluation criteria

Managing RFP Questions and Responses

You can expect to receive questions from the vendors who receive your RFP. All potential vendors must be aware of all questions and your responses. That's the law! You need to have some mechanism whereby you can answer questions concerning the RFP.

Responding to Bidder Questions

After the RFP has been distributed, you have to decide how to handle questions that will surely arise from the vendors who have received your RFP. You have three ways to handle these questions:

- **Answer questions individually** — Receive questions directly from the vendors and distribute your responses electronically to all vendors on the distribution list.

- **Hold a bidders' conference** — This is a common event. All vendors who wish to respond to the RFP must attend and ask their questions. That way every potential bidder will hear the questions and answers in real time. The bidders' conference can be held at a hotel or conference site convenient to your campus but is usually held on your campus.

- **Put your RFP online and respond to questions online** — This arrangement gives every vendor who is registered to respond to your RFP a chance to see other organizations' questions and to have a permanent record of your responses to questions posed. This process works only if you have someone constantly monitoring the web site for questions, and someone who is responsible for answering the questions. This process also eliminates the traveling burden on vendors who may be far away geographically. By going online, you level the playing field for all vendors.

The important thing is to make sure all potential bidders have the same information. Otherwise, you are subject to being accused of unfair business practices.

Vendor Evaluation

Before you even start reading the responses to your proposal, set the standards for choosing a given vendor. These criteria may be based on technical expertise, experience, or cost, but whatever criteria you use, it must remain the same for all of the vendors. If you are a public company, every vendor you've turned down will ask for a copy of the winning bid. If they think they have a better bid, all sorts of nasty things may occur (read: legal action). If, however, you have a standards chart, you can point out that everyone was rated with the same criteria and that the winner had the best overall number. By determining your criteria for vendor selection early in the process, it is easier to make a decision and then defend it if need be.

Vendor evaluation consists of creating a rule by which all RFP responses are evaluated on the same scale.

Establishing Vendor Evaluation Criteria

Vendor selection implies that you have specified a set of established criteria that vendors will be evaluated against. The main objective is to ensure that the evaluation of all responses to the RFP is consistent, objective, and comprehensive.

Although many criteria have been developed for vendor evaluation, it is important for you to first decide what the desired vendor relationship will be and define the problem to be solved. You can then develop a specific set of vendor selection criteria that will facilitate the systematic choice of a vendor. This implies that an evaluation team is involved. That team reviews baseline vendor evaluation criteria checklists, debates with the other team members about the relative importance of each criterion, and reaches consensus. This further implies that only the essential criteria are chosen for each vendor, and extraneous criteria that "might" be necessary should be eliminated. Criteria might also be classified as "must have," "should have," or "it would be nice to have," and some type of scoring algorithm should be applied to the criteria in each classification.

Several qualitative factors might also be used. They include the following:

- Corporate experience with similar work
- Financial stability
- Technical approach
- Personnel experience, skills, and competencies
- Risk management processes
- Location
- Applicable tools, templates, and processes
- References for similar work

Some type of weighted scoring algorithm should be employed to assess these qualitative factors.

Several quantitative models exist for evaluating and ranking vendors. Two models that I have used with good success and that are easy to master and administer are Forced Ranking and Paired Comparisons.

Forced Ranking

In the Forced Ranking example shown in Table 3-1, six vendors (numbered 1 through 6) and four consultants (A, B, C, and D) are doing the evaluation. The result of a Forced Ranking is a prioritized list of vendors. Each consultant must rank the six vendors from best to worst in terms of their overall satisfaction of the RFP. (A variation would be to specify the criteria and ask for the ranking based on the criteria.) In this example, Consultant A ranked Vendor 4 as best and Vendor 3 as worst. To determine the overall highest-ranked vendor, add the rankings across the rows. In this case, Vendor 2 is ranked first.

Table 3-1: Forced Ranking

	CONSULTANT					
VENDOR	**A**	**B**	**C**	**D**	**RANK SUM**	**FORCED RANK**
1	2	3	2	4	11	3
2	4	1	1	2	8	1
3	6	2	5	5	18	5
4	1	5	3	1	10	2
5	3	4	4	3	14	4
6	5	6	6	6	23	6

Paired Comparisons

Paired Comparisons is another way to create a single prioritized ranking. Here every vendor is compared against every other vendor. In the example shown in Table 3-2, Vendor 1 is compared against Vendor 2 in the first row. If Vendor 1 is preferred, a 1 is placed in row 1 under the Vendor 2 column and a 0 is placed in the Vendor 2 row under the Vendor 1 column. To determine the overall highest-ranked vendor, sum the values in each row. The highest row total identifies the highest priority vendor.

Table 3-2: Paired Comparisons

	1	**2**	**3**	**4**	**5**	**6**	**SUM**	**RANK**
1	X	1	1	0	1	1	4	2
2	0	X	1	0	1	1	3	3
3	0	0	X	0	0	1	1	5
4	1	1	1	X	1	1	5	1
5	0	0	1	0	X	1	2	4
6	0	0	0	0	0	X	0	6

Evaluating Responses to the RFP

Vendor RFP response evaluation is a structured method for assessing the vendor's ability to successfully deliver against the requirements stated in the RFP. It should be based on the execution by a team with the best knowledge of the disciplines represented in the RFP. In many cases, this will be an outside team of subject matter experts (SME). The primary deliverable from this unbiased evaluation is a ranked list. Comments are often requested regarding those vendors who meet the minimal requirements as stated in the RFP.

It is not unusual to have more than one evaluation phase. This may be necessary if there are several qualified respondents. The evaluation of vendor responses to the RFP is often used to reduce the number of viable bidders to a more manageable number, usually no more than five. These survivors will then be invited to make an onsite presentation of their proposed solutions. These presentations will often be attended by end users and others who will interact with the solution. They will evaluate each vendor's proposed solution using criteria developed specifically for this onsite presentation. The data collected here will be used to support the final selection of the winning bidder.

In most cases, the short list will contain more than one vendor, so your job of vendor evaluation is not yet done.

Vendor Selection

The result of vendor evaluation usually does not produce a single best choice. There will most likely be several competing vendors for all or parts of the work. So you have another decision to make and that is which vendor or vendors will win your business.

Selecting the vendor is a critical decision. There is no guarantee that even if you diligently follow the evaluation process, you will end up with a vendor that you are comfortable with and whom you can select with confidence. Some selection processes may result in failure. Don't feel obligated to choose one from the remaining list of contenders for your business. It is good practice to let potential bidders know that you may not award the contract after going through the process.

Vendor Contracting

When the software application is to be developed solely by the vendor, the project manager's primary job is contract management. Contract management involves the following:

- The vendor must supply you with deliverable dates so that you can determine whether the project is on time.

- The vendor should also supply a WBS detailing how the vendor breaks down the scope of the project and showing the tasks that make up the completion of a deliverable.

- The project manager should hold regular status meetings to track progress. These meetings should be formal and occur on specified dates. The status meetings should occur at least once a week, although in the early stages of the project, you may choose to have them more often. These status meetings will give you an idea of how the vendor is proceeding in fulfilling the contract, and by having them at weekly intervals, you won't allow the project to get very far off course. At most, you will need to correct only a week's worth of problems — anything longer than that can quickly become unmanageable.

In your contract, state who the contract manager will be for your organization. This is typically the project manager (which will be you if you're managing this project), but in some organizations, contract management functions are handled by a specific department or team. I prefer contract management to be in the hands of the project manager, or at least to have the project manager as part of the contract management team.

> **NOTE** If the contract is run on a deliverable basis — that is, the vendor agrees to given deliverables on certain dates — it is extremely important to state the payment mechanism. The person who signs off on each deliverable is extremely important to the vendor and should be specifically assigned in the RFP.

Making the actual selection can be very simple and straightforward, depending on the evaluation process. There are several possible scenarios to consider.

No Award

In this scenario, none of the evaluations result in a vendor who satisfactorily meets the requirements; therefore, no award will be made. In this case, you will probably want to rethink the RFP. Could you be asking for more than any vendor can reasonably provide? If so, you should consider revising the project scope.

Single Award

In this scenario, the results of the evaluation are clear, and a single vendor emerges with the highest evaluation across all criteria. In simpler cases, the evaluation criteria are designed to produce a single score, and the highest scoring vendor who meets the minimal requirements will be awarded the business. However, don't think that this is the end and you have a vendor. You still have a contract to negotiate and need vendor acceptance of that contract.

Multiple Awards

When there are multiple criteria, each with its own scoring algorithm, there may not be a clear single vendor who scored high enough across the criteria to be awarded the business. In this case, you may decide to award parts of the business to different vendors. If this possibility exists, you must make it clear in the RFP that the business could be awarded to several vendors who must then work together on the project. The RFP should require information on any similar situations in which the vendor has had experiences. If you have multiple vendors, you will obviously have an added management burden.

Types of Contracts

You might consider several types of contract structures. The four most popular contract types are briefly described in the following sections.

Fixed Price

This form of contract is best used when the requirements are well known and the buyer (that's you) knows that changes will be kept to a minimum. Although many buyers seem to always want a Firm Fixed Price (FFP) contract, it is wise to keep in mind that the supplier (a.k.a. vendor) should have the capability that is described by the Software Engineering Institute (SEI) in the Capability Maturity Model (CMM), Level 3. Only suppliers with organizational processes that are documented, trained, followed, and kept current will have a strong enough organizational measurement repository. These depositories will contain historical data based on many projects to be able to comfortably bid on FFP contracts. Of course all potential suppliers will agree to an FFP, but it is often done to get in the door and hope details can be worked out later with the buyer. It is not done from a base of data.

Time and Materials

Labor rates are established for each of the vendor's position classes that will be assigned to the project. These are stated in the RFP response and agreed to as part of contract negotiations. Time cards are kept by the vendor, and you are invoiced as agreed to in the contract's terms and conditions.

Materials are acquired by the vendor as agreed to in the contract. The necessary documentation is provided as attachments to the invoices.

Retainer

Retainer contracts specify a fixed amount per period to be paid to the vendor, with an agreed number of person days per period provided by the vendor in return for the fee. Retainer contracts are often used when a detailed Statement of Work cannot be provided. In these contracts, it is your responsibility to make periodic assignments with deadlines to the vendor.

Cost Plus

This form of contract is especially useful if you are willing to pay more for higher performance and quality but are not sure how to determine the supplier's true capability. A Cost Plus contract includes direct labor and indirect cost (overhead, actual work performed, and so on) to make up the bill rate, with other direct costs listed separately. Cost Plus puts a major emphasis on contractor performance and quality and can be used as a way to enforce standards and procedures. The award fee is negotiated at the beginning of contract and is directly tied to vendor performance. Vendor performance should be measured in terms of specific quantitative metrics so there is no argument about attainment.

Cost Plus contracts can also include penalties for not meeting acceptance criteria.

Discussion Points for Negotiating the Final Contract

This section of the RFP specifies the areas that will be discussed for the final terms and conditions of the contract following vendor selection. You do not want to present the vendors with any surprises. Some of the areas you will want to discuss in the RFP include the following:

- Work schedule
- Payment schedule
- Fees
- Personnel assigned to the contract
- Rights in data
- Other terms and conditions
- Ownership
- Warranties
- Cancellation terms

Final Contract Negotiation

Establishing and maintaining the vendor agreement provides the vendor with the project needs, expectations, and measures of effectiveness.

The vendor agreement typically includes the following:

- Statement of work for the vendor
- Terms and conditions
- List of deliverables, schedule, and budget
- Defined acceptance process, including acceptance criteria
- Identification of the project and supplier representatives responsible and authorized to agree to changes to the vendor agreement
- Description of the process for handling requirements change requests from either side

- The processes, procedures, guidelines, methods, templates, and so on that will be followed
- Critical dependencies between the project and the vendor
- Descriptions of the form, frequency, and depth of project oversight that the vendor can expect from the project, including the evaluation criteria to be used in monitoring the vendor's performance
- Clear definition of the vendor's responsibilities for ongoing maintenance and support of the acquired products
- Identification of the warranty, ownership, and usage rights for the acquired products

Vendor Management

I have always recommended that you do whatever you can to make the vendor feel like an equal partner in the project. That means including them in every team activity for which it makes sense to have them involved.

Expectation Setting — Getting Started

Starting a contract on the right foot avoids a lot of subsequent frustration for both parties. A good start-up allows the project team and contractor team working relationship to be established early on so that they can function as a unified team throughout the project. Communication needs to be established early among all relevant stakeholders in order to optimize the development environment before the implementation starts.

Conducting meetings and having face-to-face discussions are the easiest and best ways to set clear expectations and gain a mutual understanding of the requirements and expected performance. It is important to remember that the individuals who created and sent the RFP response may not be the same individuals who will actually work on the project. Therefore, it is good practice to hold some type of orientation with the vendor team at the beginning of the project to ensure that both parties share the same understanding of the project goal and objectives.

During this vendor orientation, you should provide answers to the following questions:

- For whom does the vendor work?
- What is expected of the vendor?
- What tools and facilities are available to the vendor?
- What training is available to the vendor? To your team by the vendor?
- What must the vendor deliver?
- When must it be produced?

- Who will receive the deliverables?
- How will the deliverables be evaluated?

However, if the vendor is not onsite, this orientation will pay for itself thousands of times over.

Monitoring Progress and Performance

Monitoring and reporting the progress and performance of one or more vendors takes effort, and you should not expect a vendor to manage their own reporting. The best way to think of the vendor is as a member of the project team. The activities of receiving status reports from the project members and holding project reviews to discuss progress, risks, problems, and ensuing tasks all apply to a vendor as well.

The following discussion of monitoring vendor activities is not intended to be complete or absolute, but rather should be used as a starter kit for subsequent tailoring to ensure proper attention is being devoted to the vendor based on business objectives, constraints, requirements, and operational environment.

Monitoring Requirements Change Requests

One of the most important areas to consider is the requirement change request. These will most likely come from your team and client, but you might also give the vendor the same privileges. After all, they are the experts at what they are doing and may be able to contribute to the betterment and overall success of the project. The bottom line is that requirements management is a collaborative effort of both parties.

Changes to the requirements must be controlled as they evolve over the product life cycle due to changing needs and derived requirements. All appropriate stakeholders on both sides must review and agree on the change requests to the requirements before they are applied. Approved changes to the requirements are tracked and a change history is maintained for each requirement along with the rationale for the change. Applied changes to requirements must be communicated to all stakeholders in a timely manner.

The change process is similar to the process used when no vendor is involved, except for the addition of the vendor's project impact analysis. An impact analysis is conducted on each requirements change request before negotiations take place or a decision to accept or reject the change request is made. The implication will be that a contract or schedule change may be required on the part of the vendor. Even if that is not the case and the vendor's work will not be impacted, it is recommended that you keep the vendor in the approval chain for all change requests. The vendor's approval of all change requests is necessary. Let the vendor decide if their work will be impacted. The vendor's project impact analysis report may conclude that the proposed change will not impact their work in any way, but the vendor needs to officially convey that to the project manager (you).

Monitoring the Performance of Standard Project Activities

The following key metrics need to be provided by the vendor to track actual versus planned contract performance:

- Labor hours
- Cost
- Schedule

Cost and schedule are part of the earned value analysis, which you learn about in Chapter 7.

Other performance metrics that should be tracked by both the vendor and the project manager include the following:

- Frequency of change requests over time
- Incidence of bugs
- Risks
- Issues resolution
- Staffing levels and changes by position type

Transitioning from Vendor to Client

Transitioning from the vendor's environment to your environment for integration and acceptance testing requires thought and up-front planning.

You need to determine what deliverables and/or services you expect to receive in order to successfully transition the product or product component from the vendor to you. The project manager in collaboration with the vendor should develop a high-level summary of the checklist to assist the transitioning of the deliverables:

- What do you expect to be delivered and how will you accept it?
- What environment must you provide in order to accept the vendor's deliverables?
- What support must the vendor provide during acceptance of the deliverables?
- How will problems be resolved?
- What type of maintenance agreement do you expect?
- What about future changes?

It is assumed that acceptance criteria have already been defined and agreed to.

Closing Out a Vendor Contract

Closing out the contract is often an overlooked function of the project manager. It both certifies what has been done and gives all parties a chance to deal with open issues and final payments. The project manager must be aware of all steps to be followed in the procurement process even though he or she may not be the person directly responsible for managing them. This is just another part of being a professional project manager. Consider the following as you bring a contract to a close:

- **There should be a clear understanding of when the project is finished.** When you write your RFP, state clearly the list of deliverables you expect in order for the project to be considered complete and what the final deliverable is. Failure to do this will almost always lead to cost overruns in the form of maintenance activities under the heading of project work. State what the final product of the project is to be, who is to determine if it has been delivered, and what is to be done with any open issues. Make this information as clear as possible and you will save the company thousands of dollars.

- **After the contract is closed, make sure you file all of the materials used during the project.** These materials include the original RFP, the project baseline, the scope statement, the WBS, the various plans used to manage the project, and all changes, including those that were requested but turned down. You also need to show all payments and make sure that any subcontractors on the project were paid. Confirming that subcontractors have been paid is done through the vendor, who must show that all payments have been made to the subcontractors.

- **Put all this information into a large file and keep it.** How long? I have seen instances of disputes coming up years after a project is finished. Keep it as long as the project product is in use. Ideally, keep these records permanently.

Mapping Knowledge Areas to Process Groups

As you can see in Table 3-3, Process Groups and Knowledge Areas are closely linked.

What the Mapping Means

This mapping shows how interdependent the Knowledge Areas are with the Process Groups. For example, eight of the nine Knowledge Areas are started during the Planning Process Group and executed during the Monitoring and Control Process Group. That gives clear insight into the importance of certain deliverables in the project plan and guidance as to the content of the project plan.

Table 3-3: Mapping of the Nine Knowledge Areas to the Five Process Groups

KNOWLEDGE AREAS	SCOPING PROCESS GROUP	PLANNING PROCESS GROUP	LAUNCHING PROCESS GROUP	MONITORING AND CONTROLLING PROCESS GROUP	CLOSING PROCESS GROUP
INTEGRATION	X	X	X	X	X
SCOPE		X		X	
TIME		X		X	
COST		X		X	
QUALITY		X	X	X	
HR		X	X	X	
COMMUNICATIONS		X	X	X	
RISK		X		X	
PROCUREMENT		X	X	X	X

How to Use the Mapping

The mapping provides an excellent blueprint for designing your project management approach to a project. For example, Procurement Management spans the Planning, Launching, Monitoring and Controlling, and Closing Process Groups. Therefore, a PMLC model for Procurement Management will be effective if it has components in each of those Process Groups.

Using Process Groups to Define PMLCs

Many who are new to project management make the mistake of calling the Process Groups a project management methodology. This is incorrect. However, by properly sequencing and perhaps repeating some Process Groups, you can define PMLCs that are project management methodologies. So the Process Groups are the building blocks of project management methodologies. Similarly, by selecting and adapting the processes within a Process Group, you can establish the specific processes that drive a PMLC. So the processes within a Process Group are the detailed building blocks of the phases of the PMLC.

A Look Ahead: Mapping Process Groups to Form Complex PMLCs

Five PMLCs are defined in Part II. These five PMLCs are inclusive of all the meaningful PMLCs you could form, and they completely cover the four-quadrant project landscape. So regardless of the kind of project you have to manage, you will be able to use one of the five PMLCs as the project management methodology for the project. A given PMLC can be modified to accommodate a specific project as described in Part II.

Putting It All Together

This chapter defined all of the Process Groups and listed the processes that they comprise. You know about Knowledge Areas and how they intertwine with the Process Groups. What you don't yet know is how all of these processes are put together to produce project management methodologies specific to the varying management needs of different types of projects. That is the topic of Part II.

The remaining chapters of Part I dig deeper into the Knowledge Areas and show you the many "how-to's." You will learn about the various methods that can be used to execute the processes within each Knowledge Area. In Part II, you will learn how to choose the best-fit method to execute a process, which may be a direct result of the type of project or dependent on one or more external factors.

Discussion Questions

1. Other than the five Process Groups and nine Knowledge Areas approach taken by PMI, how else might you structure your approach to defining a project management methodology for your company?

2. As far as your company's needs for a project management methodology are concerned, are any of the Process Groups incomplete? Do any of the Process Groups have superfluous processes that would not be applicable to your company? Which are they and why would they not work for you?

3. Can you think of a sixth Process Group or tenth Knowledge Area that your company would require of its project management methodology?

CHAPTER 4

How to Scope a TPM Project

Prediction is very difficult, especially about the future.
— Neils Bohr

Define the problem before you pursue a solution.
— John Williams, CEO, Spence Corp.

CHAPTER LEARNING OBJECTIVES

After reading this chapter, you will be able to:

- Understand what managing client expectations really means
- Explain the Conditions of Satisfaction (COS) development process
- Develop the COS document
- Recognize the importance of maintaining the COS throughout the entire project life cycle
- Plan and conduct the Project Scoping Meeting
- Build the Requirements Breakdown Structure (RBS)
- Use facilitated group sessions, business process diagramming, prototyping, and use cases to decompose requirements
- Define the basic parts and function of the Project Overview Statement (POS)
- Write a saleable POS for your project idea using the language of your business

Continued

CHAPTER LEARNING OBJECTIVES   *(continued)*

- Understand the role of the POS in the project management life cycle (PMLC)
- Write clear goal and objective statements
- Establish measurable criteria for project success
- Identify relevant assumptions, risks, and obstacles
- Discuss attachments to the POS and their role in project approval
- Understand the approval process for the POS

The Scoping Process Group defines all of the tools, templates, and processes needed to answer two questions: "What do you need to do?" and "How will you know you did it?" If you don't know where you are going, how will you know when and if you ever get there? If I had to pick the Process Group where most of the project failures originated, it would be the Scoping Process Group. Not only is it the most difficult of the five Process Groups, but it is also the most sloppily executed of the five Process Groups. It probably has a lot to do with the feeling that good planning is a waste of time and effort and the desire to get on with the work of the project. So many times I have seen projects get off to a terrible start simply because there never was a clear understanding of exactly what was to be done. A definition of completeness or doneness was never documented and agreed to. In this chapter, you learn all of the tools, templates, and processes needed to get you started on the right foot with a series of activities that lead to a clearly defined and understood definition of what the project is all about.

After you have learned how to put an initial project scope in place, you learn how to maintain that scope. It may change as you learn more about the solution during project execution, but that is the nature of complex projects. In my experience, if there is no change, there probably won't be a satisfactory outcome either.

Using Tools, Templates, and Processes to Scope a Project

The effective scoping of a project is as much an art as it is a science. A number of tools, templates, and processes can be used during the scoping effort, and they are all precisely defined and documented in this chapter. That is the science of scoping. Knowing your client, your organization's environment, and the market situation and how to adapt the tools, templates, and processes to them is part of the art of scoping. Virtually all of the scoping effort involves an interaction and collaboration between the client who is requesting a service or product and the project manager who is providing the service or product. That collaboration can be very informal (the "back of the napkin" approach) or very formal (a planned Scoping Meeting). In both cases, a document is prepared that answers the questions: "What do you need to do?" and "How will you know you did it?" The nature of that relationship will contribute to how the scoping effort proceeds and how successful it is likely to be.

The following tools, templates, and processes are described in this chapter:

- Conditions of Satisfaction
- Project Scoping Meeting
- Requirements decomposition
- Facilitated group sessions
- Diagramming business processes
- Prototyping
- Use cases
- Project Overview Statement
- Approval to plan the project

Managing Client Expectations

Somehow clients always seem to expect more than project managers are prepared for or capable of delivering. I have seen this expectation gap manifest itself time and time again. I believe that it is more the result of a failure to communicate than it is anything else. This lack of communication starts at the beginning of a project and extends all the way to the end. The project manager assumes he or she knows what the client is asking for and the client assumes the project manager understands what they are asking for. In many cases that is simply not true and little is done to check the validity of either of those assumptions. That stops right here! I believe that miscommunication does not have to happen. The section "Conducting Conditions of Satisfaction" describes a tool that I have used successfully for many years. It is a tool that establishes a language of communication and understanding between the project manager and the client. Understand at the outset that the tool is easy to explain and understand, but demands constant attention if it is to make a difference.

Wants versus Needs

The root cause of many communications problems originates from disconnects between what the client says they want and what they really need. If the project manager doesn't pay attention that disconnect may not be very obvious. The disconnect may come about because the client is so swept up in a euphoria over the technology (for example, they may be enamored with what they see on the Web) that they have convinced themselves they have to have it without any further thought of exactly what it is they really need.

Wants and needs are closely linked to one another but are fundamentally different. From my experience client wants tend to be associated with a solution to a problem that the client envisions. Needs tend to be associated with the problem. If wants are derived from a clear understanding of needs, then it is safe to proceed based on what the client wants, but you cannot always know that this is the case. To be safe, I always ask the client why they want what they want. By continuing this practice of asking why, you will eventually get to the root of the problem and needs will then become clear. This is not unlike a Root Cause Analysis (described in Chapter 15). The solution to that problem will be what the client really needs. Your job as project manager is to convince the client that what they want is what they really need.

The disconnect can also come about because the client does not really know what they need. In many cases, they can't know. What they need can be discovered only through doing the project. Traditional project management (TPM) forces them to specify what they want. If there is any reason to believe that what the client says they want is different from what they need, the project manager has the responsibility of sifting and sorting this out before any meaningful planning or work can be done. It would be a mistake to proceed without having the assurance that wants and needs are in alignment or can be brought into alignment. You should never start a project without knowing that the solution is in fact what will satisfy the client. That is one of the reasons for the Conditions of Satisfaction, discussed in the next section. It is a tool I have used for more than 20 years, and it has served me well.

Project Scoping Process

Figure 4-1 is a diagram of the Project Scoping Process that I use in my consulting practice. It is described in detail in this section.

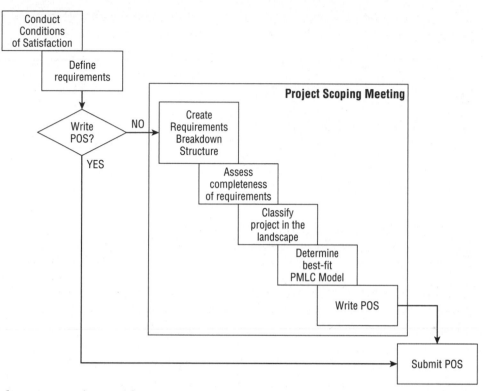

Figure 4-1: Project Scoping Process

Conducting Conditions of Satisfaction

If I had to pick one area where a project runs into trouble, I would pick the very beginning. For some reason, people have a difficult time understanding what they are saying to one another. How often do you find yourself thinking about what you are going to say while the other person is talking? If you are going to be a successful project manager, you must stop that kind of behavior. As a project manager, it is essential that you cultivate good listening skills.

To that end you should begin every scoping exercise with a Conditions of Satisfaction (COS) session. The COS is a structured conversation between the client (the requestor) and the likely project manager (the provider). Figure 4-2 illustrates the COS process.

The deliverable from the COS is a one-page document (with attachments) called the Project Overview Statement (POS). The POS is a template that is used to clearly state what is to be done. It is signed by the requestor and the provider as a record of their COS session. When the POS is approved by senior management, the Scoping Phase is complete and the project moves to the Planning Phase, which is the topic of Chapter 5.

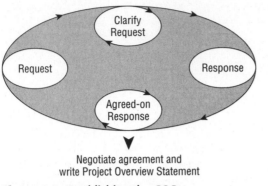

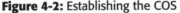

Negotiate agreement and
write Project Overview Statement

Figure 4-2: Establishing the COS

> **NOTE** The COS works well for smaller projects. It does not scale to large projects. For larger projects, a more formal process is needed (described in "The Project Scoping Meeting" section later in this chapter).

The process of developing the COS involves the following four parts:

1. **Request** — A request is made by the client.

2. **Clarification** — The provider explains what he or she heard as the request. This conversation continues until the client is satisfied that the provider clearly understands the request. Both parties have now established a clear understanding of the request in the language of the requestor.

3. **Response** — The provider states what he or she is capable of doing to satisfy the request.

4. **Agreement** — The client restates what he or she understands the provider will provide. The conversation continues until the provider is satisfied that the client clearly understands what is being provided. At this point, both parties have established a clear understanding of what is being provided in the language of the provider.

Establishing a common language with which to communicate is critically important. If you don't have that and verify that you do, you are planting the seeds of failure.

Establishing Clarity of Purpose

By the time you leave the COS session, both you and the client have stated your positions and know that the other party understands your position. You have established the beginnings of a common language with common terminology. That is critically important. You and the client will have planted the seeds for a continuing dialog. As the project work progresses, any changes that come up can be dealt with effectively because the effort to understand each other has been made up front.

The final step in the COS process is to negotiate to closure on exactly what will be done to meet the request. Obviously, some type of compromise will be negotiated. The final agreement is documented in the POS.

More than likely, the parties will not come to an agreement on the first pass. As shown in Figure 4-2, this process repeats itself until there is an agreed-on request that is satisfied by an agreed-on response. As part of this agreement, the POS should include a statement of *success criteria* that specifies when and how the request will be satisfied. It is important that this statement be very specific. Do not leave it up to interpretation whether or not the conditions have been met. An ideal statement will have only two possible results: the criteria were met or the criteria were not met. There can be no in-between answer here and no debate over the outcome. The success criteria (a.k.a. doneness criteria) will become part of the POS.

This early step of establishing and agreeing to what will be done is very important to the project's success. It is difficult to do a thorough job, especially when everyone is anxious to get to work on the project. It is also a painful process. People can be impatient; tempers may flare. You may be inclined to skip this step. ("Pain me now or pain me later" — you choose what you are willing to live with.) Even if the request seems straightforward, do not assume that you understand what the client has asked or that the client understands what you will provide, even if the request seems straightforward. Always use the COS to ensure that you both understand what is expected and that you have a language with which the two of you can communicate clearly.

Specifying Business Outcomes

As indicated in the previous section, it is a good idea to specify within the COS exactly what outcomes demonstrate that the COS has been met. The outcomes have been called success criteria, explicit business outcomes, and objectives, among other names. Whatever term you use, you are referring to a quantitative metric that signals success. That metric is discussed in more detail later in the chapter. For now just understand that it is a quantitative measure (for example, profit, cost avoidance, and improved service levels) that defines success.

Conducting COS Milestone Reviews

The COS is not a static agreement. It is a dynamic agreement that becomes part of the continual project monitoring process. Situations change throughout the project life cycle and so will the needs of the client. That means that the COS will change. Review the COS at every major project status review and project milestone. Does the COS still make sense? If not, change it and adjust the project plan accordingly.

WRITE THE POS?

Depending on the degree of complexity and uncertainty associated with the project it may be advisable that a Project Overview Statement (POS) be developed with the known information at this point. If that certainty is not present, the writing of the POS should be delayed and more project information gathered using a Project Scoping Meeting. The POS is fully described later in this chapter.

The Project Scoping Meeting

You have a variety of ways to scope a project. At one extreme is a formal multiple-day meeting and at the other extreme is scoping on the back of a napkin over a cup of coffee at the local coffee stand. Both extremes and all of the variants in between are valid. It all depends. This section suggests the best way to scope a project based on my experiences.

The Project Scoping Meeting is your first substantive encounter with the client. You may have had a COS session and agreed on a high-level scope for the project but need more detail in order to write a POS. The Project Scoping Meeting takes the COS deliverable to the next level of detail. In this meeting, the core project team will be present, as will the client, several key managers, staff, a facilitator, and representative users of the project deliverables.

Purpose

The Scoping Meeting has two purposes. The first is to draft the POS. The second is to create the Requirements Breakdown Structure (RBS). The RBS is used as further input to the POS and to help the team decide which project management approach is the best fit for this type of project.

Attendees

A Project Scoping Meeting attended by 15–20 people is large but manageable. An experienced meeting facilitator could manage a group of more than 20 people, but it requires breakout groups and their coordination. This is definitely the territory of a skilled facilitator and that is not the project manager. The project manager needs to focus on the scoping of the project, not on conducting the Scoping Meeting. The two activities require different skill sets. I prefer that the project manager draw on their project management skills and the facilitator draw on their meeting facilitation skills. Unfortunately the reality is that the project manager is usually recruited as the facilitator. If the Scoping Meeting requires more than 20 attendees, you might consider breaking the project up into two or more subprojects of lesser scope each or having more than one Scoping Meeting.

The following three groups need to be represented at the Scoping Meeting:

- **The client group** — Decision makers as well as operations-level staff should be represented. Among them should be the individual(s) who suggested the project.

- **The project manager and core members of the project team** — The core members are the experienced professionals who will be with the project from beginning to end. For larger projects, they will be the future sub-project managers and activity managers. In some cases, critical but scarce skilled professionals might also be present.

- **The facilitator group** — This group comprises two or three individuals who are experienced in conducting scoping and planning meetings. The facilitator group will have a meeting facilitator, a requirements gathering facilitator, and a position that I call a technographer. The two facilitators are often the same person. A technographer is the recording secretary for scoping and planning meetings who has solid experience using a variety of high-tech tools. Larger projects may require two such professionals.

Agenda

A typical agenda for the Scoping Meeting includes:

- Introductions
- Purpose of the meeting (led by the facilitator)
- Review COS
- Description of the current state (led by the client representative)
- Description of the problem or business opportunity (led by the client representative)
- Description of the end state (led by the client representative)
- Requirements decomposition (led by the facilitator)
- Discussion of the gap between the current and end states

- Choose the "best-fit" project management approach to close the gap (led by the project manager)
- Draft and approve the POS (whole group)
- Adjourn

For very small projects, the agenda can be accomplished in one day. It would not be unusual for larger, more complex projects to require a full work week to cover the agenda. As an example of the latter, I ran a very complex Web-based decision support system project that was initially budgeted for three years and $5M. The Scoping Meeting took 3 days. But at the end of those three days the group had a common understanding of the project and how to approach it from a process perspective. As testimony to the effectiveness of the scoping process we used, the project finished early and under budget.

Project Scoping Meeting Deliverables

As shown in Figure 4-1, the Project Scoping Meeting includes the following deliverables:

- RBS
- Assessment of completeness of RBS
- Project classification
- Determination of best-fit PMLC model
- The POS

These are described in the following sections.

Creating the RBS

Requirements definition takes place immediately following the COS session and before the POS is written. Requirements decomposition, which involves describing in detail how the requirement will be met, can take place at different times in the project life cycle:

- As input to the POS
- During the Project Scoping Meeting
- During the Project Planning Meeting

My advice is to begin requirements documentation by initially identifying the requirements with no decomposition. That is usually enough detail for POS purposes. Requirements decomposition can take place after the POS has been approved and the project is deemed feasible. Either the Project Scoping Meeting or the Project Planning Meeting will be the appropriate event at which requirements decomposition can be done. If you expect requirements decomposition to be complex, take several days, and consume too many resources, you might want to wait until after the POS has been approved and your project idea is judged to be feasible before you spend the resources needed to generate the RBS. Creating the RBS before you know if your project stands a chance at being approved will be a big waste if POS approval is not given. And so after the POS is approved and you enter the planning phase is the better time to create the RBS. Both options are shown in Figure 4-1.

The RBS is not static but in fact is quite dynamic. The details can change several times throughout the life of the project for one or more of the following reasons:

- Changes in market
- Actions of a competitor
- Emergence of new or enhanced technologies
- Organizational priorities change
- Changes in sponsors
- Learning and discovery from simply doing the project

Because of the volatility of requirements I choose not to use the IIBA definition of a requirement because it guarantees that requirements cannot be fully identified at the beginning of a project. Instead I recommend that you use my definition of requirements, which results in a complete list of requirements at the beginning of the project. This may seem like a trivial difference but it has a profound impact on assessing the resulting business value that is not evident from the IIBA definition because in that definition the requirements that generate business value are embedded in all the other requirements.

Requirements decomposition is presented in the form of a hierarchical diagram (Figure 4-3) that I call the Requirements Breakdown Structure (RBS). In its most detailed rendering it consists of the following levels of decomposition:

Requirement
    Functions
        Sub-functions
            Processes
                Activities
                    Features

As you gather and document requirements by whatever method you choose, place them in their appropriate level in the RBS. The graphical format shown in Figure 4-3 works well. Alternatively, you could present the RBS in an indented outline format. It's all a matter of taste.

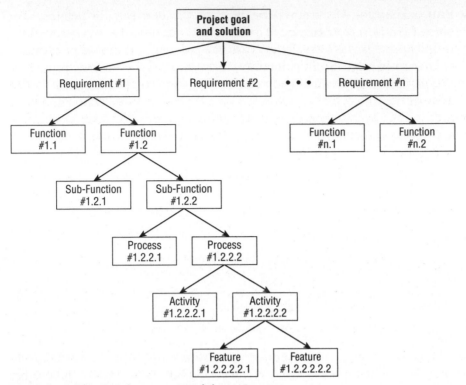

Figure 4-3: The Requirements Breakdown Structure

Each requirement may consist of one or more functions. Each function may consist of one or more sub-functions, and so on. Depending on the level of complexity the decomposition can include all or any combination of the preceding levels. The simplest requirement might only need a list of its features to describe it completely. Here's a brief description of each level:

▪ **Function** — At the discretion of the project manager, the highest level of decomposition may be at the function level. This level comprises the functions that must be performed in order for a solution to be acceptable. It is important to understand that the RBS reflects what is known about the solution at the time the RBS is first defined. This initial list of functions may or may not be complete. Neither you nor the client can be expected to know if that list is complete. You might know that it is incomplete, but you wouldn't know that it is complete. How could you? For the sake of generating the RBS, you have to proceed on the basis that the initial list will be complete. If it turns out that it is not, you will discover that as part of doing the project.

- **Sub-function** — At the next level of decomposition are sub-functions. For some functions, you may not have any idea of what those sub-functions might be and that is okay. In any case, the project team should make every effort to identify the sub-functions that further define a function. Once these sub-functions have been developed, the function they define will now be complete. This is the same as the premise underlying the WBS architecture and is very intuitive. For many adaptive projects, additional sub-functions will be discovered as part of doing the project.

- **Process** — Complex functions and sub-functions can be further described with the business processes that comprise them. These are the business processes that are commonly used in today's organizations. To make them more understandable the functions might be decomposed into sub-functions and the business processes that comprise the sub-functions then decomposed to processes.

- **Activity** — Activities are otherwise known as process steps.

- **Feature** — At the lowest level of decomposition are features. These are the visible enhancements and characteristics of the entity that they describe.

Requirements decomposition is the first and very challenging task that the project manager and client will face in the life of the project. To do this effectively is as much an art as it is a science. On the art side of the equation, the project manager will have to prepare the client to engage in the decomposition and documentation process. The attitude, commitment, willingness to be meaningfully involved, and preparation of the client are major determinants in the choice of approach. This preparation will include the choice of approach to be used and perhaps some preliminary training of the client and the core team. Some clients will be open and proactive in participating; others will not. Some will be sure of their needs; others will not. Some will be expressing their wants, which may be very different from their needs. The project team should be searching for needs.

On the science side of the equation are the many techniques that have been used successfully to decompose and document requirements. I have had good success using facilitated group sessions, prototyping, business process diagramming, and use cases. Those are the four approaches discussed later in this chapter.

It is very important to realize that requirements identification and decomposition are critical to understanding the direction of the project. It is now that the framework for the project begins to take shape.

The steps to generate requirements begin by looking at the business function as a whole. This is followed by the selection of a method or methods for gathering requirements. This effort must be planned. There are several approaches to requirements elicitation. (See Table 4-1.)

> **NOTE**   There is extensive literature on all of these methods. A particularly good reference is *Mastering the Requirements Process* by Suzanne Robertson and James C. Robertson (Addison-Wesley, 2006). The bibliography in Appendix C has a few more references you might want to check.

I single out facilitated group sessions, business process diagramming, prototyping, and use cases for a more detailed discussion because I have had the most success with them. Typically, more than one method is chosen to decompose requirements. Selecting the best method(s) for the project is the responsibility of the project manager, who must evaluate each method for costs, ease of implementation and comfort with the client, and risks. Further, selection of a particular method should be based on specific product and project needs, as well as proven effectiveness. Certain methods have been proven effective for specific client groups, industries, and products. An example of this would be using physical, three-dimensional prototypes in product development and construction. I'll come back to a more detailed discussion of these four methods of requirements decomposition later in this chapter.

Regardless of the method you use to generate the RBS, I strongly advise creating an RBS for every project for the following reasons:

- The RBS is most meaningful to the client.
- The RBS is a deliverables-based approach.
- The RBS is consistent with the Project Management Body of Knowledge (PMBOK) defined by the Project Management Institute (PMI).
- The RBS remains client-facing as long as possible into the planning exercise.
- The RBS is the higher order part of the Work Breakdown Structure (WBS). (See Chapter 5.)

Approaches to Decomposing Requirements

The most commonly used requirements decomposition methods are as follows:

- Facilitated group sessions
- Interviews
- Observation
- Requirements reuse
- Business process diagramming
- Prototypes
- Use case scenarios

Table 4-1 briefly describes the strengths and risks associated with each method.

Table 4-1: Methods for Requirements Decomposition

METHOD	STRENGTHS	RISKS
Facilitated group sessions	Excellent for cross-functional processes. Detailed requirements can be documented and verified immediately. Resolves issues with an impartial facilitator.	Use of untrained facilitators can lead to a negative response from users. The time and cost of the planning and/or executing session can be high.
Interviews	End-user participation. High-level descriptions of functions and processes are provided.	Descriptions may differ from actual detailed activities. Without structure, stakeholders may not know what information to provide. Real needs may be ignored if the analyst is prejudiced.
Observation	Specific and complete descriptions of actions are provided. Effective when routine activities are difficult to describe.	Documenting and videotaping may be time-consuming and expensive, and may have legal overtones. Confusing or conflicting information must be clarified. Can lead to misinterpretation of what is observed.
Requirements reuse	Requirements are quickly generated and refined. Redundant efforts are reduced. Client satisfaction is enhanced by previous proof. Quality is increased. Reinventing the wheel is minimized.	Requires a significant investment for developing archives, maintenance, and library functions. May violate intellectual rights of previous owner. Similarity of an archived requirement to a new requirement may be misunderstood.
Business process diagramming	Excellent for cross-functional processes. Visual communication through process diagrams. Verification of "what is" and "what is not."	Implementation of improvement is dependent on an organization being open to changes. Good facilitation, data gathering, and interpretation are required. Time-consuming.

Continued

Table 4-1 *(continued)*

METHOD	STRENGTHS	RISKS
Prototypes	Innovative ideas can be generated.	Client may want to implement the prototype.
	Users clarify what they want.	
	Users identify requirements that may be missed.	Difficult to know when to stop.
	Client-focused.	Specialized skills are required.
	Early proof of concept.	Absence of documentation.
	Stimulates thought processes.	
Use case scenarios	The state of the system is described before the client first interacts with that system.	Newness has resulted in some inconsistencies.
	Completed scenarios are used to describe state of system.	Information may still be missing from the scenario description.
	The normal flow of events and/or exceptions is revealed.	Long interaction is required.
	Improved client satisfaction and design.	Training is expensive.

Facilitated Group Sessions

This is probably the approach used in every requirements decomposition session and it often integrates one or more of the other approaches. There are a number of ways to structure these sessions that I want you to be aware of. You'll need to do a little planning to decide how best to approach the facilitated group session.

- **One single group session** — This works well for smaller projects and for projects that involve only one business group. I prefer this approach whenever possible. All involved parties hear the same discussion and conclusions.

- **Separated group sessions** — As the project gets larger you might consider breaking the project into sub-projects for the purposes of requirements decomposition. That would allow you to invite those business groups with specific expertise or interest in a particular sub-project. This approach has the added step of combining the results of the multiple sessions. Resolving differences can become an issue and some type of shuttle diplomacy may be required. Compromises are often needed to come to closure.

Business Process Diagramming

NOTE This section is adapted from Appendix K of my book, *Effective Software Project Management* (Wiley, 2006).

Often, you will choose to start identifying requirements for the project by mapping the current business process (the "As Is" process) or processes that are going to be affected. You might also want to map the business process after the solution is installed (the "To Be" process). Both of these are excellent artifacts to use as input to creating the RBS.

From the business process development perspective, gathering requirements details often begins with knowledge of the current or "As Is" business process and ends with the "To Be" business process. The gap between the "As Is" and "To Be" processes is filled with new or enhanced project deliverables. Having the "As Is" and the "To Be" business process flow diagrams is an invaluable aid in the ensuing solutions development effort.

It is an ongoing dictum of today's business that you must continuously improve your business processes. The old "If it ain't broke, don't fix it" adage no longer applies. If you aren't improving your processes and the way that they support your clients, you run the risk of losing market share. Your client should also be taking the lead in approaching your teams to demand process improvement. Conversely, they are your clients, and you should be ever watchful for ways to improve the service that your clients provide to their clients.

All organizations are under pressure to improve. The pressure can come from their clients, the competition, environmental changes, or a combination of the three. The improvements can be in their products or their processes. All too often, the client doesn't give their business to the company with the best product. When clients find that a supplier is too difficult to deal with, they will decide to use a "second best" supplier who is easier to deal with.

This also applies to internal organizations. One reason for outsourcing is a belief (frequently inaccurate) that other groups will be easier, faster, or cheaper to deal with. Internal organizations need to counter this belief by clearly demonstrating that they are continuously improving what they can deliver and their methods of delivery.

What Is a Business Process?

A business process is a collection of activities that takes one or more kinds of input from one or more different sources and produces value for the client (see Figure 4-4). The focus of the business must be to ensure that the effort of dealing with the process does not outweigh the value received from completing the process.

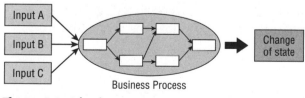

Figure 4-4: A business process

Order entry and fulfillment is a clear example of a business process. From the client's viewpoint, the process starts when the client places an order; it ends when the client receives the goods requested. There are numerous activities in between. Credit checks may be run to confirm that the client can pay for the order. Inventory is assessed to confirm you have what the client is requesting. A typical list of activities would include the following:

- Receiving the order
- Logging the order
- Verification of completeness
- Client credit check
- Determining the price
- Inventory checking
- Production request
- Order picking
- Order packaging
- Shipment

You will notice that the activity in a high-level business process may include activities that can be regarded as processes in and of themselves. Processes can be decomposed into other processes until you reach the task level where some interim component is produced. The key is to start with the client as the focus of the original process and then define the sub-processes by their contribution to added value.

Creating a Business Process Diagram

How do you diagrammatically represent a business process? You can use the standard flowchart to keep it simple and couched in symbols you are already familiar with. Figure 4-5 shows the more commonly used symbols.

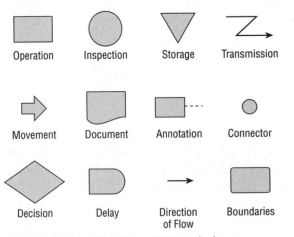

Figure 4-5: Standard flow chart symbols

The symbols shown in the figure denote the following process steps:

- **Operation** — Denotes that a change has taken place. The input is somehow changed as a result of having gone through this process.

- **Movement** — Denotes the movement of output from one process step to become the input to the next process step.

- **Decision** — Denotes that a question needs to be answered. There are two flow paths that emanate from a decision box: Yes or True and No or False. You follow one of these paths based on the decision.

- **Inspection** — Someone other than the person producing the output must inspect it for quality, conformance, or some other tangible characteristic. Often an approval is included as a successful inspection.

- **Document** — Denotes a paper document.

- **Delay** — Denotes a wait state in a process. It's usually associated with something joining a queue and waiting for the operator of the next process step to become available.

- **Storage** — Indicates that an item has been placed in storage and must wait for a release before moving to the next process step. This usually represents wasted time that must be removed from a process.

- **Annotation** — Provides added detail about some process, which is needed for clarification. It might also include the position title of the person responsible for the process.

- **Direction of Flow** — Denotes the order of process steps.

- **Transmission** — The interrupted arrow indicates when information is to be transmitted from one physical or virtual location to another.

- **Connector** — Connects the flow between two separate locations; often used as an off-page connector.

- **Boundaries** — Denotes the initiating and closing processes of a flow diagram. Usually the words START or BEGIN are associated with the initiating process, and STOP or END with the closing process.

Business Process Diagram Formats

Three common formats are used to render business process diagrams. The first (shown in Figure 4-6) is the top-down and left-to-right format. It is commonly used in program and system flow charts. The second is the "swim-lane" format (shown in Figure 4-7). It identifies the actors who participate in the business process.

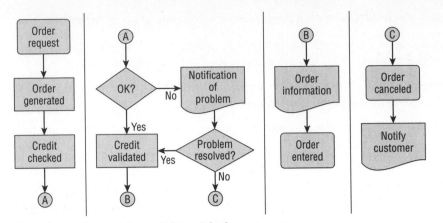

Figure 4-6: The top-down, left-to-right format

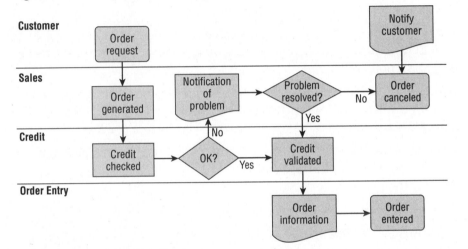

Figure 4-7: The swim-lane format

Software developers are typically most familiar with the top-down, left-to-right format. It harkens back to the early days of programming and is the standard they adopted several decades ago. It follows the logical thought patterns of software developers and is therefore their popular choice.

However, I prefer the swim-lane format when diagramming business processes. For one, it is a client-facing format. By that I mean it is intuitive to the client and represents their processes in a way that they can easily understand. Part II of this book uses swim lanes extensively.

Context Diagrams

One way to describe your process at a very high level is with the context diagram. It is a good starting point. A context diagram describes a rough process or a set of processes. It generally has only the following few components:

- A stick figure representing the external entity that is triggering the process

- A large circle representing the organization responding to the request
- A text block showing each organization or process acting to fulfill the request
- Arrows showing the rough flow between text blocks

The context diagramming process (shown in Figure 4-8) requires that the group identify one or more candidate processes. For example, a process might start with a client request or action and end with a fulfillment. The modeling activity starts by identifying those two points. You show the process start by using an arrow from the client to the organization. You show the process end by using an arrow from the organization to the client. That provides an initial bounding of the process, and the group can decide whether that particular process has enough issues to warrant more time diagramming. If the process merits more discussion, the diagramming process continues by identifying the first group to receive the request and the action sequence that the organization performs to fulfill the request. Simply put, the group uses Post-it notes and arrows to show what goes on in the organization to fulfill the request. This should be done at a high level, and the constrained area of the circle helps maintain this high-level perspective.

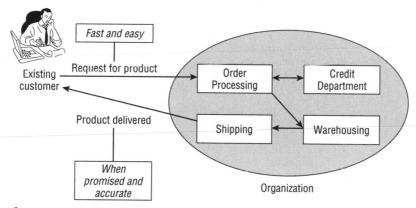

Figure 4-8: Context diagramming process

Frequently the group will make refinements as they go. The most common refinement is a clearer identification of the existing client being focused upon or the transaction being performed. For example, "client" might become "existing client" if the process is different (or should be different) for an existing client versus a new client. The group can then annotate the process with success criteria, issues, and so on.

Business Process Work Flow Diagrams

The flow chart is an intuitive tool to use when you need to identify the actual and ideal path that any product or service follows. It is a picture of steps in a process, and can be used to examine the relationship and sequence of steps; to identify redundancy, unnecessary complexity, and inefficiency in a process; and to create common visual understanding of the process flow.

Considered one of the simplest tools, the flow chart can be as basic or technically intricate as the process it is used to illustrate. Each type of process step is traditionally identified on the chart by a standardized geometric shape. A flow chart illustrates a process from start to finish and should include every step in between. By studying these charts, you can often uncover loopholes, which are potential sources of trouble. Flow charts can be applied to anything from the travels of an invoice and the flow of materials to the steps in making a sale or servicing a product.

In process improvement, flow charts are often used to clarify how a process is being performed or to agree upon how it should be performed. When a process is improved, the changes should be noted on the flow chart in order to standardize the revised flow.

Follow these steps to create a flow chart:

1. Decide on the process to be diagrammed.

2. Define the beginning and ending steps of the process, also known as boundaries.

3. Describe the beginning step using the Boundaries symbol.

4. Keep asking "What happens next?" and writing each of the subsequent steps in Operations symbols below the Boundaries symbol.

5. When a decision step is reached, write a yes/no question in a diamond and develop each path.

6. Make sure that each decision loop reenters the process or is pursued to a conclusion.

7. Describe the ending step using the Boundaries symbol. Sometimes a process may have more than one ending boundary.

Prototyping Your Solution

Many clients cannot relate to a narrative description of a system but they can relate to a visual representation of that system. For requirements decomposition purposes, the idea of a prototype was conceived several decades ago. Its original purpose was to help clients define what they wanted. By showing them a mock-up of a solution, they could comment on it and give the developers more insight into what constitutes an acceptable solution. Originally these prototypes were storyboard versions, not production versions. (Later prototypes did become production versions of the solution when used in agile projects but that is another story presented in Part II.)

Use Cases

Use cases are an excellent forum for working with the client to define the functions and features of the solution. They tell the story of how the solution will operate in the mind of the client and are documented following a specific graphic and textual format. The Unified Modeling Language (UML) and Business Process Management Notation (BPMN) are commonly used. These representations should be rendered in the language of the client and for that reason UML and BPMN have found favor with most developers. This section describes use cases in sufficient detail to get you started. The bibliography in Appendix B has several additional references for those who would like to explore use cases in more detail. Figure 4-9 depicts the position of use cases in the overall project scoping.

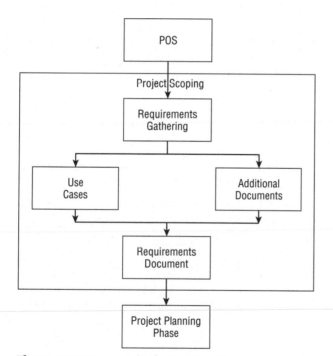

Figure 4-9: Use cases in the Scoping Phase

Project scoping can be part of the Scoping Process Group or Planning Process Group. It is a matter of procedure and protocol in the organization. In Figure 4-9, project scoping is between the Scoping Process Group, which has the POS as output, and the Planning Process Group. It will be the same regardless of where you position it in your project management process. After the use cases have been defined and documented, a single requirements document is assembled, and the project can move to the approval stage or, if the approval stage has already been reached, to the Planning Phase.

There are two artifacts in use cases: use case diagrams and use case flow of events, as described in the following sections.

Use Case Diagrams

A use case diagram is a simple way to describe how an individual interacts with a business process. It consists of one of more stick figures (the actors), ovals (the process steps), and connecting arrows (the interactions), as shown in Figure 4-10.

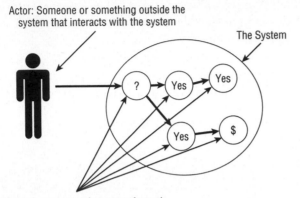

Figure 4-10: Use case diagram

An actor initiates the use case by interacting directly with the system. The system gathers information from the actor, processes it, and returns a result to the actor. In the simple example shown in Figure 4-10, the system asks the actor a question, the answer is processed by the system, and a result (money in this case) is delivered to the actor. This is the so-called "happy path." Several scenarios may spin off of this simple example. In one scenario, the actor may provide the wrong answer, and the system aborts the request. Alternatively, the system may give the actor a second opportunity to provide the correct answer. If this were an ATM scenario, it may be that the client wants to withdraw more money than is in the account, and the system will return the appropriate message — without the money, of course. In this example, there is only one actor — referred to as the *primary actor*. There may be secondary actors as well. For example, if the online bank transaction requires another actor to verify account status, that actor is called a *secondary actor*. Again, the secondary actor may be someone or something, such as another system.

This document reads like the script in a play. It is initiated with an action by the primary actor, the system responds, the actor takes another action, and this back and forth exchange continues until the use case ends. Consider the case study described in the following sidebar of an order entry transaction for a company called PDQ (Pizza Delivered Quickly). In this use case, the actor is a client who has direct access to the system. If a person (instead of a system) were taking the order from the client, he or she would be the actor and not the client.

CASE STUDY – PIZZA DELIVERED QUICKLY (PDQ)

Here is an example of an order entry use case for PDQ. The basic flow of placing an order goes like this:

1. The use case begins when the actor indicates that he or she wants to place an order.
2. The system requests order information (coupon information).
3. The actor provides valid order information.
4. The actor indicates that the order information is complete.
5. The system validates the delivery address (additional detail).
6. The system prices the order.
7. The system displays the completed order with the price.
8. The actor confirms the order.
9. The system assigns the order to the appropriate preparation location.
10. The system prioritizes the order within all store orders. This ends the use case.

Again, this use case is the so-called "happy path." There are several alternatives that could fall under this use case. They are called *scenarios*. One scenario might be that the actor changes his or her mind and cancels the order after finding out the price. Another scenario might be that the system cannot validate the address and terminates the order.

Types of Requirements

Whether you use the IIBA definition or my definition, requirements define the product or service that constitutes the deliverable of the project. These requirements are the basis for defining the needs that the client is seeking to solve a problem or to take advantage of a business opportunity. At this early stage, the client, the project manager, and their teams are tasked with going through the process of establishing the requirements baseline for the project. This process is a systematic, step-by-step effort that requires the patience and diligence of both teams. It is these requirements that will eventually be used for estimating the cost, time, and resources required to do the project. Ultimately, these requirements drive acceptance of the product or service by the client. Requirements are separated into the following four categories.

- Functional requirements
- Non-functional requirements
- Global requirements
- Product and/or project constraints

Functional Requirements

Functional requirements specify what the product or service must do. They are actions that the product or service must take, such as check, calculate, record, or retrieve. For example: "The service shall accept a scheduled time and place for delivery."

Non-Functional Requirements

Non-functional requirements demonstrate the properties that the product or service should have in order to do what it must do. These requirements are the characteristics or qualities that make the product or service attractive, usable, fast, or reliable. Most non-functional requirements are associated with performance criteria and are usually requirements that will establish the product or service boundary. Non-functional requirements can sometimes be generated by the refinement of a global requirement. Non-functional requirements are usually associated with performance criteria that set the parameters for how a system is to function. For example: "The product shall have a homemade appearance" or "The product shall be packaged so as to be attractive to senior citizens."

Global Requirements

Global requirements describe the highest level of requirements within the system or project. Global requirements describe properties of the system as a whole. During the initial stages of a project, many requirements end up being global requirements. The project manager and the team then refine them through the methods of requirement generation. *Global requirements* is a relatively new term. In the past, these have been called general requirements, product constraints, or constraining requirements. Be careful in your use of global requirements because in most cases they can be turned into non-functional requirements simply by asking the questions associated with what, why, or how. In fact, it is wise to move a global requirement to a non-functional requirement in order to gain a better focus on what the requirement really is. For example: "The system shall run on the existing network" or "The system must be scalable."

Product and/or Project Constraints

Product and/or project constraints are those requirements that, on the surface, resemble design constraints or project constraints. Design constraints are pre-existing design decisions that mandate how the final product must look or how it must comply technologically. Project constraints cover the areas of budget and schedule along with deadlines and so on. One important note here is that product constraints can be listed as global requirements, but project constraints *cannot*. For example: "The maximum system response time for any client-based transaction must not exceed 4 milliseconds" or "The total out-of-pocket cost plus five-year maintenance must not exceed $35 million."

Assessing the Completeness of Requirements Decomposition

Assessing completeness of the RBS is a subjective exercise. You might be able to tell if the RBS is complete but because you might have imperfect knowledge of the solution you might not recognize an incomplete RBS. The safe assumption is to assume that it is incomplete and proceed accordingly. To err on that side of the decision is not a serious error but to err on the other side by assuming it is complete when it is not can have serious consequences. I prefer to take the safe ground!

Project Classification

The question to answer here is whether the project should be managed by a PMLC model that is Linear, Incremental, Iterative, Adaptive, or Extreme. (See Table 4-2.) The answer is somewhat subjective and depends mostly on the degree to which you and the client see the RBS as complete.

Table 4-2: Project Characteristics as a Determinant of Which PMLC Model to Use

PMLC MODEL TYPE	WHEN TO USE IT
Linear	The solution and requirements are clearly defined.
	You do not expect too many scope change requests.
	The project is routine and repetitive.
	You can use established templates.
Incremental	Same conditions as the Linear approach, but the client wants to deploy business value incrementally.
	There may be some likelihood of scope change requests.
Iterative	You feel that requirements are not complete or may change.
	You will learn about remaining requirements in the course of doing the project.
	Some features of the solution are not yet identified.
Adaptive	The solution and requirements are only partially known.
	There may be functionality that is not yet identified.
	There will be a number of scope changes from the client.
	The project is oriented to new product development or process improvement.
	The development schedule is tight and you can't afford rework or re-planning.
Extreme	The goal and solution are not clearly known.
	The project is an R & D type project.

You'll explore each of these in more detail in subsequent chapters. In Chapter 10, I discuss the Linear and Incremental PMLC models. In Chapter 11, I discuss the Iterative and Adaptive PMLC models. In Chapter 12, I discuss the Extreme and Emertxe PMLC models. Each of these models will have other adaptations that result in special-case models. These will also be discussed in detail. The final picture is one of a rich family of models that cover the entire project landscape and fit any project situation you are likely to encounter.

You have now reached the point where a critical decision needs to be made about how to manage this project. At this point, the project management gurus would agree that you cannot say that the requirements list is complete. You can never really know that until the project is complete and all success criteria have been met. However, you *can* say that the requirements are *not* complete. Certain parts are missing, and you know they are missing. The more that is missing, the more complex the process of managing the project will be. The development manager and the client manager must make an initial decision on the best-fit PMLC based on the degree to which requirements are complete. Completeness is more of an expression of the comfort level you have with the RBS than it is any quantitative measure of completeness. It is a subjective call, and it is not a "once for the whole life of the project" decision — it can change as the clarity and completeness of the requirements changes. For example, at some point in the project life cycle, the project team may experience the great "AHA!" At last the project team sees what the complete solution looks like. Does it make sense to change the PMLC? It might. It might not. Here are some criteria to consider:

- What are the cost and time penalties for abandoning the current PMLC and changing to a different PMLC?

- Can the project team adapt to the new PMLC?

- How certain are you and your client that a change will result in a better solution?

- What is the cost versus the benefit of the change?

As you can see, gathering and documenting client requirements is extremely difficult even in the simplest of situations. Poorly defined requirements are the root cause of many project failures, so it is critical that you approach this task with the best-fit requirements gathering approach available to you. For clients, the requirements gathering approach you use is difficult because they are being asked to think about satisfying their needs using tools that they may not be familiar with. For project managers, the requirements documentation approach they choose may be difficult because they may not have made the distinction between client wants and client needs. For both parties, generating the RBS is a learning experience. How well the client and the project manager are able to learn will be the key to project success. Therefore, the choice of PMLC will be a critical success factor for that learning to take place and for successful requirements documentation.

In addition to being a good representation of the requirements, the RBS works very well as a requirements gathering approach for any project because of the following characteristics:

- It does not require a trained facilitator.
- It does not require learning one of the contemporary approaches to requirements gathering.
- It presents an intuitive approach to gathering requirements.
- It allows the client to work with the project team in an environment that is familiar to them, enabling them to stay in their own comfort zone.
- It paints a clear picture of the degree to which the solution is clearly defined.
- It provides the input needed to choose the best-fit PMLC model and the appropriate project management approach.

Determining the Best-Fit PMLC Model

The choices come from among such approaches as Waterfall, Scrum, and many, many others. Organizations will have a preference and will have skilled and experienced potential team members to adequately staff their preferences. Scrum is an extremely powerful and popular choice in many organizations, but it requires a senior level developer who can work without supervision in a self-managed situation. That puts a strain on many organizations whose developers will often be less experienced.

Based on the project characteristics, which specific PMLC model is the closest fit? This decision is made without a consideration of the environment in which it will be implemented. It is based solely on goal and solution clarity.

Based on the project environment how does that model need to be adjusted to establish the best fit model? An example is the best way to convey this information. Suppose the project is in the adaptive category and Scrum is the obvious choice. Scrum requires meaningful client involvement through their representative, the Product Owner, but such an individual cannot be identified. As an alternative an iterative approach, such as RUP or Evolutionary Waterfall, might be used. The difference being that the project manager and a senior level BA can function as co-project managers and together they can take a more proactive role that otherwise would have been done by the Product Owner.

For another example, consider a project that is best categorized as iterative and RUP would be the best-fit choice. However, past projects for that client have been disappointing because the client could not fully participate. One alternative would be to step back and use an incremental approach to compensate for the shortcomings of the client involvement and allow the project manager and BA to take up the slack. An approach I have used is to go ahead with the choice of a RUP approach but to strengthen it by holding concurrent workshops with the client to help them better understand their role and responsibilities. For example, a workshop on use cases could be helpful if run concurrently with the requirements gathering exercises.

Writing the POS

The more complexity and uncertainty associated with the project, the more likely senior management will want assurances that the approach that will be used to solve the problem or to take advantage of a business opportunity makes good business sense. A very important question will be, "Does the resulting business value exceed the total cost of the deliverables?" Validation may take the form of using the organization's templates to establish validity. You may have to simulate the deliverables by building a prototype of the solution. You can expect to provide any number of financial analyses such as cost/benefit, Return on Investment (ROI), breakeven, and cash flow analyses, among others. Some of these might accompany the POS.

The COS and the deliverables from the Project Scoping Meeting if one is held are the primary inputs you need to generate the Project Overview Statement (POS). The POS is a short document (ideally one page) that concisely states what is to be done in the project, why it is to be done, and what business value it will provide to the enterprise when completed.

The main purpose of the POS is to secure senior management's approval and the resources needed to develop a detailed project plan. It will be reviewed by the managers who are responsible for setting priorities and deciding what projects to support. It is also a general statement that can be read by any interested party in the enterprise. For this reason, the POS cannot contain any technical jargon that generally would not be used across the enterprise. After it is approved, the POS becomes the foundation for future planning and execution of the project. It becomes the reference document for questions or conflicts regarding the project's scope and purpose.

My idea for the POS originated at Texas Instruments in the early 1960s. They used a form of the POS as part of a process whereby anyone in the organization could suggest an idea for increasing efficiency, improving productivity, or seizing a business opportunity. One particular example has stayed with me over all these years. It involved a maintenance man whose only equipment was a Phillips-head screwdriver. He walked the halls of an approximately 1,800,000-square-foot building and tightened the screws that held the wall-mounted ashtrays in position. You could smoke inside the building in those days. They became loose from people or equipment bumping into them. The maintenance man had an idea for replacing these screws with another fastening device that would not work loose, and he presented his idea using a POS. The project was funded, and he was appointed project manager. The project was completed successfully, and his job was thus eliminated. (I hope he was able to move on to something a little more challenging and rewarding!) Today, several organizations use the POS or some adaptation of it.

Because the POS can be drafted rather quickly by one person, it serves to capture a brief statement of the nature of the idea. Senior management can react to the proposed idea without spending too much time. If the idea has merit, the proposer will be asked to provide a detailed plan. The idea may be conditionally accepted, pending a little more justification by the proposer. Again, the idea is pursued further if it has merit. Otherwise, it is rejected at this early stage, before too much time and too many resources are spent on needless planning.

The POS can serve other purposes as well. Here are a couple of examples.

Inherited Project — Sometimes you inherit a project. In these instances, the project has been defined and scoped. A budget, staff resources, and a completion date have also been determined. In this scenario, do you write a POS? Yes!

There are at least two reasons to write a POS when you inherit a project. The first is to become familiar with and understand the project as well as the client's and management's expectations. I can't stress enough how important it is for both the requestor and provider to ensure that what will be delivered is what the client expects.

The second reason is that the POS will become the referent for the planning team. It is the foundation on which the project plan will be built. The project team can use the POS as the tiebreaker or referent to resolve any misunderstandings. In this case, the project scope has been determined, and it is up to the planning team to ensure that the resulting project plan is within the scope of the project, as defined in the POS.

Briefing Tool — An equally important reason for writing a POS is to give your team briefing information on the project. In addition to reaching a consensus with your client on what will be done, the team members need to have an understanding of the project at their level of involvement. Think of this as a COS for the team. Here the focus is on ensuring that you (as the project manager) and the team have a common understanding of the project. The POS serves as a good briefing tool for staff members who are added after the project commences. It helps them get up to speed with their understanding of the project.

Parts of the POS

The POS has the following five component parts:

- Problem or opportunity
- Project goal
- Project objectives
- Success criteria
- Assumptions, risks, and obstacles

Its structure is designed to lead senior managers from a statement of fact (problem or opportunity) to a statement of what this project will address (project goal). Senior management is interested in the project goal and whether it addresses a concern of sufficiently high priority; therefore, they need details on exactly what the project includes (project objectives). The business value is expressed as quantitative business outcomes (success criteria). Finally, conditions that may hinder project success are identified (assumptions, risks, and obstacles). The following sections take a closer look at each of these POS components. An example POS is shown in Figure 4-11.

PROJECT OVERVIEW STATEMENT	Project Name	Project No.	Project Manager
Problem/Opportunity			
Goal			
Objectives			
Success Criteria			
Assumptions, Risks, Obstacles			
Prepared by	Date	Approved by	Date

Figure 4-11: An example POS

Stating the Problem or Opportunity

The first part of the POS is a statement of the problem or opportunity that the project addresses. This statement is fact — it does not need to be defined or defended. Everyone in the organization will accept it as true. This is critical because it provides a basis for the rest of the document. The POS may not have the benefit of the project manager's being present to explain what is written or to defend the reason for proposing the project to management. A problem or opportunity statement that is known and accepted by the organization is the foundation on which to build a rationale for the project. It also sets the priority with which management will view what follows. If you are addressing a high-priority area or high-business-value area, your idea will get more attention and senior management will read on.

Here are several examples of situations that will lead to a statement of the problem or opportunity that has given rise to this POS.

> **Known Problem or Opportunity** — Every organization has a collection of known problems. Several attempts to alleviate part of or the entire problem may have already been made. The POS gives proposers a way to relate their idea to a known problem and to offer a full or partial solution. If the problem is serious enough and if the proposed solution is feasible, further action will be taken. In this case, senior managers will request a more detailed solution plan from the requestor.

> With the business world changing and redefining itself continuously, opportunities for new or enhanced products and services present themselves constantly. Organizations must be able to take advantage of them quickly because the window of opportunity is not wide and is itself constantly moving. The POS offers an easy way to seize these opportunities.

> **Client Request** — Internal or external clients make requests for products or services, and their requests are represented in the COS. The POS is an excellent vehicle for capturing the request and forwarding it to senior management for resolution. More recently, with employee-empowerment trends, a worker may not only receive a request, but may also have the authority to act on that request. The POS, coupled with the COS, establishes an excellent and well-defined starting point for any project.

> **Corporate Initiative** — Proposals to address new corporate initiatives should begin with the POS. Several ideas will come from the employees, and the POS provides a standardized approach and document from which senior management can prioritize proposals and select those that merit further attention. A standard documentation method for corporate initiatives simplifies senior management's decision-making process for authorizing new projects.

> **Mandated Requirements** — In many cases, a project must be undertaken because of a mandated requirement, arising from market changes, client requirements, federal legislation, as well as other sources. The POS is a vehicle for establishing an agreement between the provider and the decision maker about the result of the project. The POS clarifies for all interested parties exactly how the organization has decided to respond to the mandate.

Establishing the Project Goal

The second section of the POS states the goal of the project — what you intend to do to address the problem or opportunity identified in the first section of the POS. The purpose of the goal statement is to get senior management to value the idea enough to read on. In other words, they should think enough of the idea to conclude that it warrants further attention and consideration. Several submissions may propose the same issue. Because yours will not be the only proposal that's submitted, you want it to stand out among the crowd.

A project has one goal. The goal gives purpose and direction to the project. At a very high level, it defines the final deliverable or outcome of the project in clear terms so that everyone understands what is to be accomplished. The goal statement will be used as a continual point of reference for any questions that arise regarding the project's scope or purpose.

The goal statement must not contain any language or terminology that might not be understandable to anyone having occasion to read it. In other words, no "techie talk" is allowed. It is written in the language of the business so that anyone who reads it will understand it without further explanation from the proposer. Under all circumstances, avoid jargon.

Just like the problem or opportunity statement, the goal statement is short and to the point. Keep in mind that the more you write, the more you increase the risk that someone will find fault with something you have said. The goal statement does not include any information that might commit the project to dates or deliverables that are not practical. Remember that you do not have much detail about the project at this point.

The specification of a date deserves further discussion because it is of major interest to the client and to senior management. First, and most important, you do not control the start date and therefore you cannot possibly know the end date. For example, it might be that the most specific statement you could make at this point is that you could complete the project approximately 9 to 12 months after starting. Even such a broad statement as that is fraught with risk because you do not know the particulars of the project yet. Senior management will need some type of statement regarding completion before they will give authorization to continue the project to the planning stages. Your objective is to postpone giving any fixed duration or completion date until you have completed the project plan.

Unfortunately, most managers have a habit of accepting as cast in stone any number that they see in writing, regardless of the origin of the number. The goal statement should not include a specific completion date. (I realize that this is easier said than done.) If you expect management to ask for a date, estimate the date to the nearest quarter, month, or week as appropriate, but with the caveat that the estimated delivery date will become more specific as you learn more details about the project. The first instance of that will be the project plan. It will specify the total duration of the project, not a specific end date. It is important that management understand how some of the early numbers are estimated, and that a great deal of variability exists in those early estimates. Assure them that better estimates will be provided as the project plan is built and the project work is undertaken. Leave the specific dates for the detailed planning session, when a more informed decision can be made.

George Doran's S.M.A.R.T. characteristics provide the following criteria for a goal statement:[1]

Specific — Be specific in targeting an objective.

Measurable — Establish measurable indicators of progress.

Assignable — Make the object assignable to one person for completion.

Realistic — State what can realistically be done with available resources.

Time-related — State when the objective can be achieved — that is, the duration.

In practice, I have incorporated the S.M.A.R.T. characteristics into both the POS and the project plan. The Specific characteristic can be found in the problem or opportunity statement and the goal statement (discussed previously), and the objective statements (discussed next). The Measurable characteristic is incorporated into the success criteria, discussed later in this section. The Assignable, Realistic, and Time-related characteristics are part of the project plan and are discussed in Chapter 5.

Defining the Project Objectives

The third section of the POS describes the project objectives. Think of objective statements as a more detailed version of the goal statement. The purpose of objective statements is to clarify the exact boundaries of the goal statement and define the boundaries or the scope of your project. In fact, the objective statements you write for a specific goal statement are nothing more than a decomposition of the goal statement into a set of necessary and sufficient objective statements. That is, every objective must be accomplished in order to reach the goal, and no objective is superfluous.

A good exercise to test the validity of the objective statements is to ask if they clarify what is in and what is not in the project. Statements of objectives should specify a future state, rather than being activity-based. They are statements that clarify the goal by providing details about the goal. If you think of them as sub-goals, you will not be far off the mark.

One variation that I have seen work particularly well is to state what is not in the project. When you are having trouble defining what is in the project, think of this as an added convenience for clarification. Don't get carried away with this though. I have also seen senior management add some of the "what is not in the project" objectives to the project objectives.

---

[1]George T. Doran, "There's a S.M.A.R.T. Way to Write Management Goals and Objectives," *Management Review* (November 1981): 35–36.

It is also important to keep in mind that these are the *current* objective statements. They may change during the course of planning the project. This will happen as details of the project work are defined. We all have the tendency to put more on our plates than we need. The result is that the client and subsequently the project team will often include project activities and tasks that extend beyond the boundaries defined in the POS. When this occurs, stop the planning session and ask whether the activity is outside the scope of the project; and, if so, whether you should adjust the scope to include the new activity or delete the new activity from the project plan.

The objectives might also change during the course of doing the project. This occurs in cases where the requirements are not completely and clearly defined during the scoping activities but are subsequently discovered during the project. This is quite common, so don't be too alarmed.

> **TIP** You will find that throughout the project planning activities discussed in this book, there will be occasions to stop and reaffirm project boundaries. Boundary clarification questions will continually come up. Adopting this questioning approach is sound TPM.

An objective statement should contain the following four parts:

- **An outcome** — A statement of what is to be accomplished.
- **A time frame** — A preliminary estimate of duration.
- **A measure** — Metrics that will measure success.
- **An action** — How the objective will be met.

In many cases, the complete objective statement will be spread across the POS rather than collected under the heading of "Objectives." This is especially true for the time frame and measures of success.

Identifying Success Criteria

The fourth section of the POS answers the question, "Why do we want to do this project?" It is the measurable business value that will result from doing this project. It sells the project to senior management.

Whatever criteria are used, they must answer the question, "What must happen for us and the client to say the project was a success?" The COS will contain the beginnings of a statement of success criteria. Phrased another way, success criteria form a statement of doneness. It is also a statement of the business value to be achieved; therefore, it provides a basis for senior management to authorize the resources to do detailed planning. It is essential that the criteria be quantifiable and measurable, and, if possible, expressed in terms of business value. Remember that you are trying to sell your idea to the decision makers.

No matter how you define success criteria, they all reduce to one of the following three types:

Increased revenue — As a part of the success criteria, the increase should be measured in hard dollars or as a percentage of a specific revenue number.

Reduced costs — Again, this criterion can be stated as a hard-dollar amount or a percentage of some specific cost. Be careful here because oftentimes a cost reduction means staff reductions. Staff reductions do not mean the shifting of resources to other places in the organization. Moving staff from one area to another is not a cost reduction.

Improved service — Here the metric is more difficult to define. It's usually some percentage of improvement in client satisfaction or a reduction in the frequency or type of client complaints.

In some cases, identifying the success criteria is not so simple. For example, client satisfaction may have to be measured by some pre- and post-surveys. In other cases, a surrogate might be acceptable if directly measuring the business value of the project is impossible. Be careful, however, and make sure that the decision maker buys into your surrogate measure. Also be careful of traps such as this one: "We haven't been getting any client complaint calls; therefore, the client must be satisfied." Did you ever consider the possibility that the lack of complaint calls may be the direct result of your lack of action responding to complaints? Clients may feel that it does no good to complain because nothing happens to settle their complaints.

The best choice for success criteria is to state clearly the bottom-line impact of the project. This is expressed in terms such as increased margins, higher net revenues, reduced turnaround time, improved productivity, a reduced cost of manufacturing or sales, and so on. Because you want senior management's approval of your proposal, you should express the benefits in the terms with which they routinely work.

Even if you recognize the bottom-line impact as the best success criteria, you may not be able to use it as such. As an alternative, consider quantifiable statements about the impact your project will have on efficiency and effectiveness, error rates, reduced turnaround time to service a client request, reduced cost of providing the service, quality, or improved client satisfaction. Management deals in deliverables, so always try to express your success criteria in quantitative terms. By doing this, you avoid any possibility of disagreement as to whether the success criteria were met and the project was successful.

Senior management will also look at your success criteria and assign business value to your project. In the absence of other criteria, this will be the basis for their decision about whether or not to commit resources to complete the detailed plan. The success criteria are another place to sell the value of your project. For example, one success criteria can be as follows:

This reengineering project is expected to reduce order entry to order fulfillment cycle time by 6 percent.

From that statement, management may conclude the following:

If that is all you expect to gain from this project, we cannot finance the venture.

Alternatively, they may respond as follows:

If you can get 6 percent improvement from our current process, that will be a remarkable feat — so remarkable, in fact, that we would like more detail on how you expect to get that result. Can you provide an analysis to substantiate your claim?

Subjective measures of success will not do the job. You must speak quantitatively about tangible business benefits. This may require some creativity on your part. For example, when proposing a project that will have an impact on client satisfaction, you will need to be particularly creative. There may be some surrogates for client satisfaction. A popular approach to such situations is to construct and conduct pre- and post-surveys. The change will measure the value of the project.

Listing Assumptions, Risks, and Obstacles

The fifth section of the POS identifies any factors that can affect the outcome of the project and that you want to bring to the attention of senior management. These factors can affect deliverables, the realization of the success criteria, the ability of the project team to complete the project as planned, and any other environmental or organizational conditions that are relevant to the project. You want to record anything that can go wrong.

WARNING   Be careful to put in the POS only the items that you want senior management to know about and in which they will be interested. Items that are quite specific and too detailed to be of interest to senior managers should be saved for the Project Definition Statement (PDS). The PDS list may be extensive and generates good input for the risk analysis discussed in Chapter 2. (You'll learn more about the PDS in Chapter 5.)

The project manager uses the assumptions, risks, and obstacles section to alert management to any factors that may interfere with the project work or compromise the contribution that the project can make to the organization. Management may be able to neutralize the impact of these factors. Conversely, the project manager should include in the project plan whatever contingencies can help reduce the probable impact and its effect on project success.

Do not assume that everyone knows what the risks and perils to the project will be. Planning is a process of discovery about the project itself as well as any hidden perils that may cause embarrassment for the team. Document them and discuss them.

There are several areas where the project can be exposed to influences that may inhibit project success. They are as follows:

Technological — The company may not have much or any experience with new technology, whether it is new to the company or new to the industry. The same can be said for rapidly changing technology. Who can say whether the present design and technology will still be current in three months or six months?

Environmental — The environment in which the project work is to be done can be an important determinant. An unstable or changing management structure can change a high-priority project to a low-priority project overnight. If your project sponsor leaves, will there be a new sponsor? And if so, how will he or she view the project? Will the project's priority be affected? High staff turnover will also present problems. The project team cannot get up on the learning curve if turnover is high. A related problem stems from the skill requirements of the project. The higher the skill level required, the higher the risk associated with the project.

Interpersonal — Relationships among project team members are critical to project success. You don't have to be friends, but you do have to be coworkers and team players. If sound working relationships are not present among the project team or stakeholders, there will be problems. These interpersonal problems should be called to the attention of senior management.

Cultural — How does the project fit with the enterprise? Is it consistent with the way the enterprise functions, or will it require a significant change to be successful? For example, if the deliverable from the project is a new process that takes away decision-making authority from staff who are used to making more of their own decisions, you can expect development, implementation, and support problems to occur.

Causal relationships — All project managers like to think that what they are proposing will correct the situation addressed. They assume a cause and effect relationship where one may not exist. The proposer assumes that the solution will, in fact, solve the problem. If this is the case, these assumptions need to be clearly stated in the POS. Remember that the rest of the world does not stand still waiting for your solution. Things continue to change, and it is a fair question to ask whether your solution depends on all other things remaining equal.

Attachments

Even though I strongly recommend a one-page POS, some projects call for a longer document. As part of their initial approval of the resources to do detailed project planning, senior management may want some measure of the economic value of the proposed project. They recognize that many of the estimates are little more than an order-of-magnitude guess, but they will nevertheless ask for this information. I have seen the following two types of analyses requested frequently:

- Risk analysis
- Financial analysis

The following sections briefly discuss these analysis types. Check the bibliography in Appendix C for sources where you can find more information about these topics.

- **Risk Analysis** — In my experience, risk analysis is the most frequently used attachment to the POS. In some cases, this analysis is a very cursory treatment. In others, it is a mathematically rigorous exercise. Many business-decision models depend on quantifying risks, the expected loss if the risk materializes, and the probability that the risk will occur. All of these are quantified, and the resulting analysis guides management in its project-approval decisions.

  In high-technology industries, risk analysis is becoming the rule rather than the exception. Formal procedures are established as part of the initial definition of a project and continue throughout the life of the project. These analyses typically contain the identification of risk factors, the likelihood of their occurrence, the damage they will cause, and containment actions to reduce their likelihood or their potential damage. The cost of the containment program is compared with the expected loss as a basis for deciding which containment strategies to put in place.

- **Financial Analyses** — Some organizations require a preliminary financial analysis of the project before granting approval to perform the detailed planning. Although such analyses are very rough because not enough information is known about the project at this time, they will offer a tripwire for project-planning approval. In some instances, they also offer criteria for prioritizing all of the POS documents that senior management will be reviewing. At one time, IBM required a financial analysis from the project manager as part of the POS submission. Following are brief descriptions of the types of financial analyses you may be asked to provide.

  Feasibility Studies — The methodology to conduct a feasibility study is remarkably similar to the problem-solving method (or scientific method, if you prefer). It involves the following steps:

  1. Clearly define the problem.
  2. Describe the boundary of the problem — that is, what is in the problem scope and what is outside the problem scope.

3. Define the features and functions of a good solution.

4. Identify alternative solutions.

5. Rank alternative solutions.

6. State the recommendations along with the rationale for the choice.

7. Provide a rough estimate of the timetable and expected costs. You, as the project manager, will be asked to provide the feasibility study when senior management wants to review the thinking that led to the proposed solution. A thoroughly researched solution can help build your credibility as the project manager.

Cost and Benefit Analyses — These analyses are always difficult to do because you need to include intangible benefits in the decision process. As mentioned earlier in the chapter, things such as improved client satisfaction cannot be easily quantified. You could argue that improved client satisfaction reduces client turnover, which in turn increases revenues, but how do you put a number on that? In many cases, senior management will take these inferences into account, but they still want to see hard-dollar comparisons. Opt for the direct and measurable benefits to compare against the cost of doing the project and the cost of operating the new process. If the benefits outweigh the costs over the expected life of the project deliverables, senior management may be willing to support the project.

Breakeven Analysis — This is a timeline that shows the cumulative cost of the project against the cumulative revenue or savings from the project. At each point where the cumulative revenue or savings line crosses the cumulative cost line, the project will recoup its costs. Usually senior management looks for an elapsed time less than some threshold number. If the project meets that deadline date, it may be worthy of support. Targeted breakeven dates are getting shorter because of more frequent changes in the business and its markets.

Return on Investment — The ROI analyzes the total costs as compared with the increased revenue that will accrue over the life of the project deliverables. Here senior management finds a common basis for comparing one project against another. They look for the high ROI projects or the projects that at least meet some minimum ROI.

CROSS-REFERENCE **Many books provide more detailed explanations of each of these analyses. The bibliography in Appendix C contains some suggested titles.**

Submitting the POS

After you have completed the POS, you need to submit it to your senior management for approval. The approval process is far from a formality. It is a deliberate decision on the part of senior management that the project as presented does indeed have business value and that it is worth proceeding to the detailed planning phase. As part of the approval process, senior management asks several questions regarding the information presented. Remember, they are trying to make good business decisions and need to test your thinking along the way. My best advice is to remember that the document must stand on its own. You will not be present to explain what you meant. Write in the language of the business, and anticipate questions as you review the content of the POS.

During this process, expect several iterations. Despite your best efforts to make the POS stand on its own, you will not be successful at first. Senior management always has questions. For example, they can question the scope of the project and may ask you to consider expanding or contracting it. They may ask for documentation showing how you arrived at the results that you claim in your success criteria. If financial analyses are attached, you may have to provide additional justification or explanation of the attachments.

The approved POS serves three audiences, as follows:

- **Senior management** — The approval of senior management is their statement that the project makes enough business sense to move to the detailed planning stage.

- **The client** — The client's approval is his or her concurrence that the project has been correctly described and that he or she is in agreement with the solution being offered.

- **The project team** — The approved POS serves as a message to the project team from senior management and the client that the project has been clearly defined at this high level of detail.

Approval of the POS commits the resources required to complete a detailed plan for the project. It is not the approval to do the project. Approval to proceed with the project is the result of an approval of the detailed plan. At this early stage, not too much is known about the project. Rough estimates of time or cost variables (also referred to as WAGs, for "wild a** guesses," or SWAGs, for "scientific wild a** guesses") are often requested from the project manager and the project team. You may also be asked to describe what will be done and how this will benefit the enterprise. More meaningful estimates of time and cost are part of the detailed plan.

Gaining management approval of the POS is a significant event in the life of a project. The approving manager questions the project manager, and the answers are scrutinized very carefully. Even though there isn't a lot of detailed analysis to support it, the POS is still valuable to test the thinking of the proposer and the validity of the proposed project. It is not unusual to have the project manager return to the drawing board several times for more analysis and thought as a prerequisite to management approval. As senior managers review the POS, you can anticipate the following review questions:

- How important is the problem or opportunity to the enterprise?
- How is the project related to our critical success factors (CSFs)?
- Does the goal statement relate directly to the problem or opportunity?
- Are the objectives clear representations of the goal statement?
- Is there sufficient business value as measured by the success criteria to warrant further expenditures on this project?
- Is the relationship between the project objectives and the success criteria clearly established?
- Are the risks too high and the business value too low?
- Can senior management mitigate the identified risks?

The approval of the POS is not a perfunctory or ceremonial approval. By approving the document, professionals and managers are saying that, based on what they understand the project to involve and its business value, it demonstrates good business sense to go to the next level — that is, to commit the resources needed to develop a detailed project plan.

Participants in the Approval Process

The following managers and professionals will often participate in the approval process:

- **Core project team** — At the preliminary stages of the project, a core project team may have been identified. This team will be made up of the managers, the professionals, and perhaps the client who will remain on the project team from the beginning to the very end of the project. They may participate in developing the POS and reach consensus on what it contains.
- **Project team** — Some potential members of the project team are usually known beforehand. Their subject-matter expertise and ideas should be considered as the POS is developed. At the least, you should have them review the POS before you submit it to upper management.
- **Project manager** — Ideally, the project manager will have been identified at the start and can participate in drafting the POS. Because you will manage the project, you should have a major role to play in its definition and its approval.
- **Resource managers** — Individuals who will be asked to provide the skills needed for the project are certainly important in its initial definition and

later during its detailed planning. There is little point in proposing a project if the resources are not or cannot be made available to the project.

- **Function or process managers** — Project deliverables don't exist in a vacuum. Several business or functional units will provide input to or receive output from the project products or services. Their advice should be sought. Give them an early chance to buy into your project.

- **Client** — Clients play a significant role in the PMLC. As previously discussed, the COS is a prerequisite to, or a concurrent exercise in developing, the POS. Many professionals are not skilled in interpersonal communications. Developing the COS is a difficult task.

In some situations, the client is the project manager — for example, if the development of a product or service affects only one department or in projects where the client is very comfortable with project management practices. In these situations, I encourage the client to be the project manager. The benefits to the organization are several: increased buy-in, lower risk of failure, better implementation success, and deliverables that are more likely to meet the needs of the client, to name a few. Commitment and buy-in are always difficult to get. This problem is solved when the client is also the project manager. For this approach to work, the technical members of the project team take on the roles of advisor and consultant. It is their job to keep the feasible alternatives, and only the feasible alternatives, in front of the project manager. Decision making will be a little more difficult and time-consuming. However, by engaging the client as the project manager, the client not only appreciates the problems that are encountered but also gains some skill in resolving them. I have seen marvelous learning-curve effects that pay off in later projects with the same client.

- **Senior management** — Senior management support is a critical factor in successful projects and successful implementation of the deliverables. Their approval says, "Go and do detailed planning; we are authorizing the needed resources."

Approval Criteria

The approval criteria at this stage of the project life cycle are not as demanding as they will be when it's time to approve the project for execution or addition to the organization's project portfolio. All that senior management is looking for at this point is a rough estimate of the value of the project to the organization. Their approval at this stage extends only to an approval to plan the project. That detailed project plan will give them a more specific estimate of the project costs. Knowing the actual costs, senior management can calculate the return that they can expect from the project.

Project Approval Status

Senior management may not be ready or willing to give their approval to plan the project at this point. Instead, they might take one of the following courses of action:

- They may reject the proposal out of hand. That decision will often be based on a comparison of expected benefits versus total cost coupled with a time frame as to when the benefits will be realized.

- They may request a recalibration of the goal and scope of the project followed by a resubmission to seek approval to plan the project.

- They might decide that a later resubmission is in order. In other words, they are not ready to commit to the project at this time.

- Finally, the approval may be associated with a consideration to add the project to the organization's project portfolio. This is discussed in Chapter 14 as part of the project portfolio management topic.

Putting It All Together

A clear understanding of the project scope is critical to the planning and execution phases of the project. This chapter described the COS and POS as the two basic tools for developing a joint agreement and a joint statement of scope in collaboration with the client. As you will see in later chapters, these documents are the foundation of all project management approaches.

Discussion Questions

1. Traditional project management (TPM) depends heavily on being able to clearly define what the client needs. You cannot create a detailed project plan without that information. Within the framework of the TPM, what could you do if it were not possible to get a clear definition of client needs?

2. You have run the COS by the book, and your gut tells you that the client's wants may be a bit too far-reaching. In fact, you have a strong suspicion that what they need is not what they have told you they want. What could you do?

CHAPTER 5

How to Plan a TPM Project

This report, by its very length, defends itself against the risk of being read.
— **Winston Churchill, English Prime Minister**

The man who goes alone can start today, but he who travels with another must wait 'til that other is ready.
— **Henry David Thoreau, American naturalist**

Every moment spent planning saves three or four in execution.
— **Crawford Greenwalt, President, DuPont**

The hammer must be swung in cadence, when more than one is hammering the iron.
— **Giordano Bruno, Italian philosopher**

CHAPTER LEARNING OBJECTIVES

After reading this chapter, you will be able to:

■ Understand the importance of planning a project

■ Understand the purpose of the Joint Project Planning Session (JPPS)

■ Know how to plan a JPPS

■ Know the contents of the project proposal

■ Recognize the difference between activities and tasks

■ Understand the importance of the completeness criteria to your ability to manage the work of the project

(Continued)

CHAPTER LEARNING OBJECTIVES *(continued)*

- Explain the approaches to building the Work Breakdown Structure (WBS)
- Generate a WBS from the RBS
- Use the WBS as a planning tool and reporting tool
- Understand top-down versus bottom-up processes for building the WBS
- Define a work package and its purposes
- Understand the difference between effort and duration
- Explain the relationship between resource loading and task duration
- List and explain the causes of variation in task duration
- Use any one of six task-duration estimation methods
- Understand the process of creating cost estimates at the task level
- Schedule people to project activities using a skill matrix
- Understand the process of determining resource requirements at the task level
- Construct a network representation of the project tasks
- Understand the four types of task dependencies and when they are used
- Recognize the types of constraints that create task sequences
- Compute the earliest start (ES), earliest finish (EF), latest start (LS), and latest finish (LF) times for every task in the network
- Understand lag variables and their uses
- Identify the critical path in the project
- Define free slack and total slack and know their significance
- Analyze the network for possible schedule compression
- Use advanced network dependency relationships for improving the project schedule
- Understand and apply management reserve
- Utilize various approaches to leveling resources
- Determine the appropriate use of substitute resources

How often have you heard it said that planning is a waste of time? No sooner is the plan completed than someone comes along to change it. These same naysayers would also argue that the plan, once completed, is disregarded and merely put on the shelf so the team can get down to doing some real work. As this chapter points out, these views are incorrect.

Using Tools, Templates, and Processes to Plan a Project

If you were able to do a project twice — once with a good plan and once with a poor or no plan — the project with the good plan would finish earlier, including the time spent planning. The project with a good plan has a higher probability of finishing than does the poorly planned project. The quality is better, the cost is less, and the list of benefits to good planning goes on. So why is planning often seen as not being real work? Figure 5-1 expresses my message clearer than mere words could.

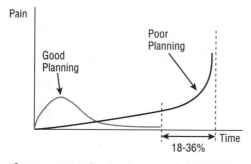

Figure 5-1: Pain curves

"Pay me now or pay me later" applies equally well to the oil change commercial as it does to project planning. When the team and management are anxious for work to begin, it is difficult to focus on developing a solid plan of action before you are pressed into service. At times it would seem that the level of detail in the plan is overkill, but it is not. The project manager must resist the pressure to start project work and instead spend the time up front generating a detailed project plan. It has been demonstrated that a poor planning effort takes its toll later in the project as schedules slip, quality suffers, and expectations are not met.

The pain curve demonstrates that proper planning is painful but pays off in less pain later in the project. To not plan is to expose yourself to significant pain as the project proceeds. In fact, that pain usually continues to increase. It would continue to increase indefinitely except that someone usually pulls the plug on the project when the pain reaches unbearable levels.

The International Benchmark Council (it has gone out of business and as far as I know has not re-emerged or passed its research to another organization) provided the data from more than 5000 completed projects that generates these two curves. The project that uses good planning finishes 18–36 percent sooner than the poorly planned project, including the time spent planning. If you want to get your management's attention, show them this curve. The pain curve is a powerful attention getter, and I strongly recommend you use it. Once you've got senior management attention, show them the support you will need to plan your newly assigned project!

In this chapter, you learn all of the tools, templates, and processes that you will need to generate good project plans. All of the material presented here is directly applicable to the Linear PLMC model. The concepts are also adaptable to all of the models discussed in Part II and are discussed there. More specifically, in this chapter you learn about the following:

- Planning and running a Joint Project Planning Session (JPPS)
- The relationship between the RBS and the WBS
- Creating the WBS
- Techniques for estimating task duration, resource requirements, and cost
- Building the initial schedule
- Analyzing the initial schedule
- Schedule compression techniques
- Writing an effective project proposal
- Gaining approval of the project proposal

The Importance of Planning

If you are to be an effective project manager, a project plan is indispensable. Not only is it a road map to how the work is scheduled, but it is also a tool to aid in your decision making. The plan suggests alternative approaches, schedules, and resource requirements from which you can select the best alternative.

NOTE Understand that a project plan is dynamic. It is a statement of intent, not a statement of fact. You expect it to change. A complete plan will clearly state the tasks that need to be done, why they are necessary, who will do what, when the project will be completed, what resources will be needed, and what criteria must be met in order for the project to be declared complete and successful. However, traditional project management (TPM) models are not designed for change, even though it is expected. Part II of this book describes project management life cycle (PMLC) models that are designed for change. One of the many advantages of these models is that change is accommodated within the process itself. Change in the TPM world is something the project manager would rather not deal with, whereas the project manager who is using the models discussed in Part II sees change as a necessary ingredient of a successful project.

There are three benefits to spending the effort needed to develop a good project plan. They are:

1. **Planning Reduces Uncertainty.**

   Even though you would never expect the project work to occur exactly as planned, planning the work enables you to consider the likely outcomes and to put the necessary corrective measures in place when things don't happen according to plan.

2. **Planning Increases Understanding.**

   The mere act of planning gives you a better understanding of the goals and objectives of the project. Even if you were to discard the plan, you would still benefit from having done the exercise.

3. **Planning Improves Efficiency.**

   After you have defined the project plan and the necessary resources to carry out the plan, you can schedule the work to take advantage of resource availability. You also can schedule work in parallel — that is, you can do tasks concurrently, rather than in series. By doing tasks concurrently, you can shorten the total duration of the project. You can maximize your use of resources and complete the project work in less time than by taking other approaches.

Just as Alice needed to know where in Wonderland she was going, the project manager needs to know the goal to be achieved by the project and the steps that will be taken to attain that goal, that is, the solution. Not knowing the parameters of a project prevents measurement of progress and results in never knowing when the project is complete. The plan also provides a basis for measuring work planned against work performed.

Using Application Software Packages to Plan a Project

Before I begin discussing the tools, templates, and processes needed for project planning, I want to spend some time on the software packages and why you might or might not use them. I have always been an advocate of using the appropriate tools to plan a project. My experiences have ranged from the back of the napkin to the use of sophisticated modeling and prototyping tools. The size and complexity of the project has a lot to do with your choice of software packages. The larger the project, the more you will need to depend on software packages. But what about small projects or projects that are done in some incremental or iterative fashion? The answer is not always clear, but the following section describes my approach.

Determining the Need for a Software Package

Project management software packages (at least those priced under $1000 per seat) are both a boon and a bust to project teams. On the boon side of the ledger, they are great planning tools and allow the project manager to investigate several alternatives without the accompanying labor of having to manually adjust the planning parameters. On the bust side, they have not been very helpful in managing resources and in fact have had some rather bizarre results.

Schedule updates are also a troublesome area. The problem lies in getting reliable estimates of percent complete and estimated time to completion from each task manager. Garbage in, garbage out. These data are essential to maintaining the project plan. On balance, the project manager has to be aware of the time savings, the time drains, and the reliability of the schedule updates in deciding whether to use a package or not. It all comes down to the value that is added for the effort that is expended. The smaller the project, the less likely it is that you will find added value in using the software package. Clearly for large or even medium-sized projects, software packages are a must.

For the types of projects that this book deals with, the answers aren't all that obvious. In these cases, project software packages can make the task of building the initial project plan a bit less labor-intensive than manual alternatives are. But even that is a matter of choice and preference. You can just as easily move sticky notes across a whiteboard as you can drag and drop task nodes across a Project Evaluation and Review Technique (PERT) chart. PERT is a graphical tool that displays the relationship between dependent tasks. For schedule updating, I have a clear preference for whiteboards and sticky notes. My reasoning is that I can get the entire team involved in the exercise, and everyone can see the alternatives much easier on the whiteboard than they can on the computer screen. For distributed teams, some compensation can be made by using web-based tools to communicate sticky note information electronically.

The best testimony I can give you is from my own experiences managing a three-year, $5M project. All I used were the planning tools discussed in the next section. That agile project was completed nine months early, successful beyond client expectations, and significantly under budget.

Project Planning Tools

The list here is very short: sticky notes, marking pens, and plenty of whiteboard space. I don't want you to think that I have taken a step backward to a time when there were no automated tools. Quite the contrary: I do use automated tools for project planning but not for execution. The tools I just mentioned happen to be my choice for some incremental, most iterative, all adaptive, and all extreme projects. These are introduced in Chapter 9 and discussed in detail in Chapters 10, 11, and 12. Agile, Extreme, and Emertxe projects account for more than 80 percent of all projects. The reason I use such simple tools is simple.

These projects all proceed in short cycles of two to four weeks. You don't need a sledgehammer to kill a mosquito! If you really have to depend on software tools, go ahead. Just remember that if you create the plan using software tools, you have to maintain it.

Sticky Notes

Sticky notes are used to record information about a single task in the project. The information that you might want to record on a sticky note includes the following:

- Task ID
- Unique task name
- Task duration
- Task labor
- Resource requirements
- Task leader
- Calculated values such as earliest start (ES), earliest finish (EF), latest start (LS), and latest finish (LF)
- Critical path (calculated)

Color-coded sticky notes offer a number of alternatives for the creative planner. For example, you can use a different color to represent each of the following:

- The type of task (critical, for example)
- Specific parts of the WBS (design, build, test, and implement, for example)
- A position on the team (a critical or scarce skill, for example)

Using sticky notes in this way is not only visually appealing, but it's very informative during resource scheduling and finalization of the project plan. With experience, the color coding becomes intuitive.

Marking Pens

For the purposes of project planning, you will need dry-erase marking pens. They come in several colors, but you will only need the black and red ones. They are used to visually display the dependencies (black marking pens) that exist among and between the project tasks or the critical path (red marking pens).

Whiteboard

The whiteboard is indispensable. Flip charts are not a good alternative. For large projects, you need to have a minimum of about 30 linear feet of whiteboard space for planning purposes. The room that provides this space will become the team war room and, if possible, should be reserved for the exclusive use of the team for the entire project. It will need to be a secure room as well.

CROSS-REFERENCE   See Chapter 6 for more on the team war room.

The whiteboard will be used to create, document, and in some cases post the following:

- Project Overview Statement (POS)*
- WBS*
- Dependency diagram*
- Initial project schedule
- Final project schedule*
- Resource schedule*
- Issues log*
- Updated project schedule*

The items shown with an asterisk (*) are permanently posted on the whiteboard and updated as required.

Portable electronic whiteboards can be used when a dedicated space is not available.

How Much Time Should Planning Take?

This is one of those "it all depends" questions. This is not a question that is easily answered because a number of variables will affect planning time. The most important variables are project complexity, solution clarity, and the availability of the team members and the client for planning meetings. The actual labor involved in building a plan for the typical small project is about one workday. Ideally that would occur in one calendar day, but peoples' schedules might make that impossible. When you have difficulty scheduling the planning team, don't revert to planning by walking around. That just doesn't work. Trust me — I learned the hard way!

As a rule of thumb the following estimates of planning time are a good guide:

Very small projects: Less than 1/2 day

Small projects: Less than one day

Medium projects: 2 days

Large projects: 3–4 days

Very large projects: 30 team members translates to a large project. The planning time can vary widely from 5 or more days to several months.

Further complicating estimating planning time are the APM, xPM, and MPx projects. For all of the PMLC models in those three quadrants planning is done iteratively over time. If you still need an estimate, here is the best I have to offer. If you know the total number of iterations involved, then consider each iteration as a very small project and multiply the number of iterations by 1/2 day.

Running the Planning Session

Consider the ideal situation first. All of the following activities are part of the planning process, and all of them are completed in one workday. This section gives you a high-level look at what these activities are. In subsequent sections, you'll learn the details of how they are to be accomplished.

In a one-day planning session for a typical small project, the planning team performs the following major activities:

- Reviews the POS for clarity
- Creates the complete WBS, including the Activity List
- Estimates task duration and resource needs
- Constructs project network diagram
- Determines critical path
- Revises and approves project completion date
- Finalizes resource schedule
- Gains consensus on the project plan

The project manager can run the planning session for small simple projects. For larger or more complex projects, it pays to have someone other than the project manager facilitate the planning meetings. To complete this planning session in one day, the project manager will have to tightly control the discussion and keep the planning team moving forward. Any briefing materials that can be distributed ahead of time will help reduce briefing time in the actual planning meeting. There should be a timed agenda, and everyone must commit to sticking to it. Ground rules need to be put in place. One time-saving alternative is to have the project manager and the client complete the Conditions of Satisfaction (COS) and Project Overview Statement (POS) ahead of time and circulate these documents to the planning team prior to the meeting.

Planning and Conducting Joint Project Planning Sessions

All of the planning activities discussed so far to create the detailed project plan take place in a Joint Project Planning Session (JPPS). I advocate and use a group process for generating the detailed project plan. The JPPS is a group session in which all of the people who are involved in the project meet to develop the detailed plan. The session can last from one to three days, and it can be work-intensive. Conflict between session attendees is common, but the final result of this meeting is an agreement about how the project can be accomplished within a specified time frame, budget, resource availabilities, and according to client requirements.

> **NOTE** My planning process shares many of the same features as Joint Requirements Planning (JRP) and Joint Applications Design (JAD) sessions. The JRP session is commonly used to design computer applications. My JPPS is robust — that is, it can be used for any type of project.

The objective of a JPPS is this: Develop a project plan that meets the COS as negotiated between the requestor and the provider, and as described in the POS and RBS. Sounds simple, doesn't it?

Unfortunately, that agreement doesn't often happen with any regularity, for many reasons. The client and the project team are generally impatient to get on with the work of the project. After all, there are deadlines to meet and other projects demanding the team member's attention. Team members don't have time for planning — there is too much work to do and too many clients to satisfy. Regrettably, at the project's eleventh hour, when it is too late to recover from a poor plan, the team and the client bow in defeat. Next time, pay more attention to the planning details. But somehow that next time never seems to come. It's time for change!

In this day and age, the virtual team seems to be the rule rather than the exception. To accommodate this type of team, the project manager usually does one-on-one planning with each team member and consolidates the results for review with the entire team participating in an online review session.

Planning the JPPS

Team planning has always been viewed as advantageous over other forms of project planning, such as the project manager planning the project by walking around gathering data for the plan. In my experience, the synergy of the group provides far more accurate activity duration estimates and more complete information input to the planning process itself. Team planning is more likely to be complete than any other form of planning. Perhaps the best advantage of all is that it creates a much stronger commitment to the project on the part of all those who lived through the pain of generating and agreeing to the complete project plan. There is a sense of ownership that participating in the planning session affords. If all else fails, it is more fun than doing planning in isolation.

I know you sometimes feel that planning is a necessary evil. It is something you do because you have to and because you can then say that you have thought about where you want to go and how you are going to get there. After they have been written, plans are often bound in nice notebooks and become bookends gathering dust on someone's shelf or in a file folder in your desk drawer. Make up your mind right now to change that! Consider the plan as a dynamic tool for managing the project and as the base for decision making, too.

Planning is essential to good project management. The plan that you generate is a dynamic document. It changes as the project commences. It will be a reference work for you and the team members when questions of scope and change arise. Make no bones about it: To do good planning is painful, but to do poor planning is even more painful. Remember the pain curves in Figure 5-1? Which one will you choose?

The first document considered in the JPPS is the POS. One may already exist and therefore will be the starting point for the JPPS. If one doesn't exist, it must be developed as the initial part of or as a prerequisite to starting the JPPS. The situation will dictate how best to proceed. The POS can be developed in a number of ways. If it is an idea for consideration, it will probably be developed by one individual — typically the person who will be the project manager. It can be departmentally based or cross-departmentally based. The broader the impact on the enterprise, the more likely it will be developed as the first phase of a JPPS. Finally, the POS may have been developed through a COS exercise. In any case, the JPPS begins by discussing and clarifying exactly what is intended by the POS. The project team might also use this opportunity to write the Project Definition Statement (PDS) — their understanding of the project. The PDS is nothing more than an expanded version of the POS, but from the perspective of the planning team.

The JPPS must be planned down to the last detail if it is to be successful. Time is a scarce resource for all of us, and the last thing you want to do is waste it. Recognize before you start that the JPPS will be very intense. Participants often get emotional and will even dig their heels in to make a point.

Before learning about how to plan and conduct a JPPS, let's take a look at who should attend.

Attendees

The JPPS participants are invited from among those who might be affected by or have input into the project. If the project involves deliverables or is a new process or procedure, then anyone who has input to the process, receives output from the process, or handles the deliverables should be invited to participate in the JPPS. The client falls into one or more of these categories and must be present at the JPPS. Any manager of resources that may be required by the project team should also attend the JPPS. In many organizations, the project has a project champion (not necessarily the project manager or client manager) who may wish to participate at least at the start.

Here is a list of potential JPPS attendees:

Facilitator — A successful JPPS requires an experienced facilitator. This person is responsible for conducting the JPPS. It is important that the facilitator not have a vested interest or bring biases to the session because that would diminish the effectiveness of the plan. It must be developed with an open mind, not with a biased mind. For this reason, I strongly suggest that the project manager not facilitate the session. If using an outside consultant is not possible, I recommend that you select a neutral party to act as the facilitator, such as another project manager.

Project manager — Because you are not leading the planning session, you can concentrate on the plan itself, which is your major role in the JPPS. Even if you receive the assignment before any planning has been done, having you facilitate the JPPS may seem to be an excellent option, but it can be the wrong choice if the project is politically charged or has clients from more than one function, process, or resource pool. You must be comfortable with the project plan. After all, you are the one who has final responsibility when it comes to getting the project done on time, within budget, and according to specification.

Another project manager — Skilled JPPS facilitators are hard to find. Because you are not a good choice for facilitator, then maybe another project manager — presumably unbiased — would be a good choice, especially if he or she has JPPS experience. If your organization has a PMO, they will likely be able to provide an experienced facilitator.

JPPS consultant — Project management consultants will often serve as another source of qualified JPPS facilitators. Their broad experience in project management and project management consulting will be invaluable. This is especially true in organizations that have recently completed project management training and are in the process of implementing their own project management methodology. Having an outside consultant facilitate the JPPS is as much a learning experience as it is an opportunity to get off to a good start with a successful JPPS.

Technographer — The JPPS facilitator is supported by a technographer, a professional who not only knows project management but is also an expert in the software tools used to document the project plan. While the JPPS facilitator is coordinating the planning activities, the JPPS technographer is recording planning decisions on the computer as they occur in real time. At any point in time — and there will be several — the technographer can print out or display the plan for all to see and critique.

Core project team — Commitment is so important that to exclude the core team from the JPPS would be foolish. Estimating activity duration and resource requirements will be much easier with the professional expertise these people can bring to the planning session. The core project team is made up of individuals (both from the client and from the provider) who will stay with the project from the first day to the last day. This does not mean that they are with the project full-time. In today's typical organization, an individual would not be assigned to only one project at a time, unless the organization is totally projectized or uses self-directed teams.

Client representative — This attendee is always a bit tricky. Face it: Some clients really don't want to be bothered. It is up to the project manager or champion to convince clients of the importance of their participation in the JPPS. I don't claim that this will be easy, but it is nevertheless important. The client must buy in to the project plan. The client won't have that buy-in if the project manager simply mails a copy of the plan. The client must be involved in the planning session. To proceed without the client's involvement is to court disaster. Changes to the project plan will occur, and problems will arise. If the client is involved in preparing the plan, he or she can contribute to resolutions of change requests and problem situations.

Resource managers — These managers control resources that the project will require. Putting a schedule together without input and participation from these managers would be a waste of time. They may have some suggestions that will make the plan more realistic, too. In some cases, they may send a representative who will also be part of the project team. The important factor here is that someone from each resource area is empowered to commit resources to the project plan. These are not commitments to provide a specific named person or room. They are commitments to provide a certain skill set or type of facility.

Project champion — The project champion drives the project and sells it to senior management. In many cases, the champion can be the client — which is an ideal situation because the client is already committed to the project. In other cases, the project champion can be the senior managers of the division, department, or process that will be the beneficiary of the project deliverables.

Functional managers — Because functional managers manage areas that can either provide input to or receive output from the project deliverables, they or a representative should participate in the planning session. They will ensure that the project deliverables can be smoothly integrated into existing functions or that the functions will have to be modified as part of the project plan.

Process owner — For the same reasons that functional managers should be present, so should process owners. If the project deliverables do not smoothly integrate into their processes, either the project plan or the affected processes will have to be altered.

A formal invitation that announces the project, its general direction and purpose, and the planning schedule should be issued by the project manager to all of the other attendees.

NOTE RSVPs are a must! Full attendance is so important that I have canceled the JPPS when certain key participants were not able to attend. On one occasion, I acted as the project manager for a client and cancelled the JPPS because the client did not think his attendance was important enough. My feedback to the client was that as soon as it was a high enough priority for him to attend, I would reschedule the JPPS. Pushback like this is tough, but the JPPS is so critically important to the ultimate success of the project that I was willing to take this strong position with the client.

Facilities

Because the planning team may spend as many as three consecutive days in planning, it is important that the physical facility is comfortable and away from the daily interruptions. To minimize distractions, you might be tempted to have the planning session offsite. However, I prefer onsite planning sessions. Onsite planning sessions have both advantages and disadvantages, but with proper preparation, they can be controlled. In my experience, having easy access to information is a major advantage to onsite planning sessions, but interruptions due to the daily flow of work are a major disadvantage. With easy access to the office made possible by cell phones and e-mail, the potential for distraction and interruptions has increased. These distractions need to be minimized in whatever way makes sense.

Allocate enough space so that each group of four or five planning members can have a separate work area with a table, chairs, and a flip chart. All work should be done in one room. In my experience, breakout rooms tend to be dysfunctional. To the extent possible, everybody needs to be present for everything that takes place in the planning session. The room should have plenty of whiteboard space or blank walls. In many cases, I have taped flip-chart paper or butcher paper to the walls. You can never have enough writing space in the planning room.

Equipment

You will need an ample supply of sticky notes, tape, scissors, and colored marking pens. For more high-tech equipment, an LCD projector and a PC are all you need for everyone in the room to see the details as they come together.

The Complete Planning Agenda

The agenda for the JPPS is straightforward. It can be completed in one, two, or three sessions. For example, an early meeting with the requestor can be scheduled, at which time the COS are drafted. These will be input to the second session, during which the POS is drafted. In cases where the POS must be approved before detailed planning can commence, there will be an interruption until approval can be granted. After approval is obtained, the third session can be scheduled. At this session (which is usually two or three days long), the detailed project plan can be drafted for approval.

Here's a sample agenda for the project planning sessions:

Session 1

1. Negotiate the COS.
2. Build the RBS.

Session 2

1. Write the POS.

Session 3 (JPPS)

1. The entire planning team creates the first-level WBS.
2. Subject matter experts develop further decomposition, with the entire planning team observing and commenting.
3. Estimate activity durations and resource requirements.
4. Construct a project network diagram.
5. Determine the critical path.
6. Revise and approve the project completion date.
7. Finalize the resource schedule.
8. Gain consensus on the project plan.

Deliverables

The deliverables from the JPPS are listed here:

Work Breakdown Structure — Recall that the WBS is a graphical or indented outline of the work (expressed as activities) to be done to complete the project. It is used as a planning tool as well as a reporting structure.

Activity Duration Estimates — The schedule, which is also a major deliverable, is developed from estimates of the duration of each work activity in the project. Activity duration estimates may be single-point estimates or three-point estimates, as discussed later in this chapter.

Resource Requirements — For each activity in the project, an estimate of the resources to perform the work is required. In most cases, the resources will be the technical and people skills, although they can also include such things as physical facilities, equipment, and computer cycles.

Project Network Schedule — Using the WBS, the planning team will define the sequence in which the project activities should be performed.

Initially, this sequence is determined only by the technical relationships between activities, not by management prerogatives. That is, the deliverables from one or more activities are needed to begin work on the next activity. You can understand this sequence most easily by displaying it graphically. The definition of the network activities and the details of the graphical representation are covered later in this chapter.

Activity Schedule — With the sequence determined, the planning team will schedule the start date and end date for each activity. The availability of resources will largely determine that schedule.

Resource Assignments — The output of the activity schedule will be the assignment of specific resources (such as skill sets) to the project activities.

Project Notebook — Documentation can be a chore to produce. But that's not the case in the five-phase PMLC described in this book, where project documentation is a natural by-product of the project work. All you need to do is appoint a project team member to be responsible for gathering information that is already available, putting it in a standard format, and electronically archiving it. This responsibility begins with the project planning session and ends when the project is formally closed.

Conducting the JPPS

The first priority of the facilitator is to create an open and collaborative environment for the planning team. There is going to be disagreement, and all members of the planning team must feel free to express their thoughts. In conducting the sessions, the facilitator must encourage everyone to fully participate. Those who are more reserved must be drawn into the conversation by the facilitator. Likewise, those who tend to dominate the conversation must be diplomatically controlled by the facilitator. Excellent meeting management skills are required. That is why a trained facilitator is preferred over a project manager when it comes to running a JPPS.

Building the WBS

The WBS is a hierarchical description of all work that must be done to complete the project as defined in the RBS. Recognize that the RBS documents in detail the deliverables needed to produce the expected business value as described in the POS. The WBS is a further decomposition of the RBS components and describes in detail how those components will be created. In other words it defines the work of the project. Several processes can be used to create this hierarchy. They are described in this section.

The Requirements Breakdown Structure (RBS) is the input to constructing the WBS. If the RBS is complete, then a traditional approach to project management can be taken and the complete WBS developed. This chapter describes how to build a complete WBS. However, in most cases the RBS will not be complete, and therefore, the WBS will not be complete, and some other project management approach will have to be taken. Those are discussed later in Chapters 10, 11, and 12, which consider all of the exceptions.

Using the RBS to Build the WBS

One of the major benefits of the RBS is that it can dramatically reduce the work and improve the effectiveness of the WBS. Figure 5-2 is the RBS graphical depiction first introduced in Chapter 4.

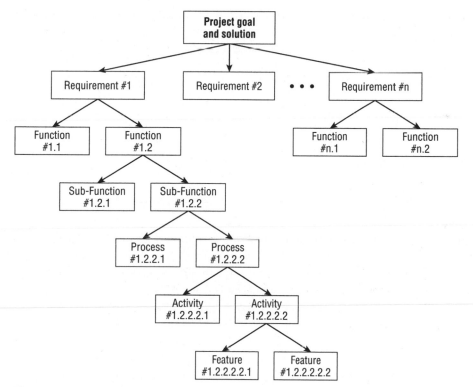

Figure 5-2: The RBS

NOTE The RBS is linked directly to the success criteria that justified the project. The WBS describes the work that must be done to satisfy the RBS. Therefore, through the RBS the WBS is tied directly to the project success criteria. This feature is not present in the traditional approaches to building the WBS.

Excluding the "Feature" level for the moment, the lowest level of decomposition in the RBS constitutes the level "n" Activities defined in the WBS in

Figure 5-3. So using Figure 5-2 as the actual RBS Function 1.1, Sub-Function 1.2.1, Process 1.2.2.1, Activity 1.2.2.2.1, and Activity 1.2.2.2.2, are the lowest level of decomposition in the RBS. The tasks needed to build these deliverables would define the WBS as shown in Figure 5-3.

Activities as shown in Figure 5-3 are simply chunks of work. The decomposition of these chunks of work continues for each chunk until the lowest level of decomposition meets the six criteria tests for completion and then no further decomposition of that chunk is needed. Although not shown in Figure 5-3 the second term is *task*. The lowest level of decomposition that meets the six completion criteria is called a task rather than an activity. The term task is used to differentiate the chunk of work it defines from all other chunks of work that are called activities. Although these definitions may seem a bit informal, the difference between an activity and a task will become clearer shortly.

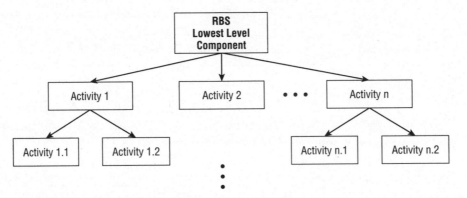

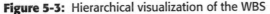

Figure 5-3: Hierarchical visualization of the WBS

The terms "activity" and "task" have been used interchangeably among project managers and project management software packages. Some think of activities as being made up of tasks, others say that tasks are made up of activities, and still others use one term to represent both concepts. In this book, I refer to higher-level work as activities. An activity is composed of two or more tasks. When the tasks that make up an activity are complete, the activity is complete.

Another term is *work package*. A work package is a complete description of how the tasks that make up an activity will actually be done. It includes a description of the what, who, when, and how of the work. Work packages are described in more detail in Chapter 6.

Decomposition to the task level is important to the overall project plan because it enables you to estimate the duration of the project, determine the required resources, and schedule the work. By following the decomposition process, activities at the lowest levels of decomposition will possess known properties that enable you to meet planning and scheduling needs.

This process of decomposition is analogous to the process many students use in school for writing research papers. Despite the teacher's extolling the value of preparing a detailed outline before writing the paper, the student chooses to do it the other way around — writing the paper first and extracting the outline from it. That won't work in project planning. You have to define the work before you set out to do it.

Those who have experience in systems development should see the similarity between hierarchical decomposition and functional decomposition. In principle, there is no difference between a WBS and a functional decomposition of a system. My approach to generating a WBS departs from the generation of a functional decomposition in that I follow a specific process with a stopping rule for completing the WBS. I am not aware of a similar process for generating the functional decomposition of a system. Veterans of systems development might even see some similarity to older techniques such as stepwise refinement or pseudo-code. These tools do, in fact, have a great deal in common with the techniques I use to generate the WBS.

Uses for the WBS

The WBS has four uses: as a thought-process tool, an architectural-design tool, a planning tool, and a project-status-reporting tool. The following sections describe how to use the WBS for each of these purposes.

Thought-Process Tool

First, and maybe foremost, the WBS is a thought process. As a thought process, it is a design and planning tool. It helps the project manager and the planning team visualize exactly how the work of the project can be defined and managed effectively. It would not be unusual to consider alternative ways of decomposing the work until an alternative is found with which the project manager is comfortable.

Architectural-Design Tool

When all is said and done, the WBS is a picture of the work of the project and how the items of work are related to one another. It must make sense. In that context, it is a design tool.

Planning Tool

In the planning phase, the WBS gives the planning team a detailed representation of the project as a collection of activities that must be completed in order for the project to be completed. It is at the lowest activity level of the WBS that you will estimate effort, elapsed time, and resource requirements; build a schedule of when the work will be completed; and estimate deliverable dates and project completion.

Project-Status-Reporting Tool

Although this is not a common use of the WBS, it has been used as a structure for reporting project status. The project activities are consolidated (that is, rolled up) from the bottom as lower-level activities are completed. As work is completed, activities will be completed. Completion of lower-level activities causes higher-level activities to be partially complete. Shading is often used to highlight completed tasks and activities. Some of these higher-level activities may represent significant progress whose completion will be milestone events in the course of the project. Thus, the WBS defines milestone events that can be reported to senior management and the client.

NOTE Trying to find a happy compromise between a WBS architecture that lends itself well to the planning thought process and the rolling up of information for summary reporting can be difficult. It is best to have input from all the parties that may be using the WBS before settling on a design. There is no one right way to do it; it's subjective. You will get better with practice.

In the final analysis, it is the project manager who decides on the architecture of the WBS and the level of detail required. This detail is important because the project manager is accountable for the success of the project. The WBS must be defined so that the project manager can manage the project. That means that the approach and detail in the WBS might not be the way others would have approached it. Apart from any senior management requirements for reporting or organizational requirements for documentation or process, the project manager is free to develop the WBS according to his or her needs and those of management. Because of this requirement, the WBS is not unique. That should not bother you because all that is required is a WBS that defines the project work so that you, the project manager, can manage it. "Beauty is in the eyes of the beholder" applies equally well to the choice of which of several approaches to building the WBS is the best choice. As project manager you have the responsibility of making that choice.

Generating the WBS

The best way to generate the WBS is as part of the JPPS. You'll learn the steps as you look at two different approaches to building the WBS in this section. Before I discuss those approaches, I want to remind you of where you are in the planning process and then offer a few general comments about procedures I have followed in my practice regardless of the approach taken.

WARNING   Do not build the WBS by walking around the workplace or e-mail space and asking participants to complete their part of the WBS. It may seem like a faster way to generate the WBS and it is much easier than conducting the JPPS, but it is a ticket to failure. You need several pairs of eyes looking at the WBS and critiquing it for completeness.

At this point in the planning process, you should have completed the RBS and have an approved POS. You may have to go back and reconsider the POS as a result of further planning activities, but for now assume the POS is complete. My technique for generating the WBS will reduce even the most complex project to a set of clearly defined activities. The WBS will be the document that guides the remainder of the planning activities.

As many as 10 to 20 participants may be involved in building the WBS, so gathering around a computer screen won't do the job. Neither will projecting the screen on an overhead LCD projector. The only way I have found that works consistently is to use sticky notes, marking pens, and plenty of whiteboard space. In the absence of whiteboard space, you might wallpaper the planning room with flip-chart or butcher paper. You cannot have too much writing space. Using butcher paper, I have even filled the four walls of the planning room and several feet of hallway outside the planning room. It is sloppy, but it gets the job done.

Converting the RBS to the WBS

This approach begins at the lowest levels of decomposition in the RBS. From that point each of these deliverables is hierarchically decomposed to one or more levels of work detail until the participants are satisfied that the work has been sufficiently defined. The completion criteria discussed later in this chapter is the guide to the decomposition exercise for this approach.

After the project work activities have been defined using this approach guided by the completion criteria, they are defined at a sufficient level of detail to enable the team to estimate time, cost, and resource requirements first at the activity level and then aggregated to the project level. Because the activities are defined to this level of detail, the project time, cost, and resource requirements are estimated much more accurately.

Because every work activity at the lowest level of work decomposition appears as a manageable activity in the project plan, there is good reason to not define work at a level that is too detailed so that it is more of a management burden than it is worth. For that reason the team should look for opportunities to "roll up" the work to less detailed levels while being cognizant of the completion criteria.

I have used and can recommend two variations of this approach: the team approach and the subteam approach. I have used both in my consulting practice.

Team Approach

Although it requires more time to complete than the subteam approach, the team approach is the better of the two. In this approach, the entire team works on all parts of the WBS. For each of the lowest levels of decomposition in the RBS, appoint the most knowledgeable member of the planning team to facilitate the further decomposition to the work level of that part of the RBS. Continue with similar appointments until the WBS is complete. This approach enables all members of the planning team to pay particular attention to the WBS as it is developed, noting discrepancies in real time.

Subteam Approach

When time is at a premium, the planning facilitator may choose to use the subteam approach. The first step is to divide the planning team into as many subteams as there are requirements in the RBS. Assigning similar requirements to the same team is okay too. Then follow these steps:

1. Each subteam begins further decomposition to the work level for the part of the RBS associated with the requirement(s) assigned to them

2. Each subteam reports its results to the entire team. The entire team is looking for overlaps between their results and the reporting subteam's, missing work, and scope boundary issues.

3. The entire WBS is approved by the team.

It is important to pay close attention to each presentation and ask yourself these questions: Is there something in the WBS that I did not expect to see? Is there something missing from the WBS that I expected to see? The focus here is to strive for a complete WBS. In cases where the WBS will be used for reporting purposes, the project manager must be careful to attach lower-level activities to higher-level activities to preserve the integrity of the status reports that will be generated.

As the discussion continues and activities are added and deleted from the WBS, questions about agreement between the WBS and the POS will occur. Throughout the exercise, the POS should be posted on flip-chart paper and hung on the walls of the planning room. Each participant should compare the scope of the project as described in the POS with the scope as presented in the WBS. If something in the WBS appears out of scope, challenge it. Either redefine the scope or discard the appropriate WBS activities. Similarly, look for complete coverage of the scope as described in the WBS with the POS. This is the time to be critical and carefully define the scope and work to accomplish it. Mistakes found now, before any work is done, are far less costly and disruptive than they will be if found late in the project.

The dynamic at work here is one of changing project boundaries. Despite all efforts to the contrary, the boundaries of the project are never clearly defined at the outset. There will always be reasons to question what is in and what is not in the project. That is fine. Just remember that the project boundaries have not yet been set in concrete. That will happen after the project has been approved to begin. Until then, you are still in the planning mode.

Using the WBS for Large Projects

For very large projects, you may be tempted to modify the preceding approach. Although I prefer to avoid modification, difficulty in scheduling people for the planning meeting may necessitate some modification. This brief section describes a modification that serves this situation well.

As project size increases, it becomes unwieldy to build the entire WBS with the all of the planning team assembled in a single planning session. My rule of thumb is to partition the project into subprojects whenever the planning team has more than 30 members. Each requirement or group of similar requirements can be assigned to a subteam. A temporary program office can be established for managing the entire project. Each subproject manager is accountable to the program office manager.

Iterative Development of the WBS

After the RBS has been built, you choose the best-fit PMLC. Depending on your feeling about the degree of completeness of the RBS, you will choose one of the six approaches: Linear, Incremental, Iterative, Adaptive, Extreme, or Emertxe. As discussed in Chapter 2, the less you know about the RBS and the less certain you are that the client has been able to define the solution, the more likely you are to choose an approach toward the Adaptive and Extreme part of the landscape. The Linear and Incremental approaches require a complete WBS. The Iterative approach can work in cases where all of the functions and sub-functions have been defined and only a few processes, activities, and features have not. These will be eventually described at the lower levels of decomposition of the WBS, but they will not be completely defined at the outset. When there are missing or incomplete functions and sub-functions, an Adaptive approach should be used, and the WBS will have large gaps that need to be defined through iteration. Finally, when even the goal is not clearly defined, very little of the WBS can be built at the beginning of the project. Both the goal and solution (functions and features) must be defined through iteration.

Six Criteria to Test for Completeness in the WBS

Developing the WBS is the most critical part of the JPPS. If you do this part right, the rest is comparatively easy. How do you know that you've done this right? Each activity must possess the following six characteristics in order for the WBS to be deemed to be complete — that is, completely decomposed. When an activity has reached that status, it changes from an activity to a task. The six characteristics that an activity must possess to be called a task are as follows:

- Status and completion are measurable.
- The activity is bounded.
- The activity has a deliverable.
- Time and cost are easily estimated.
- Activity duration is within acceptable limits.
- Work assignments are independent.

If the activity does not possess all six of these characteristics, decompose the activity and check it again at that next lower level of decomposition. As soon as an activity possesses the six characteristics, there is no need to further decompose it. As soon as every activity in the WBS possesses these six characteristics, the WBS is defined as complete. The following sections look at each of these characteristics in more detail.

> **NOTE** In 1991, Joseph Weiss and I introduced a four-criteria version of this completion test in *5-Phase Project Management: A Practical Planning and Implementation Guide* (Perseus Publishing Company, 1992). I have since continued to refine the criteria in the completion test to include the six characteristics presented here.

Status and Completion Are Measurable

The project manager can question the status of an activity at any point in time during the project. If the activity has been defined properly, that question is answered easily. For example, if a system's documentation is estimated to be about 300 pages long and requires approximately four months of full-time work to write, here are some possible reports that your activity manager could provide regarding the status:

- The activity is supposed to take four months of full-time work. I've been working on it for two months full-time. I guess I must be 50 percent complete.
- I've written 150 pages, so I guess I am 50 percent complete.
- I've written and had approved 150 pages and estimate that the remaining work will require two more months. I am 50 percent complete.

No one would buy the first answer, but how many times is that the information a project manager gets? Even worse, how many times does the project manager accept it as a valid statement of progress? Although the second answer is a little better, it doesn't say anything about the quality of the 150 pages that have been written, nor does it say anything about the re-estimate of the remaining work. You can see that an acceptable answer must state what has been actually completed (that is *approved*, not just written) and what remains to be done, along with an estimate to completion. Remember that you'll always know more tomorrow than you do today. After working through about half of the activity, the activity manager should be able to give a very accurate estimate of the time required to complete the remaining work.

A simple metric that has met with some success is to compute the proportion of tasks completed as a percentage of all tasks that make up the activity. For example, if the activity has six tasks associated with it and four of the tasks are complete, the ratio of tasks completed to total tasks is 4/6 — that is, the activity is 60 percent complete. Even if work is done on the fifth task in this activity, because the task is not complete on the report date, it cannot be counted in the ratio. This metric certainly represents a very objective measure. Although it isn't completely accurate, it is a good technique. Best of all, it's quick. A project manager and activity manager do not have to sit around mired in detail about the percentage complete. You can use this same approach to measure the earned value of an activity.

CROSS-REFERENCE Earned value is defined and discussed in Chapter 7.

The Activity Is Bounded

Each activity should have a clearly defined start and end event. After the start event has occurred, work can begin on the activity. The deliverable is most likely associated with the end event that signals work is closed on the activity. For example, the start event for systems documentation might be notifying the team member who will manage the documentation creation that the final acceptance tests of the system are complete. The end event would be notifying the project manager that the client has approved the systems documentation.

The Activity Has a Deliverable

The result of completing the work that makes up the activity is the production of a deliverable. The deliverable is a visible sign that the activity is complete. This sign could be an approving manager's signature, a physical product or document, the authorization to proceed to the next activity, or some other sign of completion. The deliverable from an activity is output from that activity, which then becomes input to one or more other activities that follow its completion.

Time and Cost Are Easily Estimated

Each activity should have an estimated time and cost of completion. Being able to do this at the lowest level of decomposition in the WBS enables you to aggregate to higher levels and estimate the total project cost and the completion date. By successively decomposing activities to finer levels of granularity, you are likely to encounter primitive activities that you have performed before. This experience at lower levels of definition gives you a stronger base on which to estimate activity cost and duration for similar activities.

Activity Duration Is Within Acceptable Limits

Although there is no fixed rule for the duration of an activity, I recommend that an activity have a duration of less than two calendar weeks. This seems to be a common practice in many organizations. Even for long projects in which contractors may be responsible for major pieces of work, they will generate plans that decompose their work to activities with a two-week or shorter duration. Exceptions will occur when the activity defines process work, as is the case in many manufacturing situations. In addition, there will be exceptions for activities involving work that's repetitive and simple. For example, if you are going to build 500 widgets and it takes 10 weeks to complete this activity, you need not decompose it into five activities with each one building 100 widgets. This type of activity requires no further breakdown. If you can estimate the time to check one document, then it does not make much difference if the activity requires two months to check 400 documents or four two-week periods to check 100 documents per period. The danger you avoid is longer-duration activities whose delay can create a serious project-scheduling problem.

Work Assignments Are Independent

It is important that each activity be independent. An activity should continue reasonably well without interruption and without the need for additional input or information until the activity is complete. The work effort could be contiguous, but it can be scheduled otherwise for a variety of reasons. You can choose to schedule it in parts because of resource availability, but you could have scheduled it as one continuous stream of work.

Related to activity independence is the temptation to micromanage an activity. Best practices suggest that you manage an individual's work down to units of one week. For example, Harry is going to work on an activity that will require 10 hours of effort. The activity is scheduled to begin on Monday morning and be completed by Friday afternoon. Harry has agreed that he can accommodate the 10 hours within the week, given his other commitments that same week. Harry's manager (or the project manager) could ask Harry to report exactly when during the week he will be working on this 10-hour activity and then hold him to that plan, but what a waste of everyone's time that would be! Why not give Harry credit for enough intelligence to manage his commitments at the one-week level? No need to drill down into the workweek and burden Harry with a micro-plan and his manager with the task of managing that micro-plan. Such a scenario may in fact increase the time to complete the activity because it has been burdened with unnecessary management overhead.

The Seventh Criterion for Judging Completeness

I've separated this from the preceding six criteria because it is not a criterion in the same sense as they are. This seventh "criterion" is pure judgment on the part of the project manager. A WBS could be defined as complete based on the preceding six criteria, yet the project manager might have a lingering doubt simply because of the way the client conducted themselves during the WBS decomposition process. Something might alert the project manager that things may not be what they seem to be. For example, perhaps the client never seemed to be fully engaged or never bought into the decomposition process. They simply went along with the exercise, but never really contributed to it. That might give you reason to suspect that scope change requests may be just around the corner and that you had better have chosen a project management approach that expects and can accommodate change, rather than one that incorrectly assumes the WBS to be complete. Better to be safe than sorry. If there is any doubt in your mind about the completeness of the WBS, choose some type of Iterative or Adaptive approach so that you will be in a position to accept scope change requests.

Exceptions to the Completion Criteria Rule

In some cases, the completion criteria do not have to be satisfied in order for the WBS to be considered complete. Two common scenarios are discussed in the sections that follow.

Stopping Before Completion Criteria Are Met

A common situation where this occurs is duration-related. Suppose the activity calls for building 100 widgets, and it takes one day per widget. The maximum duration for a task has been set at 10 days. If you follow that rule, you would decompose the activity to build 100 widgets into 10 activities. That doesn't add any value to the WBS — it only adds management time. Leave the activity at 100 days and simply ask for status at the appropriate intervals. Adding activities that simply increase management time and do not add value to the project are a waste of time.

Decomposing Beyond Completion of the Criteria

For projects of a shorter duration (for example, four weeks), it would be poor management to set the acceptable activity duration at 10 days. That would create a situation with too few management checkpoints and hence create a project that would be poorly managed. Instead, the acceptable duration limit might be set at three days, for example. Even shorter duration limits might be imposed for projects that contain surgical procedures or other processes of very short duration. If the entire surgical procedure lasts only a few hours, the acceptable duration limit might be set at a few minutes. These will always be judgment calls on your part. Do what your common sense tells you to do rather than conform to a rule that might not be appropriate given the situation.

One other situation often arises when decomposition beyond satisfaction of the completion criteria makes sense. That is with activities that are considered high risk or have a high estimated duration variance. An activity with an eight-day duration and five-day variance should raise your concern. Even though the activity has met the duration limit of 10 days, you should further decompose it in an attempt to isolate high-risk parts or the high variance parts of the activity. Again, do what makes sense.

Approaches to Building the WBS

There are many ways to build the WBS. Even though you might like the choice to be a personal one that you, the project manager, make (reasoning that because you are charged with managing the project, you should also be the one to choose the architecture that makes that task the easiest), unfortunately that will not work in many cases. The choice of approach must take into consideration the uses to which the WBS will be put. What may be the best choice for defining the work to be done may not be the best choice for status reporting.

There is no one correct way to create the WBS. Hypothetically, if you put each member of the JPPS in a different room and ask them all to develop the project WBS, they might all come back with different renditions. That's all right — there is no single best answer. The choice is subjective and based more on the project manager's preference than on any other requirements. In practice, I have sometimes tried to follow one approach only to find that it was making the project work more confusing, rather than simpler. In such cases, my advice is simply to throw away the work you have done and start all over again with a fresh approach.

The three general approaches to building the WBS are as follows:

> **Noun-type approaches** — These approaches define the deliverables of the project work in terms of the components (physical or functional) that

make up the deliverable. These are the requirements that populate the RBS. This approach is the one currently recommended by PMI. If you have generated the RBS, you are very close to having a deliverables-based WBS. Figure 5-4 shows the relationship between the RBS and the WBS. First, note that the RBS is a subset of the WBS. To put it another way, the RBS defines what must be done, and the WBS defines how it will be done.

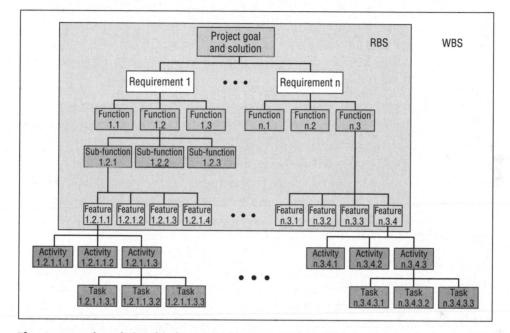

Figure 5-4: The relationship between the RBS and the WBS

Verb-type approaches — These approaches define the deliverable of the project work in terms of the actions that must be done to produce that deliverable. Verb-type approaches include the design-build-test-implement and project objectives approaches. This approach was recommended by PMI prior to the current release of PMBOK.

Organizational approaches — These approaches define the deliverable of the project work in terms of the organizational units that will work on the project. This type of approach includes the department, process, and geographic location approaches.

You have probably seen one or more of these approaches used in practice to create the WBS. The following sections take a look at each of these approaches in more detail.

Noun-Type Approaches

There are two noun-type approaches: physical decomposition and functional decomposition.

Physical Decomposition

In projects that involve building products, it is tempting to follow the physical decomposition approach. Consider a mountain bike, for example. Its physical components include a frame, wheels, suspension, gears, and brakes. If each component is to be manufactured, this approach might produce a simple WBS. As mentioned previously, though, you have to keep in mind the concern of summary reporting.

For example, consider rolling up all the tasks related to gears. If you were to create a Gantt chart for reporting at the summary level, the bar for the gears' summary activity would start at the project start date. A Gantt chart is a simple graphical representation of the work to be done and the schedule for completing it. The Gantt chart consists of a number of rectangular bars — each one representing an activity in the project. The length of each bar corresponds to the estimated time it will take to complete the activity. These bars are arranged across a horizontal time scale, with the left edge of the bar lined up with the scheduled start of the activity. The bars are arranged vertically in the order of scheduled start date. The resulting picture forms a descending stair-step pattern. That is, after all, where the detailed tasks of doing design work would occur. The finish of the bar would occur at about the project completion date. That is where testing and documentation for the gears occurs. Using the summary Gantt chart as a status reporting tool for the gears doesn't have much use. The bar extends from the beginning to the end of the timeline. The same is true of all the other physical components mentioned. Showing all of them on a summary Gantt chart would simply look like the stripes on a prison uniform.

This type of WBS is initially attractive because it looks similar to, and in fact could be identical to, a company's financial chart of accounts (CoA). A CoA is noun-oriented because it accounts for the cost of developing things such as gears and brakes. A CoA should not be confused with the WBS. The WBS is a breakdown of work; the CoA is a breakdown of costs. Most popular project-management software products provide code fields that can be used to link project task costs with accounting CoA categories.

Functional Decomposition

The WBS can also be built based on the functional components of the product. Using the mountain bike example from the preceding section, the functional components would include the steering system, gear-shifting system, braking system, and pedaling system. The same cautions that apply to the physical decomposition approach apply here as well.

Verb-Type Approaches

There are two verb-type approaches: the design-build-test-implement approach and the objectives approach.

Design-Build-Test-Implement

The design-build-test-implement approach is commonly used in projects that involve a methodology. Application systems development is an obvious example. Using the bicycle example again, a variation on the classic waterfall categories could be used. The categories are design, build, test, and implement. If you use this architecture for your WBS, then the bars on the Gantt chart would all have lengths that correspond to the duration of each of the design, build, test, and implement activities, and hence would be shorter than the bar representing the entire project. Most, if not all, would have differing start and end dates. Arranged on the chart, they would cascade in a stair-step ("waterfall") manner. These are just representative categories — yours may be different. The point is that when the detail-level activity schedules are summarized up to them, they present a display of meaningful information to the recipient of the report.

Remember, the WBS activities at the lowest levels of granularity must always be expressed in verb form. After all, this is *work*, which implies action, which in turn implies verbs.

Objectives

The objectives approach is similar to the design-build-test-implement approach and is used when progress reports at various stages of project completion are prepared for senior management. Reporting project completion by objectives provides a good indication of the deliverables that have been produced by the project team. Objectives are almost always related to business value and will be well received by senior management as well as the client. There is a caveat, however. This approach can cause some difficulty because objectives often overlap. Their boundaries can be fuzzy. If you use this approach, you'll have to give more attention to eliminating redundancies and discovering gaps in the defined work.

Organizational Approaches

The deployment of project work across geographic or organizational boundaries often suggests a WBS that parallels the organization. The project manager would not choose to use this approach but rather would use it only when forced to because of the organizational structure. In other words, the project manager has no other reasonable choice. These approaches offer no real advantages and tend to create more problems than they solve. However, they are described here in case you have no other option for building the WBS.

Geographic

If project work is geographically dispersed, it may make sense from coordination and communication perspectives to partition the work first by geographic location and then by some other approach at each location. For example, a project for the U.S. space program because of its geographic components might require this type of approach.

Departmental

Departmental boundaries and politics being what they are, you might benefit from partitioning the project first by department and then within each department by whatever approach makes sense. You benefit from this structure in that a major portion of the project work is under the organizational control of a single manager, which in turn simplifies resource allocation. Conversely, using this approach increases the need for communication and coordination across organizational boundaries.

Business Process

The final approach involves breaking down the project first by business process and then by some other method for each process. This has the same advantages and disadvantages as the departmental approach, with the added complication that integration of the deliverables from each process can be more difficult when you use this approach. The difficulty arises from process interactions at the boundaries of the involved processes. For example, at the boundary between order entry and order fulfillment how would order verification be defined? It could be part of either process. The process in which you place it will impact the customer.

Selecting the Best Approach

Again, no single approach can be judged to be best for a given project. My advice is to consider each approach at the outset of the JPPS and pick the one that seems to bring the most clarity to defining the project work.

Representing the WBS

Whatever approach you use, the WBS can be generically represented, as shown previously in Figure 5-3. The goal statement represents the reason for doing the project. At Level 1 partition the goal into some number of activities (also known as chunks of work). These chunks of work are a necessary and sufficient set that define the goal. That is, when all of these first-level activities are complete, the goal is met and the project is complete.

Partition any activity that does not possess the six characteristics into a set of necessary and sufficient activities at the next level of decomposition. The process continues until all activities have met the six criteria. The lowest level of decomposition in the WBS defines a set of activities (renamed "tasks") that will each have a task manager, someone who is responsible for completing the task.

Tasks are further defined by a work package. A work package is simply the list of things to do to complete the task. The work package may be very simple, such as getting management to sign off on a deliverable, or it may be a mini-project and consist of all the properties of any other project, except that the activity defining this project possesses the six criteria and need not be further partitioned.

CROSS-REFERENCE Chapter 6 describes how to create and use work packages.

Some examples will help clarify this idea. Figure 5-5 is a partial WBS for building a house, and Figure 5-6 is the indented outline version (for those of you who prefer an outline format to a hierarchical graph). Both convey the same information.

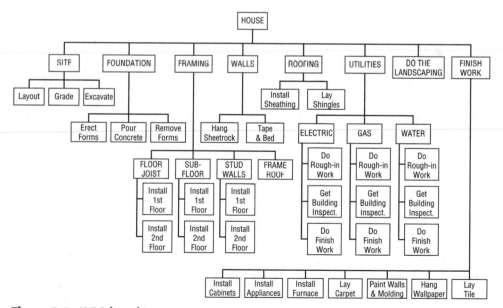

Figure 5-5: WBS for a house

1. SITE PREPARATION
  1.1   Layout
  1.2   Grading
  1.3   Excavation

2. FOUNDATION
  2.1   Erect Forms
  2.2   Pour Concrete
  2.3   Remove Forms

3. FRAMING
  3.1   Floor Joists
          3.1.1. Install First-Floor Joists
          3.1.2. Install Second-Floor Joists
  3.2   Subflooring
          3.2.1. Install First-Floor Subflooring
          3.2.2. Install Second-Floor Subflooring
  3.3   Stud Walls
          3.3.1. Erect First-Floor Stud Walls
          3.3.2. Erect Second-Floor Stud Walls
  3.4   Frame the Roof

4. UTILITIES
  4.1   Electrical
          4.1.1. Do Rough-in Work
          4.1.2. Get Building Inspection
          4.1.3. Do Finish Work
  4.2   Gas
          4.2.1. Do Rough-in Work
          4.2.2. Get Building Inspection
          4.2.3. Do Finish Work
  4.3   Water
          4.3.1. Do Rough-in Work
          4.3.2. Get Building Inspection
          4.3.3. Do Finish Work

5. WALLS
  5.1   Hang Sheetrock
  5.2   Tape and Bed

6. ROOFING
  6.1   Install Sheathing
  6.2   Lay Shingles

7. FINISH WORK
  7.1   Install Cabinets
  7.2   Install Appliances
  7.3   Install Furnace
  7.4   Lay Carpet
  7.5   Paint Walls and Molding
  7.6   Hang Wallpaper
  7.7   Lay Tile

8. LANDSCAPING

Figure 5-6: Indented outline WBS for a house

Figure 5-7 shows the WBS for the traditional waterfall systems development methodology. If you're a systems project manager, this format could become a template for all your systems development projects. It is a good way to introduce standardization into your systems development methodology.

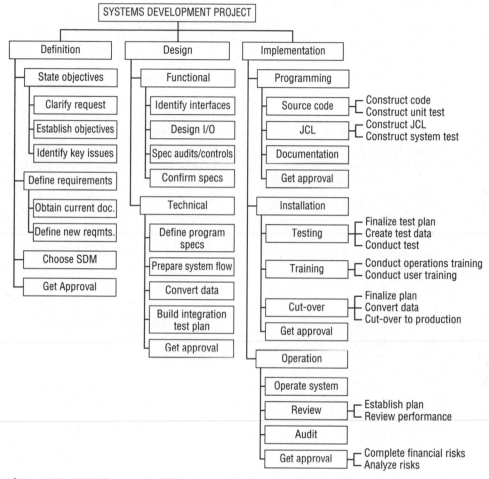

Figure 5-7: WBS for a waterfall systems development methodology

Estimating

Estimation is the one area where most project teams have trouble. For one thing, there is no consistency. One person might be optimistic, another pessimistic, and you won't know which unless you have had prior substantiating evidence of one or the other. Having the professional who will be responsible for the work also estimate the duration or labor involved is a good idea, but it isn't the answer either. Will this person be pessimistic just so the work is sure to meet the estimated deadline? The approach that I use is to have more than one person provide each estimate, as explained in this section.

Estimating Duration

Before you can estimate duration, you need to make sure everyone is working from a common definition. The duration of a project is the elapsed time in business working days, not including weekends, holidays, or other non-work days. Work effort is labor required to complete a task. That labor can be consecutive or nonconsecutive hours.

Duration and work effort are not the same thing. For example, I had a client pose the following situation: The client had a task that required him to send a document to his attorney, where it would be reviewed, marked up, and then returned. He had done this on several previous occasions, and it normally took about 10 business days before the document was back in his office. He knew the attorney took only about 30 minutes to review and mark up the document. His question was, "What's the duration?" The answer is 10 days. The work effort on the part of the attorney is 30 minutes.

It is important to understand the difference between labor time and duration time. They are not the same. Suppose an estimate has been provided that a certain task requires 10 hours of focused and uninterrupted labor to complete. Under normal working conditions, how many hours do you think it will really take? Something more than 10 for sure. To see why this is so, consider the data shown in Figure 5-8.

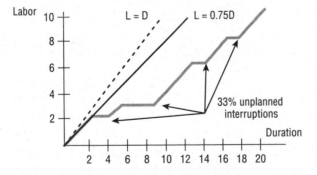

Figure 5-8: Elapsed time versus work time

If a person could be focused 100 percent of the time on a task, he or she could accomplish 10 hours of work in 10 hours. Such a person would indeed be unique, for it is more likely that his or her work will be interrupted by e-mail, cell phones or text messages, meetings, coffee breaks, and socializing. Several estimates have been made regarding the percentage of a person's day that he or she can devote to project work. Past data that I have collected from information technology (IT) professionals indicates a range of 66 to 75 percent. More recently, among the same client base, I have seen a downward trend in this estimate to a range of 50 to 65 percent. If you use the 75 percent estimate, a 10-hour task should require about 13 hours and 20 minutes to complete. That is *without* interruptions, which, of course, always happen.

For some professionals (those who provide technical support, for example), interruptions are frequent; for others (such as testing staff), interruptions are infrequent. I polled the 17-person technical support unit of a midsize IT department and found that about one-third of their time was spent on unplanned interruptions. Unplanned interruptions might include a phone call with a question to be answered, a systems crash, power interrupts, random events of nature, the boss stopping in to discuss an unrelated matter, or a personal call from your golfing buddies. Using a 75 percent estimate for focused work and a 33 percent estimate for unplanned interruptions, a 10-hour task will take approximately 20 hours to complete.

It is this elapsed time that you are interested in when estimating for each task in the project. It is the true duration of the task. For costing purposes, you are interested in the labor time (work) actually spent on a task.

> **NOTE** When estimating task duration, you have a choice to make: Do you want to estimate hours of billable labor to complete the task, or do you want to estimate the clock time required to complete the task? You will probably want to do both. The labor hours are needed in order to bill the client. The elapsed clock time is needed to estimate the project completion date. Some project managers will estimate labor and convert it to duration by dividing labor time by an established efficiency factor, typically ranging from 0.6 to 0.75.

Resource Loading versus Task Duration

The duration of a task is influenced by the amount of resources scheduled to work on it. I say "influenced" because there is not necessarily a direct linear relationship between the amount of resources assigned to a task and its duration.

Adding more resources to hold a task's duration within the planning limits can be effective. This is called "crashing the task." For example, suppose you are in a room where an ordinary-size, four-legged chair is in the way. The door to the room is closed. You are asked to pick up the chair and take it out of the room into the hallway. You might try to do it without any help, in which case you would perform the following steps:

1. Pick up the chair.
2. Carry it to the door.
3. Set the chair down.

4. Open the door.

5. Hold the door open with your foot as you pick up the chair.

6. Carry the chair through the door.

7. Set the chair down in the hallway.

Suppose you double the resources. You'll get someone to help you by opening the door and holding it open while you pick up the chair and carry it out to the hallway. With two people working on the task, you'd probably be willing to say it would reduce the time needed to move the chair out of the room and into the hallway.

Doubling the resources sounds like a technology breakthrough in shortening duration. Now double them again and see what happens. Now you've got four resources assigned to the task. It would go something like this: First, you hold a committee meeting to decide roles and responsibilities. Who's in charge? Who holds the door open? Who takes what part of the chair? The duration actually increases!

The point of this silly example is to demonstrate that there may be diminishing returns for adding more resources. You would probably agree that there is a maximum loading of resources on a task to minimize the task duration, and that by adding another resource, you will actually begin to increase the duration. You have reached the crashpoint of the task. The *crashpoint* is the point where adding more resources will increase task duration. The project manager will frequently have to consider the optimum loading of a resource on a task.

A second consideration for the project manager is the amount of reduction in duration that results from adding resources. The relationship is not linear. Consider the chair example again. Does doubling the resources cut the duration in half? Can two people dig a hole twice as fast as one? Probably not. The explanation is simple. By adding the nth person to a task, you create the need for *n* more communication links. Who is going to do what? How can the work of several people be coordinated? There may be other considerations that actually add work. To assume that the amount of work remains constant as you add resources is simply not correct. New kinds of work will emerge from the addition of a resource to a task. For example, adding another person adds the need to communicate with more people, which increases the duration of the task.

A third consideration for the project manager is the impact on risk that results from adding another resource. If you limit the resource to people, you must consider the possibility that two people will prefer to approach the task in different ways, with different work habits and different levels of commitment. The more people working on a task, the more likely one will be absent, the higher the likelihood of a mistake being made, and the more likely they will get in each other's way.

The fourth consideration has to do with partitioning the task so that more than one resource can work on it simultaneously. For some tasks, this will be easy; for others it may be impossible. For example, painting a house is a partitionable task. Rooms can be done by different painters, and even each wall can be done by a different painters. The point of diminishing returns is not an issue here. Conversely, the task of writing a computer program may not be partitionable at all. Adding a second programmer creates all kinds of work that wasn't present with a single programmer — for example, choosing a language and/or naming conventions to use, integration testing, and so on.

Variation in Task Duration

Task duration is a random variable. Because you cannot know what factors will be operative when work is underway on a task, you cannot know exactly how long it will take. There will, of course, be varying estimates with varying precision for each task. One of your goals in estimating task duration is to define the task to a level of granularity such that your estimates have a narrow variance — that is, the estimate is as good as you can get it at the planning stages of the project. As project work is completed, you will be able to improve the earlier estimates of activities scheduled later in the project.

The following factors can cause variation in the actual task duration:

Varying skill levels — Your strategy is to estimate task duration based on using people of average skills assigned to work on the task. In actuality, this may not happen. You may get a higher- or lower-skilled person assigned to the task, causing the actual duration to vary from planned duration. These varying skill levels will be both a help and a hindrance to you.

Unexpected events — Murphy's Law is lurking around every bend in the road and will surely make his presence known, but in what way and at what time you do not know. Random acts of nature, vendor delays, incorrect shipments of materials, traffic jams, power failures, and sabotage are but a few of the possibilities.

Efficiency of worker's time — Every time a worker is interrupted, it takes additional time to get back to the level of productivity attained prior to the interruption. You cannot control the frequency or time of interruptions, but you do know that they will happen. As to their effect on staff productivity, you can only guess. Some will be more affected than others.

Mistakes and misunderstandings — Despite all of your efforts to clearly and concisely describe each task that is to be performed, you will most likely miss a few. This will take its toll in rework or scrapping semicompleted work.

Common cause variation — A task's duration will vary simply because *duration* is a random variable. The process has a natural variation, and there is nothing you do can to cause a favorable change in that variation. It is there and must be accepted.

Six Methods for Estimating Task Duration

Estimating task duration is challenging. You can be on familiar ground for some activities and on totally unfamiliar ground for others. Whatever the case, you must produce an estimate. It is important that senior management understand that the estimate can be little more than a WAG (wild a** guess). In many projects, the estimate will improve as you learn more about the deliverables after having completed some of the project work. Re-estimation and replanning are common. In my consulting practice, I have found the following six techniques to be quite suitable for initial planning estimates:

- Similarity to other activities
- Historical data
- Expert advice
- Delphi technique
- Three-point technique
- Wide-band Delphi technique

The following sections describe each of these techniques in more detail.

Extrapolating Based on Similarity to Other Activities

Some of the activities in your WBS may be similar to activities completed in other projects. Your or others' recollections of those activities and their durations can be used to estimate the present task's duration. In some cases, this process may require extrapolating from the other task to this one. In most cases, using the estimates from those activities provides estimates that are good enough.

Studying Historical Data

Every good project management methodology includes a project notebook that records the estimated and actual task durations. This historical record can be used on other projects. The recorded data becomes your knowledge base for estimating task duration. This technique differs from the previous technique in that it uses a record, rather than depending on memory. To estimate the duration of a task, you extract similar tasks from the database and compute an average. That is a simple application of the database.

The historical data can be used in a more sophisticated way, too. One of my clients built an extensive database of task duration history. They use this database to record not only estimated and actual duration, but also the characteristics of the task, the skill set of the people working on it, and other variables that they found useful. When a task duration estimate is needed, they go to their database with a complete definition of the task and, with some rather sophisticated regression models, estimate the task duration. This particular client builds product for market, so it is very important to them to be able to estimate as accurately as possible. Again, my advice is that if there is value added for a particular tool or technique, use it.

Seeking Expert Advice

When the project involves a breakthrough technology or a technology that is being used for the first time in the organization, there may not be any organizational experience with that technology within the organization. In these cases, you will have to appeal to outside authorities. Vendors may be a good source, as are non-competitors who use that technology.

Applying the Delphi Technique

The Delphi technique can produce good estimates in the absence of expert advice. This is a group technique that extracts and summarizes the knowledge of the group to arrive at an estimate. After the group is briefed on the project and the nature of the task, each individual in the group is asked to make his or her best guess of the task duration. The results are tabulated and presented to the group in a histogram labeled First Pass, as shown in Figure 5-9. Participants whose estimates fall in the outer quartiles are asked to share the reason for their guess. After listening to the arguments, each group member is asked to guess again. The results are presented as a histogram labeled Second Pass, and again the outer quartile estimates are defended. A third guess is made, and the histogram plotted is labeled Third Pass. Final adjustments are allowed. The average of the third guess is used as the group's estimate. Even though the technique seems rather simplistic, it has been shown to be effective in the absence of expert advice.

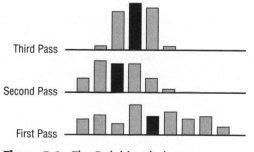

Figure 5-9: The Delphi technique

I attended an IBM business partners' meeting several years ago. One of the sessions dealt with estimating software development time, and the presenter demonstrated the use of the Delphi technique with a rather intriguing example. She asked if anyone in the group had ever worked in a carnival as a weight-guessing expert. None had, so she informed the group that they were going to use the Delphi technique to estimate the average weight of the 20 people who were in the room. She asked everyone to write his or her weight on a slip of paper. The weights were averaged by the facilitator and put aside. Each person took an initial guess as to the average weight of the people in the room, wrote it down, and passed it to the facilitator. She displayed the initial-pass histogram and asked the individuals with the five highest and five lowest guesses to share their thinking with the group; a second guess was taken and then a third. The average of the third guess became the group's estimate of the average body weight. Surprisingly, the estimate was just two pounds off the average of the individual's reported weights.

The approach the presenter used is actually a variation of the original Delphi technique. The original version used a small panel of experts (say, five or six) who were asked for their estimate independently of one another. The results were tabulated and shared with the panel members, who were then asked to submit their own second estimate. A third estimate was solicited in the same manner. The average of the third estimate was the one chosen. Note that the original approach does not involve any discussion or collaboration between the panel members. In fact, they weren't even aware of who the other members were.

Applying the Three-Point Technique

Task duration is a random variable. If it were possible to repeat the task several times under identical circumstances, duration times would vary. That variation may be tightly grouped around a central value, or it might be widely dispersed. In the first case, you would have a considerable amount of information on that task's duration as compared to the latter case, where you would have very little or no usable information on that task's duration. In any given instance of the task, you would not know at which extreme the duration would likely fall, but you could make probabilistic statements about their likelihood in any case. Figure 5-10 illustrates the point.

To use the three-point technique, you need the following three estimates of task duration:

Optimistic — The optimistic time is defined as the shortest duration one has experienced or might expect to experience given that everything happens as expected.

Pessimistic — The pessimistic time is that duration that one would experience (or has experienced) if everything that could go wrong did go wrong, yet the task was completed.

Most likely — The most likely time is that time that they usually experience.

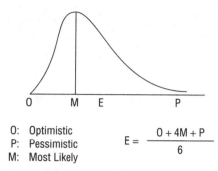

O: Optimistic
P: Pessimistic
M: Most Likely

$$E = \frac{O + 4M + P}{6}$$

Figure 5-10: The three-point technique

Then the estimated duration is given by the formula

```
(O + 4M + P) / 6
```

For this method, you are calling on the collective memory of professionals who have worked on similar activities but for which there is no recorded history.

Applying the Wide-Band Delphi Technique

Combining the Delphi and three-point methods results in the wide-band Delphi technique. It involves a panel, as in the Delphi method. In place of a single estimate, the panel members are asked, at each iteration, to give their optimistic, pessimistic, and most likely estimates for the duration of the chosen task. The results are compiled, and any extreme estimates are removed. Averages are computed for each of the three estimates, and the averages are used as the optimistic, pessimistic, and most likely estimates of task duration.

Estimation Life Cycles

A word of advice on estimating is in order here. Early estimates of task duration will not be as good as later estimates. It's a simple fact that you get smarter as the project work commences. Estimates will always be subject to the vagaries of nature and other unforeseen events. You can only hope that you gain some knowledge through the project to improve your estimates.

In the top-down project planning model, you start out with "roughly right" estimates, with the intention of improving the precision of these estimates later in the project. Both your upper management and the client must be aware of this approach. Most managers have the habit of assuming that a number, once written, is inviolate and absolutely correct regardless of the circumstances under which the number was determined. This is unrealistic in the contemporary world of project management. It may have once been appropriate for the engineer, but that is not the case with the businessperson. Figure 5-11 illustrates a typical estimation life cycle.

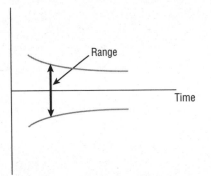

Figure 5-11: The estimation life cycle

During project planning, most task estimates are not much better than a dart throw. Of course, if the task is one that has been done several times before under similar situations, then the estimate will have a narrower variance than it would if the task had never been done before under any circumstances. As project work commences, the team will gain knowledge and understanding of the project and the work needed to deliver an acceptable solution. That includes improved estimates of future tasks in the project. After the task has begun, even more information will come to light, and the estimate (or a better estimate to completion) will be quite accurate.

Estimating Resource Requirements

By defining project activities according to the completion criteria, you should have reached a point of granularity with each task so that it is familiar. You may have done the task or something very similar to it in a past project. That recollection, or historical information, gives you the basis for estimating the resources you will need to complete the activities in the current project. In some cases, it is a straightforward recollection. In others, it is the result of keeping a historical file of similar activities. In still others, the resource estimate may be the advice of experts.

The importance of resources varies from project to project. You can use the six techniques discussed in the previous section to estimate the resource requirements for any project.

Types of resources include the following:

People — In most cases, the resources you will have to schedule are human resources. This is also the most difficult type of resource to schedule.

Facilities — Project work takes place in locations. Planning rooms, conference rooms, presentation rooms, and auditoriums are but a few examples of facilities that projects require. The exact specifications of the required facilities as well as the precise time at which each facility is needed are some of the variables that you must take into account. The project plan can provide the required details. The availability of the facilities will also drive the project schedule.

Equipment — Equipment is treated exactly the same as facilities. The availability of equipment will also drive the task schedule.

Money — Accountants will tell you that everything is eventually reduced to dollars, which is true. Project expenses typically include travel, accommodations, meals, and supplies.

Materials — The timely availability of parts to be used in the fabrication of products and other physical deliverables will be part of the project work schedule. For example, the materials needed to build a bicycle might include nuts, bolts, washers, and spacers.

People as Resources

People are the most difficult type of resource to schedule because you plan the project by specifying the types of skills you need, when you need them, and in what amounts. You do not specify the resource by name (that is, the individual you need), which is where problems arise.

There are a few tools you can use to help you schedule people.

Skills Matrices

I find that an increasing number of my clients are developing skills-inventory matrices for staff, and skill-needs matrices for activities. The two matrices are used to assign staff to activities. The assignment could be based on task characteristics such as risk, business value, criticality, and/or skill development. Figure 5-12 illustrates how the process can work.

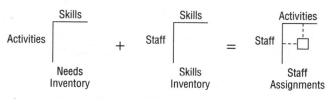

Figure 5-12: Assigning staff to activities

This process involves gathering data for the following two inventories:

- An inventory of the demand for skills needed to perform the tasks associated with specific activities. This is represented as a matrix whose rows are the activities and whose columns are the skills. These include both current and long-term needs.

- An inventory of the current skills among the professional staff. This is represented as a matrix whose rows identify the staff and whose columns represent the skills.

The columns of both matrices define the same set of skills. This gives you a way to link the two matrices and assign staff to activities. This approach can be used for on-the-job staff development. As an on-the-job development strategy, the manager would have previously met with the staff member, helped him or her define career goals, and translated those goals into skill development needs. That information can then be used in project planning to assign staff to activities so that the work they will do on the task enables them to meet those goals.

Skill Categories

This part of the skill matrix is developed by looking at each task that the unit must perform and describing the skills needed to perform the task. Because skills may appear in unrelated activities, the list of possible skills must be standardized across the enterprise.

Skill Levels

A binary assessment that simply determines whether a person has the necessary skill or doesn't is certainly easier to administer, but it isn't sufficient for project management. Skills must be qualified with a statement about how much of the skill the person possesses. Various methods are available, and companies often develop their own skill-level system.

Resource Breakdown Structure

Just as there is a Work Breakdown Structure (WBS), so also is there a Resource Breakdown Structure. Figure 5-13 gives a simple example.

The Resource Breakdown Structure is used to assist in not only resource estimation but also cost estimation. The Resource Breakdown Structure is determined by the job families, which are defined by the human resources department. That definition is simply put into this hierarchical framework and used as the basis for identifying the positions and levels that are needed to staff the project. This is then used to construct the staffing budget.

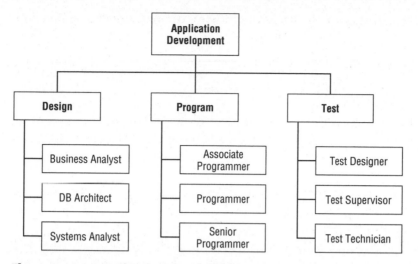

Figure 5-13: Example of a Resource Breakdown Structure

Determining Resource Requirements

The planning team includes resource managers or their representatives. At the time the planning team is defining the WBS and estimating task duration, they also estimate resource requirements.

I have found the following practice effective:

1. Create a list of all the resources required for the project. For human resources, list only the position title or skill level. Do not name specific people even if there is only one person with the requisite skills. Envision a person with the typical skill set and loading on the project task. Task duration estimates are based on using workers of average skill level, and that should be consistent with the needed resource requirements. You can worry about changing the assumption of using average skilled persons later in the planning session.

2. The project manager can provide resource requirements as part of the WBS.

You now have estimated the parameters needed to begin constructing the project schedule. The task duration estimates provide input to planning the order and sequence of completing the work defined by the activities. After the initial schedule is built, you can use the resource requirements and availability data to further modify the schedule.

Resource Planning

You need to consider several factors concerning the resources for your project. As you learned earlier in this chapter, adding resources doesn't necessarily mean that you will shorten the time needed for various activities. Adding too many people can actually add time to the project. Another factor to consider deals with the skill level of the resources.

Suppose that you are going to have a team of developers work on an application. When you are planning resources, you have to know the skill level of the potential resources. You may have to trade money for time. That means you may be able to get a lower cost by using a junior developer, but it's likely you will also find that the process takes longer. Knowing the skill sets of the available people and taking that into account when doing scheduling are critical to resource planning.

Another factor to consider is that of using existing staff on a part-time basis. At first glance, using staff on a part-time basis might seem like a good idea because you can make good decisions concerning their schedules and you will get extremely efficient use of their time. However, this isn't reality, particularly if they are coders. Development is a mental task, and what you need are knowledge workers. You can't turn a mental process on and off at will.

Similarly, scheduling people to work on two projects on the same day won't be an efficient use of resources. It takes some time for a developer to get up to writing speed. That kind of schedule may look good on paper, but it doesn't work. Give your resources a chance to get into the flow of work, and you'll be much more successful.

WHAT IF THE SPECIFIC RESOURCE IS KNOWN?

Knowing the specific resource will occur quite often, and when it does, you will be faced with some questions. Should you put that person in the plan? If you do and that person is not available when you need him or her, how will that affect your project plan? If he or she is very highly skilled and you used that information to estimate the duration of the task that person was to work on, you may have a problem. If you cannot replace him or her with an equally skilled individual, will that create a slippage that has a domino effect on the project schedule? Make your choice.

Estimating Cost

After you have estimated task duration and resource requirements, you have the data you need to establish the cost of the project. This is your first look at the dollars involved in doing the project. You know the resources that will be required and the number of hours or volume of resources needed. You can now estimate the project cost by applying the unit cost data to the amount of resources required.

When doing an estimate, you need to consider a few concepts. No matter how well you estimate cost, it is always an estimate. One of the reasons that so many projects come in over budget is that people actually believe that they have done perfect estimating and that their baseline estimate is set in stone. Remember that it is still and always will be an estimate. Anytime you are forecasting the future, as you are when you plan a project, you are dealing with some amount of uncertainty. Projects are so often over budget because the budget itself is an estimate, not an exact mathematical calculation. Even experienced cost estimators miss the mark.

With those warnings in mind, you still need to do your best to come up with a working budget for the project. Estimating can be done several ways. One method is to find an analogous project — a completed project that looks a great deal like the project you're currently planning. By using this previous project as a guideline, you'll have a reference point for the costs. The caveat that you must keep in mind is that each project is unique, which means you will have a slightly different budget for your estimate than the one from the previous project. Don't just use the same figures when you estimate, or this will come back to haunt you sometime in the project.

Another good practice in estimating is to invite subject matter experts (SMEs) to help you prepare your estimate. Ideally, these SMEs will be able to discuss their areas of expertise and give you a better handle on the estimating for your current projects.

The team should have access to a standard costing table. This table will list all resources, units of measure, and cost per unit. It is then just a simple exercise in calculating the cost per resource based on the number of units required and the cost per unit. Many organizations have a spreadsheet template that will facilitate the exercise. These calculated figures can be transferred to the WBS and aggregated up the WBS hierarchy to provide a total cost for each task level in the WBS.

The following three types of estimates are common in project management. They are often done in the sequence listed.

Order of magnitude estimate — This type means that the number given for the estimate is somewhere between 25 percent above and 75 percent below the number. Order of magnitude estimates are often used at the very beginning of the estimation process when very little detail is known about the project work and a rough estimate is all that management calls for. It is understood that this estimate will be improved over time. This estimate is often a very preliminary one and is done just to get some sense as to the financial feasibility of the project.

Budget estimate — This type can typically have a range of 10 percent over and 25 percent below the stated estimate. These estimates are generated during project planning and are based on knowing some detail about the project activities.

Definitive estimate — This type is generally the one that is used for the rest of the project. It has a range of 5 percent over and 10 percent below the stated estimate. These estimates are done frequently during project execution when new information helps further improve the range of the estimates generated during project planning.

NOTE When giving an estimate for a project, it's a good idea to have the preceding three ranges in mind. Remember that even if you tell your client that your estimate is an order of magnitude estimate, they will not remember it for the rest of the project. Protect yourself in this case by writing "Order of Magnitude" on the estimate. Doing so will at least give you something with which to defend yourself if it comes to that. Make it a point to let all concerned parties know about the different types of estimates you are providing and how those estimates are used.

Cost Budgeting

After you've done an estimate, you enter the cost budgeting phase. This is the phase when you assign costs to tasks on the WBS. Cost budgeting is actually very formulaic. You take the needed resources and multiply the costs by the number of hours they are to be used. In the case of a one-time cost (such as hardware), you simply state that cost.

Cost budgeting gives the sponsor a final check on the costs of the project. The underlying assumption is that you've got all the numbers right. Usually you'll have the cost of a resource right, but often it's tough to be exact on the total number of hours the resource is to be used. Remember that no matter what, you are still doing an estimate. Cost budgeting is different from estimating in that it is more detailed. However, the final output is still a best effort at expressing the cost of the project.

Cost Control

Cost control presents the following major issues for the project manager:

■ How often do you need to get reports of the costs? Certainly, it would be good if you could account for everything occurring on the project in real time. However, that is generally way too expensive and time-intensive. More likely, you'll get figures once a week. Getting cost status figures once a week gives you a good snapshot of the costs that are occurring. If you wait longer than a week to get cost figures, you may find that the project has spun out of control.

- How will you look at the numbers you're receiving? If you've done a cost baseline, you'll have some figures against which you can measure your costs. What you're looking for is a variance from the original costs. The two costs you have at this point are your baseline and the actual costs that have occurred on the project. The baseline was the final estimate of the costs on the project. Your job is to look at the two and determine whether management action must be taken.

> **TIP** How far off do the numbers need to be between the final estimate and your actual costs before you take some action? Usually 10 percent is the most allowed. However, if you start to see a trend of the plan going over budget or behind schedule or both — you should take a look at the reasons behind the variances before they reach the 10 percent level. See Chapter 7 for more details.

A word of advice: Keep in mind that for some projects, time is the most important constraint. Remember Y2K? In such cases, you must balance your need for cost control with the need for a definitive project ending time. There may be a trade-off in cost control for time constraints. As a project manager, you must be aware of these trade-offs and be ready to justify changes in costs to the sponsor based on other considerations such as time and quality.

Constructing the Project Network Diagram

At this point in the PMLC, you have identified the known set of tasks in the project as output from building the RBS and WBS as well as the task duration for the project. Next, the planning team needs to determine the order in which these tasks are to be performed.

The tasks and the task duration are the basic building blocks needed to construct a graphic picture of the project. This graphic picture provides you with the following two additional pieces of schedule information about the project:

- The earliest time at which work can begin on every task that makes up the project
- The earliest expected completion date of the project

This is critical information for the project manager. Ideally, the required resources will be available at the times established in the project plan. This is not very likely, and Chapter 6 discusses how to deal with that problem. But first, you need to know how to create an initial project network diagram and the associated project schedule, which is the focus of this section.

Envisioning a Complex Project Network Diagram

A *project network diagram* is a pictorial representation of the sequence in which the project work can be done. You need to follow a few simple rules to build the project network diagram.

Recall from Chapter 1 that a project is defined as a sequence of interconnected tasks. You could simply perform the tasks one at a time until they are all complete, but in most projects, this approach would not result in an acceptable completion date. In fact, it results in the longest time to complete the project. Any ordering that allows even one pair of tasks to be worked on concurrently results in a shorter project completion date.

Another approach is to establish a network of relationships between the tasks. You can do this by looking forward through the project. What tasks must be complete before another task can begin? Conversely, you can take a set of tasks and look backward through the project: Now that a set of tasks is complete, what task or tasks could come next? Both methods are valid. The one you use is a matter of personal preference. Are you more comfortable looking backward in time or forward? My advice is to look at the tasks from both angles. One can be a check of the completeness of the other.

The relationships between the tasks in the project are represented in a flow diagram called a *network diagram* or *logic diagram*.

Benefits to Network-Based Scheduling

A project schedule can be built using either of the following:

- Gantt chart
- Network diagram

The Gantt chart is the oldest of the two and is used effectively in simple, short-duration types of projects. To build a Gantt chart, you begin by associating a rectangular bar with every task. The length of the bar corresponds to the duration of the task. You then place the bars horizontally along a time line in the order in which the tasks should be completed. In some instances you will be able to schedule and work on tasks concurrently. The sequencing is often driven more by resource availability than any other consideration.

There are two drawbacks to using the Gantt chart. They are as follows:

- Because of its simplicity, the Gantt chart does not contain detailed information. It reflects only the order imposed by the manager and, in fact, hides much of that information. In other words, the Gantt chart does not contain all of the sequencing information that exists. Unless you are intimately familiar with the project tasks, you cannot tell from the Gantt chart what must come before and after what.

- The Gantt chart does not tell the project manager whether the schedule that results from the chart completes the project in the shortest possible time or even uses the resources most effectively. The Gantt chart reflects only when the manager would like to have the work done.

Although a Gantt chart is easier to build and does not require the use of an automated tool, I recommend using the network diagram. The network diagram provides a visual layout of the sequence in which project work flows. It includes detailed information and serves as an analytical tool for project scheduling and resource management problems as they arise during the life of the project. In addition, the network diagram enables you to compute the earliest time at which the project can be completed. That information does not follow from a Gantt chart.

Network diagrams can be used for detailed project planning, during implementation as a tool for analyzing scheduling alternatives, and as a control tool as described here:

Planning — Even for large projects, the project network diagram gives a clear graphical picture of the relationship between project tasks. It is, at the same time, a high-level and detailed-level view of the project. I have found that displaying the network diagram on the whiteboard or flip charts during the planning phase is beneficial. This way, all members of the planning team can use it for scheduling decisions.

Implementation — If you are using automated project management software tools, update the project file with task status and estimate-to-completion data. The network diagram is then automatically updated and can be printed or viewed. The need for rescheduling and resource reallocation decisions can be determined from the network diagram, although some argue that this method is too cumbersome because of project size. Even a project of modest size (such as one that involves about 100 tasks) produces a network diagram that is too large and awkward to be of much use. I cannot disagree, but I place the onus on software manufacturers to market products that do a better job of displaying network diagrams.

Control — Although the updated network diagram retains the status of all tasks, the best graphical report for monitoring and controlling project work will be the Gantt chart view of the network diagram. This Gantt chart cannot be used for control purposes unless you have done network scheduling or incorporated the logic into the Gantt chart. Comparing the planned schedule with the actual schedule, you can discover variances and, depending on their severity, be able to put a get-well plan in place.

CROSS-REFERENCE Chapter 7 examines progress monitoring and control in more detail and describes additional reporting tools for analyzing project status.

Building the Network Diagram Using the Precedence Diagramming Method

One early method for representing project tasks as a network dates back to the early 1950s and the Polaris Missile Program. It is called the *task-on-the-arrow* (*TOA*) *method*. As Figure 5-14 shows, an arrow represents each task. The node at the left edge of the arrow is the event that begins the task, and the node at the right edge of the arrow is the event that ends the task. Every task is represented by this configuration. Nodes are numbered sequentially, and in the early versions of this method, the sequential ordering had to be preserved. Because of the limitations of the TOA method, ghost tasks had to be added to preserve network integrity. Only the simplest of dependency relationships could be used. This method proved to be quite cumbersome as networking techniques progressed. This approach is seldom used these days.

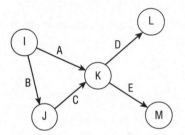

Figure 5-14: The TOA method

With the advent of the computer, the TOA method lost its appeal, and a new method replaced it. This method is called the *task-on-the-node* (*TON*) *method*, or more commonly, the *precedence diagramming method* (*PDM*).

The basic *unit of analysis* in a network diagram is the task. Each task in the network diagram is represented by a rectangle called a task *node*. Arrows represent the predecessor/successor relationships between tasks. Figure 5-15 shows an example of a project network diagram in PDM format. You take a more detailed look at how the PDM works later in this chapter.

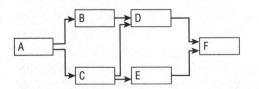

Figure 5-15: PDM format of a project network diagram

Every task in the project will have its own task node (see Figure 5-16). The entries in the task node describe the time-related properties of the task. Some of the entries describe characteristics of the task, such as its expected duration (E), whereas others describe calculated values (ES, EF, LS, and LF) associated with that task. (These terms will be defined shortly, and you'll see examples of their use.)

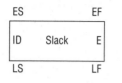

Figure 5-16: Task node

In order to create the network diagram using the PDM, you need to determine the predecessors and successors for each task. To do this, you ask: "What tasks must be complete before I can begin this task?" Here, you are looking for the technical dependencies between tasks. After a task is complete, it will have produced an output, which is a deliverable that becomes input to its successor tasks. Work on the successor tasks requires only the output from its predecessor tasks.

> **NOTE** Later, you can incorporate management constraints that may alter these dependency relationships. In my experience, considering these constraints at this point in project planning only complicates the process.

What is the next step? Although the list of predecessors and successors to each task contains all the information you need to proceed with the project, it does not represent the information in a format that tells the story of your project. Your goal is to provide a graphical picture of the project. To do that, you need to understand a few rules. When you know the rules, you can create the graphical image of the project. This section teaches you the simple rules for constructing a project network diagram.

The network diagram is logically sequenced to be read from left to right. With the exception of the start and end tasks, every task in the network must have at least one task that comes before it (its immediate predecessor) and one task that comes after it (its immediate successor). A task begins when its predecessors have been completed. The start task has no predecessor, and the end task has no successor. These networks are called *connected*. They are the type of network used in this book. Figure 5-17 gives examples of how the variety of relationships that might exist between two or more tasks can be diagrammed.

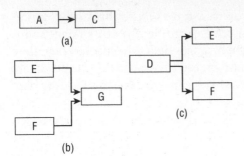

Figure 5-17: Diagramming conventions

Dependencies

A *dependency* is simply a relationship that exists between pairs of tasks. To say that task B depends on task A means that task A produces a deliverable that is needed in order to do the work associated with task B. There are four types of task dependencies, as illustrated in Figure 5-18.

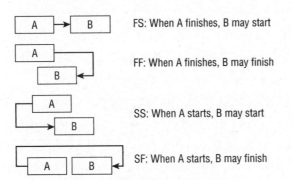

Figure 5-18: Dependency relationships

The four task dependencies shown in the figure are as follows:

Finish-to-start (FS) — This dependency says that task A must be complete before task B can begin. It is the simplest and most risk averse of the four types. For example, task A can represent the collection of data, and task B can represent entry of the data into the computer. To say that the dependency between A and B is finish-to-start means that once you have finished collecting the data, you may begin entering the data. I recommend using FS dependency in the initial project planning session. The FS dependency is displayed with an arrow emanating from the right edge of the predecessor task and leading to the left edge of the successor task.

Start-to-start (SS) — This dependency says that task B may begin once task A has begun. Note that there is a no-sooner-than relationship between task A and task B. Task B may begin no sooner than task A begins. In fact, they could both start at the same time. For example, you could alter the data collection and data entry dependency: As soon as you begin collecting data (task A), you may begin entering data (task B). In this case, there is an SS dependency between task A and B. The SS dependency is displayed with an arrow emanating from the left edge of the predecessor (A) and leading to the left edge of the successor (B). I use this dependency relationship in the "Compressing the Schedule" section later in the chapter.

Start-to-finish (SF) — This dependency is a little more complex than the FS and SS dependencies. Here task B cannot be finished sooner than task A has started. For example, suppose you have built a new information system. You don't want to eliminate the legacy system until the new system is operable. When the new system starts to work (task A), the old system can be discontinued (task B). The SF dependency is displayed with an arrow emanating from the left edge of task A to the right edge of task B. SF dependencies can be used for just-in-time scheduling between two tasks, but they rarely occur in practice.

Finish-to-finish (FF) — This dependency states that task B cannot finish sooner than task A. For example, data entry (task B) cannot finish until data collection (task A) has finished. In this case, task A and B have a finish-to-finish dependency. The FF dependency is displayed with an arrow emanating from the right edge of task A to the right edge of task B. To preserve the connectedness property of the network diagram, the SS dependency on the front end of two tasks should have an accompanying FF dependency on the back end.

Constraints

The type of dependency that describes the relationship between tasks is determined as the result of *constraints* that exist between those tasks. Each type of constraint can generate any one of the four dependency relationships. The following four types of constraints will affect the sequencing of project tasks and, hence, the dependency relations between tasks:

- Technical constraints
- Management constraints
- Interproject constraints
- Date constraints

The following sections describe each of these constraint types in more detail.

Technical Constraints

Technical dependencies between tasks arise because one task (the successor) requires output from another (the predecessor) before work can begin on it. In the simplest case, the predecessor must be completed before the successor can begin. I advise using FS relationships in the initial construction of the network diagram because they are the least complex and risk-prone dependencies. If the project can be completed by the requested date using only FS dependencies, there is no need to complicate the plan by introducing other, more complex and risk-prone dependency relationships. SS and FF dependencies will be used later when you analyze the network diagram for schedule improvements.

Within the category of technical constraints, the following four related situations should be accounted for:

Discretionary constraints — These are judgment calls by the project manager that result in the introduction of dependencies. These judgment calls may be merely a hunch or a risk-aversion strategy taken by the project manager. Through the sequencing tasks, the project manager gains a modicum of comfort with the project work. For example, revisit the data collection and data entry example used earlier in the chapter. The project manager knows that a team of recent hires will be collecting the data and that the usual practice is to have them enter the data as they collect it (SS dependency). The project manager knows that this introduces some risk to the process; and because new hires will be doing the data collection and data entry, the project manager decides to use an FS, rather than SS, dependency between data collection and data entry.

Best-practices constraints — These are based on past experiences that have worked well for the project manager or are known to the project manager based on the experiences of others in similar situations. The practices in place in an industry can be powerful influences here, especially in dealing with bleeding-edge technologies. In some cases, the dependencies that result from best-practices constraints, which are added by the project manager, might be part of a risk-aversion strategy following the experiences of others. For example, consider the dependency between software design and software build tasks. The safe approach has always been to complete the design before beginning the build. The current business environment, however, is one in which getting to the market faster has become the strategy for survival.

In an effort to get to market faster, many companies have introduced concurrency into the design-build scenario by changing the FS dependency between design and build to an SS dependency as follows. At some point in the design phase, enough is known about the final configuration of the software to begin limited programming work. By introducing this concurrency between designing and building, the project manager can reduce the time to market for the new software. Even though the project manager knows that this SS dependency introduces risk (design changes made after programming has started may render the programming useless), he or she will adopt this best-practices approach.

Logical constraints — These are like discretionary constraints that arise from the project manager's way of thinking about the logical way to sequence a pair of tasks. It's important for the project manager to be comfortable with the sequencing of work. After all, the project manager has to manage it. Based on past practices and common sense, you may prefer to sequence tasks in a certain way. That's acceptable, but do not use this as an excuse to manufacture a sequence out of convenience. As long as there is a good, logical reason, that is sufficient justification. For example, in the design-build scenario, several aspects of the software design certainly lend themselves to some concurrency with the build task. However, part of the software design work involves the use of a recently introduced technology with which the company has no experience. For that reason, the project manager decides that the part of the design that involves this new technology must be complete before any of the associated build tasks can start.

Unique requirements — These constraints occur in situations where a critical resource — such as an irreplaceable expert or a one-of-a-kind piece of equipment — is involved on several project tasks. For example, suppose a new piece of test equipment will be used on a software development project. There is only one piece of this equipment, and it can be used on only one part of the software at a time. It will be used to test several different parts of the software. To ensure that no scheduling conflicts arise with the new equipment, the project manager creates FS dependencies between every part of the software that will use this test equipment. Apart from any technical constraints, the project manager may impose such dependencies to ensure that no scheduling conflicts will arise from the use of scarce resources.

Management Constraints

A second type of dependency arises as the result of a management-imposed constraint. For example, suppose the product manager on a software development project is aware that a competitor will soon introduce a new product with similar features. Rather than follow the concurrent design-build strategy, the product manager wants to ensure that the design of the new software will yield a product that can compete with the competitor's new product. He or she expects design changes in response to the competitor's new product and, rather than risk wasting the programmers' time, imposes the FS dependency between the design and build tasks.

You'll see management constraints at work when you analyze the network diagram and as part of the scheduling decisions you make as project manager. Dependencies based on management constraints differ from technical dependencies in that they can be reversed, whereas technical dependencies cannot. For example, suppose the product manager finds out that the competitor has discovered a fatal flaw as a result of beta testing and has decided to indefinitely delay the new product introduction pending resolution of the flaw. The decision to follow the FS dependency between design and build can now be reversed, and the concurrent design-build strategy can be reinstituted. That is, management will have the project manager change the design-build dependency from FS to SS.

Interproject Constraints

Interproject constraints result when deliverables from one project are needed by another project. Such constraints result in dependencies between the tasks that produce the deliverable in one project and the tasks in the other project that require the use of those deliverables. For example, suppose a new piece of test equipment is being manufactured by the same company that is developing the software that will use the test equipment. In this case, the start of the testing tasks in the software development project depends on the delivery of the manufactured test equipment from the other project. The dependencies that result are technical but exist between tasks in two or more projects, rather than within a single project.

Interproject constraints arise when a very large project is decomposed into smaller, more manageable projects. For example, the construction of the Boeing 777 took place in a variety of geographically dispersed manufacturing facilities. Each manufacturing facility defined a project to produce its part. To assemble the final aircraft, the delivery of the parts from separate projects had to be coordinated with the final assembly project plan. Thus, there were tasks in the final assembly project that depended on deliverables from other sub-assembly projects.

NOTE These interproject constraints are common. Occasionally, large projects are decomposed into smaller projects or divided into a number of projects that are defined along organizational or geographic boundaries. In all of these examples, projects are decomposed into smaller projects that are related to one another. This approach creates interproject constraints. Although I prefer to avoid such decomposition because it creates additional risk, it may be necessary at times.

Date Constraints

At the outset, I want to make it clear that I do not approve of using date constraints. I avoid them in any way I can. In other words, "just say no" to typing dates into your project management software. If you have been in the habit of using date constraints, read on.

Date constraints impose start or finish dates on a task, forcing it to occur according to a particular schedule. In this date-driven world, it is tempting to use the requested date as the required delivery date. These constraints generally conflict with the schedule that is calculated and driven by the dependency relationships between tasks. In other words, date constraints create unnecessary complication in interpreting the project schedule.

The three types of date constraints are as follows:

No earlier than — Specifies the earliest date on which a task can be completed.

No later than — Specifies a date by which a task must be completed.

On this date — Specifies the exact date on which a task must be completed.

All of these date constraints can be used on the start or finish side of a task. The most troublesome application is the on-this-date constraint. It firmly sets a date and affects all tasks that follow it. The result is the creation of a needless complication in the project schedule and in reporting the status of the project as it progresses. The next most troublesome date constraint is the no-later-than constraint. It will not allow a task to occur beyond the specified date. Again, you are introducing complexity for no good reason. Both on-this-date and no-later-than constraints can result in negative slack. If at all possible, do not use them. There are alternatives, which are discussed in the next chapter.

The least troublesome date constraint is the no-earlier-than constraint. At worst, it simply delays a task's schedule and by itself cannot cause negative float.

Using the Lag Variable

Pauses or delays between tasks are indicated in the network diagram through the use of *lag variables*. Lag variables are best described with an example. Suppose that data is being collected by mailing out a survey and is entered as the surveys are returned. Imposing an SS dependency between mailing out the surveys and entering the data would not be feasible unless you introduced some delay between mailing surveys and getting back the responses that could be entered. For the sake of the example, suppose that you wait 10 days from the date you mail the surveys until you schedule entering the data from the surveys. Ten days is the time you think it will take for the surveys to arrive at the recipient locations, for the recipients to answer the survey questions, and for the surveys to be returned to you by mail. In this case, you have defined an SS dependency with a lag of 10 days. To put it another way, task B (data entry) can start 10 days after task A (mailing the survey) has started.

Creating an Initial Project Network Schedule

As mentioned, all tasks in the network diagram have at least one predecessor task and one successor task, with the exception of the start and end tasks. If this convention is followed, the sequence is relatively straightforward to identify. However, if the convention is not followed, if date constraints are imposed on some tasks, or if the resources follow different calendars, understanding the sequence of tasks that result from this initial scheduling exercise can be rather complex.

To establish the project schedule, you need to compute two schedules: the early schedule, which you calculate using the forward pass, and the late schedule, which you calculate using the backward pass.

The early schedule consists of the earliest times at which a task can start and finish. These are calculated numbers derived from the dependencies between all the tasks in the project. The late schedule consists of the latest times at which a task can start and finish without delaying the completion date of the project. These are also calculated numbers that are derived from the dependencies between all of the tasks in the project.

The combination of these two schedules gives you the following two additional pieces of information about the project schedule:

- The window of time within which each task must be started and finished in order for the project to be completed on schedule
- The sequence of tasks that determine the project completion date

The sequence of tasks that determine the project completion date is called the *critical path*. The critical path can be defined in the following ways:

- The longest duration path in the network diagram
- The sequence of tasks whose early schedule and late schedule are the same
- The sequence of tasks with zero slack or float (as defined later in this chapter)

All of these definitions say the same thing: The critical path is the sequence of tasks that must be completed on schedule in order for the project to be completed on schedule.

The tasks that define the critical path are called *critical path tasks*. Any delay in a critical path task will delay the completion of the project by the amount of delay in that task. Critical path tasks represent sequences of tasks that warrant the project manager's special attention.

The *earliest start* (ES) time for a task is the earliest time at which all of its predecessor tasks have been completed and the subject task can begin. The ES time of a task with no predecessor tasks is arbitrarily set to 1, the first day on which the project is open for work. The ES time of tasks with one predecessor task is determined from the *earliest finish* (EF) time of the predecessor task. The ES time of tasks with two or more predecessor tasks is determined from the latest of the EF times of the predecessor tasks. The earliest finish (EF) time of a task is calculated as ((ES + Duration) – One Time Unit). The reason for subtracting the one time unit is to account for the fact that a task starts at the beginning of a time unit (hour, day, and so forth) and finishes at the end of a time unit. In other words, a one-day task, starting at the beginning of a day, begins and ends on the same day. For example, in Figure 5-19 note that task E has only one predecessor: task C. The EF for task C is the end of day 3. Because it is the only predecessor of task E, the ES of task E is the next day, the beginning of day 4. Conversely, task D has two predecessors: task B and task C. When there are two or more predecessors, the ES of the successor (task D in Figure 5-19) is calculated based on the maximum of the EF dates of the predecessor tasks. The EF dates of the predecessors are the end of day 4 and the end of day 3. The maximum of these is 4; therefore, the ES of task D is the morning of day 5. The complete calculations of the early schedule are shown in Figure 5-19.

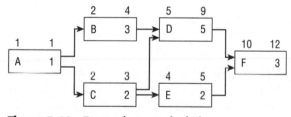

Figure 5-19: Forward-pass calculations

The *latest start* (LS) and *latest finish* (LF) times of a task are the latest times at which the task can start or finish without causing a delay in the completion of the project. Knowing these times is valuable for the project manager, who must make decisions regarding resource scheduling that can affect completion dates. The window of time between the ES and LF of a task is the window within which the resource for the work must be scheduled or the project completion date will be delayed. To calculate these times, you work backward in the network diagram. First set the LF time of the last task on the network to its calculated EF time. Its LS is calculated as ((LF – Duration) + One Time Unit). Again, you add the one time unit to adjust for the start and finish of a task within the same day. The LF time of all immediate predecessor tasks is determined by the minimum of the LS, minus one time unit, times all tasks for which it is the predecessor.

For example, calculate the late schedule for task E in Figure 5-20. Its only successor, task F, has an LS date of day 10. The LF date for its only predecessor, task E, will therefore be the end of day 9. In other words, task E must finish no later than the end of day 9 or it will delay the start of task F and hence delay the completion date of the project. Using the formula, the LS date for task E will be $9 - 2 + 1$, or the beginning of day 8. Conversely, consider task C. It has two successor tasks: task D and task E. The LS dates for these tasks are day 5 and day 7, respectively. The minimum of those dates, day 5, is used to calculate the LF of task C — namely, the end of day 4. The complete calculations for the late schedule are shown in Figure 5-20.

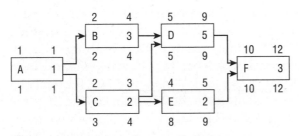

Figure 5-20: Backward-pass calculations

Critical Path

As mentioned, the critical path is the longest path or sequence of tasks (in terms of task duration) through the network diagram. The critical path drives the completion date of the project. Any delay in the completion of any one of the tasks in the sequence will delay the completion of the project. You should pay particular attention to critical path tasks. The critical path for the example problem you used to calculate the early schedule and the late schedule is shown in Figure 5-21.

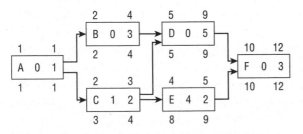

Figure 5-21: Critical path

Calculating Critical Path

One way to identify the critical path in the network diagram is to identify all possible paths through the diagram and add up the durations of the tasks that lie along those paths. The path with the longest duration time is the critical path. For projects of any size, this method is not feasible, and you have to resort to the second method of finding the critical path: computing the slack time of a task.

Computing Slack

This method of finding the critical path requires you to compute a quantity known as the task *slack time*. Slack time (also called *float*) is the amount of delay, expressed in units of time, that could be tolerated in the starting time or completion time of a task without causing a delay in the completion of the project. Slack time is a calculated number. It is the difference between the late finish and the early finish (LF – EF). If the result is greater than zero, the task has a range of time in which it can start and finish without delaying the project completion date, as shown in Figure 5-22.

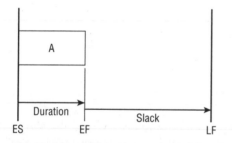

Figure 5-22: ES-to-LF window of a task

Because weekends, holidays, and other nonwork periods are not conventionally considered part of the slack, these must be subtracted from the period of slack. There are two types of slack, as follows:

Free slack — This is the range of dates in which a task can finish without causing a delay in the early schedule of any tasks that are its immediate successors. Notice in Figure 5-21 that task C has an ES of the beginning of day 2 and an LF of the end of day 4. Its duration is two days, and it has a day 3 window within which it must be completed without affecting the ES of any of its successor tasks (task D and task E). Therefore, it has free slack of one day. Free slack can be equal to but never greater than total slack. When you choose to delay the start of a task, possibly for resource scheduling reasons, first consider tasks that have free slack associated with them. By definition, if a task's completion stays within the free slack range, it can never delay the early start date of any other task in the project.

Total slack — This is the range of dates in which a task can finish without delaying the project completion date. Consider task E in Figure 5-21. This task has a free slack (or float) of four days, as well as a total slack (or float) of four days. In other words, if task E were to be completed more than three days later than its EF date, it would delay completion of the project. If a task has zero slack, then it determines the project completion date. In other words, all the tasks on the critical path must be done on their earliest schedule or the project completion date will suffer. If a task with total slack greater than zero were to be delayed beyond its late finish date, it would become a critical path task and cause the completion date to be delayed.

Based on the method you used to compute the early and late schedules, the sequence of tasks having zero slack is defined as the critical path. If a task has been date-constrained using the on-this-date type of constraint, it will also have zero slack. However, this constraint usually gives a false indicator that a task is on the critical path. Finally, in the general case, the critical path is the path that has minimum slack.

Near-Critical Path

Even though project managers are tempted to rivet their attention on critical path tasks, other tasks also require their attention. These make up what is called a *near-critical path*. The full treatment of near-critical tasks is beyond the scope of this book. I introduce the concept here so that you are aware that paths other than critical paths are worthy of attention. As a general example, suppose the critical path tasks are tasks with which the project team has considerable experience. In this case, duration estimates are based on historical data and are quite accurate in that the estimated duration will be very close to the actual duration.

Conversely, suppose there is a sequence of tasks not on the critical path with which the team has little experience, so the duration estimates have large estimation variances. Also suppose that such tasks lie on a path that has little total slack. It is very likely that this near-critical path may actually drive the project completion date even though the total path length is less than that of the critical path. This situation will happen if larger-than-estimated durations occur. Because of the large duration variances, such a case is very likely. Obviously, this path cannot be ignored.

Analyzing the Initial Project Network Diagram

After you have created the initial project network diagram, one of the following two situations will be present:

- The initial project completion date meets the requested completion date. Usually this is not the case, but it does sometimes happen.

- The more likely situation is that the initial project completion date is later than the requested completion date. In other words, you have to find a way to squeeze some time out of the project schedule.

You eventually need to address two considerations: the project completion date and resource availability under the revised project schedule. The following section is based on the assumption that resources will be available to meet this compressed schedule. Later in this chapter, the resource-scheduling problem is addressed. The two are quite dependent on one another, but they must be treated separately.

Compressing the Schedule

Almost without exception, the initial project calculations will result in a project completion date beyond the required completion date. That means the project team must find ways to reduce the total duration of the project to meet the required date.

To address this problem, you analyze the network diagram to identify areas where you can compress project duration. Look for pairs of tasks that allow you to convert tasks that are currently worked on in series into patterns of work that are more parallel. Work on the successor task might begin once the predecessor task has reached a certain stage of completion. In many cases, some of the deliverables from the predecessor can be made available to the successor so that work might begin on it.

WARNING   Changing the predecessor after work has started on the successor creates a potential rework situation and increases project risk. Schedule compressions affect only the time frame in which work will be done; they do not reduce the amount of work to be done. The result is the need for more coordination and communication, especially between the tasks affected by the dependency changes.

You first need to identify strategies for locating potential dependency changes. Focus your attention on critical path tasks because these are the tasks that determine the completion date of the project, the very thing you want to have an impact on. You might be tempted to look at critical path tasks that come early in the life of the project, thinking that you can get a jump on the scheduling problem, but this usually is not a good strategy for the following reason: At the early stages of a project, the project team is little more than a group of people who have not worked together before (I refer to them as a herd of cats). Because you are going to make dependency changes (FS to SS), you are going to introduce risk into the project. Your herd of cats is not ready to assume risk early in the project. You should give them some time to become a real team before intentionally increasing the risk they will have to contend with. That means you should look downstream on the critical path for those compression opportunities.

A second factor to consider is focusing on tasks that are partitionable. A *partitionable* task is one whose work can be assigned to two or more individuals working in parallel. For example, painting a room is partitionable. One person can be assigned to each wall. When one wall is finished, a successor task, such as picture hanging, can be done on the completed wall. That way, you don't have to wait until the room is entirely painted before you can begin decorating the walls with pictures.

Writing a computer program may or may not be partitionable. If it is partitionable, you could begin a successor task like testing the completed parts before the entire program is complete. Whether a program is partitionable depends on many factors, such as how the program is designed, whether the program is single-function or multifunction, and other considerations. If a task is partitionable, it is a candidate for consideration. You might be able to partition it so that when some of it is finished, you can begin working on successor tasks that depend on the part that is complete. After you have identified a candidate set of partitionable tasks, you need to assess the extent to which the schedule might be compressed by starting the task's successor task earlier. There is not much to gain by considering tasks with short duration times. I hope I have given you enough hints at a strategy to help you find opportunities to compress the schedule that you will be able to find those opportunities quite easily. If you can't, don't worry. The next chapter gives you other suggestions for compressing the schedule.

Assume you have found one or more candidate tasks to work with. See what happens to the network diagram and the critical path as dependencies are adjusted. As you begin to replace series (SF dependencies) with parallel sequences of tasks (SS dependencies), the critical path may change to a new sequence of tasks. This change will happen if, because of your compression decisions, the length of the initial critical path is reduced to a duration that is less than that of some other path. The result is a new critical path. Figure 5-23 shows two iterations of the analysis. The top diagram is the original critical path that results from constructing the initial network diagram using only FS dependencies. The critical path tasks are identified with a filled dot.

The middle diagram in Figure 5-23 is the result of changing the dependency between tasks A and B from FS to SS. Now the critical path has changed to a new sequence of tasks. The tasks with filled triangles illustrate the new critical path. If you change the FS dependency between tasks C and D, the critical path again moves to the sequence of tasks identified by the filled squares.

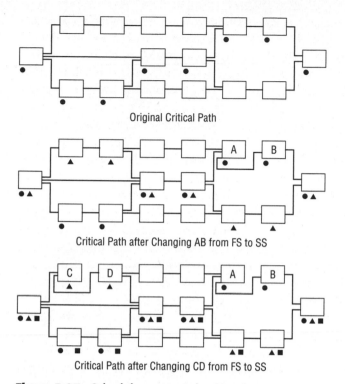

Original Critical Path

Critical Path after Changing AB from FS to SS

Critical Path after Changing CD from FS to SS

Figure 5-23: Schedule compression iterations

Occasionally, some tasks always remain on the critical path. For example, notice the set of tasks that have a filled circle, triangle, and square in Figure 5-23. They have remained on the critical path through both changes. This set of tasks identifies a bottleneck in the project schedule. Although further compression may result in this set of tasks changing, this set of bottleneck tasks does identify a set of tasks deserving of particular attention as the project commences. Because all critical paths generated to this point pass through this bottleneck, you might want to take steps to ensure that these tasks do not fall behind schedule.

Management Reserve

Management reserve is a topic associated with task duration estimates, but it more appropriately belongs in this section because it should be a property of the project network more so than of the individual tasks.

At the individual task level, you might be tempted to pad your estimates to have a better chance of finishing a task on schedule. For example, you know that a particular task will require three days of your time to complete, but you submit an estimate of four days just to make sure you can get the three days of work done in the four-day schedule you hope to get for the task. The one day that you add is padding. First, let's agree that you will not do this. Parkinson's Law (which states that work will expand to the time allotted to complete it) will surely strike you down, and the task will, in fact, require the four days you estimated it would take. Stick with the three-day estimate and work to make it happen. That is a better strategy. Now that you know padding is bad at the task level, you are going to apparently contradict yourself by saying that it is all right at the project level. There are some very good reasons for this.

Management reserve is nothing more than a contingency budget of time. The size of that contingency budget can be in the range of 5 to 10 percent of the total of all the task durations in your project. The size might be closer to 5 percent for projects having few unknowns, or it could be closer to 10 percent for projects using breakthrough technologies or that are otherwise very complex. After you have determined the size of your management reserve, you create a task whose duration is the size of management reserve and put that task at the end of the project. It will be the last task, and its completion will signal the end of the project. This management reserve task becomes the last one in your project plan, succeeded only by the project completion milestone.

What is this management reserve used for? First, the project team should manage the project so that the reserve task is not needed — though in reality, this is rarely possible. The date promised to the client is the one calculated by the completion of the reserve task. The reserve task's duration can be shortened as necessary. For example, if the critical path slips by two days, the reserve task's duration will be reduced by two days. This holds the project completion date constant.

This technique keeps the management reserve task visible and enables you to manage the rate at which it's being used. If 35 percent of the overall project time line has elapsed and 50 percent of the reserve task has been used, you know you're heading for trouble.

Second, management reserve can be used as incentive for the project team. For example, many contracts include penalties for completing milestones later than planned, as well as rewards for completing milestones ahead of schedule. Think of management reserve as a contingency fund that you do not want to spend. Every day that is left in the contingency fund at the completion of the project is a day ahead of schedule for which the client should reward you. Conversely, if you spend that contingency fund and still require more time to complete the project, this means that the project was completed later than planned. For every day that the project is late, you should expect to pay a penalty.

Writing an Effective Project Proposal

The deliverable from all the planning activities in the JPPS is the project proposal. It is the document you will forward to the senior management team for approval to do the project. In most cases, this will be the same team that approved the project for planning based on the POS. The project proposal states the complete business case for the project. This includes the expected business value, as well as cost and time estimates. In addition to this information, the proposal details what is to be done, who is going to do it, when it is going to be done, and how it is going to be done. It is the road map for the project.

> **NOTE** Expect feedback and several revisions before approval is granted. It is not the purpose of this section to spell out in detail what a project proposal should look like. The organization will have a prescribed format to follow. This section merely outlines the contents you will be expected to submit.

Contents of the Project Proposal

Each organization will have a prescribed format for its project proposal, but most proposals have sections similar to the ones listed in the sections that follow. The project proposal is a restatement of all the planning work that has been done so far.

Executive Summary

This section may not exceed one page and in most cases should be about a half page. Think of the two-minute elevator speech (if you can't summarize the project in a two-minute elevator ride, you haven't done your job) and you won't go wrong. I recommend that this section include three brief paragraphs, each describing one of the following topics:

- Business situation (expanded from the POS)
- Your project goal (expanded from the POS)
- Business value (expanded from the POS)

Now that was easy wasn't it?

If there is a strategic plan in place for your organization, you might want to add a fourth paragraph that briefly describes how your project supports that strategic plan. This will be necessary if your project is competing with other projects for a place in the project portfolio. See Chapter 14 for more details on this important topic.

Background

This is a brief description of the situation that led to the project proposal. It often states the business conditions, opportunities, and any problems giving rise to the project. It sets the stage for later sections and puts the project in the context of the business.

Objective

This is another short section that gives a very general statement of what you hope to accomplish through this project. Avoid jargon — you don't know who might have reason to read this section. Use the language of the business, not the technical language of your department. The objective should be clearly stated so that there is no doubt as to what is to be done and what constitutes attainment of the objective.

Overview of the Approach to Be Taken

For those who might not be interested in the details of how you are going to reach your objective, this section provides a high-level outline of your approach. Some mention of the PMLC model to be used would be good here. Again, avoid jargon whenever possible. Give a brief statement of each step and include a few sentences of supporting narrative. Brevity and clarity are important.

Detailed Statement of the Work

Here is where you provide a high-level summary of what will be done, when it will be done, who will do it, how much time will be required, and what criteria will be used to measure completeness. This is the road map of all the project work. Gantt charts are useful for such presentations of schedule data because they are easily understood and generally intuitive, even for people who are seeing them for the first time.

Time and Cost Summary

It is my practice to include a summary page of time and cost data. This usually works best if presented as a single high-level table. Often the data will have been stated over several pages, and it is brought together here for easy review and comment by the client.

Appendices

I recommend reserving the appendix for all supporting data and details that are not germane to the body of the proposal. Anticipate questions your client might have, and include answers here. Remember that this is detail beyond the basic description of the project work. Supporting information is generally found here.

Format of the Project Proposal

There are no hard-and-fast rules regarding the format of a project proposal. You will surely be able to find examples of successful proposals in your department or company that you can use as guides. After you have your ideas sketched out, share the proposal with a trusted colleague. His or her feedback may be the most valuable advice you can get.

Gaining Approval to Launch the Project

Getting your POS approved means that the senior management team thinks your idea addresses an important business situation and that they will give you the resources you need to develop your project plan. Your project proposal has to convince them that your approach makes good business sense and the resources you are requesting are in line with the business value that will be generated. To gain that approval, you may have to submit and revise the proposal several times. That will come about for one or more of the following reasons:

- **The cost-benefit is not in your favor** — Decompose your solution and estimate benefits by function. Perhaps you can trim the solution down by eliminating functions with unfavorable cost-benefit ratios.

- **The risks of failure are too high** — This happens often. For example, a new technology or one for which your organization is not experienced is the major contributor to high risk. Replace that technology with a more stable, well-known technology and wait for time to correct the situation.

- **The total project cost exceeds available funding** — The scope triangle would suggest trimming scope or decomposing the project into phases.

- **Other projects are competing for the same resources** — Maybe it's time to press your sponsor into service. The politics or the leverage your sponsor can bring to bear may be sufficient.

For any or all of these reasons, you may be asked to revise and resubmit your proposal.

Putting It All Together

The work of planning the project is now complete. You have written and submitted a detailed project proposal based on the project plan. To the best of your ability, you've provided a time line, budget, and resource requirements list. Approval at this stage means approval to do the project as defined in the project plan. In the next chapter, armed with an approved project proposal, project plan, and the resources to support the project, you will begin recruiting team members and putting the necessary team operating rules in place.

Discussion Questions

1. What are the advantages and disadvantages of holding a JPPS session onsite versus offsite?

2. Your planning session seems to have reached an impasse. The planning team is divided between two ways to approach a particularly difficult part of the project. Approximately two-thirds of the team members want to use a well-tested and well-understood approach. The remaining third (of which you are a member) wants to use a new approach that holds the promise of significantly reducing the time to complete this part of the project. You are the project manager and feel very strongly about using the new approach. Should you impose your authority as project manager and take the new approach, or should you go with the majority? What is the basis for your decision? Be specific. Is there anything else you might do to resolve the impasse?

3. Why is building the WBS by walking around the workspace or the e-mail space a ticket to failure?

4. The WBS identifies all of the work that must be done to complete the project. What would you do if the answer to a question posed as part of the work determines which of the two alternatives mentioned in question #2 you should pursue?

5. Under what conditions might you choose to decompose an activity that meets all of the six completeness criteria? Give specific examples.

6. Can you think of any activities that would not meet all six completeness criteria, yet need not be further decomposed? Give specific examples.

7. You have used the three-point method to estimate the duration of a task that you know will be critical to the project. The estimate produces a very large difference between the optimistic and pessimistic estimates. What actions might you take, if any, regarding this task?

8. Discuss a project on which you've worked where time was the major factor in determining the success or failure of the project. What did you do

about cost considerations? Did the sponsor(s) agree with the added cost? Was the project successful?

9. Prepare a simple budget showing an order of magnitude estimate, a budget estimate, and a definitive estimate. What did you have to do to bring each successive budget closer to the final working budget?

10. The project network diagram has been constructed, and the project completion date is beyond the management-imposed deadline. You have compressed the schedule as much as possible by introducing parallel work through changes from FS to SS dependencies, and you still do not meet the schedule deadline. What would you do? (Hint: Use the scope triangle discussed in Chapter 1.)

11. Even though all of your tasks have met the WBS completion criteria, what scheduling problems might prompt you to further decompose one or more of them, and how will that resolve the problems?

12. You are the project manager of a project to develop a new system for the company. You have two options for a resource to work on a specific programming task for your project. The task is not on the critical path, but it is somewhat complex. Your options are as follows:

    (a) One choice is Harry. He is the most skilled programmer in the company and is therefore in constant demand. As a result, he is usually assigned to several projects at the same time. He is available to your project on a half-time basis. He currently has commitments to two other projects for the remaining half of his time.

    (b) Your other choice is actually a team of two programmers, both of whom have average skills. They are recent hires into the company and have never worked together before. You have two alternatives and are free to choose whichever one you want. First, you could pick one of these programmers to work half-time on your project. Second, they could each be assigned to your project quarter-time. Regardless of which choice you make, this would be the only project they would be working on. The remainder of their time will be spent in training on company processes and systems, and orientation to company policies and practices.

    You have three alternatives from which to choose. Identify and evaluate the advantages and disadvantages of each alternative. What are the risks associated with each alternative? How might you mitigate those risks? Which choice would you make and why? Are there conditions under which one choice would be preferred over the other? Be specific.

CASE STUDY – PIZZA DELIVERED QUICKLY (PDQ)

13. The PDQ system consists of the following six subsystems:

- Pizza Factory Locator
- Order Entry
- Logistics
- Order Submit
- Routing
- Inventory Management

Pick one of these subsystems and build a complete WBS. You may have to make assumptions in order to complete this exercise. If so, just state them with your rationale.

CHAPTER 6

How to Launch a TPM Project

The productivity of a workgroup seems to depend on how the group members see their own goals in relation to the goals of the organization.
— Paul Hersey and Kenneth H. Blanchard

When the best leader's work is done, the people say, "We did it ourselves."
— Lao-Tzu, Chinese philosopher

When a team outgrows individual performance and learns team confidence, excellence becomes reality.
— Joe Paterno, football coach, Penn State University

CHAPTER LEARNING OBJECTIVES

After reading this chapter, you will be able to:

- Describe the characteristics of an effective project team member
- Understand the different roles and responsibilities of core versus contract team members
- Help contract team members become part of the team
- Establish team operating rules for problem solving, decision making, and conflict resolution
- Know the types of team meetings and when to use each type
- Establish and use a team war room
- Define scope change processes and change management processes
- Know project communications requirements and use
- Assign resources

Continued

CHAPTER LEARNING OBJECTIVES   *(continued)*

- Finalize the project schedule
- Describe the format and explain the contents of a work package
- Know when to require a work package description

The project plan has been approved, and it's time to get on with the work of the project. Before you turn the team loose, you must attend to a few housekeeping chores.

Using Tools, Templates, and Processes to Launch a Project

The major topics of this chapter are recruiting the full project team and preparing it to begin working on the project. This is an important step in the project, especially in those circumstances where the project team is coming together for the first time. At this point, they are just a group of people united by a common purpose they may know little or nothing about. It is your job as project manager to turn them into a team. The tools and templates you have at your disposal include the following:

- (Process) Recruiting the project team members
- (Template) The Project Definition Statement (PDS)
- Establishing team operating rules for:
  - (all 3) Problem solving
  - (Tool) Decision making
  - (Tool) Conflict resolution
  - (Tool) Consensus building
  - (Process) Brainstorming
  - (Tool) Team meetings
- (Process and Template) The scope change management process
- (Process) Communications management planning
- (Tool and Template) Work packages
- (Process) The resource assignment process
- (Process and Template) Finalizing the project schedule

Recruiting the Project Team

After some 40 years of practicing project management, I finally had a project management assignment that allowed me to select exactly the team I wanted. My selection received the highest priority, and I got everyone I requested — 100-percent assignment from everyone. I thought I had died and gone to heaven. What a pleasure it was to work with a team whose members were all known to me and with whom I had worked with on previous projects. They were people who made a commitment and stuck to it. You could go the bank with their commitment and know that it was sound. With that team it is no surprise that the project finished ahead of schedule and under budget. There was no staff turnover during the 27-month project. I don't expect to ever have that ideal situation again.

The reality is that most likely you will inherit team members because they are available. (I've often wondered if availability is a skill.) So this chapter starts by discussing the realities of recruiting a project team.

Project plans and their execution are only as successful as the manager and team who implement them. Building effective teams is as much an art as it is a science.

When recruiting and building an effective team, you must consider not only the technical skills of each person but also the critical roles and chemistry that must exist between and among the project manager and the team members. The selection of you as the project manager and your team members will not be perfect — there are always risks with any personnel decision.

In addition to choosing you as the project manager the project team will have two or three separate components. Clients (internal or external to the company) and the core team are required. Contract team members are required only when the project outsources segments of the project work. The project team has the following three separate components:

- Core team
- Client team
- Contract team

Be aware of the characteristics that should be part of an effective project team. The following sections describe the responsibilities of each of the three components of the project team. Also provided are a checklist that should assist you in your selection process and guidelines for organizing the project in an organization.

Core Team Members

Core team members are with the project from cradle to grave. They typically have a major role to play in the project and bring a skill set that has broad applicability across the range of work undertaken in the project. They might also have responsibility for key tasks or sets of tasks in the project.

Although the ideal assignment for Agile Project Management (APM) and Extreme Project Management (xPM) projects is full-time, that is rarely the case in today's business environment. In matrix organizations, professional staff can be assigned to more than one project at a time. This case is especially true when a staff member possesses a skill not commonly found in the staff. They will be assigned to several projects concurrently. A core team member will have some percentage of his or her time allocated to the project — it is not likely you will get them full-time.

When to Select the Core Team Members

Because the core team will be needed for the Joint Project Planning Session (JPPS), its members should be identified as early as possible. The core team is usually identified at the beginning of the scoping phase. This means that the members can participate in the early definition and planning of the project.

Selection Criteria

Because of the downsizing, rightsizing, and capsizing going on in corporate America, much of the responsibility for choosing core team members has been designated to the project manager. However, even if you're given this responsibility as the project manager, you may have little or no latitude in picking the individuals who you would like on your core team. This problem can be caused by one of the following situations:

- Most organizations have a very aggressive portfolio of projects with constantly changing priorities and requirements.

- The individual you want already has such a heavy workload that joining yet another team is not an option.

- Staff turnover, especially among highly technical and in high demand professionals, is out of control in many organizations. Because of the high demand, the turnover among these professionals is also high.

All of these situations make it difficult for the project manager to select the core dream team. For example, suppose a project manager has a choice between the A Team and the B Team. The A Team is the most skilled in a particular technology. Its members are the company's experts. Conversely, the B Team is made up of individuals who would like to be on the A Team but just don't have the requisite experience and skills. The project manager would like to have all A Team members on the core team but realizes that this is just not going to happen. Even a suggestion of such a core team would be immediately rejected by the managers of such highly skilled professionals. The politically savvy project manager would determine the project work that must have an A Team member and the project work that could get done with a B Team member, and then negotiate accordingly with the managers of these potential team members.

The project manager will have to pick his or her battles carefully, because he or she may want the A Team for critical-path tasks, high-risk tasks, and high-business-value projects, and accept the B Team for tasks and projects of lesser criticality. Be ready to horse trade between projects, too. Give the resource managers an opportunity to use non–critical path tasks as on-the-job training for their staff. Remember that they have as many staff development and deployment problems as you have project planning and scheduling problems. Trading a favor of staff development for an A Team member may be a good strategy.

I identified a list of characteristics that many project managers have offered as successful core team characteristics as a result of my project management consulting work. The list of characteristics follows shortly. For the most part, these characteristics are observed in individuals based on their experiences and the testimony of those who have worked with them. Typically, the presence or absence of these characteristics cannot be determined through interviews.

In many cases, the project manager must take a calculated risk that the team member possesses these characteristics even though the individual has not previously demonstrated that he or she has them. It will become obvious very quickly whether or not the individual possesses these characteristics. If not, and if those characteristics are critical to the team member's role in the project, the project manager or the team member's line manager will have to correct the team member's behavior.

The following characteristics have been identified by project managers as being the most important for core team members to possess:

Commitment to the project — This is critical to the success of the project. The project manager must know that each core team member places a high priority on fulfilling his or her roles and responsibilities in the project. The core team must be proactive in fulfilling those responsibilities and not need constant reminders of schedules and deliverables from the project manager.

Shared responsibility — This means that success and failure are equally the reward and blame of each team member. Having shared responsibility means that you will never hear one team member taking individual credit for a success on the project, or blaming another team member for a failure on the project. All share equally in success and failure. Furthermore, when a problem situation arises, all will pitch in to help in any way. If one team member is having a problem, another will voluntarily be there to help.

Flexibility — Team members must be willing to adapt to the situation. "That is not my responsibility" doesn't go very far in project work. Schedules may have to change at the last minute to accommodate an unexpected situation. It is the success of the project that has priority, not the schedule of any one person on the project team.

Task-oriented — In the final analysis, it is the team members' ability to get their assigned work done according to the project plan that counts.

Ability to work within schedules and constraints — Part of being a member of the team is your ability to consistently complete assignments within the planned time frame instead of offering excuses for failing to do so. Team members will encounter a number of obstacles, such as delays caused by others, but they will have to find a way around those obstacles. The team depends on its members to complete their work according to plan.

Trust and mutual support — These are the hallmarks of an effective team, and every member must convey these qualities. Team members must be trusting and trustworthy. Are they empathetic and do they readily offer help when it is clear that help is needed? Their interaction with other team members will clearly indicate whether they possess these characteristics. Individuals who do not will have a difficult time working effectively on a project team.

Team-oriented — To be team-oriented means to put the welfare of the team ahead of your own. Behaviors as simple as the individual's use of "I" versus "we" in team meetings and conversations with other team members are strong indicators of team orientation.

Open-minded — The open-minded team member will welcome and encourage other points of view and other solutions to problem situations. His or her objective is clearly to do what is best for the team and not look for individual kudos.

Ability to work across structure and authorities — In contemporary organizations, projects tend to cross organizational lines. Cross-departmental teams are common. Projects such as these require the team member to work with people from a variety of business disciplines. Many of these people will have a different value system and a different approach than the team member might be used to. Adaptability, flexibility, and openness are desirable assets.

Ability to use project management tools — The team member must be able to leverage technology in carrying out his or her project responsibilities. Projects are planned using a variety of software tools, and the team member must have some familiarity with these tools. Many project managers will require the team member to input task status and other progress data directly into the project management software tool.

Client Team

You may have no choice about who the client assigns to your team. Be cautious, however, that individuals might get this assignment merely because they aren't too busy back in their home departments. There may be a good reason why they weren't too busy. (I'll let you guess why that might be.)

When to Select the Client Team

These people need to be assigned in time to participate in the Project Kick-Off Meeting. Many of them might have been part of the JPPS, and that would be a bonus. They are probably assigned to the project for some percentage of their time rather than full time. In some cases, they might join the team when work on their area of responsibility is being done. If that is the case, they should still be identified along with others and kept informed of project status.

Selection Criteria

All you will likely be able to do is profile the skills and experiences of the client team members you will need. Perhaps specification by position title would be preferred by both the client and the project manager. Also, you would like to have client members with some decision-making authority. If not, the client members will have to return to their supervisor or manager for decisions. That can slow project progress.

Contract Team Members

The business-to-business environment is changing, and many changes are permanent. Organizations are routinely outsourcing processes that are not part of their core business or core expertise. As a result, project managers have been forced to use contract team members instead of their company's own employees for one or both of the following reasons:

- Shortage of staff
- Shortage of skills

These shortages have made it possible for a whole new type of business to grow — *tech-temps* is the name I associate with this new business opportunity. The day of the small contractor and niche market player is here to stay. To the project manager, this creates the need to effectively manage a team whose membership will probably include outside contractors. Some may be with the project for only a short time. Others may be no different from full-time core team members except that they are not company employees.

Typically, contract team members are available to work on the project for only short periods of time. A contract team member may possess a skill that is needed for just a brief time, and he or she is assigned to the project for that time only. As soon as the assigned task is completed, he or she leaves the project.

Implications of Adding Contract Team Members

Contract team members present the project manager with a number of challenges. In most systems development efforts, it is unlikely that professionals would be assigned full-time to the project team. Rather, people will join the project team only for the period of time during which their particular expertise is needed. The project manager must be aware of the implications to the project when contract professionals are used, which may include the following:

- There may be little or no variance in the time contracted team members are available, so the tasks on which they work must remain on schedule.

- They must be briefed on their role in the project and how their task relates to other tasks in the project.

- Commitment of contract members is typically a problem because their priorities probably lie elsewhere.

- Quality of work may be an issue because of poor levels of commitment. They just want to get the job done and get on with their next assignment. Often anything will do.

- Contract team members will often require more supervision than core team members.

Selection Criteria

If as a project manager, you've made the decision to buy rather than build a project team, you must determine who will get your business. Contract team members are usually employed or represented by agencies that cater to technical professionals who prefer freelancing to full-time employment. These professionals are available for short-term assignments in their area of specialization. To employ these professionals, you must make the following decisions: what process you're going to follow, who should be invited to submit information, and how you're going to evaluate the information received. The evaluation often takes the form of a score sheet. The score sheet contains questions grouped by major features and functions, with weights attached to each answer. A single numeric score is then calculated to rank vendor responses. Nonquantitative data such as client relations and client service are also collected from reference accounts provided by the vendor.

Here are the steps you might take as a project manager to engage the services of a contract team member:

1. Identify the types of skills and the number of personnel needed, and the time frame within which they will be required.

2. Identify a list of companies that will be invited to submit a proposal.

3. Write the request for proposal (RFP).

4. Establish the criteria for evaluating responses and selecting the vendor(s).

5. Distribute the RFP.

6. Evaluate the responses.

7. Reduce the list of vendors to a few who will be invited on site to make a formal presentation.

8. Conduct the on-site presentations.

9. Choose the final vendor(s), and write and sign the contract.

CROSS-REFERENCE See Chapter 3 for more details on the procurement process.

CASE STUDY – PIZZA DELIVERED QUICKLY (PDQ)

PDQ is not staffed to provide the skills and experiences needed for this project. Several outside contractors will be needed. That means the project team will consist of technically challenged PDQ personnel and technically experienced outside professionals. That is a challenging mix for the project manager to deal with effectively.

Balancing a Team

Balance is a critical success factor for any team that hopes to successfully complete its project. There are several ways to measure balance and several characteristics of the team that have been used to define balance. Take a simple example — learning styles. Learning styles are measured using an instrument, the Learning Styles Inventory (LSI), which was developed by David Kolb in 1981. Kolb identifies the following four learning styles:

- Assimilating
- Diverging
- Accommodating
- Converging

Assimilating

Assimilators are people who excel at collecting and representing data in crisp logical form. They are focused on ideas and concepts, rather than people. These individuals like to put data and information together into models that explain the situation from a larger perspective. As a result, they are more interested in something making sense logically than they are in any practical value. They are not results-oriented people. These types of individuals typically specialize in various technical fields, such as software developers.

Diverging

These individuals like to look at alternatives and view the situation from a variety of perspectives. They would rather observe than take action. Divergers like brainstorming, and they generally have a broad range of interests and like gathering and analyzing information. On a project team, these people will often display outside-of-the-box thinking and offer suggestions for approaches other than those that have already been identified.

Accommodating

These individuals are results-oriented and want to put things into practice. They are adaptive and can easily change with the circumstances. Accommodators are people persons. They are strong at implementation and hands-on tasks and are good team players. They tend to be action-oriented and more spontaneous than logical. As problem solvers, they rely on people for input, rather than on any technical analysis. On the project team, you can count on these people to help foster a strong sense of teamwork and to facilitate the coordination of team members. They are often the peacekeepers as well.

Converging

These individuals like to assemble information in order to solve problems. Convergers are the solution finders but not the solution implementers. Their strength lies in their ability to take concepts, models, and ideas and turn them into practical use. They are not particularly people-oriented and would rather work with technical tasks and problems. They are good at picking the best option among a number of alternatives. On the project team, these type of individuals will be the results-oriented members. They will drive the team into action by helping it focus on which approach to a situation is best and then mobilizing the team into action.

Now suppose you have a team that is loaded with convergers and does not have a single diverger among its members. What do you think might happen?

With no one on the team to encourage looking for alternatives (the role of the diverger), you would very likely have a rush to judgment, or "group think," as the convergers press the team into action. I have personally witnessed many situations where a single approach to a problem is presented, and the convergers on the team aggressively suggest that the team go forward with the single proposed solution without even considering whether there is an alternative. Teams involved in high-technology projects are likely to display this behavior.

A team that has balanced learning styles among its members is a team that is prepared to do a very good job at solving problems and making decisions.

CROSS-REFERENCE Learning styles are not the only point of balance. Thinking styles, conflict resolution styles, and skills and competencies are also important, but an in-depth discussion of such matters is beyond the scope of this book. For more information about balancing your project team in this manner, you can consult another of my books, *Building Effective Project Teams* (Wiley, 2001).

Developing a Team Deployment Strategy

Having balance on the team in all of the characteristics discussed in the previous section is certainly a worthy goal, but it is a goal not likely to be reached. In reality, the team is formed more according to availability than to any need to balance its membership. As a result, teams are not balanced, but they are the team nevertheless. What's a project manager to do?

First of all, the project manager had better know where the imbalance exists. What characteristics does the team have? Where are its strengths and where are its weaknesses? For example, suppose a confrontation has arisen with the client. I would much rather send an accommodator than a converger to resolve the conflict. However, there might not be an accommodator on the team. Teams are most likely to be formed and when a conflict situation arises the imbalances are discovered.

The project manager needs to determine which team members have a greater likelihood of success on which types of work assignments. Build the strategy. If you still have gaping holes, you need a team development plan. That is the topic of the next section.

Developing a Team Development Plan

After you've assembled your team and assessed each member's characteristics, you may discover several areas in which the team is noticeably weak. Although your job as project manager is not to be a career or professional development manager of the team members, you still have to get the project done, and any imbalance on the team can be a barrier to your success. As project manager, identify the high-risk areas that are not covered by at least one team member who can deal with those types of risks. As part of your risk management plan, put a development plan in place for selected members of the team.

What form might that development plan take? Here are two possibilities:

- You might want to use a conflict-resolution management behavior called *masked behavior*. Briefly, it means that you find the person on your team whose normal behavior is as close as possible to the missing behavior. That person then role-plays as though his or her normal behavior were the missing behavior.

- You might consider sensitivity training for all or some of the team. That training involves creating an awareness of the behavior that is lacking and practicing it under supervision. For example, technology professionals are generally not very good people persons. They often lack the traits of an accommodator. Sensitivity training for these team members might include listening skills, learning how to be a team player, acceptance of change, diversity training, and other related interpersonal skills training.

Conducting the Project Kick-Off Meeting

The Project Kick-Off Meeting is the formal announcement to the organization that this project has been planned and approved for execution. This meeting happens only once on each project — at the beginning of the project, after the project plan and project itself have been approved but before any work has been done. It is not only a get-acquainted meeting for the team members, but it's also your opportunity to get the project off to a good start.

The meeting signals the start of the project. It has the following two major parts.

- The sponsor-led part
- The project manager–led part

Sponsor-Led Part

The first part is basically a show-and-tell for the organization. Selected senior managers and other interested parties are invited to this brief meeting. It should last no more than 30 minutes. The project sponsor provides a brief overview of the project, why it is being done, what it will accomplish, and what business value will be derived from it. The Project Overview Statement (POS) is a good outline of what this briefing might include.

Project Manager–Led Part

The second part is an initial working session for the entire project team. This part will last for the remainder of the day. Except for small projects, the team members may not know one another, or they may have worked on the same projects but did not directly interact with one another. The project team comprises not only the development team members but also the client team members. In larger organizations, these two groups may never have had the chance to work together before. This first meeting of the entire project team can be filled with confusion about what is to be done, who is to do it, and when it must be completed. Some may be asking, "What is our project manager like and what are her (or his) expectations of me?"

Purpose of the Project Kick-Off Meeting

This is the meeting that gets the project started. You will want to make it an event to remember. Here is a sample Project Kick-off Meeting agenda:

- Introduce the sponsor to the project team
- Introduce the importance of the project by the sponsor
- Introduce the project (client)
- Introduce the project (project manager)
- Introduce the project team members to each other
- Write the PDS
- Establish the team operating rules
- Review the project plan
- Finalize the project schedule
- Write work packages

The meeting lasts until this entire agenda is completed. In mid- to large-sized projects, the meeting often lasts a full day. The first three agenda items are completed in the sponsor-led part. The remaining items are completed in the project manager–led part.

Attendees

The Project Kick-Off Meeting is usually attended by the following:

- Sponsor
- Other managers
- Project team
- Contractors and vendors

The sponsor's role is to get the project team excited about the project and its importance to the business of the organization. In larger organizations, there may be some political ramifications, so other senior-level managers may be invited by the sponsor so that they are aware of the project and its value to the organization as well. For the sponsor, this is a good way to cultivate a support group for later project portfolio decisions that may impact this project.

You might wonder why I include contractors in the attendee list. The objective is to make the contractors feel as much a part of the project as the project team. I like to include them in every project team activity that I can. If possible and if it makes sense, I try to make them feel like an equal partner. More to the point, I like them to have their own work space in the team war room. Having them attend the Project Kick-Off Meeting is a good way to start building a collaborative and supportive relationship with your contractors and vendors.

Facilities and Equipment

The Project Kick-Off Meeting includes a working meeting, and the facility needs to accommodate that purpose. Except for a brief introductory period during which several managerial-level people and the sponsor may be present, the only other attendees will be the project team, contractors, and vendors. In some cases, the first part of the meeting might take place using a theater styled layout, and the working part of the agenda might convene in a more appropriate facility with separate worktables. For larger projects, you will probably need a few breakout rooms attached to the central larger room. If a team war room is available, that would be an excellent choice.

You will need an ample supply of sticky notes, tape, scissors, and colored marking pens. Flip charts are good to have on hand for use at each worktable configuration. You can never have too much whiteboard space. For more high-tech equipment, an LCD projector and a PC are all you need for everyone in the room to see the details as they come together. The project team members should bring their laptops. You should have distributed the POS, Requirements Breakdown Structure (RBS), and project proposal to them earlier, and they should have these loaded on their laptops as well.

The Working Session Agenda

The agenda for the working session portion of the Project Kick-Off Meeting is straightforward. Here's a typical list of agenda items:

- Introduce the project team members to each other
- Write the PDS
- Review the project plan

- Finalize the project schedule
- Write work packages

Introducing the Project Team Members to Each Other

"Hi, I'm Earnest F. Forte, and I'm the Senior Business Analyst in Supply Chain Management" just isn't the introduction I'm thinking about. This part of the meeting is critical to the project manager because it is the first opportunity to begin building an open and honest relationship with and between each team member. Remember you don't have a project team yet; all you have is a group of people wondering what their manager got them into. The introductions are an open invitation to build esteem and credibility among and between all team members. The best way to do this is for you to facilitate a conversation with each team member. You will have to do some homework so that you know something about each person and why they are on the team. Engage them in a conversation that starts with your introducing them by name, position title, something about them, and why they are on the team. They will immediately begin building their self-esteem. Then ask them an open-ended question to get the conversation started. For example, a good open-ended question is "How do you see yourself contributing to this project?"

Writing the Project Definition Statement

One of the first things the project manager will want to do is make sure every team member has the same understanding of what the project is all about. There is a lot of documentation to support this exercise: COS, POS, RBS, WBS, and project proposal. All of these documents should have been distributed to every team member prior to the Project Kick-Off Meeting so the project team has a chance to review them beforehand.

Everyone will come to the Project Kick-Off Meeting with questions about the project and with a different point of view with regards to what this project is all about. That is not a good foundation on which to go forward. It is essential that everyone have the same point of view. To achieve this, I have found that having the project team draft a Project Definition Statement (PDS) is quite successful. Just as the client and the project manager benefit from the COS and the POS, the project manager and the project team will benefit from the PDS. The PDS uses the same five parts as the POS but incorporates considerably more detail. Whereas the POS is a single-page document, the PDS will be several pages. The project manager and the project team use the detailed information provided in the PDS for the following:

- As a basis for continued project planning
- To clarify the project for the project team
- As a reference that keeps the team focused in the right direction

- As an orientation for new team members
- As a method for discovery by the team

In most cases, the PDS expands on two sections of the POS. The first part is the project objectives statement. In the POS, the project objectives are written so that they can be understood by anyone who might have reason to read them. In the PDS, the situation is somewhat different. The PDS is not circulated outside the project team; therefore, the language can be technical and the development more detailed. Project objectives take on more of the look of the RBS. The purpose is to provide a description that the project team can relate to.

The second part is the assumptions, risks, and obstacles statement. The POS contains statements of assumptions, risks, and obstacles that will be of interest to senior management. For the PDS, the list will be of interest to the project team, so it will be much longer and more detailed. In my experience, the PDS list is built during the JPPS, whereas the POS list is built as part of the scoping activity of the project.

The PDS document was discussed for the first time in the second edition of this book. Since then, my consulting engagements have verified that the PDS can be used by the team to help them understand the project at their level of detail. The POS did not satisfy this need, so I developed the PDS. It is simply a variant of the POS designed specifically for the team. In implementing the PDS, I felt that it could further clarify the communications problems that often arise in the project as team members come and go. In the several cases where I have used it, the PDS has proven to be of value to the team.

Reviewing the Project Plan

Some of the project team members will be seeing the project plan for the first time, and their input is necessary. You also need to give them a chance to buy into the plan and begin thinking about their role. They will be the best objective observers you have, so don't miss an opportunity to get their input.

Finalizing the Project Schedule

The project schedule was built in the planning phase, and certain assumptions were made regarding availability. Now it's time to integrate every team member's schedules with the project schedule to present a workable schedule that meets the client's needs. Final assignments can be made, too.

Writing Work Packages

Work packages should be written for every task that is on the critical path, has a high risk of failure, has a high duration variance, or uses scarce resources. You want to protect the project as much as possible from the potential loss of a team member. Knowing how team members were going to complete their task and knowing the status of their task at the time of their loss provides good protection.

Establishing Team Operating Rules

PMBOK does not include establishing team operating rules as part of any process group. I believe that having these rules developed and agreed to by every team member is critical to project success. The rules of the engagement will help solve many project-related problems. Project teams all too often fail to define and agree on the team operating rules. This can be a real problem, especially when you are managing a multi-team project. (See Chapter 17 for a lengthy discussion of that type of situation.) These operating rules define how the team works together, makes decisions, resolves conflicts, reports progress, and deals with a host of other administrative chores. Even before the work of the project begins, the team members should agree on how they will work together. This section looks at the areas where operating rules are needed, and then covers the specifics of those operating rules.

Situations that Require Team Operating Rules

Some general situations may arise during the course of a project that will require some action on the part of the team. I have grouped them into the following six action areas:

- Problem solving
- Decision making
- Conflict resolution
- Consensus building
- Brainstorming
- Team meetings

Consider the following questions from *Managing the Project Team: The Human Aspects of Project Management, Volume 3*, by Vijay K. Verma (Project Management Institute, 1997) that must be answered at some point in the project life cycle:

- What has to be done and where? (Scope)
- Why should it be done? (Justification)
- How well must it be done? (Quality)
- When is it required and in what sequence? (Schedule)
- How much will it cost? (Budget/Cost)
- What are the uncertainties? (Risk)
- Who would do the job? (Human resources)

- How should people be organized into teams? (Communication/ Interpersonal skills)

- How will you know if you have done the job? (Information dissemination/ Communication)

Each one of these questions will engage one or more of the six action areas listed previously. The team needs to decide ahead of time how it will carry out each of the action areas — that is, the rules of engagement. Now take a look at those action areas in more detail and see what is involved on the part of the team.

Problem Solving

There will be many situations during the course of the project work in which the team will be challenged to figure out how to satisfactorily meet the client's needs while maintaining the schedule and the budget within the assigned resources. Some situations will be easily resolved, whereas others will challenge even the most creative of minds. The problem-solving process is well known, and many variations are in print. Creativity and problem solving go hand in hand. A good problem solver will think outside the box. He or she will conceive of approaches that may have been overlooked. As you will see next, each of the learning styles mentioned earlier in the chapter relates to a different part of the problem-solving model. That means the team must have all learning styles represented in order to solve problems effectively. In this section, you see how those learning styles relate to the problem-solving process.

The model that seems most appropriate for project problem solving is one put forward by J. Daniel Couger in his book *Creative Problem Solving and Opportunity Finding* (Boyd and Fraser Publishing, 1995). The model is shown in Figure 6-1.

Stimulus ⟹		Required Learning Styles
Step One	Delineate opportunity and define problem.	Assimilator
Step Two	Compile relevant information.	Assimilator
Step Three	Generate ideas.	Diverger
Step Four	Evaluate and prioritize ideas.	Converger
Step Five	Develop implementation plan.	Accommodator
		⟹ Action

Figure 6-1: Couger's Creative Problem Solving (CPS) model

Couger's process begins with an outside stimulus: Something has arisen that creates an out-of-control situation in the project and must be rectified. That launches a series of actions that clarifies the situation, identifies and assembles relevant data, gets a number of ideas and approaches on the table, and analyzes the ideas. It then selects the idea that would appear most promising as the way to rectify the situation and return it to normal. Finally, an action plan is put in place and executed (the exit point of the model is the action itself). You will see how all of the learning styles are needed to complete each step in the model. Couger identifies the following five steps that make up this problem-solving process:

Step 1: Delineate the opportunity and define the problem — This is a scoping step in which the team members attempt to establish a formulation and definition of the problem and the desired results that a solution to the problem will provide. It helps the team develop the boundaries of the problem — that is, what is in scope and what is out of scope. This step is best performed by team members who have a preference for the assimilator style. These individuals look at the problem independently of any focus on people and try to present the problem at the conceptual level and put it into a logical framework. Their penchant for collecting and concisely reporting data is an early task in this model.

Step 2: Compile the relevant information — With a definition of the problem in hand, the team can now identify and specify the data elements that are needed to further understand the problem and provide a foundation on which possible solutions can be formulated. Again, the assimilator is well suited to this task.

Step 3: Generate ideas — This step typically begins with a brainstorming session. The team should identify as many solutions as possible. This is the time to think outside the box and look for creative and innovative ways to approach a solution. Ideas will spawn new ideas until the team has exhausted its creative energies. The diverger is well suited to the tasks that take place in this step. The job of this individual is to look at the problem from a number of perspectives. Like the assimilator, the diverger also has an interest in collecting data in order to generate ideas, but he or she is not interested in generating solutions.

Step 4: Evaluate and prioritize ideas — In this step, the list of possible solutions needs to be winnowed down to the one or two solutions that will actually be planned. Criteria for selecting the best solution ideas need to be developed (that's a job for the converger), metrics for assessing advantages and disadvantages need to be developed (again, a job for the converger), and then the metrics are used to prioritize the solutions. The calculation of the metric value for each alternative and the ranking of the alternatives based on those metric values are straightforward exercises that anyone on the team can perform. This individual has the ability to take a variety of ideas and turn them into solutions. This person's work is not finished, however, until he or she has established criteria for evaluating those solutions and made recommendations for action.

Step 5: Develop the implementation plan — The solution has been identified, and it's now time to build a plan to implement the solution. This step is a whole-team exercise that draws on the team's collective wisdom for planning and implementation. When it is results that you want, call on the accommodator. His or her contribution will be to put a plan in place for delivering the recommended solution and making it happen. The accommodator is a good person to lead this planning and implementation exercise.

Although this five-step process may seem cumbersome and involved, many of the steps can often be executed in a simple and straightforward manner. Situations requiring a problem-solving effort occur frequently and are often done from start to finish by one team member. Of course, more complex situations will require several team members and the collective creativity of the whole team. The five steps should become second nature to each team member. As team members become familiar with the five steps, the steps will begin to form a commonsense sequence, and they should not be overly burdensome to anyone on the team.

Decision Making

Team members make decisions continuously as they engage in the work of the project. Some of those decisions are obvious and straightforward and may not require the involvement of other team members; other decisions are more complex and may require the involvement and active participation of the team, the client, and even people outside of the project. The three major types of decision-making models are as follows:

Directive — In this model, the person with the authority (the project manager for the project and the task manager for the task) makes the decision for all team members. Although this approach is certainly expedient, it has obvious drawbacks. The only information available is the information that the decision maker possesses, which may or may not be correct or complete. An added danger is that those who disagree or were left out of the decision may be resistant or unwilling to carry it out. A directive approach is often used when time is of the essence and a decision is needed immediately. It makes no sense to hold a committee meeting to get everyone's input before proceeding.

Participative — In this model, everyone on the team contributes to the decision-making process. A synergy is created as the best decision is sought. Because everyone has an opportunity to participate, commitment will be much stronger than in the directive approach. Obviously, there is an additional benefit to team building — empowerment of the team.

I recommend that you use this participative approach whenever possible. Because the team members have a chance to participate in the decision-making process, they will be much more committed to the decision that is made and more likely to support it during implementation. From a political perspective, the project manager is much better off using this approach than a directive approach.

Consultative — This middle-ground approach combines the best of the other two approaches. The person in authority makes the final decision, but this decision is made only after consulting with all members to get their input and ideas. This approach is participative at the input stage but directive at the point of decision making. In some cases, when expediency is required, this approach is a good one to take. Rather than having to involve the entire team, the project manager can decide whose input should be sought and then make the decision based on that input. Politically this is a very good strategy, and it can have positive effects on those whose input was sought.

Selecting the Appropriate Decision-Making Model

Selecting a model to use in a specific situation is generally a function of the gravity and time sensitivity of the pending decision. Some organizations have constructed categories of decisions, with each category defined by some financial parameters, such as the value of the decision, or by some scope parameters, such as the number of business units or clients affected by the decision. The person responsible for making the decision is defined for each decision category — the more serious the category, the higher the organizational level of the decision maker. Some decisions might be made by an individual team member, some by a task manager, some by the project manager, some by the client, and some by senior management. Yet others might require a group decision, using either a participative or a consultative approach.

Decision Making and the Learning Styles Inventory

Just as the LSI relates to the problem-solving process as discussed earlier in the chapter, it also relates to the decision-making process. Although decision making and problem solving are closely related, it is instructive for you to see just how the LSI relates to decision making as well. Problem solving cannot happen without some decisions having been made. In that sense, decision making can be thought of as a subset of problem solving.

NOTE Decision making can also occur outside of the problem-solving context. For example, suppose a project is behind schedule and the design phase is not yet complete. You could start some preliminary programming, but you risk having to rework some of this programming when the design is complete. Do you begin programming to make up lost time and take the risk, or do you

**wait for the design to be finished before you begin programming? This is
clearly a decision-making situation and not a problem-solving one.**

Decision making is pervasive throughout the life of the project. How will
the project team make decisions? Will they be based on a vote? Will they be a
result of team consensus? Will they be left up to the project manager? Just how
will the team operate?

Determining how decisions are made is only one piece of the puzzle. Another
piece is whether the team can make a decision, and if not, what they do about
it. This section takes a closer look at the decision-making environment that the
project team faces.

In their book *Organizational Behavior in Action: Skill Building Experiences* (West
Publishing, 1976), William C. Morris and Marshall Sashkin propose a six-phase
model for rational decision making. The six phases in their approach are outlined
in the list that follows. However, as I have indicated, there is a lot of similarity
between using the LSI in problem solving and in decision making, and the following list also reflects how the LSI applies to Morris and Sashkin's rational decision
making in a way similar to how it applied to Couger's problem-solving process.

Phase I: Situation definition — This phase is one of discovery for the team,
clarifying the situation to ensure a shared understanding of the decision
the team faces. Phase I requires the services of an assimilator. As part of
the process of discovery, the assimilator will collect data and information
and formulate the situation and the required decision.

Phase II: Situation decision generation — Through brainstorming, the
team tries to expand the decision space in search of alternative decisions.
This is the province of the diverger, although it is a collaborative effort
because it continues to involve the assimilator in a definition type of task.

Phase III: Ideas to action — Metrics are devised to attach a reward and
penalty to each possible decision that might be made. With the alternatives
identified, the work can be turned over to the converger in Phase III. His
or her job is to establish criteria. This person's work is complete when a
plan for implementing the decision is in place in Phase IV.

Phase IV: Decision action plan — The decision has been made, and the
development of a plan to implement it is now needed. In this phase, the
accommodator takes over and implements the decision.

Phase V: Decision evaluation — This phase is kind of a post-decision
audit of what worked and what didn't work. Some lessons learned will
be the likely deliverable as well. The team, under the direction of an
accommodator, will take an honest look at how effective the decision was.

Phase VI: Evaluation of the outcome and process — The team needs to
determine whether the decision got the job done and whether another
attempt at the situation is needed. An evaluation of the results from Phase

IV puts the work back into the hands of the assimilator. If the expected results were not attained, another round may be required.

Table 6-1 provides a summary of the six decision-making phases and the required learning styles.

CROSS-REFERENCE This discussion has been brief and is only a summary of a complex and interesting topic. The decision-making model discussed here is described in more detail in my book *Building Effective Project Teams* (Wiley, 2001).

Table 6-1: The Six Phases of the Decision-Making Process

PHASE	DESCRIPTION	LEARNING STYLE
Phase I: Situation definition	Discovery phase. The team investigates, discusses, clarifies, and defines the situation. It is important for the team to understand the root causes and evidence that led to the need for a decision.	Assimilator
Phase II: Situation decision generation	Continuation of Phase I. Characterized by brainstorming and searching for new ideas and alternatives for resolving the situation, which should lead to better options for the decision. Above all, the team needs to avoid a rush to judgment.	Diverger
Phase III: Ideas to action	Define the criteria for evaluating the alternative decisions. This involves identifying the advantages and disadvantages of each alternative. Whatever approach is used, the result should be a ranking of alternatives from most desirable to least desirable.	Converger
Phase IV: Decision action plan	Begins once the alternative is chosen. This is the planning phase for the project team. The team action plan determines tasks, resources, and time lines that are required to implement the decision. This phase requires a concerted effort to obtain buy-in from all affected parties.	Converger
Phase V: Decision evaluation	Learning opportunity for the project team. The team identifies what did and did not work, as well as areas in which it can improve and how to do so. The value of this discussion lies in the team's willingness to be honest and straightforward with one another.	Accommodator
Phase VI: Evaluation of the outcome and process	Focuses on the quality of results. The team evaluates the situation: Was the situation improved satisfactorily, or will another round be required? Was the situation defined correctly, or is revision required? Did the process work as expected, or will it need adjustment for the next attempt?	Assimilator

Conflict Resolution

The next area for which operating rules are needed deals with how the team resolves conflicts. Conflicts arise when two or more team members have a difference of opinion, when the client takes issue with an action to be taken by the project team, or in a variety of other situations involving two parties with different points of view. In all of these examples, the difference must be resolved. Clearly, conflict resolution is a much more sensitive situation than the decision-making rule because it is confrontational and situational, whereas the decision-making rule is procedural and structured. Depending on the particular conflict situation, the team might adopt one of the following three conflict resolution styles:

Avoidant — Some people will do anything to avoid a direct confrontation. They agree even though they are opposed to the outcome. This style cannot be tolerated on the project team. Each person's input and opinion must be sought. It is the responsibility of the project manager to ensure that this happens. A simple device is to ask all of the team members in turn what they think about the situation and what they suggest should be done about it. Often this approach will defuse any direct confrontation between two individuals on the team.

Combative — Some people avoid confrontation at all costs; others seem to seek it out. Some team members play devil's advocate at the least provocation. At times this is advantageous — testing the team's thinking before making the decision. At other times it tends to raise the level of stress and tension, when many team members will see it as a waste of time and not productive. The project manager must be able to identify these combative team members and act to mitigate the chances of these combative situations arising.

TIP One technique I have used with success is to put potentially combative individuals in charge of forming a recommendation for the team to consider. Such an approach offers less opportunity for combative discussion because the combative team member is sharing recommendations before others give reasons for disagreement.

Collaborative — In this approach, the team looks for win-win opportunities. The approach seeks a common ground as the basis for moving ahead to a solution. This approach encourages each team member to put his or her opinions on the table and not avoid any conflict that may result. At the same time, team members do not seek to create conflict unnecessarily. This approach is constructive, not destructive.

Further discussion of conflict resolution styles is beyond the scope of this book. You can consult several resources on the topic. Two that I have found particularly helpful are "Conflict and Conflict Management" by Kenneth Thomas in *The Handbook of Industrial and Organizational Psychology* (Wiley, 1983) and *The Dynamics of Conflict Resolution: A Practitioner's Guide* by Bernard S. Mayer (Jossey-Bass, 2000). Of particular importance are the variety of collaborative models that might be adopted.

Consensus Building

Consensus building is a process used by the team to reach agreement on which among several alternatives to follow. The agreement is not reached by a majority vote, or any vote for that matter. Rather, the agreement is reached through discussion, whereby each participant reaches a point when he or she has no serious disagreement with the decision that is about to be made. The decision will have been revised several times for the participants to reach that point.

Consensus building is an excellent tool to have in the project team toolkit. In all but a few cases, there will be a legitimate difference of opinion as to how a problem or issue should be addressed, where no clear-cut actions can be agreed upon. In such situations, the team must fashion an action or decision with which no team members have serious disagreement even though they may not agree in total with the chosen action. To use the method successfully, make sure that everyone on the team has a chance to speak. Talk through the issue until an acceptable action is identified. Conflict is fine, but try to be creative as you search for a compromise action. As soon as no one has serious objections to the defined action, you have reached a consensus. After a decision is reached, all team members must support it.

If you (as the project manager) choose to operate on a consensus basis, you must clearly define the situations in which consensus will be acceptable and convey this to your team.

Brainstorming

Brainstorming is an essential part of the team operating rules because, at several points in the life of the project, the creativity of the team will be tested. Brainstorming is a technique that can focus creativity and help the team discover solutions. In some situations, acceptable ideas and alternatives do not result from the normal team deliberations. In such cases, the project manager might suggest a brainstorming session. A brainstorming session is one in which the team contributes ideas in a stream-of-consciousness mode, as described in the next paragraph. Brainstorming sessions have been quite successful in uncovering solutions where none seemed present. The team needs to know how the project manager will conduct such sessions and what will be done with the output.

Here is a simple and quick method for brainstorming:

1. Assemble any individuals whether they are team members, consultants, or others who may have some knowledge of the problem area. They don't need to be experts. In fact, it may be better if they are not. You need people to think creatively and outside the box. Experts tend to think inside the box.

2. The session begins with everyone throwing any idea out on the table. No discussion (except clarification) is permitted. This continues until no new ideas are forthcoming. Silence and pauses are fine.

3. After all the ideas are on the table, discuss the items on the list. Try to combine ideas or revise ideas based on each member's perspective.

4. In time, some solutions will begin to emerge. Don't rush the process, and by all means test each idea with an open mind. Remember that you are looking for a solution that no individual could identify but that you hope the group is able to identify collectively.

NOTE This is a creative process, one that must be approached with an open mind. Convention and "we've always done it that way" have no place in a true brainstorming session.

Team Meetings

The project manager and the project team need to define and agree upon team meetings in terms of frequency, length, meeting dates, agenda preparation and distribution, who calls the meeting, and who is responsible for recording and distributing the minutes. The entire team needs to participate in and understand the rules and structure of the meetings that will take place over the life of the project. Different types of team meetings, perhaps with different rules governing their conduct and format, may occur.

Team meetings are held for a variety of reasons, including problem definition and resolution, scheduling work, planning, discussing situations that affect team performance, and decision making. The team needs to decide on several procedural matters, including the following:

Meeting frequency — How often should the team meet? If it meets too frequently, precious work time will be lost. If it meets too infrequently, problems may arise and the window of opportunity may close before a meeting can be held to discuss and solve these problems. If meetings happen too infrequently, the project manager risks losing control over the project. Meeting frequency will vary according to the length and size of the project. There is no formula for frequency. The project manager must simply make a judgment call.

Agenda preparation — When the project team is fortunate enough to have a project administrative assistant, that person can receive agenda items and prepare and distribute the agenda. In the absence of an administrative assistant, the assignment should be rotated to each team member. The project manager may set up a template agenda so that each team meeting covers essentially the same general topics.

Meeting coordinator — Just as agenda preparation can be circulated around to each team member, so can the coordination responsibility. Coordination involves reserving a time, a place, and equipment.

Recording and distributing meeting minutes — Meeting minutes are an important part of project documentation. In the short term, they are the evidence of discussions about problem situations and change requests, the actions taken, and the rationale for those actions. When confusion arises and clarifications are needed, the meeting minutes can settle the issue. Recording and distributing the minutes are important responsibilities and should not be treated lightly. The project manager should establish a rotation among the team members for recording and distributing the meeting minutes.

Daily Status Meetings

For some of you, this will seem like overkill and not something you want to engage in. You can already see the expressions on your team members' faces when you announce that there will be daily team meetings. I remember the first time I encountered the daily team meeting. I reacted the same way, but I quickly changed my mind, as I hope you will change yours. This is one of those "try it, you'll like it" cases.

For one thing, the meeting lasts only 15 minutes and everybody stands. The attendees are the task managers of all tasks that are open for work and are not yet completed. In other words, the scheduled start date for the task has passed, and the work on it is not yet complete. The only valid reports for such a task are as follows:

- I'm on plan.
- I am x hours behind schedule but have a plan to be caught up by this time tomorrow.
- I am x hours behind plan and need help.
- I am x hours ahead of plan and available to help with other tasks.

There is no discussion of solutions to schedule slippages. There is no taking of pizza orders for lunch or other irrelevant discussions. Such discussions are taken offline and involve only the team members who are affected by the problem or issue being raised.

You'll probably experience a learning curve for this process. My first 15-minute team meeting took 45 minutes, but the team quickly learned to bring the meeting time within the 15-minute limit and within the next few meetings were inside the 15-minute window consistently.

CASE STUDY – PIZZA DELIVERED QUICKLY (PDQ)

Due to the complexity and lack of clarity in defining the solution, daily meetings are essential. For outside contractors, this may not be their cup of tea. The challenge to the project manager is to get a firm commitment from the contractors. They must feel like part of the team for this to happen.

Problem Resolution Meetings

Problem resolution should never be handled in the team status meeting. Instead, a special meeting should be called and the attendees should include only the team members directly involved in the problem or its solution. The reason you don't deal with problems in the team status meeting is that not everyone in attendance will have an interest in or connection to the problem. You don't want to waste team members' time by having them sit through a discussion of something that does not involve them or interest them.

The problem resolution meeting should be planned around the problem-solving methodology discussed previously.

Project Review Meetings

These are formal meetings held at milestone events or other defined points in the life of the project. Oftentimes the stage gate that passes a project from one phase to another is used as the time for a project review meeting. These meetings are attended by the project manager, the client, the sponsor, stakeholders, a senior manager who officiates, and two or three technical subject matter experts (such as managers of similar projects). The project manager may invite others whose input will be valuable to the review. The meeting focuses on any variances from the plan, and identifying corrective action steps as suggested by the subject matter experts present. If this is not the first project review meeting for the project, there might also be a status review of corrective action steps recommended from previous project review meetings.

Team War Room

In the ideal setting, the team war room is the physical facility that the team owns during the lifetime of the project. Ideally all team members are co-located there, and all team meetings take place there. However, I recognize that this is not possible for all projects, so some variations are discussed in the sections that follow.

Physical Layout

Ideally, all of the walls are covered with whiteboards. Depending on the size of the team, the team war room may be one large room that accommodates everyone or several smaller rooms that are adjacent to a larger community-type room for group meetings and presentations. These adjacent rooms can double as breakout rooms. Each team member has his or her own private workspace, but there is a minimum number of partitions. A line of sight between each team member is ideal. The project artifacts are displayed so everyone has immediate access.

Variations

I realize that the preceding physical layout may seem idealistic, but several vendors and consulting companies that I have worked with make it a point to provide such facilities for their teams. A few of my clients have even designed their space with the thought of accommodating team war rooms and providing such space when the vendor cannot.

The first ideal to be sacrificed is co-location. In the global marketplace, project teams and the client are often spread over the globe. The cost of face-to-face meetings is prohibitive (travel expenses) and getting everyone to these meetings is a great waste of time (unproductive time while en route). While being geographically distributed has a few advantages (a 24-hour work day for example), it does create a logistics nightmare for the project manager and team members. In place of trying to schedule face-to-face meetings, teleconferences and even video conferences have become affordable and commonplace.

The second ideal to be sacrificed is the co-located team room. Many organizations simply do not have contiguous spaces they can release to a team for the duration of their project. Space is at a premium and has to be shared. In these situations, the project artifacts must be mobile rather than fixed. Although this may be an inconvenience, it is not a show stopper. Electronically posting the artifacts is another workaround.

The third ideal to be sacrificed is 100-percent assignment to a project. The commitments, loyalties, and priorities of the project team members may be spread over two or more projects as well as their home assignments.

Operational Uses

A well-planned team war room is not only for the use of the team as it conducts the work of the project, but it also serves other needs of the project. All scoping, planning, kick-off, status, and review meetings will take place there. Depending on the layout, parts of the space may be reserved for use by others outside the project on an as-needed and as-available basis. This will partially alleviate a space shortage problem for some organizations.

Managing Scope Changes

Regardless of the project management life cycle (PMLC) model you choose, you will have to deal with scope change requests coming from the client and from the project team. In some cases, you'll be expecting these change requests, and you'll be ready to process them. In other cases, you will not be expecting them (or at least won't want them), but that doesn't absolve you from having a way to process them. You need to have a scope change management process in place as you start the project so you can deal with both the expected and unexpected changes that will come your way.

The Scope Change Management Process

It is difficult for anyone, regardless of his or her skills at prediction and forecasting, to completely and accurately define the needs for a product or service that will be implemented 6, 12, or 18 months in the future. Competition, client reactions, technology changes, a host of supplier-related situations, and many other factors could render a killer application obsolete before it can be implemented. The most frequent situation starts with a statement that goes something like this: "Oh, I forgot to tell you that we will also need ..." or "I just found out that we have to go to market no later than the third quarter instead of the fourth quarter." Face it: Change is a way of life in project management. You might as well confront it and be prepared to act accordingly.

Because change is constant, a good project management methodology has a change management process in place. In effect, the change management process has you plan the project again. Think of it as a mini-JPPS.

Two documents are part of every good change management process: the project change request and the Project Impact Statement. Here's a brief description of what each of these documents contains:

> **Project change request** — The first principle to learn is that *every change is a significant change*. Adopt that maxim and you will seldom go wrong. What that means is that every change requested by the client must be documented in a *project change request*. That document might be as simple as a memo but might also follow a format provided by the project team. In any case, it is the start of another round of establishing COS. Only when the request is clearly understood can the project team

evaluate the impact of the change and determine whether the change can be accommodated.

Project Impact Statement — The response to a change request is a document called a *Project Impact Statement*. It is a response that identifies the alternative courses of action that the project manager is willing to consider. The requestor is then charged with choosing the best alternative. The Project Impact Statement describes the feasible alternatives that the project manager was able to identify, the positive and negative aspects of each, and perhaps a recommendation as to which alternative might be best. The final decision rests with the requestor.

One of the following six possible outcomes can result from a change request:

It can be accommodated within the project resources and timelines — This is the simplest of situations for the project manager to handle. After considering the impact of the change on the project schedule, the project manager decides that the change can be accommodated without any harmful effect on the schedule and resources.

It can be accommodated but will require an extension of the deliverable schedule — The only impact that the change will have is to lengthen the deliverable schedule. No additional resources will be needed to accommodate the change request.

It can be accommodated within the current deliverable schedule, but additional resources will be needed — To accommodate this change request, the project manager will need additional resources, but otherwise the current and revised schedule can be met.

It can be accommodated, but additional resources and an extension of the deliverable schedule will be required — This change request will require additional resources and a lengthened deliverable schedule.

It can be accommodated with a multiple-release strategy and by prioritizing the deliverables across the release dates — This situation comes up more often than you might expect. To accommodate the change request, the project plan will have to be significantly revised, but there is an alternative. For example, suppose that the original request was for a list of 10 features, and they are in the current plan. The change request asks for an additional two features. The project manager asks the client to prioritize all 12 features. He or she will give the client eight of them earlier than the delivery date for the original 10 features and will deliver the remaining four features later than the delivery date for the original 10. In other words, the project manager will give the client some of what is requested earlier than requested and the balance later than requested. I have seen several cases where this compromise has worked quite well.

It cannot be accommodated without a significant change to the project — The change requested is so substantial that, if accommodated, it will render the current project plan obsolete. There are two alternatives here. The first is to deny the change request, complete the project as planned, and handle the request as another project. The other is to call a stop to the current project, replan the project to accommodate the change, and launch a new project.

An integral part of the change control process is documentation. I strongly suggest that every change be treated as a major change until proven otherwise. To not do so is to court disaster. That means every change request follows the same procedure. Figure 6-2 is an example of the steps in a typical change process. The process is initiated, and the change request is submitted by the client, who uses a form like the one shown in Figure 6-3. This form is forwarded to the manager or managers charged with reviewing such requests. They may either accept the change as submitted or return it to the client for rework and resubmission. After the change request has been accepted, it is forwarded to the project manager, who performs an impact study.

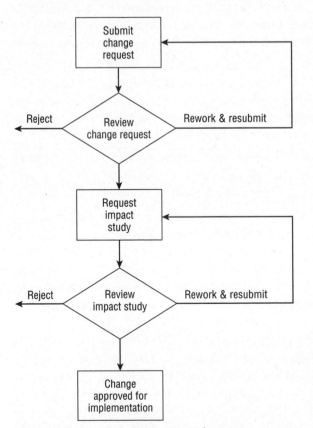

Figure 6-2: A typical change control process

Project Name
Change Requested By
Date Change Requested
Description of Change
Business Justification
Action
Approved by   Date

Figure 6-3: Change control form

The impact study involves looking at the project plan, assessing how the change request impacts the plan, and issuing the impact study, which is forwarded to upper management for final disposition. They may return it to the project manager for further analysis and recommendations or reject it and notify the client of their action. The project manager reworks the impact study and returns it to upper management for final disposition. If they approve the change, the project manager will implement it into the project plan.

Management Reserve

One way to control the abuse of client-generated scope change requests is to set up a time contingency in the budget. Just as a dollar budget has a contingency line to take care of unexpected expenditures, so also should a project schedule have a contingency for the unexpected. This is called *management reserve*. There is a good way to account for management reserve in the project schedule and there is a bad way.

Consider the bad way first. In this case, you might hear a task manager saying: "It should take about three days to complete this task, and I am going to put five days in the schedule to account for the unexpected." What's wrong with this approach? Just about everything. First, the two days of padding is hidden in the plan. The three-day task will mysteriously expand into a five-day task. That is Parkinson's Law (work will expand to the time allotted to complete it) and not at all what was intended. Second, the two days of padding is very arbitrary and will accomplish nothing more than confusing the project schedule and taking away the project manager's ability to effectively manage the schedule.

Now take a look at the good way to account for management reserve. First, add up all of the labor for all of the tasks in the project. A percentage of that total will become management reserve, and it will be tacked to the end of the project tasks as the last task before the project is complete. The percentage that you allocate to management reserve can vary. I have seen ranges from 5 to 10 percent. The same approach can be used for a sequence of tasks that lead into the critical path. Do the same calculation for that sequence and add the management reserve to the end of the sequence just before it merges back into the critical path. This idea shares a lot in common with the concept of a *buffer* in Critical Chain Project Management (CCPM). Critical Chain Project Management is discussed in detail in Chapter 10.

The client needs to know how much contingency time has been put into management reserve task. You need to explain to the client that every scope change request costs time. The time to process the request and the time to accommodate the change in the schedule make up that time. That time will be deducted from the management reserve task. When that time is spent, the only way the client will be able to make additional scope change requests is if the time is somehow replaced in the schedule. They can do that by deleting some future requirement not yet put into the solution. The time associated with that deleted requirement will be credited to management reserve.

Scope Bank

Another way to control client-generated scope change requests is to set up a Scope Bank with a deposit of time in it. In principle, this is very similar to management reserve and operates the same way. The time to process and incorporate a scope change request into the project schedule is deducted from the Scope Bank and that time is added to the project schedule. Clients can make deposits to the Scope Bank by deleting requirements from the solution. The Scope Bank will be adapted to some of the PMLC models in Part II.

Managing Team Communications

Communicating among and between technical team members does not come naturally. Technical people often simply aren't good communicators. In most cases, they would rather spend their time immersed in the technical details of what they are working on. However, for team members to be truly effective, they have to openly communicate with one another. For some, that will be difficult; for others, it is simply a matter of practice. In this section, I examine the importance and role of communications in the effective team.

Establishing a Communications Model

Getting information to the correct team members at the right time in the project usually determines the success or failure of the project. The project manager must manage the communication process as much as the technical process or risk failure. It isn't possible to manage all the communication in a project; that in itself is more than a full-time job. What the project manager has to do is examine the needs of the project team and make sure that communication occurs at the correct time and with the correct information. The following sections look at those ideas.

Timing

The timing of information can be critical. The following problems can arise if the information comes too soon or too late:

- If the information comes too far in advance of the action needed, it will be forgotten. It's almost impossible to remember information given one year in advance of its use. The project manager has to understand what the various team members need to know and when they need to know it in order to carry out their assignments. Where does this information come from? Like many other things in a project, you can find communication needs in the Work Breakdown Structure (WBS), which is discussed in Chapter 5. As you look through the tasks in the WBS, you will see that each team member has to be alerted to upcoming tasks and needs to be in communication with the other team members whose tasks take precedence over their own. The project manager can make this happen.

- A second problem in timing is getting the information needed to the project team members after they need it. Remember that project team members may need a few days to assimilate the information you give them, particularly if you're speaking about a new technology. This requires that you, as the project manager, manage the timing carefully so that all team members have as much information as possible and that you give everyone sufficient time to absorb and process the information in order to get the job done.

Content

The next communications management issue you need to be concerned about is communicating the correct information. This means you must understand what the project team members need to know to be successful. If you don't know what information the team members need, ask them. If the team members don't know, sit down with them and find out what sort of information needs to be given to the team in order to make the project run smoothly. Sometimes you will know what information is needed intuitively; other times you will have to meet with the project team to consider critical information needs. Whichever the case, you need to be in charge of getting the information to your team members at the right time and with the right content.

Choosing Effective Channels

After you have determined when the communication needs to occur for the project team to be successful and you have identified the basic communication content, the choice of how to get the information to the team members becomes important. As the project manager, you should stipulate how the team members will communicate the necessary information to each other. You have a choice among various channels through which communication can flow. The following list takes a look at each of these channels:

Face-to-face, in-person meeting — A verbal, face-to-face, in-person meeting is usually the best way to communicate. Not only can you get immediate feedback, you can see the person's reaction to information in his or her nonverbal cues. However, although this is often the best way to communicate, it's not always possible.

Videoconferencing — The cost of teleconferencing has dropped dramatically, and it is now much less expensive than traveling across the country. And don't forget the time savings. The software available to support these types of meetings has become far more accessible. Products such as NetMeeting and WebCast enable you to conduct face-to-face meetings via video and share slide presentations across the Internet. However, although videoconferencing gives team members a chance to see each other, some people are "telenerds" and don't come off very well on TV. Just be aware that videoconferencing is not the same as in-person, face-to-face communication.

E-mail — E-mail is not, I repeat *not*, the communication blessing that everyone thinks it is. It does have certain advantages: It is fast, you can read e-mail at your own speed, and I'm sure you all know people who won't respond to voice mail but will respond immediately to e-mail. However, e-mail does have the following drawbacks:

■ **Volume** — Many people get hundreds of e-mails per day. There's a pretty good chance that the e-mail you sent isn't the single most visible e-mail on the recipient's list, even if you put an exclamation point in front of it. Be aware that e-mail is so ubiquitous that it loses the visibility needed to get important information to other people simply because there is so much other e-mail "noise" out there.

- **Tone** — E-mail tends to be much shorter than voice mail, and often people misinterpret the intended tone of the message. It happens. Be aware that the tone conveyed in your e-mail message may not be the one that you would use if you had voice communication.

- **Quality** — Sending an e-mail message doesn't automatically make you a good writer. It's still difficult to send clear information to others in written form.

E-mail is very valuable, but you need to remember the caveats I just listed. Although e-mail is a nice invention, it still requires as much management attention by the project manager as any of the other channels of communication.

TIP Manage the frequency of your e-mail use. Don't overuse it, or your messages may end up being dismissed as spam. You also need to manage the distribution list for your e-mails. It's easy to just add another name to the distribution list, but you must resist doing so indiscriminately. Pretend that you only have so many e-mail coins to spend, and spend them wisely and frugally.

Written materials — These are permanent records. That's the good news. If you want to keep the records permanently, write them down. However, as with all of these channels, it requires effort to write things down well. It is also difficult for many people to write succinctly. Some use length to make up for good communication. Keep your writing short and clear, which will benefit the project team.

Phone — The phone is great if you actually get to talk to a live person rather than a recorded message, but a lot of people let the phone ring and dump you into voice mail. (Most people are now conditioned to leave a message and find themselves surprised when a human actually answers.) The phone has the same good points and pitfalls as all the other channels. Like face-to-face communication, its strength lies in the fact that you can get immediate feedback and exchange ideas quickly. As the project manager, you will be in phone meetings often, either on a one-to-one basis or in a conference call. It's important to manage these calls as you would any of the other channels of communication.

Effectively managing communications is a critical factor for successful project management. A complete treatment of this topic is beyond the scope of this book, but an example of effective communications management is certainly in order.

Suppose part of your project involves soliciting review comments from a number of people who will use the process being designed and implemented. You are going to distribute a document that describes the process, and you want these potential end users to return their comments and critique what you are proposing. What is the most effective way to distribute the document and get meaningful feedback from the recipients? For the sake of the example, assume that the document is 50 pages long. Your first impulse might be to send it electronically and ask recipients to respond by making their comments directly on the electronic version. If you are using Microsoft Word, you would request that they use the Track Changes feature. Is this the most effective way? It keeps everything in an electronic format and makes incorporating changes into the final document reasonably straightforward, but look at this request from the recipient's point of view. I know from experience that many people do not like to make edits to an electronic document. They prefer marking up a hard-copy version. Your process does not give them that option, which it probably should. The task of incorporating handwritten feedback is a little more involved than it would be with the electronic markup, but you will likely gain more and better feedback. Getting meaningful feedback is the goal, and you should use whatever means are at your disposal to ensure that happens.

What about the fact that the document is 50 pages long? Is that a barrier to meaningful feedback? I think so. If you agree, then what is the fix? My suggestion is that you dole out the document in sections. Does everyone on the distribution list need to see all 50 pages? Maybe not. Maybe you would get more meaningful feedback by parceling out the document based on level of interest and involvement in the process, rather than asking everyone to read and comment on all 50 pages.

The professional project manager is aware of the communication patterns he or she needs to manage to make it possible for the project team to be successful as a unit. The areas to manage include timing, content, and channel. Although it's probable that most project managers do a lot of the communication management on an ad hoc basis, it's important to be aware of the different areas of communication that you can manage. The skill of managing communication is just as important as any of the technical skills in project management. As a matter of fact, most surveys I've seen list project communication as the most important of all the areas to manage. By being aware of some of the components of project communication, you can be more effective as a project manager.

Managing Communication beyond the Team

To be successful as a project manager, you need to communicate not only within the team but also to various stakeholders outside of the team. Your project may seem successful to you, but unless that is conveyed to the right people outside of the team, it won't matter. The question is then "Who are those right people?"

Managing Communications with the Sponsor

The single most important communication for the whole project is the communication you have with the project sponsor. The sponsor is the person or group of people who have agreed to give you the necessary resources to complete the project, which makes the sponsor your new best friend for this project. Without sponsor involvement in all phases of the project, you will be in dire trouble. This section discusses a couple of good strategies for managing communications with your project sponsor.

The first action to take when you are about to start a project is to go to the sponsor and ask what they want to know and when they want to know it. The sponsor is the one who gets to use the information you pass on and is ultimately the person who has to justify the expenditure on your project. The sponsor may want a different type of information than you are used to giving. It doesn't matter. Sponsors pay the bills, so they should get what they want in the way of communication.

> **WARNING** Don't tell the sponsor what they're going to get. For example, don't start talking about earned value and watch the sponsor's eyes glaze over before they can tell you what they want.

A second consideration is to ensure that the sponsor gets information regularly. Status reports should be sent to the sponsor at least once a week. It's not a good idea to hold on to information concerning the project if it is important to the sponsor. Get the information to the sponsor as fast as possible if it will affect the project.

Now it's time to turn to another communication topic you need to consider as a project manager: upward communication filtering.

Upward Communication Filtering and "Good News"

Upward communication filtering is a strange form of distorting information that is found in almost any type of organizational life. It can also be called the *good news syndrome*. Unfortunately, it can kill a project as fast as any facet of bad communication management. There are two types of upward communication filtering. The first type occurs when the person who is reporting upward — for example, to a sponsor — spins the information or leaves out information so that the communication looks like nothing but good news. For example, instead of saying that a company building has burned down, the person says that everything is under control, that the fire department and insurance company have been called, and that all the people are safe. Sure, some of this is information the sponsor needs to know, but a good-news filter is something that puts a positive spin on everything, often at the expense of accuracy.

If something is going badly on a project, let the sponsor know what's going on as soon as possible. It is a good idea to talk about what you plan to do about the problem, but it never pays to filter problems from upward communication.

The second type of upward communication filtering involves withholding information. Perhaps there is a problem that you think can be resolved sometime in the future, so you withhold the current information from the sponsor, thinking that you can fix the problem. Such actions will almost always come back to bite you. Don't withhold information just because you're worried about a reaction. It's better to give all the news to the sponsor than it is to hope you can fix something that is broken, because if you can't fix the problem, it will just get worse and worse. Go ahead and tell the sponsor the truth.

Communicating with Other Stakeholders

A sponsor isn't the only stakeholder outside of the operating project team. A *stakeholder* is anyone who has an interest in the outcome of the project. The other stakeholders may be line managers of people on the team or consumers who are going to be involved in user acceptance tests. The best way to keep stakeholders informed is to send them copies of the meeting notes from your status meetings so they're aware of the project's progress. This is simple enough to do but is often overlooked. The effective project manager makes sure all people who have an interest in the project are informed. If there is a special piece of information that will affect only one stakeholder, then get the information to him or her immediately. Once again, you start this whole process by asking what the stakeholders want to know and when. Then you provide it.

Ultimately, communication occurs on a project all the time. A professor whose name I have long forgotten once said, "You can't *not* communicate." Although you can't spend all your time managing communications, you do need to be aware of the communication needs of your team and stakeholders at all times. The better you are at satisfying the communication needs of your team members and stakeholders, the better your chances of managing a successful project.

Assigning Resources

The final step to putting together the project plan is to assign the resources according to the schedule developed in Chapter 5. Up to this point, you have identified the tasks in the project and developed a schedule that meets the expected end date of the project. Now you need to determine if you can accomplish this schedule with the resources and their available dates. This section looks at tools and methods available to help you make this determination.

> **NOTE** There could be cases where the required resources' current commitments are such that they are not available according to your project schedule. In those situations, you have to revert to the original project definition, budget, time, and resource allocations to resolve the scheduling

problem, which may require additional time, budget, and resource allocation in order to comply with the requested deliverables and deliverable schedule.

Leveling Resources

Resource leveling is part of the broader topic of resource management. This is an area that has always created problems for project managers and the project schedule. Software packages that claim to do resource leveling just further aggravate the scheduling problem. Following are some of the situations that organizations have to deal with:

- Committing people to more than they can reasonably handle in the given time frame, reasoning that they will find a way to get it done but putting each of the projects they are assigned to further in harm's way

- Changing project priorities and not considering the impact on existing resource schedules

- The absence of a resource management function that can measure and monitor the capacity of the resource pool and the extent to which it is already committed to projects

- Employee turnover and promotions that are not reflected in the resource schedule

Any organization that does not have a way of effectively handling these situations will find itself in a situation analogous to the flow through a funnel, as depicted in Figure 6-4.

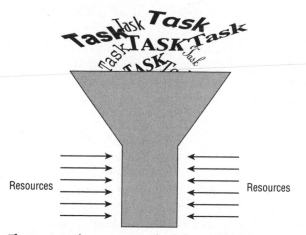

Figure 6-4: The resource scheduling problem

Figure 6-4 is a graphic portrayal of the resource-scheduling problem. The diameter of the funnel represents the total of all resources available for the project. Tasks can pass through the funnel at a rate that is limited by the amount of work that can be completed by the available resources according to the schedule of the tasks. You can try to force more into the funnel than it can accommodate, but doing so only results in turbulence in the funnel. You are no doubt familiar with situations where managers try to force more work onto your already fully loaded schedule. The result is either schedule slippage or less-than-acceptable output. In the funnel example, it results in rupture due to overload (such as requiring team members to work weekends and long hours).

The core teamwork takes place at the center of the pipeline. This center, where the tasks flow through the funnel, is the smoothest because it is based on a well-executed schedule. The work assigned to the contract team takes place along the edge of the funnel. According to the laws of flow in a pipeline, there is more turbulence at the walls of the structure. The deliverables are the completed task work. Because the diameter of the funnel is fixed, only so much completed work can flow from it.

Too many organizations believe that by simply adding more into the top of the funnel, more will come out of the bottom. Their rationale is that people will work harder and more efficiently if they know that more is expected. Although this may be true in a limited sense, it is not in the best interest of the project because it results in mistakes and compromised quality. Mistakes will be made as a direct result of the pressure from the overly ambitious schedule forced on people. In this chapter, I provide resource-leveling strategies that the project manager can adopt to avoid the situation depicted in the funnel example.

Take a step back for a moment. When you were creating the project network diagram, the critical path was the principal focal point for trying to finish the project by a specified date. The under- or over-allocation of resources was not a consideration. There's a reason for this. It is important to focus your attention on planning one portion of the project at a time. If you can't reach the desired finish date based strictly on the logical order in which tasks must be completed, why worry about whether resources are over- or under-allocated? You've got another problem to solve first. After the finish date has been accepted, you can address the problem of over-allocation, and, in some cases, under-allocation.

Resource leveling is a process that the project manager follows to schedule how each resource is allocated to tasks in order to accomplish the work within the scheduled start and finish dates of each task. Recall that the scheduled start and finish dates of every task are constrained by the project plan to lie entirely within their earliest start–latest finish (ES–LF) window. Were that not the case, the project would be delayed beyond its scheduled completion date. As resources are leveled, they must be constrained to the ES–LF window of the tasks to which they are assigned, or the project manager must seek other alternatives to resolve the conflict between resource availability and project schedule.

The resource schedule needs to be leveled for the following two reasons:

- To ensure that no resource is over-allocated. That is, you do not schedule a resource to more than 100 percent of its available time.

- You, as the project manager, want the number of resources (people, in most cases) to follow a logical pattern throughout the life of the project. You would not want the number of people working on the project to fluctuate wildly from day to day or from week to week. That would impose too many management and coordination problems. Resource leveling helps you avoid this by ensuring that the number of resources working on a project at any time is fairly constant. The ideal project would have the number of people resources relatively level over the planning phases, building gradually to a maximum during the project work phases, and decreasing through the closing phases. Such increases and decreases are manageable and expected in the life of a well-planned project.

Acceptably Leveled Schedule

As I begin this discussion of leveling resources, I want to be clear on one point. It is very unlikely, perhaps impossible, that you will develop a resource schedule that simultaneously possesses all the desirable characteristics I discuss. Of course, you will do the best you can and hope for a resource schedule that is acceptable to management and to those who manage the resources employed on your project. When a resource schedule is leveled, the leveling process is done within the availability of the resource to that project. When I discussed task estimating and resource assignments in Chapter 5, I said that resources are not available to work on a task 100 percent of any given day. Based on my clients' experiences, this number ranges from 50 to 75 percent. This value, for a typical average day, is the resource's maximum availability. In some project management software programs, this is referred to as max availability or max units. Some software applications allow this value to be varied by time period whereas others do not.

Ideally, you want to have a project in which all resource schedules can be accommodated within the resources' maximum availability. However, this may not always be possible, especially when project completion dates are paramount and may require some overtime. We're all familiar with this situation. Overtime should be your final fallback option, however. Use it with discretion and only for short periods of time. If at all possible, don't start your project off with overtime as the norm. You'll probably need it somewhere along the line, so keep it as part of your management reserve.

Resource-Leveling Strategies

You can use one of the following three approaches to level project resources:

- Utilizing available slack
- Shifting the project finish date
- Smoothing

This section describes each of these strategies in more detail.

Utilizing Available Slack

Slack was defined in Chapter 5 as the amount of delay expressed in units of time that could be tolerated in the starting time or completion time of a task without causing a delay in the completion of the project. Recall that slack is the difference between the ES–LF window of a task and its duration. For example, if the ES–LF window is four days and the duration of the task is three days, its slack is 4 – 3, or one day.

Slack can be used to alleviate the over-allocation of resources. With this approach, one or more of the project tasks are postponed to a date that is later than their ES date but no later than their LF date. In other words, the tasks are rescheduled but remain within their ES–LF window.

When you are seeking to level resources, having free slack can come in handy. Free slack, as mentioned in Chapter 5, is the amount of delay that can be tolerated in a task without affecting the ES date of any of its successor tasks. When you need to resolve the "stack-up" of tasks on the schedule, first determine whether any of the tasks has free slack. If any of them do, and if rescheduling the task to that later start date will solve the resource over-allocation problem, you are done. If moving the start date of the task does not resolve the over-allocation, you have to use total slack, and at least one other task will have its ES date delayed.

Shifting the Project Finish Date

Not all projects are driven by the completion date. For some, resource availability is their most severe constraint. On these projects, the critical path may have to be extended to achieve an acceptable resource-leveled schedule. This case could very well mean that the parallel scheduling on the task network diagram that moved the original finish date to an earlier date needs to be reversed. The start-to-start (SS) and finish-to-finish (FF) dependencies might need to be set back to the linear finish-to-start (FS) type.

In some cases, a project is of a low enough priority within the organization that it is used mostly for fill-in work. In that case, the completion date is not significant and doesn't have the urgency that it does in a time-to-market project. For most projects, however, moving the finish date to beyond a desired date is the least attractive alternative.

If you find yourself caught between over-allocated resources on a schedule that cannot be acceptably leveled and a firm, fixed completion date, you may have to consider reducing the scope of the project. For example, you might consider delaying some of the features to the next release.

Smoothing

Occasionally, limited overtime is required to accomplish the work within the scheduled start and finish dates of the task. Overtime can help alleviate some resource over-allocation because it allows more work to be done within the same scheduled start and finish dates. I call this *smoothing.* You can use smoothing to eliminate resource over-allocations, which appear as spikes in the resource loading graphs. In effect, what you do is move some of the work from normal workdays to days that otherwise are not available for work. To the person doing the work, it is overtime.

Alternative Methods of Scheduling Tasks

Rather than treating the task list as fixed and leveling resources within that constraint, you could resolve the leveling problem by considering further decomposition of one or more tasks. One of the six characteristics of a complete WBS mentioned in Chapter 5 is "work assignments are independent." That independence means that once work has begun on a task, work can continue without interruption until the task is complete. Usually, you do not schedule the work to be continuous for a number of reasons, such as resource availability, but you could if necessary.

Further Decomposition of Tasks

Resource availability, or rather the lack of it, can require some creative task scheduling on the part of the project manager. For example, suppose that a task requires one person for three days within a five-day window. There are two days of slack in the schedule for that task. In other words, the ES–LF window of the task is five days, and the task duration is three days. The project manager would prefer to have the task scheduled for its ES date, but the unavailability of the resource for three consecutive days beginning on the

ES date will require scheduling the task work to a longer period of time. One solution would be to have the resource work for three nonconsecutive days as early as possible in the five-day window. Continuing with the example, suppose that the resource is available for the first two days in the five-day window and for the last day in the five-day window. To simplify the scheduling of the resource, the project manager could decompose the five-day task into two tasks — one two-day task and one one-day task. The two-day task would then have an FS dependency on the one-day task. The scheduled start and finish dates of the two tasks would be set so that they fit the availability of the resource. Other solutions to this scheduling problem are possible but I do not discuss them here. The one I have presented is the best approach to situations similar to the example.

Stretching Tasks

Another alternative that preserves the continuity of the task work is to stretch the work over a longer period of time by having the resource work on the task at a percent per day lower than was originally planned.

The previous example can be modified to illustrate this by stretching the task. Suppose the resource is available 80 percent of each day in the five-day window, and you need four days of work. The resource is therefore available for $(0.80) \times$ five days, or four days of work, over the five-day window. You need only four days of work from the resource, so how do you schedule the work in the five-day window to accomplish the four days of work you need? The solution is to stretch the task from four days to five and schedule the resource to work on the task for those five days. Because the resource can work only 80 percent of the time on the task, the resource will accomplish four days of work over a five-day period.

In this simple example, the percentage was constant over the five days, but it might also follow some profile. For example, suppose you need the resource for three days, and the resource is available full-time for the first and second days but only half-time for the remaining three days of the five-day window. You could first split the task into two tasks — a two-day task and a one-day task. The two-day task would fully use the resource and get two days of work completed. The second task would be stretched to two days, and the resource would be assigned half-time for two days to complete the remaining day of work on the task. In other words, you got the three days of work in four days — the first two days at full-time, and the next two days at half-time. Resource availability can be the determining factor for how you can stretch a task within its ES–LF window and still get the required amount of work from the resource.

Assigning Substitute Resources

Your original estimate of task duration was based on the assumption that a typically skilled resource will be available to work on the task. That may not be possible, however, because of the unavailability of the resource. This unavailability will be especially likely in the case of scarce resources such as some of the newer technologies. In this case, the project manager needs to use another strategy. One approach would be to use less-skilled resources and add to the total number of hours requested. Here, the thinking is that a less-skilled resource would require a longer period of time to complete the task work.

WARNING   Be careful in using less-skilled resources, because there is additional risk in using a less-skilled person, and it is not clear exactly what increase in task duration is needed to account for the person with fewer skills. This strategy works only for non–critical path tasks. Using it for a critical path task would extend the completion date of the project.

Cost Impact of Resource Leveling

It should be obvious to you that resource leveling almost always stretches the schedule. For example, a stretch may occur when slack is available in the right places in the schedule. Scheduling the work of a resource over a longer period of time not only removes scheduling conflicts, but it also removes any over-allocations of that resource. To do all that, the project completion date is extended, which can have the following results:

- If the resources are billable based on the labor expended, project costs do not increase.

- If there are resources that are charged on a calendar basis, project costs will increase. Such expenses would be attributable to equipment and space on a rental agreement. In some cases, there may be increased human resources costs as well.

- If there are incentives for early completion and penalties for late completion of a project, a cost impact will be felt as well.

Finalizing the Project Schedule

The last schedule was built by the JPPS planning team. At that point, you knew the core team by name but the full project team by position titles only. Now that you have all of the named members of the project team, you have all of the information you need to finalize the project schedule. Team-member availability must be factored into the schedule. Such things as other project schedule commitments and non-project time commitments (department meetings, training, work week schedules, previously approved vacations, and so on) will impact the current project schedule.

Micro-level planning is another step in the decomposition of the tasks that are assigned to an individual. It involves a decomposition to what I call *subtasks*. In some cases, these subtasks may be a very simple to-do list or, in more complex situations, they might appear as a very small project network. Remember that you are dealing with tasks that have met the six WBS completion criteria and are therefore relatively simple tasks of short duration.

Micro-level project planning begins with the lowest-level task defined in the WBS. Because it appears in the WBS, it will have management oversight by the project manager. The responsibility for completing this task within a defined window of time will be assigned to a task manager (or team leader, if you prefer). The task may be simple enough that all of the work of completing it is done by the task manager. In more complex situations, a small team assigned to the task manager will actually complete the work of the task. I use the word *subteam* in the discussion that follows, but you should keep in mind that the team may be only one person, the task manager.

The first thing the subteam must do is to continue the decomposition that was done in building the WBS, but this decomposition will be below the task level. As indicated previously, the subtasks might be nothing more than a simple to-do list that is executed in a linear fashion. More complex tasks will actually generate a task network diagram composed of tasks and their dependency relationships. Recall that the task must meet the completeness criteria discussed in Chapter 5. These tasks will each be less than two weeks' duration, so the subtasks that make them up will be of shorter duration. The decomposition should be fairly simple and result in tasks of one to three days' duration. I would be surprised if it took more than 10 subtasks to define the work of the task.

Using a project management software package to create the micro-level plan and its accompanying schedule is overkill. My suggestion is that you define the tasks and their dependency relationships, and schedule them on a whiteboard using sticky notes and marking pens. Figure 6-5 is an example of what that whiteboard display might look like. The task consists of seven subtasks that are shown in the upper portion of the figure along with their dependencies. The lower portion of the figure shows the time-scaled schedule for the three members of the subteam. The shaded areas of the schedule are non-workdays and days when a resource is not available. Half-day time segments are the lowest level of granularity used.

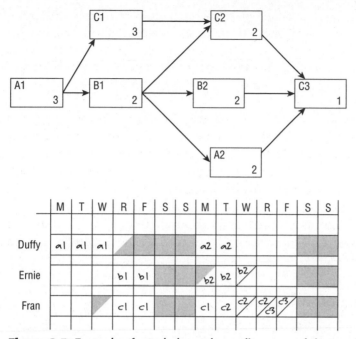

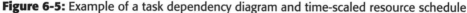

Figure 6-5: Example of a task dependency diagram and time-scaled resource schedule

TIP You might adjust to a finer timescale as the project tasks would suggest. However, I have found that to be helpful in only a very few situations.

This task is typical of others in the project plan. It is simple enough that all of the work can be done at the whiteboard. Updating is very simple. There is no need for software support, which simply adds management overhead with little return on the investment of time expended to capture and manage it.

In the next section, you learn how to develop and use work packages. What you have done so far is decompose a task into subtasks — you have a list of things that have to be done in order to complete the task. The work package describes exactly how you are going to accomplish the task through the identified subtasks. In other words, it is a mini-plan for your task.

Writing Work Packages

The work package is a statement by each task manager as to how he or she plans to complete the task within the scheduled start and finish dates. It is like an insurance policy. For the project manager, the work package is a document that describes the work at a level of detail such that if the task manager or anyone working on the task were not available (if he or she were fired, hit by a bus on the way to work, or otherwise not available), someone else could use the work package to figure out how to continue the work of the task with minimal lost time. This safeguard is especially important for critical path tasks for which schedule delays are to be avoided.

A work package can consist of one or several tasks. On the one hand, this may be nothing more than a to-do list, which can be completed in any order. On the other hand, the work package can consist of tasks that take the form of a mini-project, with a network diagram that describes it. In this case, work packages are assigned to a single individual, called a task manager or work package manager. This manager is responsible for completing the task on time, within budget, and according to specification. Sounds like a project manager, doesn't it? That person has the authority and the access to the resources needed to complete the assignment.

Purpose of a Work Package

The work package becomes the bedrock for all project work. It describes in detail the tasks that need to be done to complete the work for a task. In addition to the task descriptions, the package includes start and end dates for the task.

The work package manager (or task manager) may decide to include the start and end dates for each task in the package so that anyone who has occasion to use the work package will have a sense of how the plan to complete the work will be accomplished.

WARNING   Be careful if you adopt this approach because it encourages micromanagement on the part of the project manager. The more you say, the more you encourage objections. The trade-off, however, is protecting the project schedule. There is always a trade-off between the need for detail and the need to spend work time actually accomplishing something, not just shuffling papers.

The work package also can be adapted to status reporting. Tasks constitute the work to be done. Checking off completed tasks enables you to measure what percent of the overall task is complete. Some organizations use the percent of tasks completed as the percent of task completion. In other words, if 80 percent of the tasks are done, then 80 percent of the overall task is complete. This is a simple yet consistent measure. This simple yet effective metric serves as the basis for earned-value calculations. Earned value is discussed in detail in Chapter 7.

Format of a Work Package

I recommend that you use the following two work package documents:

Work package assignment sheet — This is a very special type of telephone directory used as a ready reference by the project manager. It contains some basic information about each work package and its manager.

Work package description report — This is a detailed description of the task plan. It contains much of the same information that is found in a project plan, but it focuses on tasks, not projects. It is therefore a much simpler document than a project plan, even though it contains the same type of information as the project plan.

Work Package Assignment Sheet

The work package assignment sheet, shown in Figure 6-6, is a report created by the team member responsible for managing the work package for the project manager only. It includes the earliest start and latest end dates for each task. This sheet is one of the few resources available to the project manager, and it should not be made available to anyone other than the project manager. For example, the project manager is unlikely to tell a task manager that a given task is scheduled for completion on July 15, when the task manager really has until August 15 because of slack. Task managers should be given only the scheduled start and end dates for their tasks.

WORK PACKAGE ASSIGNMENT SHEET		Project Name	Project No.	Project Manager	
Work Package		Schedule			
Number	Name	Early Start	Late Finish	Work Package Manager	Contact Information
A	DESIGN	03/01/08	04/01/08	ANNA LYST	
B	PROD. EVAL	04/02/08	07/02/08	HY ROWLER	
C1	PLACE.LOCATE.PT1	04/02/08	03/04/09	SY YONARA	
C2	PLACE.LOCATE.PT2	07/03/08	03/04/09	HY ROWLER	
D	PROD.FCAST	07/03/08	03/04/09	SY YONARA	
E	PROD.DELETE	03/05/09	06/02/09	HY ROWLER	
F	PROMO.REGION	03/05/09	07/06/09	TERRI TORY	
H	PRICE	08/04/09	02/05/10	HY ROWLER	
I	PLACE.DESIGN	06/05/09	08/03/10	HY ROWLER	
J	PROMO.SALES.LEAD	07/07/09	11/05/09	TERRI TORY	
G	PROMO.MEDIA	07/07/09	02/05/10	SY YONARA	
K	PROMO.SALES.RPT	10/07/09	02/05/10	TERRI TORY	
L	SYSTEM.TEST	02/08/10	05/10/10	ANNA LYST	
M	SYSTEM.ACCEPT	05/10/10	06/10/10	ANNA LYST	
Prepared by	Date	Approved by		Date	Sheet 1 of 1

Figure 6-6: Work package assignment sheet

The work package assignment sheet has limited value in smaller projects but can be invaluable in larger ones. For example, my business was once involved in a project that consisted of more than 4,000 tasks. Over the seven-year life of the project, more than 10,000 task managers were involved. This report became a phone directory that needed constant updating as team members came and went. Because of the complexity and personnel changes that accompany these large projects, the project manager needs an effective and efficient way of staying current with the project team membership, who is assigned to what, and how each team member will accomplish their work.

Work Package Description Report

A work package description report is a document prepared by the task manager in which he or she describes the details of how the work of the task will be accomplished. A very simple example of a work package description report, or statement of work, is shown in Figure 6-7.

After the project plan has been approved, it is the task manager's responsibility to generate the work package documentation. Not all tasks will require or should require work package documentation. The documentation can be limited to critical path tasks, near-critical path tasks, high-risk tasks, and tasks that use very scarce or highly skilled staff. The project manager decides which tasks need work package description reports.

The descriptions must be complete so that anyone could pick them up, read them, and understand what has to be done to complete the task. Each task must be described so that the status of the work package can be determined easily. Ideally, the task list is a check-off list. After all the tasks have been checked off as being completed, the task is completed. Each task will also have a duration estimate attached to it. In some project planning sessions, these estimates may have been supplied as a bottom-up method of estimating task duration.

Putting It All Together

This chapter discussed the team, its membership, the skills needed of the members, and the rules that the team must follow as it goes about the work of the project. Even though you have done your best to put the team together and have set and agreed on the operating rules, much is yet to be done. The team needs to learn how to work together by actually working together. Mistakes will be made, procedures will not always be followed as intended, and the first few team meetings will be clumsy. Learning is taking place, and it must be allowed to do so. The team is passing through a stage called *norming*, where it is

WORK PACKAGE DESCRIPTION

		Project Name	Project No.	Project Manager		
Work Package Name			Work Package No.	Work Package Manager	Contact Info.	Date
Start Date	End Date	Critical Path Y　N	Predecessor Work Package(s)		Successor Work Package(s)	

TASK

No.	Name	Description	Time (days)	Responsibility	Contact Info.

Prepared by	Date	Approved by	Date	Sheet 1 of 1

Figure 6-7: Work package description report

learning to work together as teams should. It is a natural phase of development. Unfortunately, you can't wait for the team to become a lean, mean machine. The work of the project must begin.

Today's contemporary project world adds other challenges. Perhaps the major challenge is that teams are seldom co-located. The members might be in different buildings, states, countries, and even continents. Holding effective meetings these days means scheduling to accommodate differing time zones. I have experienced as many as 12 time zones separating team members' locations. Teams often comprise several cultures whose work habits and social interactions are often quite different than you might be used to. Your not understanding these differences could bring disaster to the project.

The next chapter describes how to monitor and report project progress against the plan, and the changes that you can expect as the project work is done.

Discussion Questions

1. You have recently been promoted to the position of project manager. Your team consists of senior members of the technical staff, and it is time to establish the team operating rules. You expect some resistance because the team is experienced and you are a project manager who they see as still wet behind the ears. How would you go about doing this?

2. Your project managers have been able to communicate very effectively with all of your clients except one. Getting feedback from this client has always been a nagging problem. What should you do?

3. Your past projects gave the client wide berth when it came to suggesting changes at any time they saw fit. Often they expressed an unbridled enthusiasm in making frequent changes, many of which were not well thought out. Times have changed, and you need to implement effective management control. Describe your plan to implement good scope change control practices.

4. A number of your clients seem to be abusing the change request process. You have seen an increase in the number of frivolous requests. These, of course, must be researched and resolved, and that takes away from the time that your team members have to do actual project work. From a process point of view, what might you do? Be specific.

5. Discuss the concept of the work package as an insurance policy. How is it an insurance policy, and what might it contain that would make it an insurance policy?

CHAPTER 7

How to Monitor and Control a TPM Project

When you are drowning in numbers, you need a system to separate the wheat from the chaff.
— Anthony Adams, Vice President, Campbell Soup Co.

If two lines on a graph cross, it must be important.
— Ernest F. Cooke, University of Baltimore

You can't monitor and control a project by simply reading reports. You have to walk around and personally check progress.
— Robert K. Wysocki, Ph.D., President, Enterprise Information Insights, Inc.

CHAPTER LEARNING OBJECTIVES

After reading this chapter, you will be able to:

- Understand the reasons for implementing controls on the project
- Track the progress of a project
- Determine an appropriate reporting plan
- Measure and analyze variances from the project plan
- Use Gantt charts to track progress and identify warning signs of schedule problems
- Construct and interpret milestone trend charts to detect trends in progress
- Use earned value analysis (EVA) to detect trends in schedule and budget progress

Continued

CHAPTER LEARNING OBJECTIVES *(continued)*

■ Integrate milestone trend charts and EVA for further trend analysis

■ Build and maintain an Issues Log

■ Manage project status meetings

■ Determine the appropriate corrective actions to restore a project to its planned schedule

■ Properly identify corrective measures and problem escalation strategies

The project plan is a system. As such, it can get out of balance, and a get-well plan must be put in place to restore the system to equilibrium. The longer the project manager waits to put the fix in place, the longer it will take for the system to return to equilibrium. The controls are designed to discover out-of-balance situations early and put get-well plans in place quickly.

You can use a variety of reports as control tools. Most can be used in numeric and tabular form, but I suggest using graphics wherever possible. A well-done graphic is intuitive. It does not require a lengthy explanation and certainly doesn't require a lot of reading. Be cognizant of the fact that senior managers don't have a lot of time to dwell on your report. Give them what they need as succinctly as possible. Graphics are particularly effective as part of your status report to management. Senior managers generally aren't interested in reading long reports only to find out that everything is on schedule. Although they will be pleased that your project is on track, their time could have been spent on other pursuits that require their attention. When projects are not on schedule, they want to know this immediately and see what corrective action you plan to take.

Using Tools, Templates, and Processes to Monitor and Control a Project

I insist on using graphical types of status reports. And they must be intuitive to the recipient — always. Here are some of the reporting tools that I have used over the years:

■ Current period reports

■ Cumulative reports

■ Exception reports

■ Stoplight reports

■ Variance reports

■ Gantt charts

■ Burn charts

- Milestone trend charts
- Earned value analysis (EVA)
- Integrated milestone trend charts and EVA
- Project status meetings
- Problem escalation strategies

Establishing Your Progress Reporting System

After project work is under way, you want to make sure that it proceeds according to plan. To do this, you need to establish a reporting system that keeps you informed of the many variables that describe how the project is proceeding as compared to the plan.

A reporting system has the following characteristics:

- Provides timely, complete, and accurate status information
- Doesn't add so much overhead time as to be counterproductive
- Is readily acceptable to the project team and senior management
- Warns of pending problems in time to take action
- Is easily understood by those who have a need to know

To establish this reporting system, you can choose from among the hundreds of reports that are standard fare in project management software packages. Once you decide what you want to track, these software tools offer several suggestions and standard reports to meet your needs. Most project management software tools enable you to customize their standard reports to meet even the most specific needs.

Types of Project Status Reports

There are five types of project status reports: current period, cumulative, exception, stoplight, and variance. Each of these report types is described here.

Current Period Reports

These reports cover only the most recently completed period. They report progress on activities that were open or scheduled for work during the period. Reports might highlight activities completed, as well as the variance between scheduled and actual completion dates. If any activities did not progress according to plan, the report should include the reasons for the variance and the appropriate corrective measures that will be implemented to fix the schedule slippage.

Cumulative Reports

These reports contain the history of the project from the beginning to the end of the current report period. They are more informative than the current period reports because they show trends in project progress. For example, a schedule variance might be tracked over several successive periods to show improvement. Reports can be at the activity or project level.

Exception Reports

Exception reports indicate variances from the plan. These reports are typically designed for senior management to read and interpret quickly. Reports that are produced for senior management merit special consideration. Senior managers do not have a lot of time to read reports that tell them everything is on schedule and there are no problems serious enough to warrant their attention. In such cases, a one-page, high-level summary report that says everything is okay is usually sufficient. It might also be appropriate to include a more detailed report as an attachment for those who might want more information. The same might be true of exception reports. That is, the one-page exception report tells senior managers about variances from the plan that will be of interest to them, and an attachment provides more details for the interested reader.

Stoplight Reports

Stoplight reports are a variation that can be used on any of the previous report types. I believe in parsimony in all reporting. Here is a technique you might want to try: When the project is on schedule and everything seems to be proceeding as planned, put a green sticker on the top-right corner of the first page of the project status report. This sticker will signal to senior managers that everything is progressing according to plan, and they need not even read the attached report.

When the project has encountered a problem — schedule slippage, for example — you might put a yellow sticker on the top-right corner of the first page of the project status report. That is a signal to upper management that the project is not moving along as scheduled but that you have a get-well plan in place. A summary of the problem and the get-well plan may appear on the first page, but they can also refer to the details in the attached report. Those details describe the problem, the corrective steps that have been put in place, and some estimate of when the situation will be rectified.

Red stickers placed on the top-right corner of the first page signal that a project is out of control. Red reports should be avoided at all costs because they indicate that the project has encountered a problem for which you don't have a get-well plan or even a recommendation for upper management. Senior managers will obviously read these reports because they signal a major problem with the project. On a more positive note, the red condition may be beyond your control. Here's an example of when a red condition would be warranted: there is a major power grid failure on the East Coast and a number of companies have lost their computing systems. Your hot site is overburdened with companies looking for computing power. Your company is one of them, and the loss of computing power has put your project seriously behind in final system testing. There is little you can do to avoid such acts of nature.

Variance Reports

Variance reports do exactly what their name suggests — they report differences between what was planned and what actually happened. The report has the following three columns:

- The planned number
- The actual number
- The difference, or variance, between the two

A variance report can be in one of the following two formats:

- The first is a numeric format containing rows that show the actual, planned, and variance values for those variables requiring such calculations. Typical variables that are tracked in a variance report are schedule and cost. For example, the rows might correspond to the activities open for work during the report period, and the columns might be the planned cost to date, the actual cost to date, and the difference between the two. The impact of departures from the plan is signified by larger values of this difference (the variance).

- The second format is a graphical representation of the numeric data. It might be formatted so that plan data is shown for each report period of the project, denoted with a curve of one color, and the actual data is shown for each report period of the project, denoted by a curve of a different color. The variance need not be graphed at all because it is merely the difference between the two curves at some point in time. One advantage of the graphical version of the variance report is that it shows any variance trend over the report periods of the project, whereas the numeric report generally shows data only for the current report period.

Typical variance reports are snapshots in time (the current period) of the status of an entity being tracked. Most variance reports do not include data points that report how the project reached that status. Project variance reports can be used to report project as well as activity variances. For the sake of the managers who will have to read these reports, I recommend that one report format be used regardless of the variable being tracked. Your upper management will quickly become comfortable with a reporting format that is consistent across all projects or activities within a project. It will make life a bit easier for you, as the project manager, too.

Here are five reasons why you should measure duration and cost variances:

- **Catch deviations from the curve early** — The cumulative actual cost or actual duration can be plotted against the planned cumulative cost or cumulative duration. As these two curves begin to display a variance from one another, the project manager should put corrective measures in place to bring the two curves together. This reestablishes the agreement between planned and actual performance, as described in detail in the "Earned Value Analysis" section later in this chapter.

- **Dampen oscillation** — Planned versus actual performance should display a similar pattern over time. Wild fluctuations between the two are symptomatic of a project that is not under control. Such a project will get behind schedule or overspend in one report period, be corrected in the next period, and go out of control in the next period. Variance reports can provide an early warning that such conditions are likely, giving the project manager an opportunity to correct the anomaly before it gets serious. Smaller oscillations are easier to correct than larger oscillations.

- **Allow early corrective action** — As just suggested, the project manager would prefer to be alerted to a schedule or cost problem early in the development of the problem, rather than later. Early problem detection may offer more opportunities for corrective action than later detection.

- **Determine weekly schedule variance** — I have found that progress on activities open for work should be reported on a weekly basis. This is a good compromise on report frequency and gives the project manager the best opportunity for corrective action plans before a situation escalates to a point where it will be difficult to recover any schedule slippages.

- **Determine weekly effort (person hours/day) variance** — The difference between the planned effort and actual effort has a direct impact on both planned cumulative cost and the schedule. If the effort is less than planned, it may suggest potential schedule slippage if the person is not able to increase his or her effort on the activity in the following week. Alternatively, if the weekly effort exceeded the plan and the progress was not proportionately the same, a cost overrun situation may be developing.

Early detection of out-of-control situations is important. The longer you wait to discover a problem, the longer it will take for your solution to bring the project back to a stable condition.

How and What Information to Update

As input to each of these report types, activity managers and the project manager must report the progress made on all activities that were open for work (in other words, those that were to have work completed on them during the report period) during the period of time covered by the status report. Recall that your planning estimates of activity duration and cost were based on little or no information. Now that you have completed some work on the activity, you should be able to provide a better estimate of duration and cost. This is reflected in a re-estimate of the work remaining to complete the activity. That update information should also be provided.

The following list describes what should actually be reported:

Determine a set period of time and day of week — The project team will have agreed on the day of the week and time of day by which all updated information is to be submitted. A project administrator or another team member is responsible for ensuring that all update information is on file by the report deadline.

Report actual work accomplished during this period — What was planned to be accomplished and what was actually accomplished are often two different things. Rather than disappoint the project manager, activity managers are likely to report that the planned work was actually accomplished. Their hope is to catch up by the next report period. Project managers need to verify the accuracy of the reported data, rather than simply accept it as accurate. Spot-checking on a random basis should be sufficient.

Record historical data and re-estimate remaining work (in-progress work only) — The following two kinds of information are reported:

- All work completed prior to the report deadline is historical information. It enables variance reports and other tracking data to be presented and analyzed.

- The other kind of information is future-oriented. For the most part, this information consists of re-estimates of duration and cost and estimates to completion (both cost and duration) of the activities still open for work.

Report start and finish dates — These are the actual start and end dates of activities started or completed during the report period.

Record days of duration accomplished and remaining — First reported is how many days have been spent so far working on this activity. The second number is based on the re-estimated duration as reflected in the time-to-completion number.

Report resource effort (hours/day) spent and remaining (in-progress work only) — Whereas the preceding numbers report calendar time, these two numbers report labor time over the duration of the activity. One reports labor completed over the duration already accomplished. The other reports labor to be spent over the remaining duration.

Report percent complete — Percent complete is the most common method used to record progress because it is the way people tend to think about what has been done in reference to the total job to be completed. Percent complete isn't the best method to report progress, however, because it is a subjective evaluation. What goes through a person's mind when you ask him or her, "What percent complete are you on this activity?" The first thing is most likely "What percent should I be?" This is followed closely by "What's a number that we can all be happy with?" To calculate the percent complete for an activity, you need something quantifiable. Different approaches have been used to calculate percent complete, including the following:

- Duration
- Resource work
- Cost

Frequency of Gathering and Reporting Project Progress

A logical frequency for reporting project progress is once a week, usually on Friday afternoon. For some projects, such as refurbishing a large jet airliner, progress is recorded after each shift, three times a day. I've seen others that were of such a low priority or long duration that they were updated once a month. For most projects, start gathering the information around noon on Friday. Let people extrapolate to the end of the workday.

Variances

Variances are deviations from plan. Think of a variance as the difference between what was planned and what actually occurred. There are two types of variances: positive variances and negative variances.

Positive Variances

Positive variances are deviations from the plan indicating that an ahead-of-schedule situation has occurred or that an actual cost was less than a planned cost. This type of variance is good news to the project manager, who would rather hear that the project is ahead of schedule or under budget.

Positive variances bring their own set of problems, however, which can be as serious as negative variances. Positive variances can result in rescheduling to bring the project to completion early, under budget, or both. Resources can be reallocated from ahead-of-schedule projects to behind-schedule projects. Positive variances also can result from schedule slippage! Consider budget. Being under budget means that not all dollars were expended, which may be the direct result of not having completed work that was scheduled for completion during the report period.

CROSS-REFERENCE This situation is revisited in the "Earned Value Analysis" section later in this chapter.

Conversely, if the ahead-of-schedule situation is the result of the project team finding a better way or a shortcut to complete the work, the project manager will be pleased. This situation may result in a short-lived benefit, however. Getting ahead of schedule is great, but staying ahead of schedule presents another kind of problem. To stay ahead of schedule, the project manager must negotiate changes to the resource schedule. Given the aggressive project portfolios in place in most companies, it is unlikely that resource schedule changes can be made. In the final analysis, being ahead of schedule may be a myth.

Negative Variances

Negative variances are deviations from the plan indicating that a behind-schedule situation has occurred or that an actual cost was greater than a planned cost. Being behind schedule or over budget is not what the project manager or reporting manager wants to hear. Negative variances are not necessarily bad news, however. For example, you might have overspent because you accomplished more work during the report period than was planned. In overspending during this period, you could have accomplished the work at less cost than was originally planned. You can't tell by looking at the variance report. You will need the details available in the EVA reports

CROSS-REFERENCE More details are forthcoming on this topic in the "Earned Value Analysis" section later in this chapter.

In most cases, negative time variances affect project completion only when they are associated with critical-path activities or when the schedule slippage on non–critical-path activities exceeds the activity's slack. Slack is defined in Chapter 5. Minor variances use up the slack time for that activity; more serious ones will cause a change in the critical path.

Negative cost variances can result from uncontrollable factors such as cost increases from suppliers or unexpected equipment malfunctions. Some negative variances can result from inefficiencies or error. I discuss a problem escalation strategy to resolve such situations later in this chapter.

> **REPORTING AND DISPARATE PROJECT MANAGEMENT APPROACHES**
>
> Not every project will use the same project management approach. That may create reporting problems when project status reports are sent up the food chain to senior managers. You could just let the chips fall where they may and force senior managers to aggregate the data to fit their own needs. I don't see many senior managers agreeing to place that burden on their office staff. Instead a standard reporting format must be established and each project manager must be responsible for reporting status accordingly.

Applying Graphical Reporting Tools

As mentioned earlier in the chapter, senior managers may have only a few minutes of uninterrupted time to digest your report. Respect that time. They won't be able to fully read and understand your report if they have to read 15 pages before they get any useful information. Having to read several pages only to find out that the project is on schedule is frustrating and a waste of valuable time.

Gantt Charts

A *Gantt chart* is one of the most convenient, most frequently used, and easiest-to-grasp depictions of project activities that I have encountered. The chart is formatted as a two-dimensional representation of the project schedule, with activities shown in the rows and time shown across the horizontal axis. It can be used during planning, for resource scheduling, and for status reporting. The only downside to using Gantt charts is that they do not contain dependency relationships. Some project management software tools provide an option to display these dependencies, but the result is a graphical report that is so cluttered with lines representing the dependencies that the report is next to useless. In some cases, dependencies can be guessed at from the Gantt chart, but in most cases, they are lost.

Figure 7-1 shows a representation of the Cost Containment Project as a Gantt chart, using the format that I prefer. The format shown is from Microsoft Project, but it is typical of the format used in most project management software packages.

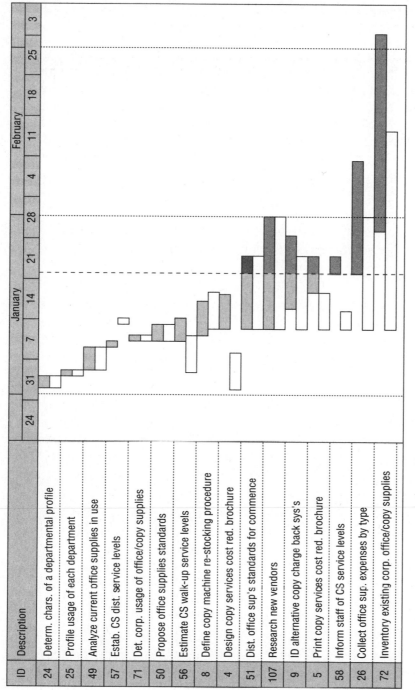

Figure 7-1: Gantt chart project status report

Stoplight Reports

As mentioned earlier in the chapter, stoplight reports are a very effective way to communicate status intuitively without burdening senior managers with the need to read anything. The explanation will, of course, be in the attached report if the managers are interested in reading the details.

Burn Charts

Burn charts are another intuitive tool that displays the cumulative consumption of any resource over time, expressed either as a percentage of the resource allocated to the project or the quantity of the resource. If you are displaying the quantity, there should be a horizontal line showing the maximum quantity of the resource available. Burn charts are very simple, but they're limited in their value. For a more sophisticated display of resource use against the plan, the earned value analysis would be used.

Milestone Trend Charts

Milestones are significant events that you want to track in the life of the project. These significant events are zero-duration activities and merely indicate that a certain condition exists in the project. For example, a milestone event might be the approval of several different component designs. This event consumes no time in the project schedule. It simply reflects the fact that those approvals have all been granted. The completion of this milestone event may be the predecessor of several build-type activities in the project plan. Milestone events are planned into the project in the same way that activities are planned into the project. They typically have finish-to-start (FS) relationships with the activities that are their predecessors and their successors.

Figure 7-2 shows a milestone trend chart for a hypothetical project. The trend chart plots the difference between the planned and estimated date of a project milestone at each project report period. In the original project plan, the milestone is planned to occur in the ninth month of the project. That is the last project month on this milestone chart. The horizontal lines represent one, two, and three standard deviations above or below the forecasted milestone date. All activities in the project have an expected completion date that is approximately normally distributed. The mean and variance of an activity's completion date are a function of the longest path to that activity from the report date. In this example, the units of measure are one month. For this project, the first project report (at month 1) shows that the new forecasted milestone date will be one week later than planned. At the second project report date (month 2 of the project), the milestone date is forecasted on target. The next three project reports indicate a slippage to two weeks late, then three weeks late, then four weeks late, and finally six weeks late (at month 6 of the project). In other words, the milestone is forecasted to occur six weeks late, and only three more project months remain in which to recover the slippage. Obviously, the project is in trouble. It appears to be drifting out of control, and in fact it is. Some remedial action is required of the project manager.

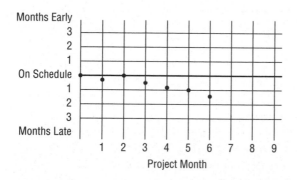

Figure 7-2: A run up or down of four or more successive data points

STANDARD DEVIATION

The variance and standard deviation of a set of data points measure the spread of the data points around the average value of the data points. The formula for calculating standard deviation of a set of n data points $x_1, x_2, \ldots x_n$ is as follows:

Variance $= \Sigma((x_i - xm) / xm)^2$

Standard Deviation = Square root of the variance, where xm is the average of the n data points.

If you want to learn more about these two metrics, refer to any elementary materials on statistics.

Certain patterns signal an out-of-control situation. These patterns are shown in Figures 7-2 through 7-5 and are described here:

Successive slippages — Figure 7-2 (shown previously) depicts a project that is drifting out of control. Each report period shows additional slippage since the last report period. Four such successive occurrences, however minor they may seem, require special corrective action on the part of the project manager.

Radical change — Figure 7-3 shows the milestone to be ahead of schedule, but it also reports a radical change between report periods. Activity duration may have been grossly overestimated. There may be a data error. In any case, the situation requires further investigation.

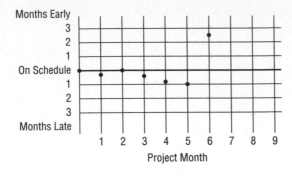

Figure 7-3: A change of more than three standard deviations

Successive runs — Figure 7-4 signals a project that may have encountered a permanent schedule shift. In the example, the milestone date seems to be varying around one month ahead of schedule. Barring any radical shifts and the availability of resources over the next two months, the milestone will probably be reached one month early. Remember that you have negotiated for a resource schedule in these two months, and now you will be trying to renegotiate an accelerated schedule.

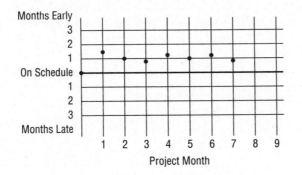

Figure 7-4: Seven or more successive data points above or below the planned milestone date

Schedule shift — Figure 7-5 depicts a major shift in the milestone schedule. The cause must be isolated and the appropriate corrective measures taken. One possibility is the discovery that a downstream activity will not be required. Perhaps the project manager can buy a deliverable, rather than build it, and remove the associated build activities from the project plan.

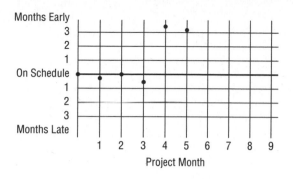

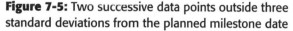

Figure 7-5: Two successive data points outside three standard deviations from the planned milestone date

Earned Value Analysis

Earned value analysis (EVA) is used to measure project performance and, by tradition, uses the dollar value of work as the metric. As an alternative, resource person hours/day can be used in cases where the project manager does not directly manage the project budget. Actual work performed is compared against planned and budgeted work expressed in these equivalents. These metrics are used to determine schedule and cost variances for both the current period and the cumulative to-date period. Cost and resource person hours/day are not good, objective indicators with which to measure performance or progress. Unfortunately, there is no other good objective indicator. Given this, you are left with dollars or person hours/day, which you are at least familiar working with in other contexts. Either one by itself does not tell the whole story. You need to relate them to each other.

One drawback that these metrics have is that they report history. Although they can be used to make extrapolated predictions for the future, they primarily provide a measure of the general health of the project, which the project manager can correct as needed to restore the project to good health.

Figure 7-6 shows an S curve, which represents the baseline progress curve for the original project plan. It can be used as a reference point. That is, you can compare your actual progress to date against the curve and determine how well the project is doing. Again, progress can be expressed as either dollars or person hours/day.

By adding the actual progress curve to the baseline curve, you can see the current status versus the planned status. Figure 7-7 shows the actual progress curve below the planned curve. If this represented dollars, you might be tempted to assume the project is running under budget. Is that really true?

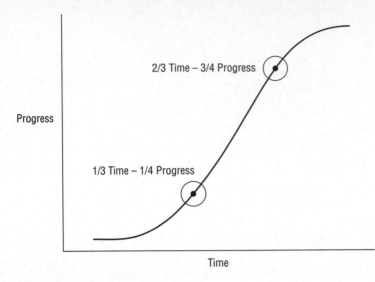

Figure 7-6: The standard S curve

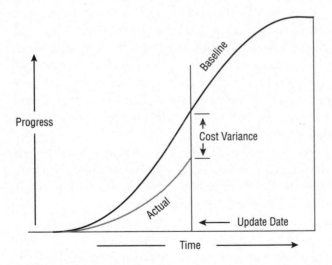

Figure 7-7: Baseline versus actual cost curve illustrating cost variance

Projects rarely run significantly under budget. A more common reason for the actual curve to be below the baseline is that activities that should have been done have not been, and thus the dollars or person hours/day that were planned to be expended are unused. The possible schedule variance is highlighted in Figure 7-8.

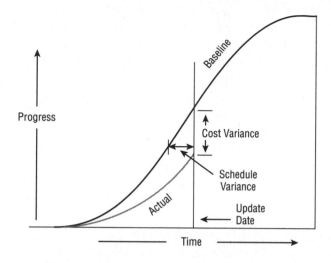

Figure 7-8: Baseline versus actual cost illustrating schedule variance

To determine actual progress schedule variance, you need some additional information. EVA comprises three basic measurements: budgeted cost of work scheduled, budgeted cost of work performed, and actual cost of work performed. These measurements result in two variance values: schedule variance and cost variance. Figure 7-9 is a graphical representation of the three measurements.

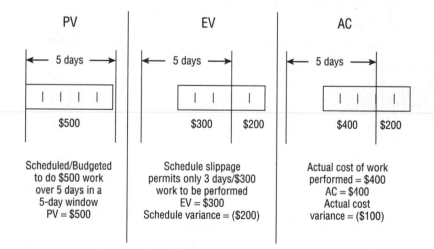

Figure 7-9: Cost and performance indicators

The figure shows a single activity that has a five-day duration and a budget of $500. The budget is prorated over the five days at an average daily value of $100. The left panel of Figure 7-9 shows an initial (baseline) schedule with the activity starting on the first day of the week (Monday) and finishing at the end of the week (Friday). The budgeted $500 value of the work is planned to be accomplished within that week. This is the planned value (PV). The center panel shows the actual work that was done. Note that the schedule slipped and work did not begin until the third day of the week. Using an average daily budget of $100, you see that you were able to complete only $300 of the scheduled work. This is the earned value (EV). The rightmost panel shows the actual schedule, as in the center panel, but now you see the actual dollars that were spent to accomplish the three days' work. This $400 is the actual cost (AC).

The PV, EV, and AC are used to compute and track two variances. The first is *schedule variance (SV)*. SV is the difference between the EV and the PV, which is –$200 (EV – PV) for this example. That is, the SV is the schedule difference between what was done and what was planned to be done, expressed in dollar or person hours/day equivalents. The second is *cost variance (CV)*. CV is the difference between the EV and the AC, which is $100 in this example. That is, (AC – EV) the cost of the work completed, was overspent by $100.

EVA TERMINOLOGY

For those who are familiar with the older cost/schedule control terminology, I have used the new terminology as defined in the Project Management Body of Knowledge (PMBOK) 2000 and as used in PMBOK 2003. The old terminology corresponds to the new terminology as follows:

- **ACWP is the actual cost (AC).**
- **BCWP is the earned value (EV).**
- **BCWS is the planned value (PV).**

Management might react positively to the information previously shown in Figure 7-7, but they might also be misled by such data. The full story is told by comparing both budget variance and schedule variance as shown in Figure 7-10.

To correctly interpret the data shown previously in Figure 7-8, you need to add the EV data shown in Figure 7-9 to produce Figure 7-10. Comparing the EV curve with the PV curve, you see that you have underspent because all of the work that was scheduled has not been completed. Comparing the EV curve to the AC curve also indicates that you overspent for the work that was done. Clearly, management would have been misled by Figure 7-7 had they ignored the data in Figure 7-9. Either one by itself may be telling a half-truth.

In addition to measuring and reporting history, EVA can be used to predict the future of a project. Take a look at Figure 7-11. By cutting the PV curve at the report date height from the horizontal axis, which has been achieved by the EV, and then pasting this curve onto the end of the EV curve, you can extrapolate the completion of the project. Note that this is based on using the original estimates for the remaining work to be completed. If you continue at the same rate you have been progressing thus far, you will finish beyond the planned completion date. Doing the same thing for the AC shows that you will finish over budget. This is the simplest method of attempting to "estimate to completion," but it clearly illustrates that a significant change needs to occur in the way this project is running.

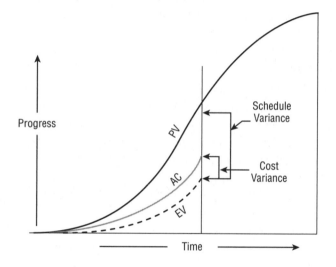

Figure 7-10: The full story

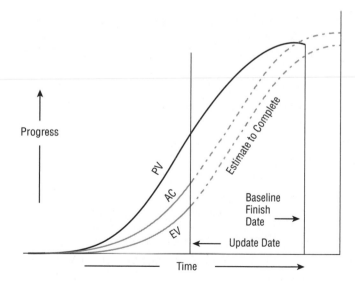

Figure 7-11: PV, EV, and AC curves

The three basic indicators yield an additional level of analysis for you. *Schedule performance index (SPI)* and *cost performance index (CPI)* are further refinements computed as follows:

$$SPI = EV \,/\, PV$$

$$CPI = EV \,/\, AC$$

Schedule Performance Index — The SPI is a measure of how close the project is to performing work as it was actually scheduled. If you are ahead of schedule, EV will be greater than PV, and therefore the SPI will be greater than 1. Obviously, this is desirable. Conversely, an SPI below 1 indicates that the amount of work performed was less than the work scheduled — not a good thing.

Cost Performance Index — The CPI is a measure of how close the project is to spending on the work performed to what was planned to have been spent. If you are spending less on the work performed than was budgeted, the CPI will be greater than 1. If not, and you are spending more than was budgeted for the work performed, then the CPI will be less than 1.

Some managers prefer this type of analysis because it is intuitive and quite simple to equate each index to a baseline of 1. Any value less than 1 is undesirable; any value over 1 is good. These indices are displayed graphically as trends compared against the baseline value of 1.

Integrating Milestone Trend Charts and Earned Value Analysis

Both milestone trend charts and earned value can easily be accommodated within the project life cycle. All of these metrics can be used to track practice-level improvements resulting from a process improvement program. After all, they are where the rubber meets the road.

NOTE This section is adapted from an earlier book of mine, *Effective Software Project Management* (Wiley, 2006).

Integrating Earned Value

At each report date, tasks that are open for work or were scheduled to be open for work can be in one of the following three situations:

- They are complete and hence have accrued 100 percent value.

- They are still open for work and hence have accrued a percentage of value equal to the proportion of subtasks completed.

- They are still open for work, and no subtasks are completed; hence, they have accrued 0 percent value.

Add all of the accrued values since the last report date to the cumulative project total. Display that data on the baseline S curve.

Integrating Milestone Trend Data

At each report date, the task managers of tasks that are open for work or were scheduled to be open for work should update the project file. The update information will indicate the following:

- The task is reported as complete as of a certain date.
- A certain percentage of the task work is complete (same as the earned value report mentioned previously) and an updated estimate to completion is given.
- No progress is reported.

If project management software is used, the software produces an updated project file with new forecasted dates for the milestones you are tracking. The presentation of the SPI and CPI data over time can be represented using the same format that was used to report milestone trend data. Three examples follow.

Figure 7-12 depicts a common situation. Here the project has gotten behind schedule (denoted by the "S" in the figure) but is under budget (denoted by the "C" in the figure). That is probably due to the fact that work that was scheduled has not been done and hence the labor costs associated with those tasks have not been incurred.

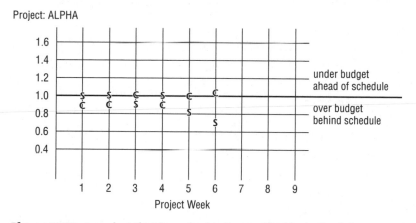

Figure 7-12: A project that is under budget and behind schedule

On rare occasions, you might experience the situation shown in Figure 7-13. The project is ahead of schedule and under budget. Less costly ways were found to complete the work, and the work was completed in less time than was planned. If this should ever happen to you, relish the moment. Take whatever kudos your client or management cares to heap on you. You deserve their accolades. They don't happen often.

Project: BETA

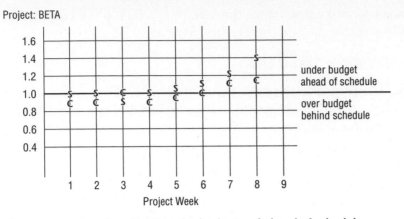

Figure 7-13: A project that is under budget and ahead of schedule

Figure 7-14 is the worst of the worst. Nothing more needs to be said.

Project: GAMMA

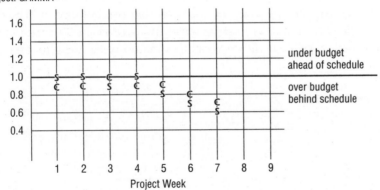

Figure 7-14: A project that is over budget and behind schedule

The same approach can be used to track a project portfolio over time, as shown in Figure 7-15.

The graph shows the SPI values of the individual projects that comprise the portfolio. This is also a useful graphic for summarizing the practice changes from your process improvement program. If a clear trend is visible at the portfolio level, it is indicative of a successful transition from process to practice.

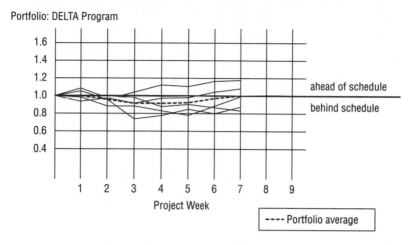

Portfolio: DELTA Program

Figure 7-15: Adapting the life cycle for a project portfolio schedule

Managing the Scope Bank

The Scope Bank was introduced in Chapter 6. I now want take a more detailed look at exactly how it can be used as a monitoring and control tool. As part of the Launching Phase, you established the scope change management process. The Scope Bank was an integral part of that process. Recall that in setting up the Scope Bank, an initial deposit of some number of days was made. Ten percent of the total labor days would be a reasonable deposit. Make sure the client understands that when this time is used, it will add to the project completion date. Your job as project manager is to make sure that this time is managed effectively. The job of the client is to make sure that this time is spent in the best way possible to improve the business value of the final deliverables. Change requests and other suggestions will be submitted, and at the appropriate time, decisions will be made on which ones will be implemented and when. The time needed to analyze the requests and the time to implement the requests is taken from the time in the Scope Bank.

Sooner or later, the balance in the Scope Bank will be zero. That means no more change requests can be accepted or acted upon without a compensating deposit being made in the Scope Bank. That deposit will come from the labor time required to implement functions and features not yet integrated in the solution. In order to make that deposit, the client must prioritize the functions and features not yet integrated in the solution with the new change requests. Some of the functions and features of lesser priority than the requested changes will be removed from the solution and become the source of the deposits.

As long as you make it clear to the client at the outset of the project how the Scope Bank is defined and managed, there should be no problems with its implementation. It is important that you keep the client up to date on the status of the Scope Bank.

Building and Maintaining the Issues Log

The Issues Log is a dynamic document that contains all of the problems that have arisen during the course of the project and have not yet been resolved. The resolution of these problems is important to the successful continuation of the project. The Issues Log contains the following information:

- ID number
- Date logged
- Description of the problem
- Impact if not resolved
- The problem owner
- Action to be taken
- Status
- Outcome

If a Risk Log is maintained, it is often integrated into the Issues Log. At each project status or team meeting, the Issues Log is reviewed and updated.

Managing Project Status Meetings

To keep close track of progress on the project, the project manager needs information from his or her team on a timely basis. This information will be provided during a project status meeting. At a minimum, you need to have a status meeting at least once a week. On some of my major projects, daily status meetings were the norm for the first few weeks, and when the need for daily information wasn't as critical, I switched to twice a week and finally to weekly status meetings.

Who Should Attend Status Meetings?

To use the status meetings correctly and efficiently, it's important to figure out who should be in attendance. This information should be a part of your communication plan.

When choosing who should attend, keep the following points in mind:

■ At first your status team may include only those team members who are needed in the planning phase. If the other team members don't need to know the information, don't make them come to a meeting and sit there without a good reason. You are going to distribute meeting minutes anyway, so the team members who aren't needed at the actual meeting will be informed about what transpired.

■ There will be times in a status meeting when two team members get into a discussion and the other people in the meeting aren't needed. If this happens, ask them to conduct a sidebar meeting so that your own status meeting can continue. A *sidebar meeting* is one in which a limited number of people need to participate, and problems can resolved more effectively away from your status meeting. Having everyone in the room listen to these sidebar topics isn't useful.

When Are Status Meetings Held?

Usually, status meetings are held toward the end of the week. Just make sure it's the same day each week. People get used to preparing information for a status meeting if they know exactly when the meeting will occur.

What Is the Purpose of a Status Meeting?

You hold a status meeting to get information to the whole team. On large projects, the participants in the status meeting may be representatives of their department. You can't have all the people on a 250-person project team come into a meeting once a week, so make sure that someone is there to represent the rest of the people in their section. The purpose of the meeting is to encourage the free flow of information, and that means ensuring that the people who need to have information to do their jobs get the information at the status meeting. Remember once again that you are going to distribute minutes of the meeting later, so that will take care of the people who aren't in attendance.

TIP The size of the project may determine the length of the status meeting, but in general I prefer a one-hour limit. This is the maximum, and an entire hour should not be necessary at every project status meeting. Good judgment is needed here — don't waste people's time.

What Is the Status Meeting Format?

Although the format of status review meetings should be flexible, as project needs dictate, certain items are part of every status meeting. I recommend that you proceed in the following top-down fashion:

1. The project champion reports any changes that may have a bearing on the future of the project.

2. The client reports any changes that may have a bearing on the future of the project.

3. The project manager reports on the overall health of the project and the impact of earlier problems, changes, and corrective actions at the project level.

4. Activity managers report on the health of activities open or scheduled open for work since the last status meeting.

5. Activity managers of future activities report on any changes since the last meeting that might impact project status.

6. The project manager reviews the status of open problems from the last status meeting.

7. Attendees identify new problems and assign responsibility for their resolution (the only discussion allowed here is for clarification purposes).

8. The project champion, client, or project manager, as appropriate, offers closing comments.

9. The project manager announces the time and place of the next meeting and adjourns the meeting.

Minutes are part of the formal project documentation and are taken at each meeting, circulated for comment, revised as appropriate, distributed, and filed in the electronic project notebook. Because there is little discussion, the minutes contain any handouts from the meeting and list the items assigned for the next meeting. The minutes should also contain the list of attendees, a summary of comments made, and assigned responsibilities.

An administrative support person should be present at the project status review meetings to take minutes and monitor handouts. This responsibility might also be shared by the project team members. In some organizations, the same person is responsible for distributing the meeting agenda and materials ahead of time for review. This advance distribution is especially important if decisions will be made during the meeting. People are very uncomfortable when they are given important information for the first time and are immediately expected to read it, understand it, and then make a decision about it.

The 15-Minute Daily Status Meeting

These short status meetings were originally introduced as a tool to monitor and control agile and extreme projects. For small projects (teams of less than 10 members), the entire project team meets frequently (every morning for about 15 minutes in the team war room, for example). For larger projects, the task leaders should meet every morning. These are stand-up meetings where status is reported. Each attendee who has a task open for work should report. Open for work means the task start date has passed and the task is not yet complete. In their reports, the meeting attendees state where they are with respect to the time line (ahead, on target, or behind) and by how many hours or days. If they are behind, they should briefly state whether or not they have a get-well plan and when they expect to be back on schedule. If anyone in the meeting is able to help, they should say so and take that conversation offline. Problems and issues are not discussed in the daily status meeting except to add them to the Scope Bank and Issues Log. Their resolution or further clarification should be dealt with by the affected parties offline. Do not use team time to discuss things that are of interest to only a few members.

Problem Management Meetings

Problem management meetings provide an oversight function to identify, monitor, and resolve problems that arise during the life of a project. Every project has problems. No matter how well planned or managed the project is, there will always be problems. Many problems arise just as an accident of nature. Consider the following scenario as an example: One of your key staff members has resigned just as she was to begin working on a critical-path activity. Her skills are in high demand, and she will be difficult to replace. Each day that her position remains vacant is another day's delay in the project. It seems like an impossible problem. Nevertheless, you (as the project manager) must be ready to take action in such cases. The problem management meeting is one vehicle for addressing all problems that need to be escalated above the individual for definition, solution identification, and resolution.

This is an important function in the management of projects, especially large projects. Problems are often identified in the project status meeting and referred to the appropriate team members for resolution. A group is assembled to work on the problem. Progress reports are presented and discussed at a problem management meeting. Problem management meetings usually begin with a review of the status of the activity that resulted in the problem, followed by a statement of the problem and a discussion to ensure that everyone has the same understanding of the problem. At that point, the meeting should move into the problem-solving process that was discussed in detail in Chapter 6.

Defining a Problem Escalation Strategy

Something has happened that put the project plan at risk. Late shipments from suppliers, equipment malfunctions, sickness, random acts of nature, resignations, priority changes, errors, and a host of other factors can lead to problems that affect deliverables, deliverable schedules, and resource schedules. The project team owns the problem and must find a solution.

This situation is very different for the project manager than the case of a change request. When a change request has been made, the project manager has some leverage with the client. The client wants something and might be willing to negotiate to an acceptable resolution. That is not the case when a problem arises on the project team. The project manager does not have any leverage and is in a much more difficult position.

When the unplanned happens, the project manager needs to determine who owns the problem and the extent of the problem, and then take the appropriate corrective measures. Those measures often include helping the owner of the problem find an acceptable solution following the escalation hierarchy discussed later in this chapter. Minor variations from the plan will occur and may not require corrective measures. There are degrees of corrective measures available to the project manager: In trying to resolve a problem, the project manager begins at the top of the escalation hierarchy and works down the hierarchy, examining each option until one is found that solves the problem.

There are three levels of escalation strategy: project team–based, resource manager–based, and client-based.

Project Manager–Based Strategies

If the problem occurs within a non–critical-path activity, it can be resolved by using available slack, which is defined in Chapter 5. One example is to reschedule the activity later in its ES–LF window or extend the duration to use some of the available slack. Note that this strategy does not affect any other activities in the project. By using slack, you affect the resource schedule for all activities that have this activity as a predecessor. Another approach is to continue the schedule compression techniques employed in defining the original project plan. This strategy can affect resource schedules just as in the prior case. The last option open to you is to consider the resource pool under your control as the project manager. Can some resources be reassigned from non–critical-path activities to assist with the problem activity?

Resource Manager–Based Strategies

After you have exhausted all the options under your control as the project manager, it is time to turn to the resource managers for additional help. This help may take the form of additional resources or rescheduling of already committed resources. Expect to make a trade-off here. For example, you might be accommodated now, but at the sacrifice of later activities in the project. At least you have bought some time to resolve the downstream problem that will be created by solving this upstream problem. If you have other projects that you are currently managing, some trades across projects may solve the problem.

Client-Based Strategies

When all else fails, you will have to approach the client. The first option would be to consider any multiple-release strategies. Delivering some functionality ahead of schedule and the balance later than planned may be a good starting point. The last resort is to ask for an extension of time. This may not be as unpleasant as it seems because the client's schedule may have also slipped and the client may be relieved to have a delay in your deliverable schedule, too.

The Escalation Strategy Hierarchy

The problem escalation strategy presented here is based on the premise that you, as the project manager, will try to solve the problem with the resources that you control. Failing to do that, you can appeal to your resource managers. As a last resort, you can appeal to the client.

One thing to note here that is very different from the change request situation discussed previously is the leverage to negotiate. As mentioned, you, as the project manager, have leverage when the client has requested a change, but no leverage when you have a project problem to solve. The client has nothing to gain and is therefore less likely to be cooperative. In most cases, the problem can be reduced to how to recover lost time. The following six outcomes are possible to this problem situation:

> **No action required (Schedule slack will correct the problem)** — In this case, the slippage involved a non–critical-path activity and it will self-correct.

> **Examine FS dependencies for schedule compression opportunities** — Recall that you originally compressed the schedule to accommodate the requested project completion date by changing FS dependencies to SS dependencies. You should use that same strategy again. The project schedule will have changed several times since work began, and there may be several new opportunities to accomplish further compression and solve the current problem.

> **Reassign resources from non–critical-path activities to correct the slippage** — Up to a point, you control the resources assigned to this project and others that you manage. You may be able to reassign resources from non–critical-path activities to the activities that have

slipped. These non–critical-path activities may be in the same project in which the slippage occurred or they may be in another project that you manage.

Negotiate additional resources — Having exhausted all of the resources that you control, you need to turn to the resource managers as the next strategy. To recoup the lost time, you need additional resources. These resources may come in the form of added staff or dollars to acquire contract help.

Negotiate multiple release strategies — This strategy involves the client. Just as in the case of a change request, you can use a multiple-release strategy to your advantage. An example will illustrate the strategy: The project manager shares the problem with the client and then asks for the client to prioritize the features requested in the project plan. The project manager then offers to provide the highest-priority features ahead of their scheduled delivery date and the remaining priorities later than the scheduled delivery date. In other words, the project manager gains an extended delivery schedule, but gives the client something better than the original bargain offered — namely, something ahead of schedule.

Request a schedule extension from the client — This is the final alternative. Although it's similar to the multiple-release strategy, it offers the client nothing in trade. The slippage is such that the only resolution is to ask for a time extension.

You, as the project manager, should try to solve the problem by starting at the top of this list of six outcomes and working down until a solution is found. By using this approach, you will first try to solve the problem with resources that you control, then with resources that the resource managers control, and finally with resources and constraints that the client controls.

Gaining Approval to Close the Project

The client decides when the project can move to the Closing Phase. This is not an arbitrary decision, but one based on the acceptance criteria initiated during project planning and maintained throughout the project. Whenever a scope change request has been approved, the acceptance criteria are updated to reflect that.

In most cases, the acceptance criteria are nothing more than a checklist that reflects the client requirements. After all of the items have been checked as satisfactorily completed, the project is ready to move to the closing activities.

Putting It All Together

Monitoring and controlling the progress of a project won't happen just because the team is committed to the project. There must be an organized oversight process put in place and understood by the client, senior management, the project manager, and all the team members. As you have seen, there are reports for all of these audiences. You have also seen that the extent to which progress reports are necessary and the amount of effort to generate them requires a reasonable balance between effort and value. Requiring too much reporting takes away from the time available to work on the project. Requiring too little reporting puts the project manager at risk of not being able to complete the project within time and cost constraints. You have also seen that there are both numeric and graphic reporting formats. Some managers prefer numeric data, whereas others prefer graphic data. The reporting system you choose must meet the needs of both types of managers.

Discussion Questions

1. What are the advantages and disadvantages of confirming the accuracy of status reports filed by your team members?

2. You correctly defined and introduced the Scope Bank to your client, who initially agreed to use it. However, the client seems to have forgotten their agreement. The Scope Bank needs a deposit in order to process a new change request, and the client insists on integrating the most recent change request without removing any functions or features not yet integrated into the solution. You are at an impasse. How will you resolve the stalemate?

CASE STUDY – PIZZA DELIVERED QUICKLY (PDQ)

The project work is soon to begin, and you are conferring with your team members to decide on reporting requirements and frequency. Take into account the stakeholders in this project and what their needs might be. Refer back to the case study background statement in this book's "Introduction" for the input you will need to answer the following questions:

3. Who are the people that you need to hear from to determine whether they are satisfied with your progress on this project?

4. How will you get information from your team and distribute it to the other stakeholders for this project?

CHAPTER 8

How to Close a TPM Project

*We judge ourselves by what we feel capable of doing,
while others judge us by what we have already done.*
— Henry Wadsworth Longfellow, American poet

We cannot afford to forget any experiences, even the most painful.
— Dag Hammerskjöld, Former Secretary General of the United Nations

---

CHAPTER LEARNING OBJECTIVES

After reading this chapter, you will be able to:

- Understand the steps needed to effectively close a project
- Develop a closing strategy
- Identify the components of project documentation
- Conduct a post-implementation audit
- Explain the significance of each post-implementation audit question

---

Closing a project is all too often a sigh of relief on the part of the development team and the client team. The punishment has finally ended, and everyone can return to their normal jobs. There are probably project responsibilities that are behind schedule and waiting for you to get started on them. Is that how you remember project closings? Or do you remember them as celebrations of success?

Using Tools, Templates, and Processes to Close a Project

By using the following tools, templates, and processes you can turn a project closing into an ordered and defined process:

- Acceptance test procedures (ATP)
- Implementation strategies
- Project documentation
- Post-implementation audit
- Final project report

Writing and Maintaining Client Acceptance Procedures

The worst time to negotiate the completion of a project is at its eleventh hour. If you wait until then, you are at the mercy of the client. A company that I worked for developed Internet and intranet solutions for their clients using fixed bid contracts. The company was very sloppy about scope change control and did not formally establish project completion criteria. As a result, the company was always facing last minute changes from the client. Profit margins were seriously eroded as a result. In fact, they had trapped themselves on more than one occasion and ended up spending more to complete projects than they received from their clients.

The message is clear. The process of writing and maintaining client acceptance test procedures begins during requirements gathering, is documented during project planning, is maintained during project execution, and is applied as the only criteria for moving to the project Closing Phase.

Closing a Project

Closing the project is routine once you have the client's approval of the deliverables. It involves the following six steps:

1. Getting client acceptance of deliverables
2. Ensuring that all deliverables are installed
3. Ensuring that the documentation is in place
4. Getting client sign-off on the final report

5. Conducting the post-implementation audit

6. Celebrating the success

This chapter describes each of these steps in more detail.

Getting Client Acceptance

The client decides when the project is done. It is your job as the project manager to demonstrate that the deliverables (whether products or services) meet client specifications. For small projects, this acceptance can be very informal and ceremonial, or it can be very formal, involving extensive acceptance testing against the client's performance specifications.

Ceremonial Acceptance

Ceremonial acceptance is an informal acceptance by the client. It does not have an accompanying sign-off of completion or acceptance. It simply happens. The following two situations fall under the heading of ceremonial acceptance:

- The first involves deadline dates at which the client must accept the project as complete, whether or not it meets the specifications. For example, if the project is to plan and conduct a conference, the conference will happen whether or not the project work has been satisfactorily completed.

- The second involves a project deliverable requiring little or no checking to determine whether specifications have been met — for example, planning and taking a vacation. A colleague of mine shared the following example with me. The project involved recommending or not recommending the renewal of a hosted IT service. There really was no client to satisfy — just a decision to be made. The project ended on a ceremonial note following the filing of the recommendation.

Formal Acceptance

Formal acceptance occurs in projects for which you and the client have written an acceptance test procedure (ATP). In many cases, especially for projects that involve computer applications development, writing an ATP may be a joint effort of the client and appropriate members of the project team. It typically is done very early in the life of the project. This ATP requires that the project team demonstrate compliance with every feature in the client's performance specification. A checklist is used and requires a feature-by-feature sign-off based on performance tests. These tests are conducted jointly and administered by the client and appropriate members of the project team.

NOTE   The ATP checklist is written in such a fashion that compliance is either demonstrated by the test or it is not demonstrated by the test. It must not be written in such a way that interpretation is needed to determine whether compliance has been demonstrated.

Installing Project Deliverables

The second step of closing a project is to go live with the deliverables. This commonly occurs in computer systems work. The installation can involve phases, cutovers, or some other rollout strategy. In other cases, it involves nothing more than flipping a switch. Either way, some event or activity turns things over to the client. This installation triggers the beginning of a number of close-out activities that mostly relate to documentation and report preparation. After installation is complete, the deliverables move to support and maintenance, and the project is officially closed.

There are four popular methods to install deliverables, and the subsections that follow discuss them.

Phased Approach

The phased approach decomposes the deliverable into meaningful chunks and implements the chunks in the appropriate sequence. This approach would be appropriate in cases where resource limitations prevent any other approach from being used.

Cut-Over Approach

The cut-over approach replaces the old deliverable with the new deliverable in one action. To use this approach, the testing of the new system must have been successfully completed in a test environment that is exactly the same as the production environment.

Parallel Approach

In the parallel approach, the new deliverables are installed while the old deliverables are still operational. Both the old and the new deliverables are simultaneously in production mode. In cases where the new system might not have been completely tested in an environment exactly like the production environment, this approach will make sense. It allows the new system to be compared with the old system on real live data.

By-Business-Unit Approach

In the by-business-unit approach, the new deliverables are installed in one business unit at a time, usually in the chronological order that the system is used. Like the phased approach, this approach is appropriate when resource constraints prohibit a full implementation at one time. Similar to the by-business-unit approach would be a geographic approach where the system is installed at one geographical location at a time. This facilitates geographic differences, too.

Documenting the Project

Documentation always seems to be the most difficult part of the project to complete. There is little glamour in writing documentation. That does not diminish its importance, however. There are at least five reasons why you need to write documentation. Those five reasons are described here.

Reference for Future Changes in Deliverables

Even though the project work is complete, there will most likely be further changes that warrant follow-up projects. By using the deliverables, the client will identify improvement opportunities, features to be added, and functions to be modified. The documentation of the project just completed is the foundation for the follow-up projects.

Historical Record for Estimating Duration and Cost on Future Projects, Activities, and Tasks

Completed projects are a terrific source of information for future projects, but only if the data and other documentation from them is archived so that it can be retrieved and used. Estimated and actual durations and costs for each activity on completed projects are particularly valuable for estimating these variables on future projects.

Training Resource for New Project Managers

History is a great teacher, and nowhere is that more significant than on completed projects. Such items as how the Work Breakdown Structure (WBS) was determined; how change requests were analyzed and decisions reached; problem identification, analysis, and resolution situations; and a variety of other experiences are invaluable lessons for the newly appointed project manager.

Input for Further Training and Development of the Project Team

As a reference, project documentation can help the project team deal with situations that arise in the current project. How a similar problem or change request was handled in the past is an excellent example, especially if the causes of the problem or change are included.

Input for Performance Evaluation by the Functional Managers of the Project Team Members

In many organizations, project documentation can be used as input to the performance evaluations of the project manager and team members.

WARNING Care must be exercised in using project documentation for performance evaluations. In some cases, a project was doomed to fail even though the team members' performance may have been exemplary. The reverse is also likely. The project was destined to be a success even though the team members' performance may have been less than expected.

Given all that documentation can do for you, to be most effective and useful, the documentation for a given project should include but not be limited to the following parts:

- Project Overview Statement (POS)
- Project proposal and backup data
- Original and revised project schedules
- Minutes of all project team meetings
- Copies of all status reports
- Design documents
- Copies of all change notices
- Copies of all written communications
- Outstanding issues reports
- Final report
- Sample deliverables (if appropriate)
- Client acceptance documents
- Post-implementation audit report

For a given project, the project manager has to determine what documentation is appropriate. Always refer back to value-added considerations. If the project has potential value for future projects, as many projects do, then include it in the documentation. Note also that the preceding list contains very little that does not arise naturally in the execution of the project. All that is added is the appointment of someone to maintain the project notebook. This job involves collecting the documents at the time of their creation and ensuring that they are in an easily retrievable form (electronic is a must).

Conducting the Post-Implementation Audit

The post-implementation audit is an evaluation of the project's goals and activity achievement as measured against the project plan, budget, time deadlines, quality of deliverables, specifications, and client satisfaction. The log of the project activities serves as baseline data for this audit. The following six important questions should be answered:

1. Was the project goal achieved?

    (a) Does it do what the project team said it would do?

    (b) Does it do what the client said it would do?

    The project was justified based on a goal to be achieved. That goal either was or wasn't achieved, and the reasons for this must be provided in the audit. This can be addressed from two different perspectives. The provider may have suggested a solution for which certain results were promised. Did that happen? Conversely, the requestor may have promised that if the provider would only provide, say, a new or improved system, then certain results would occur. Did that happen?

2. Was the project work done on time, within budget, and according to specification?

    Recall from the scope triangle discussed in Chapter 1 that the constraints on a project are time, cost, and the client's specification, as well as resource availability and quality. Here you are concerned with whether the specification was met within the budgeted time and cost constraints.

3. Was the client satisfied with the project results?

    It is possible that the answers to the first two questions are yes, but the answer to this question is no. How can that happen? Simple: the Conditions of Satisfaction (COS) changed, but no one was aware that they had. The project manager did not check with the client to see whether the needs had changed, or the client did not inform the project manager that such changes had occurred.

NOTE I remind you again that it is absolutely essential that the COS be reviewed at every major event in the life of the project, including changes in team membership, especially a new project manager, and changes in the sponsor. Reorganization of the company, acquisitions, and mergers are other reasons to recheck the COS.

4. Was business value realized? (Check the success criteria.)

   The success criteria were the basis on which the business case for the project was built and were the primary reason why the project was approved. Did you realize that promised value? When the success criteria measure improvement in profit, market share, or other bottom-line parameters, you may not be able to answer this question until some time after the project is closed.

5. What lessons were learned about your project management methodology?

   Companies that have or are developing a project management methodology will want to use completed projects to assess how well the methodology is working. Different parts of the methodology may work well for certain types of projects or in certain situations, and these should be noted in the audit. These lessons will be valuable in tweaking the methodology or simply noting how to apply the methodology when a given situation arises. This part of the audit might also consider how well the team used the methodology, which is related to, yet different from, how well the methodology worked.

6. What worked? What didn't?

   The answers to these questions are helpful hints and suggestions for future project managers and teams. The experiences of past project teams are real "diamonds in the rough" — you will want to pass them on to future teams.

The post-implementation audit is seldom done, which is unfortunate because it has great value for all stakeholders. Some of the reasons for skipping the audit include the following:

Managers don't want to know — They reason that the project is done and what difference does it make whether things happened the way you said they would? It is time to move on.

Managers don't want to pay the cost — The pressures on the budget (both time and money) are such that managers would rather spend resources on the next project than on those already completed.

It's not a high priority — Other projects are waiting to have work done on them, and completed projects don't rate very high on the priority list.

There's too much other billable work to do — Post-implementation audits are not billable work, and people have billable work on other projects to do.

NOTE I can't stress enough the importance of the post-implementation audit, which contains so much valuable information that can be extracted and used in other projects. Organizations have such a difficult time deploying and improving their project management process and practice that it would be a shame to pass up the greatest source of information to help that effort. I won't mislead you, though — actually doing the post-implementation audit is difficult because of all the other tasks waiting for your attention, not the least of which is probably a project that is already behind schedule.

Writing the Final Report

The final project report acts as the memory or history of the project. It is the file that others can check to study the progress and impediments of the project. Many formats can be used for a final report, but the content should include comments relative to the following points:

Overall success of the project — Taking into account all of the measures of success that you used, can you consider this project successful?

Organization of the project — Hindsight is always perfect, but now that you are finished with the project, did you organize it in the best way possible? If not, what might that organization have looked like?

Techniques used to get results — By referring to a project summary list, what specific things did you do that helped to get the results? Start this list at the beginning of the project.

Project strengths and weaknesses — What features, practices, and processes proved to be strengths or weaknesses? Do you have any advice to pass on to future project teams regarding these strengths and/or weaknesses? Start this list at the beginning of the project.

Project team recommendations — Throughout the life of the project, there will have been a number of insights and suggestions. This is the place to record them for posterity. Start this list at the beginning of the project.

The client should participate in the closing activities and in the post-implementation audit. Get their unbiased input and have them attest to its accuracy and validity by signing the final report.

Celebrating Success

There must be some recognition for the project team at the end of the project. This can be as simple as individual thank you notes, a commemorative mug, a T-shirt, a pizza party, or tickets to a ball game; or it can be something more formal, such as bonuses. I recall that when Release 3 of the spreadsheet package Lotus 1-2-3 was delivered, each member of the project team was presented with a videotape showing the team at work during the last week of the project. That was certainly a nice touch and one that will long be remembered by every member of the team.

Even though the team may have started out as a "herd of cats," the project they have just completed has honed them into a real team. Bonding has taken place, new friendships have formed, and mentor relationships have been established. The individual team members have grown professionally through their association with one another, and now it is time to move on to the next project. This can be a very traumatic experience for them, and they deserve closure. That is what celebrating success is all about. My loud and continual message to the senior management team is this: Don't pass up an opportunity to show the team your appreciation. This simple act on the part of senior management promotes loyalty, motivation, and commitment in their professional staff.

Putting It All Together

You have now completed all five phases of the project life cycle. I can only hope that the practical tools and techniques I have shared will provide a lasting and valuable store of resources for you to use as you grow in this exciting profession. Whether you are a full-time project manager, an occasional project manager, an experienced project manager, or a wannabe project manager, you should have found value in these pages.

I haven't finished adding to your store of project management tools and processes, however. There is much more to come in Part II of this book, which you start next.

Good luck as you continue on your journey to expand your mind with the many possibilities of effective project management!

Discussion Questions

1. I have advocated the use of a checklist as the acceptance test procedure for establishing that the project is finished. What other type of acceptance test procedure might you suggest? Be specific.

2. Can you suggest a cost/benefit approach to selling management on the value of the post-implementation audit? Be specific.

3. The post-implementation audit is vitally important in improving the practice and process of project management, yet it is always so difficult to get senior management and the client to allocate the time to authorize and participate in these audits. Knowing that, what would you as project manager do to help alleviate this problem?

Establishing Project Management Life Cycles and Strategies

The purpose of Part I was to define projects, project management, and the Process Groups. The five Process Groups and nine Knowledge Areas are the building blocks of every project management life cycle (PMLC). Chapters 4 through 8 presented the robust use of these building blocks. That completes the foundation for our further exploration of PMLC models.

Part II identifies five different PMLCs and discusses their characteristics, strategies for using them, when to use them, and how to adapt the tools, templates, and processes to each life cycle model.

Overview of Part II

Part II consists of four chapters.

Chapter 9: Complexity and Uncertainty in the Project Management Landscape

The project management landscape is defined based on two characteristics: goal and solution. They are either clearly defined or not clearly defined. That generates a two-by-two matrix into which all projects fit. In Chapter 2 these four categories were illustrated in Figure 2-1. These four categories are the landscape over which the five PMLC models that were defined in Chapter 2 are distributed. In Part II we will examine each of these five PMLC models and discuss their use in managing the complexity and uncertainty that is characteristic of the projects that populate the four-quadrant project landscape.

Chapter 10: Traditional Project Management

The simplest part of the landscape arises in cases where both the goal and the solution are clearly defined. These are what I call Linear and Incremental life cycles. Data gathered from more than 10,000 project managers around the world suggests that approximately 20 percent of all projects fall in this part of the landscape.

Chapter 11: Agile Project Management

Next in complexity are projects for which the goal is clearly defined but the solution is not. These are what I call Iterative and Adaptive life cycles. The testimonial data that I have collected from across the globe suggests that approximately 70 percent of all projects fall in this part of the landscape.

Chapter 12: Extreme Project Management

The most complex projects are those for which neither the goal nor the solution are clearly documented. These are what I call Extreme projects. Their complexity comes from the fact that through iteration it is hoped that the goal and the solution will converge to something that has business value. Pure research and development (R&D) projects would be of that type. The same testimonial data referred to above suggests that approximately 10 percent of all projects fall in this part of the landscape.

There is a fourth group of projects in the landscape. Those are the projects for which a solution is clear but the goal is not. Although at first this may seem like a nonsense category, it really isn't. Again pure R&D projects are often of this type. Consider the case where a new technology has been introduced and the question becomes, "Is there any practical use for this technology in our business?" Wal-Mart's investigation of Radio Frequency Identification (RFID) technology is one such example. For the purposes of this book, I am calling these projects extreme in reverse, or "Emertxe" projects.

CHAPTER 9

Complexity and Uncertainty in the Project Management Landscape

The design, adaptation, and deployment of project management life cycles and models are based on the changing characteristics of the project and are the guiding principles behind practicing effective project management.

Don't impose process and procedure that stifles team and individual creativity! Rather create and support an environment that encourages that behavior.

— Robert K. Wysocki, Ph.D., President, Enterprise Information Insights, Inc.

CHAPTER LEARNING OBJECTIVES

After reading this chapter, you will be able to:

- **Know how complexity and uncertainty affect the project landscape**

- **Incorporate requirements, flexibility, adaptability, change, risk, team cohesiveness, communications, client involvement, specifications, and business value into how you will choose and use a project management life cycle (PMLC) model**

- **Use the Requirements Breakdown Structure (RBS) as the key ingredient of the best-fit decision model**

You have now completed the foundation of what I will call the traditional project management process. It was once the only way projects were managed. Then along came complexity, uncertainty, and a market that demanded speed and agility. The agile age was born with the publication of the Agile Manifesto in 1991, and we have since entered the twenty-first century with a huge collection of agile project management approaches. Most of them were for software development projects and little else. In the remaining chapters of Part II I will organize all of these approaches into the landscape defined in Chapter 2 and discuss when to use them, their strengths and weaknesses, and finally how to adapt them to the variety of project management challenges that you will encounter. The material from Part I will be adapted to these unique and challenging high-risk situations. It is a project world filled with complexity and uncertainty, as described in this chapter.

Understanding the Complexity/Uncertainty Domain of Projects

The four-quadrant project landscape (Figure 9-1) is used first to categorize the project to a quadrant, and within that quadrant to select a best-fit PMLC model. But even having made that categorization and selected a best-fit PMLC model based on goal and solution clarity, you are not quite finished. Contemporary projects have become more uncertain, and along with this increased uncertainty is increased complexity. Uncertainty is the result of changing market conditions that require high-speed and high-change responses to produce a solution in order to be competitive. Complexity is the result of a solution that has eluded detection and will be difficult to find. That imposes a challenge on the project manager to be able to respond appropriately. Hence the complexity of project management increases as well. Uncertainty and complexity are positively correlated.

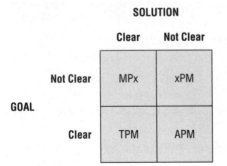

Figure 9-1: The Project Landscape

As you move through the quadrants from clarity to lack of clarity and from low uncertainty to high uncertainty, the project management processes you use must track with the needs of the project. Here's a general word of advice: As you move through the quadrants, remember that "lots is bad, less is better, and least is best." In other words, don't burden yourself and your team with needless planning and documentation that will just hinder their efforts. As my colleague Jim Highsmith said in his book *Agile Project Management: Creating Innovative Products* (Addison-Wesley Professional, 2004): "The idea of enough structure, but not too much, drives agile managers to continually ask the question, 'How little structure can I get away with?' Too much structure stifles creativity. Too little structure breeds inefficiency."

TPM projects are plan-driven, process-heavy, and documentation-heavy and hence are very structured projects. As you move to Quadrants 2 and 3, project heaviness gives way to lightness. Plan-driven gives way to value-driven, rigid process gives way to adaptive process, and documentation is largely replaced by tacit knowledge that is shared among the team members. These are some of the characteristics of the many approaches that fall in the APM, xPM, and MPx quadrants. You will learn how to choose and adapt several models and approaches that fall under the umbrella of agile.

This notion of heavy versus light is interesting. I've always felt that any project manager must see value in a project management process before they are willing to use it. Burdening them with what they will perceive as a lot of non-value-added work is counterproductive, to be avoided and will probably not be used by them in the spirit in which it was intended. This becomes more significant as the type of project you are managing falls in the PM, xPM, or MPx category. Furthermore, project managers will resist, and you will get a token effort at compliance. My overall philosophy is that the less non-value-added time and work that you encumber your project managers with the better off you will be. Replacing non-value-added work to make more room for value-added work will increase the likelihood of project success. Time is a precious (and scarce) resource for every project. You need to resist the temptation to add work that doesn't directly contribute to the final deliverables. Up to a point project managers should determine what is a value add to their project processes and documentation. Make it their responsibility to decide what to use, when to use it, and how to use it. A good manager makes it possible for his or her project managers to be successful and then stays out of their way. I'll get off my soapbox for now and get back to the discussion of project complexity and uncertainty.

DEFINITION: NON-VALUE-ADDED WORK Non-value-added work involves the consumption of resources (usually people or time) on activities that do not add business value to the final product or process.

Each quadrant of the project landscape has different profiles when it comes to risk, team, communications, client involvement, specification, change, business value, and documentation. This section examines the changing profile of each domain as a project moves from quadrant to quadrant.

Complexity and uncertainty are positively correlated with one another. As projects become more complex, they become more uncertain.

In the TPM models, you know where you are going and you know precisely how you are going to get there. The definition of where you are going is described in the RBS and how you are going to get there is described in the WBS. Your plan reflects all of the work, the schedule, and the resources that will get you there. There's no goal or solution complexity here. As soon as you move away from a clearly specified solution, you leave the comfort of the TPM world and are in the APM world, which is no longer as kind to you. The minute you have uncertainty anywhere in the project, its complexity goes up. You have to devise a plan to fill in the missing pieces. There will be some added risk — you might not find the missing piece, or when you do, you find that it doesn't fit in with what you already have built. Go back two steps, undo some previous work, and do the required rework. The plan changes. The schedule changes. A lot of the effort spent earlier on developing a detailed plan has gone to waste. By circumstance, it has become non-value-added work. If you had only known.

As less and less of the solution is known, the realities of non-value-added work become more and more of a factor. Time has been wasted. APM models are better equipped than TPM models to handle this uncertainty and the complexity that results from it. The models are built on the assumption that the solution has to be discovered. Planning becomes less of a one-time task done at the outset and more of a just-in-time task done as late as possible. There is less and less reliance on a plan and more reliance on the tacit knowledge of the team. That doesn't reduce the complexity, but it does accommodate it. So even though complexity increases across the TPM to APM to xPM to MPx landscape, you have a way to deal with it for the betterment of your client and your sanity as a project manager.

Requirements

The first place that you encounter complexity is in the RBS. As project complexity increases, the likelihood of nailing the complete definition of requirements decreases. To all observations it might look like you have defined the necessary and sufficient set of requirements that when built into the solution will result in delivering expected business value. But due to the complex interactions of the requirements that value is not realized. Perhaps a missing requirement will surface. At a more fundamental level maybe project scope needs to expand to include the additional requirements needed to achieve expected business value. In a complex software development project, the extent of the number of requirements can be staggering. Some may in fact conflict with one another. Some may be redundant when it comes to contributing to expected business value. Some will be missing. Many of these may not become obvious until well into the design, development, and even integration testing tasks.

I recall a project to develop a wage and salary administration system. The system I envisioned was way ahead of its time and would strain the available technologies and software development tools. I was the senior budget officer for the organization, business analyst, and client for the project and was responsible for facilitating the process to gather and document requirements. I was familiar with all of the conventional processes for gathering requirements and felt that I had done an exemplary job. The resulting RBS and WBS was a 70-page listing of more than 1400 functions and features. Looking back on that project I don't see how anyone could absorb a 70-page document and conclude that the WBS was complete. We assumed it was only to find out later that it wasn't.

Flexibility

As the project complexity increases, so does the need for process flexibility. Increased complexity brings with it the need to be creative and adaptive. Neither is comfortable in the company of rigid processes. APM projects are easily compromised by being deluged with process, procedure, documentation, and meetings. Many of these are unrelated to a results-driven approach. They are the relics of plan-driven approaches. Along with the need for increased flexibility in APM and xPM projects is the need for increased adaptability. Companies that are undergoing a change of approach that recognizes the need to support not just TPM projects but also APM projects are faced with a significant and different cultural and business change. For one thing, the business rules and rules of the project engagement will radically change. Expect resistance.

Flexibility here refers to the project management process. If you are using a one-size-fits-all approach, you have no flexibility. The process is the process is the process. This is not a very comforting situation if the process gets in the way of commonsense behaviors and compromises your ability to deliver value to your client. Wouldn't you rather be following a strategy that allows you to adapt to the changing situations rather than being bound to one that just gets in the way?

TPM projects generally follow a fixed methodology. The plan is developed along with a schedule of deliverables and other milestone events. A formal change management process is part of the game plan. Progress against the planned schedule is tracked, and corrective actions are put in place to restore control over schedule and budget. A nice neat package isn't it? All is well until the process gets in the way of product development. For example, if the business situation and priorities change and result in a flurry of scope change requests to accommodate the new business climate, an inordinate amount of time will then be spent processing change requests at the expense of value-added work. The schedule slips beyond the point of recovery. The project plan, having changed several times, has become a contrived mess. Whatever integrity there was in the initial plan and schedule is now lost among the changes.

APM is altogether different. APM, like all project management, is really nothing more than organized common sense. So when the process you are using gets in the way, you adapt. The process is changed in order to maintain focus on doing what makes sense to protect the creation of business value. Unlike TPM processes, APM processes expect and embrace change as a way to find a better solution and as a way to maximize business value within time and budget constraints. That means choosing and continually changing the PMLC model to increase the business value that will result from the project. Realize that to some extent scope is a variable in these types of PMLC models.

xPM projects are even more dependent upon flexible approaches. Learning and discovery take place throughout the project, and the team and client must adjust on a moment's notice how they are approaching the project.

Adaptability

The less certain you are of project requirements, functionality, and features, the more need you will have to be adaptable with respect to process and procedure. Adaptability is directly related to the extent to which the organization empowers your team to act. The ability of your team to adapt increases as empowerment becomes more pervasive. To enable your team members to be productive, senior managers need to stay out of their way as much as possible. One way to stay out of their way is to clearly define and agree with them about what they are to do and by when, but be careful not to overstep your role as an effective project manager by telling your team members how to complete their assignments. Don't impose processes and procedures that stifle team and individual creativity! This would be the death knell of an APM project. Instead, create an environment that encourages creativity. Don't encumber the team members with the need to get sign-offs that have nothing to do with delivering business value. Pick your team members carefully and trust them to act in the best interest of the client.

Risk vs. the Complexity/Uncertainty Domain

Project risk increases as the project falls in TPM, APM, xPM, and MPx categories. In TPM, you clearly know the goal and the solution and can build a definitive plan for getting there. Templates that have had the test of time are often used and any risks associated with their use are minimal. The exposure to risks associated with product failure will be low. The focus can then shift to process failure. A list of candidate risk drivers would have been compiled over past similar projects. Their likelihood, impact, and the appropriate mitigation strategies will be known and documented. Like a good athlete, you will have anticipated what might happen and know how to act if it does.

As the project takes on the characteristics of APM, two forces come into play. First, the PMLC model becomes more flexible and lighter. The process burden lessens as more attention is placed on delivering business value than on conformance to a plan. At the same time, project risk increases. Risk increases in relation to the extent to which the solution is not known. On balance, that means more effort should be placed on risk management as the project moves through APM and looks more like an xPM project. There will be less experience with these risks because they are specific to the product being developed. In xPM and MPx projects, risk is the highest because you are in an R & D environment. Process risk is almost nonexistent because the ultimate in flexibility has been reached in this quadrant but product risk is extremely high. There will be numerous product failures because of the highly speculative nature of xPM and MPx projects, but that is okay. Those failures are expected to occur. Each product failure gets you that much closer to a feasible solution, if such a solution can be found within the operative time and budget constraints. At worst, those failures eliminate one or more paths of investigation and so narrow the range of possible solutions for future projects.

Team Cohesiveness vs. the Complexity/ Uncertainty Domain

In TPM, the successful team doesn't really have to be a team at all. You assemble a group of specialists and assign each to their respective tasks at the appropriate times. Period. Their physical location is not important. They can be geographically dispersed and still be successful. The plan is sacred, and the plan will guide the team through their tasks. It will tell them what they need to do, when they need to do it, and how they will know they have finished each task. So the TPM plan has to be pretty specific, clear, and complete. Each team member knows his or her own discipline and is brought to the team to apply that discipline to the set of specific tasks. When they have met their obligation, they often leave the team to return later if needed.

The situation quickly changes if the project is an APM, xPM, or MPx project. First of all, there is a gradual shift from a team of specialists to a team of generalists. The team becomes more self-organizing, self-sufficient, and self-directing as the project moves across the quadrants. TPM teams do not have to be co-located. Although co-location would make life a bit easier for the project manager, it is not a necessity.

It is highly recommended that APM, xPM, and MPx teams be co-located. Research has shown that co-location adds significantly to the likelihood of successful completion of the project. Not being co-located creates communication and coordination problems for the project manager. One of the first APM projects that I managed had a team of 35 professionals scattered across 11 time zones. We were still able to have daily 15-minute team meetings! Despite the communications obstacle, the project was successfully completed, but I have to admit that this project added considerably more management overhead for me than there would have been if the team was co-located.

Communications vs. the Complexity/Uncertainty Domain

The Standish Group surveys over the past decade or more have found that the lack of timely and clear people-to-people communications is the most frequent root cause for project failure. I am referring here to both written and verbal communications media. The following is the current prioritized list of the top 10 reasons for project failure as reported in the Standish Group CHAOS 2010 Report.

Projects fail because of:

1. Lack of user input
2. Incomplete requirements and specification
3. Changing requirements and specification
4. Lack of executive support
5. Technology incompetence
6. Lack of resources
7. Unrealistic expectations
8. Unclear objectives
9. Unrealistic time frames
10. New technology

The first three items on the list are related to people-to-people communications, either direct or indirect.

As a project increases in complexity and heightened uncertainty, communication requirements increase and change. When complexity and uncertainty are low, the predominant form of communications is one-way (written, for example). Status reports, change requests, meeting minutes, issues reporting, problem resolution, project plan updates, and other written reports are commonplace. Many of these are posted on the project's website for public consumption. As uncertainty and complexity increase, one-way communication has to give way to two-way communication, so written communications give way to meetings and other forums for verbal communication. Distributed team structures give way to co-located team structures to support the change in communications modes. The burden of plan-driven approaches is lightened, and the communications requirements of value-driven approaches take over.

Value-driven communications approaches are the derivatives of meaningful client involvement where discussions generate status updates and plans going forward. Because projects that are high in complexity and uncertainty depend on frequent change, there is a low tolerance of written communications. In these project situations, the preparation, distribution, reading, and responding to written communications is viewed as a heavy burden and just another example of non-value-added work. It is more for historical record keeping than it is for action items. It is to be avoided, and the energy should be spent on value-added work.

Client Involvement vs. the Complexity/ Uncertainty Domain

Consider for a moment a project where you were most certain of the goal and the solution. You would be willing to bet your first-born that you had nailed requirements and that they would not change. (Yes, that type of project may just be a pipe dream, but give me the benefit of the doubt for just a moment.) For such a project, you might ask: "Why do I need to have my client involved except for the ceremonial sign-offs at milestone events?" This is a fair question, and ideally you wouldn't need the client's involvement. How about a project at the other extreme, where the goal is very elusive and no solution would seem to be in sight? In such cases, the complete involvement of the client, as a team member perhaps, but at least as a subject matter expert (SME) would be indispensable. What I have been describing here are the extreme cases in the project landscape.

TPM projects are plan-driven and team-driven projects. Client involvement is usually limited to answering clarification questions as they arise and giving sign-offs and approvals at the appropriate stages of the project life cycle. It would be accurate to say that client involvement in TPM projects is reactive and passive. But all that changes as you move into APM projects. Clients must now take a more active role in APM projects than was their role in TPM projects. For xPM projects, meaningful client involvement is essential. In fact, the client should take on a proactive role. The project goes nowhere without that level of commitment from the client.

Finding the solution to a project is not an individual effort. In TPM, the project team under the leadership of the project manager is charged with implementing a known solution. In some cases, the client will be passively involved, but for the most part, it is the team that will solve the problem. The willingness of clients to even get passively involved will depend on how you have dealt with them so far in the project. They are clearly in a followership role. If you bothered to include them in the planning of the project, they may have some sympathy and help you out. But don't count on it. Beginning with APM and extending through xPM, there is more and more reliance on meaningful client involvement. Clients move from a followership role to a collaborative role and even to a leadership role. In your effort to maintain a client-focus and deliver business value, you are dealing with a business problem, not a technology problem. You have to find a business solution. Who is better equipped to help than clients? After all, you are dealing with their part of the business. Shouldn't they be the best source of help and partnership in finding the solution? You must do whatever it takes to leverage that expertise and insight. Client involvement is so critical that without it you have no chance of being successful with xPM projects.

Meaningful client involvement can be a daunting task for at least the three reasons cited in the following subsections.

The Client's Comfort Zone

Ever since the 1950s, project managers have trained clients to take up a passive role. We trained them well, and now we have to retrain them. In many instances, their role was more ceremonial than formal. They didn't understand what they were approving but had no recourse but to sign. The sign-off at milestone events was often a formality because the client didn't understand the techie-talk, was afraid not to sign-off because of the threat of further delays, and didn't know enough about development to know what kinds of questions to ask, when to ask them, and when to push back. Now we are asking them to step into a new role and become meaningfully engaged throughout the project life cycle. Many are not poised to take up that responsibility. That responsibility is ratcheted up a notch as the project moves further into the APM quadrant toward the xPM and MPx quadrants, where less is known about the situation. The project team is faced with a critical success factor of gaining meaningful client involvement throughout the PMLC. In an xPM project, the client's involvement is even more proactive and engaging. xPM projects require that the client take a co-leadership role with the project manager to keep the project moving forward and adjusted in the direction of increasing business value.

At the same time, the clients' comfort zone is growing. They have become smarter. It is not unusual to find clients who are now more willing to get technically involved. They go to conferences where presentations often include technical aspects. They now know how to push back. They know what it takes to build solutions. They've built some themselves using spreadsheet packages and other applications tools. That has two sides. These types of clients can be supportive, or they can be obstacles to progress.

Ownership by the Client

Establishing ownership by the client of APM and xPM projects' product and process is critical. I often ensure there is that ownership by organizing the project team around co-managers — one from the developer side and one from the client side. These two individuals are equally responsible for the success and failure of the project. That places a vested interest squarely on the shoulders of the client co-manager. This sounds really good on paper, but it is not easily done. I can hear my clients saying, "This is a technology project and I don't know anything about technology. How can I act in a managerial capacity?"

The answer is simple, and it goes something like this: "True, you don't have a grasp of the technology involved, but that is a minor point. Your real value to this endeavor is to keep the business focus constantly in front of the team. You can bring that dimension to the team far better than any of the technical people on the team. You will be an indispensable partner in every decision situation faced in this project." This ownership is so important that I have postponed starting client engagements because clients can't send a spokesperson to the planning meeting. When they do, you have to be careful that they don't send you a weak representative who just isn't busy at the time or who doesn't really understand the business context of the project. Maybe there was a reason that person wasn't busy.

Client Sign-Off

This has often been the most anxiety-filled task that you will ever ask of your clients. Some clients think that they are signing their lives away when they approve a document or a deliverable. You are going to have to dispel that perception. We all know that we live in a world of constant change, high speed, and high risk. Given that, how could anyone reasonably expect that what works today will work tomorrow? Today's needs may not even come up on the radar screen next week. On no project, no matter how certain you are that you have nailed the RBS, can you expect the RBS to remain static for the length of the project. It simply won't happen. That means you had better anticipate change as a way of life in most PMLC models.

Specification vs. the Complexity/Uncertainty Domain

What does this mean? Simply put, it advises you that the choice of PMLC model should be based on an understanding of the confidence you have that the specifications have been completely and clearly defined and documented and that scope change requests will not arise from any shortcomings in the specifications documents. As specification uncertainty increases, your best choices lie first in the Iterative models that populate the APM quadrant and then in the Adaptive models that populate the APM quadrant — those that allow the solution to become more specific and complete as the project commences or that allow you to discover the solution as the project commences. If you have very little confidence that you have clearly and completely documented the specifications, then your PMLC model takes on the flavor of the research and development models that populate the xPM and MPx quadrants.

The PMLC models that require a high level of specification certainty (Linear and Incremental) tend to be change-intolerant. Consider the situation where a significant change request comes early in the project life cycle. That could render much of the planning work obsolete. A large part of it will have to be done over. That contributes to the non-value-added work time of the PMLC model you have chosen. If changes like that are to be expected, a PMLC model that is more tolerant and supportive of change should have been chosen. The non-value-added work could have been greatly diminished or removed altogether.

If you look inside the specifications document, there is more detailed information that might help you decide on the best PMLC model. Specifications are composed of the RBS and WBS. These are often displayed in a hierarchical structure that was introduced in Chapter 4 and is reproduced here as Figure 9-2.

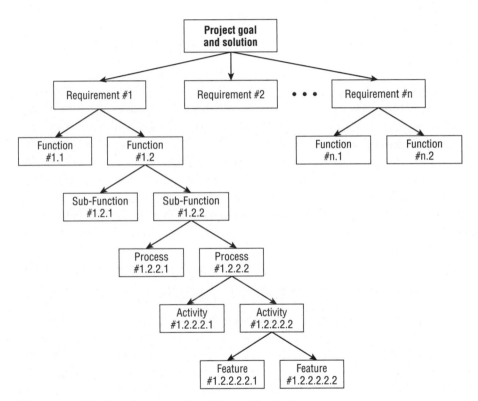

Figure 9-2: The Requirements Breakdown Structure

At the highest level are the requirements. These form a necessary and sufficient set for meeting the expected business value. The illustrated hierarchy is the complete hierarchy that even the most complex and comprehensive requirement might need in order to be clearly understood. In most cases only some subset of the hierarchy will be needed for a requirement. Remember that your objective in defining this hierarchy is so that the client and the project team will clearly understand what the requirement entails. Use your common sense in deciding what that decomposition should look like. There are no objective criteria for deciding on that decomposition.

Uncertainty at the requirements level has more impact on your choice of PMLC model than does uncertainty at the functionality level, which has more impact than uncertainty at the feature level. And despite all of your efforts to the contrary, you can still have changes on any one of these three fronts that could have significant impact on your decisions and best efforts. That's just some of the surprises you will encounter in your daily life as a project manager.

Gauging the integrity of the specification document will always be a subjective assessment. Based on that subjective assessment, you choose a PMLC model, make the appropriate adaptations, and hope you made a good decision. Time will tell.

Change vs. the Complexity/Uncertainty Domain

As complexity increases, so does the need to receive and process change requests. A plan-driven project management approach is not designed to effectively respond to change. Change upsets the order of things as some of the project plan is rendered obsolete and must be redone. Resource schedules are compromised and may have to be renegotiated at some cost. The more that change has to be dealt with, the more time is spent processing and evaluating those changes. That time is forever lost to the project. It should have been spent on value-added work. Instead it was spent processing change requests.

You spent so much time developing your project plan for your TPM project that the last thing you want is to have to change it. But that is the reality in TPM projects. Scope change always seems to add more work. Did you ever receive a scope change request from your client that asked you to take something out? Not too likely. The reality is that the client discovers something else they should have asked for in the solution. They didn't realize that or know that at the beginning of the project. That leads to more work, not less. The decision to use TPM models is clear. Use TPM models when specifications are as stable as can be. The architects of the APM and xPM models knew how stability of specifications affected choice of PMLC model and so designed approaches that expected change and were ready to accommodate it. You'll see how WBS stability and completeness impacts PMLC model choice in more detail in Chapters 10, 11, and 12.

The less you know about requirements, functionality, and features, the more you have to expect change. In TPM, you assume that you and the client know everything there is to know about requirements, functionality, and features for this project as can be known. You assume that the RBS and WBS are complete. The assumption then is that there will be little or no internal forces for change during the development project. Externally, however, that is not the case. Actions of competitors, market forces, and technological advances may cause change, but that is true for every project and can only be expected. The best the enterprise can do is maintain a position of flexibility in the face of such unpredictable but certain events.

APM is a different story altogether. Any change in the position of the project in this quadrant will come about through the normal learning process that takes place in any project. When the client has the opportunity to examine and experiment with a partial solution, they will invariably come back to the developers with suggestions for other requirements, functionality, and features that should be part of the solution. These suggestions can be put into one of two categories: either they are *wants* or they are *needs*.

Wants may be little more than the result of a steak appetite on a baloney budget. It is up to the project manager to help clients defend their wants as true needs and hence build the business case for integrating the changes into the solution. If clients fail to do that, their suggestions should be relegated to a wish list. Wish lists are seldom revisited. On the other hand, if a client demonstrates the true value of what they want, it can be transferred to a true need. It is up to the project manager to accommodate that new requirement, functionality, or feature into the solution set. It may have to be prioritized in the list of all needs not yet integrated into the solution. The COS session is the best place to make these decisions. Often you should back this up with a Root Cause Analysis (see Chapter 15). For more details on distinguishing the difference between wants and needs see *The New Rational Manager* by Charles H. Kepner and Benjamin B. Tregoe (Kepner-Tregoe Publishers, 1997).

In xPM projects, there is yet a further reliance on change to affect a good business-valued product. In fact, xPM projects require change in order to have any chance at finding a successful solution. Change is the only vehicle that will lead to a solution.

The bottom line here is that as the project type moves across the landscape, the scope change management process changes as well. Chapters 10, 11, and 12 track the changes in the scope change management process for you.

Business Value vs. the Complexity/Uncertainty Domain

This domain would seem to be trivial. After all, aren't all projects designed to deliver business value? These projects were commissioned based on the business value they would return to the enterprise. This is all true. However, TPM projects focus on meeting the plan-driven parameters: time, cost, and scope. When the project was originally proposed, the business climate was such that the proposed solution was the best that could be had. In a static world, that condition would hold. Unfortunately the business world is not static, and the needs of the client aren't either. The bottom line is this: what will deliver business value is a moving target. TPM PMLC models aren't equipped with the right stuff to assure the delivery of business value. TPM PMLC models deliver to specification within cost and time constraints.

It follows then that TPM projects deliver the least business value and that business value increases as you move from TPM to APM to xPM. At the same time, risk also increases, which means that higher-valued projects are expected in order to be commissionable as you move across the quadrants. Remember that the expected business value of a project is the product of (1 – risk) and value. Here, risk is expressed as the probability of failure, and the probability of success is therefore (1 – risk). So if you were able to repeat this project a number of times, the average business value you would realize is the product of (1 – risk) and value.

What does this mean? Simply put, whatever PMLC model you adopt for the project, it must be one that allows redirection as business conditions change. The more uncertainty that is present in the development project, the more need there is to be able to redirect the project to take advantage of changing conditions and opportunities.

As projects move through TPM, APM, and xPM, they become more client-facing. The focus changes from conformance to plan to delivery of business value. The TPM models focus on conformance to plan. If they also happen to deliver maximum business value, it would be more the result of the inevitable statistical probability that sometimes things just turn out well than the result of a clairvoyant project plan. The focus on delivery of business value is apparent in all of the APM and xPM project management approaches. It is designed into their PMLC models.

Putting It All Together

The definition of the project landscape is mine and mine alone. I like simplicity and intuitiveness, and my definition provides exactly that. It is also a definition that encompasses every project that ever existed and ever will exist, so there is no reason to ever change it! That means it can be used as a foundation for all further discussion about PMLC models. There is a certain academic soundness and theoretical base to that approach. In fact, it is the beginnings of a project management discipline. At the same time, the definition has a very simple and practical application. That base will be the foundation on which all best-fit project management approach decisions can be made. As you will see in the chapters that follow, I will be able to exploit that base from both a conceptual and applications perspective.

Using the project landscape as the foundation for managing projects, I have defined five PMLC models at the Process Group level of detail. The definitions give a clear and intuitive picture of how project management approaches can vary as the degree of uncertainty changes. Within each PMLC model, there will be a number of specific instantiations of the model. You will explore each of these in Chapters 10, 11, and 12.

Discussion Questions

1. Suppose two projects have the same expected business value. Project A has a very high estimated business value along with a high probability of failure. Project B has a much lower estimated business value along with a low probability of failure. If you could do only one of the projects, which one would you choose and under what conditions?

2. Planning APM, xPM, and MPx projects is done just-in-time, rather than at the beginning of the project as in TPM projects. How would you defend the statement that TPM projects take longer than any other project in the landscape?

3. How might your approach to risk management change as you move from the less risky TPM projects to the riskier APM, xPM, and MPx projects?

4. What might you do to increase meaningful client involvement?

5. Change is the bane of the TPM project manager and is a necessity for the APM project manager. Is the client likely to be confused about the role of change, and what would you do to mitigate that confusion?

CHAPTER 10

Traditional Project Management

Don't fall victim to forcing round projects into square project holes.
You are only courting failure. If your project isn't well-served by your
methodology, find and use a methodology that does fit the project.
— **Robert K. Wysocki, Ph.D., President, Enterprise Information Insights, Inc.**

CHAPTER LEARNING OBJECTIVES

After reading this chapter, you will be able to:

- **Appreciate and understand the history of traditional project management (TPM)**
- **Know when to use TPM**
- **Use and adapt the Linear project management life cycle (PMLC) model**
- **Explain the benefits and use of the Rapid Linear PMLC model**
- **Explain the benefits and use of the Feature-Driven Development (FDD) model**
- **Anticipate and resolve the potential problems from using a Rapid Linear PMLC model**
- **Explain the benefits of using an Incremental PMLC model**
- **Anticipate and resolve the potential problems of using an Incremental PMLC model**
- **Explain the difference between the critical path and the critical chain**
- **Identify resource constraints and know how to resolve them**
- **Use the critical chain approach to project management for single projects**

In this chapter, you learn at a very detailed level the kinds of projects that lend themselves to TPM approaches. These are the approaches that satisfy the management needs of projects whose goal and solution are clearly and completely documented. There are two different models in the traditional category — Linear and Incremental — and one variation within the Linear PMLC models — the Rapid Linear PMLC model. Critical chain analysis for resource-constrained approaches to building the project schedule is included.

What Is Traditional Project Management?

TPM is firmly rooted in the 1950s and has been around longer than any other approach to project management. In fact, I don't recall it even being called project management in those early days. Process Control System (PCS) was the label I recall. I think the name came from an old IBM program by the same name. In its most elementary form, PCS was nothing other than a sequence of phases such as define, plan, execute, and close with tasks identified within each phase. PCS depended heavily on crude programs that generated Gantt charts based on dependency relationships among tasks that the project manager defines from a functional specification, an earlier form of what we now call a requirements document. Estimates of duration allowed a schedule to be calculated and the critical path identified. These Linear approaches date back to the decades of the 1950s and 1960s. Until the early 1980s, this was the overwhelming choice of software developers. There were few alternatives at that time. Because of its longevity, it has become habit with many developers. Even though there are a number of alternatives today, developers don't give second thoughts to changing. They would rather force-fit the old when the new would be the better choice. Old habits die hard! That is unfortunate, because all of the developer's attempts to modify the Linear approach to accommodate software development projects that don't fit the conditions ultimately lead to failure or sadly disappointed clients.

Since the 1980s, the project management landscape has been radically changing. The introduction of the PC in 1981 ushered in the start of a wave of software applications to support the project manager. By the year 2000, there were more than 125 PC project management software applications on the commercial market and at least 25 mainframe packages. There is now a long list of Agile Project Management (APM) approaches and the software, documentation, and training to support them.

For the purposes of this book, I have classified the project management approaches into Traditional, Agile, and Extreme. In this chapter, I present my ideas on what constitutes TPM and how to adapt it for maximum benefit. In Chapters 11 and 12, I explore the same topics for APM and xPM.

Linear Project Management Life Cycle

The Linear PMLC model is the simplest and most intuitive of the five major models in the project management landscape. It assumes that you have as nearly perfect information about the project goal and solution as can reasonably be expected. The Linear PMLC model is based on that assumption and does not easily accommodate any deviations. Deviations such as scope change requests can cause major upheavals in the project schedule. Figure 10-1 provides a view at the Process Group level of the Linear PMLC model.

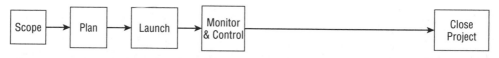

Figure 10-1: The Linear PMLC model

 The first thing to note about this model is that each Process Group must be complete before the next Process Group can begin. After a Process Group is complete, there is no returning at some later point to revise work completed in any earlier Process Group. The Linear PMLC model is definitely not a learning model, which has been the major criticism about it. All too often, the project manager will jury-rig the Linear PMLC just to accommodate learning. This means changing the project plan, which just leads to further problems like having to reschedule resources and the domino effect that has on resources already scheduled for work on other projects. The result is the addition of non-value-added work.

 The contemporary business world is one of constant change. The world isn't going to stand still just because you are managing a project. So projects that are not impacted by outside factors are the ones that are likely to succeed using a Linear PMLC model. Infrastructure projects number among those that can generally use a Linear PMLC model. Installing a network in a field office is an example of an infrastructure project. Projects that are repeated annually or more frequently can also do well with a Linear PMLC model.

Definition

The Linear PMLC model consists of the five Process Groups, each performed once in the sequence: Scoping ➢ Planning ➢ Launching ➢ Monitoring and Controlling ➢ Closing. The complete solution is not released until the Closing Process Group is executed. In the Rapid Linear PMLC model, the sequencing is followed through multiple swim lanes, with each swim lane defining a linear path. The Rapid Linear PMLC model has an integration process that the Linear PMLC model does not. The deliverables from each swim lane and the accompanying testing must be integrated in order to produce the final deliverables. This adds time to the schedule that is not present in the Linear PMLC model.

There is one feedback loop in the Linear PMLC model that is not shown in Figure 10-1, but it does not compromise the linearity of the overall model. That feedback loop describes how scope change or problem situations are received as part of the Monitoring and Controlling Process Group, and how they are processed and acted upon as part of the Planning Process Group. This added time is not accounted for in the original project plan. The result is usually an extension of the project completion date, and that has its own set of compromising problems.

Characteristics

To be used effectively, the Linear PMLC model works best with projects that have the following:

- Complete and clearly defined goal, solution, requirements, functions, and features
- Few expected scope change requests
- Routine and repetitive activities
- Use of established templates

Complete and Clearly Defined Goal, Solution, Requirements, Functions, and Features

You first have to have a clear understanding of what the project is trying to accomplish. That originally led to a statement of the project goal, which you and your client developed together. With the goal firmly established, you and the client were able to define exactly what had to be done to achieve the goal. The statement of what had to be done was detailed through a requirements gathering process that listed and documented the functions and features that spelled out the details of what had to be done. If you and the client were convinced of the completeness of the requirements document, then a Linear PMLC model was chosen for the project.

At the risk of being repetitive, I want to stress that the decision that requirements details were complete is a very subjective decision. You will never really know that requirements details were complete. On the other hand, you would probably know that some of the details were not complete or clear.

Few Expected Scope Change Requests

You are not likely to encounter a project that turns out to be totally free of any scope change requests. We live and work in a dynamic environment that is always changing. I have never encountered a change-free project in more than 45 years of managing projects. It would be presumptuous of you and your client to expect that your project will be safe from any changes. If you have any doubt, add a management reserve task to the end of the project schedule and explain to the client how it will be used. If you successfully manage the project according to the initial plan and there are no scope change requests that impact the schedule, the project will end on its originally planned date. If not, you will have a contingency to handle the changes. If you feel there will be numerous changes, but you meet all other conditions for using a Linear PMLC model, you should probably choose some other model. An Iterative PMLC model would be my most likely choice.

Routine and Repetitive Activities

Even though projects are unique, they can still be repeated. Their uniqueness comes from external factors acting on the project, your client, your team, and your organization. If you manage projects that are routine and repetitive, here are some suggestions to make life a bit easier for you and to increase the effectiveness of your management of those projects.

Build and Use a Library of Templates

This is perhaps the most valuable artifact you will generate from repetitive projects. I have helped my clients build and use templates that range from Work Breakdown Structures (WBSs) to parts of WBSs; from candidate risk events lists to detailed risk mitigation plans for a specific risk event, acceptance test criteria lists, vendor solicitation strategies, Request for Information (RFI), Request for Proposals (RFP) and Request for Quote (RFQ) outlines, project notebook outlines, curriculum design, meeting agendas, and the list goes on. If you have a WBS template, it is highly likely that the template also contains duration, resource requirements, project network diagrams, and the schedule to the WBS template. That gives you a start on a big chunk of the project plan. It requires some editing for the specifics of the project plan, but at least you have a start. And you have a start for which there is previous experience.

The next most valuable template will be risk management plans. Not only will the template identify risks for this type of project but also the mitigation plans and a historical record of outcomes.

Building a template library requires very little extra effort. You can start by simply saving in retrievable form any of the documents just mentioned that are produced as part of normal project activities. For some future project, retrieve the document and modify it for use on the current project. Add the modified document to your template library. In time you will build a variety of examples of that type of document. These become your templates. I have found with my clients that a template library has saved them time and reduces mistakes. They are also great training aids. Your Project Management Office (PMO) may already maintain a template library. If it doesn't, suggest that it start one.

But there is a caution here that you need to be aware of. Too many project managers look for silver bullet solutions, and templates can be misused. The degree of fit of a template to a project or partial project must be examined carefully. Expect to modify the template rather than use it off the shelf.

Keep and Post the History of Lessons Learned

This sounds great, but it rarely happens to any benefit. Several reasons are given for not documenting lessons learned on a project, including the following:

- Post-implementation audits are not done.
- Takes too much time to document lessons learned.
- No way to classify lessons for easy retrieval.
- No one is assigned the responsibility.
- The lessons won't apply to my projects.
- Lessons learned are not seen as useful.
- To use lessons learned would reflect badly on my reputation.
- Unbiased information is not forthcoming.
- Teams won't share mistakes and dirty laundry.

Lessons learned are most successful if posted at the time of their occurrence. Waiting until the project is over before these lessons are documented and posted is usually a waste of time.

Lessons learned can provide a powerful development opportunity. Many project managers have tried to collect and post lessons learned on a project for all to take advantage of, but few have succeeded. If you are going to try — and I strongly advise that you do — make sure you have an effective way of neutralizing the excuses listed here.

Keep a History of Estimated and Actual Task Duration

This can be a very simple history or a very complex one. It all depends on its importance to your project management practices. Most organizations would point to their inability to accurately estimate as a major weakness. They need all the help they can get, and I would suggest that their estimation history is a good resource. Here are a few ways I have helped my clients define, create, and maintain their history.

Recall that the first method that most individuals will use to estimate task duration is recollection of having done a similar task in the past and using their own experiences with similar tasks to estimate the duration of the task at hand. That's okay if you have the experience, but if you don't, your next approach will be to draw on the experiences of others. One way to do that is to refer to a recorded history of similar tasks. The trick is to identify and measure the variables that define similar tasks and index the estimates based on those variables. For the task at hand, you will need to know the value of its variables and retrieve the recorded history using that task profile. Some of the variables that you might use to define this task profile are as follows:

- Task category
- Task type
- Estimated task duration
- Actual task duration
- Software environment
- Requested skill level of the person doing the task
- Actual skill level of the person doing the task
- Work environment profile (using a scale of 1 for excellent to 5 for very poor)

Collecting and maintaining such a history file is labor-intensive. You will invest in that labor if improving task duration estimation is critical to your organization. Here are three ways that my clients have used their task history:

- Display a sample of similar tasks and average the actual duration to get an estimate for the task at hand.
- Compile a list of tasks ranked by similarity and choose a duration that fits the history.
- Generate a multiple linear regression model to estimate task duration.

The first two methods are the quickest and easiest. The third is an automated solution and may not produce estimates that are any better than those produced using the first two methods.

Keep a History of Risks, Your Mitigation Plans, and the Results

Risk history, like task duration history, can be a very simple file. The indexing variables might be any or all of the following:

- Risk category
- Risk type
- Risk description
- Mitigation plan
- Actual risk event that occurred
- Result
- Resource person

The team member who is responsible for the risk log will also have the responsibility for maintaining the risk history file. The risk log provides all of the information you need to populate your risk history file. Your PMO might support a risk history service. If it doesn't, ask it to do so.

Use of Established Templates

If used properly, the template library can really cut down on planning time, significantly increase the quality of your project management experience, and decrease the risk of project failure. There are several benefits to using templates, including the following:

- Increases standard practices
- Provides learning modules for new project managers
- Establishes an archive of project artifacts
- Provides input for process and practice improvement programs

Increases Standard Practices

If the templates are seen as valuable, they can become the foundation on which practices are formed. Learning by way of example is supported. As the templates are used, the adopters will find ways to improve them and ultimately improve the processes they support.

Provides Learning Modules for New Project Managers

Templates can be integrated into the classroom and online curriculum as learning aids for training project managers. Because you are using actual templates from the projects in your organization, they will be of maximum benefit to those attending training. They will have immediate application on the job.

Establishes an Archive of Project Artifacts

Artifacts from actual projects provide help to project managers across all Process Groups. Project managers need a simple and intuitive way to access information from past projects and find what will be helpful to them in managing their current projects. The collection of artifacts will grow quickly. That will require a good indexing and retrieval system. One of my clients has established an intake function for submissions to the archives. No one can just add stuff. All proposed submissions must go through the intake function and be screened for acceptability and indexing before they are added.

Provides Input for Process and Practice Improvement Programs

Templates are looking glasses into the Process Groups. They reflect how clients, project managers, and project teams have applied the PMLC models. Some will have done so correctly, others not. So, one of the responsibilities of the person in charge of the archive intake function is to screen contributions for compliance.

Strengths

The strengths of the Linear PMLC model are as follows:

- The entire project is scheduled at the beginning of the project.
- Resource requirements are known from the start.
- The Linear PMLC model does not require the most skilled team members.
- Team members do not have to be co-located.

The Entire Project Is Scheduled at the Beginning of the Project

For those who don't like surprises, this is the ticket. The plan is complete. The project manager and every team member know what has to be done, who will do it, and when it must be complete. There are no surprises — well, you hope not too many, and not too serious ones at that.

Resource Requirements Are Known from the Start

Not only do you know what type of resource is needed but you also know when, for how long, and what that resource is required to do. For people resources you even know the name of the person who will be assigned to the project. That allows you to complete the project budget. You will know what everything will cost and when you need to encumber the funds.

Human resource management and planning can benefit from the Linear PMLC model. Because you know from the existing project plans what skills are needed, by when, and in what numbers, you can compare this against your inventory of skills and when they will be available. The gaps will give you information training and development needs. You have an opportunity to take corrective steps to remove those skill gaps through training or otherwise plan for contracting out your needs.

The career and professional development plans of your staff can also benefit. Knowing what project opportunities lay ahead and what the development needs of your staff are, you can begin to match up possible assignments. While you would like to think that your HR department is on top of this, I really have been disappointed. Most HR management I talk to want a complete solution for all staff and not just a partial solution for project teams. The PMO appears to be a better place for that type of planning and staff development to take place.

The Linear PMLC Model Does Not Require the Most Skilled Team Members

This is the real strength of the Linear PMLC model. Because the project plan is detailed and work packages have been written for some tasks, a person of intermediate skill can do the work with minimal or no supervision. This is a real plus.

Team Members Do Not Have to Be Co-Located

Again, because the project plan is complete, the person responsible for the task can proceed with the work wherever he or she happens to be located. Some added documentation may be required. Outsourcing and the use of offshore developers are also possible alternatives.

There are strategies that you might employ when the development team is located across several time zones. For example, I have done development in the United States and passed the code to Europe and Asia for testing. The following morning, the developers in the United States had tested code at their disposal. So while having a team distributed across several time zones has its management problems, there are also some advantages to this sort of scheduling.

Weaknesses

The weaknesses of the Linear PMLC model are as follows:

- Does not accommodate change very well
- Costs too much
- Takes too long before any deliverables are produced
- Requires complete and detailed plans
- Must follow a rigid sequence of processes
- Is not focused on client value

Does Not Accommodate Change Very Well

The problem is that nearly any scope change request that is approved will create problems with the schedule. The time of the team members who have to process the request and write the Project Impact Statement is time that has to be added to the schedule. That probably results in a delayed completion of the project. That is the lesser of the two problems. The more serious problem is the adjustment to the schedules of every task that was scheduled to occur after the scope change was added to the project schedule. Literally every team member's schedule will be affected. If those schedule changes are too severe, the request might be delayed until much later in the project. I'm sure you can see the potential for adding significant management time just to accommodate the change request.

Costs Too Much

The client won't see any of the deliverables until the 11th hour in the project schedule — when the acceptance test criteria are being checked for requirements satisfaction. Usually there will be problems with acceptance. More work will have to be done, but there is no money available for that work. By that time, most of the money will have been spent.

Takes Too Long before Any Deliverables Are Produced

As I just stated, the client doesn't see any of the deliverables until very late in the project. That leaves no time for change even if the money is available. The project deadline is rapidly approaching, and the team members are scheduled to move on to other project work. This is not a problem in simple projects but all of those have already been done. In more complex projects, any additional work that has to be done to gain client acceptance will take time that has not been planned for and will come at the end of the project. The team members' attention is already turned to their next assignment.

Requires Complete and Detailed Plans

Although this may sound strange, a complete plan may be a waste of time. Before you cast your first stone, let me explain. In my early years as a project manager, I fell into the trap of always requiring complete plans. Unfortunately I don't recall even one of those plans being executed without changes being made. Every change request that is approved requires a revision in the project plan from the point where the change is inserted to the end of the project.

Take a look at how much time is wasted doing all of this replanning. Suppose there are 10 approved change requests in a 12-month project. For the sake of simplicity, also suppose that each change request requires one work day per remaining project month to revise the complete project plan and reschedule the team members out to the end of the project. Each change request is approved at the end of a project month. Table 10-1 calculates the wasted planning time.

WOW! The work scheduled for the last two project months has been replanned and rescheduled 10 times, and you spent 20 project days doing that replanning! Further to the point, notice how much of the project work in the later months of the project isn't even done. Change requests may have rendered some of that work as not needed, yet you spent all that time replanning and rescheduling it.

Table 10-1: Replanning Time

CHANGE REQUEST #	PROJECT MONTH	REMAINING MONTHS	REPLANNING DAYS	CUMULATIVE REPLANNING DAYS
1	1	11	11	11
2	2	10	10	21
3	3	9	9	30
4	4	8	8	38
5	5	7	7	45
6	6	6	6	51
7	7	5	5	56
8	8	4	4	60
9	9	3	3	63
10	10	2	2	65

If that doesn't rattle you, how about taking a look at the percentage of team work time that was spent replanning and rescheduling? Suppose the team has five members who each work half time on the project. The project is 48 weeks long, and you have five people working at 50 percent of their time. So, you have 600 person days of resources to complete the project, and you just spent over 10 percent of those days doing replanning and rescheduling. Translate that into project days, and you have just added more than five weeks to the completion date of the project — all non-value-added work time! And you still have to add the work time necessary to deliver the changes.

I hope I have given you sufficient motivation to stop and think about the impact of change on your project plan and the importance of having good scope change controls in place. I don't want you to think that I'm advocating no scope change requests, which would make no sense whatsoever. However, I *am* advocating good scope control processes.

Must Follow a Rigid Sequence of Processes

You chose to use the Linear PMLC model, so you have to play by the rules. And the rules say no going back. Remember, you chose this model because you didn't expect to have to go back.

Is Not Focused on Client Value

The Linear PMLC model is driven by the need to get the project done on time, within the budget, and according to client specifications. Nowhere does it say that you have to deliver business value. If it should happen that the delivery according to client specification is the cause of business value, then you are okay. Unfortunately I have had many clients tell me that they got what they asked for, but it didn't do what they expected. Go back to the discussion of wants versus needs in Chapter 4, and you'll find an explanation for this.

When to Use a Linear PMLC Model

Projects that have been repeated several times are excellent candidates for a Linear PMLC model. Supposedly you built a library of templates for those repetitive projects. You will have encountered and put plans in place for every identifiable risk. There will be few, if any, surprises. Simple projects of short duration that fall entirely within a single department and use no resources outside of that department are also good candidates for the Linear PMLC model.

Variations to the Linear PMLC Model

Two variations of the Linear PMLC model are worth mentioning. Both are designed to compress the project into a narrower window of time in order to deliver the solution quicker and get product and service to the market or to the end user sooner. They are as follows:

- **Rapid Linear PMLC model** — This is a client-focused model that delivers incremental functionality with business value in parallel swim lanes.

- **Feature-Driven Development (FDD) Linear PMLC model** — This is not a client-facing model. Instead it delivers parts of the solution in parallel, technically cohesive increments referred to as feature sets.

These two variations are described in the following subsections.

The Rapid Linear PMLC Model

The Rapid Linear PMLC model occurs frequently in product development projects. Figure 10-2 is a graphical description of that variation. The purpose of this variation is to finish the project as quickly as possible so as to get the deliverables implemented sooner. Usually this is done in response to pressures from marketing for early entry product introductions.

The decision to use this variation must be made during execution of the Planning Process Group. Note that planning is done once in a Rapid Linear PMLC model. The planning goal is to partition the functions and features into independent swim lanes so that the dependencies within each swim lane are high (*maximum cohesion*) and the dependencies between swim lanes are minimal or nonexistent (*minimal coupling*). This allows each swim lane to proceed independently of all other swim lanes. That minimizes the additional management time brought about by the parallel dependent swim lanes. If a cross–swim lane dependency exists and something goes wrong in one swim lane, it can adversely impact other swim lanes that are dependent upon it.

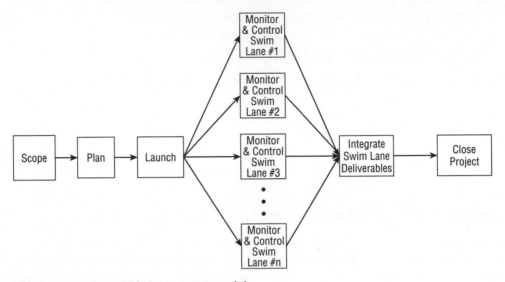

Figure 10-2: The Rapid Linear PMLC model

One of the major obstacles to minimal cohesion is resource contention across the dependent swim lanes. Using team members across swim lanes is another area where caution is needed. If one swim lane is delayed, it can delay the availability of a team member to begin work in another swim lane. Don't expect to avoid this resource contention problem altogether in the Rapid PMLC model. It won't happen. You just have to be aware of the risks and do what you can to minimize the impact.

Feature-Driven Development Linear PMLC Model

Feature-Driven Development (FDD) first appeared in *Java Modeling in Color with UML* by Peter Coad, Eric Lefebvre, and Jeff DeLuca (Prentice Hall PTR, 1999). A more comprehensive treatment of FDD can be found in *A Practical Guide to Feature-Driven Development* by Stephen R. Palmer and John M. Felsing (Prentice Hall PTR, 2002).

The high-level process view of the FDD Linear PMLC model is shown in Figure 10-3. Note that planning is done only once, so the solution must be known in order to use FDD effectively. A model of the solution is developed and used to create the functional WBS. The functional WBS contains a very detailed list of features. The features list is grouped into similar features and prioritized for development. FDD iterates on the design and building of the groups of features.

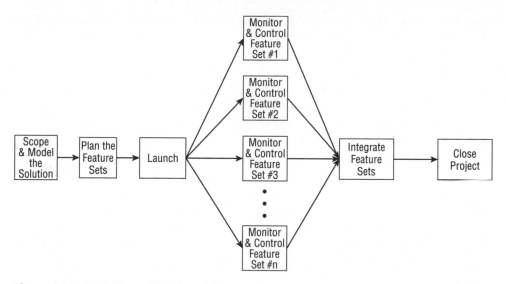

Figure 10-3: FDD Linear PMLC model

Much like the Rapid Development PMLC model, the FDD Linear PMLC model prioritizes parts of the solution. But this time it is features-driven. Just as in the Rapid Development PMLC model, you have multiple design/build swim lanes running concurrently in the FDD Linear PMLC model. It differs from the Rapid Linear PMLC model in that the releases consist of groups of features that have a technical relationship to one another rather than a functional relationship to one another. Several feature sets might have to be completed before the client is satisfied that the cumulative features list has enough business value to be released. FDD models might use concurrent swim lanes, sequential phases, or some combination of the two.

Considerations in Choosing a Variation

In choosing between the Rapid Linear model and the FDD model, you need to weigh three considerations.

Decomposing the Project Into Parallel and Independent Swim Lanes

The first objective would be to decompose the functionality into independent swim lanes. The fewer dependencies there are across the swim lanes, the easier it will be to schedule resources and work. The likelihood of cross–swim lane scheduling conflicts is reduced as the dependency between swim lanes is reduced.

Swim Lane Cohesiveness

The second objective would be to make the functions or technical features within a swim lane as cohesive as possible. Does the functionality fit together?

Does the technical dependency fit together? Do these swim lanes offer business value?

Increased Risk

The work of the project is compressed into a shorter time frame than required by the single–swim lane approach. That causes risk to increase because of such factors as scope change, resource contention, and problem resolution. There is less time to analyze and take action than in the single–swim lane approach. In addition, the opportunities to recover are fewer and more difficult than in the single–swim lane approach.

> **WARNING** There is no such thing as a free lunch. The price you pay, or the weakness of these variations, is that they increase risk of project failure. The work is compressed into a much shorter time frame, so there is less opportunity to recover from mistakes or resource scheduling problems.

Adapting and Integrating the Tools, Templates, and Processes for Maximum Effectiveness in Linear PMLCs

To successfully implement either the Rapid Linear model or the FDD model, you have to begin during the construction of your project network diagram. Your objective is to define a sequence of swim lanes where each swim lane contains the functions and features of part of the solution. In total, all swim lanes contain functions and features that combine to provide a complete solution. These swim lanes must have the following properties:

- The functions and features of a swim lane can be built independently of the functions and features of any other swim lane.
- There are no resource dependencies across swim lanes.
- There are no schedule dependencies across swim lanes.
- The total duration of each swim lane must be nearly equal.

If these properties cannot be satisfied, then at least the interactions between swim lanes must be minimized. Although this variation might seem to be very attractive given today's rush to market, some problems will arise.

There are several things to consider in creating such an aggressive schedule. By squeezing the work into a shorter time frame, you must remember that the amount of work has not decreased — it just must be completed in less time. The last parallel swim lane that is complete determines the completion date of the development project. The results of schedule compression are as follows:

- Increased management time to handle intra– and inter–swim lane issues
- Increased likelihood of resource contention

- Potential for overlooking cross–swim lane dependencies
- Less time to recover from a mistake

All of these results contribute to an increased risk of project failure. So if there is pressure to use either the Rapid Linear PMLC model or the FDD Linear PMLC model instead of the Linear PMLC model, assess the complexity and potential risk implications. You might also want to assess the skills and competencies of the project team members and the likelihood that they can adapt to such an aggressive schedule.

Incremental Project Management Life Cycle

The Incremental PMLC model is the second type of TPM approach and was originally posed as a way to get products and services to market sooner but with what has been labeled "crippled solutions." That is a solution that is not fully functional. It is designed to enable your client to gain a foothold in a new market or enhance their leverage in an existing market.

Figure 10-4 is a graphical description of the Incremental PMLC model that shows the dependent increments. The increments follow sequentially, not concurrently.

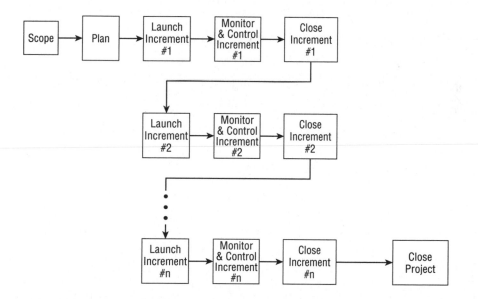

Figure 10-4: The Incremental PMLC model

Note that the sequence formed by the Launching, Monitoring and Controlling, and Closing Process Groups is repeated n times. Each repetition integrates another part of the solution until the *nth* repetition, when the final part of the solution is integrated and the project moves to the Closing Process Group.

Definition

An Incremental PMLC model consists of a number of dependent increments that are completed in a prescribed sequence. Each increment includes a Launching, Monitoring and Controlling, and Closing Process Group for the functions and features in that increment only. Each increment integrates additional parts of the solution until the final increment, where the remaining parts of the solution are integrated.

Characteristics

To be used effectively the Incremental PMLC model requires the following:

- The same characteristics as the Linear PMLC model
- A need to release deliverables against a more aggressive schedule

Strengths

The strengths of the Incremental PMLC model are as follows:

- Produces business value early in the project
- Enables you to better schedule scarce resources
- Can accommodate minor scope change requests between increments
- Offers a product improvement opportunity
- More focused on client value than the Linear PMLC model

Produces Business Value Early in the Project

Releasing a partial product or service early in the project creates market presence and value earlier than in the Linear PMLC model, hence, an earlier return on investment. From a marketing standpoint, early entry has its advantages, and the Incremental PMLC model supports that entry.

Organizational velocity is something you need to think about as you plan these increments. By *velocity*, I mean the ability of the organization to implement and absorb change. For example, if the increments are two weeks long, you are fooling yourself if you think the organization can absorb changes every two weeks. You have to support these increments, too. I see some real problems with short increments. On the other hand, increments that are too long may adversely affect your success in the market. Most of my clients plan for quarterly or semi-annual releases. Annual releases are typically version releases that take care of bugs and major product upgrades, not partial product releases.

Enables You to Better Schedule Scarce Resources

Increments are defined around function and feature dependencies, but they can also be defined around the availability of scarce resources. When a scarce resource is available only during certain windows of time, using the Linear PMLC model may create resource contention problems in that the scarce resource is needed when the scarce resource is not available. If instead, you use the Incremental PMLC model in planning the project, you could assign functions and features to an increment that will be scheduled during the available time of the scarce resource. The remainder of the increments and their schedules can be planned around the increment that is using the scarce resource. If there are several scarce resources, the same strategy can be used.

Can Accommodate Minor Scope Change Requests Between Increments

When you release a partial product or service to the end user, you had better expect that those end users will find reasons for change. Something can always be done better. While changes are not supported in the TPM category, you should expect changes when using the Incremental PMLC model. Don't ignore the likelihood of these change requests; instead, plan for them by adding a management reserve task to every increment.

TIP You must tell the client you have added management reserve and make sure they understand how this can impact the project schedule.

Offers a Product Improvement Opportunity

Releasing functions and features to the end user or client in increments gives room for feedback and possible improvements in later increments. A word of caution is needed here. Your hope is that the time between increments is very short. The longer the time between increments, the more likely you will lose team members to short-term assignments that turn out to be longer term than planned. If the time between increments is short, the end user or client will not have much opportunity for testing and feedback. You've given the end user or client an opportunity to try something out and make suggestions for change, so you had better be prepared to respond.

More Focused on Client Value Than the Linear PMLC Model

Just by giving your client the opportunity to work with a partial solution and provide feedback on improvements, you are already more client-facing than if you are using the Linear PMLC model.

Weaknesses

The weaknesses of the Incremental PMLC model are as follows:

- The team may not remain intact between increments.
- This model requires handoff documentation between increments.
- The model must follow a defined set of processes.
- You must define increments based on function and feature dependencies rather than business value.
- You must have more client involvement than Linear PMLC models.
- An Incremental PMLC model takes longer than the Linear PMLC model.
- Partitioning the functions may be problematic.

The Team May Not Remain Intact Between Increments

This may be the most serious risk created in an Incremental PMLC model that is not a serious issue in the Linear PMLC model. The longer the time between successive increments, the more likely you will lose one or more team members. If they are not busy doing some work on your project, what do you think they will be doing? Another project manager will see that your team members are not busy and request "a little bit of their time" to work on his or her project. My experience has been that this "little bit of time" always gets stretched out, and you will either lose those team members or have your project delayed waiting for them to return.

There will inevitably be some delay between the end of one stage and the beginning of the next. That delay can be dangerous because there will be a temptation to assign team members to other short-term tasks while waiting to start the next stage. The short term can extend to a longer term and compromise the next stage.

This Model Requires Handoff Documentation Between Increments

You have to assume that the team who will work on the next increment may not be the same as the team who worked on the just-completed or previously completed increments. You should also assume that you may not have face-to-face or real-time communications with those who might be assigned to future increments. Nevertheless, the new team must pick up where the old team left off.

That means the team working on the current increment must create documentation for the team that will work on the next increment. This adds time to the increment duration and hence adds time to the project completion. Fortunately, not every increment will require this additional non-value-added work.

The Model Must Follow a Defined Set of Processes

This is the same as with the Linear PMLC model.

You Must Define Increments Based on Function and Feature Dependencies Rather Than Business Value

The constraining factor in choosing the functions and features to go into an increment are the dependencies between functions and features. In most cases, the features that belong to a function should be in all increments that include this function. That would make for a more efficient use of development resources. A good start would be to build a network diagram of the functions. That will be your guide to allocating functions to increments. A simple example is shown in Figure 10-5.

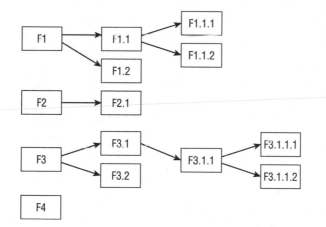

Figure 10-5: Allocating functions to increments

Suppose the client would like to have three releases of the product or service. One way to approach the partitioning would be to look at the longest dependency path and allocate that path to the three increments. The longest dependency path is the one that begins with F3. Here are some possible alternatives for allocating that longest path:

Alternative A

Increment #1: F3

Increment #2: F3.1, F3.1.1

Increment #3: F3.2, F3.1.1.1, F3.1.1.2

Alternative B

Increment #1: F3, F3.1

Increment #2: F3.2, F3.1.1

Increment #3: F3.1.1.1, F3.1.1.2

Alternative C

Increment #1: F3, F3.1, F3.2

Increment #2: F3.1.1 F3.1.1.1

Increment #3: F3.1.1.2

How would you choose the best allocation? The criteria might be resource availability, increment duration, increment risk, and/or business value. The same criteria would apply if you were trying to choose from among two or more complete allocations.

You Must Have More Client Involvement Than Linear PMLC Models

The first and primary difference in client involvement between the Linear and Incremental PMLC models is increment planning. In the Linear PMLC model, there is only one increment, and the point is moot. In the Incremental PMLC model, the client will be concerned about increment duration and business value. The development team will be concerned about compliance to the dependency relationships between increments, risk, and resource availability. It is possible that client needs will conflict with development team needs and some negotiation will have to take place.

An Incremental PMLC Model Takes Longer Than the Linear PMLC Model

The added time arises from the following:

- Delays between increments
- The need for handoff documentation between increments
- More scope change requests

- Supporting interim solutions
- The loss of team members between increments
- Integration of the latest increment deliverables

Partitioning the Functions May Be Problematic

As stated previously, you will have occasions where some negotiation will have to take place, and the results of that negotiation may require compromises by both parties. Here is where the allocation of the features may help. Developing the feature list for a particular function could be allocated to several increments, beginning with the increment where the function is developed. There will be several options to consider, and balancing the increments by allocating the feature list may present some acceptable compromises.

When to Use an Incremental PMLC

The only justification for using an Incremental PMLC model is to get a partial product, service, or process into the end user's hands faster than any alternative model. The added risks are often much higher than if a Linear PMLC model had been chosen.

> **WARNING** Resist the temptation to use the increments to solve a problem. That is not the purpose. You must have a clearly defined goal as well as a clearly defined solution to use these approaches. If the solution is not clearly defined, Iterative and Adaptive approaches will serve you better.

Adapting and Integrating the Tools, Templates, and Processes for Maximum Effectiveness in Incremental PMLCs

To successfully implement the Incremental PMLC model, you have to begin during construction of the project network diagram (just as you do for the Rapid PMLC model). Your objective is to define a set of increments so that each increment contains only the functions and features that depend on functions and features released through previous increments. When the last increment is complete, the solution is complete. These increments must have the following properties:

- The functions and features of an increment can be built independently of the functions and features that are still not integrated into the solution.
- The functions and features in any increment must provide a meaningful addition to the business value when integrated into the current solution.

- The organization can absorb the frequent changes to the solution.
- The total duration of each increment should be nearly equal.

Although this variation may seem to be very attractive given today's rush to market, some problems will arise.

The risk of failure is increased. There are several things to consider in creating such an incremental schedule. The amount of work has not decreased — it just must be completed in a shorter time frame. The last increment that is complete determines the completion date of the development project. The results of an incremental schedule are as follows:

- An increase of management time to handle between-increment issues
- An increase in the total amount of work as compared to the Linear PMLC model
- Encouraging between-increment scope change requests
- An increased likelihood of losing resources between increments
- The possibility of project delays between increments
- Potential for overlooking increment dependencies
- Handoff documentation requirements between increments

All of these results contribute to an increased risk of project failure. So if there is pressure to use the Incremental PMLC model rather than the Linear PMLC model, assess the complexity and potential risk implications. You might also want to assess the skills and competencies of potential replacement team members in anticipation of losing your original team members between increments.

Using Critical Chain Project Management

In 1984, Eliyahu M. Goldratt introduced the Theory of Constraints (TOC) in a book entitled *The Goal* (North River Press, 1992). The basic idea behind the TOC is that every organization is constrained by at least one factor. That factor ultimately constrains the activities of the organization. In projects, that constraint is often the availability of people either in terms of numbers or skills. Peter Senge, in his book *The Fifth Discipline* (Currency/Doubleday, 1994), stated that "to change the behavior of a system, you must identify and change the limiting factor," which Lawrence P. Leach, in his book *Critical Chain Project Management, Second Edition* (Artech House, 2005), called the best definition of TOC that he has heard. Still, it was not until the late 1990s that practitioners were able to link TOC to project management. Critical chain project management (CCPM) is the result of the linkage between TOC and project management. CCPM has grown in popularity and is making an impact on project success.

The second edition of this book contained a brief paragraph on CCPM. At the suggestion of several readers, I decided to expand my treatment of CCPM. That is the purpose of this chapter. I am aware that many project management practitioners and writers dismiss CCPM as just another way of managing risk, and suggest that it does not represent any new thinking about project management. It is not my purpose to settle that debate. I merely want to give some space to an idea, an approach, that all project managers will appreciate. The interested reader should consult Leach's *Critical Chain Project Management*.

What Is the Critical Chain?

As mentioned in Chapter 5, the critical path is the longest duration path through the project. It is built by considering only the task dependencies and their individual durations in an additive fashion. CCPM claims that the critical path approach to project management is flawed. Instead, CCPM claims that the focus should not be on the critical path, which is resource-independent, but on the path that is task-dependent and resource-constrained, the so-called *critical chain*. The critical chain is defined as the longest duration path through the project, if you consider both the task dependencies and the resource constraints. *Critical chain project management* is defined as the planning, scheduling, and maintenance of the critical chain throughout the course of the project. Furthermore, by giving priority to the critical chain, the project manager identifies and schedules tasks around the most constrained of the resources, increasing the probability of completing the project in less time than the critical path approach. This chapter includes a simple example to illustrate how that schedule compression happens.

In the critical path approach, resources are allocated first to the critical path, which is known to not be the optimal way to create the shortest schedule. Two concepts form the justification of the CCPM approach, described in the next two sections.

Variation in Duration: Common Cause versus Special Cause

The first concept that justifies the CCPM approach is that there are two basic kinds of variation that you experience in task duration. They are as follows:

> **Common cause variation** — This is fluctuation in task duration that results from the capacity of the system affecting that task. In other words, this type of variation occurs naturally in nature. For example, if you consider the time it takes an experienced runner to complete a 100-meter race under normal environmental conditions, you might observe times such as

9.85, 9.88, 9.92, and 9.86 seconds. The times are not all the same because the runner (the system) has only a certain capacity for repeatability. There is a natural variation in the actual execution times. Nothing can be done to affect that; it is the nature of the runner. These variations are attributable to common cause variation.

Special cause variation — Using the same example, if the runner is running against a 20-mile-per-hour wind, or at a 5,000-foot elevation, or in 100-degree heat, the recorded times will be even higher and have a greater variation from one another. Those higher recordings are the result of special causes.

NOTE You can do something to mitigate or avoid special cause variations but not common cause variations.

What do these mean to the project manager? Common cause variation is accounted for in the contingency attached to each task. Common cause variation occurs naturally and is always present. You live with that and plan accordingly. Special cause variation is dealt with as part of your risk management plan. These are the variations you can manage as project manager.

NOTE Both of these sources of variation have to be accounted for in traditional project management (TPM) and in CCPM. However, CCPM takes advantage of common cause variation through the use of the *central limit theorem* from mathematical statistics, whereas TPM essentially ignores it. The theorem states that the sum of a large number of independent observations from the same distribution has, under certain general conditions, an approximate normal distribution that steadily improves as the number of observations increases. It is this use of common cause variation and some statistical properties of variances of additive random variables that enables a CCPM project to actually complete in less time than a TPM approach, even on the same project.

Statistical Validation of the Critical Chain Approach

The second concept that lends credence to the CCPM approach is based in statistical distribution theory. Here you call on a basic concept from statistics: the variance of a sum is the square root of the sum of the variances of each of the components in the sum. The square root of the sum of squares is less than the sum itself. That may sound like gibberish to most of you, so let's take a look at how it translates to project duration. Figure 10-6 shows a sequence of four consecutive tasks. Each one has a contingency associated with it (the shaded area after the task). Contingency is defined as the difference in duration between a 50-percent probable estimate and a 90-percent probable estimate. For example, suppose that about half the time a particular activity completes in 10 hours or less. That is the 50-percent probable estimate. In addition, that same activity completes in 15 hours or less approximately 90 percent of the time. That is the 90-percent probable estimate. The difference between the two (15 − 10, or 5 hours) is the contingency.

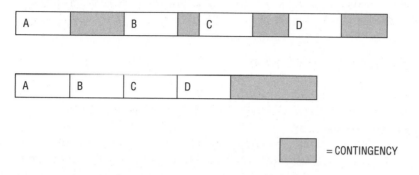

Figure 10-6: Using contingency can reduce project time

In the lower part of the figure, I have moved the contingency of each task to the end of the sequence of tasks. Note that the variance of the sum of the contingencies is less than the sum of the variances of the contingencies. Calling on that statistical property has enabled me to shorten the duration of the sequence of tasks. You might say that I haven't really done anything; I've just defined things a little differently. Not quite. I have used the average task duration as the point estimate of task duration. (A *point estimate* is a single number that represents your best guess as to the real value of the number you are trying to estimate, whereas a *range estimate* is a low and high number that you believe spans the unknown number you are trying to estimate.) The *average* is the number that the duration will exceed half of the time and be less than half of the time. Because of the variation in duration as a result of common causes, you can expect some of the tasks to take more time than their average duration and some to take less time. That variation is collected into the contingency at the end of the sequence. To bring the sequence in by the shorter time, the project manager has to manage the contingency. So what I have accomplished by collecting the contingencies at the end of the sequence is to change the focus of the project manager to that newly aggregated contingency. The contingency has been made visible, and therefore it is manageable.

A final comparison of the critical path approach versus the critical chain approach will help you understand the fundamental differences between the critical path and the critical chain approaches is one of a sequence of activities. Some of them will take longer than their estimated duration, and others will take less time. The project manager reviews the status of the contingency and decides whether to act or to let the statistical variation correct the overage.

I'll have more to say on that by way of an example in the next section, but for now it is important to see the distinction and the real strength of CCPM. The TPM project manager reacts to the performance of a single task in a sequence of dependent tasks and expends management time. The CCPM project manager dismisses that as a waste of time, reasoning that attention should be given to the sequence and not to any single task. CCPM relies on the statistical properties of a sequence of dependent tasks, whereas TPM does not.

The Critical Chain Project Management Approach

The CCPM approach is identical to the TPM approach up to the point where the project network diagram is defined and the critical path is identified. The traditional project manager would next conduct a resource-leveling exercise targeting resource usage on the critical path. At this point, the critical chain project manager develops the critical chain plan. In the discussion that follows, I describe each of the CCPM planning steps for you by way of a simple example.

Step 1: Creating the Early Schedule Project Network Diagram

Figure 10-7 shows the early schedule for a simple seven-task project. This early schedule is the same one someone using TPM might make. Note that the project duration is estimated at 16 days using the original task duration estimates, which include contingencies for each task. Figure 10-7 shows the critical path (C1–C2–C3) for a project manager using TPM, and it is the starting point for resolving any resource contention problems.

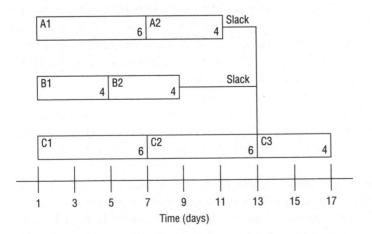

Figure 10-7: The early schedule

Step 2: Converting the Early Schedule to the Late Schedule and Adding Resources

After calculating the earliest start (ES), earliest finish (EF), latest start (LS), and latest finish (LF), a project manager using CCPM converts the task schedule to the late schedule, as shown in Figure 10-8. Note that this conversion removes the slack associated with the sequence defined by tasks A1–A2 and B1–B2. In fact, it removes all of the free slack and total slack associated with any task or task sequence in the project. Note also that the 50-percent duration estimates have replaced the original estimates, which included contingencies. In doing that, the project duration has been reduced from the original 16 days to 8 days. I have also added the three resources (Duffy, Ernie, and Fran) to the tasks to which they have been assigned. Note that there is a resource conflict with Ernie on tasks A2 and B2. In addition, note that the project duration is reduced to eight days when the contingencies are removed.

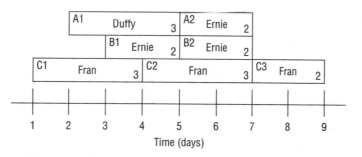

Figure 10-8: The late schedule with resource assignments

Step 3: Resolving Resource Conflicts

In general, resource conflicts are removed by beginning with the task sequence that has the least slack. After resolving that conflict, move to the task path that now has the least slack. Continue in this fashion until all resource conflicts have been resolved. In the example, the critical chain (C1–C2–C3) does not have any resource conflicts. The next task path to consider is A1–A2. In this case, Ernie would be scheduled to work on A2, which means pushing his work on B1 to an earlier date. This resolution is illustrated in Figure 10-9.

The other way to resolve the resource conflict is to have Ernie work on B2; then after Duffy has completed A1, Ernie can work on A2. This resolution is illustrated in Figure 10-10. The second option extends the duration of the project.

This simple example illustrates the major difference between TPM and CCPM. TPM uses the early schedule as the base for all management decisions. CCPM uses the late schedule. TPM focuses only on the critical path and manages in accordance with that. CCPM focuses on the paths with resource constraints and manages in accordance with the best use of the resources. It does so by using the critical path but only to identify the chains with the least slack, and prioritizing resource use based on the minimum slack paths. To protect the scarce resources, CCPM uses the concept of *buffers*, which is the topic of the next section.

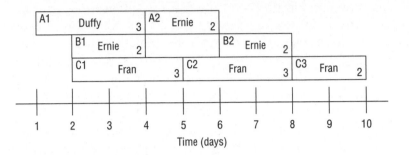

Figure 10-9: One way to resolve the resource conflict

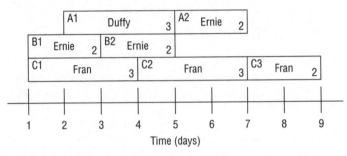

Figure 10-10: Another way to resolve the resource conflict

Establishing Buffers

Now that I have adjusted the late schedule for the resource conflicts, I can add the appropriate buffers to the project schedule. There are many different kinds of buffers and many different purposes for which they are used. I discuss and illustrate three of them with this simple project.

CROSS-REFERENCE For a complete discussion of buffers, see Lawrence P. Leach's book *Critical Chain Project Management, Second Edition* (Artech House, 2005).

Defining Buffers

Buffers are segments of time that are placed at the end of a sequence of tasks for the purpose of protecting the schedule of those tasks. Buffers can also be used to protect cost, much like a contingency for unexpected expenses in a budget. The size of time buffers is based on the total duration of the task sequence to which they are attached. Basically, the size of the buffer is determined by calculating the total of the contingencies in the tasks that make up the sequence.

Types of Buffers

Although there are others, I focus on the following three types of buffers in this chapter:

- Project buffers
- Feeding buffers
- Resource buffers

Project Buffers

The project buffer is a time buffer placed at the end of the critical chain to protect the overall project schedule. Its size can be calculated as the square root of the sum of the squared differences between the original task duration estimate and the reduced task duration estimate.

Feeding Buffers

The feeding buffer is a time buffer placed at the end of a sequence of tasks that lead into the critical chain. Its size is calculated the same way as the project buffer size.

Resource Buffers

The resource buffer is different from the previous buffers. It is not a time buffer. It is a flag, usually placed on the critical chain to alert a resource that it is needed. The flag can be placed at intervals such as one week before the resource is needed, three days before the resource is needed, or one day before the resource is needed. Because it does not contain any time interval, it does not affect the project's scheduled completion date. It serves merely to protect the critical chain.

Other Buffers

As indicated earlier, several other buffer types are used, but they relate to a multiproject environment and are beyond the scope of this overview chapter. The interested reader should consult Leach's book *Critical Chain Project Management*. Some of the other pertinent buffers found in Leach's book are as follows:

- **Capacity constrained buffer** — A buffer placed between projects to ensure a specific sequence of projects in a multiproject environment
- **Cost buffer** — A contingency added to a project or sequence of tasks to protect overall cost
- **Drum buffer** — The capacity of a single resource that is scheduled across several projects

Managing Buffers

The CCPM project manager is concerned about the starting time of a sequence of tasks, including the critical chain, but isn't concerned about the finish time of the sequences. The finishing times are not even in the CCPM project plan. Instead, the CCPM project manager manages the buffers. In managing the buffers, the CCPM project manager is protecting the actual duration sequence and hence the completion time of the project.

The TPM treats the buffer as nothing more than management reserve, which was discussed in Chapter 5. The only real similarity between a management reserve and a buffer may be in how they are managed. Managing management reserve and managing buffers can follow very similar logic. The three decision trigger points in buffer management are as follows:

- When the schedule for the sequence of tasks slips and penetrates into the first third of the buffer

- When the schedule for the sequence of tasks slips and penetrates into the middle third of the buffer

- When the schedule for the sequence of tasks slips and penetrates into the final third of the buffer

Let's take a closer look at each of these trigger points and the appropriate action that the CCPM project manager should take.

Penetration into the First Third of the Buffer

Unlike the project manager using TPM who chases every slippage on the critical path or any change in the critical path, the project manager using CCPM is looking at the performance of a sequence and is less likely to respond immediately to the first slippage. Penetration into the first third of the buffer means that the cumulative slippage in the sequence is less than one-third of the buffer. There is no defensible reason why the CCPM project manager would want to take any action.

TIP The later this occurs in the sequence, the less likely any action will be taken.

Penetration into the Middle Third of the Buffer

Penetration into the middle third of the buffer does call for some action on the part of the CCPM project manager. In this case, the correct action is to investigate the cause of the slippage and put a get-well plan in place. The earlier in the sequence the slippage occurs, the more serious the problem.

Penetration into the Final Third of the Buffer

Penetration into the final third of the buffer is serious regardless of when in the sequence it occurs. Obviously, if it is in the first third of the duration of the sequence, it is very serious. If it occurs late in the final third, there may be little that can be done. In any case, action is called for.

Figure 10-11 illustrates a matrix that can be used to determine schedule slippage severity and the need for action as a function of buffer penetration and distance into the task sequence.

		Buffer Penetration		
		First Third	**Second Third**	**Final Third**
Task Sequence Penetration	**First Third**	NO ACTION	Serious problem; immediate action required	A very serious problem exists; aggressive action is needed
	Second Third	NO ACTION	Define the problem and formulate a solution	Serious problem; implement the solution
	Final Third	Task sequence will be ahead of schedule	NO ACTION	Monitor the situation for any further penetration

Figure 10-11: Buffer penetration and action decisions

To grasp the significance of the penetration matrix, first consider the diagonal from the top-left cell to the bottom-right cell in Figure 10-11. The cells on the diagonal reflect situations where task sequence penetration is about equal to buffer penetration. The statistician would say that is what you should expect on the average. However, the further you move into task sequence penetration (moving down the diagonal), the more you should be paying attention to the team's performance on the tasks in the sequence. The nearer you are to the ending tasks in the sequence, the less likely it is that you can formulate and execute a get-well plan should things go poorly. For example, if you are in the second third of the task sequence, it might be a good idea to take a look at the problem situation and formulate an action plan in the event that things deteriorate. The problem is not serious, but it does deserve your attention. In the final third of the task sequence, all you can do is closely monitor things and take action at the slightest aberration in the task sequence schedule.

The best place to be is below the diagonal I've been discussing. You could even be experiencing a situation where the task sequence will finish ahead of schedule, and the time saved can be passed to the successor task sequence. However, you're probably more used to situations that are above the diagonal. If you are in the first third of the task sequence and have penetrated into the second third of the buffer, you have a serious problem that needs immediate investigation and solution implementation. There may be a systemic flaw in the project plan, and early intervention is needed. If the schedule continues to slip and you find that you have penetrated into the final third of the buffer, you are in real trouble, as the matrix suggests. You could be looking at a significant slippage that may impact the project buffer as well.

Track Record of Critical Chain Project Management

It was not until the 1997 publication of Eliyahu M. Goldratt's book *Critical Chain* (North River Press, 1997) that people began to see the connections between TOC and project management. CCPM has a history of more than 10 years to draw upon for its successes. Leach cites a few of them in his book *Critical Chain Project Management*. Here are brief summaries of some of those success stories.

Honeywell Defense Avionics Systems — Using critical chain concepts, a team at Honeywell was able to reduce a 13-month project schedule to 6 months, and they did finish it in 6 months.

Lucent Technologies — A project that was scheduled using CCPM was to have taken one year. Many said it couldn't possibly be done in one year. It was, with buffer to spare.

Harris Semiconductor — Harris undertook to build a new manufacturing facility using the CCPM approach. The industry standard for such facilities was 46 months to get the plant up and running to 90-percent capacity. Harris built it and brought it up to 90-percent capacity in 13 months.

Israeli Aircraft Industry — A particular type of aircraft maintenance requires three months on the average. Using CCPM techniques the maintenance team reduced the average to two weeks.

Better Online Solutions — A software package was originally planned to be released to the public in August. The TOC schedule cut it down to May 1. The actual delivery date was early April.

These stories do not in any way validate CCPM as better than TPM. It is too early to tell that, but it is a fact that there have been many successes using it. You be the judge. You decide whether or not CCPM presents a more advantageous approach for your projects than TPM. I have simply presented another way of managing resources and leave it up to the project team to decide which approach makes more sense, given the situation.

Putting It All Together

Table 10-2 summarizes what has been discussed in this chapter and shows how each Process Group relates to each PMLC model.

Schedule compression, which is listed under the Planning Process Group, is a strategy that is used to move the project completion date to an earlier date. That is done using a number of different strategies on the critical path, such as adding more skilled resources to a task to reduce its duration, or changing the dependency relationship so that two successive tasks can be overlapped and the total duration of the two tasks can be reduced by the amount of the overlap.

Table 10-2: The Relationship Between the Process Groups and the PMLC Models

PROCESS GROUP	PROCESS	LINEAR PMLC MODEL	RAPID LINEAR PMLC MODEL	FDD LINEAR PMLC MODEL	INCREMENTAL PMLC MODEL
Scoping	COS	X	X	X	X
	Project Scoping Meeting	X	X	X	X
	Requirements Gathering	X	X	X	X
	Diagram Business Process				
	Prototyping				
	Validate Business Cases				
	Procurement Mgt	X	X	X	X
	Outsourcing	X	X	X	X
	POS	X	X	X	X
Planning	Plan and run a JPPS	X	X	X	X
	Creating the WBS	X	X	X	X

Continued

Table 10-2 *(continued)*

PROCESS GROUP	PROCESS	LINEAR PMLC MODEL	RAPID LINEAR PMLC MODEL	FDD LINEAR PMLC MODEL	INCREMENTAL PMLC MODEL
	Estimation techniques	X	X	X	X
	Building the schedule	X	X	X	X
	Analyzing the schedule	X	X	X	X
	Schedule compression	X	X	X	X
	Risk Mgt Planning	X	X	X	X
	Writing the proposal	X	X	X	X
Launching	Recruit team members	X	X	X	X
	Write the PDS	X	X	X	X
	Problem solving	X	X	X	X
	Decision making	X	X	X	X
	Conflict resolution	X	X	X	X
	Consensus building	X	X	X	X
	Brainstorming	X	X	X	X
	Team meetings	X	X	X	X
	Scope change process	X	X	X	X
	Communications plan	X	X	X	X
	Work packages	X	X	X	X
	Resource assignment	X	X	X	X
	Finalizing the schedule	X	X	X	X

PROCESS GROUP	PROCESS	LINEAR PMLC MODEL	RAPID LINEAR PMLC MODEL	FDD LINEAR PMLC MODEL	INCREMENTAL PMLC MODEL
Monitoring and Controlling	Current period reports	X	X	X	X
	Cumulative reports	X	X	X	X
	Exception reports	X	X	X	X
	Stoplight reports	X	X	X	X
	Variance reports	X	X	X	X
	Gantt Charts	X	X	X	X
	MTC	X	X	X	X
	EVA	X	X	X	X
	Integrated MTC/ EVA	X	X	X	X
	Project Status Meetings	X	X	X	X
	Problem Escalation	X	X	X	X
Closing	ATP	X	X	X	X
	Implementation	X	X	X	X
	Post-Impl. Audit	X	X	X	X
	Document the Project	X	X	X	X
	Final Project Report	X	X	X	X

Additionally, this chapter has provided enough of an overview of CCPM to enable you to use it in your projects. Because the overview is brief and applied to a simple project, readers who are more serious about its application will need to dig deeper into it. Again, I heartily endorse Leach's book *Critical Chain Project Management, Second Edition* (Artech House, 2005).

Discussion Questions

1. How would you sell your client on the wisdom of using management reserve?

2. How would you go about the task of decomposing the project into meaningful business chunks in preparation for an Incremental approach? Speak to the rules you might employ.

3. You have completed the first few increments and released deliverables to the client. They are now coming to you with changes to what has been released. These changes make sense, but will cause your project to go off schedule if integrated into the future increments. What would you do?

4. List the advantages and disadvantages of using management reserve.

5. How would you manage the time between increments in an Incremental PMLC model? There is pressure for longer between-increment delays to allow the client to integrate the increment deliverables, and there is pressure for shorter between-increment delays to reduce the risk of losing a team member. How do you balance these conflicting needs? How would you manage the work of your team members between increments — that is, what would you have them do?

6. What is the impact on your risk management plan for using a Rapid Linear PMLC model instead of a Linear PMLC model — that is, what risks are added and what mitigation plans would you put in place? Be specific.

7. Assume that your organization is interested in using CCPM along with TPM. What criteria would you use to decide which approach makes more sense for a given project? You might try answering this question by considering some of the characteristics of the project that would lead you to one choice over the other.

8. You are a senior project manager in your company. You have 15 years' experience with them and a solid reputation for delivering successful projects. What might you do, acting on your own, to get your organization to appreciate the value of CCPM? What obstacles might prevent you from going forward with your plan?

CASE STUDY — PIZZA DELIVERED QUICKLY (PDQ)

9. Are there any projects in the case study that would benefit from any of the PMLC models studied in this chapter? (Remember the six subsystems defined for the case are Order Entry, Order Submit, Logistics, Routing, Inventory Management, and Pizza Factory Locator.) Defend your decisions.

Agile Project Management

Based on testimonial data collected from over 10,000 project managers from around the world, over 70 percent of projects are best managed by processes that adapt to continual learning and discovery of the project solution.

When in doubt, leave it out.

When the pain the organization is suffering from failed projects reaches some threshold, the health of the business suffers and the bottom line is affected. If all previous corrective action plans have failed, senior management is ready to listen.

— Robert K. Wysocki, Ph.D., President, Enterprise Information Insights, Inc.

CHAPTER LEARNING OBJECTIVES

After reading this chapter, you will be able to:

- Appreciate and understand the history of Agile Project Management (APM)

- Know when to use APM

- Use and be able to adapt the Iterative project management life cycle (PMLC) model and variations

- Explain the benefits and use of the Iterative PMLC model

- Anticipate and resolve the potential problems from using an Iterative PMLC model

- Know how and when to use the Prototyping Iterative PMLC model

- Know how and when to use the Rational Unified Process (RUP) Iterative PMLC model

- Use and be able to adapt the Adaptive PMLC model

Continued

CHAPTER LEARNING OBJECTIVES *(continued)*

- Explain the benefits of using an Adaptive PMLC model
- Anticipate and resolve the potential problems of using an Adaptive PMLC model
- Know how and when to use the Adaptive Software Development (ASD) PMLC model
- Know how and when to use the Adaptive Project Framework (APF) PMLC model
- Know how and when to use the Scrum Adaptive PMLC model
- Know how and when to use the Dynamic Systems Development Method (DSDM) Adaptive PMLC model

This is the key chapter of Part II. Extensive testimonial data suggests that more than 70 percent of all projects should have used some type of Agile Project Management (APM) model but didn't. Too many project managers have tried to force fit the wrong project management life cycle (PMLC) model because that is the only model approved for use by their management, or they did so in ignorance of other models that were better choices for a management approach. The poor project track record of many organizations is sad testimony of those poor management decisions.

It is my hope that you approach this chapter with an open mind to the possibilities. Many of you and the managers above you in the organization's chain of command have to unlearn some bad project management habits to make room for better project management habits.

In this chapter, you learn at a very detailed level about the kinds of projects that lend themselves to Agile approaches. As you know, these are the approaches that satisfy the management needs for projects whose goal is clearly documented but whose solution is not. Many of these projects address problems and business opportunities for which there has not been an acceptable solution put forth or the business opportunity has not been successfully exploited. These projects are characterized by high complexity and uncertainty and present the organization with a significant challenge. The fact that these high-risk projects are addressed at all means that their successful completion is critical to the business. These projects will challenge the creative abilities of the project manager, the client team, and the development team.

There are two different PMLC models in the Agile category: Iterative and Adaptive. Iterative PMLC models are appropriate for projects where most of the solution has been discovered. Only a few minor features have not been decided. In many cases, alternatives will be known but a final decision not made as to which to implement. Adaptive PMLC models are appropriate for projects where perhaps very little of the solution is known. Understanding and integrating major functions into the solution are integral to the learning and discovery part of Adaptive PMLC models.

There are several Agile models to choose from. The four popular choices for software development are Rational Unified Process (RUP), Scrum, Dynamic Systems Development Method (DSDM), and Adaptive Software Development (ASD). RUP is an Iterative PMLC model. Scrum, DSDM, and ASD are Adaptive PMLC models. These four APM models are similar in that they are designed to facilitate software solution discovery. There is a fifth Adaptive PMLC model that you will also learn about in this chapter. It is called Adaptive Project Framework (APF). It is different than the other four because it was designed for both software development and non–software development projects. Its application to product development, process design, and process improvement projects has been successfully demonstrated.

For a given Agile project, the choice of which of the two Agile PMLC model types provides a better fit will always be subjective. Many of the Agile models also work quite well on Q3 and Q4 projects. In this chapter, I will try to shed some light on the decision to use an Iterative PMLC model or an Adaptive PMLC model based on other factors that can impact project success.

What Is Agile Project Management?

APM is the new kid on the block. Its history stretches back a little more than 25 years. As recently as 2001, Agile software development was first codified through the "Agile Manifesto" (shown in the accompanying sidebar) put forth by Martin Fowler and Jim Highsmith.[1] There were 17 signers of the original Agile manifesto.

THE AGILE MANIFESTO

"We are uncovering better ways of developing [products] by doing it and helping others do it. Through this work we have come to value:

Individuals and interactions over processes and tools

Working software over comprehensive documentation

Customer collaboration over contract negotiations

Responding to change over following a plan

That is, while there is value in the items on the right, we value the items on the left more."

---

[1] Martin Fowler and Jim Highsmith. "The Agile Manifesto." *Software Development* 9, No. 8 (August 2001): 28–32.

The Agile Manifesto has been the guiding principle in all APM models, including those discussed in this book. Most of the APM models originated with software development and, as a result, are based on very specific software development practices. Prototyping and the Adaptive Project Framework (APF) are the only APM models designed for use on any type of project. Prototyping is discussed in the Iterative PMLC model section of this chapter; APF is discussed in the Adaptive PMLC model section. I'll share several APM models in some detail and show you how they map into the Iterative PMLC model and the Adaptive PMLC model.

CROSS-REFERENCE The bibliography in Appendix C has an extensive list of references to APM models.

This chapter covers several different APM PMLC models, but there are two major issues surrounding all APM projects regardless of the model used. These deserve special attention. I bring them up now so that you are aware of them as you explore the variety of models discussed in this chapter.

Implementing APM Projects

Adding more functions and features to the solution and implementing them at the same time sounds great. The client and the end user can benefit from whatever business value can be attained, experience the solution unfolding over short time periods, work with the solution, and provide valuable feedback to the developers about further additions and changes to the solution. But there is another side to this story, and that is the implementation of a constantly evolving solution. Iterations and cycles are short duration — 2 to 4 weeks is typical. The end users will give up and surrender if you expect them to change how they do their work by implementing a new solution every few weeks. How about your organization? What is its organizational velocity? Can it absorb change that fast? Most can't or won't. So what are the client and the project manager to do? Getting frequent client feedback is critical to discovering the complete solution and ultimately to project success, but the organization can't absorb change as fast as the APM models require. There is also the question of the project team's ability to support frequent releases. Training, documentation, and a support group are needed. Let's see, what release are you using again?

The following explains a way out of this dilemma that I have used with several of my clients.

Fully Supported Production Versions of Partial Solutions Are Released to the End User Quarterly or Semi-Annually

This seems to fit other organizational practices for implementing change, so it won't be viewed as anything different than what they are already doing. The input received from the end user and others who affect or are affected by the solution should still be gathered. It will be your most valuable information. There is a benefit in having longer periods to experiment and get comfortable with a new tool. You will gain valuable insight into the intuitive properties of your solution and see what the learning curve looks like.

This approach does not release the project team from the need to support the quarterly releases. I mention that so that you will remember to incorporate in your project plan the effort and support time that will have to be provided.

Intermediate Versions Are Released to a Focus Group Every 2–4 Weeks

You don't stand idly by and wait for end-user feedback from the quarterly releases. That flies in the face of delivering business value early and often. Instead, assemble a focus group of staff and managers who are respected by their peers and who have earned the right to critique the solution. You should ask them to commit to reviewing and critiquing every version of the solution. You will need to take advantage of any learning curve effects from having the same focus group members reviewing the evolving solution. The focus group should have some of the client members of the project team on it as well as a few other key end users. A focus group of 10 members is a good working group, but use your judgment on the size. The decision model you choose to use might also influence size — for example, do you need an odd number for voting? The project team will work very closely with the focus group on every version of the solution — both those that are released quarterly to end users and those that are not released. The documentation, training, and support needed by the focus group to understand the non-released solutions will be minimal. If you choose the focus group members to be a representative sample of all user groups, they can also provide limited support to the end users for the quarterly and semi-annual production versions. That way they can become a conduit from the end users back to the project team.

Co-Located APM Project Teams

Every proponent of APM approaches advises using small co-located teams of highly skilled professionals who are assigned 100 percent to the project and who can work without supervision. That's a nice goal to strive for but not too practical or likely in today's business environment. I haven't encountered a single example of a co-located team among my clients for at least five years. And the likelihood that I will is decreasing.

Most of the Iterative and all of the Adaptive PMLC models require a team of highly skilled professionals. The Adaptive project teams that do use highly skilled professionals are self-organizing teams and work effectively without supervision. One of my colleagues is managing an APM project and has never seen nor is she ever likely to see her teammates. She didn't even have the option of selecting them, and none of them are assigned to her project 100 percent. They were available, and they are distributed across the country. There is no money in the project budget for team members to travel. She has their pictures taped to her computer. It is obvious that the success of her project rests on team members knowing what has to be done and getting it done with little or no supervision. Openness and honesty are her critical success factors.

The reality is that the skills in most demand are in short supply and so the availability of individuals who possess those skills to work on a project is a problem. Out of necessity these professionals are assigned to multiple projects. That raises two management problems that must be attended to.

Cross-Project Dependencies

Consider this scenario. Harry is your only data warehouse design professional. When he finishes the data warehouse design on the Alpha Project, he is scheduled to begin the data warehouse design on the Beta Project. This raises the following management questions:

- Is Harry overcommitted?
- If Project Alpha is delayed, what is the impact on Project Beta?
- Who decides the project priority if there is a scheduling conflict with Harry?
- Can Harry's work on Project Alpha be overlapped with his work on Project Beta?
- What if Harry leaves the company?

These are difficult and complex questions to answer. But they must be answered. Your risk management plan is a good place to look for most of the answers.

Project Portfolio Management

Many of the situations that gave rise to the preceding questions can be mitigated through a project-portfolio management process. The decisions to approve a project for the portfolio can be based on a Human Resource Management System (HRMS). That system should include the skills inventory of all professionals, their current and future commitments, and their availability for additional project assignments. Unfortunately, not many organizations have such systems in place. Instead, they add a project to the portfolio based on its business value. That is all well and good, but not sufficient.

What is sufficient and what you might want to adopt is the Graham-Englund Model,[2] which answers the following four questions:

- What should we do?
- What can we do?
- What will we do?
- How will we do it?

The answer to the first question is a list of potential projects prioritized usually by business value. The answers to the next two questions can be based solely on the skills inventory and the availability of those skills over the planning horizon of the portfolio and the scheduling needs of the projects in the portfolio. The effective management of the contents of the project portfolio depends on access to a solid HRMS. There are commercially available software systems for portfolio management under a variety of resource constraints. For maximum effectiveness, this HRMS should be housed in a Project Management Office (PMO).

Co-location of the project team members is strongly advised in the Iterative PMLC model and required in the Adaptive PMLC model, but in its absence, Agile projects can still survive and succeed. The challenge is to deliver sound management of such projects despite the challenges of physical separation and time differences.

I developed APF under similar constraints. My team comprised 35 senior professionals spread across 12 time zones. The project was to design and implement an integrated software development PMLC process for Internet/intranet applications for outside clients under a fixed bid contract — a tall order even under the best of circumstances. With some logistical problems that had to be solved before the project started, we were able to hold daily 15-minute team meetings! Of course, there was some juggling of meeting times to minimize the torture inflicted on any one team member.

There are all kinds of technologies to help. Web meetings, instant messaging, and electronic whiteboards are all cost-effective alternatives. Some members of the APF development team cobbled together slide presentations and distributed them ahead of time to all who would be attending a daily team meeting or other meeting they were hosting. Another member built a simple dashboard so all team members could quickly post the status of work

---

[2] Robert J. Graham and Randall L. Englund, 1997. *Creating an Environment for Successful Projects: The Quest to Manage Project Management*. San Francisco: Jossey-Bass Publishers.

in process for presentation at the daily meetings. It wasn't fancy, but it got the job done. The bottom line is that distributed APM teams can be made to work. It just takes a little effort and some creativity. Above all, the value added from these tools needs to be balanced against the time to create and maintain them. Burdening an Agile project with non-value-added work is something to be avoided.

Iterative Project Management Life Cycle

On the certainty/uncertainty line, the models are aligned from Linear to Incremental to Iterative to Adaptive to Extreme. Both the Iterative and Adaptive models have been proposed to address the difficulty many project managers face when they try to clearly decompose requirements and are unable to do so. In some cases that difficulty arises from the client not having a clear picture of their needs and in other cases from the solution not being known. In either case, some type of APM approach is called for.

Definition of the Iterative PMLC Model

An Iterative PMLC model consists of a number of process groups that are repeated sequentially within an iteration with a feedback loop after each iteration is completed. At the discretion of the client, the last process group in an iteration may release a partial solution.

Iterative approaches are used when you have an initial version of the solution, but it is known to fall short in terms of features and perhaps functions. The iterative cycles are designed to select and integrate the missing pieces of the solution. Think of the Iterative PMLC model as a variant of production prototyping. The intermediate solutions are production ready, but they might not be released by the client to the end user until the final version is ready. The intermediate versions give the client something to work with as they attempt to learn and discover additional needed features. The client would choose to release a partial solution to the end user in an attempt to get input from them on further solution detail.

Figure 11-1 is the process group–level view of the Iterative PMLC model.

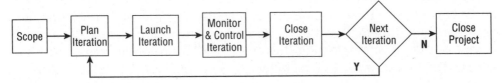

Figure 11-1: Iterative PMLC model

The Iterative PMLC model requires a solution that identifies the requirements at the function level but might be missing some of the details at the feature level. In other words, the functions are known and will be built into the solution through a number of iterations, but the details (the features) are not completely known at the beginning of the project. The missing features will come to light as the client works with the most current solution in a prototyping sense. The Iterative PMLC model is a learn-by-doing model. The use of intermediate solutions is the pathway to discovering the intimate details of the complete solution.

The Iterative PMLC model embraces several types of iteration. Iteration can be on requirements, functionality, features, design, development, solutions, and other components of the solution. An iteration consists of the Planning, Launching, Monitoring and Controlling, and Closing Process Groups. Closing an iteration is not the same as closing the project.

The Iterative PMLC model kicks in when one of the following occurs:

- Most but not all of the solution is clearly known.

- You might otherwise have chosen the Incremental PMLC model but have a strong suspicion that there will be more than a minimum number of scope change requests.

- You might otherwise have chosen the Adaptive PMLC model but are concerned about lack of client involvement.

Most of the Solution Is Clearly Known

Some of the details of the solution are missing. The alternatives to how those details (that is, features) might be added to the solution are probably known up to a point. All that remains is to give the client a look at how those features might be deployed in the solution and get their approval on which alternative to deploy or their recommendations for further change. This is the simplest of the Iterative situations you will encounter. Production prototype approaches are the usual choice. The Prototyping PMLC model is discussed later in this chapter. As far as the project team knows, all of the functions and sub-functions have been identified and integrated into the current solution. As features are added, there could be changes in how the functions and sub-functions are deployed in the solution, and hence, further changes are recommended. This is the nature of an Iterative approach. It continues in this vein until the client says you are done or until time and/or money is exhausted. The Prototyping PMLC model is ideal for such situations.

Likely to Be Multiple Scope Change Requests

This may just be a hunch, or this client's reputation is one of having made many changes in past projects. It's better to be safe than sorry. The off-the-shelf

Incremental PMLC model does not leave room in the project schedule for receiving and processing scope change requests. Rather than risking the consequences, choose an Iterative PMLC model that does leave room in the project schedule for client and end-user feedback or the accommodation of scope change requests.

Concern about Lack of Client Involvement

Coming from the Adaptive PMLC model side of the project landscape, if you have chosen to use an Iterative PMLC model, there are some risks you need to know about. You will have some degree of meaningful client involvement but not to the degree that you feel you will need it. Rather than depending on meaningful client involvement, you will have to guess at what the complete solution will be. The more involved the client is, the less you will be dependent on guessing. You might be good at guessing or just lucky, but you will still be guessing. The more knowledge your team has of the client systems and processes, the better off you will be.

If there is more than one client group, such as different departments all having to utilize the same solution, you are going to have to deal with complications. The first one is coming to closure on the final solution. This is so difficult that you should plan for considerable opposition. A single solution is possible, but it has to accommodate different requirements for each client group. You may have even come to closure on a requirement, but not on its representation in the solution. Those differences might begin with different user views and extend to different features and even different functions. The solution design is going to be more complex but still achievable.

Scoping Phase of an Iterative PMLC Model

The Scoping Phase of the Iterative PMLC model takes on a bit more complexity than the Scoping Phase of the Linear or Incremental PMLC models, and it requires decisions that are not part of Linear or Incremental PMLC models. The key input for your decision to use an Iterative PMLC model is the requirements definition expressed by the Requirements Breakdown Structure (RBS). You and the client will review and discuss the RBS, paying particular attention to how complete you both think it is. Except in the simplest of situations, neither you nor the client can ever know for certain that the RBS is complete. This will always be a subjective decision. My advice is to err on the side of deciding that an RBS is less complete rather than more complete. That is, choosing an Iterative PMLC model rather than a Linear PMLC model or choosing an Adaptive PMLC model rather than an Iterative PMLC model is the safer ground.

Planning Phase of an Iterative PMLC Model

Planning is done at two levels in the Iterative PMLC model. The initial Planning Phase develops a high-level plan without much detail. The reason is that the full detail is not known at the initial stage. The functionality is known, and its design and development can be planned across any number of iterations. There are two ways to structure the high-level plan in the Iterative PMLC model.

The Complete Plan for Building the Known Solution

The first iteration in this plan may be of long duration in order to accommodate building a production version of the entire but incomplete known solution. If you feel that this iteration will be too long, then you might consider using a tool to model the solution instead. You will use that model throughout the entire project and create the production version of the complete solution at the end of the project.

To create this plan, use the Planning Process Group as defined in Chapter 3 and remember that you do not have a complete solution.

The Partial Plan for the High-Priority Functions

For this approach, you will begin the partial plan by prioritizing the functions and features in the initial RBS. The rule for prioritization will most likely be business value so that the deliverables from an iteration can be released to the end user, if the client so chooses. Alternatively, the prioritization might be based on risk or complexity: high-risk functions at the top of the list or high-complexity functions at the top of the list. By developing these functions early in the project, you ensure the successful completion of the project. In some cases, all the known functions and features will be developed in the first few iterations. Later iterations then drill down to possible areas for further identification and development of features. This is probably the most efficient of all the development alternatives you might consider. Yet another strategy would be to develop the high-risk parts of the system first. That removes one of the major variables that could adversely affect the project if left to a later iteration. A final rule may be to satisfy as many users as possible with your choice of functions or features.

Within each iteration, you might have concurrent swim lanes — each developing a different piece of functionality or expanding on its features. The determining factor is the resource pool from which you are drawing your team members. If you need to compress the development time frame, you can structure the project much like you would in the Linear PMLC model when you move from the Linear PMLC model to the Rapid Linear PMLC model or the FDD Linear PMLC model by adding concurrent swim lanes, each developing a different part of the solution.

Iterations are designed to help the client choose additional features or feature detail by having them and the end user spend some time working with the current partial solution. An iteration will present the user with alternatives from which to choose what will be added to the solution in preparation for the next iteration. Presumably those newfound features or feature detail are then prioritized and added to the next version of the solution. This game plan suggests that iterations be kept to two or less weeks. I have managed projects where the new prototyped solution was produced overnight.

Launching Phase of an Iterative PMLC Model

There is a significant difference between the project team for a Traditional Project Management (TPM) project and the project team for an APM project. Table 11-1 summarizes those differences.

Table 11-1: Differences Between a TPM Project Team and an APM Project Team

CHARACTERISTIC	TPM PROJECT TEAM	APM PROJECT TEAM
Size	Could be very large	Usually less than 15
Skill level	All levels	Most skilled
Location	Co-located or distributed	Co-located
Experience level	Junior to Senior	Senior
Position responsibility	Requires supervision	Unsupervised

The team profile for an Iterative PMLC model can be somewhat relaxed, whereas the profile for the Adaptive PMLC model should be adhered to as closely as possible.

In addition to the team differences that you have to consider, there is one major difference in the way scope change is dealt with. In TPM projects, there must be a formal scope change management process. That is not the case in an APM project. There is no need for a formal scope change management process in an APM project, because all of the learning and discovery that takes place during an iteration in an APM project is saved (in a Scope Bank, for example) and reviewed between iterations. The items in the Scope Bank are prioritized for integration into the solution in a later iteration.

Monitoring and Controlling Phase of an Iterative PMLC Model

In the Iterative PMLC model, the Monitoring and Controlling Phase begins to change. Because of the speculative nature of the iterative strategy, much of the heavy documentation and status reporting gives way to more informal reporting. Much of that formalism becomes non-value-added work and begins to burden the team with tasks that do not bring them any closer to the final solution. You want to be careful to not overload the architects and developers with those types of tasks. Let them remain relatively free to pursue the creative parts of the project. During the between-iteration reviews, you should review the status and progress of solution definition and make any needed adjustments.

Closing Phase of an Iterative PMLC Model

The Closing Phase for the Iterative PMLC model is similar to the Closing Phase for the TPM PMLC model in that there are client-specified criteria that must be met in order for the iteration or cycle deliverables to be considered complete. Those criteria were specified during iteration planning. Each iteration has closing criteria, but only regarding the iteration deliverables for that cycle. The only difference is that the project might end (all of the time and or money has been used), and there might still be features not integrated into the solution. These are noted in the final report and are to be considered whenever the next version of the solution will be commissioned.

Lessons learned take on an additional dimension. What did the team and the client learn about doing projects following the Iterative PMLC model? How can the approach be improved for the next iteration or project?

Characteristics

The characteristics of an effective Iterative PMLC model are as follows:

- The solution is known, but not to the expected depth (that is, features are not complete).
- It often uses iconic or simulated prototypes to discover the complete solution.

The Solution is Known, but Not to the Expected Depth

In simpler applications of the Iterative PMLC model, features may not be clearly defined. Should you do it this way or that way? These alternatives are presented to the client for deciding on which way is best by their criteria. They might choose to engage the end user in that decision. In more complex cases an iteration might explore and try to uncover possible alternatives.

Often Uses Iconic or Simulated Prototypes to Discover the Complete Solution

In more complex cases that require solution discovery a modeling approach would be the quick and efficient approach. Such situations often use an Adaptive PMLC model instead of an Iterative PMLC model. The decision as to which PMLC model is best is almost always subjective and dependent on factors other than solution clarity.

Strengths

The strengths of the Iterative PMLC model are as follows:

- The client can review the current partial solution for suggested improvements.
- Scope changes can be processed between iterations.
- You can adapt it to changing business conditions.

Client Reviews Current Partial Solution for Improvement

There is no substitute to experiencing and using a partial solution for the client. Narratives, process flow diagrams, and fancy graphics are nice, but they don't do the job for many clients and end users. They need to see and try out your suggested solution. This continual review by the client tends to keep the solution aligned with business needs.

Can Process Scope Changes Between Iterations

Although the simple Iterative models can receive and process scope change requests between iterations, you should try to stay in control by presenting the client with alternatives and ideas at each iteration. There will be cases where the client sees improvements in the solution that you didn't see. That will result in their proposing scope changes you will have to deal with. Process those requests between iterations, and if approved, integrate the changes into a future iteration.

Adaptable to Changing Business Conditions

I've already mentioned the fact that the world isn't standing still because you are managing a project. Except for projects that are internal and are unaffected by external factors, you have to be ready to accommodate the need for changes outside of your immediate control. If you choose a change-intolerant model such as the TPM models, you place the project at risk if the need for change arises.

Weaknesses

The weaknesses of the Iterative PMLC model are as follows:

- It requires a more actively involved client than Linear and Incremental PMLC models require.
- It requires co-located teams.
- The implementation of intermediate solutions can be problematic.
- The final solution cannot be defined at the start of the project.

Requires a More Actively Involved Client Than TPM Projects

The higher the likelihood of change the more you need active client involvement to make good business decisions regarding that change. Along with that involvement is the need for client ownership of the project. If you don't have both the involvement and ownership, the project is in harm's way. Clients who are only casually involved often get off plan with requests for wants rather than validated needs. The focus must continually be on real business value.

Requires Co-Located Teams

Having co-located teams is usually not possible, and this places a high-change project at great risk. I have managed high-change projects when the team was globally distributed, but they required much more management overhead than otherwise would have been the case. In high-change projects, real-time communications is a project management necessity. So if co-location is not possible, you had better spend a lot of time developing your communications management plan, especially the internal team and client communications components.

Difficult to Implement Intermediate Solutions

I commented on this at the beginning of this chapter. What is the capacity of your organization to absorb change, and what is your capacity for supporting intermediate solutions? Quarterly implementation of partial solutions is about as frequent as most organizations can accommodate. You have to keep the provision of support requirements in mind as well.

Final Solution Cannot Be Defined at the Start of the Project

The final solution is variable. The less you know about the solution at the beginning, the more unexpected it may be at the end. You might have started out thinking you were going to solve the entire problem, but you ended up solving only a part of it because the time or budget ran out. Or maybe parts of the problem turn out to be intractable, and you just have to live with the best you can do.

Types of Iterative PMLC Models

Several software development models map quite well into an Iterative PMLC model. Models that are Iterative by my definition are Prototyping and RUP. Scrum and DSDM are viewed by some as Iterative and by others as Adaptive. For my purposes, I have chosen to classify Scrum and DSDM as Adaptive. Also in the Adaptive category are Adaptive Software Development (ASD) and Adaptive Project Framework (APF). All of these models work across the Agile landscape — some better than others, depending on a number of other factors.

Prototyping PMLC Model

Prototyping has been around since the days of the pharaohs. Engineers and the construction industry use prototypes on most projects. Early prototypes were physical models built to scale. Other prototypes include iconic models and simulated models. The kind of prototype that is used in the Iterative PMLC model is called a *production prototype*. A production prototype is a working version of the known solution. It evolves as the project team learns more about the solution from using the current prototyped solution. The deployment of intermediate solutions is the decision of the client.

It should be obvious that the meaningful involvement of the client is critical to the success of APM approaches. The client works with a version of the solution and provides feedback to the project team as they envision further enhancements and changes to improve the solution. This process continues as version after version is put in place. The Prototyping PMLC model doesn't really have a rule that says you are finished and can move to the Closing Phase. At some point in time, the client will have spent enough money or time or is satisfied that all requirements have been met and the solution is as good as it is going to get. The project then moves to the Closing Phase. Also note that this model always presents the client with a production-ready version of the system. Succeeding versions merely add to the features and functions.

Iterative PMLC models are definitely in the learn-and-discover category. In the Prototyping Iterative PMLC model shown in Figure 11-2, the learning and discovering experience is obvious. With each iteration, more and more of the depth of the solution is revealed and implemented. That follows from the client and developers having an opportunity to experiment with the current solution and collaborate on further enhancements.

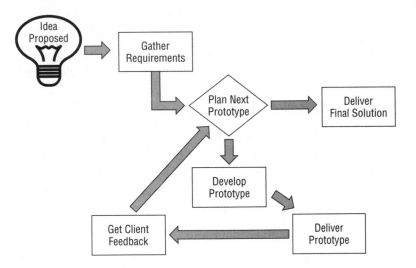

Figure 11-2: Prototyping model

The discovery of additional features is a process that fully engages the client in meaningful exchanges with the developers. Both client and developers work with the prototypes — sometimes independently and sometimes in collaboration. Collaboration usually follows periods where they work independently. The collaboration would be done in an effort to decide how to go forward with new or redefined features in the next and subsequent iterations.

The Prototyping Iterative PMLC model reaches some distance into Quadrant 2 because it can embrace learning and discovery even under conditions when not much of the solution is known. At some point on the uncertainty axis, it will make more sense to use an Iterative approach called Rational Unified Process (RUP), and then use an Adaptive PMLC model at the outermost point on the uncertainty axis.

As Figure 11-3 shows, the Prototyping model is an example of the Iterative PMLC model.

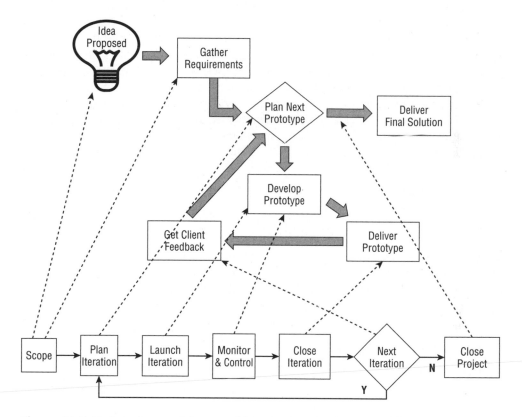

Figure 11-3: Prototyping model mapped into the Iterative PMLC model

The iteration is defined by the sequence Plan Next Prototype, Develop Prototype, and Deliver Prototype. Get Client Feedback includes the client commenting on the current prototype and the client deciding with the development team how to proceed. The next step could be another iteration or accepting the current prototype as the final solution. If the prototype is a product prototype, the final solution can be implemented. If it is an iconic or simulated solution, then a Linear PMLC model can be used to create the production version. In this case, the RBS can correctly be assumed to be complete.

**CASE STUDY – PIZZA DELIVERED QUICKLY (PDQ):
ORDER ENTRY SUBSYSTEM**

Because this is the first experience many PDQ employees will have with participating in a systems design project, Pepe has decided to begin the project with the simplest of the six subsystems — Order Entry. The employees will be most familiar with the current order-entry process and will easily relate to an automated version. Pepe has a good grasp of the current order-entry process and has decided to start with the Prototyping PMLC model. As added insurance he has decided to offer a one-day workshop to the employees who are currently responsible for receiving orders.

There is an important lesson here that Pepe teaches. When in doubt about the knowledge or understanding of your client with respect to any process you are going to use and that they will have to participate in, don't assume any prior knowledge. Begin with the most basic approach you can. In this case, a workshop is perfect. You can even run the workshop in parallel with the actual prototyping exercise on the automated order-entry process. Starting slow and building meaningful client involvement is always a good strategy.

Rational Unified Process (RUP)

RUP is a completely documented process for building a software system in an iterative fashion. An extensive library of books and Internet resources are available on the topic. A good starting point is the book by Stefan Bergstrom and Lotta Raberg entitled *Adopting the Rational Unified Process: Success with the RUP* (Addison-Wesley, 2004). The bibliography has several other reference texts on RUP.

The essential phases in a RUP approach are as follows:

- Inception
- Elaboration
- Construction
- Transition

Inception

Inception has as its objective the definition and concurrence of all the stakeholders as to the scope of the software development project. The scope is bounded by a number of use cases that define the functions that the software system must perform. Initial systems architecture is developed using these critical use cases. Cost, schedule, and risk are also estimated as a preparation for the Elaboration Phase.

Elaboration

Elaboration is the engineering phase of a RUP project. It is here that the details of the problem and its solution are formed and the architecture is finalized. That permits more refined estimates of time, cost, and risk. Prototypes are often built as an aid to the design considerations, more detailed functionality, and features.

Construction

In the Construction Phase, the current design is turned into a working system. If this is phase has been repeated, then the most recent designs are integrated into the current solution and a more enhanced solution is turned over to the client.

Transition

Transition turns over a solution that the client and end user can put into production. It need not be a complete solution, but it does need to have sufficient business value to be released to the end user by the client. Later minor enhancements will be made to integrate features defined but not integrated.

All four of these phases are embedded within each of the stages shown in Figure 11-4. The stages are not explicitly shown in the figure, however.

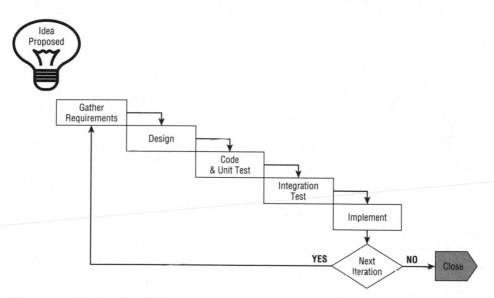

Figure 11-4: Rational Unified Process

RUP is probably the most well known of the Iterative software development processes. It adapts quite well to a process approach that is documentation-heavy or to one that is documentation-light. The foundation of RUP lies in the library of reusable code, requirements, designs, and so on. That library will have been built from previous project experiences, which means that RUP can have a long payback period. The library must be sufficiently populated to be useful from a Return On Investment (ROI) perspective. Four to five completed projects might be enough to begin to see some payback.

RUP can be used over the APM quadrant of the project landscape. When complexity and uncertainty are low but the solution is not fully defined, RUP is viewed as a heavy process. It requires considerable documentation, especially for code reuse. On the other hand, an organization that has considerable RUP experiences to draw upon can deploy a lighter RUP version across many projects.

As Figure 11-5 shows, RUP is an example of the Iterative PMLC model.

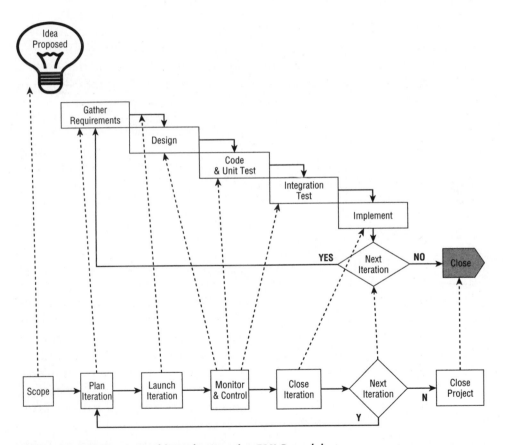

Figure 11-5: RUP mapped into the Iterative PMLC model

Note that a RUP iteration begins with gathering requirements and ends with implementation of the resulting solution. You can almost interpret a RUP iteration as defining a complete Linear PMLC model. A RUP iteration is commonly defined around one or more related use cases, so that dictates the process to be followed for gathering requirements.

When to Use an Iterative PMLC Model

In addition to what I have already discussed about the use of Iterative PMLC models, there is one application that I want to present. I have used Iterative PMLC models for just about every continuous process-improvement project I have ever managed. It is clearly the best-fit choice for the following reasons:

- Intuitive to the client
- Easily engages the client
- Immediate feedback on the effect of solution change
- Tolerant of assessing and evaluating the impact of alternatives
- No fixed deadline for completion

Intuitive to the Client

The client is kept in the safety of their own work environment, where they can see the solution unfold and have an opportunity to practice with it and to offer their acceptance of it. The solution evolves rapidly from iteration to iteration. The differences between the alternatives that you present can be compared with respect to how they work and are represented in the solution. The client becomes an active decision maker in the process, and that is what you want to happen.

Easily Engages the Client

In my experiences with the Prototyping Iterative PMLC model, I have seen the client get very actively involved, and even excited, about seeing their solution evolve. As long as you are using a production prototype, you are safe working within the constraints of client excitement. When you are using iconic or simulated prototypes, the situation is very different. The time between iterations is often very short because you are not building a production version, and the client tends to minimize the effort required to go from an iconic or simulated solution to the real solution. They are disappointed when you tell them it will be six months before they will see and be able to deploy the production version.

Immediate Feedback on the Effect of Solution Change

On a recent project, I decided to use a simulated prototype approach to brainstorm possible solutions and was able to create a successive version of the solution in a matter of hours, and even minutes in some cases, not days or weeks. The simulated solution looked just like the production solution, but there was no logic generating screen after screen. It looked real to the client. I could feel the electricity in the air as the client really got into the process. Ideas were flowing freely, and the developers were able to respond quickly.

Tolerant of Assessing and Evaluating the Impact of Alternatives

In my experience with prototypes, I have gotten the most benefit out of using them on process-improvement projects. In this context, the time between iterations is long enough to implement a process change and let it operate long enough to measure the impact of the change on process performance. Process improvement projects are usually continuous improvement projects. There are target performance metrics that you would like to see in an improved process and you continue with iterations until the performance is reached or determined to be at its best.

No Fixed Deadline for Completion

The stopping rule for a prototyping project is usually qualitative, not quantitative. The solution either meets or does not meet client requirements, or the money runs out. The number of iterations is variable. Iteration timeboxes are usually not specified. But short duration timeboxes are good.

Adaptive Project Management Life Cycle

The Adaptive models are more appropriate for projects involving higher levels of uncertainty and complexity than the Iterative models. In that sense, they fill a void between the Iterative and Extreme models. Adaptive models are more useful than Iterative models in those situations where very little is known about the solution. Keep in mind that solution discovery is still the focus of these models. Each iteration in the Adaptive models must address not only task completion for newly defined functions and features but also further solution definition through function and feature discovery. It is the discovery part of the Adaptive PMLC models that sets them apart from the Iterative PMLC models.

Definition

An Adaptive PMLC model consists of a number of phases that are repeated in cycles, with a feedback loop after each cycle is completed. Each cycle proceeds based on an incomplete and limited understanding of the solution. Each cycle learns from the preceding cycles and plans the next cycle in an attempt to converge on an acceptable solution. At the discretion of the client, a cycle may include the release of a partial solution.

Unlike the Iterative PMLC model where some depth of the solution is not known (features, for example), the Adaptive PMLC model is missing both depth and breadth of the solution. Figure 11-6 depicts the Adaptive PMLC model for projects that meet the conditions of an incomplete solution due to missing features and functions.

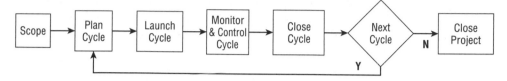

Figure 11-6: Adaptive PMLC model

With the exception of using the term "cycles" in place of "iterations," the Process Group–level diagram for the Adaptive PMLC model is identical to the Iterative PMLC model. But the similarity ends there.

The four Adaptive models you will study here are Adaptive Software Development (ASD), Adaptive Project Framework (APF), Dynamic Systems Development Method (DSDM), and Scrum. All four are in popular use. Except for APF, the other models are used almost exclusively for software development. ASD, DSDM, and Scrum were built for that application. APF was built to be applicable to any type of project. For that reason, I offer a more in-depth discussion of APF. All four models thrive on learning, discovery, and change. In time, and with enough cycles, you hope that an acceptable solution will emerge.

In the Adaptive PMLC model, as with other Agile approaches, the degree to which the solution is known might vary over a wide range from knowing a lot but not all (projects that are a close fit for the Iterative PMLC models) to knowing very little (projects that are a close fit for the Adaptive PMLC models). The less that is known about the solution, the more risk, uncertainty, and complexity will be present. To remove the uncertainty associated with these projects, the solution has to be discovered. That will happen through a continuous change process from cycle to cycle. That change process is designed to create convergence to a complete solution. In the absence of that convergence, Adaptive projects are frequently cancelled and restarted in some other promising direction.

NOTE That cancellation is not a sign of failure but instead is the result of discovering that the solution is found by pursuing a different line of attack. To take advantage of this feature of Adaptive models, give some consideration for the trip wires that you establish for detecting an out-of-control situation.

The success of Adaptive PMLC models is leveraged by expecting and accommodating frequent change. Change is the result of learning and discovery by the team and, most importantly, by the client. Because change will have a dramatic impact on the project, only a minimalist approach to planning is employed. Planning is actually done just in time and only for the next cycle. No effort is wasted on planning the future. The future is unknown, and any effort at planning that future will be viewed as non-value-added work. All Quadrant 2 approaches are designed to minimize non-value-added work.

Compared to the Iterative PMLC model, the Adaptive PMLC model requires more involvement with the client. As you will learn in the discussion of specific Adaptive PMLC models, clients have more of a directive role in the project than they do in the Linear, Incremental, and even Iterative PMLC models. Four Adaptive PMLC models are discussed later in this chapter in the order of increasing client involvement: ASD, APF, DSDM, and Scrum. Once you have decided that an Adaptive PMLC model is a best fit for your project, you can choose the specific model based on your expected involvement with the client. Without their meaningful involvement, the Adaptive PMLC model project has little chance of success. To be meaningful, the client must be fully involved in the decisions to go forward with the project and in what direction. I have had projects where the client was the primary decision maker, and I was there to keep the project pointed in the right direction. Some clients have the confidence and leadership skills to assume this role; others do not, and the more traditional role of the project manager is employed.

Scoping Phase of an Adaptive PMLC Model

The Scoping Phase of the Adaptive PMLC model is a high-level activity because not much is known about the solution. The missing functions and features have to be discovered and learned through repeated cycles much like the Iterative SDPM strategy. For the Adaptive PMLC model, the scoping activities merely set the boundaries and the high-level parameters that will be the foundation on which you proceed to learn and discover. As part of the Scoping Phase deliverables, you will document requirements, as you know them; functionality, as you know it; and features, if you know any. In addition, you will specify the number of cycles and cycle length for the first cycle. If you have enough insight into the solution, you might tentatively map out the cycle objectives at a high level. A partial high-level Work Breakdown Structure (WBS) can help complete this exercise.

Planning Phase of an Adaptive PMLC Model

At this point in the Adaptive PMLC model, planning is done for the coming cycle. High-level planning was done as part of the Scoping Phase. Based on the known functionality and features that will be built in the coming cycle, a detailed plan is developed. This plan utilizes all of the tools, templates, and processes that were defined for the Planning Process Group.

Remember that the typical cycle timebox is 2–4 weeks. So the tools, templates, and processes you use to plan a cycle don't have to be that sophisticated. An Agile project I recently managed was a $5M three-year project. I used sticky notes, marking pens, and whiteboards for every cycle plan. The project was completed ahead of schedule and under budget! I could have used a project management software package, but I have found that the overhead associated with their use was like killing mosquitoes with a sledge hammer.

NOTE The sticky notes often included clarification information that was preserved in the documentation for future use.

Launching Phase of an Adaptive PMLC Model

The Launching Phase will be the same as discussed in the Iterative PMLC model. The launch activities will include establishing team operating rules, the decision-making process, conflict management, team meetings, and a problem-solving approach. The only difference will be defining the approach that will be used to establish subteams and their work plan to accommodate concurrent swim lane tasks.

Monitoring and Controlling Phase of an Adaptive PMLC Model

As you move from the Iterative PMLC model to the Adaptive PMLC model, there is a marked shift from formality to informality when it comes to this phase. That move to informality makes room for the marked increase in creativity that the team is called upon to deliver. Creativity and formality are not comfortable bedfellows. You need to give the team and the client the best opportunity you can to be successful and that means relaxing the need for status reporting and strict control of the schedule. The nature of these projects is that they are focused on delivering value rather than being focused on meeting time and cost criteria.

The monitoring and controlling functions pertain to the cycle build tasks. A cumulative history of project performance metrics should be maintained. These metrics should inform the project team about the rate at which convergence to an acceptable solution is occurring. Frequency of changes, severity of change, and similar metrics can help. As part of that control function, the team collects whatever learning and discovery took place and records it in the Scope Bank. All change requests go into the Scope Bank as well. No changes are implemented within a cycle. All changes and other learning and discovery are reviewed at the checkpoint. The review results in placing newly discovered functions and features into a priority list for consideration at the next or some future cycle.

One metric that I have found useful is to track the size of the Scope Bank over each cycle. Figure 11-7 shows three trends in Scope Bank size that I have seen in my client engagements.

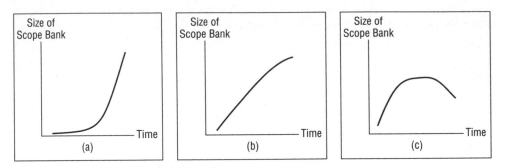

Figure 11-7: Tracking Scope Bank size

Increasing at an Increasing Rate

This is the trend displayed in Figure 11-7(a). It indicates a client whose involvement has increased over time, and it indicates that the solution is diverging. Changes beget changes, and those changes beget even more changes. Although it is good to have increased client involvement, it comes too late. If you see a pattern like this, it's too late for any corrective action to be taken. Your intervention should have come much earlier so that you would have a chance to work with the client to increase their involvement earlier in the project. The solution would have been to put some trip wires in place as early warning signs that client involvement is below expectations.

Increasing at a Decreasing Rate

Figure 11-7(b) shows that the size of the Scope Bank is increasing at a decreasing rate. That may be a good sign in that the size of the Scope Bank may eventually turn to an actual decrease. That fact that it is still increasing is not good. Like panel (a), it might be indicative that the solution is diverging. I would wonder if it weren't too late.

Decreasing at an Increasing Rate

Figure 11-7(c) is the desired trend. It shows an exemplary level of client involvement and good solution convergence.

Closing Phase of an Adaptive PMLC Model

The Closing Phase produces the typical artifacts: lessons learned, validation of success criteria, and so forth. In addition to those, you might have items left in the Scope Bank that were not included in any cycle build. These are to be documented and held for the next version of the solution.

Characteristics

The characteristics of an effective Adaptive PMLC model are as follows:

- Iterative structure
- Just-in-time planning
- Critical mission projects
- Thrives on change through learning and discovery

Iterative Structure

An Adaptive PMLC model is structured around iterations that are designed to find and complete the solution. Each Adaptive PMLC model finds and defines that solution in a different way.

Just-in-Time Planning

For all of the Adaptive PMLC models, planning is confined to the next iteration. There is no speculation on what might be in the solution and then planning for it. That would turn out to be a potential waste of time.

Critical Mission Projects

Because of the complexity and uncertainty associated with an Adaptive project, these projects are high risk. With that high risk comes high business value. They are undertaken because their successful completion is critical to the enterprise.

Thrives on Change through Learning and Discovery

Learning and discovery sets Adaptive projects apart from Iterative projects. The learning and discovery can come about only with the client being heavily involved in the project. There is an increasing dependence on that involvement as you move across the Adaptive landscape from the ASD Adaptive PMLC model to the Scrum Adaptive PMLC model.

Strengths

The strengths of the Adaptive PMLC model are as follows:

- Does not waste time on non-value-added work
- Avoids all management issues processing scope change requests

■ Does not waste time planning uncertainty

■ Provides maximum business value within the given time and cost constraints

Does Not Waste Time on Non-Value-Added Work

One of the biggest wastes in the Linear and Incremental PMLC models is the creation of a complete project plan that will change several times before the project is complete. Table 10-1 in Chapter 10 gave a hypothetical example that showed how easy it was to waste 10 percent of the project time constantly repeating the rescheduling of tasks in the outer part of the schedule. The Adaptive PMLC models do not suffer from this waste. These PMLC models plan what is known to be in the solution, and they do that planning just in time. There is no wasted time. In fact, if a project could be done twice — once using a Linear PMLC model and once using an Adaptive PMLC model — the one using an Adaptive PMLC model would always finish sooner and deliver a better solution at less cost. No exceptions.

Avoids All Management Issues Processing Scope Change Requests

In the Adaptive PMLC models, there is no formal scope change management process. What otherwise would have been a scope change request in a Linear or an Incremental PMLC model is simply a note to the Scope Bank in the Adaptive PMLC models. That item is considered and prioritized along with other functionality and features yet to be integrated into the solution. Best of all, it does not take time away from the team's work. It is imbedded in the planning time spent between cycles.

Does Not Waste Time Planning Uncertainty

No one can know the future, so why waste time guessing what it might be and then planning for it? I have encountered many project managers who have a project that clearly fits an APM model, but they force-fit it to a TPM model. If that has been your practice in the past, stop it right now. You will save yourself many heartaches and project failures. Spend your time planning the certainty part of the project, and leave the uncertainty to the future (you will discover it in good time).

Provides Maximum Business Value within the Given Time and Cost Constraints

At the completion of each cycle, the entire project team will consider what is still missing from the solution and how it might be discovered and integrated.

Those missing pieces should be prioritized based on business value and their discovery should be investigated. So, every cycle ends with a more complete solution than the previous cycle, and the new solution has maximum business value at that point in time. If the project should be cancelled for any reason, the client will walk away with the best that could have been done for the effort, time, and money expended. That is not the case with any project that uses a Linear PMLC model and most projects that use an Incremental PMLC model.

Weaknesses of the Adaptive PMLC Model

The weaknesses of the Adaptive PMLC model are as follows:

- Must have meaningful client involvement
- Cannot identify exactly what will be delivered at the end of the project

Must Have Meaningful Client Involvement

You know that the Iterative PMLC models benefit from client input. That is a passive type of input. You show the client something, they give it thumbs up or down, and you go on to the next iteration. In an Adaptive PMLC model, that involvement changes from passive to active. The entire project team collaborates on the current solution. The responsibility for suggesting the next version of the solution is shared equally among the client members and the developer members of the project team. Clients must be fully engaged and must accept responsibility for the project along with the development team. Client involvement increases across the Adaptive PMLC models in the following order: ASD, APF, DSDM, and Scrum. In the Scrum Adaptive PMLC model, there is no project manager. The development team is a self-organized team. If you are more comfortable having a named project manager, the closest in a Scrum project is the client. A client is called the Product Owner in a Scrum project. Each Scrum project has a Scrum Master assigned to the project. For now consider the Scrum Master as a project administrator and compliance officer. See the "Scrum" section later in the chapter for a more thorough discussion of the roles that are represented on the Scrum team.

Cannot Identify Exactly What Will Be Delivered at the End of the Project

The Linear and Incremental thinkers have a real problem with not knowing what will be delivered. In the early days of Agile projects, I vividly remember prospective clients saying, "You mean I am going to give you $500,000 and six months, and you can't tell me what I am going to get?"

"That's right," I said, "but you are going to get the most business value that you and I can deliver for that money and time. You came to me with an unsolved problem that had to be solved, and we are going to do our best to solve it with the money and time you are willing to invest."

Types of Adaptive PMLC Models

There are four Adaptive PMLC models that I would like to bring to your attention. There are others, but these four are more popularly used. Three are used primarily for software development: ASD, DSDM, and Scrum. The fourth is APF, which I developed for use on any type of agile or extreme project. I've ordered my presentation of the four based on the extent to which meaningful client involvement is needed. They all require meaningful client involvement, but I put ASD at the low end and Scrum at the high end.

Adaptive Software Development (ASD)

The first Adaptive model I want to take a look at is the ASD PMLC model. ASD is fully described in a book by James A. Highsmith III titled *Adaptive Software Development: A Collaborative Approach to Managing Complex Systems* (Dorsett House, 1999). The description in this section is a brief adaptation of his presentation.

ASD has three phases, as shown in Figure 11-8: Speculate, Collaborate, and Learn.

Speculate

The Speculate Phase is nothing more than a guess at what the final goal and solution might look like. It might be correct, or it might be far from the mark. It really doesn't make much difference in the final analysis because the self-correcting nature of ASD will eventually lead the team to the right solution. "Get it right the last time" is all that matters. All of the tools, templates, and processes of the Scoping Process Group are used as part of Project Initiation. A preliminary guess at the objectives of each cycle is recorded in this phase as well.

Collaborate

After the Speculate Phase has been completed, it is time to take stock of where the team and client are with respect to a final solution. What great discoveries did the team and the client make? All tools, templates, and processes of the Launching Process Group and the Monitoring and Controlling Process Group are typically used during Concurrent Component Engineering.

Learn

What was learned from the just completed phase, and how might that redirect the team for the next phase?

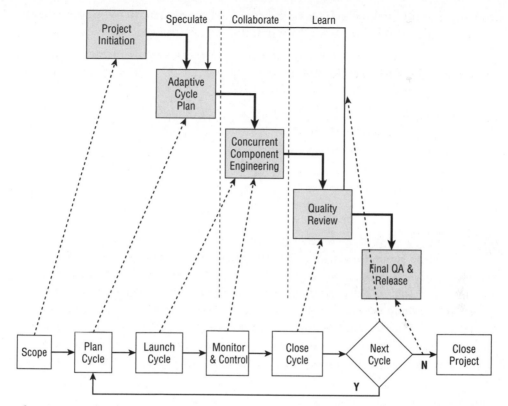

Figure 11-8: The three phases of ASD

You might have noticed in Figure 11-8 that each of these three phases encompasses different activities. The following list takes a brief tour inside each of these three phases and explains the activities that go on there.

- **Project Initiation** — The objective of the Project Initiation Phase is to clearly establish project expectations among the sponsor, the client, the project team, and any other project stakeholders. This would be a good place to discuss, agree upon, and approve the Project Overview Statement (POS). For a project of long duration (more than six months), it might be a good idea to hold a kick-off meeting, which might last two to three days. During that time, requirements can be gathered and documented and the POS written.

- **Adaptive Cycle Plan** — Other deliverables from the kick-off meeting might include the project timebox, the optimal number of cycles and the timebox for each, and objective statements for each cycle.

  Every cycle begins with a plan. These plans are high-level. Functionality is assigned to subteams, and the details are left to them to establish. This is at odds with TPM, which requires organized management oversight against a detailed plan. ASD is light when it comes to management processes.

- **Concurrent Component Engineering** — Several concurrent swim lanes are established for each functionality component. Each subteam is responsible for some part of the functionality.

- **Quality Review** — This is the time for the client to review what has been completed to date and revise accordingly. New functionality might emerge and is reprioritized for consideration in later cycles.

- **Final QA and Release** — At some point, the client declares the requirements met, and there is a final acceptance test procedure and release of the product.

WARNING Adaptive models can accommodate quite a wide range of situations where some or even all of the solution cannot be defined. Although the majority of projects will fall into this class, do not be too quick to make that judgment. Consider the project and what is known about the goal and solution. Perhaps an Adaptive model is the best choice. Even if that is the starting model, continue to ask yourself whether it is the most appropriate model. As the project matures and more of the solution becomes evident, it might make sense to switch to one of the other models in the Linear, Incremental, or Iterative class.

Adaptive Project Framework

The Adaptive Project Framework (APF), which I developed in 2003-4, unlike most of the approaches in Quadrant 2, is not limited to software development. Although it is beyond the scope of this book to discuss this in detail, APF is equally at home with software development, process improvement, product development, and research and development projects. APF was first used on product design and process design projects. The interested reader can see my book on the topic, *Adaptive Project Framework: Managing Complexity in the Face of Uncertainty* (Addison-Wesley, 2010).

The fundamental concept underlying APF is that scope is variable, and within specified time and cost constraints, APF maximizes business value by adjusting scope at each iteration. It does this by making the client the central figure in deciding what constitutes that maximum business value. At each iteration, the client has an opportunity to change the direction of the project based on what was learned from previous iterations. This constant adjustment means that an APF project's course is constantly corrected to ensure the delivery of maximum business value in the eyes of the client. In other words, change is embraced, not avoided. Planning takes on a whole new meaning in APF. Initial APF planning is done at a high level and is component-based or function-based, as opposed to initial TPM planning, which is activity-based and task-based. APF planning at the micro level is done within iterations. It begins with a mid-level component-based or function-based WBS and ends with a micro-level activity-based and task-based WBS. I like to think of it as just-in-time planning. The underlying strategy to APF planning is not to speculate on the future — it's a waste of time. *When in doubt, leave it out!* At each iteration, plan for what you know to be factual. So, planning is done in chunks, where each chunk represents work that will only require a few weeks, and it will be completed in the next cycle. Like a production prototype, APF produces a partial but workable solution, so even if the project is terminated prematurely, business value is generated.

What Is the Adaptive Project Framework?

For businesses that have only recently realized the pain of not having a project management process in place and are struggling to adapt traditional practices advocated by the SEI and PMI to nontraditional projects, I say, *"Stop wasting your time!"* It's time to pay attention to the signals coming from the business environment and discover how projects can succeed in the fast-paced, constantly changing, and high-quality demands of the new business model. This is definitely not your father's project management. I don't even use the word *management*. APF represents a shift in thinking about projects and how they should be run. I like to think of APF as the infrastructure upon which you build and continuously revise the recipe for managing your project. Here are a few observations on APF:

- It is a new mind-set — one that thrives on change rather than one that avoids change.
- It is not a "one size fits all" approach — it continuously adapts to the unique character of the specific business situation as it learns more about that business situation.
- It utilizes a just-in-time planning approach.
- It adapts tools and processes from TPM and Extreme Project Management (xPM) to the special needs of APF.
- It is based on the principle that you learn by doing.
- It guarantees "if we build it, they will come."
- It seeks to "get it right" every time.
- It's client-focused and client-driven.
- It is grounded in a set of immutable core values.
- It ensures maximum business value for the time and dollars expended.
- It is a framework that has squeezed out all of the non-value-added work that it possibly could.

- It meaningfully and fully engages the client as the primary decision maker.

- It creates a shared partnership with shared responsibility between requestor and provider.

- It is a framework that works — 100 percent of the time! No exceptions!

Do I have your attention? APF is new. APF is exciting. APF works. APF has been adopted as the de facto standard in several client companies. I urge you to step outside the comfort zone of Traditional Project Management and try APF. Be assured that I have not abandoned TPM. As discussed in Chapter 10, there are many projects for which TPM is a good fit. It has several tools and processes that make sense even with the type of project for which APF was designed. Many of those tools and processes have been incorporated into APF.

APF Core Values

You might have noticed that one of the characteristics of APF mentioned in the previous section is that APF is grounded in a set of immutable core values. This means that APF is more than just a framework — it represents an entirely new way of thinking about clients, how best to serve them, and how to add significant business value to the enterprise at the same time. Through its core values, APF establishes a collaborative environment within which the client and the development team can work effectively to create business value for the enterprise. This way of thinking is embodied in the following six core values:

- **Client-focused** — The phrases "walk in the shoes of the client" and "always do what is right for the client" express what it means to be client-focused. This is the most important of the core values. The needs of the client must always come first as long as they are within the bounds of ethical business practices. This can never be compromised. More than simply keeping it in mind, being client-focused must be obvious through your interactions with one another and with your clients. And this doesn't mean a passive acceptance of whatever the client might request. Client-focused also means that you have clients' best interests at heart, obligating you to challenge ideas, wishes, and wants whenever you believe challenge is called for. As a project manager, you need to do the right things for the right reasons and to always act with integrity.

  How you and your team relate to the client will be different depending on the client's understanding and comfort with the tools, templates, and processes you use. Some will be very comfortable based on your prior project experience with them. Others will need to be led along the way. You have to be ready to be adaptive. Always!

- **Client-driven** — Engage the client in every way that you can. You want them to have significant meaningful involvement, to have the sense that they are determining the direction that the project is taking. Remember, it's their money, and they have the right to choose how it will be spent. At the extreme, this would mean having the client take on the role and responsibilities of the project manager. This will not happen very often, but you should look for opportunities to make it happen. The more likely situation will have co-project managers — one from the client and you. In this effective arrangement, a clear and established co-ownership exists, and you both share equally in the success and failure of the project. Research tells me that this is a key to successful implementation. I maintain constant vigilance on keeping projects client-driven and have based my 20+ year consulting practice on this core value.

- **Incremental results early and often** — Deliver a working application to the client as early as possible, especially in cases where the real solution for the client has not yet surfaced despite all best efforts. The functionality of the first iteration of the application may be very limited, but it should deliver business value and give the client an early feel for what the final deliverables will be. Giving the client an opportunity to work with something concrete is always better than asking them to react to some vague concept described in a complex specification document. If you can put something in front of the client early in the project and repeat it often, they get a sense of belonging and ownership — they become engaged in the project. You should clearly sense the degree to which they are engaged very early in the project. That's an important part of your strategy to grow and sustain their meaningful involvement. In later iterations, you can lengthen the cycle and not risk losing the client's interest.

- **Continuous questioning and introspection** — When you build a solution iteratively, you have more chances for creativity and more opportunity to adjust as better and more valuable features or functions are discovered. The client and the project team should always be looking for improvements in the solution or the functionality offered both as the cycle build proceeds and as they look back at previous cycles. All of this learning and discovery comes together in the Client Checkpoint Phase, where the client and the project team propose, discuss, and approve changes in a spirit of openness. Neither party should be afraid to offer or challenge an idea or the real value of some present or future deliverable. Teams and clients should understand that if any one of them has an idea and doesn't share it, it's dereliction of their responsibility to the team.

- **Change is progress to a better solution** — One of my colleagues is often heard saying: "You're always smarter tomorrow than you are today." He is referring to improving estimates over time, but his comment applies to APF as well. APF starts with the client and you agreeing on a definition of what is needed and what will be delivered. Your efforts will be good and in earnest, but remember that all you have done to this point is take the best guess you can as to what will be done. This guess might turn out to be very good, but that is not important. What is important is that working with the deliverables from the first cycle gives both parties a better picture of what should be delivered and, because of their experiences with early deliverables, makes them smarter as they move to uncover the solution going forward in the next cycle.

▪ **Don't speculate on the future** — Someone once said: "If you don't know the future, why waste time planning for it?" APF strips out all non-value-added work. Planning is done just in time. It focuses on what is known about the solution, not on what is not known. It discovers a new function or feature, and then plans how to build and integrate it into the solution. When in doubt, leave it out. APF is designed to spend the client's money on business value not on non-value-added work.

Figure 11-9 is a graphic portrayal of how the APF is structured. The next five short sections dig deeper into each of the five phases of APF shown in the figure: Version Scope, Cycle Plan, Cycle Build, Client Checkpoint, and Post-Version Review.

First note the basic structure of APF. There are four StageGates denoted by the decision diamonds at the right side of each phase. These are decision points that allow passage to the next phase. They are as follows:

▪ **StageGate #1** — Approval to begin planning the project

▪ **StageGate #2** — Approval to plan the first cycle

▪ **StageGate #3** — Approval to conduct the client checkpoint

▪ **StageGate #4** — Approval to close the project

Version Scope

The Version Scope (Figure 11-10) is the kick-off of an APF project. A rough idea of the needs is documented, and a high-level plan is constructed as to how the project will go forward. The Version Scope might be completed in a matter of hours, or it might take several days. It all depends on the level of complexity and uncertainty present in the project.

There are two major parts to Version Scope: a defining part and a planning part. The defining part can effectively be completed by two parties: a requestor and a provider. These may each be single individuals or small groups that represent the two parties. In either case, the critical factor is that they not only represent their constituency, but they speak for and can make decisions for their constituency. The planning part is not unlike the early stages of TPM planning. It should be attended by the stakeholders and core project team. The difference here is that the version plan is not a detailed plan. It does not provide a detailed definition of the work to be done or of a schedule to be followed. Those details are part of the cycle plan.

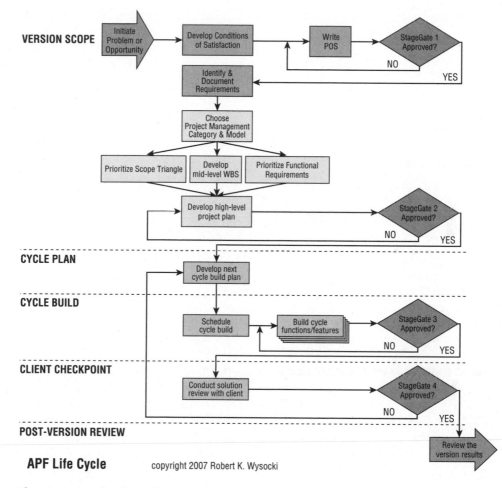

APF Life Cycle   copyright 2007 Robert K. Wysocki

Figure 11-9: Adaptive Project Framework

There are eight deliverables from Version Scope, as listed here:

- Conditions of Satisfaction (COS)
- Project Overview Statement (POS)
- Requirements Breakdown Structure (RBS)
- Prioritized scope triangle
- Prioritized functions

- Mid-level Work Breakdown Structure (WBS) and dependencies
- Cycle timebox
- Number of cycles

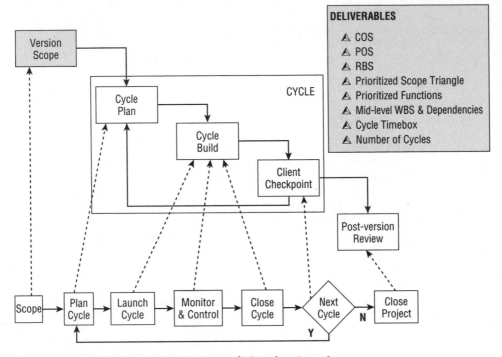

Figure 11-10: Adaptive Project Framework (Version Scope)

The result of generating the COS or RBS is the input to the decision as to what PMLC model will be used: Linear, Incremental, Iterative, Adaptive, or Extreme TPM. For this example, I have already decided that Adaptive PMLC model is the choice, so the next step is to write the POS. The five components of the scope triangle along with the known functions are prioritized. The next deliverable from Version Scope is a prioritization of the variables that define the scope triangle (time, cost, resources, scope, and quality). This prioritization will be used later as an aid to decision making and problem solving during the Cycle Build Phase.

The next deliverable from Version Scope is a prioritized list of the functionality that has been requested and agreed to in the COS or the RBS. Both you and the client recognize that this list may change but at this point in the project the list reflects the best information available.

The next deliverable from Version Scope is the mid-level WBS. For planning purposes, a mid-level WBS is one that shows a one-level decomposition of each functional requirement. Generally such a WBS would have a two- or three-level decomposition. The number of levels is not important. What's important is that you have at least one level of decomposition for each functional requirement. At this point, any more WBS detail is not considered useful. The reason for that will become clear in the Cycle Plan Phase. The traditionalist would have a problem with this because the entire foundation of traditional project planning and scheduling is based on having a complete WBS. I contend that the time spent creating a complete WBS at this stage is largely a waste of time. Why plan for the future when you don't know what it is? In this case, the piece that is missing is you are not exactly sure how you are going to deliver the functionality. You do know what functionality has to be delivered and are using that firm information to generate the mid-level WBS, but not the complete WBS. The complete WBS will eventually be generated when you know enough to do so. That will happen as the result of several iterations of Cycle Plan ➤ Cycle Build ➤ Client Checkpoint. You will generate the WBS when you need it and not before, but when you do generate it, you will know that it is correct and not a guess.

The next deliverable from Version Scope is a prioritized list of the known functions and features of the current partial solution. Business value is the typical choice for the prioritization variable. This criterion would say that high business value has the highest priority and low business value has the lowest priority. Why is that? From a business perspective, this criterion makes perfect sense. Get the most business value into the solution ASAP and start to reap some of the benefits.

Finally, a preliminary decision on cycle timebox length and number of cycles gives some structure to the entire project.

You are probably wondering why you would want to do this or even what it means to prioritize the scope triangle. First, recall the scope triangle, originally introduced in Chapter 1 and shown again in Figure 11-11.

Figure 11-11: The scope triangle

Prioritization Approaches

Before I leave this topic, I need to discuss what the prioritization of the scope triangle looks like. There are three variations I have used extensively. They were introduced in Chapter 3 but are repeated here to reinforce their importance in

APF decision making. They are briefly described in the following sections by way of examples.

Forced Ranking

The first approach is called Forced Ranking. This approach is best explained by way of an example. Suppose there are six functions and a panel of four managers to rank the functions. They can use any criteria they wish, and they do not have to describe the criteria they used. The results of their rankings are shown in Table 11-2.

Table 11-2: Example of a Forced Ranking

MANAGER FUNCTION	A	B	C	D	RANK SUM	FORCED RANK
1	2	3	2	4	11	3
2	4	1	1	2	8	1
3	6	2	5	5	18	5
4	1	5	3	1	10	2
5	3	4	4	3	14	4
6	5	6	6	6	23	6

The individual rankings from each of the four managers for a specific function are added to produce the Rank Sum for each function. Low values for the Rank Sum are indicative of functions that have been given high priority by the managers. For example, Function 2 has the lowest Rank Sum, so it's the highest priority function. Ties are possible. Ties can be broken in a number of ways. I prefer to use the existing rankings to break ties. For example, taking the tied function with the lowest rank score and moving it to the next lowest forced rank breaks a tie.

Paired Comparison

Paired Comparisons are a bit more labor intensive. Table 11-3 shows an example of six functions that are to be ranked. To do that, each function will be compared to every other function. For example, say you are comparing Function 2 (designated by row 2) to Function 3 (designated by column 3). If you think Function 2 is more important than Function 3, place a 1 in row 2 column 3 and place a 0 in row 3 column 2. In this example, Function 3 was more important than Function 2. Add the scores across the columns to calculate the Sum for each Function. The highest Sum is the highest Ranked Function. So in this example, Function 4 has the highest rank, and Function 6 has the lowest rank.

Table 11-3: Paired Comparison

	1	2	3	4	5	6	SUM	RANK
1	X	1	1	0	1	1	4	2
2	0	X	1	0	1	1	3	3
3	0	0	X	0	0	1	1	5
4	1	1	1	X	1	1	5	1
5	0	0	1	0	X	1	2	4
6	0	0	0	0	0	X	0	6

MoSCoW

The third prioritization is called MoSCoW. You may not be familiar with the acronym, but you are familiar with the rule. It's your "Must Haves," "Should Haves," and "Wouldn't It Be Nice to Haves" categories. It's your A, B, or C bucket. Here there are four buckets, where *M* stands for Must Haves, *S* stands for Should Haves, *C* stands for Could Haves, and *W* stands for Wouldn't It Be Nice to Haves. Every function is assigned to one and only one bucket. Be careful with this one because there is a temptation to make everything a "must have." To prevent that from happening, you might put a rule in place that every bucket must have at least 20 percent of the functions in it. Adjust the percentage to suit your taste.

Scope Triangle Ranking Matrix

However you decide to prioritize the five variables in the scope triangle, you should represent them in matrix form as shown in Table 11-4. This ranking tells the team what the client is willing to sacrifice or do if a problem occurs. In the example in Table 11-4, the most critical variable for this project is time. There is something compelling the client to get the solution ASAP, so time is least likely to be a negotiating point for resolving a problem. Cost, on the other hand, is the variable most likely to be a negotiating point for the client. Their first point of departure from the current plan would be to increase the budget.

Table 11-4: Scope Triangle Ranking Matrix

PRIORITY VARIABLE	CRITICAL				FLEXIBLE
	(1)	(2)	(3)	(4)	(5)
Scope				X	
Quality			X		
Time	X				
Cost					X
Resource Availability		X			

Every project will have its own matrix. It is important that you collaborate with the client on what their rankings are for this project. Do this during the Version Scope Phase and revisit it during the Client Checkpoint Phase. Changes in the business climate could affect this matrix.

You have probably guessed by now that more than one version of the solution is expected. In this version, the solution is constrained to the maximum business value that can be delivered within the time and cost constraints. If the client is willing to spend more money and give you more time and feels that additional business value can be created, you will do a second version. However, that doesn't pertain to this version, so any future versions of the solution don't need to be considered at this point. Information will be gathered during this version that will inform management about any further enhancements they might want to consider in future versions. These are the normal releases you see in products, services, and systems.

Version Budget and Timebox

In APF, the budget and timebox are fixed by the client or senior management. Because of the volatility of an APF project, I would try to keep a version timebox to less than nine months, which is less than your fiscal year if funding decisions are of concern. Any longer and you invite many of the problems that plague the traditionalist. There are no rolling schedules. There is no going back to the well for another budget increase. One of the objectives in an APF project is to maximize business value under fixed time and cost constraints. *Period!* The business validation of your proposed project is based on those two constraints. This is a very different approach to the project than the traditionalist would take. As long as the client is satisfied that the maximum business value has been attained for the time and dollars expended, the project was successfully completed. If the client and the project team pay attention, this result can be achieved every time. No exceptions! Unfortunately the maximum business value they attained may not meet the success criteria, but that is an issue for the client to deal with and should not determine the success or failure of the APF approach. Whatever didn't get done in this version will have to be left for the next version or not be done at all. Hence, you have another reason for keeping the project scope to a feasible minimum and the timebox to less than nine months. That will reduce the need to extend schedules or obtain more dollars. It will also reduce the financial loss to the organization as compared to the traditional approach. With APF, you can kill a bad project much earlier than you can with the traditional approach, and that accounts for the dollar savings.

Write the Project Overview Statement

The negotiated COS agreement provides the input you need to generate the POS. You learned about both of these in Chapter 3. Recall that the POS is a short document (ideally one page) that concisely states what is to be done in the project, why it is to be done, and what business value it will provide to the enterprise when completed. It should be signed by the requestor and the provider.

Generate the RBS

If the project passes the first StageGate, you will be authorized to plan the project. Generating the RBS is the key to what kind of planning will be needed. If you are comfortable that the RBS is relatively complete and there will be few if any scope change requests, you can use all of the Planning Process Group tools, templates, and processes to build a complete project plan. If you are not sure or if frequent change is expected, you need to tailor the Planning Process Group tools, templates, and processes to accommodate your chosen PMLC model.

Generate the Mid-Level Work Breakdown Structure

The mid-level WBS identifies the functionality that is known and that will be built in this version. It does not show what tasks have to be done to build that functionality. To complete the WBS down to that level would be to define work that might never be done. In APF, you don't know enough about the future to spend the time creating the full WBS to that level of detail. Over the course of all of the cycles, you may end up generating the complete WBS, but you don't know that for sure. In APF, you will build the WBS detail when you need it. However, at this point, you simply decompose the WBS to a level where you can reasonably estimate the time and resources needed for each piece of functionality. These are not top-down estimates, nor are they bottom-up estimates. You simply need a reasonable guesstimate.

In some applications, my clients have used the mid-level WBS to temporarily assign functionality to cycles. Although this is a best guess at this point, it does give the client useful information on release strategies.

Determine the Number of Cycles and Cycle Timeboxes

This can be as simple or as complex as you care to make it. You don't need to make a lifetime project out of this step, so for a first pass I suggest that you think in terms of four-week cycles and simply compute how many of them you can fit into the version timebox. Later on, when you assign functionality to each cycle, you may want to adjust cycle length to accommodate the build process. If you want to be a little more sophisticated, take a look at the durations of the prioritized functionality and determine cycle length from that data. In this approach, you may vary cycle length so as to accommodate functionality durations of varying lengths. If you want to get even more sophisticated, take a look at dependencies between pieces of functionality and sequence the development effort across cycles with those dependencies in mind. There are a number of ways to proceed here, so it would be counterproductive to give you a formula.

I have found that cycle length is driven more by the client's need for delivering business value sufficient to release cycle deliverables to the end user for implementation. In any case, it will be a balance between meeting client needs consistent with technical needs.

Assign Known Functions to Cycles

Using the established priorities, simply map the functions into the cycles and then step back and ask the following questions about what you have just done:

1. Based on the dependencies between functions and the resources available, does this assignment make sense?

2. When we finish the first few cycles, will we have a working version of part of the final solution?

3. Can we improve on this assignment if we vary cycle length for the early cycles?

4. Does this assignment fully utilize our resources in the early cycles?

There is no substitute for common sense, and you always want to do what is right for the client. Don't plan the details out to the last cycle. You really have no idea what will take place in the next cycle, let alone the late cycles. Focus on the first few cycles and do what makes sense for them. You can worry about the later cycles in due time.

Write Objective Statements for Each Cycle

These objective statements are more for the benefit of the client. If possible, you should tell them what they can expect at each cycle. They need to know that these objectives are not cast in stone. There are so many variables that this list will surely change. The objectives have to make business sense, and that means you may need some further modification of the assignments to each cycle as a result of the client's reviews and comments on your plan so far. You also want to make sure that the client can do something productive with the deliverables from each cycle. Those deliverables are your key to further modifications of the version scope that will be discussed at the client checkpoint at the end of each cycle.

Cycle Plan

The Cycle Plan (Figure 11-12) will be repeated a number of times before this project finishes. Each Cycle Plan begins with a decision as to what items from the prioritized Scope Bank will be developed during the coming cycle. Many of the Planning Process Group tools, templates, and processes are used to develop the Cycle Plan.

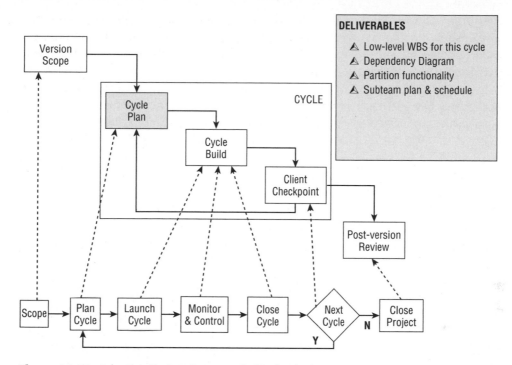

Figure 11-12: Adaptive Project Framework (Cycle Plan)

Develop the Micro-Level WBS for the Cycle Contents

Extract from your mid-level WBS the functionality that will be worked on during the coming cycle. It is that part of the WBS that will become the basis of your Cycle Plan and which you will decompose down to the micro-level.

CROSS-REFERENCE To create this micro-level WBS, I suggest you follow the process discussed in Chapter 5. It is not described again here.

Micro-Managing an APF Project

Remember that every activity that you define in the micro-level WBS must be managed. That opens up the possibility of micro-management. You want to ensure that the final decomposition isn't at such a granular level that you are forcing yourself to be a micro-manager. You should understand at the outset that micro-management is the bane of an APF project. Best APF practices suggest that you manage an individual's work down to units of one week.

Consider this scenario. Harry is going to work on an activity that will require 10 hours of effort. The activity is scheduled to begin on Monday morning and be completed by Friday afternoon. Harry has agreed that he can accommodate the 10 hours within the week given his other commitments during that same week. Now, Harry's manager (or the project manager) could ask Harry to report exactly when during the week he will be working on this 10-hour activity and then hold him to that plan. What a waste of everyone's time that would be! Why not give Harry credit for enough intelligence to make his commitments at the one-week level? No need to drill down into the work week and burden Harry with a micro-plan and his manager with the burden of managing to that micro-plan. The net result of this micro-management may, in fact, be to increase the actual time to complete the activity because Harry has been burdened with the need to comply with the unnecessary management overhead brought upon him by his manager. The exemplary APF project manager will place more confidence in the team member knowing that the processes are in place to ensure plan attainment. Harry, being the good team player that he is, will report daily on status and let the project manager know if there are any issues or concerns regarding his meeting his commitments for delivery. It is more valuable to the project to have the APF project manager spend time encouraging that behavior from Harry than it is to waste the time micro-managing Harry. If it should happen that Harry doesn't deliver against the commitment, the project manager will certainly have a conversation with him about future assignments and how his progress will be monitored. As you can see, APF defines a structured framework that gives maximum latitude to the team members.

Once the micro-level WBS has been deemed complete and all activity durations have been estimated, print the unique name of each activity and its duration on a separate sticky note. For added efficiency, you might color-code the sticky notes. Each function gets a different color. You will see the value of this later in the phase. If you are still using project management software, enter the name of each activity and its duration into the package. Print the PERT diagram, which will produce a columnar display of the activities because no dependencies have been specified. You can then cut out each activity node and tape each one to a sticky note. You will then be at the same place in the planning exercise as the sticky-note folks.

The cycle planning effort might go something like this:

- Extract from the WBS the functions to be built in the coming cycle and any features or other decomposition you have for them.

- Complete the extracted WBS down to the task level using the WBS completion criteria from Chapter 5.

- Establish the dependencies among these tasks and build the dependency network diagram.

- Partition the tasks into independent meaningful groups and assign teams to each group.

- Each team will develop a plan and schedule for the completion of their tasks within the cycle timebox and budget constraints.

Note that this planning effort is low-tech. Software is optional. There is no critical path to calculate and manage. The traditionalist would have a problem with this. Their approach is based on managing the critical path. You could certainly calculate one here, but I believe that is overkill. The cycle is so short that too much planning and analysis leads to paralysis. You don't need to clutter the cycle with non-value-added work. The only tools you should need are whiteboards, sticky notes, and marker pens. The team war room should work fine. The team can post their plans, work schedules, issues lists, and so on, and have their daily 15-minute updates, weekly status meetings with the client, and problem-solving sessions here. APF, and the other Agile approaches, place more responsibility on people and less on process. I am much more comfortable giving people their assignment and letting them figure out the best way to accomplish it. If process is needed, they can make that decision. This is not reckless abandon, but because you have created a mid-level WBS, prioritized functionality, and built a Cycle Plan, this is a well-structured approach.

The Cycle Plan Phase works best as a team event, but I realize that some project managers might have taken just a few team members aside and built the Cycle Plan. For that reason, I have left the remaining details of the Cycle Plan for this phase. Building the Cycle Plan is definitely a team event. You completed the Cycle Plan Phase with a first pass at the cycle build schedule. You start the Cycle Plan Phase by completing the last details of the schedule. The variables that you have to factor into the schedule are the specific team members you will have and what their schedules look like. For a typical APF project, the team members are assigned full-time to the project. For that reason, the scheduling problems should be minimal.

Create the Micro-Level Schedule and Finalize Resource Assignments

To finish scheduling the cycle build activities, you need to factor in the specific availabilities of the team members as well as the dependencies that exist between tasks. To continue building the cycle schedule, first lay out the color-coded sticky notes on a scaled time line and be mindful of the dependencies between the tasks. You will need this in order to continue with scheduling and resource assignment.

Before you continue creating the low-level schedule, check to see if the initial schedule and resource assignments will allow the team to build the functionality assigned to this cycle within the cycle timebox. You can do this by inspecting the scaled time line you just created. If the current schedule doesn't fit within the cycle timebox, look for alternative resource assignments that will bring the schedule inside the cycle timebox. Look for resources that are not assigned for periods of time. They can either take over a task or help another resource complete a task earlier than currently scheduled. Adding a resource to the task assumes the work of the task can be partitioned to accommodate multiple resources. What you are doing is resource leveling in a way that makes more sense than the approach taken by most software tools.

At another spot on the whiteboard, prepare a grid that shows the time line on a daily basis across the columns and has one row allocated to each resource. Show all seven days on this grid. In a crunch situation, you may need to schedule work on the weekend. Next, superimpose the calendars of each resource on the grid. For any workdays or half-workdays that a resource will not be available for cycle build work, indicate this unavailability in the corresponding cell or half-cell. Half-day units are the smallest unit of time that you are going to build your plan around. Smaller units just create non-value-added work and begin to border on micro-management. After you have done this, you end up with your resource calendar for this cycle.

Once you have met the cycle timebox constraint, you are ready to move the information to the grid. For each resource, simply transfer the information to the grid that shows what task that resource is working on, what day they expect to start it, and what day they expect to end it. Take care that you don't violate any dependency relationships between tasks. Every morning you will have a team status meeting at which time you compare what was completed the previous day with what the grid had scheduled for that day. Any adjustments to the plan are made on the grid. Resources can be moved to meet schedule delays. You still have the sticky note network diagram on the whiteboard, so you will be able to see if schedule delays will cause any other delays downstream in the plan and adjust accordingly. Figure 11-13 gives an example of what these grids might look like.

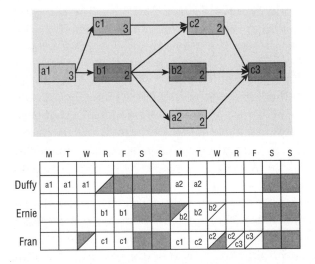

Figure 11-13: A resource-loaded cycle schedule

The example is a two-week schedule for a cycle that has seven tasks. All of this information can be put on a whiteboard and changed as needs arise. It is simple, but it conveys all of the information that you need for a real project. It can be scaled upward for larger projects. The dependency diagram is scaled to the time line shown in the grid. This is a useful representation because it allows you to plan without the fear of violating any of the dependencies between sub-functions. The legend that I have used is fairly intuitive. The grayed out days or half-days are days when the resource is not available or days that are not workdays.

Let me point out a few important points about Figure 11-13. First, when scheduling a resource, try to keep that resource busy for consecutive days. This makes it easier if you need to replace an individual on the team. Second, notice when a resource is not busy. For example, Duffy is available for a half-day on Thursday of the first week. Even though this is early in the cycle, it may provide a resource that can help either Ernie or Fran or help the team recover from a slippage or a problem. Finally, note that in the second week, Duffy and Ernie are available to perhaps help Fran complete c2 when Fran is unavailable on Wednesday afternoon. If that can be scheduled, c3 may be able to be completed early. This means that the cycle would be completed ahead of schedule. Alternatively, that staffing adjustment might provide a way to make up for earlier slippages.

This grid should be permanently displayed in the team war room. It will be the focal point of daily team meetings. As status is being reported, the team can refer to this schedule and make any changes to the latter parts of the schedule. The most important benefit is that this is visible and accessible to the team. The only negative that you have to worry about is there is no backup for this approach. The fact that the team war room is reserved for the exclusive use of the team and is secure will mitigate most of the risk, but not all of it. I have made it a practice to have one of the team members, when he or she is not otherwise busy, update an electronic version of the war room or take a digital photo of the schedule and any other irreplaceable information. Because this is only for backup, it doesn't need to be saved in a high-powered software application. A word processor, spreadsheet package, or electronic whiteboard will do just fine. I have even used Visio on occasion.

The reason that this approach works is that the cycle length is short. The example cycle is only two weeks long, but even if it were three or four weeks long, the same approach will work. Even though I have used project management software packages extensively, I still find this low-tech approach to be far more intuitive than any software display. The entire team can see what's going on and can see how to resolve scheduling problems in a very intuitive manner. Most important of all is that the maintenance effort is negligible. Try it. This would never do well in TPM. For one thing, the network diagram would take up too much real estate and is generally not available from the software package. Not because it can't be generated. We all know that it can, but the labor to create it just doesn't justify it. Resource balancing is the other side of the coin. On the whiteboard, it is easy. In a software package, who knows what will happen when you try to level resources. I want to see the problem, and most software packages just don't measure up.

Write Work Packages

By inspection, you will be able to identify the critical tasks. The aficionados will want to use a software tool to locate the critical path. That's fine, but don't let the tool do the thinking for you. The cycle is so short that you could probably generate the critical path manually in less time than it takes to input the data, extract the pertinent data, and transfer it to your working format. Your choice. For every critical task in the cycle plan, it is a good insurance policy if the person responsible for the task develops a brief step-by-step description of what he or she plans on doing to complete the task within the allotted time. If you lose that person or have to reassign the task, the person who takes over can read the work package and hopefully can continue working on the task with minimal loss of time. You might also want to create work packages for high-risk tasks or tasks for which there is little experience among the team members. I have tended to write work packages for tasks that require a scarce resource. If I lose that resource, perhaps I can replace it with less-skilled resources and depend on the work package to help them over the tough spots.

Cycle Build

The functionality to be built in this cycle is input and a detailed plan put together for the cycle. It is usually a whiteboard, sticky note, marking pen type of plan. The Cycle Build ends when the timebox expires, not before and not after. Any tasks not complete are reconsidered and reprioritized in the next Cycle Plan. See Figure 11-14.

Detailed planning for producing the functionality assigned to this cycle is prepared. The cycle work begins, work is monitored throughout the cycle, and adjustments are made as necessary. The cycle ends when its time has expired. Any functionality not completed during this cycle is returned to the Scope Bank and reprioritized for consideration in a later cycle. No changes are allowed within a cycle. This is a real strength of APF. During a cycle, the team is focused on the planned deliverables. There are no distractions. All changes and ideas for adding functions or features to the solution are saved in the Scope Bank for consideration along with other functionality during the Client Checkpoint.

During the Cycle Build Phase, I recommend that you review how the team is working and how the APF Adaptive PMLC model is working. Real teamwork is a critical success factor in APF. There is a lot of worker empowerment threaded throughout APF. I think if you count the frequency of the use of the word "I" as compared to the use of the word "we," you will have a pretty good metric for measuring team strength. The formula would be as follows:

```
Team Strength = number of We's/(number of I's plus number of We's)
```

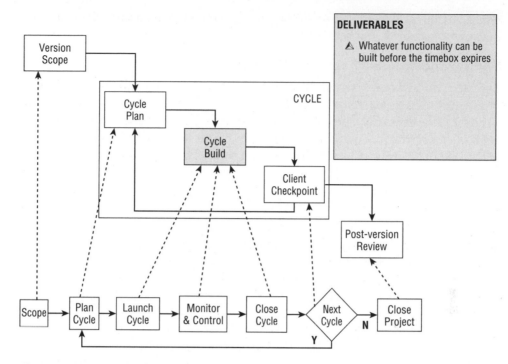

Figure 11-14: Adaptive Project Framework (Cycle Build)

Ideally, this number should be hovering around 1. The APF team needs to work in an open and honest environment for this to happen. This means that every team member must be forthright in stating the actual status of their project work. To do otherwise would be to violate the trust that must exist between and among team members. The project manager must ensure that the working environment on the project is such that team members are not afraid to raise their hand, say they are having trouble, and ask for help. To do otherwise would be to let your teammates down.

Build Cycle Functionality

Work is now underway to build the functionality prioritized for this cycle. Even though the cycle is short and the build is not very complex, things will not go according to plan. About this time, the APFist is thankful that not a lot of time was spent planning and takes the unexpected in stride. Something unexpected is sure to happen. A person gets sick or leaves the company, a vendor is late in shipping, ships the wrong hardware, or goes out of business. These are the same kinds of risks that the traditionalist faces, but for them the results are far more catastrophic than they are for the APFist.

DEFINITION: APFIST An APFist is any professional who subscribes to the processes and practices of APF.

Monitor and Adjust the Cycle Build Schedule

The team will have team status meetings every morning — no exceptions. The meeting should not last more than 15 minutes. Everyone is standing, and everyone gives their status. If they are behind schedule, they should briefly state their get-well plan. Major issues are posted to the Issues Log and are taken offline by the affected persons so as not to waste the time of the entire team. Those who are ahead of the planned schedule become a resource for the others.

Ending the Cycle

A cycle may end for any of the following reasons:

- The timebox expires.
- All swim lanes complete early.
- A major problem occurs.

Timebox Expires

This cycle build ends when the timebox expires — not before, and not after. Any tasks not complete are returned to the Scope Bank for re-prioritization for consideration in a later cycle.

I hear task managers pleading: "If we only had two more days, we could complete our tasks." You will be tempted, but you must resist giving in. While you are using an Adaptive model, some rules are inviolate. Other task managers will have finished their assigned work. Should they take a few days off while waiting for the delinquents to catch up? I don't think so.

All Swim Lanes Complete Early

No reason to let the clock run out here. Go to the Client Checkpoint and solve any scheduling problems that early cycle termination might have caused.

A Major Problem Occurs

These are showstopper problems. The competition has just introduced a product that surpasses what you are trying to develop. A business decision is needed: to go forward anyway or to abort the project and go back to the drawing board.

Depending on the severity, the APFist will either finish the current cycle or for the really major problems, he or she will terminate the current cycle and immediately move into the Client Checkpoint and plan for the next cycle. In rare cases, the project manager may jointly decide with the client to cancel the version and start all over, if at all. Note that the minimum amount of time and money was wasted in the APF approach as compared to the traditionalist approach.

Client Checkpoint

The Client Checkpoint (Figure 11-15) is really the heart of APF. It is here that the team and the client spend valuable time looking at what was done, reflecting on what was discovered and learned since the last checkpoint, and planning the Integrative and Probative Swim Lanes for the next cycle. As you will see, this introspection with the client and project team fully engaged is a very thorough process. If properly done, it is unlikely that anything significant will be missed.

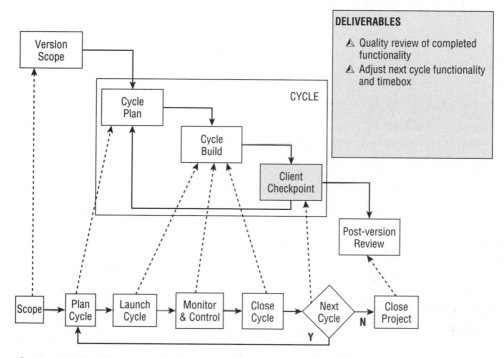

Figure 11-15: Adaptive Project Framework (Client Checkpoint)

One of the greatest benefits from this approach is the meaningful and continuous involvement of the client. They are the decision maker in all going-forward activities, and they are doing it with full knowledge of what has taken place to date. They understand where business value can be achieved by changes in functionality, and they are in a position to take action. APF allows the client to engage in the project even to the level of operating as a co-project manager. They will be a constant reminder to the team of the business aspects and value of what they are doing and what changes should be made to protect that business value. This is a very important point to remember. It ensures that what is eventually built will meet client needs.

Because cycle length is so short and is so controlled, there is little that can go wrong that is not discovered quickly and easily corrected. Within the cycle itself, not even a day goes by that the team doesn't take stock of where it is compared to where it planned to be and adjusts accordingly. Because of the structure of APF, few dollars and little time will be wasted.

Following the completion of the previous cycle, there are several inputs to consider as the client and the team look forward to the next cycle. They are as follows:

- Functionality completed in the previous cycle
- Functionality planned but not completed in the previous cycle
- Functionality originally planned for this cycle
- Functionality planned for all the cycles beyond the next one
- All learning and discovery that took place in all previous cycles
- Any changes that took place in the business environment during the previous cycles
- The extent to which the current solution is converging on the final solution
- The current contents of the Scope Bank

The entire project team should spend whatever time they need in frank and honest conversation considering all of these factors and then agreeing on what will be done in the next cycle. Do not underestimate the value that can come from the sharing of learning and discovery. That will be your most important information as it helps both parties understand what this solution is really all about and what should be offered as a final solution. This is no trivial task.

The Updated Contents of the Scope Bank

The updated Scope Bank is the cumulative depository of all the ideas and proposed changes that were generated during the previous cycles. Some of these ideas and/or changes were incorporated in later cycles, and some were not. In any case, the current contents are all of the items not previously acted upon. There may be cases where any ideas learned or discovered in all previous cycles but not yet incorporated in the solution may now be viable.

Armed with the updated Scope Bank, the project team can now identify the contents of the next cycle. The following steps are suggested:

1. Review the COS and make any adjustments to solution requirements.
2. Prioritize the items in the Scope Bank.
3. Identify and prioritize Probative Swim Lane contents.
4. Identify and prioritize Integrative Swim Lane contents.
5. Select the items to be developed in the next cycle.
6. Determine the next cycle timebox.

During the cycle build, both the client and the project team would have benefited from several discovery and learning episodes. Variations to the version functionality would surface, alternative approaches to delivering certain functionality would have been suggested, and the client would have learned how best to proceed with the further definition of the solution. All of this is recorded in the Scope Bank and must be considered along with the functionality that had originally been assigned to the coming cycle. The result is a revised prioritization of the deliverables assigned to the coming cycle. The most important thing to remember is not to speculate on the future. I don't dismiss this planning task as being an easy exercise. It definitely isn't that.

DEFINITION: APF SWIM LANES An APF swim lane is a dependent sequence of tasks that are part of a cycle and are undertaken to produce a specific deliverable. In a given cycle, there may be several swim lanes scheduled concurrently. There are two types of swim lanes in an APF cycle. They are as follows:

- **Integrative Swim Lanes** — These swim lanes are designed to integrate additional functions and features into the current solution.
- **Probative Swim Lanes** — These swim lanes are designed to discover and learn about potential functions and features that might be integrated into the solution in a later cycle.

NOTE Concurrent swim lanes should be defined so that there is maximum dependency between the tasks in a swim lane (maximum cohesion) and minimal dependency between tasks in separate swim lanes (minimal coupling).

Consider for a moment the balance between Integrative Swim Lanes and Probative Swim Lanes in a single cycle. The decision to spend team members' time on Probative Swim Lanes instead of Integrative Swim Lanes isn't at all an obvious decision. It will be a subjective call in any case. You need to compare the marginal value of adding another Probative Swim Lane against that of adding another Integrative Swim Lane. This comparison will obviously be very subjective. To help make that decision, you might consider the relative sizes of the candidate lists for those two swim lanes. Remember that the Probative Swim Lanes are what feed the Integrative Swim Lanes. You need to maintain a healthy balance between the sizes of the two lists. If you know very little about the solution, the Probative Swim Lane list should be long relative to the Integrative Swim Lane list. This will occur in the early cycles of the project, and priority will be given to including Probative Swim Lanes over Integrative Swim Lanes in the next cycle. In later cycles, the Integrative Swim Lane list should grow larger than the Probative Swim Lane list. This is indicative of the project converging to the final solution. Priority will be given to the contents of the Integrative Swim Lane list. Figure 11-16 gives some examples.

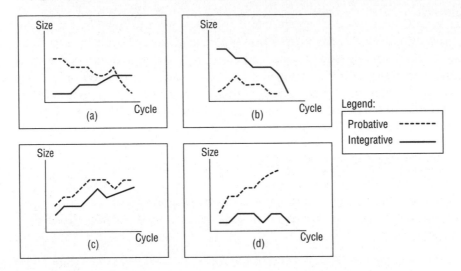

Figure 11-16: Probative versus Integrative Swim Lane size over time

The size of the two lists is a simple concept, but there is a lot of information here and a lot of guidance for future cycle content.

Figure 11-16(a) can be interpreted in either of the following ways:

- The solution is nearly complete except for the remaining function and feature integrations.

- The solution is not nearing completion, and there are very few ideas forthcoming as to how to further define the missing parts of the solution.

Figure 11-16(b) paints a different picture and can be interpreted as follows:

- Both lists are decreasing and the solution may be very near completion, so few new Probative Swim lanes are needed.

- The solution is not nearing completion, and there are no new ideas forthcoming.

Figure 11-16(c) is the sign of a healthy project. The list of functions and features to be integrated is growing as is the list of ideas for future function and feature exploration. The Probative Swim Lanes are producing good results.

Figure 11-16(d) has the following two interpretations:

- The solution is nearing completion, but the missing parts continue to be elusive. The increasing number of ideas is not producing any meaningful additions to the solution.

- The project may be spinning out of control. Few ideas are producing any tangible results.

CASE STUDY – PIZZA DELIVERED QUICKLY (PDQ): CLIENT CHECKPOINT PROBLEMS

Because this was the first APF project ever undertaken at PDQ, Pepe decided to hire an outside consultant to coach the team through the process. He had read and understood this book but felt that an expert was needed, and he wasn't an APF expert. That was a wise choice because it allowed Pepe to focus on the content, not the process. At first he noticed some reluctance on the part of the client to offer ideas and criticisms. He dismissed this reluctance as just an early reaction to a new role for the client, but it continued through the first few cycles and could no longer be ignored. Pepe decided to hold a major project review in an attempt to get the root causes of the client's lack of meaningful involvement on the table. It worked, and he learned that the client was just overwhelmed with the process and somewhat threatened by the new technologies that were being introduced. He suggested to the consultant that a project review be held in a workshop format and focus on the client's reluctance. That also worked, and the client soon began to participate as expected.

Post-Version Review

In the Version Scope Phase, you and the client developed measurable business outcomes that are the rationale on which the project was approved in the first place. These outcomes are, in essence, the success criteria defined in the POS in that the project is considered a success if, and only if, these outcomes are achieved. This is not at all how TPM measures project success. There is more than just meeting the triple constraints. Client satisfaction must be at the top of the list. All other constraints are of lesser importance. In many cases, these outcomes cannot be measured for some time after the project has been completed. Take the case of the project impacting market share. It won't happen next Tuesday. It may happen several quarters later, but the time frame is part of the success criteria statement as well.

Accordingly, the main focus of the Post-Version Review is to check how you did with respect to the success criteria; to document what you learned that will be useful in the next version, such as how well APF worked on this project and how well the team used APF; and to begin thinking about the functionality for the next version (see Figure 11-17).

The budget and/or time allotted to this version have been spent. Some functionality that was planned to be completed in the last cycle may not have been completed for this version. The Scope Bank is not empty.

In summary, the following three questions are yet to be answered:

- Was the expected business outcome realized?
- What was learned that can be used to improve the solution?
- What was learned that can be used to improve the effectiveness of APF?

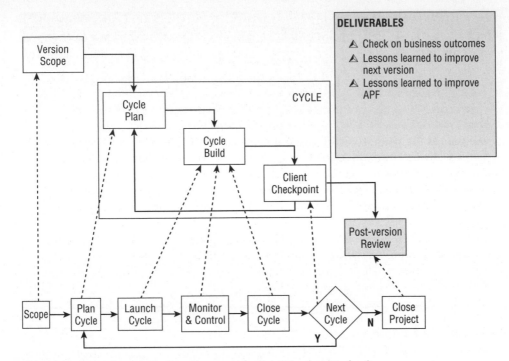

Figure 11-17: Adaptive Project Framework (Post-Version Review)

Was the Expected Business Outcome Realized?

The business outcome was the factor used to validate the reason for doing the project in the first place. If it was achieved, chalk that one up on the success side of the ledger. If it wasn't, why not? Can something further be done to achieve that outcome? If so, that will be input to the functional specifications for the next version. If not, kill the project right now. No need to send good money after bad money. There is also a lesson here for all project managers. If projects are limited in scope and they fail and there is no way to rescue them, then you have reduced the dollars lost to failed projects. The alternative of undertaking larger projects is that you risk losing more money. If there is a way of finding out early that a project isn't going to deliver as promised, cut your losses. The same logic works from cycle to cycle. If you can learn early that a version will not work, kill the version and save the time and cost from the later cycles. The traditional approach would find out after all the money was spent and time used up and then have a great deal of trouble killing the project. After all, with so much money tied up in this project, the traditional approach would mean you would be reluctant to just kill it. You would want to try to save it. How pitiful and futile. TPM is structured so that it isn't until very late in the PMLC that you discover the project won't yield the expected results. Even if the project is killed at that point, most of the dollars will have already been spent, not to mention the time that was lost pursuing a losing cause.

Just as the traditionalist conducts a post-implementation audit at the end of the project, the APFist conducts a Post-Version Review at the end of the current version (Figure 11-17). There are a number of similarities, but there are also differences. The traditionalist is looking for final closure on the project while the APFist is looking for ways to further increase the business value of the solution. In other words, the APFist is never looking for final closure but is always looking for more business value. The version just completed is just another step toward increasing business value. In that sense, APF is quite like the production prototype in that it consists of a never-ending cycle of repeated solution improvements. The only ending that is ever encountered is to stabilize the solution as the best that can be achieved. At least for the foreseeable future, the solution will be the one used. In time, there may be reason to retire the solution altogether.

What Was Learned That Can Be Used to Improve the Solution?

You know that learning and discovery were very important parts of the Client Checkpoint Phase because it led the client and the team to adjust the cycle plans going forward. Similarly, in the Post-Version Review Phase, the client and the team consider all discovery and learning experiences with a view toward the next version's functionality (assuming that there will be a next version). This information is the major input to the Version Scope Phase for the next version. The analysis of this information will be the major part of the business validation of that next version.

What Was Learned That Can Be Used to Improve the Effectiveness of APF?

So far the lessons learned have focused on the solution (a.k.a. product) of the just-completed version. The other type of lessons learned focuses on the process that was followed to create the solution, answering such questions as "How well did APF work?" and "How well did the client and the team follow APF?" In answering these questions, the client and the team will offer suggestions for improvement of the process and the practice of the process. As you can see, APF has a built-in, continuous, quality-improvement process.

Adapting APF

As its name implies, APF is adaptive. You have seen that in several ways: specifying the number of cycles, determining cycle length, changing functionality priorities at each client checkpoint, and building in changes (add new, modify existing, or delete) in functionality at each client checkpoint. I have also shown how APF not only anticipates these adaptations but expects them. But APF is far more adaptable than just the situations I have enumerated. There are three adaptations that I want you to be aware of, and these are the topic of this short section.

You will probably find other reasons to adapt APF. Feel free to do that. APF is not a rigid structure to be followed without question. For me the bottom line has always been to do what is right for the client. It's all about organized common sense. If you are asked to do something that flies in the face of some established process or procedure, you need to take a serious look at the process or procedure. It may not be serving your needs.

Adaptation: Proof-of-Concept Cycle

There will be situations where the business case has not been sufficiently made to get approval to build the first version. Much like you have used prototyping to help with client definition of functionality, you can use the same concept by making the first cycle of APF a proof-of-concept cycle. That could entail the creation of a prototype, a feasibility study, the writing of use cases, storyboarding, or any other activity to demonstrate business value. It is very important that you not drag this activity out too long. Client interests and the interests of the approving manager will wane. You need to strike quickly while the iron is hot.

Adaptation: Revising the Version Plan

There will be situations where the initial Version Scope missed the mark. That will be evidenced by a significant number of discoveries and lessons learned coming in the first few cycles without much in the way of tangible results being produced. These can create a big disconnect between the original direction of the project and the corrected one that is now indicated. In other words, to continue on the course suggested by the current Version Scope is a waste of time and money. Remember that you built a mid-level WBS and are making your cycle plans around that WBS. Too many changes brought on by learning and discovery may render much of the WBS out of sync. The need to revise the version plan is clearly a subjective decision. I would err on the side of revision rather than sticking with a plan that may be heading in the wrong direction. The APFist is hard-pressed to do anything that may be a waste of the client's time or money. The APFist would conclude that the plan is off course and should be abandoned immediately. The correct action is to revise (or even replace) the current version plan and basically start over. At this early point in the project, do not be afraid to kill the plan. In almost every case I can think of, you will be making the correct decision.

Adaptation: Embedding APF in Other PMLC Models

APF can be embedded in other PMLC models. For example, suppose the solution is completely known except for one module. You can use a Linear PMLC model for the project except for that one module. That module will require using APF. Build the WBS treating that APF module as a task for the time being. Execute the Planning Process Group to develop a project schedule. From that schedule, you can determine the earliest start (ES) and latest finish (LF) timebox for the

APF module. Within that module, execute the APF project to find the missing solution. I've had the occasion to use this approach with a few clients, and all I can say is that it works!

Implementing APF

There are two approaches to implementing APF: bottom-up or top-down.

Bottom-Up Approach to Implementing APF

Don't expect your management to enthusiastically embrace APF. You will most likely have to stick your neck out, take a chance, and prove that it has business value. Any strategy that I can envision will be a grassroots initiative. You will be putting yourself in harm's way! You will have to take the risk, so pick a demo project that you have great confidence you can bring in successfully. Make sure the team and the client are on board with you, too. If you can get a sponsor who has respect and clout in the organization, that will help considerably. It will be your only chance to convince senior management that APF has a place in your organization. If you fail, you can forget about APF for a while.

For some project managers, implementing APF will require a leap of faith. I often hear comments like: "You mean you don't know what solution you are going to deliver to the client until the project has ended?" Although that is partially true, the real payoff is that what is delivered is what the client decided they needed, and to the best of the client and the team's ability, what is delivered has maximum business value for the time and money expended. Furthermore, the client decided to be actively involved in the project from beginning to end. Is there some other way that could have happened other than through APF? I don't think so.

Top-Down Approach to Implementing APF

When the pain the organization is suffering from failed projects reaches some threshold and all previous corrective action plans have failed, senior management is ready to listen. Two recent clients came to me for this very reason. If this book had been published at that time, it would have given them a roadmap to understanding the contemporary project management landscape.

Value of APF to Organizations

The value is obvious: time is saved and costs are avoided. Additionally, the solution is the best that can be attained given the constraints.

> **NOTE** In the most complex projects, if an acceptable business solution can be found, APF can find it when other approaches might not.

Dynamic Systems Development Method (DSDM)

DSDM is what the Linear PMLC model would look like in a zero-gravity world. Feedback loops are the defining features that separate DSDM from the Linear PMLC model. DSDM is an Iterative model, but it can be used in situations where even less of the solution is specified than in other Adaptive PMLC models. The feedback loops help guide the client and the project team to a complete solution. The business case is included as a feedback loop so that even the fundamental basis and justification of the project can be revisited.

The following is a list of the nine key principles of DSDM as indicated in Jennifer Stapleton's *DSDM: Dynamic Systems Development Method* (Addison-Wesley, 1997):

1. Active client involvement is imperative.

2. DSDM teams must be empowered to make decisions.

3. The focus is on frequent delivery of products.

4. Fitness for business purpose is the essential criterion for acceptance of deliverables.

5. Iterative and incremental development is necessary to converge on an acceptable business solution.

6. All changes during development are reversible.

7. Requirements are baselined at a high level.

8. Testing is integrated throughout the life cycle.

9. A collaborative and cooperative approach between all stakeholders is essential.

Note that the characteristics in the list are quite similar to those I have previously identified as good practices.

Figure 11-18 is the Adaptive DSDM PMLC model.

The distinguishing feature of the DSDM is the incremental release and implementation of a production system at the end of each cycle. Note that repetition of the Design & Build and Functional Model iterations all follow an implementation phase. DSDM delivers business value to the client as part of its overall process design. Other approaches might do the same as a variation, but DSDM does it as part of the design of the approach itself.

Figure 11-19 shows that DSDM maps directly into the Adaptive PMLC model.

DSDM cycles can begin anywhere in the model. Even after implementation, the client may decide that the solution doesn't deliver the needed business value. Some other solution approach is needed, so another idea is entertained, starting with a feasibility study. Essentially the project is started over by following a different direction to seek out an acceptable solution. Repeating the feasibility study requires extensive client involvement.

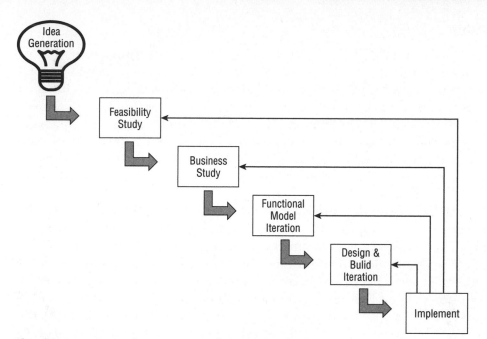

Figure 11-18: Dynamic Systems Development Method

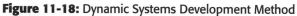

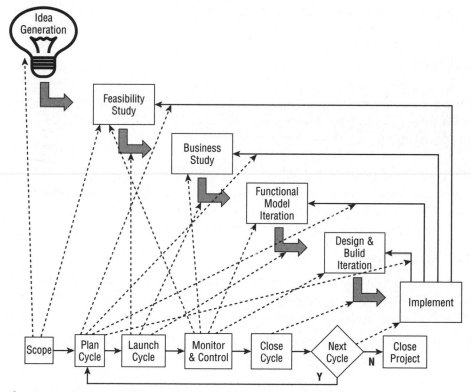

Figure 11-19: DSDM mapped into the Adaptive PMLC model

Scrum

Scrum is a term taken from rugby. A scrum involves the team as a unit moving the ball downfield in what would appear to be a chaotic fashion. Of all the Iterative approaches, Scrum would seem to define a chaotic development environment. The Scrum software development team is self-directed, operates in successive one-month iterations, holds daily team meetings, continuously offers the client demos of the current solution, and adapts its development plan at the end of each iteration. For a complete discussion on Scrum and software development, refer to *Agile Software Development with Scrum* by Ken Schwaber and Mike Beedle (Prentice Hall, 2001).

Of all the development models discussed in this book, Scrum is clearly the most client-driven approach. It is the client (called Product Owner in Scrum terminology) who defines the functions and features that the team prioritizes into phases and builds a phase at a time in 30-day cycles. In a Scrum project the Product Owner is the closest person on the team to being a project manager. The process allows the client to change functions and features as more of the solution depth is uncovered through the previous iterations. Depending on the working definition you are using for Scrum, it might be a strict application of the Iterative approach as defined herein or it might border on the Adaptive approach.

The Scrum process flow is shown in Figure 11-20, and the sections that follow explain the parts of the flow.

Idea Proposed

The original idea for the system might be vague. It might be expressed in the form of business terms. A function-level description can be developed as part of the Scoping Phase, but not to the depth of detail that the client requires. It is not likely to be expressed in system terms.

Developing and Prioritizing a List of Functionality

The Product Owner is responsible for developing this list, which is called the Product Backlog. It helps the team understand more detail about the idea and helps them form some ideas about how to approach the project.

Sprint Planning Meeting

This is an eight-hour meeting with two distinct four-hour parts. In the first part, the Product Owner presents the prioritized Product Backlog to the team. This is the opportunity for the team to ask questions to clarify each piece of functionality. In the second part, the team commits to the functionality it will try to deliver in the first Sprint. The team then spends the remaining four hours developing the high-level plan as to how it will accomplish the Sprint. The work to be done is captured in the Sprint Backlog. The Sprint Backlog is the current list of functionality that is not yet completed for the current Sprint.

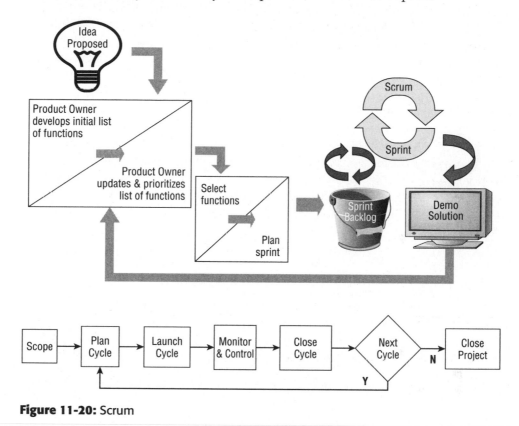

Figure 11-20: Scrum

DEFINITION: SPRINT A Sprint is the 30-day development cycle of the Scrum PMLC model.

Demo Sprint Functionality

At the end of the Sprint, the team demos the solution to the client; functionality is added or changed; and the Product Backlog is updated and reprioritized for the next Sprint. This entire process continues until the Product Backlog is empty or the client is otherwise satisfied that the current Sprint version is the final solution.

Scrum has often been characterized as a methodology that does not require a project manager. In fact, the position of project manager does not exist, but the role does. It is subsumed primarily into a self-directed and self-organized team with some oversight responsibility resting on the shoulders of the Scrum Master. The Scrum Master simultaneously functions as coach, advisor, mentor, at times as an administrator, and finally as compliance monitor for the Scrum Team. Scrum has been characterized as organized chaos, and it does seem quite disorganized at first glance.

Figure 11-21 shows how Scrum maps directly into the Adaptive PMLC model.

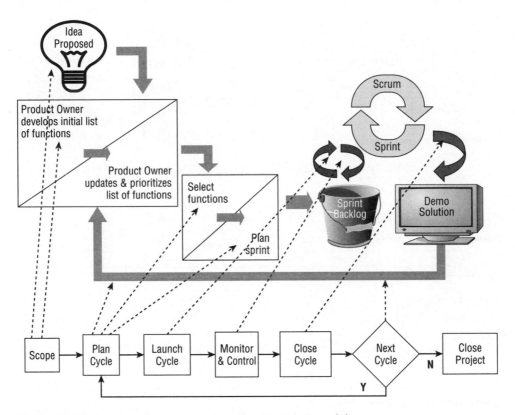

Figure 11-21: Scrum mapping into the Adaptive PMLC model

Scrum is rapidly becoming popular among software developers. Developing software using Scrum fits the psyche of the senior developer. To the casual observer, it looks like chaos, but out of that chaos comes working systems. The developers are free to choose from the Sprint Backlog whatever chunk of the solution they would like to work on next in the cycle. Once a chunk of the solution is being worked on by one of the team members, it is removed from the Sprint Backlog. All team members agreed during the four-hour Sprint planning meeting to build all of the functionality that was allocated to the current Sprint. Senior developers are motivated by the challenge to do so. The Product Owner just has to stay out of their way. The Scrum developers are senior-level professionals and do not need supervision.

Scrum offers the professional an opportunity to be creative, which is one of its major strengths.

When to Use an Adaptive PMLC Model

Even if you are convinced that an Adaptive approach makes the most sense, you need to be confident in that decision. Here are three questions that might help you confirm your decision:

- Have you or a trusted colleague had successful Adaptive project experience with this client before?
- If this is the first Adaptive experience for this client, are you confident that they will be meaningfully involved throughout the entire project?
- Has the client appointed a qualified and respected co-project manager for this project?

Has the Client Had Successful Adaptive Project Experience Before?

If yes, get a debriefing from any of your colleagues who have had direct experience with that client on an Adaptive project. What are the strengths and weaknesses of the client? What works with them and what doesn't work? If it was experience with you, then go back and relive past projects with them in as much detail as you can recall. The project notebook (you did keep one, didn't you?) will be a great help in bringing back experiences long forgotten. There may be some clues in their behavior. You might learn about things to do and things not to do. You need to understand the client and how they behave in as much detail as you can possibly gather.

If no, then you need to prepare the client for their role and responsibility in the project. First, as co-project manager they share equally with you in the authority and responsibility over and for the project. This may be a strange role for them but it is a necessary role. You may have to sacrifice some old habits and ways of doing business. Relinquishing or sharing authority is a big step for you, but you have to do it if you expect to succeed.

Will This First-Time Adaptive Project Client Be Meaningfully Involved?

The first Adaptive experience for a client is a big step into the unknown for them. Perhaps for the first time in their careers, they will have a shared project responsibility, and that will be strange turf for them. You need to understand this and prepare them for it. I have built a model to do just that, which I share with you here.

Review the Six Questions from Chapter 2

Here they are again in case you have forgotten them:

- What business situation is being addressed?
- What do you need to do?
- What will you do?
- How will you do it?
- How will you know you did it?
- How well did you do?

I use these as the foundation for every client engagement. They are non-threatening, they make sense, and every client can relate to them. Once upon a time, I did some pro bono work for my church. I volunteered to manage the annual church bazaar. That was a real learning experience for me. I was able to use my project management skills, but I did not use any technical terminology. Some of the team members had been doing the same thing for the bazaar for 20 years. Telling them they need to do it differently doesn't work. (Try volunteering sometime if you really want to test your abilities!)

Provide a Brief Overview of the Adaptive PMLC Model

If you have chosen a specific model already, share it and the reasons you have chosen it for this project. How will the client be better off from the project team having used it? Take a clue from the preceding subsection and don't use any project management jargon unless you know your client will be comfortable with it.

Continuously Review the Model during the Project

Repetition is a good teacher. Don't assume the client will remember and understand what you said way back at the beginning of the project. Lead them through the use of each tool, template, and process on a just-in-time basis. Examples taken from other projects in your organization may also be helpful.

Has the Client Appointed a Qualified Co-Project Manager?

Despite all you have done to plan and orient the client team, the wrong choice of a co-project manager can kill the project. The person must be respected in their business unit so that people will believe and listen to him or her. Don't depend on the manager of that business unit to make the right choice. Brief the unit manager on your needs and the importance of making a correct decision on the position. If possible, review candidates with the unit manager and jointly arrive at a decision.

Adapting and Integrating the APM Toolkit

The APM PMLC models define a world that is a fascinating challenge to the chefs and an overwhelming problem for the cooks.

The chefs will consider the current characteristics of the project goal and solution; reach into their tools, templates, and processes for the best fit; and adapt it to the project. In many cases, their creativity will be brought to bear on their management needs.

The cooks will try to use an APM PMLC model right out of the box and fail. I'll give them the benefit of the doubt and allow that they may well pick the best-fit tool, template, or process and then try to force fit it to the project. Frustration and high failure rates are the predictable result.

If you are going to be a chef, you have to be flexible and discerning about what you are doing. There is no substitute for thinking, and you must be thinking all of the time to stay on top of an APM project. Therefore, I'm going to describe some typical situations that demand flexibility and adaptability.

This section gives you a quick look at each part of the APM PMLC model to see how you might use Process Group tools, templates, and processes to best advantage in an APM project.

Scoping the Next Iteration/Cycle

The Scoping Process Group includes the following:

- Eliciting the true needs of the client
- Documenting the client's needs
- Negotiating with the client how those needs will be met
- Writing a one-page description of the project
- Gaining senior management approval to plan the project

The first three items embody the COS and the RBS, and getting this right is critical. Remember you are exploring the unknown in an APM project. The project is a critical mission project, and you can't afford to leave any stone unturned at this definition stage. You might want to consider doing a Root Cause Analysis if there is any doubt about the client confusing wants and needs. Remember, wants are often associated with how the client sees the solution to a problem; they may not have even conveyed to you. Needs are what you need to begin crafting a solution. With respect to the RBS, err on the side of deciding that it is not complete. That will lead you to choose a more appropriate APM PMLC model.

The POS will be the template that sells your goal and objective statements to the approving manager. Most importantly, it must use language that anyone who reads it will understand. It must be based on facts that anyone who reads it will nod in agreement (the Problem/Opportunity Statement described in Chapter 4). The success criteria must clearly state the quantitative business value that will result from the successful completion of the project. You will not be present to defend the POS. It must stand on its own merit.

Planning the Next Iteration/Cycle

The Planning Process Group includes the following:

- Defining all of the work of the project
- Estimating how long it will take to complete the work
- Estimating the resources required to complete the work
- Estimating the total cost of the work
- Sequencing the work
- Building the initial project schedule
- Analyzing and adjusting the project schedule
- Writing a risk management plan
- Documenting the project plan
- Gaining senior management approval to launch the project

Most of these tools, templates, and processes are part of the Traditional approach to planning a project, and they can be used as described in Chapter 5. The only difference is that you are planning for a two to four week horizon. Err on the side of using as little technology as makes sense. Burdening yourself with an automated project plan may be overkill in that you inherit the maintenance of that plan as well. APM projects are much higher risk than TPM projects, so you need to pay particular attention to your risk management plan. Give one of your team members the responsibility of managing that plan. As part of the daily 15-minute team meeting, review and update the risk management plan.

Launching the Next Iteration/Cycle

The Launching Process Group includes the following:

- Recruiting the project manager
- Recruiting the project team

- Writing a project description document
- Establishing team operating rules
- Establishing the scope change management process
- Managing team communications
- Finalizing the project schedule
- Writing work packages

These processes will be done once in the APM project. You will not need a scope change management process. The Client Checkpoint will incorporate the evaluation and response in the form of a re-prioritized functions and features list.

Monitoring and Controlling the Next Iteration/Cycle

The Monitoring and Controlling Process Group includes the following:

- Establishing the project performance and reporting system
- Monitoring project performance
- Monitoring risk
- Reporting project status
- Processing scope change requests
- Discovering and solving problems

My best advice is to avoid making any changes to the iteration or cycle plan in midstream. Do what you planned inside the planned timebox. Ideas and suggested changes will arise during the iteration or cycle plan. This is only natural, because an APM project is a learning and discovery project. Post the ideas and suggestions in the Scope Bank, and then wait for the iteration or cycle close and checkpoint to decide how to handle them.

Closing the Next Iteration/Cycle

Unlike a TPM project where the schedule can slip or be changed, that doesn't happen in an APM project. The cycle timebox is cast in stone. It is never extended to accommodate one of the swim lanes whose schedule has slipped. The iteration or cycle may be closed if all swim lanes are complete ahead of schedule.

Deciding to Conduct the Next Iteration/Cycle

This is not part of any TPM PMLC model. It is unique to APM and xPM. The client is the driver of this decision process. The current solution and its history along with the Scope Bank are the inputs. If the metrics you are collecting suggest that the solution is converging on the goal, there is good reason to continue with another iteration or cycle.

You need to keep in mind the following aspects of this decision-making process:

- The client manages the decision process.
- The client must be fully engaged in the process.
- The atmosphere must be completely open and honest.
- The decision must be based on expected business value.
- The solution must be converging to a solution that aligns with the goal.

Closing the Project

The Closing Process Group includes the following processes:

- Gaining client approval of having met project requirements
- Planning and installing deliverables
- Writing the final project report
- Conducting the post-implementation audit

An APM project ends when one of the following occurs:

- The time and budget are expended.
- An acceptable solution with the expected business value is found.
- The project is abandoned.

All of the processes in the Closing Process Group are conducted in an APM project just as they would be in a TPM project. The Scope Bank in an APM project will still have some suggestions and ideas for solution enhancement when the project is ended. These as well as experiences with the current solution will become the business justification for the next version.

Putting It All Together

Using Iterative and Adaptive PMLC models can be among the most challenging and fulfilling experiences you might have as a project manager. To whet your appetite, I showed you Prototyping, RUP, ASD, APF, DSDM, and Scrum. You saw how they were the same and how they differed. You saw how conditions could change your choice of model and how best to use it. You now know how to use each model, even though there is much more to learn about each one. There are many more choices for those who are interested. See the bibliography in Appendix C for suggestions of where to look. There is always something new to learn. Learning to be successful with Agile projects is as much an art as it is a science.

Agile projects are definitely calling upon you to be a chef and not a cook. I have given you enough detail to start you on your journey to being a chef. I hope you have the courage to start and stay steadfast on that journey.

Discussion Questions

1. Your Agile project has been progressing smoothly and until now, there have been few surprises. Without any warning, the client manager (your co-project manager) suddenly leaves the company and is replaced by a subordinate. The new manager isn't willing to have his people participate at the level of the prior manager, and you feel that this will seriously impact the project. What actions would you take and why? If you had identified losing the client manager in your risk management plan, what would your mitigation strategy have been?

2. All of the ideas that are suggested come from the development team and not from the client team. You have correctly concluded that the final product will not be as good as it could have been if the client had been more involved. How would you address this situation and why? If you had identified poor client involvement in your risk management plan, what would your mitigation strategy have been?

CASE STUDY – PIZZA DELIVERED QUICKLY (PDQ)

3. You are managing the Inventory Management subsystem project. Generate the RBS and choose the model you will use. Rank order the specific models from best fit to worst fit, and state your rationale for that ranking. Select from the Linear, Incremental, Iterative, and Adaptive PMLC models. Be specific.

4. Referring to the case study, which subsystems would you develop using an Agile model? Be specific as to which model you would choose and why. List any advantages or disadvantages that will result from your decision.

5. What sort of approach would you use for an Agile project if your client wasn't willing or able to participate? What are the strengths and/or weaknesses of your choice?

6. What sort of approach would you use if your client was getting so involved with the project that it was adversely affecting the team's productivity? What are the strengths and/or weaknesses of your choice?

7. You are considering volunteering to manage a critical but very challenging project that has all the makings of an Adaptive project. You've been

reading this book and have learned a great deal about Adaptive projects, and this one is fully that. Above all else, you want it to be successful, but your organization doesn't support Adaptive projects. What are you going to do? You've always risen to challenges and walking away from this one isn't an alternative.

8. Clients are always reluctant to get too involved in planning. What might you do to sell them on the idea that their full involvement in APF is needed for this effort to succeed?

9. Clearly, the Monitoring and Controlling Phase is very dependent upon the people on your team. APF gives team members great discretion in completing their work. If you were managing an APF project, how would you balance your need to know against the need to empower team members to do their work? Be specific.

10. Compare what happens with a TPM project and an APF project when a team member is taken off the team and no longer available. What are the impacts on each approach? Which approach is least affected by such a change? To do this comparison, you will be considering a full TPM plan versus an APF cycle plan.

11. A member of your team is a systems analyst from the old school and just cannot adjust to APF. Her problem is that the client has decision-making authority over the direction that your software development project is taking and that the client is, shall we say, technically challenged. How would you handle this dilemma?

12. You are the project manager over one of your company's first APF projects. You are having trouble getting the client's involvement. What would you do?

13. You have completed your first APF project. Compare and contrast the TPM and APF approaches when both of them reach this same point.

14. Suppose a project should have used a TPM approach, but you used APF. Comment on what might be different. Would the traditional approach have given you a better outcome? Why or why not? Be specific.

15. Under your leadership, your organization has spent considerable effort to adopt a traditional approach to project management. It has reached Maturity Level 3 — that is, there are fully documented project management processes and templates, and everyone is following them. PMBOK is the recognized standard. You have earned a good reputation among your management colleagues. You have noticed a number of projects where the client has requested and gotten approval for several changes throughout the project. These have cost significant money and time, the loss of e-business market share, and the subsequent loss of revenues.

As Director of the Project Support Office, you have come to realize that APF is the approach that should have been taken on this project. You are convinced that by using APF these types of projects could have been completed earlier, at less cost, and with a much better end results. What strategy would you suggest to introduce and institutionalize APF in your company? What obstacles do you foresee?

16. You are a senior project manager in your company. You have 15 years' experience with them and a solid reputation for delivering successful projects. What might you, acting on your own, do to get your organization to appreciate the value of APF? What obstacles might prevent you from going forward with your plan? How do you feel about stepping outside the box?

CASE STUDY – PIZZA DELIVERED QUICKLY (PDQ)

17. Generate the RBS for the PDQ factory location software application. Comment on the missing or partially defined functions and features. In generating the RBS consider such questions as these: How many factory locations should there be? Where should they be? What criteria should be used to evaluate a location? How many more delivery trucks will be needed?

CHAPTER 12

Extreme Project Management

Clearly no group can as an entity create ideas. Only individuals can do this. A group of individuals may, however, stimulate one another in the creation of ideas.
— Estill I. Green, former vice president of Bell Telephone Laboratories

CHAPTER LEARNING OBJECTIVES

After reading this chapter, you will be able to:

- **Know when to use Extreme Project Management (xPM) or Emertxe Project Management (MPx)**
- **Use and adapt the Extreme PMLC model**
- **Explain the benefits and use of the INSPIRE Extreme PMLC model**
- **Anticipate and resolve the potential problems of using an Extreme PMLC model**

In this chapter, you learn at a very detailed level the kinds of projects that lend themselves to Extreme xPM PMLC models. The vast majority of these are research and development (R&D) projects. For projects in Quadrant 3, the goal is a best-guess and usually reflects the proposer's idea of an ideal end state that the project should attain. Two different project management life cycle (PMLC) models are discussed in this chapter. I don't intend to be flippant about this, but the first model, xPM, is a Quadrant 3 model for projects that have a goal in search of a solution. The second model, MPx, is a Quadrant 4 model for projects that have a solution in search of a goal. Don't worry — I haven't lost my mind. See Chapter 2 for a refresher on the four quadrants.

What Is Extreme Project Management?

Extreme Project Management (xPM) is the least structured and most creatively managed of the five models that define the project management landscape presented in Part II. Extreme projects are at the furthest corner of the landscape where uncertainty and complexity are at their highest levels. Because of that, the failure rates of Extreme projects are the highest among all types of projects. The reason for the high comparative failure rate follows from the nature of the Extreme project. These projects are searching for goals and solutions where none have been found before. To converge on a goal and solution with business value is often a hunt in a dark room for something that doesn't exist in that room but might in another room, if you knew where to find that other room.

Extreme Project Management Life Cycle

The Extreme PMLC model is the most complex of the five major models in the project management landscape. Figure 12-1 is a graphical representation of the Extreme PMLC model. The first thing to note about the model is that the phases repeat all Process Groups in a linear fashion. (I call these *phases* in this model to distinguish them from *increments, iterations,* and *cycles* used in the models discussed earlier in the book.) If the decision is made to go to the next phase, that phase begins with the scoping of the changed direction for the project. The reason for this is that the just-completed phase may suggest that the solution can be found by taking the project in an entirely different direction than originally planned. By repeating the Scoping Phase, you may find that the goal may change due to the new direction the project will take.

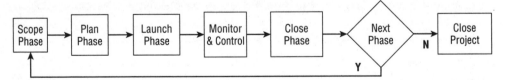

Figure 12-1: Extreme PMLC model

Definition

Extreme PMLC models consist of a sequence of repeated phases with each phase based on a very limited understanding of the goal and solution. Each phase learns from the preceding ones and redirects the next phase in an attempt to converge on an acceptable goal and solution. At the discretion of the client, a phase may release a partial solution. A phase consists of the five Process Groups, each performed once in the sequence Scoping ➤ Planning ➤ Launching ➤ Monitoring and Controlling ➤ Closing. In effect, a phase is a complete project life cycle much as it is in the Incremental PMLC model, but with an option to release a partial solution at the completion of each phase.

The following section gives a high-level overview of the four components that constitute the INSPIRE Extreme PMLC model. As such, it is a good starting point for the executive or manager who simply needs to become familiar with the xPM approach.

Characteristics

The best way to define an Extreme project is to consider its characteristics, which are discussed in the following sections. These characteristics will strike fear into the hearts of most, if not all, project managers. Make no mistake, Extreme projects are extremely challenging. Many will be cancelled before they are completed. For those that are run to completion, what they deliver may not at all reflect what you thought they would deliver. And then there is the question of the business value delivered. You may have found a $10,000 solution to a $1,000 problem. In other words, the actual goal achieved may be quite different from the goal that was originally envisioned. That is the nature of Extreme projects, and that is where I begin the investigation of how xPM applies to them.

High Speed

The types of projects that are suited to xPM are groundbreaking, innovative, critical to an organization's future, and otherwise very important to their sponsors. That means that the results are wanted ASAP. Fast is good, and if your project can keep up this pace, you will be around tomorrow to talk about it. Slow is bad, and if that's the pace of your project, you will be looking for something else to do with the rest of your life. Getting to market faster is a critical success factor in every Extreme project business endeavor.

High Change

The uncertainty about the goal or the solution means that as the project is under way, learning and discovery will occur, just as in APF projects. However, this happens with more regularity and frequency in xPM than in APF projects. The APF changes can be thought of as minor in comparison. The changes in an Extreme project may completely reverse the direction of the project. In some cases, the changes might mean canceling the current project and starting two or more projects based on the prior learning and discovery. For example, R & D projects are Extreme projects, and a discovery in one cycle through the five phases may cause the team and the client to move in a totally different direction in the next and later cycles.

High Uncertainty

Because an Extreme project is innovative and research-oriented, no one really knows what lies ahead. The direction chosen by the client and the project team might be 180 degrees out of phase with what they should be doing, but no one knows that at the beginning of the project. Furthermore, the time to complete the Extreme project is not known. The cost to complete an Extreme project is not known either. In short, there will be a lot of trial and error and a lot of false starts and killed projects.

Strengths

The strengths of the Extreme PMLC model are as follows:

- Keeps options open as late as possible
- Offers an early look at a number of partial solutions

Keeps Options Open as Late as Possible

You don't want to miss any chances of finding a solution amidst all of the options you are investigating. Any idea that generates a Probative Swim Lane must be pursued until there is no possibility that it can contribute to the solution. In planning an Extreme project, the project team will brainstorm possible solutions or solution components and prioritize the options. Starting at the top of the list, the team will launch Probative Swim Lanes in a further search. To eliminate a possible solution at this point means it will be replaced by an option of lesser priority. You don't want to do that unless you are absolutely sure the possible solution is, in fact, not feasible.

Offers an Early Look at a Number of Partial Solutions

All of the options that were prioritized are being considered. One of them might spark an idea for several others not on the priority list. Remember that you are on a search for a solution that up until now has been elusive. If the solution were that simple, it would have already been discovered.

Weaknesses

The weaknesses of the Extreme PMLC model are as follows:

- May be looking for solutions in all the wrong places
- No guarantee that any acceptable business value will result from the project deliverables

May Be Looking for Solutions in All the Wrong Places

The early phases are critical. If you can legitimately eliminate all of the prioritized options, then you should kill the project and start over in another direction.

No Guarantee That Any Acceptable Business Value Will Result from the Project Deliverables

Even if you find a solution and clarify the goal that the solution satisfies, the project may still fail. The solution may satisfy a goal that doesn't have sufficient business value, or the solution may be too costly for the goal it satisfies.

INSPIRE Extreme PMLC Model

By its very nature, an xPM project is unstructured (see Figure 12-2). xPM and Agile Project Management (APM) projects are both variations of the same theme: the learning and discovery of the solution during successive iteration, cycles, or phases moves the project forward. The INSPIRE Extreme PMLC model is an idea that I adapted from the Flexible Project model introduced in 2000 by Doug DeCarlo in his eXtreme Project Management Workshop. As Figure 12-2 illustrates, INSPIRE consists of four stages, which I am calling INitiate, SPeculate, Incubate, and REview (hence the acronym INSPIRE). The Launching Phase occurs between SPeculate and Incubate, where the normal activities described in Chapter 2 are conducted. Similarly, the Closing Phase occurs between Incubate and Review, and the same activities described in Chapter 2 are conducted.

INSPIRE is an iterative approach, just as all of the Adaptive PMLC models are iterative. INSPIRE iterates in an unspecified number of short phases (one- to four-week phases are typical) in search of the solution to some goal. It may find an acceptable solution, or it may be cancelled before any solution is reached. It is distinguished from APM models in that the goal is unknown, or at best, someone has a vague, but unspecified, notion of what the goal consists. Such a client might say, "I'll know it when I see it." That isn't a new revelation to the experienced project manager — they have heard that many times before. Nevertheless, it is the project manager's job to find the solution (with the client's help, of course).

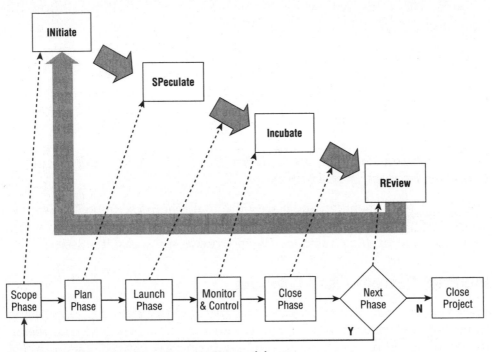

Figure 12-2: The INSPIRE Extreme PMLC model

APM models are further distinguished from INSPIRE in that INSPIRE requires the client to be more involved within and between phases, whereas the APM models require client involvement between cycles. Drug research provides a good example of the Extreme project. Suppose, for example, that the goal is to find a cure for the common cold. This is a wide-open project. Constraining the project to a fixed budget or fixed time line makes no sense whatsoever. More than likely, the project team will begin by choosing some investigative direction or directions and hope that intermediate findings and results will accomplish the following two things:

- The just-finished phase will point to a more informed and productive direction for the next and future phases. In other words, INSPIRE includes learning and discovery experiences just as the Agile models do.

- Most important of all, the funding agent will see this learning and discovery as potentially rewarding and decide to continue the funding support.

There is no constrained scope triangle in INSPIRE as there is in Traditional Project Management (TPM) and APM projects. Recall that TPM and APM projects have time and funding constraints that are meaningful. "Put a man on the moon and return him safely by the end of the decade" is pretty specific. It has a built-in stopping rule. When the money or the time runs out, the project is over. INSPIRE also has stopping rules, but they are very different. The two INSPIRE stopping rules are as follows:

- The first rule says that the project is over when a solution is found. If the solution supports a goal that has sufficient business value, the project is deemed a success, and the solution is implemented. If the solution does not support a goal that has sufficient business value, the project is deemed a failure, and it's back to the drawing board for another try (perhaps).

- The second rule says the project is over when the sponsor is not willing to continue the funding. The sponsor might withdraw the funding because the project is not making any meaningful progress. It is not converging on an acceptable solution and goal. In other words, the project is killed. Failure!

The next sections take a high-level look at the four components of INSPIRE.

INitiate

INitiate is a mixture of selling the idea, establishing the business value of the project, brainstorming possible approaches, forming the team, and getting everyone on board and excited about what they are about to undertake. It is definitely a time for team building and creating a strong working relationship with the client.

At this point, someone has an idea for a product or service and is proposing that a project be commissioned to investigate and produce it. Before any project will be launched, management must be convinced that it is an idea worth pursuing. The burden of proof is on the requestor. He or she must document and demonstrate that there is business value in undertaking the proposed project. The Project Overview Statement (POS), which you used in both TPM and APM projects, is the documentation I recommend to sell the idea. There are some differences, however, in the INSPIRE version of the POS.

Defining the Project Goal

Unlike the goal of an Agile project, the goal of an Extreme project is not much more than a vision of some future state. "I'll know it when I see it" is about the only statement of the project goal that could be made, given the vague nature of the goal as envisioned at this point in time. It has all the characteristics of an adventure in which the destination is only vaguely defined. You have to understand that the goal of an Extreme project unfolds along the course of the project life cycle. It is not something that you can plan to achieve — instead, it is something that you and the client discover along the way. That process of discovery is exciting. It will call upon all of the creative juices that the development team and the client team can muster. Contrast this to the project goal in an Agile project. In an Agile project, the goal is known — it's the solution that evolves as the project unfolds. In general, the client is more directive in an INSPIRE project, whereas the team is more directive in an Agile project.

At this early stage, any definition of the project goal should be a vision of the future. It would be good at this point to discuss how the user or client of the deliverables will use the product or service. Don't be too restrictive. Keep your options open (or "keep your powder dry," as one of my colleagues would say). Forming a vision of the end state is as much a brainstorming exercise as it is anything else. Don't close out any ideas that may prove useful later.

INSPIRE Project Overview Statement

An example will help ground some of these new ideas. Suppose the project is to find a cure for the common cold. As discussed in earlier chapters of this book, the POS is a critical document in both the TPM and APM approaches. It is also critical in xPM projects. However, because the goal is known in both TPM and APM projects but is not known in xPM projects, there will be some differences in the POS. These differences are best illustrated by way of example. Figure 12-3 is the POS for the project to find a cure for the common cold.

The following brief descriptions of the INSPIRE POS elements will help you understand the differences between this type of POS and the one that's used in TPM or APM projects.

Problem or Opportunity Statement

There's nothing unusual here. This is a very simple statement of a problem that has plagued healthcare providers and moms since the dawn of civilization.

Goal Statement

This particular project is taking a calculated (or maybe wild a**) guess that they can establish a preventative barrier to the occurrence of the common cold. Unlike the goal statements in TPM and APM projects, no time frame is specified. That would make no sense for such a research project.

Objective Statements

These objective statements identify broad directions that the research effort will take. Notice that the format does not fit the S.M.A.R.T. characteristics defined in Chapter 4. In most cases, these objective statements will provide some early guidance on the directions the team intends to pursue. Unlike TPM and APM projects, these objective statements are not a necessary and sufficient set of objectives. Their successful completion does not ensure goal attainment. In fact, some of them may be discarded based on learning and discovery in early phases. Think of them as guideposts only. They set an initial direction for the project. Because the goal is not clearly defined, you can't expect the objective statements to play the role that they do in TPM and APM projects.

PROJECT OVERVIEW STATEMENT	Project Name Common Cold Prevention Project	Project No. 02 - 01	Project Manager Carrie deCure
Problem/Opportunity There does not exist a preventative for the common cold.			
Goal Find a way to prevent the occurrence of the common cold.			
Objectives 1. Find a food additive that will prevent the occurrence of the common cold. 2. Alter the immune system to prevent the occurrence of the common cold. 3. Define a program of diet and exercise that will prevent the occurrence of the common cold.			
Success Criteria The solution must be effective for persons of any age. The solution must not introduce any harmful side effects. The solution must be affordable. The solution must be acceptable to the FDA. The solution must be easily obtained. The solution must create a profitable business opportunity.			
Assumptions, Risks, Obstacles The common cold can be prevented. The solution will have harmful side effects.			

Prepared By Earnest Effort	Date 2-14-2011	Approved By Hy Podermick	Date 2-16-2011

Figure 12-3: POS for the project to find a cure for the common cold

Success Criteria

The goal statement might do just as well as any success criteria, so this part of the POS could be left blank. In this case, you have set bounds around the characteristics of an acceptable cure. Success criteria are a quantitative measure of goal attainment, and you don't know what the final goal will be in an xPM project.

Assumptions, Risks, and Obstacles

There is no difference between xPM, TPM, and APM projects when it comes to this section. The statements given in the example lean heavily toward assumptions. Having to make such assumptions happens to be the nature of this project. I have already discussed how risk increases as your project moves along the continuum from certainty to uncertainty. Some of that risk will be reflected in this section of the POS.

Establishing a Project Timebox and Cost

Contrary to an APM project, an INSPIRE project is not constrained by a fixed time frame or cost limit. It is best to think of the time and cost parameters as providing the project team with guidance about the client's expectations. It is much like having the client say, "I would like to see some results within N months, and I am willing to invest as much as $X to have you deliver." In reality, at each REview, the decision to continue or terminate is made. That decision isn't necessarily tied to the time and cost parameters given earlier by the client. In fact, if exceptional progress toward a solution is made, then the client may relax either or both of the time and cost parameters. In other words, if the progress to date is promising, more time and/or money may be placed at the team's disposal.

Establishing the Number of Phases and Phase Length

In the beginning, very short phases are advisable. I recall an xPM project in which the first few phases were very exploratory. With the collaboration of the client, we were searching for a feasible direction. For this project, the first few phases were one to three days in length. In the early phases, new ideas are tested, and many will be rejected. Proof of concept may be part of the first few phases. The team should not be committing to complex activities and tasks early on. As the team gains a better sense of direction, phase length may be increased. Specifying phase length and the number of phases up front merely sets expectations as to when and how frequently REview will take place. At each occurrence of a REview, phase length and perhaps the number of phases remaining may be changed to suit the situation. In an exploratory project, it would be a mistake to bind the team and the client to phases that do not relate to the realities of the project. Remember that flexibility is the key to a successful INSPIRE project. Cycle and iteration length in an APM project are more stable than phase length is in an xPM project.

Trade-Offs in the Scope Triangle

Despite the fact that INSPIRE is unstructured, it is important to set the priorities of the variables in the scope triangle. As project work commences and problems arise, which variable or variables are the client and the team willing to compromise? As discussed in Chapter 1, the five variables in any project are as follows:

- Scope
- Quality
- Cost
- Time
- Resource availability

In Chapter 11, you saw the scope triangle ranking matrix (see Table 11-4). It showed which of these variables is least likely to be compromised. Which would you choose to compromise first if the situation warranted it? The answer should depend on the type of project. For example, if the project involves conducting research to find a cure for the common cold, quality is the least likely to be compromised, and time might be the first to be compromised. But what if you knew that a competitor was working on the same project? Would time still be the first variable to compromise? Probably not. Cost might take its place, because time to market is now a critical success factor.

Scope is an interesting variable in Extreme projects. Consider the example of finding the cure for the common cold again. Hypothetically, what if you knew that the competition was also looking for a cure for the common cold, and that being first to market would be very important? In an earlier phase, the team discovered not a cure for the cold but a food additive that arrests the cold at its current stage of development. In other words, the cold will not get worse than it was at the time the additive was taken. The early discovery also holds great promise to morph into the cure that you are looking for, but you need time to explore it. You feel that getting the early result to market now may give you a strategic barrier to entry, give the competition reason to pause, and buy you some time to continue toward the original goal. Therefore, the scope is reduced in the current project, and it is brought to a successful completion. A new project is commissioned to continue on the path discovered in the earlier project.

SPeculate

This component defines the beginning of a new phase and will always start with a brainstorming session. The input will be either a blank slate or output from the previous INitiate ➤ SPeculate ➤ Incubate ➤ REview cycle. In any case, the project team, client, and final user of the product or service should participate in the brainstorming session. The objective of this session is to explore ideas and identify alternative directions for the next Incubate phase. Because an INSPIRE project has a strong exploratory nature about it, no idea should be neglected. Several directions may eventually be pursued in parallel in the next phase. Phase length, deliverables, and other planning artifacts are defined in the SPeculate stage as well.

CASE STUDY – PIZZA DELIVERED QUICKLY (PDQ): LOGISTICS SUBSYSTEM

The Logistics subsystem is very complex. Although it may not seem obvious at first, the complexity begins with the goal statement. You probably prefer a goal statement that says something about the time from order entry to order fulfillment. Do you want to minimize this time? That is certainly what the pizza customer has in mind. Or would you rather minimize the time from when the order was ready to be delivered until the time it is delivered? That is certainly what PDQ has in mind for delivery of a quality order. Your choice for which PMLC model to use is between APF and INSPIRE. Either model will work just fine. The choice might depend on which approach the client is most comfortable with.

The word *speculate* conjures up deep thinking, carrying out due diligence on several alternatives, choosing one or more of those alternatives, and then simply taking your chances. You should hear yourself saying, "I wonder if this would work?" That is what the SPeculate stage of INSPIRE is all about.

Defining How the Project Will Be Done

The initial sense of direction for the team to take in the first phase of an INSPIRE project can vary considerably. A good approach is to use the POS objective statements as a guide. The POS can continuously be updated to reflect the current view of the project, and its objective statements can serve as a guide to what will be done. In later phases, the team and the client will have the benefit of learning and discovery from the prior phases. For the sake of discussion, I want to treat these two situations separately. In this section of the chapter, assume you are planning the first phase.

Conditions of Satisfaction

The Conditions of Satisfaction (COS) was described in detail in Chapter 4 and will not be repeated here. Although the COS is a tool that produces a required deliverable in TPM and the APM, its use in xPM is optional. The COS loses its value as the goal becomes more and more elusive. If the client has only a vague idea about the goal, no amount of discussion about needs and deliverables will clarify the situation for either party, and the other planning artifacts described in the text that follows may be more useful in the initial SPeculate stage.

If you choose to use the COS in your INSPIRE project, think of it as more of a brainstorming process. The project team and the client can investigate ideas en route to generating a list of what will be done in this phase.

Scenarios, Stories, and Use Cases

The technical perfectionist would probably define these terms as different from one another, but for the purposes this discussion, they are the same. All three can be defined as descriptions of how an end user might use the application. Because the application may be feature-rich, there usually will be several such descriptions. If done correctly, these descriptions will be comprehensive regarding how the application can be used. The descriptions can then be prioritized and assigned to the appropriate development phases. There is no practical limit to the number of such situations that are documented. In the case of technology projects, such as website development, the client may be more comfortable telling you how they envision someone using the deliverable and what they can do at the website than they would be trying to help you write a functional specification or generate the Requirements Breakdown Structure (RBS). The advantage in using scenarios, stories, and use cases is that the view you are building is from the end user's perspective, not from the technology perspective. That will raise the client's comfort level because they are on familiar ground during the exercise.

Prioritizing Requirements

The collection of scenarios, stories, and use cases provides insight into the requirements that the deliverable should meet. For the client, it is far easier to prioritize the collection than it is to prioritize the requirements. Prioritization is the next step in the SPeculate stage. There are several ways to produce a prioritized list of items in the collection.

CROSS-REFERENCE Chapter 11 discusses three such methods: Forced Ranking, Paired Comparisons, and MoSCoW. Refer to Chapter 11 for the details on these methods.

Here are other aspects of the prioritization that need to be considered:

■ There can be a great number of items in the collection, so approaches like Forced Ranking are not practical. Forced Ranking doesn't scale very well. A compromise approach might involve grouping the items based on their relationship to specific functions and then prioritizing between and within the functions. The strategy here would be to assign all of the items related to a specific function to a subteam for their consideration and development. Several subteams could be active in any given phase.

■ Depending on how well the goal is understood, it might be wise to plan the initial SPeculate stage so that as many options and alternatives as possible can be investigated. The strategy here is to eliminate those alternatives that show little promise earlier rather than later in the project. That enables more resources to be brought to bear on approaches that have a higher probability of success.

- Where appropriate, prototypes might be considered as part or all of the first-phase deliverables. Here the strategy is to prioritize items in the collection or functions by not spending too much time developing the real deliverable. Familiarizing the client with the prototype may provide sufficient information to enable not only a reduction in the number of items in the collection, but also a prioritization of items or functions that show promise. A good example is a typical business-to-consumer (B2C) application. The prototype will show the various ways that a client can interact with the application. Upon examination, the client adds to this list or deletes from the list as they experience what the client would experience when interacting with the application.

Think of the first phase or two as exploratory in nature. Their purpose is to discover the directions that show promise and focus later phases on them.

Identifying the First-Phase Deliverables

After the prioritization is done, it is time to decide how much of that prioritized list to bite off for the initial phase. Remember that you want shorter phases in the early part of the project, which suggests that you limit the first-phase deliverables to what you can reasonably accomplish in a week or two.

> **NOTE** By taking this approach, you are keeping the client's interest up, which is important. APM projects follow the same strategy. Once the client has been fully engaged in the project, later phases can be lengthened.

Because your team resources are limited, you have to face the question of depth versus breadth of deliverables. In other words, might it be better to extend the breadth to accommodate more functions by not delving deep into any one function until a later phase? Produce enough detail in each function in this initial phase to get a sense of further direction for the function. You may learn from only a shallow look at a function that it isn't going to be part of the final solution. This shallow look enables you to save labor that would have been spent on a function that will be discarded, and to spend it on more important work.

Go/No-Go Decision

Because the initial phase can be purely exploratory, the sponsor must have an opportunity to judge the soundness of the initial phase plan and decide whether it makes sense to proceed. It is entirely possible that the original idea of the client cannot be delivered with the approach taken in the first phase, and the first phase leads the client to the decision that the idea doesn't make any sense after all. Some other approach needs to be taken, and that approach is not known at this time. The go/no-go decision points will occur at the end of each phase.

Decisions to stop a project are more likely to occur in the early phases than in the later phases. You should expect later phases to benefit from earlier results that suggest that the project direction is feasible and should be continued.

Planning for Later Phases

Later phases will have the benefit of output from a REview to inform the planning activities that will take place in the SPeculate stage that follows. Each REview stage will produce a clearer vision and definition of the goal. That clearer vision translates into a redirection of the project, which translates into a new prioritized list of deliverables for the coming Incubate stage. The newly prioritized deliverables list may contain deliverables from previous phases that were not completed, deliverables that have not yet been part of an Incubate stage, and deliverables that are new to the project as a result of the learning and discovery that occurred in the most recently completed Incubate stage. In any case, the revised prioritized deliverables list is taken into consideration as the team plans what it will do in the coming Incubate stage. It is now in the same position as it was in the very first SPeculate stage. What follows then is the assignment of deliverables to subteams, and scheduling the work that will be done and who will do it.

Incubate

Incubate is the INSPIRE version of the Cycle Build Phase in APF. There are several similarities between the two models and some differences as well. Consider the following points:

- Even though the Incubate stage has a prioritized list of deliverables that are to be produced in this phase, INSPIRE still must maintain the spirit of exploration. It is a learning and discovery experience that may result in mid-phase corrections arising from that exploration. This would not happen in an APF project.

- Conversely, an APF project does benefit from learning and discovery as it proceeds with the Cycle Plan, but it does not vary from that plan. The learning and discovery are input to the Client Checkpoint, and that is where plan revisions take place.

These points reflect an important distinction between INSPIRE and APF. Subteams, working in parallel, will execute the plan developed in the previous SPeculate stage. The environment has to be very open and collaborative for SPeculate to be successful. Teams should be sharing ideas and cross-fertilizing discoveries and learning moments with one another. This is not just a time to execute a plan; it is a time for exploration and dynamic interchange. Mid-phase corrections with the collaboration of the client are to be expected as the subteams learn and discover together. New ideas and a redirection or clarification of the goal is likely to come from these learning and discovery experiences as well.

Assigning Resources

The Incubate stage begins with an assignment of team members to each of the deliverables that have been prioritized for this phase. The assignment should take place as a team exercise. That team involvement is important because of the exploratory nature of INSPIRE. Team members need to express their interest in one or more deliverables and share their ideas with their fellow team members. This assignment time can also be an opportunity for team members to recruit others who share their same interests and would like to develop the deliverable with them. The project manager should not pass up the opportunity to create a synergy among team members with similar interests, as well as between subteams that will be working in parallel on different deliverables. Any opportunity to create a collaborative work environment only increases the team's chances of success. You see then the importance of a co-located xPM team. The excitement generated from the spontaneous sharing of ideas can only come from a co-located xPM team.

Establishing a Phase Plan

With the subteams in place and with their assignments made, the subteams can plan how they will produce the deliverables assigned to them. Deciding how a team produces the deliverables is exactly the same as discussed in Chapter 5. In fact, many of the same tools discussed in Chapter 5 can be used to help establish a phase plan here with equal effectiveness. For example, Chapter 5 presents the phase plan as a time-sequenced whiteboard diagram showing a day-by-day schedule of what is going to be done and by whom.

NOTE However, never forget the differences of a phase plan in INSPIRE. In INSPIRE, the team has to be ready for changes at any time. Exploration will often bring the team to a point where a change of direction makes sense. When these situations arise, the team needs to collaborate with the client and decide how to go forward.

Collaboratively Producing Deliverables

Collaboration goes to the very essence of INSPIRE. Collaboration between subteams must occur. The example given earlier is one such instance. I spoke earlier in the chapter about the exploratory nature of an Extreme project. Because the project is exploratory, no one has a lock on the solution. Even the goal is somewhat elusive. That means the goal and the solution can be attained only through a solid team effort — a collaborative effort. There is a great deal of similarity between INSPIRE projects and brainstorming. One idea may not be of much value when taken individually. However, combine it with one or more other ideas and suddenly there is value. Co-location can make this exchange possible. The quote at the beginning of the chapter from Estill I. Green, former vice president of Bell Telephone Laboratories, is relevant here: "Clearly no group can as an entity create ideas. Only individuals can do this. A group of individuals may, however, stimulate one another in the creation of ideas."

REview

REview in INSPIRE is very similar to the Client Checkpoint Phase in the APF. All of the learning and discovery from the just-completed Incubate stage are brought together in another brainstorming session. During the REview stage, the project team will share their answers to questions such as the following:

- What did you learn?
- What can you do to enhance goal attainment?
- What new ideas arose and should be pursued?
- What should you do in the next phase?

The most important decision is whether or not the project will continue. This is a client decision. Have the results to date met with their expectations? Is the project moving toward an acceptable solution? These answers will determine whether or not the project continues to the next phase or is cancelled. APF and INSPIRE share this go/no-go decision point at the completion of each phase. APF is less likely to result in a cancellation, because so much more is known about the solution. Conversely, INSPIRE is so exploratory and research-based that cancellations are far more likely.

Each phase of an INSPIRE project ends with a review of the just-completed Incubate stage. It is a meeting attended by the client and the project team. The purpose of the REview stage is to reflect on what has just happened and what learning and discovery have taken place. The output is a definition of the next phase's activities.

Applying Learning and Discovery from the Previous Phase

Early in the sequence of phases, the client and the team should expect significant findings and major redirections of further efforts. As the project moves into later phases, the changes should diminish in scope because the project team should be converging on a more clearly defined goal and an acceptable solution to reach it.

NOTE This part of the INSPIRE process differs from APF. In APF, the goal has always been clearly defined — it is the solution that becomes clearer with each passing APF cycle. In an INSPIRE phase, both the goal and the solution become clearer.

Revising the Project Goal

The first order of business is for the client and the project team to revisit the previous goal statement from the prior REview stage. Ask the following questions:

- What has happened in the just-completed Incubate stage?
- What new information do you have?
- What approaches have you eliminated?
- What new discovery suggests a change in goal direction and definition?
- Are you converging on a more clearly defined goal that has business value?

This revision of the project goal is an important step and must not be treated lightly. The client and the team need to reach a consensus about the new goal, and you then need to update the POS with a revised goal statement.

Reprioritizing Requirements

The second order of business is for the client and the project team to revisit deliverables and requirements. The following questions should be asked here:

- How does the new goal statement affect the deliverables list?
- Should some items be removed?
- Should new items be added?
- How is the functionality embedded in the new goal statement affected?

The answers to these questions enable the client and the project team to reprioritize the new requirements. Update the POS to reflect any changes in the objective statements.

Making the Go/No-Go Decision for the Next Phase

Will there be a next INitiate ➢ SPeculate ➢ Incubate ➢ REview phase? Equivalently, the question could be this: Are you converging at an acceptable rate on a clearly defined goal and acceptable solution? The client will consider this question in the face of the money and time already spent. Does it make business sense to continue this project? The updated POS is the input to this decision.

What Is Emertxe Project Management?

If you haven't already guessed it, Emertxe (pronounced *e-murt-see*) is Extreme spelled backwards. And indeed an Emertxe project is an Extreme project, but done backwards. Rather than looking for a solution, you are looking for a goal. Pardon my play on words, but it was the best way to name these types of projects.

The Emertxe Project Management Life Cycle

The Emertxe PMLC model looks exactly the same as the Extreme PMLC model. Everything that was said previously about the Extreme PMLC model applies unchanged in the Emertxe PMLC model.

The differences have to do with the intent of the project. The Extreme PMLC model starts with a goal that has great business value and searches for a way (a solution) to deliver that business value. The solution may require a change in the goal. If that revised goal still has great business value, the project ends. The Emertxe PMLC model starts with a solution and no goal. The question to be answered by the Emertxe PMLC model is this, "Is there a goal that this solution can reach, and does that goal have business value?"

The commonality is that both PMLCs strive to gain a simultaneous convergence of goal and solution, but from different perspectives — one to find a solution, the other to find a goal.

When to Use an Emertxe PMLC Model

The Emertxe PMLC model should be your model of choice in any project that seeks to find business value through the integration of a new technology into a current product, service, or process. There are two major types of projects that call for this model to be used: R & D projects and some problem-solution projects.

Research and Development Projects

This is the most obvious application. You are considering how, if at all, a new technology provides business value to your organization. The search for the goal might lead your team in obvious directions, or it could be very elusive.

Problem-Solution Projects

In most cases, you would initially choose to use APF for these types of projects. The solution of a critical problem is sought. The goal will therefore be clearly and completely stated, and you start out on a journey to find and define a complete solution. Not long into the project, you and the client come to the conclusion that a complete solution to the problem as stated doesn't seem too likely. You could abandon the project, but that might not be an acceptable resolution. Perhaps the next question should be this: What problem can you solve? Now the goal is not clearly stated. Congratulations, you now meet the conditions of an Extreme project, but you are using an Adaptive model. Do you change models or continue on the present course? Would there be any noticeable difference between the two models given the present situation? You know that APF is Adaptive. Can you adapt APF to fit this situation?

The answers are really quite simple. Continue with your present strategy of introducing Probative Swim Lanes to complete the current solution to the extent that you can. Change your APF cycle strategy to introduce more Probative Swim Lanes in an attempt to find other solution alternatives or other alternatives to reinforce the current solution. There will not be any noticeable change of models. You can call what you are doing Adaptive or Extreme — it doesn't make any difference.

Using the Tools, Templates, and Processes for Maximum xPM Effectiveness

The key here is to create an environment in which the project team can freely exercise their creativity without the encumbrance and nuisance of non-value-added work. The agilist would say that this should be an environment that is light or lean versus heavy.

This section gives you a quick look at each part of the Extreme PMLC model to see how the process group tools, templates, and processes might be used or adapted to the best advantage of the xPM project team.

Scoping the Next Phase

The Scoping Process Group includes the following:

- Eliciting the true needs of the client
- Documenting the client's needs
- Negotiating with the client how those needs will be met
- Writing a one-page description of the project
- Gaining senior management's approval to plan the project

A loosely structured COS for the next phase is the starting point. Hold off on any attempt at specificity. That is not the nature of an xPM project. If this phase is among the first few phases of the project, expect them to focus on a general investigation of high-level ideas about a solution. There might be several concurrent ideas to explore in an attempt to further define possibilities. These are very preliminary ideas and must be treated as such. After some possibilities are identified, more Probative Swim Lanes might be launched to drill down into the feasibility of these ideas. A POS might be drafted that will remain valid for a few phases, but expect it to be superseded quickly and often. The approval to actually plan the phase will be a client approval.

Planning the Next Phase

The Planning Process Group includes the following:

- Defining all of the work of the project
- Estimating how long it will take to complete the work
- Estimating the resources required to complete the work
- Estimating the total cost of the work
- Sequencing the work
- Building the initial project schedule
- Analyzing and adjusting the project schedule
- Writing a risk management plan
- Documenting the project plan
- Gaining senior management's approval to launch the project

Planning is a two-level process in xPM projects. The first level is to satisfy senior management's requirements and get approval to do the project. After that approval is granted, planning can move to the phase level. Planning at the phase level isn't much more than just deciding what Probative Swim Lanes make sense and can be completed inside the phase timebox. So the little bit of detailed planning that is done is done at the swim-lane level. The subteam will plan what is to be done and who will do it. Don't burden them during the early phases with needless planning documents and reports. Leave them free to approach their swim-lane tasks in a way that makes sense for them. Detailed dependency diagrams are usually not prepared. However, there should be a lot of verbal communication among the team members as to the status of their swim lanes.

xPM projects are very high risk, and a solid plan is needed. Just as in the case of APM projects, you should appoint a team member to be responsible for monitoring the plan. The plan itself can take on different characteristics than planning in all other types of projects. Here is an application of risk planning that I have used with success. To the extent that you can identify the requirements or functions that the solution should have, prioritize that list from most risky to least risky as far as implementation is concerned. The early phases should focus on this list from top to bottom. If you can resolve the risky requirements or functions, then you can resolve other requirements or functions further down the list. Of course, the list will change as new learning and discovery takes place. Always attack the riskiest parts of the project first.

Launching the Next Phase

The Launching Process Group includes the following:

- Recruiting the project team
- Writing a project description document
- Establishing team operating rules
- Establishing the scope change management process
- Managing team communications
- Finalizing the project schedule
- Writing work packages

My comments here are exactly the same as they were in the APM project (see Chapter 11). You do each of these things once and then forget about it. You don't need a scope change process either. Use the Launching Phase to decide how to handle what otherwise would have been scope change requests.

Monitoring and Controlling the Next Phase

The Monitoring and Controlling Process Group includes the following:

- Establishing the project performance and reporting system
- Monitoring project performance
- Monitoring risk
- Reporting project status
- Processing scope change requests
- Discovering and solving problems

If you are able to use the daily 15-minute team meeting effectively, I don't see a need for much more in the way of monitoring and controlling. I remain pretty steadfast in not interfering with the creative process. As a project manager, your major responsibility is to facilitate the team and stay out of their way.

Closing the Phase

The same comments as I offered for the APM project in Chapter 11 are appropriate here.

Deciding to Conduct the Next Phase

Again the client drives this decision process. The temptation is to hang on to the project much longer than makes sense. If there isn't measurable progress toward an acceptable solution after the first few phases, think seriously about abandoning the project and restarting it in a different direction. Save the time and budget for more fruitful pursuits.

Closing the Project

The Closing Process Group includes the following:

- Gaining client approval of having met project requirements
- Planning and installing deliverables
- Writing the final project report
- Conducting the postimplementation audit

The same comments as I offered for the APM project in Chapter 11 apply here.

Putting It All Together

This concludes Part II of this book, which provided you with up-close and detailed descriptions of the five model types that populate the project-management landscape. You are now ready to take on the challenges and start out on your journey to become a chef. I just want you to keep an open mind as you assess a project and choose a PMLC model appropriate to the situation. Keep all of the variables in mind as you make those assessments and choices.

Discussion Questions

1. What are the similarities and differences between an Adaptive PMLC model and an Extreme PMLC model? Be very specific.

2. If your choice of PMLC model could be either Adaptive or Extreme, which would you choose and why? Are there any conditions that would clearly suggest one model over the other? State your rationale.

CASE STUDY – PIZZA DELIVERED QUICKLY (PDQ)

3. For the case study, the Logistics subsystem development project will use INSPIRE. The POS is shown here as an accompanying figure. If you were the approving manager, what questions might you ask? Revise the POS so that it addresses the questions you would ask.

PROJECT OVERVIEW STATEMENT	Project Name PDQ Logistics Sub-system	Project No. 09-04	Project Manager Pepe Ronee

Problem/Opportunity
In order to be competitive in the home delivery business the customer order must be delivered within 30 minutes of order entry.

Goal
Minimize order entry to order delivery time.

Objectives
1. Assign an order to a production location in order to ensure 30-minute order entry to order delivery time.   2. Assign an order to a delivery van in order to ensure 30-minute order entry to order delivery time.

Success Criteria
95% of orders meet the 30-minute order entry to order delivery time requirement as measured during the fourth month of operations.

Assumptions, Risks, Obstacles
Production capacity is not sufficient to meet the 30-minute constraint.   Delivery capacity is not sufficient to meet the 30-minute constraint.   Pizza factory locations are not sufficient in number and/or location to meet the 30-minute constraint.

Prepared By Pepe Ronee	Date 4/03/2011	Approved By Dee Livery	Date 4/05/2011

Logistics subsystem POS

4. Can APF be used on an extreme project? Why? Why not? Be specific.

5. In the formation stages of a project, are there any distinct advantages to using xPM over APF for an extreme project? If so, identify them.

6. In the formation stages of a project, are there any distinct disadvantages to using APF over xPM for an extreme project? If so, identify them. In considering your answer, think about what is really known versus what may be only speculation and how that might create problems.

7. Is APF or xPM more likely to waste less of the client's money and the team's time if the project were killed prior to completion? To answer the question, you have to consider when the decision to kill the project is made in APF projects versus when it is made in xPM projects and what is known at the time the decision is made. Defend your position with specifics.

Building an Effective Project Management Infrastructure

Annual surveys conducted by the Standish Group report on the top 10 reasons for project failure. At or near the top of every list since the surveys began is lack of senior-management support. You might think of that support as pertaining only to individual projects, but it also extends to the infrastructure that is put in place to support projects. A new category called User Involvement was added for the first time to the 2007 survey, and it topped the list as the major factor for project success.

From Parts I and II you have gained a fundamental understanding of the complexity and uncertainty of the contemporary project management environment. Next in the order of importance is the infrastructure needed to support that environment. That is the purpose of Part III.

Overview of Part III

Part III consists of three chapters.

Chapter 13: Establishing and Maturing a Project Support Office

A Project Support Office (PSO), which is also known as a Project Management Office (PMO), consists of organizational units that are put in place to support project managers and teams. They can offer a bare minimum of support services or up to 50 different support services. This chapter defines the PSO; describes its mission, objectives, support functions, structure, and placement in the organization; and discusses how to establish a PSO.

Chapter 14: Establishing and Managing a Project Portfolio Management Process

A Project Portfolio Management Process (PPMP) is put in place by senior management to ensure the best investment of money and people in the projects that are undertaken by the enterprise. This chapter discusses that process in detail. The role and responsibility of the PSO in this process is also discussed.

Chapter 15: Establishing and Managing a Continuous Process Improvement Program

Putting a project management methodology in place is the beginning of a long journey that will never end. The care and feeding of that methodology will occupy the enterprise for as long as it does business. To do that successfully requires the establishment of some type of process improvement program. This chapter discusses a four-phase model for establishing such a program. The role and responsibility of the PSO in this process is also discussed.

CHAPTER 13

Establishing and Maturing a Project Support Office

There is nothing more difficult to take in hand, more perilous to conduct, or more uncertain in its success, than to take the lead in the introduction of a new order of things.

— Machiavelli, The Prince

CHAPTER LEARNING OBJECTIVES

After reading this chapter, you will be able to:

- **Describe a Project Support Office (PSO)**
- **Understand the signs that you need a PSO**
- **Know the missions, objectives, and structures of the PSO**
- **Know the functions performed by the PSO**
- **Know how to establish a PSO**
- **Understand the challenges to establishing a PSO**
- **Know how to grow and mature your PSO**

Your organization has put a project management framework in place. It is a highly adaptive framework that embraces projects in all four quadrants. You know that that framework adapts to every type of project. Teams are beginning to use it. However, you are not satisfied. Your expectation was that with everyone using a project management methodology, a higher percentage of projects would be successfully completed. So far there has been no measurable impact on project success. What can you do?

One of the most important organizational contributions to the success of project management has been the Project Support Office (PSO). But this will be a very special version of a PSO given the project situation. It is established to support project teams and reduce the risk of project failure. The PSO has several different names and variations in terms of mission, objectives, functions, organizational structure, and organizational placement. These can become quite overwhelming for someone who is not familiar with the concept and its practice. In this chapter, I intend to help you understand all aspects of the PSO, help you recognize the signs that you should establish one, help you establish one, and help you assure that it is contributing to project success.

NOTE Senior-level management is really the target audience for this chapter. If you are in a position to propose this type of PSO, take the initiative. If you are not, at least you have the ammunition when that opportunity arises.

Background of the Project Support Office

Early in the life cycle of any process, there are always the early adopters who stumble onto it and are eager to give it a chance. Their enthusiasm may prove to be contagious, and soon others begin using the process, too. At some point, senior management begins to take notice because the various ways of understanding of the process is creating problems. Not everyone understands the process the same way, and there are many levels of expertise with the tool — while some misuse it, others don't take its use seriously.

If this sounds like the history of project management in your organization, you have plenty of company. Senior management instinctively knew they needed to do something about the problem, and the first reaction was to send people away for some project management training. Usually the choice of training was made by the appropriate middle manager. There was no coordination or integration across business units. Every business unit was doing their own thing (Maturity Level 1) with little thought of standardization or enterprise-wide process design and implementation. This by itself didn't result in much improvement.

As a further attempt to solve the problem, senior management introduced some standards and common metrics found in project management. A project management process was crafted and introduced with a lot of fanfare. All were expected to use it. Some did, some didn't (Maturity Level 2). Some still held on to their old ways and managed projects the way they had been doing it all along. While all of this was going on, projects continued to be executed. There were often so many projects under way simultaneously and so much confusion that management recognized that the problem had not gone away. More dramatic action was needed. There was no way to manage across projects within the organization because of redundancy, wasted resources, and the lack of managed standards, and there was no leadership in making project management an asset to the organization. Effective project management was a recognized need in the organization, but most organizations were a long way away from satisfying that need. Senior management held high expectations that by having a standardized project management methodology, the success rate of projects would increase. Considerable effort was spent getting a methodology designed, documented, and installed, but somehow it had little impact on project success rates. In fact, it was a big disappointment. Senior management realized that having a methodology wasn't sufficient. Something more was needed, and soon that something appeared: the Project Support Office (PSO). Project Management Office (PMO) is the name commonly given this organization, but I prefer PSO. The PSO created an opportunity to put an organizational entity in place that ensured compliance (prerequisite to attaining Maturity Level 3). Project success would surely follow. Indeed, the PSO functions like an insurance policy to protect the adoption and spread of the methodology.

There are at least four reasons why an organization would choose to implement a PSO. They are as follows:

- As the organization grows in the number and complexity of the projects in its portfolio, it must adopt formal procedures for managing the volume and diversity of projects. To do this, the organization establishes the procedures that are followed for initiating, proposing, approving, and managing projects. These procedures are discussed in Chapter 14. This is a critical part of Maturity Level 3 and the prerequisite to achieving Maturity Level 4.

- With increased volume comes a need for more qualified project managers. Those who would like to become project managers will need to be identified and trained. Those who are already project managers will need additional training to deal effectively with the increased project complexity. The PSO that I am recommending is the depository of the organization's skills inventory of current and developing project managers. Because managers using the PSO are aware of the types and complexity of current and forthcoming projects, the PSO is the entity that is best prepared to identify the training needs of project managers and their teams. The HR department is the primary beneficiary of this information.

- A lack of standards and policies leads to increased inefficiencies and compromises productivity. The increasing failure rate of projects is testimony to that fact. Through the establishment and enforcement of standards and practices, the PSO can have a positive impact on efficiency and productivity. Chapter 16 discusses prevention and intervention strategies for so-called "distressed projects."

- The increased complexity and number of projects places a greater demand on resources. It is no secret that the scarcity of information technology (IT) professionals has become a barrier to project success. The same can be said about the need for more and better qualified business analysts (BAs). By paying attention to the demand for skilled project teams and the inventory of skilled team members, the PSO can maintain the proper balance through training. That requires a close collaboration between the PSO and HR regarding the training function.

Defining a Project Support Office

Several varieties of PSOs are in use in contemporary organizations. Each serves a different purpose. Before you can consider establishing a PSO in your organization, you have to understand these differences. The purpose of this section is to describe those variations and ascertain what form is best suited for your organization. A good working definition of a Project Support Office is as follows:

DEFINITION: PROJECT SUPPORT OFFICE A Project Support Office (PSO) is a temporary or permanent organizational unit that provides a portfolio of services to support project teams that are responsible for a specific portfolio of projects.

The next three sections look at each of the major components of the PSO definition.

Temporary or Permanent Organizational Unit

Among the various forms of PSOs, some are temporary structures and some are permanent. That determination is made based on the types of projects that they support, as follows:

Temporary — PSOs that are temporary are usually called Program Offices, and they provide the administrative and other support needs of a group of projects that are related by purpose or goal. When those projects are completed, the Program Office is disbanded. Many government projects have Program Offices affiliated with them. They are generally long-term arrangements and involve millions or billions of dollars of funding.

Permanent — PSOs that are permanent are called by various names, as discussed in the "Naming the Project Support Office" section later in the chapter. The first name that you are probably familiar with is Project Management Office (PMO). These early versions of the PSO provided a range of support services for projects grouped by organizational unit, rather than goal or purpose. The IT Department was the first functional unit the PMO was attached to and remains the primary application area.

Portfolio of Services

In a recent survey of 502 PMOs, Brian Hobbs and Monique Aubry identified 27 functions that the surveyed PMOs provided.[1] I've taken those 27 functions and grouped them into the six service areas that I recommend as follows:

- Project Support
  - Report project status to upper management
  - Provide advice to upper management
  - Participate in strategic planning
  - Identify, select, and prioritize new projects
  - Manage archives of project documentation
  - Manage one or more portfolios
  - Manage one or more programs
  - Provide interface between management and customer
  - Allocate resources between projects
  - Implement and manage database of lessons learned
  - Implement and manage risk database
  - Provide networking and environmental scanning
- Consulting and Mentoring
  - Coordinate between projects
- Methods and Standards
  - Develop and implement a standard methodology
  - Monitor and control project performance
  - Implement and operate a project information system
  - Develop and maintain a project scoreboard
  - Conduct project audits
  - Conduct post-project reviews
  - Monitor and control performance of PMO

---

[1] Hobbs, Brian and Monique Aubry. (2010). *The Project Management Office (PMO): A Quest for Understanding*. Newtown Square, PA: Project Management Institute, ISBN 978-1-933890-97-5.

- Software Tools
  - Provide a set of tools without an effort to standardize
- Training
  - Develop competency of personnel, including training
- Project Managers
  - Provide mentoring for project managers
  - Promote project management within organization
  - Execute specialized tasks for project managers
  - Recruit, select, evaluate, and determine salaries for project managers
  - Manage benefits

These six groups define what I believe should be the services offered by the fully functional PSO of the future. The full-service PSO offers services aligned with the six major functions just listed. These are the services that the current and future PSOs should be supporting. They are briefly described in the following sections. Not every PSO will provide all six functions. Deciding on the services to be offered by a PSO is the responsibility of senior management. I would advise that all six functions be included in your PSO organization because they are critical to fully supporting the complex project environment.

The fully functional PSO of the future serves these six major service areas. Here is a brief description of the six purposes of the PSO of the future. Unless otherwise stated these services extend across all project types in all four quadrants. As the PSO provides that support, there may be differences by project type.

Project support — This includes preparing proposals, gathering and reporting weekly status information, maintaining the project notebook, and assisting with the post-implementation audit.

Consulting and mentoring — Professional project consultants and trainers are available in the PSO to support the consulting and mentoring needs of the project teams. In this capacity, they are a safe harbor for both the project manager and team members.

Methods and standards — This includes such areas as project initiation, project planning, project selection, project prioritization, Work Breakdown Structure (WBS) templates, risk assessment, project documentation, reporting, software selection and training, post-implementation audits, and dissemination of best practices.

Software tools — The evaluation, selection, installation, support, and maintenance of all the software that supports project work is part of this function.

Training — Training curriculum development and training delivery may be assigned to the PSO, depending on whether the organization has a centralized training department and whether it has the expertise needed to develop and deliver the needed programs.

Project manager resources — Here the PSO provides a resource to project managers for advice, suggestions, and career guidance. Regardless of the organizational structure in which the PSO exists, the project manager does not have any other safe place to seek advice and counsel. The PSO is ideally suited to that role. A variety of human-resource functions are provided. Some PSOs have project managers assigned to them. In these situations, the project managers are usually assigned to complex, large, or mission-critical projects.

Specific Portfolio of Projects

I have already identified one type of portfolio — one that contains projects that have a link through their goals and purposes. In other words, collectively these projects represent a major initiative to accomplish some overall common purpose. The PDQ case study is a good example of a small project portfolio of six development subprojects that are all linked by a common purpose. A good example of a large portfolio was the U.S. space program. Think of a single project as something that will accomplish a part of a greater overall mission. Thousands of such projects made up the space program. Together all of the projects represented a single focus and common purpose. As stated previously, these projects form a program and are administered under a Program Office. When the goal of the projects that are part of the program is accomplished, the Program Office is disbanded.

Another portfolio of projects that you can identify is one that organizes projects under a single organizational unit and is funded from the same budget, such as IT. The IT department's PSO will be a permanent structure that supports all IT projects now and into the future.

Yet another specific portfolio that deserves mention is made up of projects that are funded out of the same budget. They may have no other relationship with one another other than the fact that they share a finite pool of money or human resources. These projects are often linked through a PSO. Such a PSO will be primarily interested in ensuring the proper expenditure of the dollars in the budget that funds all of these projects. These PSOs generally have a project portfolio management process in place to manage the budgets for their projects. Chapter 14 takes up this topic.

Naming the Project Support Office

So far I have casually used the label PSO. In my experience, many different names have been used to identify the organizational unit that provides the functions just described, and you may have encountered some of these alternative terms for what I am calling the PSO. Some of these alternative names for a PSO used by my clients are as follows:

- Project Office
- Program Office
- Project Management Office (PMO)
- Project Control Office
- Project Management Community of Practice (PMCoP)
- Project Management Group
- Project Management Center of Excellence (PMCoE)
- Enterprise PMO
- Directorate of Project Management (commonly used in Europe)
- Development Management Office
- IT Project Support
- Mission Central (probably only one occurrence)

Some of these names are clearly attached to an enterprise-level unit, whereas others are more specific to the group they serve. An interesting one is the last one — Mission Central. A recent client for whom I designed and implemented a project management methodology and the accompanying PSO was troubled by the word *management* and, in fact, wasn't too happy with the term *project* either. To that client, the term "management" suggested a kind of oversight or control function that wasn't intended. In addition, the term "project" had been overused in the company and carried a lot of baggage that needed to be left behind. They needed a name for this new entity they were commissioning. A naming contest was initiated by the chairman, who also selected the winning entry: Mission Central.

Despite the misgivings of the client just described, I have nevertheless chosen to use the name PSO for a reason. In my experience, the most successful project support units are those that are characterized as providing both proactive and reactive support services. They are ready to respond to requests for help in any way that the project manager or team members may need. These PSOs also have a responsibility to see that the organization practices effective project management. That happens through the provision of a standard methodology, training and documentation to support its widespread use, and a formal review function to monitor compliance.

However, I have had experience with PSOs that send a very different message. These are the units that have more of a monitoring-and-enforcement mission. They are seldom called a PSO and are more likely to be named PMO, Project Control Office, or simply Project Office. Such units have a spy-like air about them and are unlikely to produce the usage that the organization expects.

Establishing Your PSO's Mission

If you have decided that a PSO will be established, the first order of business is to determine the mission of your PSO. The following list gives some examples of possible mission statements:

- Provide overall management and administrative support to the Alpha Program.

- Establish and monitor compliance with the project management methodology.

- Provide a comprehensive portfolio of support services to all project managers on an as-requested basis.

The first statement is the typical mission statement of a Program Office. It provides administrative support for a program, which comprises a group of projects related to something called the "Alpha Program." This type of mission statement will be very common in organizations that operate large programs consisting of many projects.

The second statement is a very limited mission statement. Often such a statement doesn't find much favor with project managers. Even though this mission statement is not popular, it is necessary in any PSO that is worth the price. A standard must be established, and there must be compliance with that standard, but it doesn't have to be couched in terms that suggest a military-like enforcement. Including strong support services in the mission statement will go a long way toward satisfying the project manager who is desperate for support and can live with the compliance monitoring and with the standard.

The third statement is more to my liking. It seems to be more supportive of the things a project manager is looking for in a PSO. This is my choice, and its purpose fits comfortably with a name like Project Support Office. A PSO will still have some of those military-like functions to perform, but the mission statement suggests that they are surrounded by and dominated by a comprehensive list of support services. It seems to define a package that can be sold to project managers as well as to senior managers.

Framing PSO Objectives

Assume that you have adopted the third statement in the preceding list as the mission statement of your PSO. (I use the name PSO from this point forward in the discussion.) Because the PSO is a business unit, its objectives should be framed in business terms. The following list illustrates some examples:

- Help project teams deliver business value.

- Increase the success rates of projects by 5 percent per year until it reaches 75 percent.
- Reach PMMM Level 4.

The first statement is a bit vague in that it passes the business reason for the PSO to the project teams. However, this places the responsibility for achieving business value on the shoulders of the client. That is as it should be. The project manager and project team are the facilitators. The client has to define value and make it happen. The PSO is not responsible for business value. If you want to hold the toes of the PSO to the fire, then either the second or third statement will do the job. They are very specific and can be easily measured.

NOTE PMMM in the third statement stands for Project Management Maturity Model. It is discussed later in this chapter.

Exploring PSO Support Functions

The six functions mentioned earlier in the chapter and discussed in the following sections are fairly inclusive of those that a PSO might offer. A word of caution is in order, however. It would be a mistake to implement all of the listed functions at once even if that is the ultimate goal of your PSO. Introducing a PSO into the organization is asking management to absorb quite a bit. You will have a much better chance of success if the functions are prioritized on the basis of the contribution they can make or on the ease of implementation and introduced a few at a time. I will have more to say about this later in the chapter when I discuss the challenges of implementing a PSO. For now I will simply define what each of these functions involves and leave for later the discussion of implementation.

Project Support

This function encompasses all of the administrative support services that a PSO might offer to a project or program manager and the project teams. They are as follows:

- Schedule updating and reporting
- Time sheet recording and maintenance
- Report production and distribution
- Report archiving
- Report consolidation and distribution
- Project notebook maintenance

The PSO project support services are an attempt on the part of the PSO to remove as much non-value-added work from the project team as it can and place it in the PSO. Obviously, you would rather have the project team focused on the work of the project and not be burdened by so-called "administrivia." More important, the PSO staff will be much more knowledgeable about how to provide these services because they will be very familiar with the tools and systems that support them. A goal of the PSO is to provide these non-value-added services at a lower cost than would be incurred if done by the project team. More to the point, the PSO staff members who will actually provide the service need minimal office skills, whereas the project team members' skill set is not likely to include the skills appropriate to provide these services. Therefore, the service will be provided by a less costly employee who is appropriately positioned and trained for the assignment.

Apart from supporting project teams, the PSO also has an administrative role to play in supporting project portfolio management. Chapter 14 explores this role in detail.

Some organizations allow budgeting for administrative support that would be assigned to the project team. Usually the needed support is calculated by taking some percentage (10–15 is common) of the total labor planned for the project. For example, if a 12-month project has 5,000 hours of direct labor, 10 percent of that would be 500 hours of administrative support spread across the 12 months of the project, which is approximately 10 hours per week.

Consulting and Mentoring

The PSO professional staff members are available to project teams and project managers on an as-requested basis. They stand ready to help with any specialized assistance. The following is a list of the consulting and mentoring services they can supply:

- Proposal development support
- Facilitating requirements gathering meetings
- Facilitation of project planning sessions
- Risk assessment
- Project interventions
- Mentoring and coaching project managers
- Mentoring senior management

The PSO professional consultants are the most experienced project managers in the company. Their experiences are broad and deep. Because they have heard and seen most situations, nothing will surprise them. They are qualified to help the project manager even in the most complex of circumstances.

TIP One practice that I have seen in a few PSOs is to rotate these consultants through the PSO. Think of it as a sabbatical from the front lines. Although the executive wants the best people in the field, there is the risk of burn-out, and taking them off the front lines and into the PSO for some deserved R&R time makes them available to all teams and to ongoing process improvement initiatives. Another benefit of this rotation is that it continually infuses new ideas and best practices into the PSO as well as back out into the field through the support given by these consultants.

The PSO staff is uniquely positioned to gather and archive best practices from around the company. That makes them particularly valuable as resources to project teams. Those resources are made available to teams through the PSO professional consultants.

One service that I believe is particularly valuable is the facilitation of project planning sessions. The PSO consultant is the ideal person to conduct a project planning session. That relieves the project manager from the facilitation responsibility and enables that manager to concentrate on the project plan itself. The PSO consultant can concentrate on running a smooth planning session. This PSO consultant will have better planning facilitation skills than the project manager by virtue of the fact that he or she has conducted far more planning sessions. It is a win-win situation.

One other useful practice that I have seen is to not have the PSO consultants actually assigned to the PSO. Acting as virtual PSO consultants, they are out in the field running projects but have particular areas of expertise that they are willing to make available to others as needed. The PSO simply becomes the clearinghouse and matchmaker for such services. With this setup, confidentiality is critical. Project managers are not likely to bare their souls to these consultants and mentors if what they say will be the topic of conversation in the lunchroom the next day.

Methods and Standards

Methods and standards represent a service that every PSO must provide. A good Return On Investment (ROI) from a PSO will not happen without a standard methodology and a means of monitoring and enforcing it. The following list contains the services included in this function:

- Collaboratively developing project management processes
- Establishing, monitoring, and enforcing standards
- Project selection for the portfolio
- WBS construction
- Project network diagram development

- Maintenance of a tools and processes library
- Bid preparation
- Risk assessment
- Status reporting
- Scope change management process
- Documentation
- Change orders

The establishment, monitoring, and enforcement of standards are major undertakings for a newly formed PSO. Perhaps more than any other task that the PSO will perform, this one affects the culture and operation of the organization. As I discuss later, a plan to put standards in place must involve as many stakeholders as possible. I am talking about a cultural change in every business unit that is involved with projects and project management. The affected parties must have an opportunity to be involved in establishing the project management processes and the standards to which they will later be held accountable or the whole effort will be for naught.

Project selection for the portfolio should extend all the way from recommending projects to the portfolio for senior-management consideration to providing complete portfolio-management support for senior management. Chapter 14 discusses process design and portfolio management in detail.

Risk assessment should be an area of constant attention by the PSO staff. They have oversight of all projects and are in the best position to assemble a library of risks and mitigation strategies to be shared across all projects. Lessons learned from other risk management efforts are valuable lessons. Asking project managers to contribute to such a library and to use its contents when planning new projects is wishful thinking. Someone must be in charge of this asset and make it useful to others. The only place where such responsibility should be placed is the PSO.

Software Tools

Every PSO should be looking for productivity improvements. As teams become dispersed, it is essential that they remain productive. In this technology-crazed business environment, you can't let time and distance erect barriers to performance. The PSO is the only organizational unit that can provide the support needed for the ever-changing set of tools available on the market. It is responsible for soliciting, evaluating, selecting, and contracting with vendors of these tools. The following list describes the software services that the organization depends on the PSO to provide:

- Software evaluation
- Software selection

- Software acquisition and licensing
- Vendor negotiations
- Software training
- Software management and maintenance

Training

Training in project management has probably been around longer than any other methodology an organization is likely to have. Unfortunately, senior managers incorrectly assume that the solution to their high rate of project failure can be found by giving everyone some training in project management. They are looking for that silver bullet, and there simply isn't one to be found. What has happened in many organizations is that several different project management training courses have been taken by the professional staff. Accordingly, there is no central approach that they follow as a result of their training. In a sense, everyone is still doing his or her own thing (Maturity Level 1). Some follow the approach they were taught, others do what they have always done, and yet others teach themselves. Under the PSO, all of that needs to change.

NOTE To have maximum impact on the practice of project management in the organization, a project management curriculum must be built around an established project management methodology. You simply can't do it any other way.

One school of thought says that if you teach concepts and principles effectively, project managers will be able to adapt them to whatever situation they encounter. That sounds good in theory, but it usually doesn't work. I have found that most project managers don't want to think and typically convey this type of message: "Just tell me what I am supposed to do. I'm not interested in the concepts and theory." That's a truly unfortunate attitude, but it's reality; you can't change it very easily. If you happen to attend one of my workshops, you will hear me say "I'm going to teach you how to think like a project manager so don't look for any recipes or task lists from me. I'll teach you how to build those for yourself."

The trends are clear. To be an effective project manager means that you must be a chef (able to build recipes) and not just a cook (routinely follow recipes). You have to be firmly grounded in the principles and concepts of project management. Every project is different, as is the best approach to managing those unique projects. The effective project manager takes the project characteristics and the environment (both internal and external) into account, and chooses and continuously adapts a best-fit project management life cycle (PMLC) model for the entire life of the project.

With all of this in mind, the PSO and the organization's training department must jointly assume the responsibility of designing and implementing a curriculum that is aligned with the organization's project management methodology. Furthermore, the PSO must assume whatever responsibility the training department is unwilling or unable to assume. Whatever the case, the job must be done. The following list describes the training services that the PSO should be prepared to assist with:

- Project management basics
- Advanced project management
- Project Management Professional (PMP certification exam preparation)
- Specialized topics
- Support of the training department
- Development of courses and course content
- Delivering courses
- Project management training vendor selection

When it comes to project management training, the relationship between the training department and the PSO must be collaborative. The development of the project management curriculum should involve both the curriculum development experts from the training department and the subject matter experts from the PSO. The curriculum can be delivered either by the PSO or by the training department. If it is to be done by the training department, then the curriculum design must have followed a facilitative design. That relieves the training department from having to find trainers who have practical project management expertise, which is difficult at best. In most cases I have seen, the trainers are project management subject matter experts, and this is the preferred method. There is no good substitute for frontline experience by the trainer — no amount of book knowledge can replace experience.

Staffing and Development

In the absence of a Human Resources Management System (HRMS) administered out of an HR department, both project staffing and professional development of project managers is often the responsibility of the PSO. This might be done in collaboration with an HR department that administers an HRMS, but it must be done. Staffing projects with qualified project managers and team members is critical and complex and the HRMS must have the capability of providing that support.

Project Manager Resources

The final function in the PSO as I see it includes a number of human resource services revolving around project managers. The following list is quite comprehensive — it encompasses assessment, development, and deployment services:

- Human resource development
- Identification and assessment of skills
- Selection of team members
- Selection of project managers
- Assessment of project teams
- Professional development
- Career guidance and development

This function is delivered in one of following ways:

- In some cases, project managers will be assigned to the PSO. They then receive their project assignments from the PSO.
- The more common arrangement is for the project managers to be assigned to a business or functional unit. Even in this case, the PSO can still make project assignments and deliver the human resource services listed under this function.

Project Team Members

Even when the PSO is responsible for assigning project managers, it is unlikely that they will have that responsibility for team members. That rests with their functional manager. However, I am aware of enterprise-level PSOs in strong matrix organizations that do have a responsibility for maintaining the inventory of available skills and competencies as an aid for staffing project teams for projects in the portfolio. These same PSOs will often have a training and professional development responsibility that may extend to team members as well. That would place some joint responsibility on the shoulders of the project manager to assign team members according to their skill profiles and in line with their professional development plans. This establishes a collaborative environment between a functional manager, the PSO, and the project managers to act in the best interests of the individual.

Projects provide a lucrative source of development opportunities but are often overlooked as such. They offer on-the-job as well as off-the-job opportunities. For example, suppose that Larry is the best planner among the current project managers. Curly is a new project manager whose planning skills are less than nominal. Moe wants to become a project manager, but knows very little about project planning. If Curly could attend one of Larry's planning sessions, it would be an on-the-job training experience, because Curly is improving a skill needed for his current job assignment. If Moe could attend one of Larry's planning sessions, it would be an off-the-job training experience, because Moe is acquiring a skill needed for a future position. The development part of a great HRMS would have the capacity to bring the Larrys, Curlys, and Moes together. I am not aware of any commercial HRMS that has that capacity.

Projects also provide another interesting on-the-job development opportunity that I have used with great success. A person who aspires to be a professional will always rise to a challenge. I knew that more than 35 years ago and used it as the foundation of a program to reduce the annual turnover in the IT department that I managed from 27 percent to 6 percent in three years. My strategy was as follows: If I give you an assignment that aligns with your professional development plan and that you are qualified to complete except for one skill that you do not have, and I give you the opportunity to learn that skill and apply it to complete your assignment, you will rise to the challenge. You learn the skill and master it with succeeding assignments. Then I repeat the process with a new assignment that you can do except for a missing skill. You get the picture. I implemented that strategy and reduced turnover as stated. Specifically, I was able to grow a computer operator into an applications programmer, a data entry clerk into an operations shift supervisor, and an applications programmer into a systems programmer. Those career-development stories and others were the sole reason for the significant improvement in retention.

NOTE The valuable development lesson for me from the experience I just mentioned was that if you can align a person's career and professional development interests with his or her job assignment, you can give that person a solid reason to remain in your employ. So my advice is to find out what each of your team members want to be when he or she grows up, and then help them along that journey through their project assignments. Not only will you have a committed and motivated team member, but you will also have a person whom you have helped along his or her life's journey.

Selecting PSO Organizational Structures

Different organizations have taken various approaches to the structure and placement of the PSO. In this section, I comment on my experiences with each of the structures I have seen in practice.

Virtual versus Real

A *virtual PSO* performs all of the functions of any other PSO, except that its staff is allocated to the business units. These virtual members of the PSO are available only when their services are needed. They do not perform any routine functions.

Other than a director and perhaps an administrative support person, the virtual PSO does not have any other budgeted staff. Professional staffs from the business units that are involved with projects have agreed to volunteer their services to the PSO on an as-needed basis. This is not a permanent volunteer position. These individuals, who are generally project managers themselves, agree to serve for some period of time and are then replaced. In many cases, they volunteer to provide only a specified type of service or services.

A *real PSO* does have a budgeted staff of professionals, which probably includes several senior-level project managers. They perform several routine functions, such as PMLC process improvement programs, project reviews, training design, training delivery, and software evaluations. The project reviews are a good way to coach other project managers, monitor the adoption of the methodology, and uncover best practices. Their strength will probably be that they offer a healthy dose of project support services to project teams on an as-requested or as-needed basis.

Proactive versus Reactive

The proactive PSO aligns very closely with the real PSO, and the reactive PSO aligns closely with the virtual PSO. The real PSO can be proactive because it has the staff to take leadership roles in a variety of projects to improve project management processes and practices. Conversely, the reactive PSO does not have the staff and does well to just respond to requests for help from project managers and team members.

The PSO can be both proactive and reactive. Its proactive role will extend to monitoring and compliance activities. Its reactive role will extend to supporting project managers and teams on an as-requested basis.

Temporary versus Permanent

What I have called Program Offices in this chapter are the only temporary form of PSO that I know of. They may be very short-lived, and as soon as their portfolio is complete, they are disbanded. Or, they may be very long-lived and continuously add new projects to their portfolio. All other examples of PSOs are permanent and service an ever-changing list of projects.

Program versus Projects

I have already defined programs as collections of related projects. The related projects always have some dependencies between them, so there is a need for an oversight organization such as a PSO. Significant resource management problems will arise because of the inter-project dependencies, and only oversight from the vantage point of a PSO can be effective in resolving such difficulties.

Enterprise versus Functional

PSOs can be attached at the enterprise level or functional level as follows:

- At the enterprise level, they must provide services to all disciplines. They are generally well-funded and well-staffed. They have visibility at the project portfolio level and at the senior management level and may be involved in strategic roles.

- At the functional level, they generally service the needs of a single discipline. They are generally not as well funded or as well staffed as their enterprise-level counterpart.

Hub-and-Spoke

The hub-and-spoke structure is an example of a PSO that is both enterprise-wide and functionally based. In very large organizations, the PSO may be organized in a hierarchical form. The hub is where the enterprise-level unit (also known as the central office) is housed. It is a high-level PSO that sets project management policy and standards for the enterprise. If only the hub form is in place, then all of the functions of the PSO will reside there. In time, as the organization grows in its maturity and dependence on the PSO, these functions may be carried out at the business unit or division level by regional PSOs (the spokes), who take their process and policy direction from the central PSO. The hub is typically staffed by high-level project executives whose focus is strategic. At the end of a spoke is a regional or functional PSO, which has operational responsibilities for the unit it represents. Obviously, the hub-and-spoke configuration works best in those organizations that have a more mature approach to project management. It is not a structure for organizations new to project management. Those organizations should focus on a hub structure first and then expand to the spokes as their practice matures.

Understanding the Organizational Placement of the PSO

There are three organizational placements for the PSO, as shown in Figure 13-1.

At the enterprise level, a PSO is usually called by some name like Enterprise PSO (EPSO) that suggests it serves the entire enterprise. I have seen the following two variations of EPSOs:

- **Centralized** — In this version, the EPSO provides all of the services to all project teams corporate-wide that any PSO would provide.

- **Decentralized** — This version (a.k.a. hub-and-spoke) often has a policy and procedure responsibility with satellite PSOs providing the actual functions in accordance with the established policy and procedures.

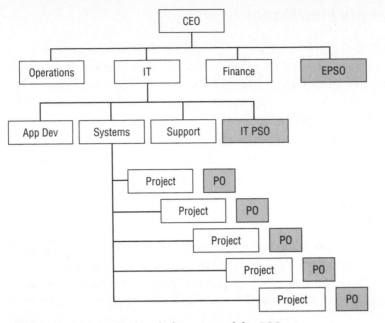

Figure 13-1: Organizational placement of the PSO

Both models can be effective. The size of the organization with respect to the number of projects needing support is the best determinant of structure, with the decentralized structure favoring the larger organization. There really are no hard-and-fast rules here.

The PSO can also serve the needs of a significant part of the enterprise — such as at the division or business-unit level. The most common example is the IT division. Here the PSO serves the needs of all the IT professionals in the organization (IT PSO in Figure 13-1, for example). Because this PSO is discipline-specific, it will probably offer project support services tailored to the needs of the IT projects. It may also offer services specific to the needs of teams that are using various systems development processes. In other words, a division-level PSO may offer not only project management support services, but also services specific to the discipline.

The PSO can also serve the needs of a single program. As shown in Figure 13-1, there may be several of these programs even within a single division. This is a common occurrence in the IT division. These PSOs are temporary. When the program that this type of PSO supports is completed, the PSO is disbanded. A past client of mine used this structure quite effectively. Whenever the team size exceeded 30, the client formed a PSO. The project was decomposed into subprojects, with each subproject having a project manager. The project managers were accountable to the program director and were part of the PSO staff of this project. For every 30 team members thereafter, another layer of project managers was added. The PSO was staffed by the program director, a program assistant, and one administrative assistant. The program assistant worked directly with each project manager in a coaching and mentoring role. The administrative assistant helped the project managers and their teams with the typical administrative functions. Team size varied from three to six. When the project was complete, the 30 or more members returned to their home departments.

REFERENCE Chapter 17 has much more to say about the challenges of managing these types of multi-team projects.

Determining When You Need a Project Support Office

However you slice it, the PSO is established for the sole purpose of improving the processes and practices of project management for the group of projects and project managers over whom it has a stewardship responsibility. The PSO is an investment, and its ROI is measured in terms of cost avoidance. That cost avoidance is a direct result of a significant reduction in project failures for which the PSO is held directly responsible and accountable.

The Standish Group Report

The reasons for project failure have been investigated and reported in detail for several years. One of the most thorough research efforts into the reasons for project failure is the work of the Standish Group. Beginning in 1994 and repeating every two years, they have conducted interviews of 300+ C-level IT executives. The objective of these surveys is to discover and prioritize the reasons why IT projects fail. CHAOS 2010 is their most recent report. According to this study, the top ten reasons why IT projects fail were the following:

1. Lack of user input
2. Incomplete requirements and specification
3. Changing requirements and specification
4. Lack of executive support
5. Technology incompetence
6. Lack of resources
7. Unrealistic expectations
8. Unclear objectives
9. Unrealistic time frames
10. New technology

After reviewing the major functions that the PSO provides, you can see that a PSO is uniquely positioned to mitigate each of these 10 reasons for project failure. In fact, it is the only organizational entity that is so positioned. I want to examine each of these reasons and see exactly what the PSO could do to mitigate it.

Lack of User Input

I would have phrased this as "meaningful client involvement." You have already learned how the importance of meaningful client involvement changes as the project type moves from Linear to Incremental to Iterative to Adaptive to Extreme. The PSO can do the following three things to assure that this involvement is present in every project:

- Provide a client document that describes how their involvement changes over the project landscape and over time for a specific PMLC model.
- For each of the five PMLC models, offer a project manager workshop on how to attain and sustain client involvement over the project landscape.
- Offer client workshops that focus on the client's role and responsibility in projects over the project landscape.

I hope that you are beginning to see the complexity of delivering effective project management. It's interesting that the industry says projects are unique, and that the same project can never occur again under the same set of circumstances. I would argue that the management of each project is also unique. Without some guidance as to how to choose the best-fit management approach, the situation becomes chaotic. If every project is managed differently, there wouldn't be any lessons to learn. But that is not the case. I have given you the rules of the engagement based on a logical and intuitive definition of the project landscape so that you can choose a best-fit PMLC model. In that sense, the process is repeatable because it is based on a set of rules. You are learning to be a chef rather than just a cook. Your pantry is stocked with all of the tools, templates, and processes you need to be an effective project manager. Everything in your pantry will have been vetted by and is supported by the PSO.

Despite the complexity of choosing best-fit models, the project landscape I have defined is very simple. There are four quadrants (TPM, APM, xPM, and MPx), and there are five PMLC model types (Linear, Incremental, Iterative, Adaptive, and Extreme) that span these four quadrants. They form an ordered set with respect to solution clarity, and within each model type, any number of specific PMLC models might be used for a specific project (for example, Standard Waterfall, Rapid Development Waterfall, Dynamic Systems Development Method (DSDM), Scrum, Adaptive Project Framework (APF), and several others).

Incomplete Requirements and Specification

All of the simple projects have been done. What is left are projects that must be done in the face of complexity and uncertainty and that means requirements that can no longer be completely defined and documented at the beginning of the project. Some of those requirements simply cannot be known at the beginning of the project. The PSO cannot do much to change the reality; all it can be asked to do is mitigate some of the operational problems associated with gathering requirements.

First, the PSO can build an arsenal of requirements gathering tools and train people to utilize them effectively. Even though it is assumed the requirements will be incomplete, the gathering effort needs to be as comprehensive as possible so that the requirements will be as complete as possible. Second, the PSO can review and improve all of the project management approaches to be best prepared to deal with incomplete requirements. That means to refine the processes of learning and discovery in the agile and extreme project management landscape.

Changing Requirements and Specification

As the PSO designs and implements the project management processes, attention needs to be paid to the fact that change is a way of life in the complex project world. The project management processes should be built to respond to what is known to be part of the solution and to be flexible in accommodating change without the attendant loss of integrity of the plan. That means avoiding wasting time on what might be part of the solution and spending the planning effort on what is known to be part of the solution. Building a project management methodology based on the future is not a good expenditure of project resources.

Lack of Executive Support

Executive support is always a necessity if the project is to be successful. The PSO needs to represent the project in a favorable light up into the organization and let project managers focus their efforts on the project.

Technology Incompetence

The PSO will need to have a good sense of the inventory of skills and competencies among all potential team members. That will enable them to advise and suggest technical approaches to the project. Maybe the latest and greatest technology may not be the best business approach, and the PSO would be in the best position to make that assessment.

Lack of Resources

The PSO should be the keeper of the skills and competencies inventory and should play an integral role in assigning staff to projects. By having management responsibility for the career and professional development plans of project managers and other project support staff, the PSO will be able to make recommendations in line with staff development needs.

Here is where the PSO can shine either indirectly through training or directly through coaching and mentoring project managers and their team members. Training can be offered at the PMLC model level, Knowledge Area level, or process level. Introductory, intermediate, and advanced courses are commonplace. Delivery systems range from books to instructor-led education to computer-based education, as well as in a variety of blended models.

Unrealistic Expectations

The world of complex projects has brought on a great deal of uncertainty. We are dealing with projects where the deliverables may not produce the expected business value that justified doing the project in the first place. The cause and effect relationships are clouded or nonexistent. The PSO needs to nurture a project culture that says we are going to do the very best we can within the time, cost, and resource constraints to deliver the most business value possible.

Unclear Objectives

The agile processes designed and implemented by the PSO should have built-in protections against this situation arising. If an objective is unclear, remove it from the project plan until the process of learning and discovery in agile iterations clarifies the objective. At that point put it back in the project plan.

Unrealistic Time Frames

The PSO is a respected and impartial player in the project life cycle. When the occasion calls for it, the PSO needs to be a support of the project manager and the project plan. If unrealistic time frames are being pushed on the project manager, the PSO needs to speak up in defense of the project manager.

New Technology

The PSO should take the position that all new technologies need to be vetted and the personnel prepared to fully utilize the technology before the technologies are incorporated into projects. The downside is that project risk increases.

It is the PSO that needs to put a program in place to accept new technologies and to make senior management aware of the risks.

Spotting Symptoms That You Need a PSO

The following symptoms provide you with clues that you might need a PSO:

Project failure rates are too high — This symptom is all too familiar to me. Reports show project failure rates of 65 to 70 percent and higher, regardless of how failure is defined. That is simply unacceptable. Many of the reasons for these high numbers are probably found in the list of the top-10 reasons for project failure from the Standish Group Chaos 2010 report. Reasons that relate to the project management approach that was used — namely, user involvement, clear business objectives, minimized scope, standard infrastructure, and formal methodology — can be addressed by choosing the correct approach (TPM, APF, xPM, or MPx). It is my contention that by choosing the appropriate approach, the organization can make a serious impact on failure rates.

Training is not producing results — I am not aware of any systematic study of the root causes of training ineffectiveness. Possible causes are inappropriate materials, inappropriate delivery, no follow-through on behavioral changes after training, or no testing of skill acquisition. Training needs to be taken seriously by those who attend the training. Attendees must be held accountable for applying what they have learned, and there must be ways to measure that application. I am amazed at how many training professionals and curriculum designers are not familiar with Kirkpatrick's model. The interested reader can consult Donald L. Kirkpatrick's *Evaluating Training Programs, Second Edition* (Berrett-Koehler, 1998). In my experience, project reviews that are held at various milestones in the life of the project are excellent points at which to validate the application of training. If clear evidence isn't shown that training has been applied, some corrective action is certainly called for.

HR project staff planning isn't effective — Organizations need to do a better job of defining the inventory of project staff skills and the demand for those skills by projects. A concerted effort is needed to match the supply to the demand and to make better staffing assignments to projects. The PSO is the best place for this responsibility to be carried out. Without question, the Graham-Englund Selection Model should be used (see Chapter 14).

Best practices are not leveraged — The PSO is the best place to collect and distribute best practices. Project status meetings and project reviews are the places to identify best practices. The PSO, through some form of bulletin board service or direct distribution to the project managers, is the best place to distribute that information. In the absence of that service, the collection and distribution of best practices isn't going to happen.

There is little or no control over the project portfolio — Many senior managers don't know the number of projects that are active, nor do they fully understand the resource availability. Unknowingly, they overcommit. They haven't made any effort to find out about or be selective of those projects that are active. That behavior has to change if there is any hope of managing the project work in the organization. The PSO is the clear choice for stewardship of that portfolio. At the least, it can be the unit that assembles project performance data and distributes it to the decision makers for their review and action.

No consistency in project reporting — Without a centralized unit responsible for the reporting process, consistent and useful reporting isn't going to happen. Again, the PSO is the clear choice to establish the reporting structure and assist in its use.

There are too many resource scheduling conflicts — Most organizations operate with some form of matrix structure. Project resources are assigned from their functional unit at the discretion of that unit's manager. In such situations, resource conflicts are unavoidable. The individuals who are assigned to projects are torn between doing work for their functional unit and doing work for the project to which they have been assigned. If you're a seasoned project manager, most likely none of this is news to you. One solution to resource scheduling conflicts is to use the PSO as the filter through which project staffing requests and staffing decisions are made. The major benefit of this approach is that it takes the project manager off the hot seat and puts the responsibility in the PSO, where it can be more equitably discharged.

There is a gap between process and practice — This is a major problem area for many organizations. They may have a well-documented process in place, but unless they have an oversight-and-compliance process in place as well, they are at the mercy of the project manager to use or not use the process. The PSO is the only unit that can close this gap. The PSO puts the process in place with the help of those who will be held accountable for its use. The PSO, through project performance reviews, can determine the extent of the gap and put remedial steps in place to close it.

Figure 13-2 shows a self-assessment that you can use to help determine if you need a PSO.

In the list below check all the boxes that describe your organization.

☐ Project failure rates are too high.
☐ The project management methodology is not widely adopted.
☐ Scope change requests are out of control through the project.
☐ One resource pool is staffing multiple projects.
☐ There is lack of project management expertise in needed areas.
☐ Several vendors and contractors are used across projects.
☐ There is a need to consolidate reports and metrics.
☐ Time to market is a critical success factor.
☐ Total project costs are too high.
☐ The resource pool is not aligned with staffing needs.
☐ Training is not impacting project performance.
☐ The HR project staffing plan is not effective.
☐ You have trouble leveraging best practices.
☐ You don't have control of the project portfolio.
☐ There is no consistency in project status reporting.
☐ There are too many resource scheduling conflicts.
☐ There is noticeable gap between documented process
    maturity and actual practice maturity.

6 or more checked boxes: PSO highly advised
10 or more checked boxes: PSO a necessity

Figure 13-2: PSO readiness assessment

Establishing a PSO

When you are planning for a PSO, four critical questions must be answered. One of them deals with defining a desired future for your organization's PSO — the goal, so to speak. To reach that goal, however, you have to assess where you currently are with respect to it. The answer to that question identifies a gap between the current state and the future state. That gap is removed through the implementation plan for your PSO. This is the definition of a standard gap analysis. The four major questions, then, arranged chronologically, are as follows:

- Where are you?

- Where are you going?

- How will you get there?

- How well did you do?

Before you attempt to answer these questions, you need a foundation for answering them. The Software Engineering Institute (SEI) at Carnegie Mellon University provides just the foundation you need. Its five-level model, described in the next section, also gives you a foundation on which you can plan for the further growth and maturation of your PSO.

PSO Stages of Maturity Growth

Over the past 20+ years, SEI has developed and maintained a maturity model for software engineering. It has gained wide support and become the de facto standard of the software development community. The model was originally called the Capability Maturity Model (CMM) and more recently the Capability Maturity Model Integrated (CMMI). It has recently been adapted to project management in the form of a Project Management Maturity Model (PMMM). I will use the five maturity levels of the PMMM to answer two of the questions: Where are you and where are you going?

Figure 13-3 offers a graphic depiction and brief description of each of the maturity levels of the PMMM.

PSO Maturity Levels

Level 1
Ad hoc support but no training from the PSO.

Level 2
Defined PM processes with reactive support from the PSO and introductory training.

Level 3
Integrated use of defined PM processes with PSO oversight, proactive support, and more training.

Level 4
PSO manages the project portfolio as an integral part of all business processes and more extensive training.

Level 5
Continuous improvement of all PSO services and processes.

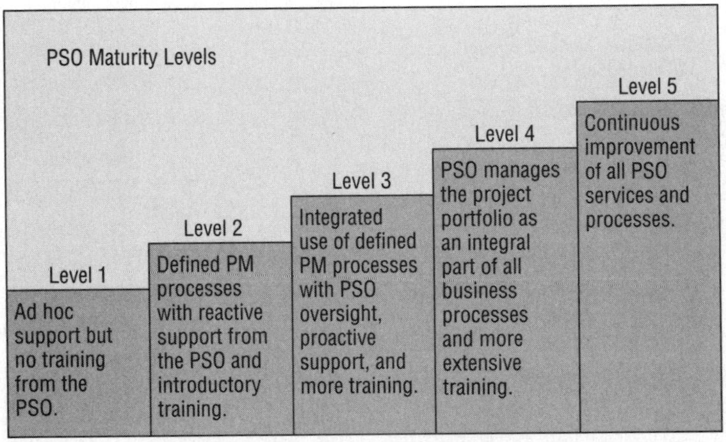

Figure 13-3: Project management maturity levels

Level 1: Initial

At Level 1, everyone basically does as he or she pleases. There may be some processes and tools for project management, which some people may be using on an informal basis. Project management training is nonexistent, and help may be available on an informal basis at best. There doesn't appear to be any signs of organization under project management.

Level 2: Repeatable

Level 2 is distinguished from Level 1 in that a documented project management process is available. It is used at the discretion of the project manager, and some training is available for those who are interested. Initially, the only sign of a

PSO is through some part-time support person who will help a project team on an as-requested basis. In time, senior management will commission a PSO and give it very basic monitoring and control responsibilities.

Level 3: Defined

The transition from Level 2 to Level 3 is dramatic. The project management processes are fully documented, and project management has been recognized as critical to business success by senior management. A formal PSO is established, staffed, and given the responsibility of ensuring enterprise-wide usage of the methodology. Enforcement is taken seriously, and a solid training curriculum is available. There is some sign that project management is being integrated into other business processes.

Level 4: Managed

At this level, successful project management is viewed as a critical success factor by the organization. A complete training program and professional development program for project managers is in place. The PSO is looked upon as a business, and project portfolio management is of growing importance. The project portfolio is an integral part of all business planning activities. The PSO director has a seat at the business strategy table and may have the title of VP PSO.

Level 5: Optimized

At Level 5, the PSO is the critical component of a continuous quality-improvement program for project management. Progress in the successful use of project management is visible, measured, and acted upon.

REFERENCE See Chapter 15 for a complete discussion of Continuous Process Improvement Programs.

Planning a PSO

You can now put the pieces of a plan together. Based on what I have discussed so far, your plan to establish a PSO might look something like what is shown in Figure 13-4. Before you can begin the activities shown in Figure 13-4, however, you have to write the Project Overview Statement (POS) for the PSO.

REFERENCE For a more detailed discussion of the components of a POS and what goes into writing one, see Chapter 4.

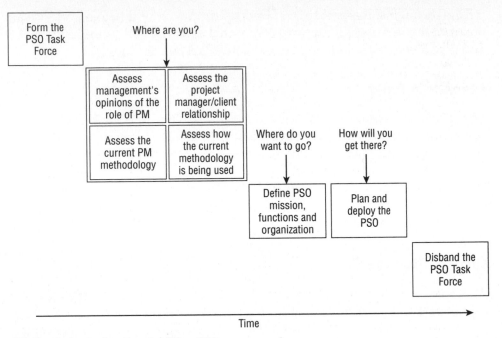

Figure 13-4: A plan to establish a PSO

The POS

Shown in Figure 13-5 is an example POS for a PSO implementation project submitted by Sal Vation.

The following sections take a quick look at what Sal submitted.

Problem/Opportunity

Note that the statement describes a business condition that needs no defense or further clarification. Anyone, especially the executive committee, who reads it will understand it and agree with it. The importance of this statement will determine whether or not the reader continues to the goal statement. In this case, the situation is grave enough that continued reading is a foregone conclusion.

Goal

The statement is clean and crisp. It states what will be done and by when. Note that it is phrased so that the project is expected to deliver results before the expected completion date. Sal recognizes the importance of early results to the executive committee and doesn't want the stated time line to shock them and perhaps jeopardize the project's approval.

PROJECT OVERVIEW STATEMENT	Project Name PSO Implementation	Project No. PSO.001	Project Manager Sal Vation

Problem/Opportunity

  To restore our lost market share, we must quickly develop our capabilities in the customized furnishings business but are unable to because our project management processes cannot support the needs of the product development teams.

Goal

  Provide a fully mature and comprehensive portfolio of project management support services to all project teams in less than four years.

Objectives

  1. Provide off-the-shelf and customized project management training.
  2. Develop and document a standard project management process to support all of our project teams with special focus on product development teams.
  3. Establish a projects review process to monitor and enforce compliance with our project management processes.
  4. Establish a portfolio management process for all customized projects.
  5. Create a professional development program for all project managers.
  6. Design and implement a continuous quality improvement process for project management.

Success Criteria

  1. Over 50% of all PMs will receive basic training by the end of 2011 Q1.
  2. Project quarterly success rates will increase from current 35% to 70% by 2011 Q3.
  3. At least 90% of all projects begun after 2011 Q3 will use the new O & P project management process.
  4. 100% of all PMs will receive training in the O & P project management process by the end of 2011 Q4.
  5. 90% of all PMs will have a professional development program in place by 2011 Q4.
  6. The PSO will reach maturity level 2 no later than Q3 2011, maturity level 3 no later than Q4 2012, maturity level 4 no later than Q2 2014, and maturity level 5 no later than Q4 2014.
  7. Market share will be restored to 100% of its highest level no later than Q4 2014.

Assumptions, Risks, Obstacles

  1. Business unit managers will resist change in their operating procedures.
  2. The customized furnishings market is not as strong as forecasted.
  3. Project managers will continue to practice their old ways.

Prepared By Sal Vation	Date 1/3/2011	Approved By Del E. Lama	Date 1/6/2011

Figure 13-5: An example POS for a PSO implementation project

Objectives

The objective statements expand and clarify the goal statement and suggest interim milestones and deliverables.

Success Criteria

Sal has expressed the success criteria in specific and measurable quantitative terms. This is very important. In this case, the criteria will help the executive committee understand the business value of the project. It is the single most important criteria Sal can present to them at this time to help them decide whether the project is worth doing.

Assumptions, Risks, Obstacles

Sal has called to the attention of the executive committee anything that he feels can potentially compromise the success of the project. These statements serve the following two purposes:

- They highlight for senior managers some of the potential problems that they might be able to mitigate for the project team.
- They provide some risk data for the financial analysts to estimate the expected return on the investment in a PSO.

The executive committee will consider the success criteria versus risk to determine the expected business value that can result from this project. In cases where other projects are vying for the same resources, the analysts would have a comparable statistic to use to decide where to spend their resources.

This is just a high-level risk identification. During project planning, you will document a detailed risk management plan.

Planning Steps

Sal will eventually get approval to move into the details of project planning in anticipation of getting executive committee approval of the plan so that he and his team can get to work. Sal might expect a few iterations of the POS before he gets that approval to proceed with planning. In my experience, senior managers often question success criteria, especially with reference to its validity.

Forming the PSO Task Force

The PSO task force forms the strategy group for this project. They are to be considered members of the project team. Their membership should include managers of business units that will be affected by the PSO. The size of the enterprise determines how many members there will be. A task force of five or seven members should work quite well, whereas a task force of 15 would be counterproductive. If voting will be used to make decisions, having an odd number of members will avoid tie votes. If an even number is used, the chairperson should have the tie-breaking vote. Without the support and commitment of each task force member, the PSO is unlikely to succeed. Because many of the task force members' operations are likely to be affected by the PSO, they must be a part of its mission and have an opportunity to be heard as decisions are made on the mission, functions, and services the PSO will provide.

Measuring Where You Are

Several metrics have been developed to quantitatively measure the maturity level of your project management processes. I have developed one such metric that consists of more than 800 yes or no questions. (The interested reader should consult me at rkw@eiicorp.com for details on this proprietary product.) These questions cover all five maturity levels for all project management processes identified by PMI in their Project Management Body of Knowledge (PMBOK). Figure 13-6 shows the results of a recent assessment for one of my clients. The data on each of the processes have been aggregated to the Knowledge Area level.

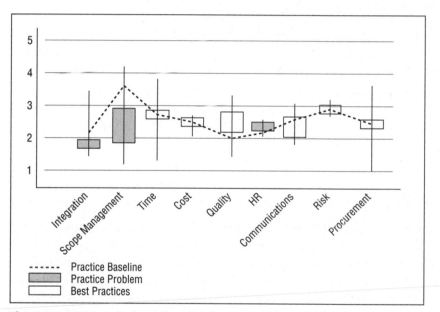

Figure 13-6: Maturity-level data for nine Knowledge Areas of PMBOK

This one graphic conveys a lot of information about this organization's project management maturity levels. First of all, the dashed line shows the maturity level of each knowledge area as documented in the organization's project management methodology. The box-and-whisker plots are maturity-level data reflecting how project management was practiced in several projects that were reviewed in the same quarter. A box-and-whisker plot is a summarized view of the data points for each project on a single Knowledge Area. Each box displays the middle 50 percent of the data. The endpoints of the whiskers denote the extreme data points. The color coding denotes the status of the Knowledge Area. A gray box indicates a process whose practice is significantly below the maturity level of the baseline process. In fact, 75 percent of the data points fall below the process maturity level. A white box indicates a process whose practice is significantly above the maturity level of the baseline process — 75 percent of the data points fall above the process maturity level. For example, take a look at the Scope Management Knowledge Area. The projects that were reviewed demonstrate a maturity-level range from a low of 1.2 to a high of 4.1. The middle half of the data points range from 1.8 to 2.9. The Scope Management Knowledge Area was assessed at a maturity level of 3.5.

Any maturity level below target or above target indicates an area that needs further investigation. The investigation should look for solutions to the less-than-nominal maturity and take the necessary corrective steps to raise the level of maturity of that Knowledge Area. In cases where the Knowledge Area is found to be performing above a nominal level, the investigation should try to reveal the reasons for that exemplary performance and for ways to share their findings (a.k.a. best practices) with other project teams.

In determining where the organization is with respect to project management, there are two threads of investigation. They are as follows:

- The first is the organizational environment in which the PSO will function. This involves assessing the opinions of the managers whose business units will be impacted. Oftentimes this can be done with face-to-face interviews of key managers.

- The second is an attempt to assess the current relationship between project managers and the clients they serve. In this case, the clients will be internal business units and external customers who buy their products.

An assessment tool I developed at Enterprise Information Insights, Inc., has been quite successful in practice: the Project Manager Competency Assessment (PMCA). It is an assessment of a project manager's project management competencies. (Contact me at `rkw@eiicorp.com` for information about how to acquire the tool.) Figure 13-7 shows an example of a PMCA report.

This PMCA reports findings in four major areas (business competency, personal competency, interpersonal competency, and management competency) as they relate to the individual's project management behaviors. A total of 18 competencies are spread across these four areas. Each one uses a box-and-whisker plot to summarize the opinions of the assessors. In this case, there were eight assessors. The endpoints of the box-and-whisker plots denote the extreme data points. The hollow rectangle is the middle half of the data. The small filled rectangle is the average of all assessors. The bolded vertical line is the individual's self-assessment. In Figure 13-7, the individual has a higher self-assessment of herself than do the managers who provided the competency data. This is especially evident in business awareness, business partnership, initiative, conceptual thinking, resourceful use of influence, and motivating others. This person should be advised to take a close look at how she sees herself relative to how others see her. This self-inflated phenomenon is not unusual. I have seen it time and time again in many of these assessments. People are simply not aware of how they affect others. As a group, this project manager's interpersonal competencies are held in high regard by her fellow workers. However, her personal competencies — particularly in the areas of initiative, conceptual thinking, and self-confidence — may be problematic.

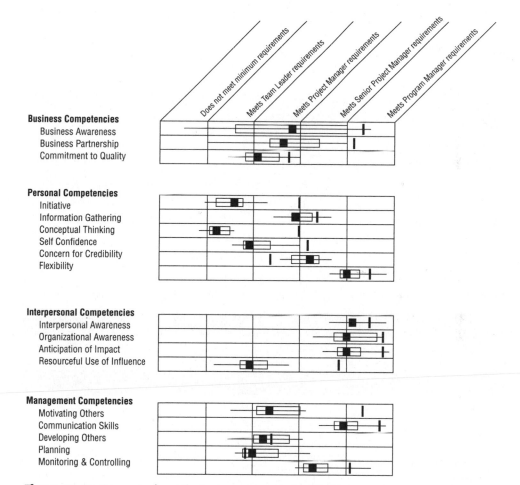

Figure 13-7: An example project manager competency assessment

If either of these two assessments — the maturity level of your project management processes or the project manager competency assessment — uncovers problems, an intervention may be needed prior to any further PSO planning. For the purposes of this exercise, the assessments have shown that the organization is ready to move forward and strongly supports the creation of a full-service PSO.

The next step is to take a look at the existing methodology. There are two areas of investigation, as described here:

- The first is to assess the maturity level of the project management processes that are in place. This can be done by using commercially available tools, such as the Project Management Maturity Assessment (PMMA).

- The second area of investigation is to assess how project teams are using that methodology. Again, there are commercially available tools for this assessment, such as the Project Management Competency Assessment (PMCA).

NOTE   Readers can contact me at `rkw@eiicorp.com` for more information on PMMA, PMCA, and similar assessment tools.

For this example, assume the assessments show that the organization is at Level 1 maturity both in terms of project management processes and the practice of those processes.

Establishing Where You Want to Go

The future of the organization in the example seems to rest on its ability to restore market share. As expressed in the POS, Sal has as a long-term goal the achievement of Level 5 maturity in the PSO. His strategy will be to achieve that in phases, with each phase providing business value to the organization. The PSO is expected to be a full-service PSO. Its mission, functions, and organization are given in Table 13-1.

Table 13-1: Example PSO Mission, Functions, and Organization

MISSION
To provide the project management services and support needed to establish a market leadership position for the organization in the customized furnishings business
FUNCTIONS
All project administrative services
Project management processes to support all project types
Comprehensive software for all phases of product development
A customized and complete PM training curriculum
A professional development program for project managers
ORGANIZATION
A revolving staff of consulting project managers
An enterprise-wide unit attached to the president's office
EPSO director will be a three-year renewable appointed position

---

ORGANIZATION

Permanent staff consists of:

Project administrator to deliver support services
Manager of methods and tools
Senior project manager consultant
Project manager consultant
Curriculum development specialist
Senior trainer
Trainer

The long-term goal of the PSO is to ensure project success. It should be obvious that goal means the attainment of at least Level 3 maturity. Without a documented process in place and in use by all teams, it is unlikely that there will be any measurable increase in the rate of project success.

However, casually stating that Level 4 maturity is the goal of the PSO is not appropriate. That is clearly a business decision. Attaining Level 4 maturity is a big step. It is very costly in terms of the extent of change in the organization. I would liken that change to the evolution of the enterprise to a projectized organizational structure. To move from Level 4 to Level 5 is a matter of implementing a continuous quality-improvement process within the PSO. Efforts to reach maturity Levels 4 and 5 can often be done in parallel. That is far less traumatic and usually involves not much more than establishing a solid project review process and making a concerted effort to capture and implement best practices from the organization's projects, as well as projects external to the organization.

Refer back for a moment to the data in Figure 13-6 and you'll see that, because the middle half of the data points all fall below the average of 3.5, Scope Management needs some improvement. Such an area is where a continuous quality-improvement effort would focus. The results of a continuous quality improvement effort in Scope Management might look something like the hypothetical data displayed in Figure 13-8. Note that not only has the process baseline maturity level improved from 3.5 to 4.1 during the period from 3/2008 to 12/2008, but the mid-range of the maturity level of the practice has moved from (1.8–2.9) to (3.9–4.3). The maturity level of the practice of Scope Management has increased significantly, and its range has decreased. This is a marked improvement! If this organization had set as its goal to increase the Scope Management maturity level of its process and its practice to 4.0, it would have achieved that goal.

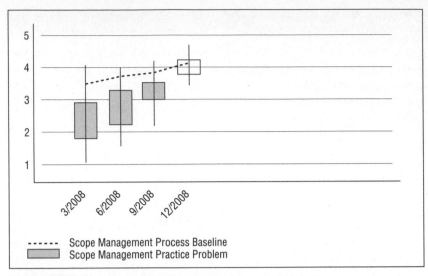

Figure 13-8: Continuous quality improvement of Scope Management

Establishing How You Will Get There

It goes without saying that the lower your current project management maturity level is, the more challenging it will be to move to Level 3 or higher. Level 3 is where the PSO can really begin to make an impact on the practice of project management. It is at this level that the organization has fully bought into project management. Teams must use it, and the PSO is monitoring that usage. Best practices are identified through project reviews and folded back into the methodology. All signs are positive. Figure 13-9 gives a brief description of what actions should be taken to move from one level to the next.

Current PSO Maturity Level	Characteristics of PSOs at This Maturity Level	Initiatives that Will Move the PSO to the Next Maturity Level
INITIAL (1)	• Some defined PM processes are available. • Informal support to teams as requested. • No PM training is available.	• Assemble a task force to establish a PM process. • Document the PM process. • Make PM training available.
REPEATABLE (2)	• A documented PM process is in place. • Part-time support to teams is available. • Limited PM training is available.	• Establish programs to increase PM process usage. • Establish a full-time PSO staff to support teams. • Monitor and enforce compliance. • Increase available PM training.
DEFINED (3)	• Fully documented and supported PM process. • Full-time support to teams is available. • All project teams are using the PM process. • PM processes are integrated with other processes. • More extensive PM training is available.	• Projects are made part of the business plan. • Put project portfolio management in the PSO. • Give the PSO an active role in project staffing. • Offer more extensive training. • Create a career development program in the PSO. • Staff project managers in the PSO.
MANAGED (4)	• PSO is responsible for professional development. • Complete PM training is available. • Project portfolio is managed as a business.	• PSO begins to identify and adopt best practices. • Metrics are defined to track process quality. • Project reviews are used to monitor compliance.
OPTIMIZING (5)	• A continuous improvement process is in place. • There is measured improvement in project success.	

Figure 13-9: How to move to the next maturity level

Sal's plan consists of four milestone events. Each milestone event signifies the attainment of the next level of maturity. The first milestone event is complete when the organization has reached Maturity Level 2 in the PSO. Milestone events Two, Three, and Four are similarly defined. Within each phase are a number of deliverables that add business value. These deliverables have been prioritized to add business value as soon as possible. Figure 13-10 describes the high-level plan through all four phases.

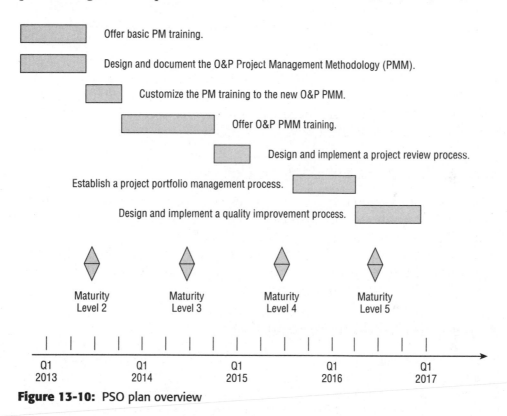

Figure 13-10: PSO plan overview

Facing the Challenges of Implementing a PSO

Too many executives have the impression that a PSO is mostly a clerical function and that establishing one is not too difficult. Nothing could be further from the truth. J. Kent Crawford provides a compelling discussion of some of those challenges in *The Strategic Project Office: A Guide to Improving Organizational Performance* (Marcel Dekker, 2001). According to Crawford, the challenges to implementing a PSO are as follows:

- Speed and patience
- Leadership from the bottom up
- A systems thinking perspective

- Enterprise-wide systems
- Knowledge management
- Learning and learned project organizations
- Open communications

Speed and Patience

Effectively deploying a PSO can require two to five years for full implementation. That is a long time. According to the Standish Group research, the longer the project is, the higher the probability of project failure. The way out of this apparent dilemma is to plan the PSO deployment in stages. Begin by prioritizing the support functions according to the level of need, and partition their deployment into stages. Each stage must deliver visible and measurable value to the process and practice of project management.

Leadership from the Bottom Up

A popular approach to putting a PSO in place is a bottom-up strategy. At the department or project level, you must demonstrate value by showing the results that a department-level PSO can achieve. Then, by way of example, others in the organization will see that success and ask how they can achieve it in their own areas. This grassroots effort will be contagious, and it is one of the keys to a successful PSO implementation over time.

A Systems Thinking Perspective

This goes to the very heart of a PSO contributing at the corporate level. At some point in the implementation of the PSO, senior managers will begin to see how an effectively managed project portfolio can contribute to corporate goals. Senior managers begin to think about the portfolio and not just the projects that comprise it. This transition from Level 3 to Level 4 maturity is the result of a major discovery by senior management as they begin to think in terms of a systems perspective.

Enterprise-Wide Systems

This characteristic is clearly one of a Level 4 organization. The integration of the project data into the other corporate databases provides senior managers with the tools they need to make enterprise-wide business decisions where projects are the strategic components of their business plans. Making this jump from a single-project focus to a strategic-portfolio focus is the sign of a Level 4 PSO.

Knowledge Management

To drive thinking to the enterprise-wide level requires sophisticated corporate databases, standardization of data capture, and the applications systems to extract knowledge from information. Even today, only a few organizations have implemented something as simple as a database of best practices and lessons learned. Part of the reason for the lack of this kind of database is because modern project management is in its infancy. It is only about 50 years old. Standards exist at the project level, but there are few standards at the portfolio level.

Learning and Learned Project Organizations

Most organizations have not taken the education and training of project managers very seriously. That fact has to change if the PSO is expected to make an impact on project success. A comprehensive curriculum with a variety of delivery approaches is needed. Currently, career and professional development programs for project managers are few and far between. The PSO is positioned to deliver, but senior management must first make the commitment and provide the needed resources. In addition, it would be very helpful if senior management could avail themselves of a one-day briefing to understand project management from their perspective. Most project management–training vendors offer one-day programs focusing on what the executive needs to know about project management.

Open Communications

Communications between and among projects and from first-line managers through to executive levels must be open and free. The PSO can establish and maintain the channels of communications and offer support for report preparation and distribution.

The PSO of the Future

In the short-term the PSO will evolve into a support organization for business projects, programs, processes, and portfolios — the four Ps that appear in what I have previously named the BP^{4}SO.[2] So far we have seen glimpses into that probable future.

---

[2] Wysocki, Robert K. (2011). *Executive's Guide to Project Management: Organizational Processes and Practices for Supporting Complex Projects.* (New York, NY: John Wiley & Sons.)

The professionals who support the BP^{4}SO will have some level of expertise in four different disciplines (project management, business analysis, information technology, and business processes). The integration of all four of these entities is future-oriented and certain to be part of your successful contemporary organization someday. For now, the best strategy is to make decisions that will accommodate that integration when it occurs.

Think of the BP^{4}SO as the PSO of the future. It does not exist today but by my estimation the trends I see portend of just such an entity emerging in the foreseeable future. My message to you is to begin laying the foundation for it by designing your PSO and putting a plan in place so that it can begin evolving into the BP^{4}SO of the future.

Hub-and-Spoke BP^{4}SO

In preparation for the BP^{4}SO, the PSO hub-and-spoke organizational structure introduced earlier in this chapter is probably the only organizational structure that makes good long-term business sense.

Figure 13-11 illustrates the final form of the demand-driven evolution of the PSO hub-and-spoke structure to the BP^{4}SO of the future. The BP^{4}SO will be implemented in several phases. Initially the Enterprise BP^{4}SO will be established and serve the support needs of the enterprise. As demand grows division level BP^{4}SOs will be established and offer support services as needed by the division. These support services might encompass all four disciplines. Once a second division has established, its BP^{4}SO Communities of Practice will begin to appear in order to establish communications links between divisions.

As demand in a division increases the spoke that feeds that division is established. The initial discipline of the Enterprise BP^{4}SO will probably be PM because of the strong historical roots of the PMO. There is already a growing trend in establishing a Community of Practice (COP) and Center of Excellence (COE) in BA so that will most likely be the second discipline that is integrated into the BP^{4}SO. That will give the BP^{4}SO a strong generalist orientation in PM and BA. From that point the IT and BP disciplines can be added as demand grows for specialists in the division BP^{4}SOs.

At some point in time, usually when two or more division BP^{4}SOs are in place, COPs for all four disciplines will emerge. They may support all four disciplines in an integrated model or support single disciplines as the BA COP now does. These will be the only direct communications link between division-level BP^{4}SOs. A sharing of best practices will develop, as will training, consulting, and other support services that can be shared. Some of these can continue to be offered by the Enterprise BP^{4}SO.

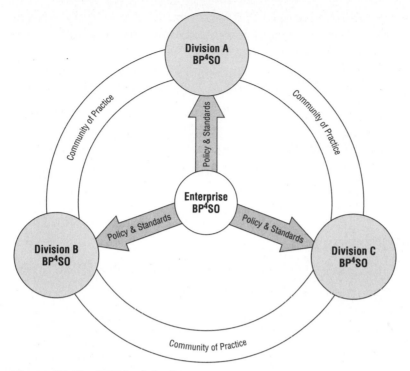

Figure 13-11: BP⁴SO of the future

Staffing the BP⁴SO

For me the only staffing strategy that makes sense is to rotate project managers and business analysts between the Enterprise BP⁴SO, division-level BP⁴SOs, and their home business unit. That accomplishes three very important things:

- They maintain a professional relationship and credibility with their peers in their home business unit.

- They seed their home business unit with practices and techniques used elsewhere in the enterprise BP⁴SO and the division-level BP⁴SOs.

- When they return to a BP⁴SO, they bring best practices back from their home business unit and pick up some clues about improving existing tools, templates, and processes.

Most attempts at spreading best practices across the organization have been a disappointment. "My project is different" and "Not invented here" are the major obstacles.

Rotations are a great way to reward a professional and give them a chance to recharge themselves. This is especially important after a really tough assignment. The rotation can happen in two ways:

- Between projects, when they are "on the beach," they can be assigned special projects within the BP⁴SO. These would be short-term projects.

- They can periodically take a sabbatical from their business unit to be assigned a major project within the BP⁴SO or simply provide consulting support across the organization. These could be competitive assignments awarded based on a proposal. The proposal could be unsolicited or a response to an RFP from the BP⁴SO. These are great ways for the BP⁴SO to do process improvement projects.

Other Considerations

There are three support areas that I see becoming more central to the role of the PSO of the future. They are briefly discussed below.

Portfolio Support

Many PSOs already provide this support to portfolio managers. That will increase and strengthen. The PSO of the future will provide project proposal intake services, evaluation, alignment, and prioritization services to the portfolio managers.

Assigning Project Managers

The PSO of the future will maintain the skills and competencies inventory of existing and "wanna-be" project managers. This coupled with their current and future assignments will be the input that guides assigning project managers to new projects.

Career and Professional Development of Project Managers

This support service must be centralized, and the PSO is the logical home for such a service. The project management subject matter expertise resides in the PSO and not in the HR department. The PSO will have its eye on the trends in projects and is in the best position to give advice on areas of need for skilled project professionals. Chapter 18 provides more details on what this career and professional development support service might look like.

Putting It All Together

In this chapter, I introduced the PSO, discussed its roles and responsibilities, and provided a plan for establishing one. The five-level Capability Maturity Model (CMM) is a good way to measure the maturity of your current PSO, and it provides a sound basis for a continuous quality improvement program.

Discussion Questions

1. Given that your existing PSO, which has been supporting TPM, is now going to support TPM, APM, xPM, and MPx projects, what would you do about organizational structure, staffing, and support functions provided? Be specific and back up your suggestions with valid reasons.

2. Senior management will always ask what business value they will realize from the PSO. How would you measure the Return On Investment for your PSO? (Be careful — this is a trick question.)

CHAPTER 14

Establishing and Managing a Project Portfolio Management Process

He who attempts too much seldom succeeds.
— **Dutch proverb**

A good way to outline a strategy is to ask yourself: "How and where am I going to commit my resources?" Your answer constitutes your strategy.
— **R. Henry Miglione, Oral Roberts University,**
An MBO Approach to Long-Range Planning

CHAPTER LEARNING OBJECTIVES

After reading this chapter, you will be able to:

■ **Understand current practices in corporate project portfolio management and how they are applied**

■ **Know how to deliver explicit business value through a strategically aligned project portfolio**

■ **Adapt the concepts and practices of project portfolio management to agile project portfolio management**

Organizations that invest in information technology (IT) projects — whether hardware-focused, software-focused, or both — must have a plan for that investment. The dollars needed to fund these projects almost always exceed the dollars available, so the organization is faced with a decision as to which projects should be funded, funded partially, or not funded at all. Is this a short-term decision that looks only at the coming budget cycle, or is there some long-term strategy that spans multiple budget cycles? How can the funding agency determine whether an IT investment is a good investment? Can some criteria be applied? The answers to these questions are simple in some cases and extremely difficult in others. This chapter uses a process life cycle approach that traces the life of a project through the portfolio management process, beginning with the project proposal and extending to the completion, termination, or postponement of the project.

Introduction to Project Portfolio Management

In this first section, I set the foundation for an exploration of project portfolio management. While everyone knows what a project is, not everyone may understand that not all projects should come under the purview of the portfolio management process. Defining the types of projects that will be considered for the project portfolio is a very basic tenet for every portfolio. You need to have a clear understanding of what a portfolio is, and in some situations more than one portfolio is advised. I want to make sure everyone is on the same page before I launch into the depths of a portfolio management discussion. In this section, I present a conceptual overview of the portfolio management process. Subsequent sections describe each part of the process in detail.

I first want to take another look at the idea of a project. The definition of a project comes from earlier discussions in this book, but not all projects belong in the portfolio. The word *portfolio* probably conjures up several different ideas. I have a simple definition that will put everyone on the same page.

What Is a Portfolio Project?

In Chapter 1, I defined a project in the following way:

> *A project is a sequence of unique, complex, and connected activities having one goal or purpose that must be completed by a specific time, within budget, and according to specification.*

This is a technical definition, and it tells you quite a bit about the type of work that can legitimately be called a project, but when you are dealing with a portfolio, it doesn't tell the whole story. Because you are constructing a portfolio of projects, you need to define the types of projects that qualify for inclusion in the portfolio. Not all projects will be managed as part of a portfolio. What about small, routine projects that are done as part of normal business operations within a single department or business unit using its own people resources? Certainly they will not fall under the enterprise portfolio management process, but they might be part of the business unit's portfolio and, hence, follow some defined process for inclusion. They are already included in the operations budget of their respective business units. Conversely, how big, complex, and expensive does the project have to be before you will consider it for the portfolio? No matter how specific you are in establishing the qualification criteria, a certain amount of subjectivity will be involved. For example, consider complexity in the case of the selection and purchase of a desktop computer. If you are technically savvy, the purchase of the computer is a simple task and would not be considered a project. If you are technically challenged, however, then the purchase of a computer clearly is a project and, at least for you, a complex one at that.

That said, it seems clear that you would want to set a minimum effort, cost, and even value to those projects that will be considered for inclusion in the portfolio. These are certainly subjective calls on your part, but you must be able to make a case for a project that will be proposed for the portfolio and one that won't.

NOTE What about capital budget projects? Regardless of their dollar value, some organizations require that all capital budget projects be approved and constitute a line item in the capital budget. In effect, the capital budget is a portfolio of projects, whereby each project defines a piece of capital equipment that the requestor is asking to purchase.

What Is a Project Portfolio?

The simple definition of a project portfolio is as follows:

A project portfolio is a collection of projects that share some common link to one another.

The operative phrase here is "share some common link to one another." I want to explore that idea in more detail. The previous note about capital budgets described one example of projects that share a common link. That link could take many forms. At the enterprise level, the link might be nothing more than the fact that all the projects belong to the same company. Although that may be true, it is not too likely the kind of link you are looking for. Some more effective and specific links might be the following:

- The projects may all originate in the same business unit or functional area (such as IT).
- The projects may all be new product development projects.
- The projects may all be funded out of the same budget or from the same resource pool.

Whichever way you choose to define the link, one thing is almost certain: Whatever resources you have available for those projects will not be enough to meet all project requests. Some choices have to be made, and that is where project portfolio management takes over.

To further complicate the situation, you might need to establish different types of portfolios. For example, all of the capital projects with a value above $500 could form a portfolio. More specifically, the portfolio could cover only technology capital projects above $500. Systems development projects longer than six months with a total cost above $500,000 might be another type of portfolio. At this point in the discussion, you can see that whatever portfolios you choose to establish, they will consist of projects that share similar characteristics.

What Is Project Portfolio Management?

Credit for establishing the field of modern portfolio theory belongs to Henry Markowitz, an economist at Baruch College, City University of New York. He first presented his theory in the *Harvard Business Review* in 1959. In later years, he was awarded the Nobel Prize in Economics for his discoveries. It wasn't until the 1990s that his theories were extended from the investment portfolio to the project portfolio. Many of the approaches I talk about later in this chapter have their conceptual roots in his earlier works.

The working definition of project portfolio management for this book is as follows:

Project portfolio management includes establishing the investment strategy of the portfolio, determining what types of projects can be incorporated in the portfolio, evaluating, and prioritizing proposed projects, constructing a balanced portfolio that will achieve the investment objectives, monitoring the performance of the portfolio, and periodically adjusting the contents of the portfolio in order to achieve the desired results.

The Project Portfolio Management Life Cycle

No matter how you slice and dice it, the Project Portfolio Management life cycle consists of the following five phases:

1. Establish
2. Evaluate
3. Prioritize
4. Select
5. Manage

These phases are delineated with shaded boxes in Figure 14-1. In this diagram, I have embedded a generic project in the phases to illustrate the principles involved and the possible courses of action that a project may take over the course of its life. All of the discussions that follow in the remaining sections of this chapter are based on this diagram.

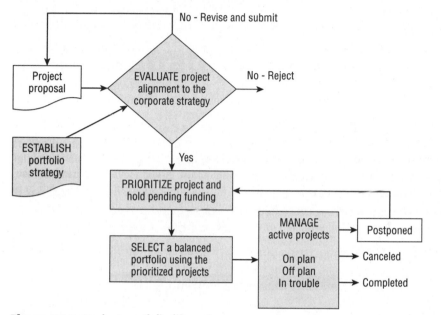

Figure 14-1: Project portfolio life cycle

Also shown in Figure 14-1 is the changing status of a project as it moves through this life cycle. Note that there are eight different stages that a project may be in during this life cycle. These stages are as follows:

Proposed — A proposed project is one that has been submitted to the portfolio with a request that it be evaluated regarding its alignment to the portfolio strategy. A project that does not meet the alignment criteria may be either rejected out of hand or returned to the proposing party for revision and resubmission. Projects that are returned for revision are generally only in minor noncompliance, and by following the suggested revisions, they should meet the alignment criteria.

Aligned — A proposed project is aligned if it has been evaluated and determined to be in alignment with the portfolio strategy. Once its alignment has been determined, the project will be placed in one or more funding categories for future consideration. At this stage, the proposing parties should begin preparing a detailed plan. The plan will contain information that helps the portfolio manager make a final determination regarding project funding and, hence, inclusion in the portfolio.

Prioritized — An aligned project is prioritized if it has been ranked along with other projects in its funding category. This is the final stage before the project is selected for the portfolio. If its priority is high enough in its category, it will be funded and included in the portfolio.

Selected — A prioritized project has been selected if it is in the queue of other prioritized projects in its funding category and is awaiting funding authorization. This is a temporary stage, and funding is certain at this point.

Active — A selected project is active if it has received its funding authorization and is open for work. At this stage, the project manager is authorized to proceed with the recruiting and assignment of team members, scheduling of work, and other activities associated with launching the project.

Postponed — An active project is postponed if its funding authorization has been temporarily removed. Such projects must return to the pool of prioritized projects and be selected once again in order for its funding authorization to be restored. The resources allocated to a postponed project are returned to the funding category from which they originated. The resources may be reassigned to the postponed project later or may be allocated to the next project in the queue of that funding category.

Canceled — An active project is canceled if it has failed to demonstrate regular progress toward its successful completion, or if priorities have been altered and the project is no longer at a high enough priority in its funding category to be continued. Depending on the stage in which the project was canceled, there may be unspent resources. If so, they are returned to the funding category from which they originated. Those funds then become available for the next project in the queue of that funding category.

Completed — A project is completed if it has met all of its objectives and delivered business value as proposed.

A project may find itself in any one of these eight stages as it proceeds through the five phases of the Project Portfolio Management life cycle. The following sections of this chapter cover each one of the five phases in more detail.

ESTABLISH a Portfolio Strategy

The first step in portfolio management is deciding the strategy for the portfolio. That strategy is an investment strategy. That is, how will the enterprise's funding be spread across the portfolio? Once this investment strategy is in place, the enterprise will have a structure for selecting the investment opportunities that will be presented in the form of project proposals. This is really a type of strategic planning phase in which the portfolio manager or the portfolio management team decides how it will allocate its project budget to various general categories of project investment.

NOTE I use the term *portfolio manager* to represent the decision-making body, whether it is one individual or a team.

Several models are easily adapted to this phase. In this chapter, I examine the following five popular models:

- Strategic Alignment Model
- Boston Consulting Group (BCG) Products/Services Matrix
- Project Distribution Matrix
- Growth versus Survival Model
- Project Investment Categories Model

Each model has desirable characteristics that meet the organization's need for good investment strategies. The strategy itself is determined by the dollar or resource investment (people, machines, facilities, and so on) that the company is willing to make in each of the funding categories defined by the various models. Once this strategy is in place, a final question must be answered: Which projects will be funded in each of these categories? The answer to that question is found in the next three phases of the model.

Prior to releasing the investment plan, the following two questions should be answered by the portfolio manager:

- Will projects be partially funded in order to include more projects in the portfolio, or will projects be funded only at the level of their request?
- If an investment category has excess resources after project funding decisions have been made, can those resources be reallocated to other investment categories without compromising the portfolio strategy, and if so, how will they be reallocated?

If possible, it is good to make these decisions before the situations arise. The rules need to be clear so that all parties are informed ahead of time.

Strategic Alignment Model

The first model is the Strategic Alignment Model. This model makes good sense because it attempts to align projects with the direction the enterprise has decided to follow. In other words, it aligns projects with the things that are important to the enterprise. Figure 14-2 graphically depicts this model.

Value/Mission

The *value/mission* is a very brief statement of why the enterprise exists. This could define an end state that the enterprise hopes to achieve or simply be a statement of how the enterprise views the business it is in. Whichever form is used, this statement is unlikely to change, at least not in the foreseeable future.

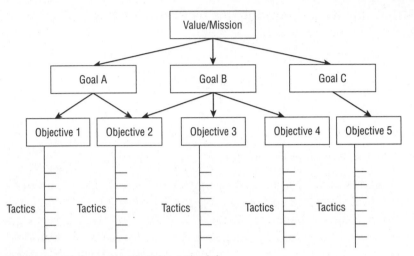

Figure 14-2: Strategic Alignment Model

Goals

To achieve its end state or accomplish its mission, the enterprise has to engage in certain major efforts. These are likely to be multiperiod or multiyear efforts designed to accomplish major results. They might never be attainable (eliminating world hunger, for example), or they might be achievable over long periods of time (finding a cure for cancer or a preventative for the common cold, for example). Any of these are good examples of goal statements. The important thing to remember is that they must be stated in a fashion that links them directly to one or more of the corporate objectives.

Objectives

There will be many approaches to the realization of each goal. Each approach is called an *objective*, which might be a one-year effort or span several years. Again, take the example of the preventative for the common cold. Objectives might include investigating possible food additives, modifying the immune system, or finding a drug that establishes immunity to the cold. All three of these objectives can launch a number of tactics.

Tactics

Tactics are the short-term efforts, usually less than one year in duration, designed to meet one or more objectives. These are the projects that will be proposed for the portfolio. A project that relates to only one objective will be less attractive to the portfolio manager than a project that relates to several objectives. Similarly, a project that relates to a lower priority objective will be less attractive than a project that relates to a higher priority objective. You will see how this works in the "SELECT a Balanced Portfolio Using the Prioritized List" section later in this chapter.

How Are You Going to Allocate Your Resources?

The application of this model is quite straightforward. The enterprise must decide what resources will be allocated to each goal and to the objectives that support that goal. With that decision made, the enterprise accepts project proposals from its various departments regarding what projects they wish to undertake and how those projects relate to the goals and objectives of the enterprise. Obviously, there won't be much interest in supporting projects that do not further the goals of the enterprise.

Boston Consulting Group Products/Services Matrix

The BCG Matrix is a well-known model that has been used for several years. It defines four categories of products/services based on their growth rate and competitive position, as shown in Figure 14-3.

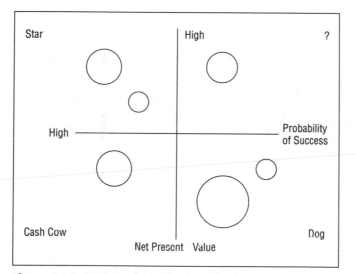

Figure 14-3: BCG Products/Services Matrix

Cash Cows

These are well-established products/services that have a strong market share but limited growth potential. They are stable and profitable. Projects that relate to cash cows are important to the organization because the company will want to protect that investment for as long as it maintains that market position.

Dogs

Because these products/services are not competitive and have little or no growth potential, any projects related to them should not be undertaken. The best thing an organization can do with dogs is phase them out as quickly and painlessly as possible. Don't throw good money after bad!

Stars

These are products/services that have strong market positions and clearly strong growth potential. Projects related to stars are good investment opportunities. Stars are the future cash cows.

?

The question mark represents the starting point of the model. Products/services that are untested in the market but appear to have strong growth potential are worthy of spending research and development (R & D) dollars. Projects linked to those efforts are good investment opportunities. The objective is to turn them into stars and then cash cows.

How Are You Going to Allocate Your Resources?

The answer to this question depends on the current market position of the enterprise, the business outlook, and a variety of other considerations. Except for the dogs, the other three categories will have some level of investment. If the industry is stable, such as cement manufacturing, more resources might be spent on the cash cows to ensure that they maintain their market position, fewer resources will be allocated to the stars because the enterprise will always want to keep some growth opportunities in the pipeline, and even fewer on the ? category because the industry isn't in the R & D mode. In a volatile, high-growth, high-tech industry, the allocations might be very different. More resources will be spent on the stars and ? projects and fewer on the cash cows. Cash cows have a very short useful life, and any investments in them are risky.

Project Distribution Matrix

Simple, yet elegant in its simplicity, the Project Distribution Matrix, shown in Figure 14-4, says that there must be a mix of projects in the portfolio. This mix will be dictated by the skills inventory of those who work on the projects, as well as the needs of the organization to attain and sustain market share. It can be used in conjunction with the models shown previously to ensure that a healthy mix is present in the project portfolio. The Project Distribution Matrix is similar to the Strategic Alignment Model in that it defines a rule for classifying projects. The rule is a two-way classification, as shown in the figure.

Project Focus	New	Enhancement	Maintenance
Strategic			
Tactical			
Operational			

Figure 14-4: Project Distribution Matrix

New, Enhancement, or Maintenance

The columns of the matrix classify projects according to whether they are New, Enhancement, or Maintenance, as follows:

New — A new project is one that proposes to develop a new application, process, or product.

Enhancement — An enhancement project is one that proposes to improve an existing process or product.

Maintenance — A maintenance project is one that simply proposes to conduct the normal care and feeding of an existing operation, which could include fixing errors that have been detected or otherwise updating some features that have become obsolete or are part of a process that has been changed.

Strategic, Tactical, or Operational

The rows of the matrix classify projects based on their role in the enterprise, as follows:

Strategic — A strategic project is one that focuses on the strategic elements of the enterprise. Applications that extract basic data from businesses, society, and the economy and translate that data into policy formulation are examples of strategic projects.

Tactical — Tactical projects are projects that look at existing processes and procedures and propose ways to make improvements by changing or replacing one or more of these processes or procedures.

Operational — Operational projects are those that focus on existing processes and try to find ways to improve efficiency or reduce costs.

How Are You Going to Allocate Your Resources?

The application of this model is quite straightforward. The enterprise that has defined a project classification rule must now decide what resources will be allocated to each of the nine categories shown in Figure 14-4. With that decision made, the enterprise accepts project proposals from its various departments as to what projects they wish to undertake. A feature of this model is that it can be tied to the resource pool of skilled employees. The required skills across each of these nine categories shown in Figure 14-4 are different. To some extent, that may dictate how much emphasis is placed on each category. The enterprise will want to use its available skills, so the relative priority of each category can help or hinder that effort.

NOTE The Graham-Englund Selection Model (discussed later in this chapter) incorporates available staff capacity based on skills as part of its selection strategy.

Growth versus Survival Model

This way of categorizing projects is the simplest of all presented here. Projects are either focused on growth or survival. *Growth projects* are those that propose to make something better in some way. Obviously, these are discretionary projects. *Survival projects* are the "must-do" projects. These projects must be done or the enterprise will suffer irreparable damage. In short, survival projects are projects that must be done, and all other projects are growth projects.

If the budget is in a contracting phase, you will probably allocate most of your resources to the survival category. Conversely, if you are in an expansion phase, you will allocate most of your resources to the growth category.

Project Investment Categories Model

The Project Investment Categories Model is a close kin of the financial investment portfolio. It identifies categories of investments. These categories define types of projects, just as a financial portfolio defines types of investment instruments. In the case of projects, you define the following categories:

Infrastructure — Projects that strengthen the hardware, software systems, and facility brick and mortar projects that support the business

Maintenance — Projects that update existing systems or products

New products — Projects that propose entirely new products or services

Research — Projects that investigate new products, services, or systems to support the business

Each type of project will receive some percentage of the resource pool.

This model operates just like the BCG Products/Services Matrix discussed earlier in the chapter. Both models require the portfolio manager to establish a distribution across existing and new products and services. The distribution will most likely be directly related to whether the enterprise is in a growth or maintenance posture with respect to its upcoming investment strategy.

Choosing Where to Apply these Models

Depending on the particular application that you have in mind, you will want to choose the most appropriate model. This section helps you consider some of the possibilities.

Corporate Level

If your organization has an enterprise-wide project management office that has management responsibility for the project portfolio, then your choice of model is limited to the BCG Products/Services Matrix or the Strategic Alignment Model. Both of these are good candidates, because they focus on the strategic goals of the organization at the highest levels and can directly relate a single project to how well it aligns with defined strategies. That provides a basis for prioritizing a project.

Functional Level

At the corporate level, dollars are allocated to strategic initiatives that affect the entire organization, whereas at the functional level — the IT department, for example — the situation can be quite different. Resources are allocated to operational- or tactical-level projects. Rather than allocate dollars, it is more likely that the resource to be allocated is professional staff. In that case, the Project Distribution Matrix, Growth versus Survival Model, or Project Investment Categories Model will do the job.

> **NOTE** Later in this chapter, I discuss the Graham-Englund Selection Model. It doesn't fit into the framework of the other models, so I treat it separately. In fact, the Graham-Englund Selection Model is built around the allocation of professional resources to prioritized projects as its basic operating rule. That makes the Graham-Englund Selection Model a good choice for functional-level projects.

EVALUATE Project Alignment to the Portfolio Strategy

This evaluation is a very simple intake task that places a proposed project into one of several funding categories as defined in the model being used. The beginning of the project intake process involves determining whether the project is in alignment with the portfolio strategy, and placing it in the appropriate "bucket."

These buckets are defined by the strategy that is used, and each bucket contains a planned dollar or resource amount. After all of the projects have been placed in buckets, each bucket is passed to the next phase, where the projects that make up a bucket are prioritized.

This intake process can take place in one of the following ways:

- The person proposing the project does the evaluation.
- The intake person does the evaluation.

It can work well either way. If the person proposing the project does the evaluation, he or she needs a clear definition of each funding category in the portfolio strategy. The project proposal may be returned to the proposer for clarification or revision before being placed in a funding category. Some procedures may ask the proposer to classify the project, in which case this intake process is nothing more than an administrative function. This places the burden on the proposer and not on the portfolio manager. However, there is the possibility of biasing the evaluation in favor of the proposer. The bias arises when the proposer, having such intimate familiarity with the proposal, evaluates it subjectively, rather than objectively. There is also the strong likelihood that these types of evaluations will not be consistent across all projects. Having an intake person conduct the evaluations ensures that all proposals are evaluated using a consistent and objective criteria.

In other cases the process is more formal, and the project proposal is screened to specific criteria. This formal evaluation is now a more significant process and may involve the portfolio manager or a portfolio committee. Projects that do not match any funding category are returned to the proposer and rejected with no further action specified or requested. If the portfolio manager does the evaluation, the problem of bias largely disappears. In this scenario, the proposer must follow a standard procedure for documenting the proposed project. This topic is revisited in the "Preparing Your Project for Submission to the Portfolio Management Process" section later in this chapter.

The deliverable from this phase of the process is a simple categorization of projects into funding categories.

PRIORITIZE Projects and Hold Pending Funding Authorization

The first tactical step in every portfolio management model involves prioritizing the projects that have been shown to be aligned with the portfolio strategy. Recall that the alignment places the project in a single funding category. It is those projects in a funding category that you prioritize. When you are finished, each funding category will have a list of prioritized projects. Dozens of approaches could be used to establish that prioritization. Some are nonnumeric; others are numeric. Some are very simple; others can be quite complex and involve multivariate analysis, goal programming, and other complex computer-based algorithms. My approach here is to identify methods that can easily be implemented in the public sector and do not require a computer system for support, although sometimes a simple spreadsheet application can reduce the labor intensity of the process. This section describes the following six models:

- Forced Ranking
- Q-Sort
- Must-Do, Should-Do, Postpone
- Criteria Weighting
- Paired Comparisons
- Risk/Benefit

Forced Ranking

Forced Ranking was introduced in Chapters 3 and 11. A further example is shown here. This approach is best explained by way of an example. Suppose 10 projects have been proposed. Number them 1, 2, … 10 so that you can refer to them later. Suppose that the portfolio management team has six members (A, B, … F), and they are each asked to rank the 10 projects from most important (1) to least important (10). They can use any criteria they wish, and they do not have to describe the criteria they used. The results of their rankings are shown in Table 14-1.

Table 14-1: Forced Ranking of 10 Projects

PROJECT #	A	B	C	D	E	F	RANK SUM	FORCED RANK
1	2	5	3	2	1	6	19	2
2	4	3	2	7	9	10	35	6
3	7	4	9	8	6	3	37	7
4	1	8	5	1	2	2	19	3
5	3	6	8	4	7	5	33	5
6	8	9	10	9	10	8	54	9
7	5	1	1	3	3	4	17	1
8	6	2	4	5	4	1	22	4
9	10	10	7	10	8	9	54	10
10	9	7	6	6	5	7	40	8

The individual rankings from each of the six members for a specific project are added to produce the rank sum for each project. Low values for the rank sum are indicative of projects that have been given high priority by the members. For example, Project 7 has the lowest rank sum and is therefore the highest priority project. Ties are possible. In fact, the preceding example has two ties (1 and 4, 6 and 9). Ties can be broken in a number of ways. For example, I prefer to use the existing rankings to break ties. In this example, a tie is broken by taking the tied project with the lowest rank score and moving it to the next lowest forced rank. For example, the lowest rank for Project 1 is 6, and the lowest rank for Project 4 is 8. Therefore, the tie is broken by giving Project 1 a rank of 2 and Project 4 a rank of 3.

Forced Ranking works well for small numbers of projects, but it does not scale very well.

Q-Sort

In the Q-Sort model (see Figure 14-5), projects are first divided into two groups: high priority and low priority. The high-priority group is then divided into two groups: high priority and medium priority. The low-priority group is also divided into two groups: low priority and medium priority. The next step is to divide the high-priority group into two groups: very high priority and high priority. The same is done for the low-priority group. The decomposition continues until all groups have eight or fewer members. As a last step, you could distribute the medium-priority projects to the other final groups.

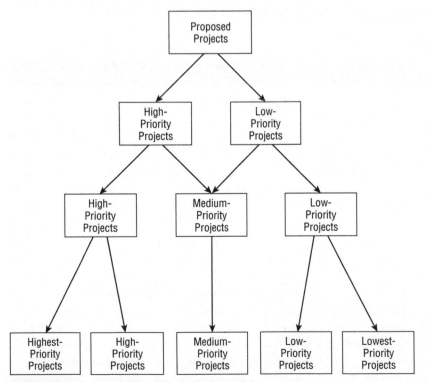

Figure 14-5: An example of the Q-Sort model

The Q-Sort method is simple and quick. It works well for large numbers of projects. It also works well when used as a small group exercise using a consensus approach.

Must-Do, Should-Do, Postpone

This approach (and variations of it such as MoSCoW) is probably the most commonly used way of ranking. As opposed to the forced rank, in which each individual project is ranked, this approach creates a few categories, such as Must-Do, Should Do, and Postpone. The person doing the ranking only has to decide which category the project belongs in. The agony of having to decide relative rankings between pairs of projects is eliminated with this approach. The number of categories is arbitrary, as are the names of the categories.

TIP I prefer to use the naming convention "Must-Do, Should-Do, Postpone" rather than categories like high, medium, and low or A, B, and C. The names avoid the need to define what each category means.

This method is even simpler than Q-Sort. If the number of projects is large, you may need to prioritize the projects within each of the three groups in order to make funding decisions.

Criteria Weighting

There are literally hundreds of criteria-weighting models. They are all quite similar, differing only in the minor details. I give one example of criteria weighting, but several others apply the same principles. A number of characteristics are identified, and a numeric weighting is applied to each characteristic. Each characteristic has a scale attached to it. The scales usually range from 1 to 10. Each project is evaluated on each characteristic, and a scale value is given to the project. Each scale value is multiplied by the characteristic weight, and these weighted scale values are added. The highest result is associated with the highest-priority project.

Figure 14-6 shows a sample calculation for one of the proposed projects for the portfolio. The first column lists the criteria against which all proposed projects for this portfolio will be evaluated. The second column lists the weight of that criterion (higher weight indicates more importance to the scoring algorithm). Columns 3 through 7 evaluate the project against the given criteria. Note that the evaluation can be given to more than one level. The only restriction is that the evaluation must be totally spread across the levels. Note that the sum of each criteria is one. Using the Contribute to Goal B row as an example, multiply the rating (0.2) times the value of "Very Good (8)" to get a score of 1.6, and then multiply the rating of (0.8) times the value of "Good (6)" to get a value of 4.8. Add the values 1.6 and 4.8 to calculate the total rating of Contribute to Goal B as 6.4, shown in column 8. So the eighth column is the sum of the levels multiplied by the score for that level. This process is totally adaptable to the nature of the portfolio. The criteria and criteria weight columns can be defined to address the needs of the portfolio. All other columns are fixed. The last two columns are calculated based on the values in columns 2 through 7.

Criteria	Criteria Weight	Very Good (8)	Good (6)	Fair (4)	Poor (2)	Very Poor (0)	Expected Level Weight	Expected Weighted Score
Fit to Mission	10	1.0					8.0	80.0
Fit to Objectives	10	0.2	0.6	0.2			6.0	60.0
Fit to Strategy	10			1.0			4.0	40.0
Contribute to Goal A	8				1.0		2.0	16.0
Contribute to Goal B	6	0.2	0.8				6.4	38.4
Contribute to Goal C	4		0.5	0.5			5.0	20.0
Uses Strengths	10				0.6	0.4	1.2	12.0
Uses Weaknesses	10	0.7	0.3				7.4	74.0
								340.4

Figure 14-6: Criteria weighting

Paired Comparisons Model

The next scoring model is called the Paired Comparisons Model. In this model, every pair of projects is compared. The evaluator chooses which project in the pair is the higher priority. The matrix in Figure 14-7 is the commonly used method for conducting and recording the results of a paired comparisons exercise.

First note that all 10 projects are defined across the 10 columns and down the 10 rows. For 10 projects, you have to make 45 comparisons. The 45 cells above the diagonal contain the comparisons you make. First, Project 1 is compared to Project 2. If Project 1 is given a higher priority than Project 2, then a "1" is placed in cell (1, 2) and a "0" is placed in cell (2, 1). If Project 2 had been given a higher priority than Project 1, then you would place a "0" in cell (1, 2) and a "1" in cell (2, 1). Next, Project 1 is compared to Project 3, and so on, until Project 1 has been compared to all other nine projects. Then Project 2 is compared to Project 3, and so on. Continuing in this fashion, the remaining cells are completed. The final step is to add all the entries in each of the 10 rows, producing the rank for each project: the higher the score, the higher the rank. The rightmost column reflects the results of those calculations. Note that Project 7 had the highest overall priority.

	1	2	3	4	5	6	7	8	9	10	SUM	RANK
1	X	1	1	0	1	1	0	1	1	1	7	2
2	0	X	0	0	1	1	0	0	1	1	4	6
3	0	1	X	0	0	1	0	0	1	1	4	5
4	1	1	1	X	1	1	0	0	1	1	7	2
5	0	0	1	0	X	1	0	0	1	0	3	7
6	0	0	0	0	0	X	0	0	1	1	2	8
7	1	1	1	1	1	1	X	1	1	1	9	1
8	0	1	1	1	1	1	0	X	1	1	7	2
9	0	0	0	0	0	0	0	0	X	0	0	10
10	0	0	0	0	1	0	0	0	1	X	2	9

Figure 14-7: An example of paired comparisons

NOTE This Paired Comparisons Model is a quick and simple method. Unfortunately, it doesn't scale very well. For example, 100 projects would require 4,950 comparisons.

Risk/Benefit

The final scoring model is the Risk/Benefit Matrix. There are many ways to do risk analysis, from subjective methods to very sophisticated mathematical models. The one I am introducing is a very simple quasi-mathematical model. Risk is divided into five levels (1, 2, ... 5). Level 1 has a very low risk (or high probability of success), and level 5 has a very high risk (or very low probability of success). Actually, any number of levels will do the job. Defining three levels is also quite common. In this model, you assess two risks: the risk of technical success and the risk of business success. These are arranged as shown in Figure 14-8.

Each project is assessed in terms of the *probability of technical success* and the *probability of business success*. The *probability of project success* is estimated as the product of the two separate probabilities. To simplify the calculation, the graph shows the results of the computation by placing projects in one of the following three shaded areas:

- **Lightly shaded** — These projects should be funded.

- **No shading** — These projects should be considered.

- **Darkly shaded** — These projects should be referred back to the proposing agency unless there is some compelling reason to fund them.

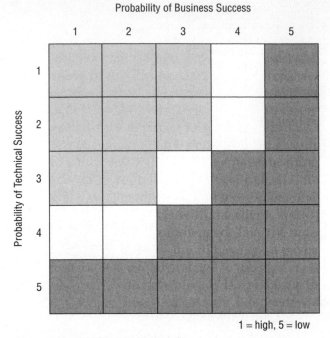

Probability of Business Success

1 = high, 5 = low

Figure 14-8: Risk/Benefit Matrix

When you have a large number of projects, you need to prioritize those that fall in the lightly shaded cells. A good way to do this would be to prioritize the cells starting in the upper-left corner and working toward the center of the matrix.

SELECT a Balanced Portfolio Using the Prioritized List

You might think that because you have a prioritized list in each funding category and you know the resources available for those projects, the selection process would be simple and straightforward, but it isn't. Selection is a very challenging task for any portfolio management team. The problem stems from the apparent conflict between the results of evaluation, the ranking of projects from most valuable to least valuable, and the need to balance the portfolio with respect to one or more variables. These two notions are often in conflict. As a further complication, should partial funding of projects be allowed? You will examine this conflict in the "Balancing the Portfolio" section later in this chapter.

There are several approaches to picking the project portfolio. As you have already seen, this chapter deals with five portfolio strategies and six prioritization approaches. That gives you 30 possible combinations for selection approaches, and many more could have been covered. From among the 30 that I could examine, I have focused on the following three:

- Strategic Alignment Model and Weighted Criteria
- Project Distribution Matrix and Forced Ranking
- Graham-Englund Selection Model with the Project Investment Categories and the Risk/Benefit Matrix

This section shows the results of combining the previous sections into an approach for selecting projects for the portfolio. Based on your choice of model, you make a statement about how your resources will be allocated. Each one of these models generates "buckets" into which resources are distributed. The buckets that contain more resources have a higher business value than those with fewer resources. These buckets represent the supply of resources available to the projects that are demanding those resources. It would be foolish to expect a balance between the supply of resources and the demand for them. Some buckets will have more resources than have been requested, whereas others will not have enough resources to meet demand. This section explains how to resolve those differences to build a balanced portfolio.

Balancing the Portfolio

Unfortunately, there isn't a perfect or best way to build a balanced portfolio. There are basically the following two approaches, and neither one ensures an optimal solution:

- The first approach is to make one master list of prioritized projects. However, if you simply use that prioritized list of projects with any of the models presented so far, you may end up with less than satisfactory results. For example, you could end up funding a number of short-term, low-risk projects with low organizational value. Alternatively, you could end up funding all long-term, high-risk projects with high organizational value. In either case, the resulting portfolio would not be representative of the organization's strategy. In other words, you could end up with a portfolio that is not at all in line with the corporate strategy.

- The second approach, and the one that I have taken here, is to separate projects into buckets, and then prioritize the projects that have been placed in each bucket. Although this certainly gives you a balanced portfolio, it may not give you the best portfolio. Some buckets may have been very popular choices for proposed projects, and a very good project may not have reached high enough on the priority list to be funded. Yet that project may be a much better alternative than some project in another bucket that did receive funding. It's basically the luck of the draw.

Which approach should you take? I recommend the second, for the following two reasons:

- Prioritizing a single list, which may be long, is far more difficult than working with several shorter lists. The work can be divided among several persons or groups in the second case, but not in the first case. Furthermore, when you first align projects with funding categories and then prioritize within funding categories, you are working not only with a smaller number of projects, but with a group of projects that are more homogeneous.

- Once the projects have been aligned within funding categories, the portfolio manager may then allocate the resources across the funding categories. That avoids situations in which there could be a wide variance between the resources that are being requested and those that are being offered in each category. The caution here is that the portfolio manager may try to honor the requests and abandon any portfolio strategy. You can't have it both ways.

The examples given in the sections that follow illustrate some of these ideas. These are but a few of the many examples I could give, but they are sufficient to illustrate some of the ways to mitigate against such outcomes and ensure a balanced portfolio that reflects the organization's investment strategy.

Strategic Alignment Model and Weighted Criteria

In this section, I use the Strategic Alignment Model to select projects for the portfolio. Figure 14-9 shows one variation that you might use.

Each objective is weighted with a number between 0 and 1. Note that the sum of the weights is 1. These weights show the relative importance of each objective compared against the others. Below each objective is the budget allocated to that objective. The total budget is $20M. Ten projects are being considered for this portfolio. The proposed budget for each is shown with the project number. The total request is for $25M. In this example, a project may be associated with more than one objective. You can do that by assigning to each project objective pair a weight that measures the strength of the relationship of that project to that objective. This weight is the result of evaluating the alignment of the projects to the objectives. The sum of the weights for any project is 1.0. To establish the priority order of the 10 projects, multiply the objective weight by the project weight and add the numbers. The result of that calculation is shown in the Score column for all 10 projects in the example. The higher the project's score, the higher the project should be on your list of projects to fund. In this example, Project 7 is the top-priority project, with a score of 0.300. Project 10 is the tenth priority, with a score of 0.120.

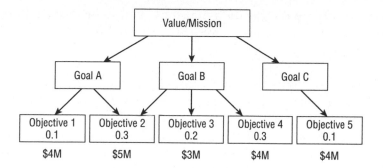

Budget Proposed								Score	Award
P#1	$2M	0.6 $1.2M		0.4 $0.8M				0.140	$2.0M
P#2	$2M	0.3 $0.6M	0.2	0.1 $0.2M		0.4 $0.8M		0.150	$1.6M
P#3	$4M	0.4 $1.6M	0.6 $2.4M					0.220	$4.0M
P#4	$1M	0.3 $0.3M	0.2 $0.2M		0.5 $0.5M			0.240	$1.0M
P#5	$3M				0.8 $2.4M	0.2 $0.6M		0.260	$3.0M
P#6	$4M		0.7		0.3 $0.3M			0.160	$0.3M
P#7	$3M		0.8 $2.4M		0. $0.6M			0.300	$3.0M
P#8	$3M			0.3 $0.9M		0.7 $2.1M		0.130	$3.0M
P#9	$1M		0.2	0.2 $0.2M	0.2 $0.2M	0.4 $0.4M		0.200	$0.8M
P#10	$2M	0.8 $0.3M		0.2 $0.4M				0.120	$0.7M

Figure 14-9: Achieving balance with the Strategic Alignment Model

The awards to the projects are made by starting with the highest-priority project, which in the example is Project 7. The request is for $3M. Of that amount, 80 percent will come from the budget for Strategy 2 and 20 percent will come from Strategy 4. That reduces the budget for Strategy 2 from $5M to $2.6M and for Strategy 4 from $4M to $3.4M. The process continues with the next highest-priority project and continues until the budget for each strategy is allocated or there are no more requests for resources. In some cases, a project may receive only partial funding from a funding category. For example, Project 10 should have received $1.6M from Strategy 1, but when it came up for funding, there was only $0.3M left in that budget. Following the example to its completion results in the allocations shown in Figure 14-9. The requests total $25M, the budget totals $20M, and the allocations total $19.4M. The remaining $0.6M should not be redistributed to projects that did not receive their requested support. These resources are held pending performance of the portfolio and the possible need to reallocate resources at some later date.

This section gives you but one example of applying an adaptation of criteria weighting to the Strategic Alignment Model to produce a portfolio selection approach. This model is probably the best of those discussed in this chapter because it enables the portfolio manager to express the enterprise strategy in a direct and clear fashion through the weights chosen for each objective. It also shows how the proposed projects relate to that prioritization through the weighted scores on each objective. The model provides management with a tool that can easily adapt to changing priorities and that can be shared with the organization.

Project Distribution Matrix and Forced Ranking Model

To further illustrate the process of creating a portfolio selection approach, next I combine the Project Distribution Matrix and the Forced Ranking Model. Assume that the total dollars available for Major IT Projects is $20M and that the dollars have been allocated as shown in Figure 14-10. I'll use the same 10 projects from the previous section with the same funding requests. The projects are listed in the order of their ranking within each funding category.

Project Focus	New	Enhancement	Maintenance
Strategic	Budget $3M	Budget $3M P#2 $2M P#10 $2M P#6 $4M	Budget $3M
Tactical	Budget $3M P#1 $2M P#4 $1M P#9 $1M	Budget $2M	Budget $1M P#3 $4M
Operational	Budget $1M	Budget $2M P#8 $3M	Budget $2M P#7 $3M P#5 $3M

Figure 14-10: Project Distribution Matrix with budget and funding requests

The first thing to note in this example is that the investment decisions do not line up very well with the funding requests from the 10 projects. There is a total of $9M in four funding categories, with no projects aligned in those categories. Your priorities as portfolio manager were expressed by your allocation of funds to the various funding categories. However, the project proposals do not line up with that strategy. Are you willing to make any budget changes to better accommodate the requests? You should, but with the stipulation that you do not compromise your investment strategy. Legitimate changes would be to move resources to the left but in the same row, or up but in the same column. If you agree that that is acceptable, then you end up with the allocations shown in Figure 14-11. $3M was moved from the Strategic/Maintenance category to the Strategic/Enhancement category, and $1M was moved from the Operational/New category to the Tactical/New category. Any other movement of monies would compromise the investment strategy.

Project Focus	New	Enhancement	Maintenance
Strategic	Budget $3M	Budget $6M P#2 $2M P#10 $2M P#6 $4M	
Tactical	Budget $4M P#1 $2M P#4 $1M P#9 $1M	Budget $2M	Budget $1M P#3 $4M
Operational		Budget $2M P#8 $3M	Budget $2M P#7 $3M P#5 $3M

Figure 14-11: Project Distribution Matrix with adjusted budget and funding requests

After the allocations have been made, you are left with the matrix shown in Figure 14-12. The balances remaining are also shown in Figure 14-12. These monies are to be held pending changes to project status as project work is undertaken.

Project Focus	New	Enhancement	Maintenance
Strategic	Budget $3M	P#2 $2M P#10 $2M P#6 $2M	
Tactical	P#1 $2M P#4 $1M P#9 $1M	Budget $2M	P#3 $1M
Operational		P#8 $2M	P#7 $2M P#5 0

Figure 14-12: Project Distribution Matrix showing budget balances and funding decisions

Graham-Englund Selection Model and the Risk/Benefit Matrix

In the examples shown thus far, the only resource I have been working with is money. However, one of the most important resources, at least for IT projects, is people. Staff resources are composed of professionals of varying skills and experience. As you consider the portfolio of projects, you need to take into account the ability of the staff to deliver that portfolio. For example, if the portfolio were largely new or enhanced strategic applications, you would draw heavily on your most experienced and skilled professionals. What would you do with those who have fewer skills or experience? That is an important consideration, and the Graham-Englund Selection Model approaches project selection with that concern in mind. Basically, it works from a prioritized list of selected projects, and staffs them until certain sets of skilled and/or experienced professionals have been fully allocated. In other words, people, not money, become the constraint on the project portfolio. Several related challenges arise as a result. I will briefly discuss some of the issues and staffing concerns that this approach raises.

The Graham-Englund Selection Model is a close parallel to the models previously discussed, but it has some interesting differences. I added it here because of its simplicity and the fact that it has received some attention in practice. Figure 14-13 illustrates an adaptation of the portfolio project life cycle to the Graham-Englund Selection Model.

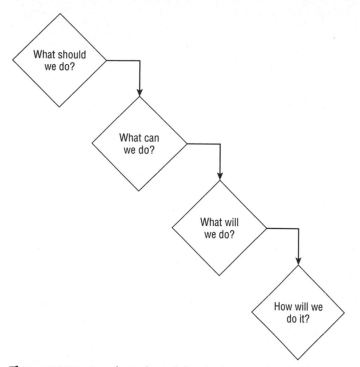

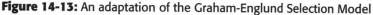

Figure 14-13: An adaptation of the Graham-Englund Selection Model

What Should We Do?

The answer to this question is equivalent to establishing the portfolio strategy. In the case of the Graham-Englund Selection Model, you are referring to the IT strategy of the organization. The answer can be found in the organization's values, mission, and objectives — it is the general direction in which they should be headed consistent with who they are and what they want to be. It is IT's role to support those goals and values. IT will do that by crafting a portfolio of projects consistent with those goals and values. Think of answering "What should we do?" as the demand side of the equation. You will use the project investment categories (infrastructure, maintenance, new products, and research) to identify the projects you should undertake. These categories loosely align with the skill sets of the technical staff and will give you a basis for assigning resources to projects. In fact, any categorization that allows a mapping of skills to projects will do the job. I have kept it simple for the sake of the example, but this approach can get very complex.

Figure 14-14 shows a list of the 10 projects and the skilled positions needed to staff them. The second column gives the number of staff members in each position that are available for these 10 projects. Again, I have kept the data simple for the sake of the example.

	# Available	P#1 I	P#2 I	P#3 M	P#4 M	P#5 M	P#6 N	P#7 N	P#8 N	P#9 R	P#10 R
Senior Project Manager	2	X					X				
Project Manager	3		X	X				X	X	X	
Associate Project Manager	2				X	X					X
Systems Architect	4	X	X				X	X	X	X	
Database Architect	4	X	X				X	X	X	X	
Senior Programmer	2	X	X				X				
Programmer	3	X	X				X	X	X		
Associate Programmer	2			X	X	X					X
Test Technician	5	X	X	X	X	X	X	X	X		

Figure 14-14: Project staffing requirements

A variation that might be incorporated is to replace the Xs in the figure with the percent (%) allocation required. That can be somewhat helpful. But schedule constraints add to the complexity, and %s may not be much better than Xs in the long run.

What Can We Do?

The answer to this question is found by comparing project requirements to the organization's resource capacity. Current commitments come into play here, because the organization must look at available capacity rather than just total capacity.

> **NOTE** Dealing with the issue of what your organization can do raises the important issue of having a good human resource staffing model in place — one that considers future growth of the enterprise, current and projected skills inventories, training programs, career development programs, recruiting and hiring policies and plans, turnover, retirements, and so on.

Think of answering "What can we do?" as the supply side of the equation. Figure 14-14 lists the projects that can be done with the staff resources available. Under each project number is the type of project (I = infrastructure, M = maintenance, N = new product, and R = research). However, it does not say which projects will be done. Not all of them can be done simultaneously with the available staff resources, so the question as to which ones will be done is a fair question.

What Will We Do?

The list of projects given in Figure 14-14 is longer than the list of projects you will do. The creation of the "will-do" list implies that some prioritization has taken place. Various criteria such as Return On Investment (ROI), break-even analysis, internal rate of return, and cost/benefit analysis might be used to create this prioritized list. In this example, I use the list that results from the Risk/Benefit Matrix, as shown in Figure 14-15.

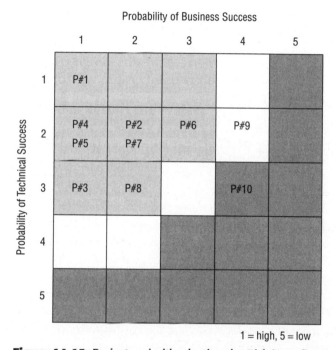

Probability of Business Success

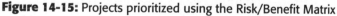

1 = high, 5 = low

Figure 14-15: Projects prioritized using the Risk/Benefit Matrix

The priority ordering of the projects based on the probabilities of success is P#1, P#4, P#5, P#2, P#7, P#3, P#6, P#8, P#9, and P#10. If you staff the projects in that order, you will be able to staff Projects 1, 4, 5, 2, and 7. At that point, you will have assigned all resources except one senior project manager. Projects 3, 6, and 8 did fall in the acceptable risk categories, but no resources are left to staff them.

However, this example is oversimplified. You have assumed that a person is staffed 100 percent to the project. That is unlikely. In reality, a scarce resource would be scheduled to work on projects concurrently to enable more projects to be active. In practice, you would sequence the projects, rather than start them all at the same time. Projects have differing durations, and this difference frees up resources to be reassigned. In any case, the example has shown you how the process works.

How Will We Do It?

Answering this question is roughly equivalent to the selection phase in the portfolio project life cycle. In the case of resource management, "How will we do it?" is just a big staffing and scheduling problem. By scheduling scarce resources across the prioritized list, you are placing more projects on active status — that is, they will be placed in the portfolio. Detailed project plans are put in place, and the scheduling of scarce resources across the projects is coordinated. Performance against those plans is carefully monitored, because the resource schedule has created a dependency between the projects. The critical chain approach to project management offers considerable detail on scheduling scarce resources across multiple projects. The interested reader should refer back to Chapter 10 of this book, which covers Critical Chain Project Management (CCPM) in more detail, and consult the book *Critical Chain Project Management, Second Edition* by Lawrence P. Leach (Artech House, 2005).

Balancing Using Partial Funding or Staffing of Projects

Earlier in the chapter, I asked whether partial funding would be allowed. The tentative answer to the question of partial funding or partial staffing is yes, because it yields a couple of key benefits: It puts more projects into active status, and it gives you a better chance to control the risk in the portfolio. If a partially funded project doesn't meet minimum expectations, it can be postponed or canceled and the remaining resources reallocated to other partially funded projects that do meet expectations. There is one major drawback that the portfolio manager must contend with: The delivery date of the partially funded projects will be extended into the next budget cycle. That may mean a delay in getting products or services into the market, thereby delaying the revenue stream. That has obvious business implications that must be taken into account.

MANAGE the Active Projects

In this last phase, you continuously compare the performance of the projects in the portfolio against your plan. Projects can be in one of three statuses: *on plan*, *off plan*, or *in trouble*. You will see how that status is determined and what action you can take as a result. Here, the challenge is to find performance measures that can be applied equitably across all the projects. The following two come to mind:

- Earned value
- Milestone trend charts

These performance measures are discussed in more detail later in this section.

To bring closure to the final phase, projects can be postponed, canceled, or, believe it or not, completed, and you will see exactly how each of these endings affects the portfolio going forward.

At this point, the project is under way. Regardless of the effort that was expended to put a very precise and complete plan in place, something will happen to thwart those efforts. In the 35 years that I have been managing projects, not a single project went according to plan. That wasn't due to any shortcomings on my part — it is simply a fact of life that unforeseen things will happen that will have an impact on the project. Corrective actions will have to be taken. This section introduces two reporting tools that enable an apples-to-apples comparison of the status of projects in the portfolio. The first tool is applied at the portfolio management level, and the second tool is applied at the project level.

Project Status

As mentioned, there are three categories for the status of active projects: on plan, off plan, or in trouble. The following sections take a look at each of these states and how that status might be determined.

On Plan

Even the best of plans will not result in a project that stays exactly on schedule. A certain amount of variance from the plan is expected and is not indicative of a project in jeopardy. The threshold between on plan and off plan is a subjective call. I offer some guidelines for this variance in the "SPI and CPI Trend Charts" section later in this chapter.

Off Plan

Once a project crosses that threshold value, it moves from on plan to off plan. For a project to be off plan is not unexpected, but getting that project back on plan is expected. If the project manager cannot show the corrective action that will be taken to get the project back on plan and when that event is likely to occur, there is a problem, and the project has now moved to in-trouble status. The project can also move to in-trouble status if it passes a second threshold value that separates off plan from in trouble.

In Trouble

Regardless of the way in which a project reaches the in-trouble condition, the implications are very serious. To be in trouble means that there is little chance the project can be restored. Serious intervention is required, because the problem is out of control and out of the range of the project manager's abilities to correct it. However, just because a project is in trouble doesn't necessarily mean that the project manager is at fault. There may be cases where freak occurrences and random acts of nature have put the project in this category, and the project manager is unable to put a get-well plan in place and is asking for help that goes beyond his or her range of authority. The portfolio manager is considering canceling the project unless there is some compelling reason why that action should not be taken. A new project manager will not necessarily rectify the problem.

The Role of the Project Manager

Obviously, one of the project manager's key responsibilities is the status of the project. While there are many reasons why a project may drift out of plan, it is the responsibility of the project manager to institute corrective measures to restore the project to an on-plan status. The extent to which the project manager meets that responsibility will be obvious from the future status of an off-plan project.

The project manager can also be a cause of an off-plan status. That can happen in a number of ways. In my experience, one of the major contributing factors is the failure of the project manager to have a good system of cross-checking and validating the integrity of the task status being reported by the team. If the project manager does not have a visible process for validating task status, then that is a good indication that scheduling problems are sure to occur.

The second behavioral problem that you see is the failure of the project manager to establish a repeatable and effective communications process. The first place to look for that is in constant questioning from the team members about some aspect of the project that affects their work for which they have little or no knowledge. There should be full disclosure by the project manager to the team. That process begins at planning time and extends through to the closure of the project.

Reporting Portfolio Performance

Two well-known reporting tools can be used to compare the projects across a portfolio and assess the general performance of the portfolio as a whole: earned value and milestone trend charts. Both of these were discussed in detail in Chapter 7, and that discussion is not repeated here. What I will do is take those two reporting tools and show how they can be applied to measuring the performance of the portfolio.

Schedule Performance Index and Cost Performance Index

The schedule performance index (SPI) and cost performance index (CPI) measure earned value as follows:

SPI — This is a measure of how close the project is to performing work as it was actually scheduled. If the project is ahead of schedule, its SPI will be greater than 1; if it is behind schedule, its SPI will be less than 1, which indicates that the work performed was less than the work scheduled.

CPI — This is a measure of how close the project is to spending on the work performed compared to what was planned for spending. If you are spending less on the work performed than was budgeted, the CPI will be greater than 1. If not, and you are spending more than was budgeted for the work performed, then the CPI will be less than 1.

These two indices are intuitive and provide good yardsticks for comparing the projects in a portfolio. Any value less than 1 is undesirable; any value over 1 is good. These indices are displayed graphically as trends compared against the baseline value of 1.

SPI and CPI Trend Charts

The milestone trend charts introduced in Chapter 7 are adapted here to fit the SPI and CPI trends. This section tracks the SPI and CPI over time using the criteria established in Chapter 7. At the risk of repetition, I want to impress upon you the flexibility and power of the integration of SPI and CPI with the milestone trend charts.

Some examples will help. Consider the milestone trend chart for the hypothetical project shown in Figure 14-16. The trend chart plots the SPI and CPI for a single project at weekly reporting intervals. The heavy horizontal line has the value 1. That is the boundary value for each index. Values above 1 indicate an ahead-of-schedule or under-budget situation for that reporting period. Values below 1 indicate a behind-schedule or over-budget situation for that reporting period. Over time these indices tell an interesting story about how the project is progressing or not progressing.

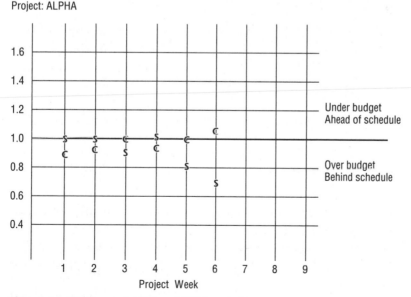

Figure 14-16: Example SPI and CPI trend chart

Figure 14-16 shows that beginning with Week 5, the schedule for Project ALPHA began to slip. The slight improvement in the budget may be explained by work not being done, and hence the cost of work that was scheduled but not done was not logged to the project. This type of relationship between schedule and cost is not unusual.

Spotting Out-of-Control Situations

Certain patterns signal an out-of-control situation. Some examples of this sort of situation are shown in Figures 14-17 through 14-20 and are described in this section.

Figure 14-17 depicts a project schedule slowly slipping out of control. Each report period shows additional slippage since the last report period. Four such successive occurrences, however minor they may seem, require special corrective action on the part of the project manager.

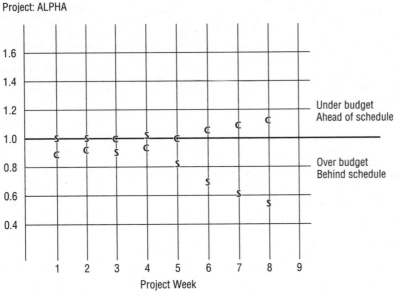

Figure 14-17: A run up or down of four or more successive SPI or CPI values

Figure 14-18 shows a minor over-budget situation. While this may not be significant by itself, that situation has persisted for the last seven report periods. The portfolio manager can fairly ask the project manager why he or she hasn't corrected the situation. The situation isn't serious, but it should have been fixed by now. There may be extenuating circumstances that occurred in the first few weeks of the project that have persisted without any possibility of correction. The CPI and SPI are fairly stable despite their negative performance.

Project: ALPHA

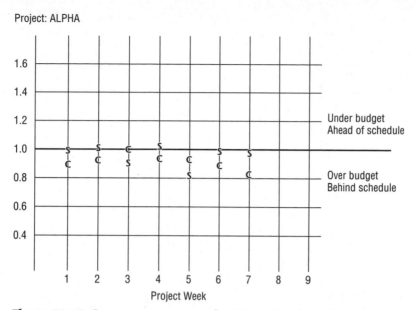

Figure 14-18: Seven or more successive SPI or CPI values above or below 1

Figure 14-19 shows both the SPI and CPI trending in the same direction. The fact that the trend is negative is very serious. Not only is the schedule slipping, there are consistent cost overruns at the same time. If the situation were reversed and the trend were positive, you would obviously have a much better situation. In that case, not only would the project be ahead of schedule, but it would also be running under budget. Figure 14-20 illustrates that scenario.

Project: ALPHA

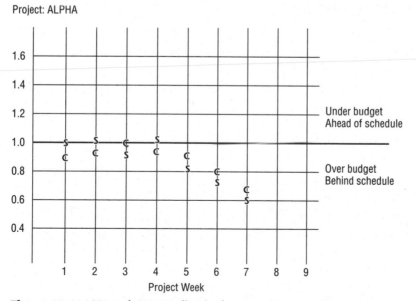

Figure 14-19: SPI and CPI trending in the same negative direction

Project: ALPHA

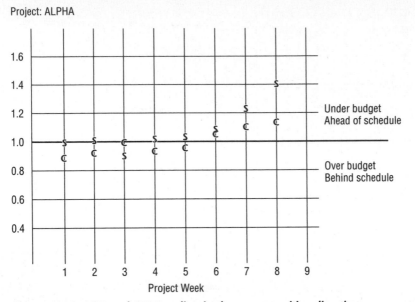

Figure 14-20: SPI and CPI trending in the same positive direction

> **NOTE** Don't be too quick to congratulate the project manager, because it may not be his or her heroic efforts that created such a positive trend. If the duration estimates were too generous and the labor needed to complete the activities was less than estimated, then the project may be ahead of schedule and under budget through no special efforts of anyone on the team. Nonetheless, give the project manager the benefit of the doubt — he or she may indeed have been heroic.

Whether a project is trending to the good or trending to the bad, a good portfolio manager investigates to find out what has happened.

These same data plots can be used to show how the portfolio is performing with respect to both schedule and cost. Figure 14-21 illustrates the hypothetical data for the BETA Program Portfolio. It consists of five projects that all began at the same time. The solid lines are the SPI values for the five projects over the seven-week reporting period. The heavy dotted line is the portfolio average. Although the portfolio has been behind schedule for the entire seven weeks, it is trending upward and has nearly reached an on-schedule situation. The same type of plot can show budget performance for the portfolio as well.

Portfolio: BETA Program

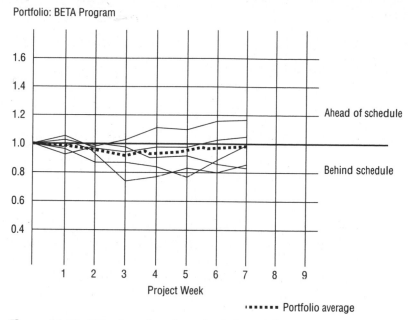

Figure 14-21: SPI values for a hypothetical portfolio

Closing Projects in the Portfolio

Best practices include acceptance criteria — agreed upon by the client and the project manager during project planning — that clearly state when the project is considered finished. This acceptance criteria usually takes the form of a checklist of scope items or requirements. When all items on the checklist have been checked off as completed, the project is deemed finished. The work of the project, however, is not yet complete. What remains is what I call a *post-implementation audit*. This section examines the activities and contents of a post-implementation audit and discusses why it is so important that one be done.

Attainment of Explicit Business Value

Each project was proposed based on the value it would return to the enterprise if it were funded and completed successfully. Was that value achieved? This is a question that may not be answerable until some time after the project is complete, but it is a question that deserves an answer. This proposed value was the justification for the project and a major factor in placing the project in the portfolio in the first place.

Lessons Learned

Following are several questions that might be asked about a project just completed:

- Were the project goals and objectives achieved?
- Was the project work done on time?
- Was the client satisfied with the project results?
- Was the explicit business value (as defined in the success criteria) realized?
- What modules were learned about your project management methodology? What worked? What didn't work?
- How well did the team follow the methodology?

All of these questions are important and should be answered. In some cases, the particular nature of the project may render some questions more important than others, but that does not excuse the project team from answering all of them. Some of the most important information about the project management process can be found in these answers, so they should be shared with all other project teams.

Roles and Responsibilities of the PSO in Portfolio Management

The Project Support Office (PSO) is an essential ingredient in any portfolio management process. Their role is supportive to two audiences: the project sponsor and the portfolio manager.

Project Sponsor

The PSO is safe harbor for the project sponsor in that it helps the project sponsor and project manager prepare the project proposal for submission to the portfolio process and then helps shepherd the proposal through the process. There will likely be several cycles of revision and review before the portfolio manager can make a good business decision with respect to the business value of the proposed project. The PSO is in the unique position of being helpful to that process more than any other.

Portfolio Manager

The PSO provides the administrative support function for the portfolio manager. In that capacity, the PSO is generally charged with the responsibilities described in the following subsections.

Proposal Intake and Evaluation

One-stop shopping for project proposal submission and evaluation with respect to alignment to the portfolio strategy is a must. This brings consistency to the process. As part of the intake process, the project sponsor should make his or her assessment of that alignment. This often takes the form of citing which strategic objectives the proposed project addresses and how they are addressed. It is, however, the final responsibility of the PSO to make that formal determination.

Project Prioritization

Having done the intake evaluation as stated previously, the PSO is now in the best position to choose the ranking process that is appropriate and to execute that process. Any one of the ranking models discussed earlier in this chapter can be used, but the PSO must convey to the project sponsor which model they are going to use for this purpose.

Selection Support to the Portfolio Manager

The portfolio manager makes the final decisions as to which projects are placed in the portfolio. The PSO supports the portfolio manager with any further data or analyses that might be required.

Monitoring and Reporting to the Portfolio Manager

Monitoring and reporting project performance to the portfolio manager is an administrative function provided by the PSO. The PSO is responsible for gathering and validating project performance reports and consolidating them to the portfolio level. Dashboard-type reports are commonly used here. This type of report gives the portfolio manager the capacity to drill down into specific projects and discover reasons for anomalies or use other cross-project performance metrics of interest to the portfolio manager. There are several commercial software applications on the market to support these activities.

Facilitate Project Review Sessions

Formal project review sessions are major Stage Gates in the life cycle of every project in the portfolio. These may be quarterly, or they may occur more often for short-duration projects. The project review is conducted to assess project status against the project plan. Various project-specific metrics are used to assist in that analysis. Risk, issues, and problems are discussed with various mitigation strategies suggested or reviewed from previous project reviews. While these project reviews provide excellent data into the portfolio process, they are also designed to help the project manager. The project review board should be chaired by a PSO member and include two or three senior project managers and perhaps a client manager. In the interest of fairness and impartiality, the senior project managers on the project review board should not be managing projects from the same portfolio.

Preparing Your Project for Submission to the Portfolio Management Process

Now that you understand the portfolio management process, you should have a pretty good idea of what you need to do to prepare your project proposal for submission and consideration as part of a portfolio. Your organization may require you to follow a prescribed procedure for proposing your project. If not, I suggest that you prepare your project proposal in one of the following ways:

- Adapt the POS, which was discussed in detail in Chapter 4. The POS will work quite well but may need some additional information, such as cost and time estimates, that is traditionally not part of the POS.

- Try a two-step approach. Submit the POS first to determine the alignment of your project, and then prepare a detailed project plan to submit time and cost data to the prioritization and selection phases.

- Develop an entirely new submission process based on the five-phase portfolio management process.

The next three sections describe each one of these options.

A Revised Project Overview Statement

As discussed in detail in Chapter 4, the POS is a short document (ideally one page) that concisely states what is to be done in the project, why it is to be done, and what value it will provide to the organization when completed.

When it is used in the portfolio management process, the main purpose of the POS is to have the portfolio committee evaluate the project and determine whether it is in alignment with the corporate strategy. Later, it will be reviewed by the managers who are responsible for setting priorities and deciding what projects to support in the portfolio. For this reason, the POS cannot contain any technical jargon that generally would not be used across the enterprise. Once approved, the POS becomes the foundation for future planning and execution of the project. It also becomes the reference document for questions or conflicts regarding project scope and purpose.

Parts of the POS

The POS has the following five component parts:

- Problem/opportunity statement
- Project goal
- Project objectives
- Success criteria
- Assumptions, risks, and obstacles

Recall that its structure is designed to lead the reader from a statement of fact (problem/opportunity) to a statement of what this project will address (project goal). Given that senior management is interested in the project goal and that it addresses a concern of sufficiently high priority, they will read more detail about exactly what the project includes (project objectives). The organizational value is expressed as quantitative outcomes (success criteria). Finally, a summary of conditions that may hinder project success are identified (assumptions, risks, and obstacles). The following list looks at each of these parts more closely as they apply to the project portfolio process:

Problem/opportunity statement — The first part of the POS is a statement of the strategic objectives that the project is addressing. If appropriate, the statement should come directly from the company's strategic plan or be based on the portfolio strategy. This is critical, because it provides a basis for the rest of the document. It also sets the priority with which the portfolio manager will view what follows. If you are addressing a high-priority area or a high-value area, your idea will get more attention and the reader will read on.

Project goal — The second section of the POS states the goal of the project: what you intend to do to address the strategic objectives identified in the previous section. The purpose of the goal statement is to get senior management to value the idea enough to read on. In other words, they should think enough of your approach to the corporate strategy to conclude that it warrants further attention and consideration. Several other proposals will pertain to the same objectives. Because yours will not be the only one submitted, you want it to stand out among the crowd.

The goal statement must not contain any language or terminology that might not be understandable to anyone having occasion to read it. In other words, no techie talk allowed. It is written in the language of the organization so that anyone who reads it will understand it without further explanation from the proposer. Under all circumstances, avoid jargon.

Keep the goal statement short and to the point. Keep in mind that the more you write, the more you increase the risk that someone will find fault with something you have said. The goal statement does not include any information that might commit the project to dates or deliverables that are not practical. Remember that you don't have much detail about the project at this point.

Project objectives — The third section of the POS presents the project objectives. Here is your chance to show more breadth to your project and bind it even tighter to one or more of the strategic objectives.

Success criteria — The fourth section of the POS answers the question "Why do we want to do this project?" It is the measurable explicit business outcome that will result from doing the project. It sells the project to the portfolio manager. This may be the most important part of the POS. The portfolio manager is trying to maximize the value that can be generated from the portfolio. Every project has to contribute to that value.

The question that you have to answer is this: What business value will result from successfully completing the project? The answer to this question will be a statement of the explicit business outcome to be realized. It is essential that the criteria be quantifiable and measurable, and, if possible, expressed in terms of business value. Remember that you are trying to sell your idea to the portfolio manager.

As an added value statement, consider quantifiable statements about the impact your project will have on efficiency and effectiveness, error rates, reduced turnaround time to service a client request, reduced cost of providing service, quality, or improved client satisfaction. Management deals in deliverables, so always try to express success criteria in quantitative terms. By doing this, you avoid any possibility of disagreement later as to whether the success criteria were met and the project was successful. The portfolio manager will look at your success criteria and assign organizational value to your project. In the absence of other criteria, this success criteria will be the basis for his or her decision regarding whether or not to place the project in the portfolio.

Assumptions, risks, and obstacles — The fifth section of the POS identifies any factors that can affect the outcome of the project and that you want to bring to the attention of the portfolio manager. These factors can affect deliverables, the realization of the success criteria, the ability of the project team to complete the project as planned, or any other environmental or organizational conditions that are relevant to the project. Record anything that can go wrong. Be careful, however, to put in the POS only those items that you want senior management to know about and in which they will be interested.

The project manager uses this section to alert the portfolio manager to any factors that may interfere with the project work or compromise whatever contribution the project can make to the organization. Do not assume that everyone already knows what risks and perils to the project exist. Document them and discuss them.

POS Attachments

The best way I have found to provide the important time and cost information with your POS is through one or more selected attachments. As part of their initial evaluation and prioritization of your project proposal, portfolio management may want some measure of the economic value of the proposed project. They recognize that many of the estimates are little more than a guess, but they will nevertheless ask for this information.

> **TIP** I recommend giving range estimates rather than point estimates. You don't have enough detail at this point to do any better.

In my experience, I recommend that you consider adding one of the following two types of analyses to your POS:

Risk analysis — In my experience, this is the most frequently used attachment to the POS. In some cases, this analysis is a very cursory treatment. In other cases, it is a mathematically rigorous exercise. Many business decision models depend on quantifying risks, expected loss if the risk materializes, and the probability that the risk will occur. All of these are quantified, and the resulting analyses guide the portfolio manager in decisions on project approval. Risk management is discussed in detail in Chapter 3 and briefly in Chapter 4.

Financial analyses — Some portfolio managers may require a preliminary financial analysis of the project. Although such analyses are very rough because not enough information is known about the project at this time, they will still be useful. In some instances, they also offer criteria for prioritizing all of the POS submissions that the portfolio manager will be reviewing. Some of the possible analyses are feasibility studies, cost/benefit analyses, and breakeven analyses. These are all discussed in Chapter 4.

A Two-Step Submission Process

The first step in the two-step submission process is to submit the POS as described in the previous section. Once the alignment decision has been made and the project is aligned with the portfolio strategy, the second step can be taken. The second step is to prepare and submit the detailed project plan. The plan can contain information that would be useful for later decisions, but this information is generally not provided unless it will be used. The strategy in the two-step process is to do the extensive planning work only if the project is deemed to be in alignment with the portfolio strategy. An added benefit to the two-step process is that *how* the project is aligned may also be useful information for the planning work. In my experience, the planning effort can take a number of directions, and knowing specifically how the project relates to the portfolio strategy can produce better and more targeted business value.

A New Submission Process

If you are going to fashion a new submission process based on the five-phase portfolio management process, I advocate a single submission that contains all of the information needed to take the project up to the SELECT stage of the project portfolio life cycle. What information is needed to reach that point? Here is a list for your consideration:

Project name — This should be a name that provides some indication of what the project is all about. Don't use code names like XP.47.

Sponsor name — This is the name, position title, and business unit affiliation of the sponsoring individual.

Project manager name — Add this if known.

Project funding category — This will attach the project to some part of the portfolio strategy. In some cases, multiple categories may be given.

Project goal — This will be the same type of statement you would have used in the POS for this project.

Project objectives — This will be the same type of statements you would have used in the POS for this project.

CASE STUDY – PIZZA DELIVERED QUICKLY (PDQ)

The entire PDQ project could be viewed as a program consisting of several dependent projects. Once the component parts of the project have been identified through the initial changes, including those introduced by Dee, the project might be represented as shown in Figure 14-22.

If one views this as a program consisting of six projects — one for each subsystem — there are a number of ways to approach finding the solution. The Order Entry and Inventory Management subsystems should be available as commercial off-the-shelf products. A Request for Information (RFI) or Request for Proposal (RFP) can reach that conclusion quickly. The other subsystems are quite different. All four require some form of heuristic algorithms as part of their solutions. The difficulty with each of these is that order preparation can be at one of three sites. The stores and the pizza factories are fixed in place, whereas the pizza vans are moving locations. The same moving location problem complicates the Routing subsystem. So these four subsystems are highly interdependent, and an optimal solution may not be possible. That is why a heuristics approach may be the best approach.

CASE STUDY — PIZZA DELIVERED QUICKLY (PDQ)

As far as a portfolio approach is concerned, this could be viewed as two separate submissions. One would be for the Order Entry, Order Submit, and Inventory Management subsystems. Together they provide an operational solution for the current store situation. The other would be the Logistics and Routing projects that deal with the complexities added by one moving component — the pizza vans that prepare pizzas and that can also deliver pizzas. Even that solution could be done in stages. The first stage would incorporate the pizza factories as just another fixed location for preparation. The second stage would add the pizza vans as moving preparation locations. The Adaptive Project Framework (APF) works well regardless of the approach taken.

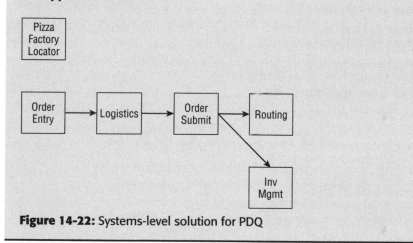

Figure 14-22: Systems-level solution for PDQ

Explicit business value — This is a very important piece of the submission. Here you have to establish the business value for this project. Make a quantitative statement about increased revenue, decreased cost, or improved service. It must be a measurable metric.

Risks — When combined with project cost and explicit business value, this gives financial analysts the grist for their mill. This is where the true business validation of the project is made or lost.

Estimated total project cost — You do not have a detailed project plan at this point, so all that you can give is a range estimate.

Estimated project duration — You do not know when the project will begin, so you cannot give a completion date. The statement you want to make here is something like, "This project will be completed eight months after the start date," or even better, "This project can be completed in six to nine months following its start date."

Agile Project Portfolio Management

As maturing organizations begin to implement Agile Project Management (APM), they need to consider how their current portfolio management process needs to be revised in order to accommodate APM, xPM, and MPx projects. At the time I was writing this edition of the book, there wasn't very much literature on Agile Project Portfolio Management. *Agile Portfolio Management* by Jochen Krebs (Microsoft Press, 2008) was the only book that I could find in print that deals with this topic.

Agile Project Portfolio Management is a logical consequence of the agile movement. Agile projects are those that are continuously redirected to take advantage of the learning and discovery about the solution that arises from the work of the project. Extend that same concept to the portfolio. At regular intervals the contents of the portfolio are changed and redirected to take advantage of the learning and discovery that arises from the performance of projects in the portfolio and from new project initiatives.

Agile Project Portfolio Management includes establishing the investment strategy of the portfolio, determining what types of projects/programs can be incorporated in the portfolio, evaluating alignment of the proposed projects to the strategy, prioritizing proposed projects/programs, constructing a balanced portfolio that will achieve the investment objectives, monitoring the performance of the portfolio, and at regular intervals adjusting the contents of the portfolio in order to maintain alignment to the strategy and achievement of the desired results.

NOTE *Agile* refers to the contents of the portfolio not to the type of projects in the portfolio. Projects of any type can be part of an agile project portfolio.

Just as an APM or Extreme Project Management (xPM) project is continuously adjusted to deliver maximum business value, so should the agile project portfolio be adjusted. This means that at periodic review points, every project in the portfolio is evaluated to ensure that the contents of the portfolio are always aligned with the objectives of the portfolio. This also means that project priorities can change from review to review. Projects in the portfolio might be re-scoped, put on hold, delayed, stretched out over a longer time horizon, or outright canceled. New projects might be brought into the portfolio at these review points, too. The objective at these project review points is to adjust the projects in the portfolio that will be active for the next period and that produce the greatest expected business value of any combination of active projects. The portfolio will then contain new projects, projects postponed at some previous review point, as well as continued and continuing projects from the previous review for the next period.

Projects can change their status at any time. For example, if an active project becomes distressed, it may make no business sense to continue the project. So, it is canceled or postponed. In either case, the unused resources for that project now become available for projects being considered for the next portfolio review.

The agile project portfolio life cycle looks very similar to the project portfolio life cycle previously depicted in Figure 14-1. Figure 14-23 is the agile project portfolio life cycle.

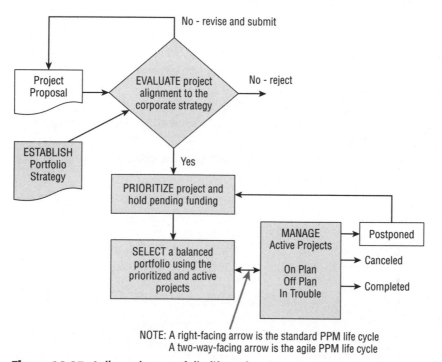

Figure 14-23: Agile project portfolio life cycle

The only difference between Figure 14-1 and Figure 14-23 is the two-way arrow linking "MANAGE active projects" to "SELECT a balanced portfolio using the prioritized and active projects." The agile project portfolio life cycle inputs the active projects to the SELECT activity. This means that the active projects must contend with the new projects for priority in the next portfolio. Creating a single prioritized list containing active projects from the just-completed portfolio cycle with new projects is a complex decision. New projects do not have a performance or business value history. Active projects do. One criterion that might be used is expected business value in the next portfolio cycle. For active and new projects, business value is a subjective estimate. Active projects do have a history of estimated versus actual business value, which may be used to adjust estimated business value for the next portfolio cycle.

Integrating a PMLC Model into the Agile Project Portfolio Management Process

In order to accommodate the Agile Project Portfolio Management (APPM) process you will need to define a very high-level PMLC that embraces the projects in all four quadrants. Whatever form your portfolio management process takes, it will have to be modified to align with some type of cyclical pattern. The cycles can be monthly, quarterly, semi-annual, or even annual. Either a quarterly or semi-annual portfolio cycle length will probably fit your organization's needs. Arguments can be put forth for longer as well as shorter cycles. This Executive Report assumes a quarterly portfolio cycle length. APM projects will have shorter duration iterations, but those projects can be planned so that several iterations can fit into a single cycle.

Figure 14-24 is a high-level PMLC model that can be adapted to any type of project and is one that fits a cyclical APPM process.

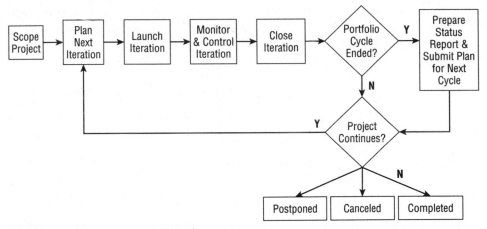

Figure 14-24: A PMLC model for the APPM process

This high-level PMLC model accommodates all four major project types (TPM, APM, xPM, and MPx) and will integrate directly into the APPM shown in Figure 14-23. There are some minor adjustments, however. First, the APPM process is cyclical, so to be compatible with it all projects in the portfolio must follow some type of cyclical model. That is true for all APM, xPM, and MPx projects, but not for all TPM projects. Within TPM approaches the Linear PMLC model does not fit but the Incremental PMLC model does. Any project that would otherwise use a Linear PMLC model will have to be planned using an Incremental PMLC model. The only other consideration is to have the completion of iterations of the project PMLC model align with the completion of the portfolio cycles of the APPM process. That has implications to PMLC iteration planning and is not a major obstacle.

The APPM life cycle consists of the following five phases and shown by the shaded boxes in Figure 14-23:

- ESTABLISH
- EVALUATE
- PRIORITIZE
- SELECT
- MANAGE

Prior to releasing the human resource investment plan, two questions should be answered by the portfolio manager:

- Will projects be partially staffed in order to include more projects in the portfolio, or will projects be staffed only at the level of their request?
- If an investment category has excess resources after project staffing decisions have been made, can those resources be reallocated to other investment categories without compromising the portfolio strategy, and if so, how will they be reallocated?

If possible, it is good to make these decisions before the situations arise. The rules need to be clear so that all parties are informed ahead of time.

This approach puts both new and active projects on the same metric for prioritization decisions, but the decision to be made is still not obvious. There is some value in having a team stay together on an active project rather than splitting the team up to staff a new project. That suggests building a tentative list of projects to be included in the coming portfolio and then staffing all active projects in the coming portfolio first. Staffing can then move to the new projects until the next project on the prioritized list cannot be staffed. Figure 14-25 graphically portrays how that staffing model might work.

Once the active projects that have been tentatively placed in the portfolio for the next portfolio cycle have been staffed, the prioritized list of new projects will be staffed as shown in Figure 14-25. This approach avoids the complications of trying to create an unbiased metric that can be used fairly on both new and active projects to create a single prioritized list of new and active projects.

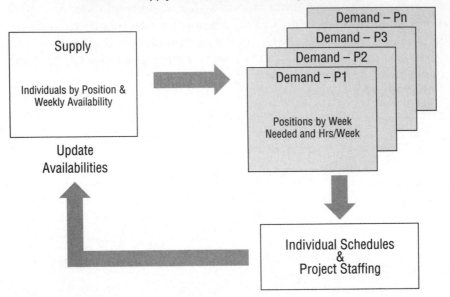

Figure 14-25: Portfolio staffing model

Challenges of Managing Agile Portfolios

The contents of the agile portfolio are at risk at the end of every portfolio cycle. That raises a number of challenges for portfolio managers and those who submit project proposals for consideration. Among those challenges are:

- Choosing between continuing a project for another cycle or postponing it and replacing it with a new or previously postponed project

- Postponing projects risks losing team members if the project should later be returned to active status

- Changing portfolio contents from one cycle to another may lead to a higher probability of project failure due to increased thrashing and missed windows of opportunity

- Comparing the expected business value of a traditional project against an agile project is like comparing apples to oranges

Handling High Change and High Speed

Change is constant in the contemporary business world. Most would agree that change is changing at an increasing rate. Factor into that the constant technology changes and market changes, and most organizations will have a very difficult time keeping up and maintaining their competitive position. If they don't leverage the technology quickly or at all, someone else will, and they will lose market share and market position. That translates to having a portfolio management process that can adapt and respond intelligently and quickly to unexpected change. That is the purpose of an agile approach to project portfolio management.

Managing Complexity and Uncertainty

High change and high speed are positively correlated with increasing complexity and uncertainty. The contents of the portfolio at any point in time represent the portfolio manager's best guess at how to leverage projects to exploit the near-term future. No one knows the future so there is the accompanying risk to the portfolio that you have decided on the wrong course of action. If you had had perfect knowledge of the future, the portfolio would have been properly constructed to return maximum business value for the investment. No one has that knowledge, so all you can do is make best guesses and make the appropriate decisions as to the contents of the portfolio. Those decisions will be made on a regular basis, say quarterly. On a quarterly basis the contents of the portfolio may be changed for the coming quarter and that process repeated without end.

Nurturing Creativity

Because the contents of an agile portfolio can change at regular intervals, that change will affect the creative environment needed to support the projects. On the one hand agile and extreme project teams may not be fully committed to a complex and uncertain project if the threat of postponement or cancelation looms on the horizon. Conversely, the agile or extreme project team may be even more committed to success and exemplary performance in order to protect the continuation of their project as much as they can. Both scenarios impact creativity and the project manager will need to pay particular attention to evidence of the impact.

SELECT a Balanced Portfolio

You might think that because you have a prioritized list in each support category and you know the resources available for those projects, the selection process would be simple and straightforward, but it isn't. Selection is a very challenging task for any portfolio management team. The problem stems from the apparent conflict between the results of evaluation, the ranking of projects from most valuable to least valuable, the need to balance the portfolio with respect to one or more variables, and the availability of skilled professionals. These factors are often in conflict with one another. As a further complication, you may decide that partial staffing of projects makes sense. Partial staffing extends the total duration of the project and can increase the risk of project postponement or failure.

There are several approaches to picking the project portfolio. I've chosen to focus on the Graham-Englund Selection Model (Figure 14-26).

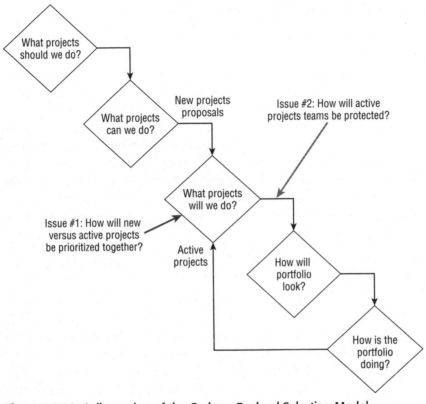

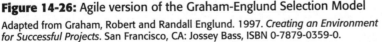

Figure 14-26: Agile version of the Graham-Englund Selection Model

Adapted from Graham, Robert and Randall Englund. 1997. *Creating an Environment for Successful Projects.* San Francisco, CA: Jossey Bass, ISBN 0-7879-0359-0.

Very few organizations use a complete project selection process for their portfolio. Many are based on dollars available in the portfolio and ignore staffing. Once the projects have been allocated to the Risk versus Business Value Project Distribution Matrix and you have generated Table 14-1, you will have a prioritized list of projects. Then the Graham-Englund Model can be used to determine how many of the projects, starting at the top of the list, can be staffed. Staffing constraints may affect priorities when lower priority projects can be staffed when higher priority projects may not have the available staffing.

What Should We Do?

The answer to this question is equivalent to establishing the portfolio strategy. In the case of the Graham-Englund Selection Model, you are probably referring to the IT strategy of the organization. The answer can be found in the organization's values, mission, and objectives; it is the general direction in which they should be headed consistent with who they are and what they want to be. It is the role of IT to support those goals and values. IT will do that by crafting a portfolio of projects consistent with those goals and values. Think of answering "What should we do?" as the demand side of the equation. You will use the project class (new, enhancement, maintenance) and the project type (strategic, tactical, and operational) to identify the projects you should undertake. These categories loosely align with the skill sets of the technical staff and will give you a basis for assigning resources to projects. In fact, any categorization that allows a mapping of skills to projects will do the job. I have kept it simple for the sake of the example, but this approach can get very complex. One complexity arises when the full-time equivalent (FTE) schedule commitments of a staff member are plotted against the project requirements and schedule for those skills.

What Can We Do?

The answer to this question is found by comparing project requirements to the organization's resource capacity. Current commitments come into play here, as the organization must look at available capacity, rather than just total capacity.

Dealing with the issue of what your organization can do raises the important issue of having a good human resource staffing model in place — one that considers future growth of the enterprise, current and projected skills inventories, training programs, career development programs, recruiting and hiring policies and plans, turnover, retirements, and so on.

Think of answering "What can we do?" as the supply side of the equation in Figure 14-26.

What Will We Do?

There are adjustments that can be made to allow more projects to be done. For example, if the bottleneck is the programmer staff, an adjustment of required programmers by level might be relaxed to allow lower-level programmers to fill project requirements.

How Will We Do It?

Answering this question is roughly equivalent to the selection phase in the portfolio project life cycle. In the case of resource management, "How will we do it?" is just a big staffing and scheduling problem. By scheduling scarce resources across the prioritized list, you are placing more projects on active status; that is, they will be placed in the portfolio. Detailed project plans are put in place, and the scheduling of scarce resources across the projects is coordinated. Performance against those plans is carefully monitored because the resource schedule has created a dependency between the projects. A critical chain approach could be used here. Consult the book *Critical Chain Project Management* by Lawrence Leach (Artech House, 2000).

MANAGE Active Projects

In this last phase, you continuously compare the performance of the projects in the portfolio against your plan. Projects can be in one of three statuses: *on plan*, *off plan*, or *in trouble*. These were discussed earlier in this chapter. You will see how that status is determined and what action you can take as a result. Here, the challenge is to find performance measures that can be applied equitably across all the projects. Two come to mind:

- Earned value
- Milestone trend charts

A detailed discussion of these was given earlier in this chapter.

Available Human Resources

If you increase the task variety assigned to an individual, you increase the risk of failure of all the tasks assigned to them. That applies to changing project assignments, too. To the extent possible you should try to keep a team intact. If the project is continued to the next cycle, that should not be a problem unless the project has moved further down in the prioritized list. The model may assign some or all of the team members to the higher priority projects, leaving less-skilled staff for the continuing project. Despite the simplicity of the expected business value approach, there will be subjective decisions regarding staff assignments.

Closing Projects in the Agile Portfolio

Best practices include acceptance criteria, agreed upon by the client and the project manager during project planning, that clearly state when the project is considered finished. These acceptance criteria usually take the form of a checklist of scope items or requirements. When all items on the checklist have been checked off as completed, the project is deemed finished. The work of the project, however, is not yet complete. What remains is what I have called a *post-implementation audit*. See Chapter 8.

Because the agile portfolio can contain any type of project, there are some added considerations. Those projects that are APM, xPM, or MPx deal with varying degrees of uncertainty. That means that the cycle-to-cycle expected business value may or may not be realized. In judging the short-term delivered value the portfolio manager cannot ignore the long-term expectations. They will change as a function of short-term delivered value. How to prioritize such projects is difficult and usually reduces to subjective decisions. That is the nature of uncertainty, and the portfolio manager just has to deal with it.

Putting It All Together

This chapter showed you a model for Project Portfolio Management and described several contemporary tools and processes that you might employ to implement it. In effect, I have given you a starter kit for building your own Project Portfolio Management Process. If you are a project manager and have to submit your project to a portfolio committee for approval, you now have a strategy for doing that, along with some hope for success.

This chapter has also outlined a Project Portfolio Management life cycle using an agile strategy. At regular intervals, say quarterly, the performance of each project in the portfolio is assessed against the planned performance for the just completed cycle. Adjustments to the project contents will be made in order to maximize the expected business value from the next cycle of the portfolio. Adjustments can be of several types:

- Some active projects will be continued for the next cycle
- Some active projects will be canceled
- Some active projects will be judged complete
- Some new projects will be added to the portfolio for the next cycle

Care must be taken to not change the contents of the portfolio more than common sense would suggest. Too much variation in contents from cycle to cycle can turn out to be counterproductive.

Discussion Questions

1. In what ways, if any, would Traditional Project Management (TPM), APM, and xPM projects affect your project portfolio management process? Be specific.

2. What criteria (time, cost, value, and so on) must a sequence of activities meet in order to qualify as a project for the portfolio?

3. What types of data will you need in order to evaluate, prioritize, and select projects for the portfolio?

4. An APM Project Portfolio Management Process differs from the TPM Project Portfolio Management Process in that in the agile version a project could have a change of state for no reason other than a competing project has a higher likelihood of delivering greater business value. So what are the advantages and disadvantages of using an agile versus traditional process for managing the project portfolio?

5. Your company has recently implemented an agile portfolio management process. You are the portfolio manager and are constantly getting complaints about the number of projects that are postponed at each quarterly review only to be restarted at the next quarterly review. How do you respond?

CHAPTER 15

Establishing and Managing a Continuous Process Improvement Program

Become addicted to constant and never-ending self improvement.
— Anthony J. D'Angelo, *The College Blue Book*

We're supposed to be perfect our first day on the job and then show constant improvement.
— Ed Vargo, major league baseball umpire

Continual improvement is an unending journey.
— Lloyd Dobens and Clare Crawford-Mason, *Thinking About Quality*

In today's business climate, there is no difference between standing still and going backwards.
— Robert K. Wysocki, Ph.D. President, Enterprise Information Insights, Inc.

CHAPTER LEARNING OBJECTIVES

After reading this chapter, you will be able to:

- Understand the differences between project management processes and practices
- Know what process and practice maturity is all about
- Be able to explain the five levels of maturity
- Understand and be able to construct the Process Quality Matrix (PQM) and the Zone Map
- Have a working knowledge of the Continuous Process Improvement Model (CPIM)
- Know the benefits of having a CPIM
- Be able to diagram a business process
- Know how to use and interpret the eight tools for business process analysis

Once an organization implements a project management methodology and even takes the next step by putting a Project Support Office (PSO) in place to support it, the road to a mature project management environment has just begun. I have never had a client who put a project management life cycle (PMLC) model in place and didn't quickly come to the realization that a process improvement program would have to follow closely on the heels of that implementation. That's just some of the baggage that goes along with effective project management. The discipline is constantly undergoing change and improvement. Effective complex project management is a work in process and will be that way for the foreseeable future. Get used to it!

Almost from the beginning, there should be a continuous effort to improve the *practice* and the *process* of project management. This should be an ongoing effort that really has no end. Indeed, the post-implementation audit that follows every project at its completion includes this effort through its lessons-learned section.

In this chapter, I present a Continuous Process Improvement Model (CPIM) for project management that I developed and have been using for more than 20 years with a high level of client satisfaction. It is based on an adaptation of the process quality matrix, which was introduced by Maurice Hardaker and Bryan K. Ward in 1987 ("How to Make a Team Work," *Harvard Business Review*, Nov.–Dec.) as a business process improvement tool. I've taken their model and adapted it to project management process improvement. The model defines where you are, can be used to define where you would like to be, and gives you some guidance on how you might go about getting there. It is a practical and easily implemented program that requires no special training. In my consulting practice I run a two-day CPIM workshop and that prepares the client with a working knowledge of the process specific to their organization and how to implement it.

Understanding Project Management Processes and Practices

Every effective project management process and CPIM must consider two aspects of project management: its process and its practice.

The Project Management Process

First, there is the project management process itself, which answers the following questions:

- How was it developed?
- How complete is it?
- How is it documented?

- How is it supported?
- How is it updated?

The answers to all five of these questions are critical to the quality of the project management process. I want to take a quick look at each one of these questions.

How Was It Developed?

There are two common approaches to developing a project management process: do it yourself or commission a task force to do it. The first approach is unacceptable. You may be the best project manager your organization has ever had, but if you develop the project management process in the back room and deploy it to the organization like Venus on the half-shell, don't expect a broad base of endorsement. It's the "not invented here" syndrome.

The second approach is the only one that makes sense to me. The task force should consist of representatives from each of the constituencies that will use the project management process. The constituency group should include each class of project managers and business analysts as well as any relevant resource managers. The PSO should provide the task force manager.

How Complete Is It?

Every PMLC model should include tools, templates, and processes from which the project manager can select what works for him or her. The specific characteristics of the project should guide in that selection. Experience and feedback on its use are a good measure of completeness. If the project teams are force-fitting or using their own stuff, that's a good sign that the project management process is not complete.

How Is It Documented?

About 20 years ago, one of my clients had just completed the documentation of their new project management process and asked me if I would review it for them. I agreed. They escorted me into a room that had one long table and a chair. On the table was a set of manuals that extended to about 10 linear feet. My review was very short. I told them that if they expected anyone to actually use this, they had better find some other way of packaging it.

At the other end of the spectrum, another client had built a website to house the documentation. It consisted of three levels of detail: executive, reference, and tutorial. The executive level was usually a one-page, intuitive graphic with links to the reference level. The reference level consisted of a few graphics with one or two pages of descriptive information with links to the tutorial level. The tutorial level consisted of detailed instructions on how to use the tool, template, or process. At this level, the best-practices library was housed. The user could drill down to their level of interest and have only what they needed displayed on the screen. That worked!

How Is It Supported?

Training (online and instructor-led), coaching, and mentoring should be available, especially with respect to the process changes.

How Is It Updated?

The PSO should be the steward of the PMLC model process documentation. Through project reviews and other feedback from the team and the client, the PSO gathers ideas and suggestions for improvements. These should be reviewed by the task force, and revisions written as appropriate. At regular intervals (initially quarterly and later semi-annual) updates should be published.

The Practice of the Project Management Process

Second, there is the practice of the project management process, which answers the following questions:

- Are all project managers required to use the process?
- Can project managers substitute other tools, templates, and processes as they deem appropriate?
- Is there a way to incorporate best practices into the practice of the project management process?
- How are project managers monitored for compliance?
- How are corrective action steps taken to correct for noncompliance?
- How are project manager practices monitored for best practices?

Again, I want to take a quick look at each one of these questions.

Are All Project Managers Required to Use the Process?

The best project management process ever developed is of no use if only a few project teams are using it. If the PMLC model process was developed correctly and is stable, complete, and supported, this is a reasonable prerequisite for its use. The more successful implementations I have seen allow the project manager to deviate from the documented tool, template, or process if the nature of the project is such that that deviation makes sense. In such cases, the project manager simply needs to document that they are not using it and why. There may be occasions where modification makes sense. Again they should document the change and why it was made. This documentation should be archived in a best practices file.

Can Project Managers Substitute Other Tools, Templates, and Processes as They Deem Appropriate?

There will be some tools, templates, and processes that are required because they are needed elsewhere in the organization — a Project Overview Statement (POS), for example. I have a client whose PMLC model consists of 43 processes, of which only 13 are required. The remaining 30 processes are optional. If any of the 13 required processes are not used or changed, the reason must be documented.

Is There a Way to Incorporate Best Practices into the Practice of the Project Management Process?

If the toolkit for your PMLC model documentation is complete, there should be no reason for this deviation. However, allowing the possibility that a new employee brings a better mousetrap, you should allow this deviation. Again, justification is needed. In the case of a tool, template, or process that is new to the organization, some documentation of it should be required. That allows the task force or PSO to vet it for possible inclusion.

How Are Project Managers Monitored for Compliance?

The project review is the best opportunity to formally review compliance. These reviews should be scheduled quarterly or at significant milestones. If there is evidence of noncompliance, corrective action steps can be suggested and the status of those corrective action steps checked at the next project review. Some observations on compliance might be made informally during mentoring or coaching sessions with the team, followed by more formal suggestions by the project review board.

How Are Corrective Action Steps Taken to Correct for Noncompliance?

At project reviews, specific corrective action steps are directed to the project manager. It is expected that the project manager will be compliant at the next project review. These are serious situations and should be treated very formally. Continued noncompliance is a serious infraction.

How Are Project Manager Practices Monitored for Best Practices?

If a project manager believes his or her tool, template, or process is better than what is in the toolkit, it won't be secret for very long. This project manager will tell his or her colleagues, who will try it out and then tell their colleagues, and so on — that is, as long as it is clear that they are welcome to suggest improved approaches. If the PSO has created an environment where deviations are not tolerated, best practices may never see the light of day.

The answers to all six of the preceding questions are critical to attaining and maintaining the quality of the practice of the project management process.

Process and practice interact in several ways to create a complex network of dependent issues to be considered in any quality improvement program. For example, the project review data may show that project managers are practicing project management at a level of maturity below that of the process maturity. There are several reasons why that may be the case. For example, the training program may be weak and not available to very many project managers, or the project managers do not feel that the process meets their needs, so they continue to use their own tools and templates.

The reverse situation is also possible. Consider the case where project managers are performing at a maturity level above that of the process. That's not really as strange as it might seem. I have encountered this situation in many client engagements. The project managers might have brought with them tools, templates, and processes that are much better for their client than those documented in their organization's project management process. I would expect that the process, however it might be documented, allows the project manager the freedom to do what makes the most sense for their project and their client. This does not mean rigid conformance to a process, but rather, it allows the responsibility and authority to deviate where it makes sense. Any organization that expects its project managers to be successful must give them an opportunity to be a chef and not just a cook! One of my clients allows project managers to skip over certain processes if they don't feel they are relevant to their needs. All they have to do is state why they skipped the process. As long as you can give good reasons for not using or following a process there is no problem. Rigid adherence to process is not the best approach. Rather, the flexibility to know what is the best and the authority to execute against it is the mark of a chef. My approach is to let the nature of the project, the project team, and the enterprise culture and environment suggest the best-fit approach. This is the foundation on which the Traditional Project Management (TPM), Agile Project Management (APM), and Extreme Project Management (xPM) models covered in Part II of this book are defined and adapted so that they can deliver maximum impact on the business.

Defining Process and Practice Maturity

The Capability Maturity Model Integrated (CMMI) supersedes the Capability Maturity Model (CMM), which was first introduced by the Software Engineering Institute (SEI) at Carnegie Mellon University in 1987. These models have become the de facto standard for measuring the maturity of any process or steps in a process. There are several models in practice, and with the exception of the PMI Organizational Project Management Maturity Model (OPM3), they all have the CMM or CMMI as their conceptual foundation. Most models define five levels of maturity, which are described in this section as they pertain to project management processes and practices.

Level 1: Ad Hoc or Informal

Basically everyone is managing projects their own way. They may be using tools, templates, or processes that they developed, discovered, or borrowed and have been in their toolkits for years. There may be some common practices in the organization, but these are not fully documented or supported — just expected. I have often seen organizations provide a collection of templates as suggestions, not requirements. In effect the "what should be done" is stated, but not the "how to do it." The PMBOK has many of these characteristics and leaves it to the organization to specify the "how."

Level 2: Documented Processes

At Level 2 maturity, the tools, templates, and processes for managing projects have been defined and documented. Level 2 is an interesting level of maturity, not so much in terms of what the documentation says, but how it was put in place. Obviously, the motivation for doing the documentation is that the organization expects its project teams to implement the documented processes. It is beyond the scope of this book to talk about how the documentation was created, but let me just say that if you expect someone to use your stuff, you had better give them an opportunity to participate in its development. Producing a process that is fully matured at birth is a sure sign of eventual failure. If you intend to develop your project management process in the back room and then spring it on your project managers, don't expect to have a willing audience. This must be a team effort to have a chance at success.

Level 3: Documented Processes That Everyone Uses

The migration from Level 2 to Level 3 maturity is a big step. At Level 3, documented processes are supported and monitored for compliance. Compliance comes in many forms. It could be rigid enforcement of standards, and that would be unfortunate. In the spirit of this book and the Part II models, compliance should be a demonstration of sound judgment and decision making when it comes to the use of the validated tools, templates, and processes that define the project management processes.

Training and a healthy dose of support must be available if you are to succeed in migrating to Level 3. In addition, consulting and advisory services should be delivered through your PSO. The PSO has to be open to suggestions for improvement from the field and have a formal process in place for receiving and acting upon those suggestions.

Level 4: Integrated into Business Processes

This is best described by saying that project management has a seat at the business decision making and planning table. At Level 4, effective project management is recognized as a critical success factor and a strategic asset to the organization. It is considered to be part of every business process or decision and a contributor to business value.

You would be correct if you conclude that to move from Level 3 to Level 4 maturity is a major step for any organization. Very few have successfully made that transition. It takes a top-down commitment and strong leadership from the corporate-level (C-level) managers. The C-level managers must understand their role in successful project management and embrace it as an integral part of the business process. At the operational level, Level 4 requires a project portfolio management process housed in a full-service PSO.

Much can be said about the organization that has reached Level 4 maturity. Project managers will have become very skilled in the business processes, and business analysts will have become skilled in project management. In this environment, project management is fully integrated into the business of the organization.

I can foresee a new professional emerging from the integration of project management and business processes. I call this the Business Analyst/Project Manager (BA/PM) professional. Interested readers can consult the *Business Analyst Times* (www.batimes.com), where I recently published a seven-article series (beginning with the May 1, 2008 issue) on the BA/PM professional. These articles got the attention of the International Institute of Business Analysis (IIBA), and I am collaborating with them to further define the BA/PM professional. See Chapter 18 for a more detailed discussion of the BA/PM.

Level 5: Continuous Improvement

Maturity Level 5 is the pinnacle of integrating project management into the business. There is a formal and continuous program in place for process and practice improvement. It runs throughout the entire project life cycle. It formally begins during project execution, and continues through to the post-implementation audit and lessons-learned exercises at the end of the project. There will be occasions where an APM or xPM project team will create solutions or processes that are above the maturity level of the tools, templates, and processes in place. At Level 5 maturity, there is a way to capture these "best practices" and integrate them into the recommended tools, templates, and processes. At Level 5, every project team is constantly on the lookout for problems and offers suggestions for improvement. Capturing and archiving these suggestions is part of an organized and managed process for the continual improvement of the project management processes and the practice of those processes.

Measuring Project Management Process and Practice Maturity

The best practices, tools, templates, and processes described in this section have been integrated to design a system for measuring process and practice maturity. This system is the major input to the CPIM described later in this chapter.

The Process Quality Matrix and Zone Map

The Process Quality Matrix (PQM) and the Zone Map shown in Figure 15-1 are the key data collection tools for CPIM.

My version of the PQM consists of 12 columns and one row for each process or process step. Note here that the PQM is a very robust tool. Any process can be represented in the rows that define the PQM. In my consulting experiences the process steps for the client's systems development life cycle have been a common application.

In the example shown in Figure 15-1, the first 10 columns are the 10 prioritized critical factors (CF) that cause IT project failure as defined by the Standish Group in their report CHAOS 2010. This list should always reflect the latest CHAOS report. The list of CFs is usually the Standish Group–prioritized list of reasons for project failure, but there are other options, too. So these 10 columns of the PQM are robust, as is the number of columns. The 11th column contains a correlation factor that is computed from the data in the first 10 columns of the PQM, which will be discussed later. The 12th column will contain a maturity level factor computed from a maturity assessment. The rows define process steps (such as the steps in a systems development life cycle) or, as used in this process improvement program, the processes defined by the Project Management Institute (PMI) in their PMBOK. All of the contents of the PQM are user defined. It can be customized to meet any client requirements. I have had occasion to use it in a variety of contexts.

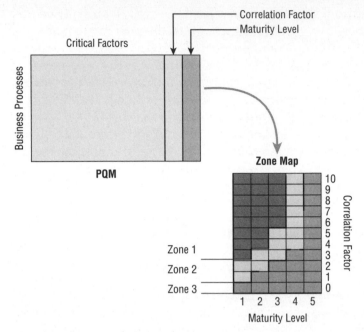

Figure 15-1: PQM and Zone Map

To complete the entries in columns 1–10, identify which processes are affected by which CFs, and mark each with a filled box as shown in Figure 15-2. This exercise is usually done once and used in repeated maturity assessments. The total number of CFs that affect performance of each process is entered in column 11. That number will range from 0 to 10: the higher the number, the stronger the relationship between the process and the CF. Column 12 will contain an assessed process maturity level, which, in this example, is a scale of 1–5 as measured by the Project Management Maturity Assessment (PMMA). Any numeric maturity assessment can be used to generate the data in column 12.

DEFINITION: PROJECT MANAGEMENT MATURITY ASSESSMENT (PMMA)

PMMA is a consultant-based proprietary interview tool to assess project management process maturity and project management practice maturity.

The numeric data in columns 11 and 12 is then transferred to a *Zone Map* as shown in Figure 15-3. The Zone Map is one of the basic tools used to drive the process improvement program. Column 11 identifies the Zone Map row, and column 12 identifies the Zone Map column. In the example shown in Figure 15-3, four processes (P35, P36, P40, and P44) were given a Level 3 maturity value and are related to five CFs. This is reflected by the P35, P36, P40, and P44 in the cell that lies at the intersection of the column labeled 3 and the row labeled 5 in the Zone Map.

		1	2	3	4	5	6	7	8	9	10	#	GR
Integration Management	P01 Develop Project Charter	■	■		■			■	■	■	■	7	3.21
	P02 Develop Preliminary Project Scope Statement	■	■		■			■	■	■	■	7	2.11
	P03 Develop Project Management Plan	■	■	■	■			■	■	■	■	8	1.33
	P04 Direct and Manage Project Execution	■			■	■	■	■	■	■		7	3.30
	P05 Monitor and Control Project Work	■			■	■	■	■	■		■	7	2.89
	P06 Integrated Change Control	■	■	■	■	■	■	■	■	■		9	1.44
	P07 Close Project	■	■	■	■		■		■	■	■	8	1.88
Scope Management	P08 Scope Planning	■	■		■		■	■	■			6	1.66
	P09 Scope Definition	■			■		■	■	■			5	2.22
	P10 Create WBS	■		■	■				■	■	■	6	3.33
	P11 Scope Verification	■	■	■	■		■		■			6	2.11
	P12 Scope Control	■	■	■	■	■	■	■	■	■		9	2.21
Time Management	P13 Activity Definition	■	■	■			■	■	■	■	■	8	1.11
	P14 Activity Sequencing		■				■		■			3	3.01
	P15 Activity Resource Estimating		■	■	■	■	■					5	2.21
	P16 Activity Duration Estimating					■	■	■	■	■	■	6	2.45
	P17 Schedule Development	■		■			■	■		■		5	1.66
	P18 Schedule Control			■		■	■	■	■	■	■	7	2.81
Cost Management	P19 Cost Estimating			■			■		■			3	2.75
	P20 Cost Budgeting	■			■		■		■	■		5	2.21
	P21 Cost Control	■	■	■			■	■	■	■	■	8	3.50
Quality Management	P22 Quality Planning	■	■	■				■	■	■		6	4.21
	P23 Perform Quality Assurance	■		■	■		■			■		5	3.51
	P24 Perform Quality Control						■			■	■	3	3.91
HR Management	P25 Human Resource Planning			■	■		■	■	■	■	■	8	3.75
	P26 Acquire Project Team		■	■	■	■	■		■	■	■	8	3.80
	P27 Develop Project Team		■	■	■	■	■	■	■	■	■	9	3.55
	P28 Manage Project Team	■			■	■	■		■			5	3.00
Comm. Management	P29 Communications Planning	■			■							2	3.51
	P30 Information Distribution						■					1	2.90
	P31 Performance Reporting	■	■	■	■		■		■			6	1.75
	P32 Manage Stakeholders	■		■	■	■	■	■	■			7	3.00
Risk Management	P33 Risk Management Planning		■			■		■	■	■		5	2.21
	P34 Risk Indetification		■		■			■			■	4	3.75
	P35 Qualitative Risk Analysis		■			■		■	■	■		5	3.51
	P36 Quantitative Risk Analysis		■			■		■	■	■		5	3.21
	P37 Risk Response Planning		■						■	■		3	3.91
	P38 Risk Monitoring & Control		■				■		■			3	4.01
Procurement Management	P39 Procurement Planning	■	■	■	■			■	■	■		7	3.51
	P40 Solicitation Planning			■		■		■	■	■		5	3.21
	P41 Solicitation			■		■			■	■		4	3.00
	P42 Source Selection			■	■		■	■	■	■		6	2.81
	P43 Contract Administration			■	■	■	■	■	■	■		7	2.75
	P44 Contract Close-out			■	■	■			■	■		5	3.55

CRITICAL FACTORS

CF1 Lack of user input
CF2 Incomplete rqmts spec
CF3 Changing rqmnts spec
CF4 Lack of exec support
CF5 Tech incompetence
CF6 Lack of resources
CF7 Unrealistic expectations
CF8 Unclear objectives
CF9 Unrealistic time frames
CF10 New Technology

Figure 15-2: A completed PQM

The Zone Map has three zones of interest. The boundaries of each zone are permanent. Beginning in the upper-left corner is Zone 1, the most critical zone. Any processes that fall in this zone should receive a high priority in the process improvement program. The focus of that process improvement program should be to revise the process so as to minimize the impact of the CFs that are related to that process. Even in Zone 1, the processes that are closest to the upper-left corner are the most critical among Zone 1 processes. So in this example,

P06 Integrated Change Control has a maturity of 1.44 and is impacted by 9 CFs. It is in most need of process improvements to minimize the impact of those 9 CFs. P12, P03, and P07 processes are next in most need of process improvement. Generally processes with lower maturity levels should have a higher priority for process improvement programs than processes affected by the same number of CFs. There are a total of 28 processes that fall in Zone 1, and these should be dealt with before any process improvement efforts are expended on the processes that fall in Zone 2. Zone 2 identifies processes that should be monitored. This zone runs roughly diagonally through the Zone Map and should receive the next level of attention for improvement based on available time and resources. There are 13 processes that fall in Zone 2. Finally, Zone 3, which runs along the rightmost columns and bottom rows, would not be of interest in the process improvement program. There are only 3 processes that fall in Zone 3. By taking into account the process maturity level and the correlation factor, processes can be ranked according to the priority needs for improvement programs.

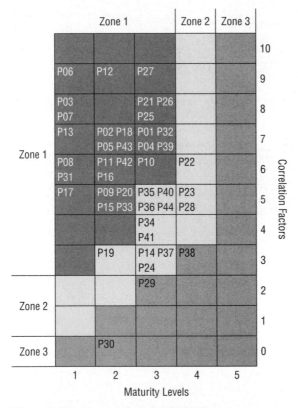

Figure 15-3: A completed Zone Map

Figure 15-4 tells a much more important story. This figure shows the Zone Map for the seven Integration Management processes. Integration Management consists of processes P01 through P07, and all of these processes fall in Zone 1. P06, P03, and P07 should be the highest priority processes for improvement programs. The same is true of Scope Management, which consists of processes P08 through P12. They also all fall in Zone 1. These two Knowledge Areas will get the high-priority attention of the CPIM. Figure 15-4 reflects this Integration Management information in a much more intuitive format.

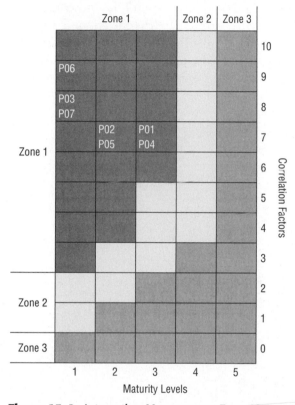

Figure 15-4: Integration Management Zone Map

In addition to the Zone Map, I have developed a graphic tool to help identify Knowledge Areas and processes within Knowledge Areas for improvement initiatives. An example of this tool is shown in Figure 15-5.

This is an intuitive plot of the process maturity levels for each of the nine Knowledge Areas (the dotted line) and the distribution of practice level maturity data from a 20-person sample of project managers (the box-and-whisker icon). The data in Figure 15-5 is from an actual client assessment and would have been gathered using the PMMA. The box-and-whisker icon for each Knowledge Area summarizes the data for that Knowledge Area. The end points of the vertical lines are the extreme practice maturities as drawn from the sample of project managers. The box represents the inter-quartile range (the middle 50 percent of the data points). I use a rule that says if the inter-quartile range falls entirely below the process maturity level (as is the case for Integration and Scope in this example), the associated process should have a high priority for an improvement initiative. That configuration says that 75 percent of the observed practice maturity data lies below the process level maturity for that Knowledge Area. This is a serious situation and requires immediate attention. If the inter-quartile range lies entirely above the process maturity level (Quality and HR in this example), that process should be targeted as a place to look for potential best practices among the project managers in the sample. In this situation, 75 percent of the observed practice maturity data lies above the process level maturity. In most cases that I have seen, this suggests that the process is not very good and project managers have substituted their own processes. Again, this is serious and immediate attention is required.

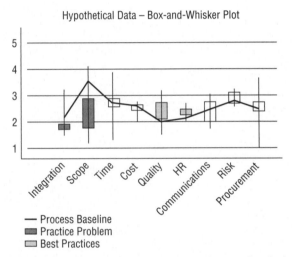

Figure 15-5: Process and practice maturity level plots

What Process Has Been Defined So Far?

Thus far, this chapter has defined the tools needed to conduct the analytical foundation in preparation for the Assessment and Analysis Phase of the CPIM (as you will see in Figure 15-6 later in the chapter). The following sections sum up the process to this point.

Step 1: Define the Process

Define an initial PQM using the PMBOK processes and the 10 CFs from the 2010 Standish Group CHAOS Report. Under the optional guidance of a trained consultant, discuss each process with reference to its relationship to one or more of the CFs. Those relationships define the PQM, which is the basis for prioritizing process-improvement initiatives.

Step 2: Validate and Finalize the PQM

The initial PQM needs to meet the needs of the PSO organization. The PQM will be reviewed with the PSO management team and modified as appropriate.

Step 3: Establish Correlations

In collaboration with the PSO, establish the correlations between the 44 project management (PM) processes and each CF. The 44 PM processes need to be correlated with CFs. This exercise should be facilitated by a trained consultant.

Step 4: Establish Metrics

Establish metrics to measure process performance on a project-by-project basis. The PMMA scorecard that I developed will be used to measure the maturity level of each process as practiced on a project-by-project basis. The use of the scorecard at the project level can also be used to identify the PSO's best practices to further improve process quality.

Step 5: Assess Project Managers against the PMMA

Audit a representative sample of project managers using the PMMA. This is the data needed to establish the practice baseline of project management.

Step 6: Assess Maturity Levels

Assess current maturity levels for all 44 processes. Based on the results of Step 5 and a review of the current organization's processes, determine the current maturity level of all PM processes. This will become the baseline against which future process improvements can be benchmarked.

Step 7: Plot Results on the PQM Zone Map

Plot the results on the PQM Zone Map in order to identify processes in need of improvement. The assessed maturity levels of all 44 processes are automatically transcribed into a Zone Map. The Zone Map is a high-level graphic view of the general maturity level of the organization's PM process. At the next level of detail, produce the Knowledge Area plot previously shown in Figure 15-5. You might even display the process maturity levels within a Knowledge Area in the same box-and-whisker plot for further identification of potential process and practice improvement areas.

Using the Continuous Process Improvement Model

As Figure 15-6 illustrates, CPIM is a four-phase model. I developed it specifically to be applied to the improvement of project management process and practice, but it can be applied to any type of business process. It is a way of life in organizations that want to attain and sustain a competitive position in fast-paced information-age industries.

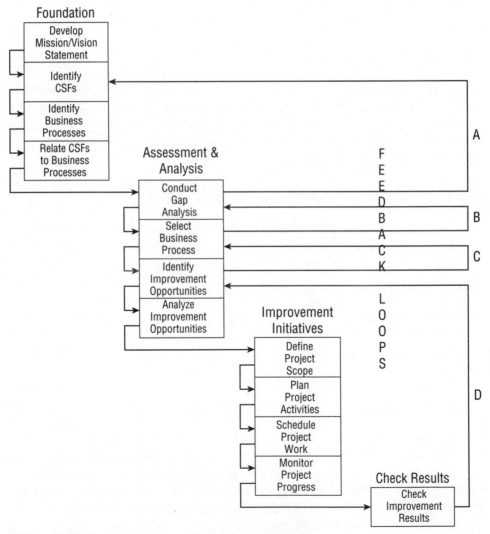

Figure 15-6: Continuous Process Improvement Model

Phase 1: Foundation

The purpose of the Foundation Phase is to establish the overall structure of the CPIM. It begins at the highest level of definition in the organization and relates that to the processes that drive the business of the enterprise. It consists of the following four activities executed in sequence:

1. Develop mission/vision statement.
2. Identify CFs.
3. Identify business processes.
4. Relate CFs to business processes.

Develop Mission/Vision Statement

The mission and vision statements will come from the most recent version of the strategic plan of the enterprise. If such statements do not exist, they need to be developed. That development is outside the scope of this book. In their absence the CPIM has no foundation on which to be undertaken. Using mission and vision as the foundation of the CPIM assures that the PMLC models align with the purpose and direction of the enterprise.

Identify CFs

What are those few factors on which the success of the enterprise depends? In completing this part of the PQM there is considerable latitude. For example, I once was engaged by a hospital to implement a quality improvement program for patient services. In place of the CFs they had identified six quality metrics that were established to measure the level of patient care provided. These metrics all had a threshold value set that the administration felt had to be achieved if the hospital was to be successful.

Identify Business Processes

Further to the point is what can be done to ensure they happen? The bottom-line question here is what processes are adversely affected by the realization of the CFs? Again, there is a great deal of latitude in how this part of the PQM is used. For example, a hospital's quality-improvement program identified all of the departments and the processes they used that had direct contact with patients in providing any patient care. Everything from the meal service to blood sampling to taking vitals was included. I have also used departments, process steps, and business processes. The PQM is quite adaptable. You decide what defines the rows and columns.

Relate CFs to Business Processes

If a business process (or whatever you are using to define the rows of the PQM) affects a CF (or whatever you are using to define the columns of the PQM), place an indicator of that relationship in the corresponding row/column intersection. That produces a PQM like the one previously shown in Figure 15-2. To complete column 11 in the example, simply count the number of CFs that can impact a business process. That is the correlation factor. For the example in Figure 15-2, it is a number ranging from 0 to 10. The entries in column 12 will be the assessed maturity level of each business process or process step.

Phase 2: Assessment and Analysis

The purpose of the Assessment and Analysis Phase is to identify several areas for potential improvement of process and practice. It consists of the following four activities executed in sequence:

1. Conduct gap analysis.
2. Select knowledge area or PM process
3. Identify improvement opportunities.
4. Analyze improvement opportunities.

Conduct Gap Analysis

At the completion of an improvement program for a process, the Zone Map should be updated. Because of the just completed improvement program, one or more processes will be changed and perhaps occupy different cells in the Zone Map. That will change the relative priorities of the remaining processes.

In collaboration with senior management, you will have established the target maturity levels for each Knowledge Area or a process within a Knowledge Area. The difference between the targeted maturity level and the actual maturity level is the *maturity gap*. You might want to superimpose the target maturity levels on Figure 15-5 for a complete graphical picture of where you are versus where you want to go.

Select Knowledge Area or PM Process

Pick the Knowledge Area, PM process, or PM process step that is most in need of an improvement initiative. For example, it might be a process or process step that exhibits one of the following characteristics:

- It has the largest gap.
- It has the lowest maturity level.
- It would be the most easily improved.

If staffing permits, you might pick more than one process or process step and run concurrent improvement programs. Be careful that the processes or process steps are not dependent upon one another, or you may be working at cross-purposes. For example, suppose that Scope Management is the Knowledge Area chosen for improvement. Project Scope Management has a significant implementation gap as viewed by the gap between process and practice, and the documented Knowledge Area is below the targeted maturity level.

Identify Improvement Opportunities

First, you choose process, practice, or both process and practice. Next, what is it about the process and/or practice that needs to be improved, and by what amount? You will need a quantitative metric to measure progress. That will be part of monitoring and controlling. The selected process will need both a process and a practice improvement initiative.

Analyze Improvement Opportunities

Here brainstorming can be of help. Get all of the ideas on the table. For the example given in Figure 15-5, you might identify the following process and/or practice improvement initiatives:

1. Improve scope process communications.
2. Clarify and simplify scope documentation.
3. Develop and deliver scope training.
4. Confirm the accuracy and completeness of the scope change control process.

There are several ways that you might consider prioritizing these four initiatives — expected contribution to maturity improvement, ease of correction, cost, time, value, and so on. For example, use value and effort as two criteria. Table 15-1 is the result for the four initiatives.

Table 15-1: Improvement Initiative Prioritization

		VALUE		
		HIGH	**MEDIUM**	**LOW**
	HIGH			
LEVEL OF EFFORT	**MEDIUM**	#3	#4	#2
	LOW		#1	

Would you choose initiative #3, and if so, why? Or would you choose initiative #1? Why? Perhaps you could do both #1 and #3 concurrently. Each of these initiatives is independent of the other initiatives, so there won't be a conflict between them.

Phase 3: Improvement Initiatives

The purpose of the Improvement Initiatives Phase is to plan and conduct the improvement initiatives. It consists of the following four activities executed in sequence:

1. Define the project scope.
2. Plan project activities.
3. Schedule project work.
4. Monitor project progress.

You should recognize this as the Linear PMLC model. A few comments on each phase of that model are in order.

Define the Project Scope

Continuing with the example, you have identified four potential improvement initiatives. Depending on your team resources, you might consider these to be done sequentially as would be the case for an Incremental PMLC model, or you might do all of them in concurrent swim lanes as in the Rapid Linear PMLC model. In some cases, you might use an Iterative PMLC model and do each initiative in separate iterations, adjusting the next iteration as results are realized.

Plan Project Activities

You must have a detailed plan for each improvement initiative you decide to do and the way you decide to do it. Use the Planning Process Group tools, templates, and processes as appropriate.

Schedule Project Work

Create the final project schedule and begin the project work. Complete all improvement initiatives. If any ideas arise during the project, save them for consideration in the next cycle of improvement initiatives. You don't want to confound your current efforts with other efforts, and you want to measure the impact of the current initiatives.

Monitor Project Progress

Use the appropriate Monitoring and Controlling Process Group tools, templates, and processes. For example, you might use a Monitoring and Controlling metric to track the results of each initiative.

Phase 4: Check Results

The Check Results Phase consists solely of an analysis of the results of the Improvement Initiatives done during Phase 3. After a suitable period of time has elapsed, the results of the improvement initiatives are checked against the desired improvement. Did the process or practice maturity improve to the targeted level? If so, you are done with this process and can select another business process (Feedback Loop D followed by Feedback Loop C) for an improvement initiative. If not, look for other improvement initiatives (Feedback Loop D) for this business process.

The CPIM is cyclical, as depicted by the feedback loops (look again at Figure 15-6). Feedback Loop A occurs when there have been significant process changes, and the relationship between CFs and processes may have changed. Feedback Loop B occurs when a business process may have changed and affected the gap analysis. Feedback Loop C simply continues the priority scheme defined earlier and selects another business process for improvement. Feedback Loop D usually involves continued improvement efforts on the same business process. The results of the current project may not have been as expected, or new improvement ideas may have arisen while the current project was being conducted.

Defining Roles and Responsibilities of the PSO

The PSO is the home of Continuous Process Improvement Programs with respect to project management processes and practices. In a Level 5 organization, that responsibility extends to all business processes, and the PSO takes on an enterprise-wide role. The BA/PM professional is the key staff resource in driving those improvement programs.

Assuming that the PSO is part of the project review process, a BA/PM professional is in an excellent position to identify process and practice problem areas and opportunities for improvement initiatives. I have participated with my clients in these project reviews and found a number of opportunities for improvement initiatives. Poor, inadequate, or inconvenient scheduling of training has been a common problem. Difficulty understanding process documentation or incomplete documentation has been another frequently occurring problem area.

Realizing the Benefits of Implementing a CPIM

The PSO will most certainly be involved in most improvement projects. It is in their best interest to do so for a number of reasons. At the completion of a CPIM initiative, the PSO should have realized the following benefits for the PM processes and practices:

- An improved ROI for the project management process
- The capability to significantly reduce the risk of project failure as a result of the improvement program
- Institutionalized continuous process improvements
- Leadership in the PM CPIM
- A documented approach that the PSO organizations will need to achieve higher PM maturity levels
- A process for identifying and acting on the weakest part of organization's PM capability

Applying CPIM to Business Processes

Business processes are another application area for a CPIM. The tools, templates, and processes are quite different than they are in the case of a process or practice improvement initiative for a PMLC model. For organizations that aspire to Level 5 maturity, knowledge of business process improvement is essential.

The business process targeted for an improvement initiative will have been identified already. Its performance is less than nominal, and that is the reason it will undergo a CPIM project. Often, you will choose to start identifying requirements for the project by mapping the current ("As Is") business process or processes that are going to be affected. You might also want to map the business process after the solution is installed ("To Be" process). This is assuming you know the To Be solution. If you know only parts of the To Be solution, you will have to use an APM PMLC model for the process improvement project. Both the As Is and To Be processes are excellent artifacts to use as input to the requirements-gathering process.

From the systems development perspective, the process of gathering requirements often begins with knowledge of the current or As Is business process and ends with the To Be business process. That gap is filled with new or enhanced project deliverables. The As Is and To Be business process flow diagrams will be invaluable aids in the ensuing solutions development effort.

It is an ongoing dictum of today's business that you must continuously improve your business processes. The old "If it ain't broke, don't fix it" adage no longer applies. If you aren't continuously improving your processes and the way that they support your clients, you run the risk of losing market share. Your client should also be taking the lead in approaching your teams to demand process improvement. Conversely, they are your clients, and you should be ever watchful for ways to improve the service they deliver to their customers.

All organizations are under pressure to improve. The pressure can come from the client, the competition, environmental change, technology change, or some combination of the four. The improvements can be in the client's products or processes. It is all too often the case that the client doesn't give their business to the company with the best product. When clients find that a business is too difficult to deal with, they will decide to use second best, a supplier who is easier to deal with.

This also applies to internal organizations. One reason for outsourcing is a belief that external groups will be easier, faster, or cheaper to deal with. Internal organizations need to counter this belief by clearly demonstrating that they are continuously improving products and processes to the degree that their performance is competitive with external (outsourced) groups.

Characteristics of Business Processes

The more you understand business processes, the more you can improve them. To do that, you must clearly understand the following characteristics of business processes:

- **Flow** — The method for transforming input into output.
- **Effectiveness** — How well client expectations are met.
- **Efficiency** — How well resources are used to produce an output.
- **Cycle time** — The time taken for transformation from input to final output.
- **Cost** — The expenses of the entire process.
- **Boundaries** — How and where each process crosses from one function (or organization) into another. Each boundary equals a handoff, which often requires a Service Level Agreement (SLA) to ensure a smoothly running process. If a single process crosses two or more functions and the total end-to-end handoff, boundaries, and SLAs are not addressed, there is a large risk that improvements made to one piece of the process will cause unintended problems in other parts of the same process, thus defeating the purpose of the continuous improvement effort.
- **Non-value-added time** — The time between process steps when no work is done on the product or service.

Except for effectiveness and efficiency, these items are self-explanatory.

Process Effectiveness

Process effectiveness is how well the process meets the requirements of the client. It measures the quality of the process. Effectiveness is also how well the output of the process meets the input requirements of internal clients and how well the inputs from the suppliers meet the requirements of the process.

The effectiveness of every process can be improved. The direct result of increased effectiveness is happier clients, improved sales, and an increase in market share.

The first step in bringing about an improvement in process effectiveness is to identify the most important effectiveness characteristics. Effectiveness characteristics are indicators of how well the process is functioning. The goal is to be sure that the output meets the client requirements.

The following are some typical indicators that a process lacks effectiveness:

- Unacceptable product and/or service
- Client complaints
- High warranty costs
- Decreased market share
- Backlog
- Redoing completed work
- Rejected output
- Late output
- Incomplete output

During the walkthrough, the team should be constantly looking for and identifying effectiveness characteristics.

Process Efficiency

The achievement of process efficiency is for the primary benefit of the client. Typical efficiency characteristics include the following:

- Cycle time per unit of transaction
- Resources per unit of output
- True-value-added cost percentage of total process cost
- Poor quality cost per unit of output
- Wait time per unit of transaction (usually at a boundary point)

During the walkthrough, the team should be looking for ways to measure efficiency.

> **NOTE** Cost is an extremely important aspect of the process. Every organization should be looking for ways to control costs within their operations. The cost of a process is an accountability issue that should be analyzed. By controlling costs, you will be able to increase your bottom line.

Streamlining Tools

Streamlining is the trimming of waste and excess in order to improve performance and quality. There are 11 tools for streamlining, as described in the following subsections.

Bureaucracy Elimination

Remove unnecessary administration tasks, approvals, and paperwork.

Duplication Elimination

Remove identical activities that are performed at different parts of the process. Be careful here that you don't create backlogs going from multiple stations to a single station.

Value-Added Assessment

Evaluate every activity in the business process to determine its contribution to meeting client requirements. Real-value-added activities are the ones that the clients would pay you to do.

Simplification

Reduce the complexity of the process.

Process Cycle-Time Reduction

Determine ways to compress cycle time to meet or exceed client expectations. Here are some ways that you can reduce cycle time:

- Use parallel instead of serial activities where possible
- Change the sequence of activities
- Reduce interruption
- Improve timing
- Reduce output movement
- Closer proximity of related work stations

Error Proofing

Make it difficult to do the activity incorrectly. Error proofing is the process of eliminating the opportunity to create errors. This can be accomplished in many ways. For example, you can automate a data entry process to remove the human-error factor. Barcoding and scanning are other ways to reduce errors. Everyone has a tendency to make errors; therefore, the more you can automate a process, the greater likelihood that a careless error will not occur.

Upgrading

Make effective use of capital equipment and the working environment to improve overall performance. Upgrading refers to improving not only your technology or office equipment, but also your personnel. Continuous learning is the norm in today's business world. Organizations that provide training and educational incentives will reap large dividends in the long run due to increased profit and higher employee morale.

Simple Language

Reduce the complexity of the way you write and talk, making your documents easy to comprehend by all who use them. Simplifying the language of your documentation and training manuals will increase effectiveness. Some organizations become burdened by wordy reports and memos. Documentation should be written in simple language for a particular audience.

Standardization

Select a single way of doing an activity and have all employees do the activity that way all the time. Standardization of work procedures is important to ensure that all current and future employees use the best way to perform activities related to the process. When each person is doing the activity differently, it is difficult (if not impossible) to make major improvements in the process. Standardization is one of the first steps in improving any process, and it's accomplished by the use of procedures. These standardization procedures should have the following characteristics:

- Be realistic, based on careful analysis
- Clarify responsibilities
- Establish limits of authority
- Cover emergency situations
- Not be open to different interpretations
- Be easy to understand
- Explain each document, its purpose, and its use
- Define training requirements
- Define minimum performance standards

Supplier Partnership

The output of the process is highly dependent on the quality of the inputs the process receives. The overall performance of any process improves when its suppliers' input improves.

All outputs require inputs, and in many cases, these inputs come from outside suppliers. The first step in this streamlining process is to analyze the inputs to determine their necessity in the process. An organization can lower costs and increase efficiency by eliminating inputs that are not needed. The next step is to work with suppliers to make sure that the inputs are being delivered on time and are of the highest quality.

Big-picture Improvement

This technique is used when the first 10 streamlining tools have not provided the desired results. It is designed to help the process improvement team look for creative ways to drastically change the process. There comes a point in time when you have to be willing to step back and look at the big picture of the process. By looking at the big picture, you examine the process from the perspective of what you would do if you abandoned the old way of doing things and started from scratch.

Watching Indicators of Needed Improvement

You need to define and track several metrics in order to discover process improvement opportunities. Some of the situations you will want to detect are as follows:

- Excessive wait time between process steps
- Backlog at a process step
- Idle workstations in the business process
- Frequent rework
- Excessive non-value-added work
- Errors and mistakes
- Frequent exception situations

For example, an order placement process might have a number of disconnects such as the following:

- Sales reps take too long to enter orders.
- There are too many entry and logging steps.
- The same level of credit checking is done for existing and new clients.
- Credit checking is done before order picking.

Any of these would be a good candidate for a process improvement project.

Documenting the "As Is" Business Process

One approach to identifying the process improvement goals is to develop a clear understanding of how the process is currently functioning (As Is) and how the process could work in the future (To Be). Knowing the gap between the present and the future is input to a plan to change the process (that is, to remove the gap).

The As Is process is nothing more than a picture of how things are currently working. If you were talking about a hotel, you could build a model of the workflow associated with a guest obtaining a room, using hotel facilities, and checking out of the hotel.

For an old hotel with no automated systems, the steps would be manual and highly dependent upon the accuracy of individuals. Having this set of data alone can make some areas prime candidates for improvement.

There is a tremendous temptation to skip the As Is process. People will say they know the process and what needs to be changed. If you skip this step, the team doesn't gain an increased understanding of how the process really works. Without that understanding, you have a very real chance of negatively impacting the client.

Envisioning the "To Be" State

This model is a picture of how the process *could* work. The same work may be done, but the flow might be very different. In some cases, tasks in the As Is state might be eliminated entirely. The intent of this model is to get people to talk about how it could be. This is sometimes done by having the subject matter experts explain how they would do things if they were building a brand-new process unconstrained by the way you have always done things. This is frequently referred to as the "green field" approach. Another approach is to have people identify areas where they would like to change the current system to do things differently.

Defining the Gap between "As Is" and "To Be"

The difference or "delta" between an As Is process and a To Be process shows the opportunities for improvement. It involves building a comparison of the two so that the differences can be categorized. Some tasks might be eliminated entirely. Some tasks might be done faster than they were before. Some tasks that had been sequential might be done in parallel. Others might be done to a higher level of quality. Some opportunities for eliminating the gap might include the following:

- Eliminate some tasks
- Speed up some tasks

■ Introduce parallelism

■ Increase quality

Defining a Business Process Improvement Project

The continuous improvement of business processes should be a high priority for every contemporary organization. Every time a process is executed, a wealth of data and information is produced as a by-product. This data and information has great value in helping the process managers identify and isolate areas where improvement can be made. A business process improvement (BPI) project uses that data and information as input to programs designed to improve the process under consideration. This is represented graphically in Figure 15-7.

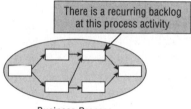

There is a recurring backlog
at this process activity

Business Process

Figure 15-7: A business process improvement project

The goal of a BPI project is to eliminate or at least reduce the effect resulting from process activities that are preventing the process from performing up to its potential.

Figure 15-7 shows that a backlog exists at a process activity. You might conclude from this diagram that the backlog is the result of two upstream process activities delivering output to a single process activity that is not staffed to handle the volume. What seems like a simple solution — namely, adding staff — might solve the backlog problem at that process activity but create another backlog at the following step. The backlog is just transferred, and the efficiency of the total process is not changed at all. This illustrates a common problem — subprocess maximization that may or may not positively affect the total process. In fact, it could reduce the efficiency of the total process. Each of the activities in a business process could make the overall process cumbersome to deal with. The goal of business process improvement is to eliminate (or at least reduce) the pain coming from the activities that are doing the most damage, and this also implies that there may be one or more precursor projects that have determined the sources of pain, confusion, and/or chaos.

Beyond a single process improvement project, there are continuous process improvement programs. By definition, continuous programs do not end. They focus on a complete process or on a super-process made up of several dependent processes. Their improvement goal is often an ideal end state, which for all practical purposes will never be reached, but it is a worthy goal nevertheless.

Enterprises that are at Level 3 maturity but desire to reach Level 4 will need to develop a BA/PM professional staff and put a CPIM in place for all business processes. The BA/PM professional assures that the PMLC model used for the business processes makes sense and that the CPIM business process initiatives can be managed successfully.

Using Process Improvement Tools, Templates, and Processes

The tools I prefer are graphic rather than tabular. The tabular reports give the details if those are needed for further analysis. The graphic reports are intuitive and convey the necessary quality information at a glance. As part of their PMBOK standards, the PMI recommends some basic tools of quality. I've added a tool to the list that I have found particularly useful. With this addition to the current PMI list of tools, the complete list includes the following:

- Fishbone diagrams and Root Cause Analysis
- Control charts
- Flowcharting
- Histograms
- Pareto analysis
- Run charts
- Scatter diagrams
- Statistical sampling (not discussed here)
- Inspection (not discussed here)
- Approved change requests review (not discussed here)
- Force field analysis

Fishbone Diagrams and Root Cause Analysis

The fishbone diagram (a.k.a. cause-and-effect diagram, a.k.a. spider chart, a.k.a. Ishikawa diagram) is a versatile and intuitive tool. It can graphically present cause-and-effect relationships and root causes. Figure 15-8 is a template of the fishbone diagram. The fishbone diagram can be used when you need to identify, explore, and display the possible causes of a specific problem or condition. It is most commonly used after data compilation and is very effective after an affinity exercise. Teams that are empowered to work on improvement-based projects or are searching for root causes may find this tool helpful. It methodically provides the answer to the general question, "What could be contributing to this problem?" After the general cause is identified, begin asking why. By continuously investigating the why for each cause, the root cause may be more concisely identified.

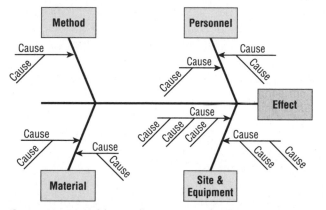

Figure 15-8: Fishbone diagram template

The fishbone diagram can be used to display the hierarchy of causes of a problem. The true root cause of a problem is not always the obvious option. If you react only to symptoms of a problem, you will need to continually modify your process. Once a root cause is identified (Figure 15-9), resolution of the root cause could provide a permanent fix for a series of annoying problems.

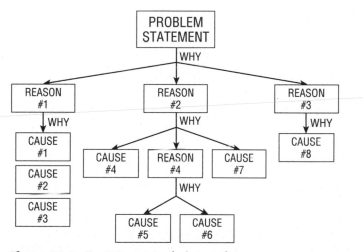

Figure 15-9: Root Cause Analysis template

Fishbone diagrams are drawn to clearly illustrate the various causes affecting a process by sorting out and relating the causes. For every effect, there are likely to be several major categories of causes. From this well-defined list of possibilities, the most likely causes are identified and selected for further analysis. When examining each cause, look for things that have changed — deviations from the norm or patterns. Look to cure the cause, not the symptoms.

After a cause-and-effect diagram has been created, the next step is to identify the causes that have the strongest impact on the effect. Often there is existing data that can be used to examine the cause-and-effect relationships, or additional data can be gathered at a reasonable cost and in an acceptable time frame.

If it is not possible to collect data to verify a cause-and-effect relationship, it may be necessary to use process knowledge to select a process variable that is suspected to have a strong influence on a quality characteristic. Once the variable is identified and a way to improve it has been selected, a small pilot test of the process change is conducted, and the results are observed. A successful pilot test provides evidence that there is a cause-and-effect relationship between the process variable and the quality characteristic.

To ensure that you have analyzed a problem fully and correctly, check the proposed root cause against the test criteria listed in Table 15-2. To be a true root cause it must pass all tests. These are listed in Table 15-2.

Table 15-2: Fishbone Root Cause Test

FISHBONE ROOT CAUSE TEST CRITERIA	YES/NO
Dead End You ran into a dead end when asking, "What caused the proposed root cause?"	
Conversation All conversation has come to a positive end.	
Feels Good Everyone involved is happy, motivated, and emotionally uplifted.	
Agreement All agree it is the root cause that keeps the problem from being resolved.	
Explains The root cause fully explains why the problem exists from all points of view.	
Beginnings The earliest beginnings of the situation have been explored and understood.	
Logical The root cause is logical, makes sense, and dispels all confusion.	
Specific Your statement of the reason gets to the point of the trouble without generalizations.	

FISHBONE ROOT CAUSE TEST CRITERIA	YES/NO
Control The root cause is something you can influence, control, and deal with realistically.	
Hope Finding the root cause has returned hope that something constructive can be done about the situation.	
Workable Suddenly, workable solutions that deal with the symptoms begin to appear.	
Stable A stable, long-term, "once and for all" resolution of the situation now appears feasible.	

Control Charts

Control charts track a metric over time. Various patterns that suggest in-control or out-of-control situations are defined. For both situations, some form of follow-up analysis should be done to identify the root causes. The milestone trend chart shown in Figure 15-10 is an example of a control chart.

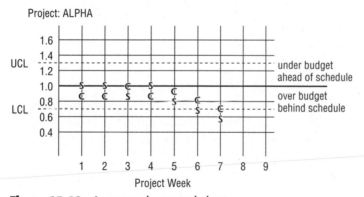

Figure 15-10: An example control chart

Flowcharting

When you need to identify the actual and ideal path that any product or service follows in order to map process quality and identify deviations and improvement opportunities, the flowchart is another tool that can be beneficial in mapping process quality and performance. It is a picture of steps in a process and can be used to examine the sequence of steps and the relationship between them; to identify redundancy, unnecessary complexity, and inefficiency in a process; and to create a common understanding of the flow of the process.

The flowchart (Figure 15-11) is considered one of the simplest tools. It can be as basic or technically intricate as the process it is used to illustrate. Each type of process step is traditionally identified on the chart by a standardized geometric shape. A flowchart illustrates a process from start to finish and should include every step in between. By studying these charts, you can often uncover loopholes, which are potential sources of trouble. Flowcharts can be applied to anything from the travels of an invoice and the flow of materials to the steps in making a sale or servicing a product.

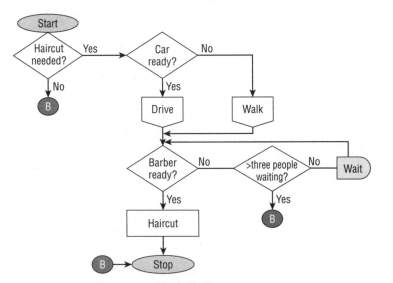

Figure 15-11: An example flowchart

In process improvement, flowcharts are often used to clarify how a process is being performed or to agree upon how it should be performed. When a process is improved, the changes should be noted on the flowchart in order to standardize the revised flow.

Follow these steps to create a flow chart:

1. Decide on the process to be diagrammed.

2. Define the beginning and ending steps of the process, also known as boundaries.

3. Describe the beginning step using the Boundaries symbol.

4. Keep asking. "What happens next?" Write each of the subsequent steps using the appropriate symbols.

5. When a decision step is reached, write a yes/no question in a diamond and develop each path.

6. Make sure that each decision loop reenters the process or is pursued to a conclusion.

7. Describe the ending step using the Boundaries symbol. Sometimes a process may have more than one ending boundary.

Histograms

Histograms are probably the most intuitive and flexible of the eight tools presented here. Categories and subcategories for classifying frequency data can be created. Figure 15-12 is a common form of histogram, where the horizontal axis is the data class and the vertical axis is the frequency of observations in each data class. The darker colored bar denotes the average of all the data.

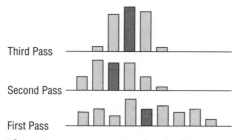

Third Pass

Second Pass

First Pass

Figure 15-12: An example of a histogram

A popular use of the histogram is as an intuitive display of frequency from most frequent to least frequent. This type of histogram is used in Pareto analysis, which is described in the next section.

Pareto Analysis

Pareto analysis is a very simple technique that helps you choose the most effective changes to make.

It uses the *Pareto principle* — the idea that by doing 20 percent of the work, you can generate 80 percent of the advantage of doing the entire job. Pareto analysis is a formal technique for finding the changes that will provide the biggest benefits. It is useful when many possible courses of action are competing for your attention.

The steps to conducting a Pareto analysis are as follows:

1. To start using the tool, write out a list of the changes you could make. If you have a long list, group it into related changes.

2. Score the items or groups. The scoring method you use depends on the sort of problem you are trying to solve. For example, if you are trying to improve client satisfaction, you might score on the basis of the number of complaints eliminated by each change.

3. Tackle the change that has the highest score first. This change will provide the biggest benefit if you solve it.

4. The options with the lowest scores will probably not even be worth bothering with — solving these problems may cost you more than the solutions are worth.

There is always the danger that you will spend a lot of time and money chasing down minor problems while ignoring major problems. Pareto analysis is also referred to as the 80/20 rule. Analysis of data frequently shows that 80 percent of problem occurrences are caused by 20 percent of problem causes. A Pareto analysis produces a histogram showing how many results were generated by each identified cause. If you order this by frequency of occurrence, you can see which problems to attack first. For example, if there were 1,000 failures in a printed circuit, and these are assigned to 15 different causes, which should you attack first? Without some vehicle to help in this selection, it can turn into a duel of personal preferences. If you gather data about how many failures are associated with which cause, it might look like what's shown in Figure 15-13. The graphic display of the data is shown in Figure 15-14.

ID	Cause	# of Failures
A		35
B	Late arrival	250
C		15
D		8
E		36
F		25
G		15
H		14
I	Missing part	350
J	Access	150
K		7
L		5
M		18
N		30
O		42
		1000

Figure 15-13: Raw data for Pareto analysis

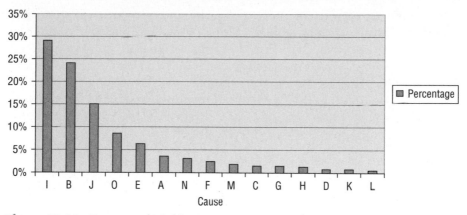

Figure 15-14: Pareto analysis histogram

Run Charts

Milestone trend charts were discussed in detail in Chapter 7. They are quite flexible and can be formatted for a single milestone or multiple milestones. As is true of many of the tools I am offering you, the milestone trend chart is quite intuitive and simple to generate. At a glance, you can see the history of the event you are tracking. The degree to which it is above or below the nominal value and whether it is tracking toward success or failure are also obvious. The run chart (Figure 15-15) can quickly focus your attention on events that need further investigation.

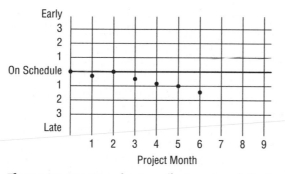

Figure 15-15: Run chart – milestone trend chart

Scatter Diagrams

Scatter diagrams originated in the field of statistical analysis. They were used to detect dependent or correlated variables. Underlying the scatter diagram is a mathematical model of the relationship between two variables: a dependent variable, which is represented on the vertical scale, and an independent variable, which is represented on the horizontal scale (see Figure 15-16). Understand that the intention is not to convey a cause-and-effect relationship. This is a common mistake. The scatter diagram merely depicts how the values of two different variables vary from one another. In the example shown in the figure, it would be incorrect to assume that the "total project labor hours" value in any way cause the "# days late" value. The relationship may in fact be causal, but that is not intended nor assumed by the scatter diagram.

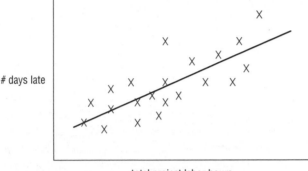

Figure 15-16: Scatter diagram

Force Field Analysis

Force field analysis is a pictorial representation of countervailing forces that act on an event to either support its occurrence or not support it. Figure 15-17 is the template and Figure 15-18 is an example of its application.

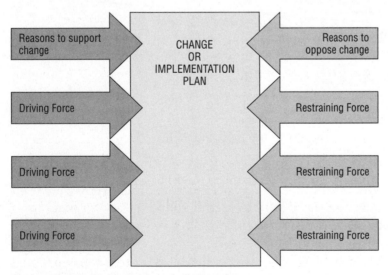

Figure 15-17: Force field analysis template

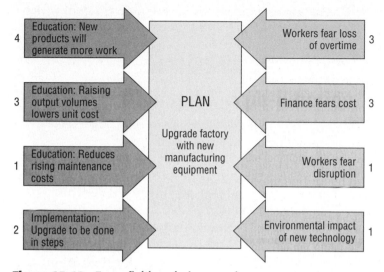

Figure 15-18: Force field analysis example

If your intention is to support the occurrence of an event, then you would take actions to support the driving factors and to reduce the restraining factors.

When you need to understand and identify the factors effecting any decision, change, or action, this tool can help build consensus on results found in the fishbone diagram.

A force field analysis is a planning tool for understanding and strategizing about the forces that will drive and restrain any change or implementation plan. It does not illustrate a solution merely through the values. You should use it in the team environment to arrive at areas of consensus based on the team's objectives. It is also a foundation for negotiation.

To conduct a force field analysis, follow these steps:

1. Convene a team that has an appreciation of the human dynamics involved and the effect the change will have. If a project team has developed the change, consider using a representative from the target group for the analysis.

2. Describe the desired change or a barrier to the change at the center/top of the force field diagram.

    (a) List all forces for change in the left-most column, and all forces against change in the right-most column.

    (b) Assign a score to each force, from 1 (weak) to 5 (strong).

    (c) Draw a diagram showing the forces for and against change. Show the size of each force as a number next to it.

3. Consider each restraining force in turn and develop a possible solution to overcome or reduce the effect of this force. These are the driving forces that will act to overcome the resistance.

4. Sort the driving forces according to priority based upon the following:

    (a) Their ability to affect more than one restraining force

    (b) The size of the impact (large, medium, or small)

    (c) Ease of implementation

    (d) Response time for effect to take place

5. Incorporate the driving forces in the order of the impact you expect from them into the project implementation action plan.

Use of the force field analysis helps to gain team consensus. In a consensus, the various points of view of each member of the team are considered, discussed, compared, and discussed again until everyone sees all sides of the picture. Ultimately, team consensus leads to a decision that all team members agree on and creates buy-in.

Anytime you implement change, you affect people. By definition, you now have forces supporting and opposing that change. A force field analysis helps identify the forces that resist change as well as those that support the change. This enables you to develop strategies to overcome resistance. Fundamentally, you should do this when implementing any change that involves or affects people.

Trigger Values

You should establish trigger values for all of your quantitative metrics. Trigger values serve as early warning signs that indicate the project is heading for an out-of-control situation and some form of corrective action will soon be needed. A trigger value could be a single number such as the frequency of an event in the reporting period, or it could be a trend such as four successive data points moving in the same direction. Figure 15-19 shows an example of a trigger value.

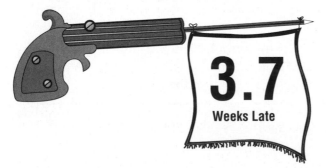

Figure 15-19: Trigger values

Putting It All Together

All of the efforts spent in designing, documenting, and implementing TPM, APM, and xPM models are for naught if there isn't a CPIM to back them up. I have never participated in a design project that has produced a finished process at its implementation. Lessons learned, project reviews, and other such assessment events are critical input to process and practice improvement. All that is needed is a formal and continuous process for improvement. In this chapter, you learned about just such a process. Now you just need the perseverance to make it happen.

Discussion Questions

CASE STUDY – PIZZA DELIVERED QUICKLY (PDQ)

1. For the case study, construct the As Is and the To Be business processes for the Order Entry subsystem. You may have to make some assumptions about the "As Is" process, but just state your assumptions and move on.

   Following is an example of an order entry use case for PDQ that you can use to help you answer the preceding question.

Basic Flow of Placing an Order

1. This use case begins when the actor indicates they want to place an order.
2. The system requests order information (coupon information).
3. The actor provides valid order information.
4. The actor indicates that the order information is complete.
5. The system validates the address (additional detail).
6. The system prices the order.
7. The system displays the completed order with the price.
8. The actor confirms the order.
9. The system assigns the order to the appropriate preparation location.
10. The system priorltizes the order.
11. The use case ends when the system prioritizes the store orders.

2. Construct a PQM for a business process that you are familiar with. You can leave column 12 empty.

3. Document the As Is state and your ideas for the To Be state for a business process familiar to you that you believe should be improved.

Managing the Realities of Projects

In my 20-plus years of running my own project management consulting practice I have encountered two types of projects that deserve special mention. The first is distressed projects. These have largely been ignored in the literature. There is one book on the market, and it was published in 2001. The other is multiple team projects. These projects are often encountered in large organizations or organizations that have independent business units, each with their own project management processes and practices. I am not aware of any books or even chapters in books devoted to the management of multiple team projects.

The final chapter focuses on professional development. Having to effectively manage complex projects means having a cadre of project managers and business analysts who are ready to collaborate on all types of projects each with its own unique set of challenges. To be successful means having an environment that promotes creativity. Both generalists and specialists are needed to make this happen.

Overview of Part IV

Part IV consists of three chapters.

Chapter 16: Prevention and Intervention Strategies for Distressed Projects

This chapter discusses distressed project prevention and intervention strategies. I describe many of my experiences with such situations. You will see that by judiciously applying what has already been presented in this book, you will have taken a big step towards preventing projects from becoming distressed. But even at best, some projects are destined for the distressed pile. Maybe that was built in from the start, and no one noticed or could tell. In any case, what do you do when the project has become distressed, and without some significant intervention, will likely fail? That is the second major topic in this chapter.

Chapter 17: Organizing Multiple Team Projects

This chapter discusses three models that are used in the industry to manage projects where two or more independent teams are involved and each team has its own project management tools, templates, and processes. The question is how to organize and manage such projects. The three alternative structures mentioned in this chapter work better for some projects than others. I examine the alternatives and when to use each one.

Chapter 18: Managing the Professional Development of Project Teams

There are several objectives that a professional development program must meet. Basically they all revolve around balancing the supply of experienced and trained project managers and team members across the demand for such professionals over time. This is a daunting challenge. The situation and a potential solution are described in this closing chapter.

CHAPTER 16

Prevention and Intervention Strategies for Distressed Projects

The best-laid schemes o' mice an' men, gang aft a-gley, and leave us naught but grief and pain, for promised joy.
— Robert Burns, Scottish national poet

CHAPTER LEARNING OBJECTIVES

After reading this chapter, you will be able to:

- **Recognize a potentially distressed project**
- **Understand why projects become distressed**
- **Implement prevention strategies**
- **Use the tools, templates, and processes for preventing distressed projects**
- **Understand and apply the intervention steps for a distressed project**
- **Conduct a Root Cause Analysis for a distressed project**
- **Understand the roles and responsibilities of the Project Support Office (PSO) with respect to distressed projects**

Despite the project team's best efforts, some projects are destined for problems. Sometimes it's the team's fault, and sometimes it's just the roll of the dice. What is important is to protect the project against the unexpected and to have early warning signs in place to minimize the impact of the coming problems. Having a solid risk management plan is also important. These are the *prevention strategies*. But the inevitable still happens, and sometimes you are left with a project that is in trouble, one you need to save as best you can. These are the *intervention strategies*. Forming and executing prevention and intervention strategies is the focus of this chapter.

What Is a Distressed Project?

Whenever the performance of a project falls outside nominal values, it is judged to be a project in distress. How it got to that state is a question that needs answering. Most important is knowing how to establish an early warning system and prevent a project from becoming distressed. But understand that even the best efforts will not be 100 percent effective, and a project can still become distressed. The question then becomes: How can it be returned to a state of normalcy — if at all? The following characteristics are symptomatic of a distressed project;

The project has exhibited a performance trend that, if continued, will result in its failure. I define two metrics in this chapter that capture the cumulative history of the project with respect to progress against time. Whenever the cumulative history of one or both of those metrics exhibits certain trends, it suggests that the project is out of control, and the reason for the trends needs to be identified and a decision needs to be made as to how to proceed. If left unchecked, the trend will continue, and failure is almost a certainty. A growing schedule slippage is one such trend that, if continued, will lead to failure. For a software development project an unresolved bug list that continues to grow and/or whose average resolution time increases is a signal that the project may be heading toward a distressed condition.

The project's performance has exceeded one or more metric values and is a high risk for failure. I will define several metrics and trigger values that can be used to track the general health of a project. When any one of these metrics exceeds its trigger value, the project is at high risk for failure. That sets off a series of activities designed to identify the source of the anomaly and the corrective action that needs to be taken. A significant schedule slippage due to a bad estimate, a mistake, and serious vendor delays are three such events that may result in project failure.

The project has recently experienced some significant change that may result in failure. Oftentimes these changes are related to personnel or other major organizational shifts. Even though the project performance metrics do not indicate any problem, the environmental change may be sufficient to throw the project off course. A change of sponsor and a loss of critical resources are two such changes that may result in a distressed condition and eventual project failure.

If any of the preceding situations happen, it should immediately trigger a project intervention process designed to discover the reasons for the distressed condition, fix the condition, and re-plan the project going forward. That process is discussed in detail later in the chapter.

Why Projects Become Distressed or Fail

Many studies have been done over the years that attempt to discover the reasons for project failure. The failure rates for information technology (IT projects) are documented to range from 70 percent and higher! That level of performance has persisted for several years with no sign of any meaningful change for the better. The industry hasn't found an effective strategy for reducing that failure rate. I believe that many of the reasons for this are related to the methodology that is being used. Traditional project management (TPM) is the default approach and seems to be outside the mainstream of contemporary project types. Data that I have collected from all corners of the globe suggest that only 20 percent of projects fall into the TPM quadrant, but the approaches to managing the projects remain relatively unchanged. TPM approaches are forced upon such projects for lack of an alternative, which is not much more than a failure waiting to happen.

From interviews conducted with my clients and my own consulting experiences with them, a number of factors emerge repeatedly as possible reasons why their projects become distressed or fail. The following subsections discuss these reasons.

Poor, Inadequate, or No Requirements Documentation

As I discussed in several previous chapters, it is impossible to generate complete requirements documentation at the beginning of a project. That is no excuse for doing a sloppy job. Once requirements have been generated following the definition I suggested in Chapter 2, ask yourself what your level of confidence is that you have done the best job possible. You should be reasonably certain that you have identified the necessary and sufficient set of requirements and only their detailed decomposition is suspect. You can employ a number of Agile Project Management (APM) project management life cycle (PMLC) models if requirements documentation is less than satisfactory or if you expect a high rate of change.

Inappropriate or Insufficient Sponsorship

Some sponsors take their job of sponsorship seriously. Others do not. As project manager, you should keep the project very visible to your sponsor. Sending an e-mail once a week is not sufficient. I would try for face-to-face meetings if there is any doubt about your sponsor's attentiveness to the project. You will certainly sense inattentiveness when they are sitting across the desk from you. Sending them informal notes of project happenings just to keep them connected is another tool I have used on occasion. You have to keep them excited about the project and how it is going to contribute value to the organization. If there is some way for you to make them look good to their management as a result of this project, doing so would be a smart move on your part. I look for added value opportunities and communicate those face to face with the sponsor.

Complexity of Requirements Not Recognized

Don't assume that the project is simple. That thinking leads to a sloppy job of requirements gathering and documentation. You are heading for trouble if you can't get requirements done correctly, realize what you have or don't have, and then choose the best-fit PMLC model.

Your risk management plan must anticipate the unusual and have the appropriate mitigation plans in place. As requirements become more complex or less complete and clearly documented, the risk of the project becoming distressed goes up.

Unwillingness to Make Tough Decisions

How easy it is to get a project approved, and how hard it is to pull the plug on the most distressed of projects. If you want to get the sponsor's attention, recommend terminating their hopelessly distressed project. But be careful that you don't hurt your own reputation in the process. You needn't be defensive, just honest.

Some projects have a very powerful sponsor. They may defend the project beyond reason, but few are willing push back or take them on. The president of your company will often be the major culprit here. If you are going to take him or her on, you had better do your homework. A good example of this situation would be my experience with the president of a company where I was the CIO. We had a very complex hardware implementation project underway, and it was in trouble mostly due to vendor delays. I presented two alternatives to the president. He was a tough boss and told me that I didn't do my homework. There was a third alternative I had not considered. He told me to combine the two alternatives I had proposed into a third and report back. I later learned that this was merely a stalling tactic on his part because he wasn't comfortable making a decision at that time. There was no feasible third alternative. We later decided to follow the first alternative I had presented.

Lag Time between Project Approval and Kick-Off

Getting a project approved is one thing. Getting it started is another. If the time between approval and startup is too long and the completion date is firm, project risk goes up. Any date-dependent tasks are compromised by the delay, so avoid using those in your project schedule if possible. You are also at some risk of losing team members due to the delay, especially those who have scarce skills that you need but so do others.

No Plan Revision after Significant Cuts in Resources or Time

Budget cuts, staff cuts, and shorter deadlines are not unusual. Under those circumstances, many project plans are not changed. Despite your pleas, senior management says something like this: "You'll figure out how to do it anyway. You always have." Most project managers are helpless to do anything here except keep quiet. Many do not have the tools to push back with an intelligent business argument.

Estimates Done with Little Planning or Thought

Far too many project managers don't take estimation seriously. They throw some numbers at the plan, and if no one objects, the numbers stay. The correct strategy is to get estimates from staff members who have done the tasks before or will be assigned to do the task on this project. Unless they have been a credible source in the past, you will want some validation of the estimates they provide. Getting a second opinion from someone who is not on the project can be a good validation strategy.

Overcommitment of Staff Resources

This continues to be a major problem. Projects are often approved without assessing staff availability. You may have the skills needed, but the people with those skills are already committed to other projects and cannot work your project into their schedules. Dealing with this situation effectively requires a Human Resources Management System (HRMS) with skills inventories and staff scheduling capability.

Inconsistent Client Sign-Off

Some clients will fully participate in acceptance procedures and not be forced to sign off until they are completely satisfied that their requirements have been met and expected business value achieved. If they have been meaningfully involved throughout the project, that's a good sign that they will be meaningful participants in the acceptance procedures, and their signature is testimony that requirements have been met. Not all clients are like this, however. Some might sign off simply to get the project out of the way and get on with their business. Others might not really understand the project and sign off in ignorance rather than risk being exposed.

No Credibility in the Baseline Plan

If the baseline plan has undergone several revisions and changes at management's and the client's request, there may be serious doubt that it can be achieved. Estimates that are made and then changed to accommodate a tight deadline are sure signs of a weak plan and one that is destined for trouble. What may have been a solid and well-thought-out plan initially has undergone so many changes and patchwork fixes that it is now a jumbled mess and lost its credibility with the team.

Unmanageable Project Scope

APM projects expect change and are structured to accommodate it, but there still must be vigilance over scope change. Tracking the frequency and cumulative number of additions to the Scope Bank are two metrics you should have in place. Over the cycles of the APM, a healthy project will show convergence. If changes are requested at an increasing rate, that is a sign of a project out of control. TPM projects do not expect scope change requests, so some control over the number and frequency must be in place. Management reserve is an effective tool and should be included in every TPM project plan.

Managing Distressed Projects

In general, there are two types of strategies for dealing with distressed projects. Every project that becomes distressed was once not in distress, and there are prevention strategies to minimize the likelihood of projects becoming distressed. Despite your diligence, the prevention strategies might not work due to prevailing conditions beyond your control, and your project will still become distressed. If this happens, there are intervention strategies that you can use. This section describes both strategy types.

Prevention Management Strategies

Prevention strategies are proactive practices and processes that you can employ to significantly reduce the number of projects that become distressed. For the typical company situation, you may be able to enhance some of the processes covered previously in this book to decrease the likelihood of a project becoming distressed. These enhancements are briefly discussed in the next subsection.

Again, it is not possible to eliminate all projects from falling into the distressed category, but you can significantly reduce their numbers. In establishing your prevention strategies, you have to take your efforts to the next level. Considering the high failure rate of projects, I suggest that you take some of the actions described in this section with every project. If for some reason you find these efforts burdensome to do on every project, you might consider them as part of your risk management plan and be more selective in how you apply them.

Using Tools, Templates, and Processes to Prevent Distressed Projects

Although there is no guarantee that prevention strategies will actually prevent a project from becoming distressed, they are your best protection against such an outcome. In this section, I discuss some specific prevention strategies you might use to reduce the likelihood of a project becoming distressed.

You learned about the following six processes earlier in this book, which are also irreplaceable tools for formulating prevention strategies:

- Requirements gathering
- Work Breakdown Structure (WBS) construction
- Dynamic risk management process
- Scope change management process
- Milestone trend charts
- Earned value analysis

These processes are briefly discussed in the following subsections with a focus on prevention strategies.

Requirements Gathering

Knowing that complete requirements documentation is difficult if not impossible at the beginning of the project, you should take extra care in identifying the list of requirements. As project complexity increases, the task is even more difficult mostly due to the dependence between requirements becoming more complex. Factor the client into that experience, and the difficulty increases even further. The client may be relatively inexperienced in identifying requirements and doesn't seem to engage in the process with the enthusiasm and commitment you would like. Perhaps a workshop approach makes sense. All of these factors suggest using a PMLC model that is closer to the APM, Extreme Project Management (xPM), and Emertxe Project Management (MPx) end of the project landscape than you might have otherwise selected. Err on the side of being more suspect of the completeness and accuracy of the requirements. As the project commences, you may find reason to move back toward the Adaptive and even Iterative end of the landscape and use a different PMLC model.

The issue to consider here is completeness and clarity of the Requirements Breakdown Structure (RBS) and what PMLC model is the best fit for such a project. Be cautious in your choice of PMLC model. Make sure you are not backing yourself into a corner by making assumptions about solution content and committing to something that won't work. Err on the side of pessimism rather than optimism, and you will be on safer ground. Say that all signs suggest that the project can be managed using a Linear or Incremental PMLC model. For this project, the safe ground might be to use an Iterative PMLC model regardless of your confidence in the defined solution. You may have some history working with this client on previous projects. That will be a big contributor to your decision on the best-fit PMLC model.

If the project has never been done before (for example, one that involves the development of a new system), you might do requirements decomposition using two completely different approaches and use the results to cross check and confirm that decomposition. Once requirements decomposition has been confirmed, consider simulating the solution by building a quick prototype (not a production prototype) around the confirmed RBS. Test your prototyped solution with a broad audience of end users to further confirm the requirements.

WBS Construction

If the project is closer to the TPM end of the landscape, the Work Breakdown Structure (WBS) becomes the foundation of your choice of PMLC model. Generating a clear and complete WBS is the most difficult part of the project planning process. Building the WBS is a very intense and tiring exercise. You and the planning team will find yourselves rushing just to get the exercise over. Resist that temptation. If you felt rushed at the end, come back to the WBS a few days later. Share what you have with a trusted colleague and get that person's opinion. Objectivity is important here. Don't be afraid to criticize your work. If you don't get this part right, the risk of project failure increases.

Having a complete and correct WBS is critical to the success of a Linear or Incremental PMLC model. The entire project plan is based on the assumption that you have a complete WBS. Whatever difference there is between your WBS and a complete WBS will probably be reflected in the number of scope change requests you get. Processing those scope change requests will seriously compromise the project plan. Recall from the pain curve discussed in Chapter 5 that the maximum pain occurs in the generation of the WBS. Doing it right is just plain hard work, but you have to get it right. Don't shortchange the exercise. Do it right!

I have found that the following three strategies help me complete the WBS effort as painlessly as possible:

- Use all of the project team members and client representatives that have been identified. You need as much expertise and as many pairs of eyes as you can assemble. Bring them together in one place for a single planning meeting. Any other approach is a distant second in terms of effectiveness.

- Put the initial version of the WBS aside for a few days and come back to it with a critical eye. There will be enough loss of memory about what you did, and you should be able to approach validating it with a bit more objectivity. It's amazing how many logic faults you will find.

- Defend the WBS in front of a few respected peers who did not participate in building the WBS. They can be far more objective than you or the planning team and may find some problems with your WBS that you couldn't see.

Dynamic Risk Management Process

A lot of risk management plans gather dust on the shelf of the project manager. They were completed as part of project planning and never looked at again. Those plans that are referred to are referred to after the fact. That's too late. Effective risk management is probably your best weapon to protect the project from becoming distressed, but it has to be monitored continuously for any changes that might suggest heightened attention to one or more risks. Remember, as the project type moves from TPM toward xPM, project risk increases, and so should the intensity of your risk management efforts.

The first thing I would do is assign one of the senior members of the project team as manager of risk for the project. This individual's assignment begins with building the risk management plan during project planning. There should be a metrics-driven risk monitoring and control process included in the risk management plan. Use tight control values around these metrics to alert the team to early warning signs of changing conditions. Every team meeting should include an update on risk and recommended actions given the state of the project.

Scope Change Management Process

Scope change is the bane of the TPM project, and lack of it is the bane of APM, xPM, and MPx projects. In either case, you must have a well-defined and well-managed change management process in place. And most importantly, it must be understood and accepted by the client. In the case of TPM projects, the process must put some controls on the frequency and number of change requests. In the case of APM, xPM, and MPx projects there is a certain level and frequency of change requests that must happen, and you must put metrics in place to track that cumulative history.

Scope change is an area that often gives rise to most project problems. It doesn't really make a difference whether this is the result of doing a poor job on gathering and documenting requirements or dealing with a client who has lots of ideas. If there is no management control exercised over the frequency of scope change requests, there are going to be problems. The time to process a scope change request comes from the value-added work time of the team members, which means an aggravated schedule, errors, and ultimately, schedule slippage. The seeds of distress have been planted.

Here is an example from the case study of a change control process that you might put in place for a Linear or Incremental PMLC model. Recall that for these projects, the solution is clearly known and documented. There should be few scope change requests.

CASE STUDY – PIZZA DELIVERED QUICKLY (PDQ): ORDER ENTRY SUBSYSTEM

The requirements of the Order Entry subsystem were gathered through a series of use cases. Client participation was exemplary even though it was the first time PDQ employees had engaged in such an activity. There was an online Order Entry Screen, so customers could go directly to the system to enter their orders and pay with a credit card. That was easily defined. A one-stop entry was created for telephone orders that replaced the need for customers to call the store they preferred to use. The order would then be routed to the Logistics subsystem and assigned to the appropriate production facility (store, pizza factory, or pizza van). The Order Entry subsystem was estimated to require 32 days for development, testing, and deployment. That completion time was firm, because an outside consulting company had been hired to develop the Logistics subsystem beginning 36 days after the start of the Order Entry subsystem. The Logistics subsystem was dependent on the Order Entry subsystem, and work on it could not begin until the Order Entry subsystem was deployed. Pepe discussed the criticality of the schedule with the Order Entry project team and the client. He proposed a management reserve of three days to accommodate unexpected change requests.

Having management reserve is an effective insurance policy to protect the start time of related systems. In its absence, there is a strong likelihood of schedule slippage being passed on to the dependent systems. Without a management reserve, the Logistics subsystem in this example would likely be in a distressed condition even before it started.

Milestone Trend Charts

The milestone trend chart introduced in Chapter 7 is one of the few metrics that I know of that looks ahead in the project schedule for expected slippages and warns the project manager ahead of time that there may be problems later in the schedule if established trends persist. This information is made available early enough in the project time line to give the project team time to analyze and correct any anomalies. The milestone trend chart is an excellent early warning system and should be part of every monitoring and control process.

Milestone trend charts are of recent vintage. I introduced them in 1995. As a protection against potentially distressed projects, you might want to consider establishing very conservative trigger values, trends, and control limits that hint of potential distressed projects. Some examples are shown in Figure 16-1 and Figure 16-2.

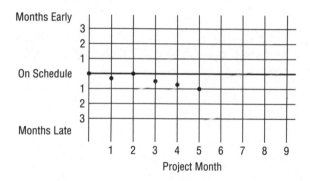

Figure 16-1: Conservative trend patterns to signal potentially distressed projects

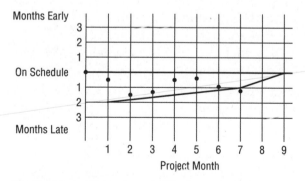

Figure 16-2: Tighter control limits as an early warning of a potentially distressed project

Figure 16-1 is one example where tightening the trend pattern will get the attention of the project manager sooner rather than later. Recall that a trend in the same direction for four or more consecutive report periods signals a potential problem that could lead to a distressed project. For good reason, you might tighten that to three or more as shown in Figure 16-1. If a project displays this type of pattern, look deeper into the causes and fix them.

Figure 16-2 is an example of tightening control limits using trigger values that dictate a potentially distressed project as you reach the outer schedule of the project. The solid line in the Late section of this project shows a control limit that ranges from 8 weeks late by reporting month 1, to 4 weeks late by reporting month 7, and then to 2 and 0 weeks late for the two remaining months of the project. The issue here is that the closer you get to the scheduled project completion date, the less likely you are to be able to make up serious slippages. A two-week slippage in the first month of a nine-month project is nowhere near as serious as a two-week slippage in the last four weeks of a project. Sooner or later you can't get there from here. This is the reason for tightening the control limits as you move to the outer part of the project schedule. Without that tightening, you will reach a point where the slippage cannot be made up, and the project will fail to meet the scheduled completion date.

Earned Value Analysis

Tracking trends in schedule performance index (SPI) and cost performance index (CPI) values and displaying them in the form of a milestone trend chart is one of the most intuitive metrics that I know of for early warnings of cost or schedule problems.

Earned value analysis, also called earned value management (EVM), has been used in the federal government for nearly 50 years. Only recently has it become popular in the private sector. It was discussed in detail in Chapter 7.

As you may recall from Chapter 7, actual cost (AC), earned value (EV), and planned value (PV) yield one additional level of analysis The SPI and CPI are further refinements. They are computed as follows:

$$SPI = EV / PV$$
$$CPI = EV / AC$$

Schedule Performance Index

As you saw in Chapter 7, the SPI is a measure of how close the project is to performing work as it was actually scheduled. If the SPI is greater than 1, the project is ahead of schedule. Obviously, this is desirable. An SPI value below 1 would indicate that the work performed was less than the work scheduled — hence, the project is behind schedule. The trend in SPI values tracked over time will be an indicator of problems.

Cost Performance Index

As you saw in Chapter 7, CPI is a measure of how close the project is to spending on the work performed to what you planned to spend. If the CPI is greater than 1, you are spending less than was budgeted for the work performed. If you are overspending for the work performed, the CPI will be less than 1.

Trend plots (like the milestone trend charts) are intuitive displays of the project history with respect to schedule and cost variances from plan. These indices are displayed graphically as trends compared against the baseline value of 1.

Just to refresh your memory, the earned value terminology has changed recently. I am using the terminology as defined in PMBOK. The old terminology compares to the new terminology as follows:

- Actual Cost of Work Performed (ACWP) is now called the actual cost (AC)
- Budgeted Cost of Work Performed (BCWP) is now called the earned value (EV)
- Budgeted Cost of Work Scheduled (BCWS) is now called the planned value (PV)

Integrating Milestone Trend Charts and Earned Value

Using both milestone trend charts and the EV for a project provides you with yet another early warning sign of potential distress. Chapter 7 gave several graphical examples of how the milestone trend chart format could use the SPI and CPI trend data to alert the project team of potential distressed project situations. To use these graphical tools, you should establish boundaries for the plots. Any trend line outside of the boundaries would trigger some form of corrective action to be taken.

Intervention Management Strategies

Despite all of your protections against a project becoming distressed, it may still happen. Depending on the seriousness of the situation, you may postpone any further work on the project while corrective actions are formulated and implemented in a revised project plan. For less serious situations, and because of resource constraints and previous schedule commitments, you might continue the project work while a resolution is defined and implemented.

Intervention occurs when the project has been deemed to be in distress. Intervention is a four-step process as defined in Figure 16-3.

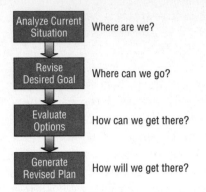

Figure 16-3: The intervention process

I answer each of the four questions shown in the figure in the sections that follow.

Analyze Current Situation: Where Are We?

Once a project has been determined to be distressed, the current status of the deliverables should be determined. A chart like the one shown in Figure 16-4 will be helpful. This is the starting point for further analysis and eventual re-planning of the distressed project.

DELIVERABLE	COMPLETE	STATUS	COMMENTS
A	Yes		Completed 2 days late
B	No	3 days behind	Error in specification
C	No	6 days behind	Key resource not available
D	No	12 days behind	Key resource not available
E	No	12 days behind	Not yet open for work

Figure 16-4: Current deliverables status

The next question to be answered is just how serious this out-of-control situation is. If it's not serious, maybe it will self-correct. If it's serious, some intervention may be needed. How do you know what must be done and what form that intervention might take? That is the topic of this section. There are several ways to approach the analysis of the situation. The most useful tool for analyzing causes of distressed projects is Root Cause Analysis.

Knowing that an undesirable situation exists is the starting point for Root Cause Analysis. Root Cause Analysis was discussed in detail in Chapter 15. Root Cause Analysis is represented as a hierarchical chart and is very intuitive. Starting from the top, the structure and terminology of Root Cause Analysis is as follows. At the top is the problem statement. The only restriction is that it must be a single problem. It must be clearly stated. Avoid jargon or terminology that might not be understood by anyone who might have the occasion to read it. The second level consists of one or more reasons that might have brought about the distressed condition. You must have the assurance that the reasons you state really are the reasons and not someone's conjecture. The reasons should be commonly accepted by the organization so that they do not need to be defended. The next several levels are "why" questions. There may be more than one "why" question per reason and more than one answer per "why" question. The answer to one "why" question gives rise to one or more additional "why" questions. At some point in this hierarchy, an answer becomes a statement for which no further "why" question makes sense. That statement is a root cause. You can expect to discover several root causes for the distressed condition.

In the experience I have had helping my clients manage distressed projects, there seems to be a pattern as to the road to defining a root cause. These are identified and briefly discussed in the following sections.

On the Road to Root Causes – Project Conception

Innocently buried in the Idea Generation Phase of several of the agile PMLC models discussed in Chapter 11 are the seeds of the project distress factors. These factors include the following:

- The project is based on an unrealistic business case.

- The project is based on executive leverage.

- The client cannot clearly define objectives.

- The project is based on state-of-the-art and immature technology.

- There is lack of client ownership.

- The client's funding or timescale is unrealistic.

- There is a failure to decompose the project into smaller feasible steps.

The first three factors are usually associated with wants, not needs. That reinforces your questioning of the client as to why they want what they want. If that is not defensible for any of the first three factors listed here, you have the makings of a distressed project. You need to take remedial action right then, during project inception, to avoid the possibility of the project becoming distressed later for any one or more of these three factors.

If the project will use the latest and greatest technology, you might not be equipped from a staffing perspective, and the project will be exposed to staff shortages or become too dependent on outside vendors. I have always stressed the importance of meaningful client involvement, and that involvement increases as you move from TPM to APM to xPM projects. As I have already discussed, the latest results from the Standish Group in their CHAOS 2010 survey report lists lack of User Involvement as the major reason for project failure. As I have commented in several places, for several years now, and at the risk of being repetitive, I can't stress enough the importance of meaningful client involvement. The extent to which you will or will not have meaningful client involvement is the driving factor in your choice of a best-fit PMLC model. I have had cases where the best-fit PMLC model required more client involvement than I could expect from my previous projects with the client. Workshops either before or during the project are highly recommended. Take the time to prepare the client for their roles and responsibilities. It will have good payback. When funding and time are unrealistic, it is usually related to the project scope being out of line with the time and cost. As you have already learned from the scope triangle presented in Chapter 1, scope, time, and cost are a dependent set. Specify any two, and the third is defined. This factor is usually a result of the client specifying all three and expecting a satisfactory result. It will never happen!

The size of the project is positively correlated with risk. The longer the project, the higher the risk of its becoming distressed. Project duration should be less than a calendar year and not span more than one fiscal year. If you have durations that are longer than that, I strongly advise decomposing them to more manageable lengths.

On the Road to Root Causes – Project Planning and Initiation

There is always the impatience to get going, and planning takes the back seat. Because of the high change environment that most projects find themselves in, many say that planning is just a waste of time. If that is the attitude of your client and your team, you have a problem and had better deal with it up front. Otherwise, your reward will be failure or at least a distressed condition. Here are some of the planning related reasons I have seen for distressed conditions on projects:

- Unrealistic cost, time, and capability estimates
- Failure to clearly define requirements
- Poor client/team relationships
- Poor scoping activities
- Lack of meaningful client involvement
- Poor WBS specification

- Unreliable risk management plan
- Poor planning
- Failure to clearly define roles and responsibilities

The first factor may be more related to the organization's steak appetite on a baloney budget. Capability is a human resource issue, and too many organizations overlook capability and the availability of skilled human resources when they approve a project. Resource contention, too much task variety, and mistakes are the result. All of these contribute to the occurrence of distressed projects. The Graham-Englund Model that I discussed in Chapter 14 must be used in deciding whether or not to add a project to the portfolio. Too many clients and teams do not give the attention to requirements gathering that they should. They are too quick to accept a requirement without the due diligence needed. The temptation to say "We'll deal with the details later in the project" is planting the seeds for distressed conditions. Take the time up front to do your best. It is worth the investment. During the Launching Phase, spend the time to build the project team and that means the client members as well as the development team. Their work environment needs to be open and honest, and you have to do whatever you can to establish that environment. Again it is worth the investment of time up front. As you move from TPM to APM to xPM projects, the WBS becomes less of a factor to initial planning, but that doesn't mean you can slack off on your efforts to build the WBS. Many of the APM and xPM PMLC models require a partial high-level WBS during the Scope Phase and partial detailed WBSs for the functions and features chosen for a cycle or iteration. If you can't get the WBS correct, the entire project plan or cycle plan is not built on a solid foundation. Risk management becomes more important as you move from TPM to APM to xPM projects, and your efforts to do risk management planning and monitoring should be heightened.

On the Road to Root Causes – Solution Definition

Many projects do not start out with a complete solution definition, so there is a high risk of project failure. These projects are complex, and there is a great deal of uncertainty associated with them. Here are some of the reasons I have seen repeatedly on these APM and xPM projects:

- Failure to apply appropriate scope management
- Poor choice of a technical platform or architecture
- Starting a phase prematurely
- Poor choice of requirements definition approach
- Poor preparation for requirements definition
- Lack of proper review

- Lack of skilled resources
- Poor standards deployment
- Poor requirements traceability

In any APM or xPM project, processing scope changes is relegated to the checkpoint that occurs at the completion of each iteration, cycle, or phase. These checkpoints are the heart and soul of every APM and xPM project, and must be taken seriously. The decision to continue and in what direction is the most important decision you have to make in these types of projects. You need to have the meaningful involvement of your client as well as the flexibility and ability to support a variety of requirements gathering approaches. The characteristics and experiences you have had with the client are major determinants in deciding how to gather requirements. Don't take the client outside of their comfort zone if you can help it. If you have to, make sure they are properly prepared to do so. That probably means training either beforehand or concurrent with the requirements gathering exercise itself.

On the Road to Root Causes – Solution Development

TPM, APM, and xPM projects all have potential problems as they try to develop the solution. Here are some of the frequently occurring reasons that I have observed:

- Technology advances overtaking the project
- Lack of proper change control
- Inadequate training and supervision
- Inadequate client review
- Poor management of outside contractors
- Lack of formal testing and integration approaches

The project is underway, and a new technological breakthrough is announced. You can ignore it and continue as planned, or you can stop the project and re-plan. What do you do and why? Whichever decision you make, there are cost implications. Adopting a new technology into a project that is already underway can be disastrous. Your capability to adopt the new technology is probably limited, because you will not have had previous experience with it. You may need to use outside consultants. On the other hand, ignoring the new technology can have severe market implications if your competitors have adopted the new technology and you haven't, because they will now have a competitive advantage in your markets. Client review is critical in APM and xPM projects. That review must be open and honest. If the client is unwilling or unable to push back, or if you can't push back, bad decisions are going to be made. The project will become distressed.

On the Road to Root Causes – Solution Implementation

I've seen so many examples of clients not taking the time to plan and implement the solution. All they are doing is laying the foundation for failure. Here are some reasons that I can recall:

- Inadequate client or end user training and support
- Catastrophic failure with no mitigation plan
- Missing a critical go-live date

The Closing Phase of any project should include implementation of the deliverables and handoff to the maintenance and support functions. This is part of the WBS, so it must be part of the project proposal. The establishment of a user training and support function in advance of implementation and handoff is often an afterthought rather than part of the project plan. To avoid catastrophic failure after implementation, some project plans include a warranty period — three months is typical. At the end of the warranty period, the deliverables are formally released to maintenance and support. That makes for a good mitigation plan.

Revise Desired Goal: Where Can We Go?

Taking all of the previous root causes into consideration, the project team needs to figure out whether they will go forward with the project, and, if so, how to go forward. The first step in that decision is to revise the original project goal. That might be straightforward or very complex given the extent of distress in the project and the criticality of the project. Maybe the project should be decomposed into several shorter-duration projects. Maybe the project should be abandoned and restarted at a later date in an entirely different direction. The process defined in this section of the chapter can work for all extremes — from minimal change to totally revised projects.

The Workshop

One highly recommended option is to hold a workshop to redirect the project. Analysis of a distressed project is a group activity. Speed is of the essence, because the project is in trouble and may still continue in that direction while the intervention process is underway. The following list describes how the ideal workshop environment should be configured:

- Hold the workshop offsite at a comfortable hotel.
- Have a good restaurant nearby.
- Book a large room with lots of whiteboard space.
- Have several flip charts.

■ Have breakout rooms for private discussions.

■ Use an experienced outside facilitator.

■ Agree on the ground rules.

Remember that the project may be on hold while you and the project team try to figure out how to get it back on track, so the workshop needs to be planned and executed quickly. The workshop itself will probably be a tense session. The project is distressed for some reason or reasons, and the client will probably have to give up or postpone getting some features and functions. They won't be happy, especially if they see this distressed condition as your fault.

The Process of Revising the Original Goal

In order to revise the project goal, you follow the process depicted in Figure 16-5. The sections that follow discuss the process depicted in the figure.

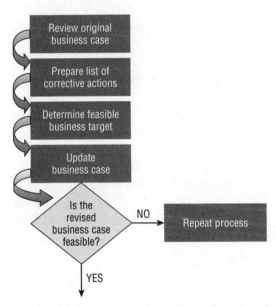

Figure16-5: The process of revising the original goal

Reviewing the Original Business Goal

Requirements descriptions must be reviewed to determine if they are essentially complete and relatively stable. As in all projects, there are both fixed requirements and evolving requirements. Fixed requirements are nice — straightforward and relatively easy to satisfy. Evolving requirements are much more delicate and are usually those that drive the project outside its boundaries. To go one step further, you and the client must determine whether or not there are any high-level requirements that need further refinement or if there are any requirements in the TBD (to be determined) category. These must either be defined or eliminated, because undefined requirements are difficult to track at best and tend to yield scope creep. There are three parts to the process of reviewing the original business goal, as follows:

- Reviewing the original business case
- Defining the current business needs
- Realigning the business case to current business needs

Reviewing the Original Business Case

In order to get the project approved for planning and then approved for execution, you and the client had to prepare a Project Overview Statement (POS) and project proposal. What did you do to justify that the project had acceptable business value to proceed with it?

Defining the Current Business Needs

There is no reason to expect the current business situation to be the same as it was when the project was originally defined and planned. The project itself is different than was planned simply because it has drifted into a distressed situation. The business climate has changed as well. These two factors influence the project going forward and must be accounted for in the revised project goal.

Even if only a few weeks or months have passed since the project began, there is a high probability that the world is different now than it was before. That opens the potential for a change in business needs. Document the current business needs and compare those to the original business needs. The variance between the two has to be resolved in order to update the business case.

Realigning the Business Case to Current Business Needs

How does the variance between the original and current business needs impact the original business case? Revise the business case if senior management requires such revision so that the revised business case aligns with the current business needs.

Taking all of these factors into consideration, the original business goal is revised to reflect the current situation.

Preparing a List of Corrective Actions

Depending upon where the project was in the PMLC model when it became distressed, you can take different actions to resolve the causes that led to the distressed condition. They are listed and briefly commented on in the following sections.

Corrective Actions – General

These are global corrective actions that apply across the entire PMLC model. They include the following:

- Strengthen, replace, or reorganize management where needed
- Implement improvements in the deployment and test environment where needed
- Consider redistributing work to commercial off the shelf (COTS) vendors

Corrective Actions – Requirements

It almost goes without saying that these corrective measures will result in a restriction of functions and features. The list of possible corrective actions includes the following:

- Establish a client-based scope change request process.
- Remove functionality where the business case is weak.
- Prioritize functionality (MoSCoW).
- Review requirements for any package customization.
- Prioritize functionality by business unit and remove functions as required.

Corrective Actions – Design/Develop/Integrate

These corrective actions apply inside the iterations, cycles, and phases. They include the following:

- Review the solution for more use of commercial off the shelf (COTS) software.
- Partition the project work into swim lanes for schedule compression.
- Consider incremental releases.
- Simplify interfaces to external applications.

Corrective Actions – Testing and Implementation

Although these could have been included in the general corrective actions list, I chose to separate them because they are quite different. This list includes the following:

- Consider incremental user testing.
- Use pilots for early release.

Evaluate Options: How Can We Get There?

The process for evaluating options is shown in Figure 16-6.

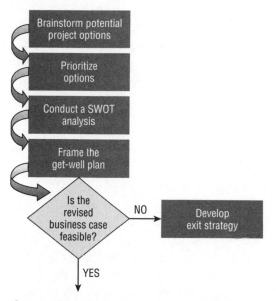

Figure 16-6: The process of evaluating options

Brainstorm Potential Project Options

This step involves the client and the project team. It begins with a review of the Root Cause Analysis results. For each identified root cause, brainstorm a list of possible remedial actions. Then identify the possible project options given that the remedial actions have been taken.

Prioritize Options

The client and the project team must now arrange the options in priority order. The priority is based on the business value of each option.

Conduct a SWOT Analysis

The prioritized list of options is now subjected to a Strengths, Weaknesses, Opportunities, Threats (SWOT) analysis. The SWOT analysis should address the following areas:

- The degree of PSO support offered to the project team throughout the PMLC model for this option
- The skill and competency profile of the team with respect to this option

- The degree to which the client has been meaningfully involved in the project and will be able to support this option
- The contents of the Scope Bank related to this option

Frame the Get-Well Plan

How are you going to approach the revised project? Will you use the same PMLC model as originally used, or is there some reason to reconsider that decision? If there is a PMLC model that will deliver intermediate results more often than the current model, you should consider switching to it. This might require the revision of timeboxes and deliverables allocated to each increment, iteration, cycle, or phase.

Is the Revised Business Case Feasible?

The answer to this question determines whether or not the project will go forward in its revised version. Just as the original business case was used to commission the project, the revised business case is needed to continue the project as revised. In its revised form, it may not make business sense to continue the project, and it will be terminated. Conversely, the possibility of continuing the project in some other revised form may make sense, so the project team will return to the drawing board to craft another revision. Scope reduction is often the way out. In other words, the revised business case addresses only part of the requirements. The unmet requirements from this version may be left for a later version.

If the revised business case does make business sense, then approval is granted to proceed to the Planning Phase. This is exactly the position of a project that was proposed following the normal process — submission of a POS.

Generate Revised Plan: How Will We Get There?

Using the results of the SWOT analysis, put together a high-level plan showing milestones, what will be delivered, and by when. The plan should also include the budget impact on both the client and the project team.

The three steps for creating a new plan to bring the distressed project back to health are the same steps you used to first plan and launch a project. They are as follows:

1. Prepare a revised project plan.
2. Get management acceptance of the revised plan.
3. Prepare to restart the project.

Prepare a Revised Project Plan

This activity begins with the revised business case and updated deliverables list as input to the planning steps that consist of building the WBS (deliverables-based);

estimating the duration, resource requirements, and labor; creating dependency diagrams; and scheduling. The revised plan should be prepared as a collaborative effort with the client fully participating. Their buy-in is essential, and you won't get it if they are not part of the process.

Get Management Acceptance of the Revised Plan

Management won't be too happy about this whole experience. The original goal will probably not be met. A compromise is offered in the revised plan. Management's approval here is no different than it was for the project when it was first proposed. The only difference is that management now has a bad taste in their mouth over the failure to-date on this project, so they won't be as easy to convince this time. Their support is the highest-priority critical success factor for any project intervention.

Prepare to Restart the Project

The launch activities for an intervention are the same as those for a first-time project launch. Hopefully the same team is in place, so team operating rules are already in place. These rules may need to be tightened because of the higher risk that this distressed project will be exposed to. Some of the important tasks include making sure of the following:

- The team's skills and competencies are correctly aligned with the revised project plan

- There are clearly defined and assigned roles and responsibilities for each team member

- A revised risk management plan is in place and assigned to a team member

- A more finely tuned monitoring system is in place to detect minor trends in schedule or cost variances

An Intervention Process Template

For those of you who like to use templates here is one that I have found particularly useful as a starting point for an intervention. In the absence of details on the project situation, it helps structure your thinking as you begin an intervention. It is an eight-step template:

Step 1: Determine sponsor expectations and intervention directive. In an intervention project sponsors are the people who requested your assistance. They have decided that the project is in distress. That conclusion may be based on their own criteria or on the project having met certain enterprise conditions that establish the project as a project in distress. As part of your initial meeting with the sponsors, they should share what they expect you to do based on what they perceive the situation to be. Do not consider this a definitive statement. I usually view these as more of their opinion rather than the results of any scientific investigation. It may be appropriate to consider suspending further work on the project until you have conducted a more thorough analysis.

Step 2: Define problem(s) and assign owner(s). Understand that the project team and especially the project manager will almost always be in a defensive mode. You have to determine the problem(s) and they are the closest to the problem, so proceed with care and understanding. You should try to validate any information they give you. Each problem should have a person assigned as owner. That person may be a team member or someone outside the team. While the owner of the problem is ultimately responsible for solving the problem, that person will have your assistance.

Step 3: Assemble an intervention team and establish intervention process. The intervention team should be kept small. Four to six members should be sufficient for most interventions. You will be the manager of the intervention team and should have the authority to pick your team. If it makes sense, the project manager should be one of your team members. At this point you should have enough details on the problem(s) to modify the rest of the template. That should be done in collaboration with your intervention team.

Step 4: Conduct Root Cause Analysis and Force Field Analysis. These are staple tools of any Six Sigma toolkit and are discussed in Chapter 15.

Step 5: Develop corrective action plans. The corrective action plans can take many forms. They could be process or practice related. A process step might have to be modified due to conditions that are present in the project. From a practice perspective some short-term training might be needed to correct a performance problem.

Step 6: Revise project scope. The remaining time and budget might constrain the original scope and render continuing the project a bad business decision. That will be for the sponsors to consider but you will have to provide input to their decision process. So begin with a statement of the revised scope. This may have to be further revised as you prepare the project plan.

Step 7: Revise project plan and deliverables. Armed with the revised scope, prepare a new project plan. This may take a few iterations in order to meet the budget and deadline constraints.

Step 8: Gain sponsor approval and authorization to continue the project. The sponsors have to make a business decision as to whether or not the project should continue. If it does continue, the trip wires that signal pending distress need to be tightened. Having had performance problems that led to the first distressed condition, it is likely that the situation will repeat itself if not closely watched.

Interventions are not easy. The entire project team and even the client are put in defensive mode. If you are the intervention team manager, you have to be very careful how you interact with the team. To the extent you can, you have to make them your allies. In general, the closer you can keep them to you the better off you will be.

Roles and Responsibilities of the PSO with Respect to Distressed Projects

Every project in the project portfolio should have several milestone events at which a project review takes place. The reviews can be powerful tools for early detection and corrective actions. First of all, the Project Support Office (PSO) needs to take project reviews very seriously. The project review may be the first opportunity to spot signs of a project potentially becoming distressed and to take corrective steps. For the astute project manager, this should not be a surprise. He or she would already be aware of the potential distressed condition and have taken the appropriate steps. At this early stage, ask the project manager to discover why the condition exists and put preventive measures in place to prevent a recurrence. The senior project managers on the project review panel will be able to offer a number of possible corrective measures. At the next project review, focus on the effectiveness of the steps taken by the project manager. Has the early warning sign been neutralized? If not, step up the intensity of the corrective measures.

The worst thing would be to do nothing and hope the situation will self-correct. It won't, so why take the risk? This reminds me of team members who practice hope creep. I talked about that in Chapter 1. Recall that hope creep is the situation where a team member falls behind schedule but doesn't report it. Their hope is that they will get caught up by the next status report date. That might happen, but it is not too likely. If you suspect that this might be going on under the table, check it out. You want your team members to be open and honest. Hiding problems is not good behavior for any of your team members or for you. That behavior lets the whole team and your client down. Rely on the project review panel. They should be committed to using their own experiences and problem-solving skills to help you succeed.

When the project has reached a distressed state, project reviews take on a heightened sense of importance and action. Recall that the project review is chaired by the PSO Director and attended by a review panel whose members are other senior-level project managers. Depending on the nature of the distressed condition, the membership of the review panel may be changed to include expertise focused on the problem situation. The distressed project review is not just a formality. It begins with the intervention process previously depicted in Figure 16-6, with the added involvement of the PSO through the review panel. I want to take a closer look at what that involvement might include.

The reports that track early warning signs would have alerted the PSO Director to a pending problem and the potential distressed situation, indicating that some preemptive action is called for. So even before the project becomes distressed, a special session of the project review team might have been called. The focus of that review is prevention, and the project manager would be expected to present the get-well plan to restore the project. The project review team might offer revisions or alternatives. The next session of the project review would be scheduled, and the status of the project would again be placed under close scrutiny. The focus is still on prevention.

Despite all of that attention and support, the project may still fall into a distressed condition. The project review panel now becomes fully engaged in the intervention process for that project. It is critically important that that review panel intervention does not add time to the intervention process. Their support must be facilitative, not punitive.

Time is not on your side. The project may be on hold pending an approved plan to move forward, so the review panel should not add to the time needed to complete the intervention process. Instead, the panel should work collaboratively with the project team. For example, adding status reports would not be a good idea. That adds report preparation time and report presentation time. A better approach would include a level of involvement where the status is known just by the nature of the review panel's involvement. For example, one of the review panel members could be assigned to the project team for the duration of the intervention process. This panel member would be responsible for reporting project performance and status back to the entire review panel until there has been some disposition of the project.

In addition to the project review role, the PSO should be constantly aware of project performance — not through progress reports, but by walking around and observing. There is no substitute for stopping in on a project manager or team meeting and just observing what is taking place. These informal visits can help build a relationship with the project manager and the team, and can be a good source of information that won't show up on any progress reports or during a project review.

Analyzing the Current Situation

The added value of the review panel is that they provide an objective viewpoint of monitoring the analysis activities. Because the review panel members are outsiders, they may look at the Root Cause Analysis a bit differently and spot something that the project team would have otherwise overlooked. Also, the review panel may observe something that triggers a thought of a past experience they had and a suggestion for what they did that might help this project. Several ideas should be forthcoming from the review panel members.

Revising the Desired Goal

All of the workshop planning and facilitating can be done by a representative from the review panel. Presumably, he or she would have previous experience with these types of workshops and can relieve the project manager to focus on the problem at hand.

The revised goal might be reduced in scope for this version, with a second version fulfilling the remaining requirements of the original goal. Reducing scope will reduce the risk of failure of a project that has gone distressed once and is a likely candidate for going into a distressed state again.

Evaluating the Options

The project manager should seek the advice of the PSO in the evaluation of the options. An outsider without preconceived ideas about what should be done will be the best critic. If the PSO concurs with the evaluation and the resulting prioritization of alternatives, a project plan can be built.

Generating the Revised Plan

The review panel can appoint one of their members or someone else who has experience facilitating project planning sessions. This will relieve the project manager of that responsibility so that he or she can focus on the project itself. To the extent possible, do not put an aggressive plan together. That is only asking for a repeat of the distressed condition. The team will already feel the pressure from the earlier problem. Don't plant the seeds of another problem.

Putting It All Together

Preventing projects from falling into a distressed state is clearly where your efforts should be placed. This translates to simply paying attention to every phase of the PMLC model. It's easy to shortchange the process steps, but you will pay for your negligence sooner or later. Do it right so you won't have to do it over again! Rework wastes time, and an APM or xPM project manager can't afford to waste time on non-value-added work.

Discussion Questions

1. Define the metrics you would put in place as early warning signs that an Adaptive Project Framework (APF) project is heading for a distressed condition. Create at least one metric for each of the five phases of an APF project. Be specific and include your trigger values.

CASE STUDY – PIZZA DELIVERED QUICKLY (PDQ)

2. For the Order Entry subsystem, define an early-warning SPI tracking metric with trigger values and a supporting graphic display.

3. Despite the team's heroic efforts to keep the Order Entry subsystem on schedule, it has fallen behind and used the management reserve. You are now expected to be two days late. The Logistics subsystem can no longer start on schedule, and the contractors are booked to start. What are you going to do?

CHAPTER
17

Organizing Multiple Team Projects

The productivity of a work group seems to depend on how the group members see their own goals in relation to the goals of the organization.

— Paul Hersey, California American University, and Kenneth H. Blanchard, University of Massachusetts

CHAPTER LEARNING OBJECTIVES

After reading this chapter, you will be able to:

- Define the multiple team (multi-team) project situation
- Know the different types and complexity of multi-team projects
- Understand the challenges presented by multi-team projects

In larger organizations, it is not unusual for projects to draw independent teams from across the organization. These teams often come with their own tools, templates, and processes, which they expect to be using to complete their work on this project. In fact, with the added need for globalization affecting nearly every application, most, if not all, projects will involve more than one team. This chapter examines this unique but growing situation and explores several ways to scope, organize, plan, and manage such projects.

What Is a Multiple Team Project?

The multi-team projects that populate the project portfolio of large organizations are unlike any other development projects found today. If you organize business initiatives around client groups and business units, any project that crosses client lines gives rise to a multi-team project. The temptation is to let each team act on its own, with some integrating activity at the end to "glue" everything together, and hope that that approach will work. That is not the approach I recommend. My approach is more deliberate and planned, as you will see.

A more formal definition of a multi-team project is given in Figure 17-1.

A multiple team project is any project that requires the collaboration and involvement of two or more independent teams.

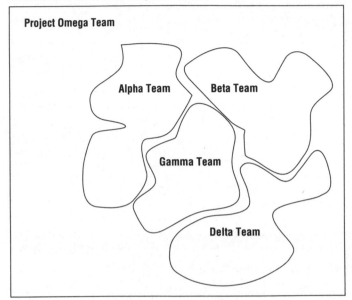

Figure 17-1: Definition of a multi-team project

This is a simple definition, but it can serve your purposes quite well. In large companies this structure can occur quite frequently, but even in smaller companies it happens, too. For example, the IT department has its own methodology for doing software development. The mechanical engineering department has its own methodology for doing new product development. Teams from both departments are brought together to develop a new product with a significant software component. The IT team has decided that this is an Agile Project Management (APM) project and will use the Adaptive Project Framework (APF) adaptive project management life cycle (PMLC) model. The engineering department has used a Linear PMLC for over 20 years and has no intention of doing it any differently. You are the project manager. What would you do? I leave this unanswered here and have included it in the "Discussion Questions" section at the end of the chapter. Once you understand the three different organizational and management approaches you will be better prepared to answer this question.

Challenges to Managing a Multiple Team Project

For many years, the focus in project management has been on the effective management of the project team. Its members were selected based on their expertise relative to the requirements of the project; requirements were gathered and documented; a project plan was built and executed; and client change requests were proposed and acted upon in the best interest of the enterprise.

Then along came companies like Walmart with its unique information systems client-centric structure. Its IT Department was organized into independent teams. Each team focused exclusively on a specific line of business or client group, and was able to satisfy their requirements for new and enhanced applications systems. These teams were very effective in meeting their client's specific needs. The IT teams became experts in the client's line of business. In meeting the specific business systems needs of their client group, each team created its own project management methodology with the tools, templates, and processes needed to support their client's line of business. Many of the team members were in fact the Business Analyst/Project Manager (BA/PM) professionals, which are discussed in Chapter 18. At the time they were my client, Walmart's Information Systems Department had more than 250 such teams. Whenever projects involved more than two teams, you can imagine the potential conflicts between methodologies that could occur. The approach used to manage such situations is the focus of this chapter. With so many companies expanding into global markets, their growth as well as the added complexities of gaining and sustaining itself in the world markets, projects are taking on a different character. Most projects now involve integrating two or more independent teams for their effective execution. In mission-critical, enterprise-wide, and other complex cases, several teams must be brought together in order to successfully deliver the expected results. Depending on the maturity of the team processes, integrating independently developed processes could be simple or it could be very complex. Being able to do this effectively without sacrificing the corporate culture and increasing project risk presents new challenges to the project manager. I am not aware of any publications that treat the management of these multi-team projects. This chapter is the first published work on this topic.

As a project manager, you are only concerned about a single project, but when you have multiple independent teams working on that project, it seems as though there are really multiple projects to be managed. The reality is that you are managing a single project and that has to be made clear to all of the involved teams if you are to be successful on these very complex endeavors. In all such projects, there will be several project managers (one from each team and perhaps one who has overall responsibility for the project). It is the job of these project managers to build the management infrastructure that will be responsible for the overall project. The situation presents the project managers with several challenges. I examine them in this chapter.

In today's project management environment, the pace of business initiatives and the lack of resources require many project managers to manage concurrent, multiple, and dependent projects. In years gone by, this scenario was reserved for senior-level project managers. Today, project managers of all experience and competency levels are called on to manage multiple efforts simultaneously. The following suggestions can help multi-project managers keep their head "in the midst of the storm" and establish a consistent methodical approach amongst the inherent chaos of multi-project team management. The emotional maturity of the project manager will surely be put to the test.

To get your creative juices flowing, the following sections raise a number of issues and considerations. These are things you need to think about as you consider possible management structures for your multi-team project.

Working with Teams from Different Companies

Projects that require the participation of two or more organizations are the source of the most complex type of multiple team projects. These range from projects that involve a team from your organization and a team from a contractor's organization to projects that are a collaborative effort from two or more independent companies. The contractor will want to impose their project management process on yours and that can create conflicting processes. How you deal with those eventualities should be part of the terms and conditions of the contract.

Working with Fiercely Independent Team Cultures

Walmart employs more than 10,000 IT professionals who are organized into more than 250 independent teams. Each team serves a single line of business or client group and has their own project management methodology designed specifically for their client. For this client, the structure works very well, until a project involving two or more teams comes along. Recognizing that there can be all sorts of complications in merging the work of two or more teams into a single project, how do you organize and manage such efforts? I have coined the term *fiercely independent* to characterize this project phenomenon. It seems that the more mature the processes, the more fierce the independence. Although that independence may have served clients well, it doesn't necessarily scale to projects that involve multiple lines of business or client groups. This is a reality that larger or global companies face; therefore, it's a problem that must be dealt with. That is the sum and substance of this chapter.

Working with Different Team Processes

Each of the three models you are going to read about in this chapter requires a different level of integration across the teams. One of those levels involves the integration of processes. A major methodology decision is whether you will establish one process or establish a process that consolidates the deliverables from several processes. Another area of integration deals with human resource management. Is the entire project team to be managed as a single team or as independent teams, each with its own human resource needs and management process? As you begin to think about the organizational structure of your project team, you have to weigh the importance of integration to the successful operation of the team and the project.

Accommodating Competing Priorities

The team members are typically not assigned 100 percent to the multi-team project. They have competing priorities for their time. They most often choose to give priority to their client rather than to the multi-team project. Balancing those competing and often conflicting priorities can be a significant challenge. In cases where the project is a very large enterprise-wide project, its members may be assigned 100 percent. That also can influence your choice of a project management structure.

Communicating within the Team Structure

The extent to which the multiple teams are integrated determines the importance of communications within the entire project team. The more layers of communication you have to deal with, the more likely there will be problems.

Establishing a Project Management Structure

Team independence has spawned a number of project management approaches and structures. Multi-team projects are complex and therefore a challenge to manage effectively. A team structure must be chosen that best meets the needs of the multi-team project and any operative constraints at play. That structure can be relatively loose or very tight. The nature of the project influences the choice. The chosen structure is going to have significant impact on the resulting management overhead.

Establishing One Project Management Life Cycle

The first step in establishing consistency and order in a multi-team project environment is to establish a definitive life cycle for the project. Whether this is one life cycle or several depends on the processes used to support the several client groups involved. Perhaps a custom-designed PMLC model is called for. Life cycles generate certain patterns of thinking among the project teams. This becomes very important when your time will be monopolized by multi-team demands. Not having the time to micro-manage personal behaviors, you need to establish a useful mindset in the project team. Using definitive life cycles and phases is a safe and "low-energy level" way of instilling these behaviors and outlook. But that means a change in process for many of the teams.

The project life cycle should be established at the inception of the project, be documented, and become part of the working project schedules. The phases should be used as high-level summary tasks in the actual project plan. It is also a good idea to distribute a definition of the individual phases, their significance, the roles and responsibilities required for each, and the clear intent of each phase prior to project kick-off or planning.

If multiple projects are serving the same end or result, it may be in your best interest as the project manager to "sell" them to senior management as a strategy versus individually disconnected projects. Other contributing projects, not under your auspices, may also be included under the strategy. When you classify a group of projects as a strategy, it is far more possible for you to do the following:

- Appoint a strategy director. This person, by title, would be responsible for coordinating and securing cross-functional resources, strategic decisions, and general project leadership.

- Establish a consistent life cycle or methodology across multiple teams under the strategy.

- Appoint a shared administrative staff for projects under the strategy.

- Utilize joint risk analysis and joint resolution strategies.

- Perform proper project scoping. This means work is apportioned properly to the team it belongs with; therefore, a more efficient use of resources is achieved.

- Take advantage of the strength that follows from numbers. The project managers under the strategy benefit from the collective experience and intuition of the project manager. Information sharing is more easily implemented due to the strategy nature of the work.

Building an Integrated Project Plan and Schedule

The overall project schedule is perhaps the most important part of the project plan. The range or integration possibilities go from not integrated to fully integrated. Furthermore, integration can be put in place at various depths (milestones, activities, and/or tasks). What level is appropriate for the project and to what extent should that integration span the entire project?

Defining a Requirements Gathering Approach

Several variables have to be coordinated in order to effectively identify, document, and validate client requirements. The first variable is the client. Several client groups are involved, so their requirements have to be gathered and consolidated with those of the other client groups. The second variable is the approach to gathering requirements. There are a number of alternatives, and each client group may have its preferred approach in which they are experienced and which they expect to be using.

The decision as to the approach or approaches to be used is one consideration, but an equally important one is the structure of the requirements gathering exercise. Will it be done as a single group or as multiple groups, or as individual client groups? If done in separate groups, how will these potentially conflicting lists be consolidated? If separate, you must become a shuttle diplomat. That may be a role you have never experienced before! A discussion question at the end of this chapter gives you a chance to develop a strategy for resolving conflicting requirements.

Establishing a Scope Change Management Process

Any request for a scope change can, and probably will, affect several client groups. Project Impact Statements and the approval process are considerably more complex than in single-team projects. Will you establish a Scope Change Control Board to manage all scope change requests? That might work fine for Traditional Project Management (TPM) projects, but what about Agile Project Management (APM) or Extreme Project Management (xPM) projects? Or to really craft a demonic example, what if part of the project were to be done using a TPM model and part using an APM model? Now what does your scope change management process look like? The answer to that is also relegated to the "Discussion Questions" section at the end of the chapter. Here's a chance to exercise your creative juices!

Defining the Team Meeting Structure

Multi-team project structures usually result in additional layers of project management, hence the need for additional team meetings. This structure should be carefully worked out and agreed to by all parties. The danger is that you will have a meeting overload, taking team members from the real work of the project.

Establishing Manageable Reporting Levels

Multi-team project management requires high levels of energy and focus over extended periods of time. To achieve this, you must consider what reporting levels are required on your projects in order for you to do the following:

- Maintain control over the scope and progress of the project
- Maintain control in the time available, with realistic reporting requirements

Milestone reporting is a way to maintain control over the project, yet minimize the amount of time spent in gathering and analyzing the data.

Consider the following issues when establishing the project reporting requirements:

- What are the levels of project complexity and urgency?
- What are the levels of project risk, both overall and within each phase?
- What is the skill level of the person who will be gathering and reporting data?
- How much time will you need to analyze data after it is reported?
- Is there a clear change management policy in place?
- Is there a clear communication protocol set for the project team?

After answering these questions, decide on reporting levels that will yield results and the detailed information required for management decisions. This must be done in a balanced approach, considering the amount of time required from the project team to gather the information and the amount of time required from you to analyze the reporting data.

Sharing Resources across Teams

If the team is structured as a single integrated team, this is a non-issue. If your team is structured as several independent teams, you may have a problem. In this situation, you should get the up-front commitment from each team leader that the use of all team resources is going to be based on a collaborative decision-making process. The actual process for sharing resources has to be jointly developed and approved.

The more complex and uncertain the project, the more likely there will be scarce skills. If this is the case, you should use a team structure that makes the sharing of those scarce skills as easy as possible.

Staffing across the PMLC

It is very likely that each team might have a phase or process within a phase that has been particularly effective in their previous projects. This project can benefit not only from using that phase or process, but also from having a member of that team manage that effort. That will not only benefit the current project but also contribute to the morale of the team that contributes that phase or process.

These decisions should be made during the planning phase. There may be integration issues to resolve ahead of time.

Searching Out Your Second

Who will represent you and speak for you in your absence? Is this one person or several people depending on the situation? The multi-team project has enough management complexity built in to warrant some help. If the total team size is above 30, you might consider having some administrative support in the form of an associate manager. This person could act on your behalf.

Classifying Multiple Team Projects

The types of project situations that give rise to multiple teams range from the simple to the very complex. There are six types of situations, as listed in Figure 17-2.

# of Teams	Update or Enhance	New	Global	Level of Complexity
Two	X		X	Medium Complexity
Two		X	X	High Complexity
Multiple	X			Low Complexity
Multiple	X		X	Medium Complexity
Multiple		X		Medium Complexity
Multiple		X	X	Very High Complexity

Figure 17-2: Types of multiple multi-team projects

Two Teams

There are only two cases to consider here. One team has the responsibility for the application, product, or service that is to be enhanced. The other team (if it actually is a team) is responsible for defining, documenting, and integrating the globalization requirements.

Update or Enhance and Global

The simpler of the two cases involves enhancing an existing application, product, or service that is already a global application. Because the requirements have already been built from previous versions of the application, only the new requirements (which must also be deployed globally) present any difficulties for the teams. The PMLC model used by the development team will usually be able to integrate global requirements into their model.

New and Global

This case is the more complex one because it involves gathering requirements that must be globally deployed. Because of cultural, economic, legal, and other considerations, this process could be very difficult. Each culture might be treated like another client. That adds complexity and potential requirements conflicts to the process. I look closely at the requirements gathering and agreement process later in the chapter.

Multiple Teams

There are four cases to consider here. More than two teams are involved in the application. If the application also must be deployed globally, then you encounter the most complex of multi-team situations.

Update or Enhance

Although moderately complex, this is the simplest of the four multi-team situations. Requirements gathering and resolving potential requirements conflicts for the new functionality and features are the complicating factors. I look closely at the requirements gathering and agreement process later in the chapter.

Update or Enhance and Global

Because several application areas are involved in the updating and enhancing, these projects tend to be complex. Requirements agreement for the new functionality must be agreed to and must be considered for global deployment.

New

These projects are generally of medium to high complexity. The level of complexity is based on the dependency of the new system to existing systems across multiple client groups. This follows from the likelihood that individual client systems are going to be impacted differently by the new application. It also introduces the possibility that the requirements of the new application might conflict with those of existing client applications.

New and Global

These are the most complex of the six cases. The same discussion that was used for two teams working on a new application for global deployment applies to this case. The added complexity is due to the fact that this is a new application and all functionality must be defined by and agreed to by all parties.

Now I want to turn your attention to the organizational structures that I have seen in my client base.

Project Office Structure

It is a common practice in organizations to establish a Project Office (PO) to manage large or mission-critical projects. Such a structure is temporary and exists only to serve the needs of large or mission-critical projects. Some organizations will even establish a PO whenever the team size reaches a certain number (for example, 30 is the rule used by one of my clients). The PO is just another layer of management, to whom the individual project managers report. The PO provides general management support, coordination, and basic administrative services to each of the project managers.

DEFINITION: PROJECT OFFICE A Project Office (PO) is a temporary management structure established to coordinate and support the work of several independent teams who are concurrently working on the same single project that has task dependencies across the team structure.

NOTE Do not confuse a Project Office (PO) with a Project Management Office (PMO) or Project Support Office (PSO). PMOs and PSOs are permanent organizational structures that support the needs of all projects of a certain type.

First note that the PO is a temporary structure. It is managed by a program manager and exists only to serve the needs of the individual teams who are working on the same project. Once the project is complete, the PO is disbanded.

Project Office Characteristics

As illustrated in Figure 17-3, the PO structure is very simple.

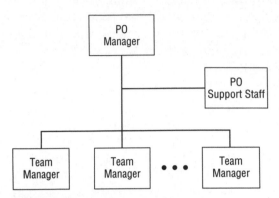

Figure 17-3: Project Office structure

This structure scales very well to large projects. The support staff ranges from a minimum of a single part-time administrative person (provided by the PMO in some cases) to a practical maximum of several full-time PO administrators and associate managers.

The roles and responsibilities of the PO Manager and support staff are as follows:

- Organize and manage the entire project
- Develop the high-level project plan in collaboration with team managers
- Integrate and coordinate the project plans of each team
- Maintain the overall project schedule
- Monitor and manage resource use
- Prepare and distribute project status reports
- Plan and conduct team meetings
- Process scope change requests
- Solve problems escalated from the individual teams
- Negotiate and solve problems between teams

The following subsections discuss each of these in more detail.

Organize and Manage the Entire Project

The PO Manager must bring together multiple teams under one management structure. These teams are accustomed to operating independently, but they must now operate under a common set of procedures and processes. This is best accomplished through an organizational meeting attended by the project leads from each team. A new set of team operating rules will come from this meeting, which all team leads have agreed to support and follow.

Develop the High-Level Project Plan in Collaboration with Team Managers

The PO Manager should collaborate with the team leads to draft the high-level project plan. Each team lead can then take that high-level plan as input and work with their team to complete their part of the project plan.

Integrate and Coordinate the Project Plans of Each Team

There will be a number of inter-plan dependencies that will have to be accounted for and built into a master project schedule. That work will be led by the PO Manager in collaboration with all of the project leads.

Maintain the Overall Project Schedule

Once the project has been launched, the PO Manager will be responsible for monitoring project performance and progress. Adjustments to the project's master schedule will have to be made as tasks are completed (ahead of or behind schedule).

Monitor and Manage Resource Use

Resource management is a critical responsibility of the PO Manager. Adjustments will have to be made to accommodate approved scope change requests and solve other schedule-related problems.

Prepare and Distribute Project Status Reports

Project status reports should be submitted by the project leads and consolidated by the PO Manager for submission to the various stakeholder groups, clients, and senior management.

Plan and Conduct Team Meetings

At the highest level, there should be frequent (perhaps daily) meetings chaired by the PO Manager and attended by the project managers. The project managers, at their own discretion, should hold meetings (probably daily) with their team members.

Process Scope Change Requests

This is a complex activity that must be managed by the PO Manager or a designated associate. You should expect that every change request will impact the schedule and resources of every team. The PO Manager is responsible for receiving, processing, and closing all scope change requests. This is no small task, because both the master schedule and resource allocation must be considered. Given that there are cross-team dependencies, this task must be dealt with using the most intense due diligence.

Solve Problems Escalated from the Individual Project Teams

There will be many situations where a project manager is unable to resolve a problem. Cross-team dependencies will lie at the root of many of the problems. These are beyond the authority of the project manager and must be escalated to the PO Manager for resolution.

Negotiate and Resolve Problems between Teams

Some problems may involve two or more teams. In the event that they are not able to resolve the problem among themselves, it will have to be escalated to the PO Manager.

Project Office Strengths

The strengths of the PO approach are as follows:

- Coordinates the work of several independent teams
- Scales to large projects
- Managed from a single integrated plan
- Integrates resource management control
- Allows teams to maintain their practices

Coordinates the Work of Several Independent Teams

The PO Manager is basically a coordinator. He or she is responsible for gluing together the deliverables and artifacts from independent teams. This coordination should be minimally invasive of each team's processes and practices. Teams prefer this approach to learning and using different processes and practices, which is a real strength of the PO structure.

On the flip side is the burden placed on the PO Manager. There will be some benefit from getting teams to agree on how their artifacts are reported to the PO Manager. For example, if the PO Manager can convince the teams to report project performance data in a common format, it can cut the administrative time needed to consolidate that information.

Scales to Large Projects

As the project grows in size, the size of the PO also grows. There will be a need for increasing the size of the administrative support group as well as the PO management structure. Installing layers of management will be a requirement for very large projects. There is no practical limit on the size of a PO. Early in my project management career, I was acquainted with a PO that managed a seven-year hardware/software systems design, development, and deployment project that had more than 10,000 team members organized into several smaller POs, programs, and projects. Obviously, there were several layers of management.

Managed from a Single Integrated Plan

This will have to be a high-level plan. The Work Breakdown Structure (WBS) will be defined to a few levels of detail and then the individual teams left to plan their own work below that level subject to certain start and end dates for their deliverables. In effect the PO Manager would be managing the deliverables just as she would manage independent contractors.

Integrated Resource Management Control

To some extent, each team manager will provide staff support across the team structure. The changing needs of the project will dictate how much support is to be provided. During the planning phase, the process for sharing staff resources should be agreed to.

Allows Teams to Maintain Their Practices

The PO structure is minimally invasive of each team's independence. They are free to proceed with their work on the project using the tools, templates, and processes most familiar to them.

Project Office Weaknesses

The weaknesses of the PO approach are as follows:

- Requires management across disparate practices
- Requires team members to manage competing priorities
- May involve a cumbersome scope change management process

Requires Management across Disparate Practices

When a team member is not allowed to use a tool, template, or process they are familiar with and have had good success with, there are sure to be problems. If you are going to force this situation on part of your team, make sure you have no reasonable alternative. It might be better for you to bear the burden of having to consolidate differing practices than to force compliance. Weigh the advantages of compliance versus consolidation. I have found several cases where the competing tool that a team member suggests may in fact be better. In those cases, I have given the team member the responsibility of leading that part of the project, with all teams using his or her approach. This is good for morale, too!

Requires Team Members to Manage Competing Priorities

A team member's annual performance review and raise comes from the manager of his or her home department. When given a choice between competing priorities and all other things are equal, what choice do you think they will make? Unless you have something to offer in return, you will always be fighting an uphill battle for priorities. In some cases, I have helped the client develop a process to receive performance input from the PO Managers they have worked with.

May Involve a Cumbersome Scope Change Management Process

There will have to be a single scope change management process. A formal process managed by a Scope Control Board will have to be established, and all teams must be required to use it. Each team will have some responsibility for analyzing the impact of the change on their project plan as well a role in the approval of changes requested by other teams. Keep in mind that some scope change requests can have major impact on the plans of several projects.

When to Use a PO

The PO is the least disruptive of current project management practices across the enterprise, so it would be the preferred model for the teams participating in a multi-team project. In a very mature enterprise, it may make sense politically to use this structure. At the same time, it places a significant coordinating burden on the shoulders of the PO Manager. The PO Manager's role is seen as coordinating rather than having direct management responsibility over the team managers. That places the PO Manager in a position where their skills as leaders and negotiators are called into service.

As project complexity and uncertainty increase, the PO structure loses its appeal. In APM or xPM projects, any organizational barriers that can be removed or avoided should be. Using a PO structure for such projects would contradict this goal. If the team size is less than 30, the PO structure can still be made to work for simpler APM projects, but there is a better choice. The PO structure works best for Linear and Incremental projects. You have to make room for creativity and flexibility, and inheriting as many project management practices as there are teams is unnecessarily burdensome on the project manager and increases the risk that a solution will not be discovered. For APM and xPM projects, the Super Team structure discussed later in this chapter is generally the better choice.

Core Team Structure

Now it's time to turn to a structure that originates from an idea I got while doing some consulting work for Walmart. I call it the Core Team (CT) structure, which is the name they used. The name makes sense to me. Originally, it was a structure they used for critical and complex projects. It was not a structure designed for multi-team projects, but I have redefined it to fit such projects.

DEFINITION: CORE TEAM A Core Team (CT) is a temporary team comprising a small number of subject matter experts (SMEs) chosen and managed by the CT Manager. These SMEs consult, advise, and support the CT Manager and the teams assigned to the project.

Core Team Characteristics

The idea of a Core Team is a term coined by Walmart and is used here in the same sense as it is used at Walmart. As Figure 17-4 illustrates, the CT structure is very simple.

The CT represents the recognized resident expertise assigned to the project. Collectively, the expertise of the CT members covers the business units and systems that support them. The project manager is not the resident expert. The CT has the respect and credibility of the individual project teams, and represents the subject matter expertise available to those teams. In fact, CT members will often be from some of the same client groups and business lines as the individual project teams themselves. They have earned the right to speak on the project, and when they do, people listen! Their responsibility spans the entire multi-project arena, from the CT Manager down to the individual teams and the members.

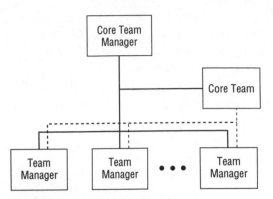

Figure 17-4: Core Team structure

The roles and responsibilities of the CT and the CT Manager are as follows:

- Advise each team on technical matters
- Provide subject matter expertise on enterprise systems and processes
- Support each team as requested and as needed
- Collaborate with and advise the CT Manager as requested
- Negotiate and help resolve inter-team problems

The following subsections discuss each of these in more detail.

Advise Each Team on Technical Matters

CT members are the recognized expertise in the company for the project they are supporting. As such, they are the best-fit advisors for the teams. Their opinions are highly respected. They speak with authority, and their advice is taken. Having that respect will be an important factor in the resolution of inter-team conflicts and problems. They offer technical support for the existing systems and development support for new or updated systems related to their assigned project.

The technical support services that a CT member can offer a project team include the following:

- Technical review of solution design
- Code review
- Problem resolution

- Conflict resolution
- Dependent systems technical impact analysis

Technical Review of Solution Design

The more complex and uncertain the project is, the more another pair of eyes should be involved. Members of the CT should be asked for their opinions. Will the new solution work seamlessly with the existing systems that it depends upon or that depend upon it? This is critical. As mentioned earlier, you might solve your immediate problem, but in so doing, you may create new problems with upstream or downstream systems.

Code Review

This is just a good quality control measure, especially for new systems. Most developers would include this as a good practice in their code development toolkit. If you are dealing with an APM or xPM project, it is even more important.

Problem Resolution

Problems in APM or xPM projects are big issues. Remember, you are dealing with solutions that have eluded the organization in the past and their discovery is not going to be easy. You will have to call upon all of the creativity available to you, and that means the CT.

Conflict Resolution

The CT, because it has earned the credibility and respect of the entire team, is best positioned to resolve conflict situations, especially conflicts that are technology-based. A CT member can assume the role of an arbitrator or mediator, hear both sides, offer his or her best professional advice, and hopefully resolve the conflict. Project managers are not able to do this because of their lack of technical expertise.

Dependent Systems Technical Impact Analysis

The project team may not have the depth of technical understanding of all dependent systems, but the CT will. They were recruited for that reason. Don't pass up any opportunity to have them review your solution.

Provide Subject Matter Expertise on Enterprise Systems and Processes

The members of the CT need to have expertise that reaches across the entire organization or at least the part of the organization impacted by the project. When questions arise from the teams about those business systems and processes, the CT is expected to provide the answers. The buck stops with the CT. Above all, they will understand the business impact of this project on other systems and processes and advise accordingly.

Support Each Team as Requested and as Needed

The CT is a resource available on an as-requested basis to all of the teams working on the multi-team project. The CT members act as coaches, mentors, and facilitators. The CT monitors team performance and may intervene as required. In the event of inter-team problems and issues, they will act as arbitrators. On occasion, they may be asked to represent one of the teams to the CT Manager.

Collaborate with and Advise the CT Manager as Requested

When the CT Manager needs technical or content help, the CT stands ready. The CT Manager will often invite input from the CT on critical decisions under consideration. The CT can be the eyes and ears of the CT Manager as they work with individual teams. For many projects that use the CT structure, the project manager is not required to have subject matter expertise as he or she would in other multi-team structures. Instead, the project manager will rely on the CT that has been recruited to provide that expertise.

Negotiate and Help Resolve Inter-Team Problems

Because the level of integration between the individual teams is low in the CT, there will be a number of inter-team problems to resolve. These problems will range the entire project life cycle and will require quick resolution. Schedule and resource conflicts are common in this structure. Because of their credibility, CT members can be instrumental in resolving these problems.

Core Team Strengths

The strengths of the CT approach are as follows:

- Enables the CT Manager to select CT members
- Provides the best available advice to the CT Manager
- Coordinates the work of several teams
- Lends support and credibility to the decisions of the CT Manager
- Assigns CT members 100 percent to this project
- Takes advantage of the most experienced SMEs
- Allows teams to retain their business unit practices

Enables the CT Manager to Select CT Members

Sounds like heaven doesn't it? In my 40+ years as a project manager, I have only had one project where I could pick the team. It was an APF project and was a booming success. I had a budget of $5M and a three-year schedule. I came in $1.5M under budget and nine months early. My 35-person team comprised professionals that I had worked with before. They were the kind of people who made a commitment, and you could go to the bank knowing they would meet their commitment. In a sense, the Core Team is just like that group of professionals I chose. As CT Manager, you are not much more than a coordinator. Your Core Team will be your technical link to the project teams.

Provides the Best Available Advice to the CT Manager

Your Core Team will be your most trusted advisors. You will be able to share your deepest concerns with them, and they will treat these concerns in confidence.

Coordinates the Work of Several Teams

Through the Core Team, you will be able to coordinate the work of the individual teams. When there is a problem, you can draw upon the Core Team to find a solution and help implement it.

Lends Support and Credibility to the Decisions of the CT Manager

If the individual teams know that you have collaborated with the Core Team, and that the Core Team has endorsed the decision you have made, you will be on firm ground.

Assigns Core Team Members 100 Percent to This Project

Having Core Team members assigned 100 percent to your project gives you a big advantage. You own this resource and can use it to maximum benefit without fear of raising schedule conflicts. Obviously, the Core Team structure is chosen for only the most important of projects. It is costly for an organization to commit its best and brightest to a project full-time. Therefore, it will only do so for projects that have high business value, are complex, and must be successfully completed.

The reality is that 100 percent assignment doesn't happen even in the case of many mission-critical projects. There are some things that the CT Manager can do in these cases. Because the CT Manager is hand-picking the Core Team, part of the conditions of appointment might be getting the commitment of the Core

Team member that he or she will give this project high priority in dealing with important issues that arise. The Core Team member's services will be limited to a few hours at most for even the most difficult of problems. He or she can certainly be available for telephone or Internet support to the CT Manager and any project team member on specific issues and questions. There is also the possibility of having two Core Team members share a 100 percent assignment.

Takes Advantage of the Most Experienced SMEs

The Core Team members are the recognized expertise in the enterprise. Your team members will know this and will respect the decisions and perspectives of the Core Team. The Core Team members will have great influence on the project. They will greatly impact all conflicts, issues, and problems.

Allows Teams to Retain Their Business Unit Practices

Just as in the PO structure, the Core Team structure preserves the processes and practices of each team. When that presents a problem, you will have the Core Team to help resolve any impasse. You don't have that buffer or leverage with the PO structure.

Core Team Weaknesses

The weaknesses of the Core Team approach are as follows:

- May not scale to the larger projects
- Does not necessarily integrate individual team plans
- Must manage across disparate practices
- May have to deal with divided loyalties
- Repeatedly uses the same SMEs

May Not Scale to the Larger Projects

As the size of the project increases, the size of the CT will have to increase to retain the needed coverage. Once the CT comprises about 10 professionals, it becomes dysfunctional. Some other structure is needed.

Does Not Necessarily Integrate Individual Team Plans

Just as in the PO structure, an integrated project plan exists only at a high level. The detailed plans are left to each team. The alignment of those plans is under the purview of the CT. They can offer constructive suggestions to each team to improve the alignment of their plans with those of other teams and with the overall project. The Core Team can be very effective in this role.

Must Manage across Disparate Practices

The CT structure inherits the same process and practice management problems as the PO structure. Consolidating processes and practices at the summary level can be problematic. You do have whatever leverage the CT can provide.

May Have to Deal with Divided Loyalties

Team members still owe their allegiance to their home department. The CT won't have much impact on that. Your ability as a leader will be put to the test. When I have been in these situations, I tried to put something of value on the table for the individual team members. Broadening their experiences or enabling them to learn a new skill through on-the-job training (OJT) is about all I had to offer. If the incentive was related to their professional development plan, it tended to help. This approach worked for some individuals, but not for everyone.

Repeatedly Uses the Same SMEs

The same SMEs are repeatedly chosen for CT membership, which doesn't provide development opportunities for future CT members. This can be a real problem. Your CT can help by identifying potential CT members among the teams assigned to your project and offer them some challenges to hone their skills as a future CT member. If the cadre of actual CT members is small, the cost to the organization for using the CT structure is large. Your SMEs will be assigned 100 percent to CT structured projects and will not be available to help out in other places. More professionals will have to rise to the ranks of CT membership. An OJT program will necessarily be part of that mix. Somehow your organization is going to have to strike a balance.

When to Use a CT

As the complexity and uncertainty of a multi-team project increases, your decision becomes whether to use the CT or Super Team structure. The size of the project is a limiting factor in using the CT structure. In my experience, CT structures are used for mission-critical projects, so the business case becomes the driving factor. The cost to the resource pool is so great that only a mission-critical project can justify this structure. CT structures can be used for Linear, Incremental, and Iterative projects.

Super Team Structure

For multi-team projects in which team size is not a deterrent to successful project performance, a Super Team (ST) structure can work quite well. It does require that the project manager be experienced in managing large (even very large) projects. This is not a job for the faint of heart. The team will have one person leading it (a senior member of one of the teams). In most cases, there will be at least one other management layer within the team. These subproject leads will be responsible for some of the deliverables. It would be a mistake to organize the subprojects along strict client-centric lines. This smacks of the PO structure. The structure of the project should suggest how those subprojects might best be defined. Using the concept of maximum cohesion and minimum coupling would be a best practice that has good application here.

DEFINITION: SUPER TEAM A Super Team (ST) is a temporary management structure used for a single project that integrates several independent teams into a single team managed by a senior-level project manager and supported by several subproject managers.

Having a single team structure means that all of the tools, templates, and processes in the five process groups can now be used. As the project size increases, the following things happen:

- The COS is replaced by a more formal requirements gathering process.
- The planning process applies here without revision.
- An experienced facilitator should prepare and conduct the planning session.
- The ST Manager focuses on plan contents, not on plan creation.
- The skill and competency profile of every team member will be needed.
- Intermediate levels of project management personnel will be needed.
- Project management software will be needed for planning and resource management.
- A technographer (once called a stenographer, but has since been upgraded by technology to a technographer) will be indispensable.

Super Team Characteristics

As shown in Figure 17-5, the ST structure is very simple.

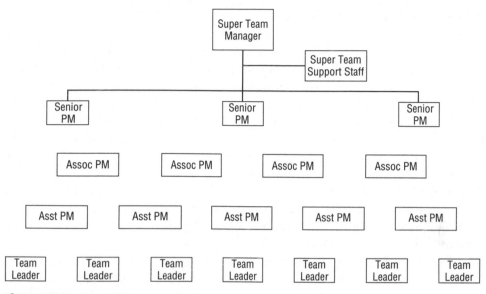

Figure 17-5: Super Team structure

This is a very dynamic structure that can easily expand or contract as a project's size increases or decreases. So you should be asking: "How big is big enough?" Here are some factors that I have used successfully in my consulting practice to help my clients decide whether or not to use the ST structure.

The first factor is the size of the support team. To compute the number of full-time equivalent (FTE) positions you need on your support team, add up all of the estimated labor time associated with the tasks from the WBS. Take a percentage of that number. In my experience, this is in the range of 7–20 percent. The percentage increases as the size of the project increases. For example, suppose the project duration is 12 months, and the total labor hours are estimated at 50,000. Ten percent of 50,000 hours is 5,000 hours spread across twelve months. That averages 416 hours per month. The average work month has 160 hours, so you will need about 2.6 FTE positions to support your administrative needs on the project. Some organizations don't think like this when it comes to staffing, so you may have a selling job to do. Somebody has to pick up an estimated 2.6 position duties. Look around you. The team members are your resource, and what you can't or shouldn't do yourself someone on the team will have to do. Look for administrative duties that you can pass on to others on the team. Rotate those duties around. Don't make the mistake of thinking that one team member should do all the meeting minutes, for example.

The second factor is the size of the team and the disposition of the senior, associate, and assistant project managers. Again from my experiences, the number 30 is the key to calculating the need for a structural change. Every team increase of 30 members triggers another structural change to the management of the project. The structural changes are bottom-up changes. For example, my preferred disposition of 30 team members would be to teams of five or six members, so the 30 team members would be split into five or six teams. Say five for the sake of the example. As the ST Manager, I can handle five direct reports, so I don't need any other project managers yet. You should also set the maximum number of direct reports any one project manager should have. For a team of 30, that number would be six, which is acceptable. As for the number of ST support staff needed, you can calculate that following the discussion in the previous paragraph. As overall project team size increases, you add to the subteams until you need more subteams, in which case you need at least one Assistant Project Manager (PM) to cover the increased management needs. There is no exact formula that I can give you, because it is basically a judgment call on your part. What makes sense for the project should be the final guide.

The roles and responsibilities of the ST Manager and the team leaders are as follows:

- Organize and manage the project
- Develop the project plan
- Maintain the overall project schedule
- Monitor and manage resource utilization
- Prepare and distribute project status reports
- Plan and conduct team meetings
- Process scope change requests

The following subsections discuss each of these in more detail.

Organize and Manage the Project

There should be one ST Manager for the ST structure. This individual must have solid experience managing large and complex projects. The ST Manager must gain each team's approval of the operating rules that bind the teams into a single working unit. In the ST structure, individual teams lose their identity. They are fully integrated into a single project team. A major organizational task is to decide how the scoping and planning tasks will be organized and managed.

Develop the Project Plan

The senior members from each team should work as a single team to draft the high-level project plan. Working with a smaller number of associates for this initial step is sufficient. Once the infrastructure has been established, the full planning team can be assembled to work out the remaining details. The planning task can easily get out of hand, so careful preparation will be required to make sure the plan is kept on track and doesn't waste the time of the team.

Maintain the Overall Project Schedule

Once the project has been launched, the team leads will be responsible for monitoring project performance and progress. The ST Manager is accountable for the entire project and should receive periodic status reports from the team leads.

Monitor and Manage Resource Utilization

Resource management is a critical component of the project. As required, resources will have to be shared across the teams. Adjustments will have to be made to accommodate approved scope change requests and solve other schedule-related problems.

Prepare and Distribute Project Status Reports

Project status reports should be submitted by the team leads to each other and to the ST Manager. These reports will have to be consolidated by the ST Manager for submission to the various stakeholder groups, clients, and senior management.

Plan and Conduct Team Meetings

At the highest level, there should be frequent (perhaps daily) meetings of the team leads chaired by the ST Manager. Each team lead may also choose to hold meetings (probably daily) with their own team members.

Process Scope Change Requests

This is a complex activity that must be managed by all of the team leads. You should expect that every change request will impact the schedule and resources of every team. The team leads are responsible for receiving, processing, and closing all scope change requests. This is no small task, because both the master schedule and resource allocation must be considered. Given that there are cross-team dependencies, this task must be dealt with using the most intense due diligence.

Super Team Strengths

The strengths of the ST approach are as follows:

- Manages from a single integrated source
- Scales to large projects
- Integrates resource management control
- Standardizes on a set of tools, templates, and processes

Manages from a Single Integrated Source

The baggage of managing across disparate teams is not an issue here, but there are still management problems to attend to. You will need to deploy a time-tested PMLC and management style for this project, which could be very large. If you haven't depended on technology to help with the management burden in the past, you will have to now. Human resource management decisions can be overwhelming on even a moderately sized project. Of the three models, this one is least affected by the process and practice baggage that team members might bring with them. The team members will expect to comply with the processes in place for projects of this magnitude.

Scales to Large Projects

Similar to the PO structure, the ST structure really has no practical limit to the size. Although larger teams are often structured within a PO structure, that is not necessary. The project can be decomposed into several subprojects and those subprojects into sub-subprojects, and so on. Those layers of management also fulfill a reporting and planning role.

Integrates Resource Management Control

All team members are accountable to the ST Manager through a number of management layers. This allows the managers to utilize team resources to the maximum. It also creates many opportunities for professional development through OJT assignments.

Standardizes on a Set of Tools, Templates, and Processes

The full range of TPM, APM, and xPM models and their supporting tools, templates, and processes are available. This is a chef's delight!

Super Team Weaknesses

The weaknesses of the ST approach are as follows:

- The difficulty in establishing standardization
- Team members have to decide among competing priorities

The Difficulty in Establishing Standardization

As project manager of an ST project, you have all of the responsibility and authority to select best-fit approaches. You must be very cautious about how you actually exercise that authority. I firmly believe that the recipients of the standardization should participate in deciding what that standardization will include. As I said earlier, don't expect your team to claim ownership just because you directed them to do so. Give them a chance to be part of the process, and they will automatically have ownership of it.

Team Members Have to Decide among Competing Priorities

The home department is a strong draw. That is where your team members get paid, and that is where they grow professionally. This is a strong bond. So when it's time to decide which of two competing tasks they will work on, guess which one gets picked?

The ST structure works for all sizes of multi-team projects. All you need in order to use it is the agreement of the key team leaders to abide by the standards. You should tell them that the standards to be used will be their decision under your guidance. I recall one such project where one of the team leaders had been very successful with a particular approach to requirements gathering. He presented his argument to the other team leaders and won them over. With the support of the other team leaders, he was given the responsibility to manage that part of the project. The message that I want to convey to you is that the entire team needs to participate in establishing those standards. Delegate the management of project phases or processes to team leaders who have earned the right to have those responsibilities. This can be a great motivational tool, too.

When to Use an ST

The ST structure is adaptable to several different project types, regardless of the total team size. It should be the structure of choice for APM and xPM projects. If the organization is at Level 3 maturity, the ST structure is the obvious choice.

This doesn't mean it is the default choice, but when you are in doubt, you should use the ST structure.

Putting It All Together

Multi-team projects are a phenomenon of the twenty-first century. As project management processes and practices become more pervasive in the enterprise, the likelihood of multi-team projects increases. Depending on their project management maturity levels, business units may have developed their own project management processes. When these come together in multi-team projects, management difficulties often arise. This chapter discussed those situations.

The literature is void of any suggestions as to how to manage these types of projects. With the exception of the three models discussed in this chapter, you will find very little else to help. The three models that I presented here are models that I have personally seen in use or recommended to my clients.

In this chapter, I discussed the following four factors that affect your choice of a best-fit project structure:

- **Project management maturity** — Either a PO or CT structure is recommended for organizations at Level 1 and 2 maturity, where business units have developed and firmly established their own project management methodologies. Organizations at Level 3 through 5 can use any structure with good results. These will comprise teams whose differences between methodologies will be minimal.

- **Complexity and uncertainty** — As complexity and uncertainty increase, the best-fit structure changes from PO to CT and finally to ST.

- **Total team size** — As team size increases, the best-fit structure changes from CT to ST to PO.

- **Criticality** — As criticality increases, the best-fit structure changes from PO to ST to CT.

Some combination of these four factors will be present on every project, and they are not independent factors. So the choice of best-fit structure may still be a subjective decision. For example, say an organization at Level 2 maturity has a highly complex and uncertain project with a small team, and the project's success is very critical to the enterprise. Based on the preceding list, this combination of factors suggests that either an ST or a CT structure should be used. The final choice will be subjective, but it should be based on additional information about the organization, its culture, client profile, and staff skills. If the client has a history of being meaningfully involved in projects, then an ST organizational structure would be a good choice. As another example, if the teams have well-developed tools, templates, and processes in place and make a strong case for using them, then a CT structure might be a better choice.

Discussion Questions

1. The IT department has its own methodology for doing software development. The engineering department has its own methodology for doing new product development. Teams from both departments are brought together to develop a new product with a significant software component. The IT team has decided that this is an APM project and will use the APF Adaptive PMLC model. The engineering department has always used a Linear PMLC and has no intention of doing it any differently. You are the project manager. What would you do? Be specific.

2. You have decided to gather requirements for the new sales management system by client group. There are five independent client groups, each involved in different noncompeting lines of business. All five are profitable and well-positioned for the future. Knowing that there will be conflicting opinions about requirements, how will you resolve those differences? Be creative and be specific.

3. What if part of the multi-team project were to be done using a TPM model and part using an APM model? Design the scope change management process you would use. What factors did you have to take into account as you designed this process? What risks were considered, and what do you recommend should be done about them? Be specific.

CASE STUDY – PIZZA DELIVERED QUICKLY (PDQ)

4. For the case study, suppose you had six independent teams, each working on a different subsystem. Given what you know about this project, how would you structure the project team? What are the strengths and weaknesses of your choice? What are some potential risks, and how would you plan for them?

CHAPTER 18

Managing the Professional Development of Project Teams

I must not rust.
— Clara Barton, Founder, The American Red Cross

It is the first of all problems for a man to find out what kind of work he is to do in this universe.
— Thomas Carlyle, Scottish essayist and historian

CHAPTER LEARNING OBJECTIVES

After reading this chapter, you will be able to:

- Understand the four component parts of a career and professional development plan
- Develop your own personalized career and professional development plan
- Monitor and progress along your own career path
- Understand the PM and BA position family
- Know why the future project manager skill profile will include business analysis, business process management, and information technology disciplines

It is my sincere wish that I have helped you start on the journey to becoming the chef I talked about earlier. For me, becoming a great project manager is a passion, and I have made it my life's journey, too. The fact that project management is organized common sense means that that journey can be successful and fulfilling for me and for my clients. It can be that way for you, too. I've spent over 40 years on my journey, and I'm still learning how to be a greater project manager.

I've shared my journey with you in the chapters and pages of this book. I've captured my life experiences as a maturing project manager, consultant, trainer, and author. I give them to you as your survival kit. Learn to use them well, and they will serve you well.

Do you remember those six questions that every project management process must answer? Here they are again:

1. What business situation is being addressed?
2. What do you need to do?
3. What will you do?
4. How will you do it?
5. How will you know you did it?
6. How well did you do?

These apply equally well to managing your life's journey to becoming a great project manager, and I can illustrate just how to do that.

My latest crusade is chronicled in the last major section of this chapter. I have a message for those of you who hold the future of project management in your hands, and I'm using this opportunity to make my case to you.

What Career and Professional Development Situation Is Being Addressed?

You are a business, and your business situation and your goal is to become a great project manager. You might be reading this book as a student working on your degree, and you're happy to have gotten to this page because it means your "course" is nearly finished. If so, treat yourself to the rewards of having finished and read on for just a few more pages. Or you might be a struggling apprentice project manager and need a lot of guidance on your journey — read on. If you've been a project manager for many years, but there are still a number of nagging problems in your practice of this noble profession that you hope to resolve through this book, you too should read on. And finally, if you are an experienced project manager and need to update your approach to managing complex projects, this is a must-read book.

What Do You Need To Do?

The map of your journey has four parts.

Experience Acquisition

Your organization might have defined a project manager position family. Here's one you can use in case they haven't:

1. Team Member
2. Task Manager
3. Activity Manager
4. Associate Project Manager
5. Project Manager
6. Senior Project Manager
7. Program Manager
8. Director of Project Management

Adapt this position family to your situation and find out what it takes in the way of experience and skills to move up in this position family from wherever you are to wherever you want to go.

On-the-job Training

Take stock of the requirements of your current position. How do your skills match up with those of the position you now hold? Where are your weaknesses with respect to performing your job roles and responsibilities as well as you can? Prioritize these development needs and start looking for training opportunities to address them.

Off-the-job Training

What skills and competencies do you need for that next position? Addressing these is essential to moving forward on your journey. Look for assignments that will give you an opportunity to acquire some of those skills and competencies. You might also find a project manager who is particularly good at a skill or competency you need and volunteer to help them or join their team if possible. Then watch how they do it and learn from their example.

Read, read, and read. There is a vast amount of literature on every aspect of project management, and you have to become familiar with it. Wander through the Internet, and you will find whatever topic you are looking for. The bibliography (Appendix C) that I have prepared for you is a good place to start.

Professional Activities

If you expect to be a great project manager, you have to get involved in the profession. Join the Project Management Institute (PMI) or any one of a number of other project management professional societies. Attend chapter meetings and trade shows. Get to know the people who have risen in the profession, and let them get to know you. Just participate, and you will be rewarded.

There are a number of ways to participate more directly. I've always preferred to give talks on the things I'm working on. It definitely isn't the same old stuff. I have introduced the Adaptive Project Framework (APF) and discussed distressed projects, multi-team projects, and portfolio management as well as several other topics at PMI chapter meetings all over New England. I've also spoken at PMI chapter conferences in Trinidad, Ohio, California, and New Jersey. This is a terrific way to get to know professionals with similar interests. Career days are another way to get involved. You can be on either side of the desk here. You might be looking for a career or interested in advising someone else on their career. I've held elected positions in several chapters at all levels. This is a great way to get to know other project managers in your area.

What Will You Do?

Start by writing your own professional development plan with the four parts I just described. Get one or more mentors who can help you with that exercise and then ask them for their guidance along your journey.

How Will You Do It?

You've planned the work, now work the plan. Pay attention to your surroundings. Always have your plan in mind and seize any opportunity to meet any development needs. Look for assignments that will give you an opportunity to advance your plan. Volunteering is a good way when the job assignments aren't there. Your plan has all four of the parts I just defined. Work them all! Always!

How Will You Know You Did It?

Make sure your manager knows about and approves your plan. You need his or her involvement in this journey, too. You will get a lot of personal satisfaction of accomplishment, and the recognition and rewards from your manager will be testimony to your growth and development.

How Well Did You Do?

You are a business, and if you paid attention to yourself like you would a business, you will do well! You have my best wishes for a successful career as a great project manager. Go with confidence.

Where Do You Go from Here? — A New Idea to Consider

My recent publishing activities include discussion of a completely new professional — the Project Manager/Business Analyst (PM/BA). I really believe that the industry needs such a professional, and I have written about it extensively. The following text is adapted from some of my earlier writings.

I consider this to be a good start on a long journey to completely define a new professional. Don't look upon it as merely having a single person with both Certified Business Analyst Professional (CBAP) and Project Management Professional (PMP) designations. That is not my intent. I am talking about a professional who truly integrates business analysis and project management. In that sense, the PM/BA professional is almost like a generalist who is prepared to fully support the business and process needs of a Level 5 maturity business unit or enterprise. I am aware of a number of professionals who meet both of these criteria, but there is not a formal definition of the PM/BA position. The following sections are my attempt to fill that gap and offer some sustainable career goals for such professionals.

The PM/BA Position Family

The PM/BA position family is a rich family of professional positions that spans the project management profession and the business analysis profession. It is a unique integration of the skill sets that comprise each of the professional positions in this family. I see that family as consisting of the following six position types:

- PM/BA Team Member
- PM/BA Task Manager
- PM/BA Associate Manager
- PM/BA Senior Manager
- PM/BA Program Manager
- PM/BA Director

The ordering of PM and BA could also be BA/PM. The two are equivalent except for minor organizational alignment. The PM/BA is primarily a project manager, and the BA/PM is primarily a business analyst. For any given organization, there will be multiple position titles within each position type. Let me offer the next level of detail for each of these position types. Years ago, I had the opportunity to consult with the British Computer Society on the development and implementation of their Professional Development Program. A few years later, I had the occasion to develop an Internet-based decision support system for information technology (IT) career development for one of my clients. That system was called CareerAgent. In defining the BA/PM family of professionals, I integrated the CareerAgent model into the earlier work for the British Computer Society. Much of what I define here takes advantage of the deliverables from both of those engagements. The result is Figure 18-1.

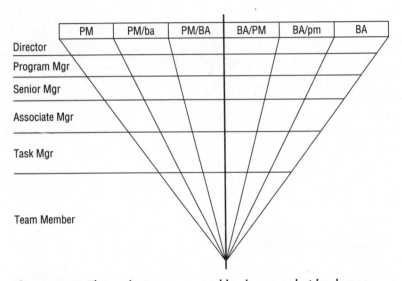

Figure 18-1: The project manager and business analyst landscape

Figure 18-1 is a career landscape and is interpreted as follows. Six vertical sectors define the PM and BA skill and competency profile of the professional. For example, a PM/ba position type has minimal business analysis skills and competencies, whereas the PM/BA has advanced business analysis skills and competencies. The six horizontal slices define the BA/PM career path illustrated in Figure 18-2. The height of the horizontal slices is an indication of the number of specific position titles in each cell. The higher the slice, the more position titles there are within that cell. The three left and three right sectors are mirror images of one another and identify professionals who are either project managers (PM) or business analysts (BA) with the accompanying skills and competencies needed for their positions. For example, the PM/ba position family includes project managers with minimal business analyst skills, whereas the PM/BA position family includes project managers with extensive business analyst skills. Therefore, all of the sectors between PM and BA are professionals with some combination of project management and business analyst skills and competencies. Most project managers would have some business analyst skills and competencies, and most business analysts would have some project management skills and competencies. The PM, PM/ba, and PM/BA position families have a project management focus. The same interpretation holds for the BA sector. The primary focus of positions in this sector is business analysis, and many business analysts have some project management skills and competencies.

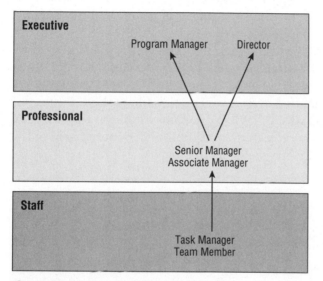

Figure 18-2: The BA/PM position family

In the middle two sectors are the PM/BA and BA/PM position families. These are the senior professionals that I envision emerging into the mainstream of project management and business analyst professional pursuits in the next few years. They are fully qualified to manage projects and manage business analysis engagements. The skill and competency profiles of the BA/PM and PM/BA are equivalent, and in some organizations, they may be the same. Their primary orientation is either as a project manager (PM/BA) or as a business analyst (BA/PM). I believe that the major career opportunities of the future are for the PM/BA or BA/PM professionals.

Figure 18-2 provides a high-level look at the career path model that underlies the six rows of the PM/BA landscape. At the staff level, there are two positions.

Team Members are at the entry level. These professionals will have an entry-level skill and competency profile that qualifies them to be a team member in a project (PM) or business analysis (BA) effort. As they gain experience, they will move up to the Task Manager level, where they will be qualified to supervise the work of a task, perhaps with the support of other Team Members.

At the professional level, there are two positions. The junior of the two is the Associate Manager. Individuals in these positions are qualified to manage small, simple projects. Through experience, they progress to the Senior Manager level. They are now qualified to manage even the most complex projects.

The executive level positions are of two types. One is the Program Manager. This position is both a consultant-type position as well as a manager of project managers working on a collection of projects having some relationship with one another. The other position is the Director. This individual is a "people manager" and is at the highest level of the six-position family.

First let me clarify my use of the word *project* in the following position descriptions. I use it in a very general sense. It refers to business analysis efforts as well as projects not encompassing business analysis activities. At this level, the position descriptions are structured to simultaneously embrace both the project manager and the business analyst. That has put some strain on the choice of language, and I beg your patience with that. In time, and with the help of the readers, we will converge on an acceptable taxonomy.

Team Member

This is an entry-level position into either a project management or business analysis effort.

Key Indicators

- Relevant two- or four-year specialized education at entry
- May have relevant but limited part-time or internship experience
- May have previous experience in at the entry level outside the BA/PM position family
- Limited experience (12–18 months) in a related position

Essential Characteristics

- Operates within a structured and routinely supervised environment
- After initial training, uses methods, procedures, and standards applicable to assigned tasks

- Demonstrates rational and organized approaches to tasks
- Has developed sufficient oral and written communication skills to conduct effective dialogues with colleagues and superiors
- Is able to absorb and apply new technical information rapidly when it is systematically presented
- Within a short time horizon, is able to plan, schedule, and monitor his or her own work

Task Manager

This is the upper-level staff position for individuals who are familiar with the scope of their tasks. Task Manager responsibilities extend to tasks within a project. There may be Team Members assigned to these tasks who receive guidance and supervision from the Task Manager. This position is distinguished from the Team Member position by the depth and complexity of their technical knowledge base and the extent to which supervision is required. This position implies a high degree of accountability for self-controlled work.

Key Indicators

- Fully trained Team Member
- Relevant experience in a related position (two to four years)

Essential Characteristics

- Operates within a largely unsupervised environment but within a clear accountability framework
- Is familiar with, uses effectively, and can select appropriately from applicable methods, procedures, and standards
- Is able to function productively and meet time and quality targets using available tools, templates, and processes with reference to others only by exception
- Can assume team leader responsibilities for the work of less-skilled professionals
- Demonstrates both formal and informal communications ability, orally and in writing, when dealing with all colleagues and clients
- Is able to rapidly absorb new technical information as required
- Demonstrates a systematic, disciplined, and analytical approach to problem solving

- Has a good appreciation of the wider field outside his or her own specialization and has developed a good broad understanding of computer systems and techniques
- Understands how the specific role relates to his or her relevant area of employment, to its clients, and to the employing business as a whole

Associate Manager

This is the more junior of two levels in the professional category. It will normally be achieved after clear evidence is available of full competence in a specialized role. At this level, full technical accountability for work done and decisions made is expected. The ability to give technical or team leadership will have been demonstrated as well as a high degree of technical versatility and broad industry knowledge. The Associate Manager will often manage major parts of projects and be responsible to the project manager or have project management responsibilities for simple projects.

Key Indicators

- 12–18 months experience as a Task Manager
- Recognized as a professional by his or her peers
- Is capable of successfully managing simple projects
- Does not have direct management responsibility for staff

Essential Characteristics

- Takes responsibility either for substantial technical decision making or for teams of staff. In the latter case, he or she demonstrates the basic qualities associated with team leadership and project management.
- Is thoroughly familiar with the available tools, templates, and processes associated with specialization, and possesses adequate technical depth to make correct choices from alternatives in all areas.
- Is able to apply selected tools and techniques in such a way as to meet set targets of cost, time, quality, and performance.
- Is able to communicate effectively both formally and informally with all those with whom working interfaces arise.
- Shows initiative and makes time available to ensure general competencies are up to date and in line with their development.
- Possesses a clear understanding of the relationship of any specialized role to the context in which the work is carried out. More generally, this

understanding applies to the employer's business and the needs of those who will use the end product.

Senior Manager

This is the upper of two levels in the professional category. It will normally be achieved after two to four years of experience as an Associate Manager and when clear evidence is available of full competence in a specialized role. At this level, full technical accountability for work done and decisions made is expected. The ability to provide technical or team leadership will have been demonstrated as well as a high degree of technical versatility and broad industry knowledge. The Senior Manager will manage complex projects and often be responsible for managing the activities of Associate Managers who function as subproject managers.

Key Indicators

- Two to four years of experience in an Associate Manager position
- Recognized as a professional by his or her peers
- Is capable of successfully managing complex projects
- Will often have direct management responsibility for project staff

Essential Characteristics

- Has demonstrated a basic understanding of the consulting role and has acted in such capacity as requested.
- Demonstrates mastery of the qualities associated with team leadership and project management.
- Is thoroughly familiar with the available tools, methods, procedures, and/ or equipment associated with his or her specialization, and possesses adequate technical depth to make correct choices from alternatives in all these areas.
- Is able to apply selected tools and techniques in such a way as to meet set targets of cost, time, quality, and performance.
- Is able to communicate effectively both formally and informally with all those with whom working interfaces arise.
- Shows initiative and makes time available to ensure general competencies are up to date and in line with their development.
- Possesses a clear understanding of the relationship of any specialized role to the context in which the work is carried out. More generally, this understanding applies to the employer's business and the needs of those who will use the end product.

Program Manager

This position represents the level associated with the mature, relevantly experienced, and fully capable professional. Such a person is fully accountable for work quality as a technical specialist. He or she possesses the background knowledge and experience to make informed and responsible decisions, which are both technically sound and take the needs of the organization fully into account. The Program Manager will be expected to advise and coach professional-level staff and is respected for his or her ability to do that.

Key Indicators

- None or very limited consulting experience at entry
- Has previous experience offering informal advice and support to less-qualified professionals
- Has peer recognition in a defined area of expertise
- Usually works unsupervised, with support from peers as requested

Essential Characteristics

- Has defined responsibility for all technical decision making within the scope of his or her specialization, and is expected to recognize and take appropriate action with respect to any safety-related applications within that scope
- Shows mature qualities of leadership in meeting targets of time, cost, quality, and performance within projects of substantial value to his or her employer
- Communicates effectively, both orally and in writing, with subordinates, colleagues, clients, and customers at all levels of seniority
- Shows mature understanding of the relationship of his or her specialization and/or project responsibilities to the undertaking as a whole, and is able to propose solutions within the scope of his or her expertise
- Shows initiative and makes time available to ensure general competencies are kept up to date and in line with industry developments

Director

This is the most senior management-level position in the BA/PM position family. It is the level occupied by the most-senior manager of a business function or unit in organizations where operating effectiveness (and possibly survival) is heavily dependent on the function or unit and where large numbers of practitioners are deployed. A wide and deep practical knowledge base is called for, accompanied by mature management qualities.

Key Indicators

- Serves as the director of a critical business unit or function in a large organization
- Has frequent visibility and direct contact at the board level
- Advises and leads the organization in strategic initiatives within his or her area of responsibility

Essential Characteristics

- Has defined responsibilities and authority for decision making or an advisory function with a direct bearing on the work of a business unit or major function
- In carrying out these responsibilities, recognizes and ensures that all appropriate actions are taken with respect to any safety-related applications within the scope of their position
- Has a technical background of sufficient depth and breadth to be able to recognize and successfully exploit opportunities for effective development or usage of his or her area of expertise, and lead and manage fully experienced reporting managers
- Demonstrates a high level of presentation skills applicable to all levels of audience
- Plays a senior role in formulating strategy and policy
- Has specific management responsibility for a specialized activity, which normally includes full budgetary and policy implementation authority for a significant overall function or a significant segment of a larger unit

Using the PM/BA Landscape for Professional Development

The playing field for the career and professional development of the BA and the PM was previously shown in Figure 18-1. There are 36 distinct cells in this landscape, and all BA and PM position configurations fall somewhere in this landscape. The landscape therefore can be used for career planning and professional development. Each cell will contain one or more position titles, and each position title will have a skill and competency profile defined for it. An individual's career history can be represented in this landscape by a sequence of connected cells. An individual's professional development plan is represented in the landscape with a planned sequence of connected cells. An example of a career path is shown later in the chapter.

Each cell in the landscape will have a minimum skill and competency profile defined for all positions in that cell. In order for an individual to be in this cell, he or she must possess the minimum skill and competency profile for the cell that they occupy or would like to occupy. For professional development planning, the individual will be in some particular cell and have career aspirations to move to another position in the same cell or to a position in another cell (usually this will be an adjoining cell). The skill and competency profile of the current and desired positions or cells can be compared, and the differences will identify the skill and competency gaps. The training and experience needed to remove those gaps and to qualify an individual to move to a position in the desired cell can be defined. The implications to the training department planning are obvious, as are the applications to human resource management.

What Might a Professional Development Program Look Like?

This is a big topic and would require more than the scope of this section allows. However, as an introduction to this topic, this section briefly defines the four parts that I think a good professional development program should include. This model is very similar to the model developed by the British Computer Society. It comprises the following components:

- **Experience acquisition** — Further experience mastering the skills and competencies needed in the current position

- **On-the-job training** — Training to increase the proficiency of skills and competencies needed in the current position

- **Off-the-job training** — Training to increase the proficiency of skills and competencies needed in the desired future position

- **Professional activities** — A combination of reading, professional society involvement, conference attendance, and networking with other professionals

Every position in every cell will have a minimum skill and competency profile required for the position. To qualify for a specific position, the individual must first define the skill and competency gap between his or her current and desired position, and then build a professional development program using the preceding four components to remove that gap. Completing such a program will enable the individual to move to the desired position when a vacancy arises.

This individual should have a mentor assigned to him or her to help with plan development and other career advice.

Since you now have a BA/PM generic position family defined and a career path for that family, Figure 18-1 takes on more meaning. An example will help. Figure 18-3 shows an individual whose current position is in the PM/ba Task Manager cell. This person is a professional project manager with minimal business analysis skills and competencies. This is a very common position. Recognizing the importance and value of having stronger business analysis skills, this person has a short-term goal to move to a position in the PM/BA Task Manager cell. He or she will build a plan in his or her Professional Development Program (PDP) to accomplish this short-term career goal. His or her PDP will focus on improving his or her business analysis skill and competency profile from that of a PM/ba Task Manager to that of a PM/BA Task Manager.

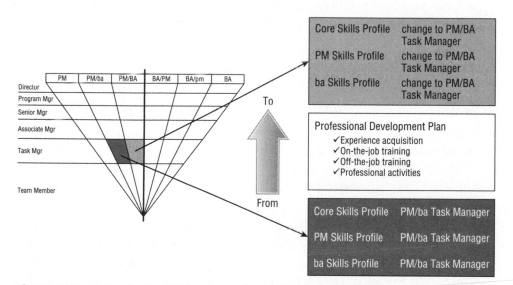

Figure 18-3: Using the BA/PM landscape for a short-term professional goal from ba to BA skills and competencies at the same position level

The PDP for this person might contain the following strategies.

Experience Acquisition

- Seek out project assignments that have more of a business analysis focus than you are accustomed to.

- Support professionals who are at a more senior level than you and have a business analysis skill that you need to improve in order to better meet current position requirements.

On-the-job Training

- Look for opportunities to observe and support the business analysis work of PM/BA professionals.

- Take courses (on- or off-site) to enhance the business analysis skills required of your current position.

Off-the-job Training

- Take courses (on- or off-site) to add business analysis skills that will be required by your targeted position in the PM/BA Task Manager cell.

- Look for opportunities to observe and support a professional who is practicing the business analysis skills you will need in your targeted position.

Professional Activities

- Read books and journal articles on topics relevant to your targeted position in the PM/BA Task Manager cell.

- Attend meetings and conferences offering seminars and workshops relevant to your targeted position in the PM/BA Task Manager cell.

Using the PDP

In my experience, an individual's PDP covers an annual planning horizon, including at least semi-annual status meetings with a mentor and/or as-needed meetings that the individual requests.

Figure 18-4 illustrates an example of a more complex situation than what was depicted in Figure 18-3. Here the change is to a higher-level position (Task Manager to Associate Manager). A career change like this may take some time to accomplish. Not only will the person need to acquire additional experience to qualify for the higher-level position, but he or she will also need to increase his or her business analysis experience and skill and competency profile to qualify for the higher-level position's business analysis requirements.

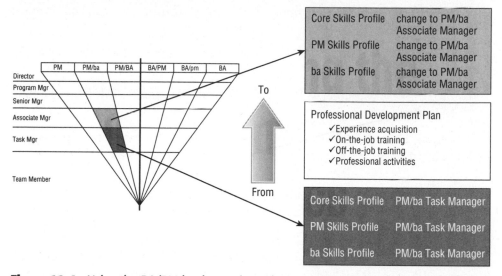

Figure 18-4: Using the BA/PM landscape for a short-term professional goal at a higher level position

Figure 18-5 is the most complex. Here the professional is seeking a higher level position (Task Manager to Associate Manager) and a more developed business analysis skill and competency profile (ba to BA)

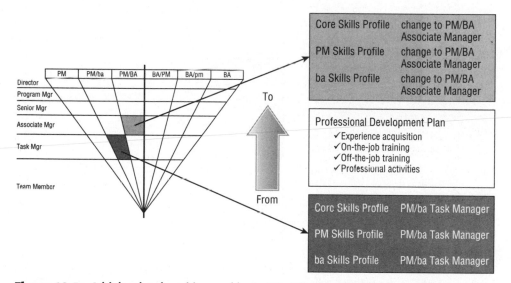

Figure 18-5: A higher level position and ba to BA skill and competency profile

A better professional development plan for the example in Figure 18-5 might be to use one of the following two-step strategy paths:

- PM/ba Task Manager ➢ PM/BA Task Manager ➢ PM/BA Associate Manager
- PM/ba Task Manager ➢ PM/ba Associate Manager ➢ PM/BA Associate Manager

You should choose the strategy that will give you the best opportunity for advancement based on the actual promotion opportunities available to you.

Career Planning Using the BA/PM Landscape

A section of the PDP should be devoted to long-range career planning. The BA/PM landscape is a tool that can aid in the planning process. Figure 18-6 illustrates a career path leading from a position in the BA Team Member cell to a position in the BA/PM Senior Manager cell. The CareerAgent System that I mentioned earlier in this chapter included a decision support system that helped the individual plan their career path down to the position title level within the cells. It mapped out a training and development sequence leading from position to position across the BA/PM landscape until the final career goal had been reached.

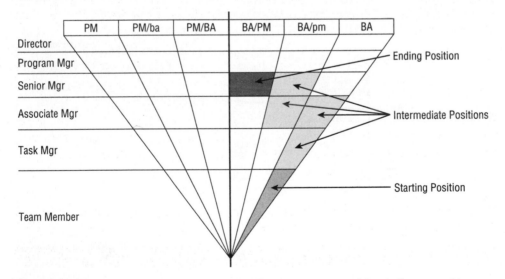

Figure 18-6: A career path from a position in the BA Team Member cell to a position in the BA/PM Senior Manager cell

As the plan is executed, it will most likely change. Several paths connect the BA Team Member position family to the BA/PM Senior Manager position family. Along the way, circumstances and changing interests might result in a change in the targeted position family. Several factors will influence the plan and suggest revisions that are more compatible with the changing business environment and that offer more career growth and professional development opportunities.

An Even Newer Idea to Consider

The Standish Group has been tracking the reason for project failures for several years now. Its 2010 report listed the top ten reasons projects become challenged (shown in Table 18-1). Based on my research into effective complex project management I have defined the disciplines needed by a complex project manager to be:

- Project Management (PM)
- Business Analysis (BA)
- Business Process Management (BPM)
- Information Technology (IT)

Table 18-1 maps these disciplines to the ten causes of project failure. Notice how important the roles of the BA and BPM are in mitigating so many of these reasons. For the first time meaningful client involvement (expressed as user input) was at the top of the list. We've always had client involvement but until quite recently it amounted to little more than signing an arcane functional specification document under threat of project delay if the document was not promptly signed. That characterized the relationship between the techie and the client in the 1950s and even into the 1960s. The techie's toolkit has evolved and now includes Joint Applications Design (JAD), Rapid Applications Development (RAD), prototyping, requirements gathering, use case scenarios, business process diagramming, and a host of other processes that bring the client into active involvement beginning with the scoping phase of the project and continuing through to completion and implementation. The BA has been instrumental in facilitating the meaningful involvement of the client and surely helped increase the likelihood of complex project success.

Table 18-1: Top 10 Prioritized Reasons for Complex Projects to be Challenged (Standish Group CHAOS Report 2010)

REASON	PM	BA	BPM	IT
Lack of user input		X		
Incomplete Requirements and Specifications			X	
Changing Requirements and Specifications			X	
Lack of Executive Support	X			

Continued

Table 18-1 *(continued)*

REASON	PM	BA	BPM	IT
Technology Incompetence				X
Lack of Resources	X			
Unrealistic Expectations			X	
Unclear Objectives			X	
Unrealistic Time Frames	X			
New Technology				X

Complex projects are characterized by a high degree of uncertainty and risk. We know that these projects cannot succeed without meaningful client involvement. How to attain that involvement and maintain it over the project life cycle is not an easy matter. Each of the four disciplines is a critical part of that effort, and that effort extends over the entire project life cycle. The best advice I have to offer is for all complex project team (CPT) members to use the language of the client. Anything else will take the client further outside of their comfort zone. It is not realistic to expect the client to adopt the language of the PM or the IT professional.

Table 18-2 is the RASCI Matrix for the responsibilities of each professional over the life of the project. RASCI is an acronym that stands for Responsible, Approves, Supports, Consults, and Informs. The combined skill profiles of the four disciplines must be sufficient to meet all project responsibilities. In this book those skills might be shared between professionals or those skills might be possessed by a single professional, one who has everything needed to effectively execute the project.

Table 18-2: PM, BA, BPM, and IT RASCI Matrix

PROJECT PHASE	DELIVERABLE	PM	BA	BPM	IT
Scoping	Problem Definition	R	R	C	C
	Solution Validation	R	R	C	C
	Project Overview Statement	R/A	S	A	I
	Requirements Elicitation	S	R	A	I
Planning	PMLC Selection	R/A	S	S	C
	Work Breakdown Structure	R/A	S	S	S
	Project Plan	R	S	S	C
Launching	Team Operating Rules	R	I	I	I
	Requirements Change Request	S	R	A	I
	Scope Change Management	R	C	A	I
	Risk Management	R	S	I	I

PROJECT PHASE	DELIVERABLE	PM	BA	BPM	IT
Monitoring/ Controlling	Performance Reporting	R	S	I	S
	Communications Management	R	S	I	I
Closing	Acceptance Test Procedure	C	R	A	S
	Deliverables Installation	R	S	A	S
	Post-Implementation Audit	R	S	S	S

LEGEND
R = Responsible
A = Approves
C = Consults
I = Informs
S = Supports

As you will note in the preceding table the deliverables are either the responsibility of the PM or the BA. Their performance goals are different. The PM focuses on process, time, cost, and resource management. The BA focuses on the deliverables from the process and meeting client needs, requirements, and expected business value. These can be at odds with one another, but it is that healthy contention that produces success. The goal of their project is to find a solution that meets the expected business value that initially justified doing the project. That project goal is the driving force that helps the PM and BA resolve the contention between their performance goals.

If you are a member of the senior management team (SMT), you should consult my recent book *Executive Guide to Project Management: Organizational Process and Practices for Supporting Complex Projects* (John Wiley & Sons, 2011).

Putting It All Together

Obviously this is a work in progress. I have participated in the development of similar structures for the IT professional but not for the BA/PM professional (or PM/BA if you prefer). Much remains to be done. I would welcome a partner from the BA side to work with me in this challenging and valuable pursuit. It is my hope that I have launched this effort in a direction that ultimately will make sense across the entire BA and PM professional landscape. I would certainly like to hear your thoughts on the BA/PM professional (or the PM/BA professional, if you prefer). I'm sure we could have a lively discussion. I promise to respond personally to every e-mail and to incorporate your points of view.

If you are interested in discussing a possible collaboration, you can reach me directly at rkw@eiicorp.com.

Discussion Questions

1. Beginning with your current position, identify your short-term career goal to be achieved in the next 12 months and write your professional development plan (be specific). It should consist of four parts:

   ▪ Experience acquisition

   ▪ On-the-job training

   ▪ Off-the-job training

   ▪ Professional activities

2. The project manager of the future will be an individual whose skills profile includes not only project management but also business analysis, business process management, and information technology. Comment on the likelihood that this four discipline profile can be built through a program of planned experiences only. Outline your program.

Glossary of Acronyms

Knowledge is of two kinds. We know a subject ourselves, or we know where we can find information upon it.

— Samuel Johnson, English lexicographer and essayist

All of the acronyms used in this book are collected together here in one place for your reading convenience.

AC	Actual Cost
ACWP	Actual Cost of Work Performed
ADC	Aid to Dependent Children
APF	Adaptive Project Framework
APM	Agile Project Management
APPM	Agile Project Portfolio Management
ASAP	As Soon As Possible
ASD	Adaptive Software Development
ATP	Acceptance Test Procedure
B2B	Business to Business
B2C	Business to Customer
BABOK	Business Analysis Body Of Knowledge
BA/PM	Business Analyst Project Manager
BCG	Boston Consulting Group

BCWP	Budgeted Cost of Work Performed
BCWS	Budgeted Cost of Work Scheduled
BPI	Business Process Improvement
BPM	Business Process Manager
BPMN	Business Process Management Notation
CBAP	Certified Business Analyst Professional
CCPM	Critical Chain Project Management
CIO	Chief Information Officer
CMM	Capability Maturity Model
CMMI	Capability Maturity Model Integrated
CoA	Chart of Accounts
COS	Conditions Of Satisfaction
COTS	Commercial Off the Shelf Software
CPI	Cost Performance Index
CPIM	Continuous Process Improvement Model
CSF	Critical Success Factor
CT	Core Team
CV	Cost Variance
DSDM	Dynamic Systems Development Model
E	Expected Task Duration
EF	Early Finish of a Task
EPM	Effective Project Management
EPSO	Enterprise Project Support Office
ES	Early Start of a Task
EV	Earned Value
EVA	Earned Value Analysis
FDD	Feature-Driven Development
FF	Finish to Finish Task Dependency
FFP	Firm Fixed Price
FS	Finish to Start task dependency
FTE	Full-Time Equivalent
GPS	Global Positioning System

HRMS	Human Resource Management System
IIBA	International Institute of Business Analysis
INSPIRE	INitiate, SPeculate, Incubate, REview
IRR	Internal Rate of Return
IT	Information Technology
JAD	Joint Application Design
JPPS	Joint Project Planning Session
LCD	Liquid Crystal Display
LF	Late Finish of a Task
LS	Late Start of a Task
LSI	Learning Styles Inventory
MoSCoW	Must Have, Should Have, Could Have, Wouldn't it be Nice to Have
MPx	Emertxe Project Management
MTC	Milestone Trend Chart
NASA	National Aeronautics & Space Administration
OJT	On the Job Training
OPM3	Organizational Project Management Maturity Model
PC	Personal Computer
PCS	Process Control System
PDM	Precedence Diagramming Method
PDP	Professional Development Plan
PDQ	Pizza Delivered Quickly
PDS	Project Description Statement
PERT	Project Evaluation and Review Technique
PM/BA	Project Manager Business Analyst
PMBOK	Project Management Body Of Knowledge
PMCA	Project Manager Competency Assessment
PMCoE	Project Management Community of Excellence
PMCoP	Project Management Community of Practice
PMI	Project Management Institute
PMLC	Project Management Life Cycle

PMM	Project Management Maturity
PMMA	Project Management Maturity Assessment
PMMM	Project Management Maturity Model
PMO	Project Management Office
PMP	Project Management Professional
PO	Project Office
POS	Project Overview Statement
PQM	Process Quality Matrix
PSO	Project Support Office
PV	Planned Value
QA	Quality Assurance
R&D	Research & Development
R&R	Rest and Recuperation
RAD	Rapid Application Development
RASCI	Responsible, Approves, Supports, Consults, Informs
RBS	Requirements Breakdown Structure
RFI	Request For Information
RFID	Radio Frequency Identification
RFP	Request For Proposal
RFQ	Request For Quote
ROI	Return On Investment
RUP	Rational Unified Process
Scrum	Scrum is not an acronym
SDLC	Systems Development Life Cycle
SEI	Software Engineering Institute
SF	Start to Finish Task Dependency
SLA	Service Level Agreement
SME	Subject Matter Expert
SPI	Schedule Performance Index
SS	Start to Start Task Dependency
ST	Super Team
SV	Schedule Variance

SWAG	Scientific Wild A** Guess
SWOT	Strengths, Weaknesses, Opportunities, Threats
TBD	To Be Determined
TOA	Task On the Arrow
TON	Task On the Node
TPM	Traditional Project Management
UML	Universal Modeling Language
WAG	Wild A** Guess
WBS	Work Breakdown Structure
xPM	Extreme Project Management

What's on the Website?

He who would search for pearls must dive below.
— **John Dryden, English poet**

The website has been established to provide a ready source of useful information about the book's contents. It is designed to bring you quickly to some supporting materials for your reference and further study, or for your use in presentations and other learning experiences. I've had numerous requests from faculty who have adopted my book to provide materials to support them in class. I've tried to respond as best I can.

You can access the website at `www.wiley.com/go/epm6e`.

Course Master File

This file contains the following:

- A PowerPoint file for every chapter
- Class exercises

The PowerPoint files contain the slides I use for my lectures. There is one file for every chapter. Every figure in the book has an accompanying slide with the figure number at the lower right of the slide for student reference. I've also added a number of slides that help with the flow of the lecture. Feel free to add, delete, or modify to suit your needs.

The class exercise file is a collection of more than 30 exercises that I have used with great success in the past. They are designed to get the class involved. Many are focused on how a tool, technique, process, or best practice might be used or adapted to the student's environment. These exercises are rendered in the same format as the chapter lecture slides. Incorporate them into the chapter course file as you see fit.

A Note on the Answer File for the Discussion Questions

Each chapter ends with a few discussion questions that might be used by instructors to create a dialogue with the class or for use with written assignments. It is hoped that these questions are thought-provoking. There are no right answers, although there are plenty of wrong answers. An answer file has been created for instructors. Just e-mail me at `rkw@eiicorp.com`, identify yourself as a legitimate instructor or faculty member, and I'll send you the answer file. I'd love to hear from you and learn how you are using the book and its materials.

Bibliography

Ignorance never settles a question.
— Benjamin Disraeli

Those who have read of everything are thought to understand everything,
too; but it is not always so — reading furnishes the mind only with
materials of knowledge; it is thinking that makes what is read ours.
We are of the ruminating kind, and it is not enough to cram ourselves
with a great load of collections; unless we chew them over again,
they will not give us strength and nourishment.
— John Locke

The books listed in this appendix represent a collection of current publications from my project management library. Nearly all the books included here were published in the past 10 years. The few exceptions are titles that were written by leaders in our field or that made a particularly valuable contribution to the field. They are classics. All of these books will be of particular interest to professionals who have project management responsibilities, are members of project teams, or simply have a craving to learn about the basics of sound project management. The focus of many of the books is systems and software development, although several also treat the basic concepts and principles of project management. Also included are books on closely related topics that I found to be of value in researching and writing this book. You might find value in them, too.

For your ease in finding specific sources, I arranged the bibliography topically according to the major areas covered in the book.

Defining and Using the Project Management Process Groups

Lambert, Lee R., and Erin Lambert. 2000. *Project Management: The CommonSense Approach.* Columbus, OH: LCG Publishing. (ISBN 0-9626397-8-8)

Traditional Project Management

Bainey, Kenneth R. 2004. *Integrated IT Project Management: A Model-Centric Approach.* Boston, MA: Artech House. (ISBN 1-58053-828-2)

Berkun, Scott. 2005. *The Art of Project Management.* Sebastopol, CA: O'Reilly Media. (ISBN 0-596-00786-8)

Blaylock, Jim, and Rudd McGary. 2002. *Project Management A to Z.* Columbus, OH: PM Best Practices, Inc. (ISBN 0-9719121-0-6)

DeGrace, Peter, and Leslie Hulet Stahl. 1990. *Wicked Problems, Righteous Solutions.* Englewood Cliffs, NJ: Yourdon Press Computing Series. (ISBN 0-13-590126-X)

DeMarco, Tom. 1997. *The Deadline: A Novel About Project Management.* New York: Dorsett House. (ISBN 0-932633-39-0)

DeMarco, Tom, and Timothy Lister. 1999. *Peopleware, Productive Projects and Teams.* 2nd ed. New York: Dorsett House. (ISBN 0-932633-43-9)

Dettmer, H. William. 1997. *Goldratt's Theory of Constraints: A Systems Approach to Continuous Improvement.* Milwaukee, WI: ASQ Quality Press. (ISBN 0-87389-370-0)

Fleming, Quentin W. 1992. *Cost/Schedule Control Systems Criteria.* Chicago: Probus Publishing. (ISBN 1-55738-289-1)

———. 1992. *Subcontract Planning and Organization.* Chicago: Probus Publishing. (ISBN 1-55738-463-0)

Fleming, Quentin W., and Loel M. Koppelman. 2000. *Earned Value Project Management, Second Edition.* Newtown Square, PA: Project Management Institute. (ISBN 1-880410-27-3)

Friedlein, Ashley. 2001. *Web Project Management: Delivering Successful Commercial Web Sites.* San Francisco: Morgan Kaufmann Publishers. (ISBN 1-55860-678-5)

Goldratt, Eliyahu M. 1997. *Critical Chain.* Great Barrington, MA: North River Press. (ISBN 0-88427-153-6)

Goldratt, Eliyahu M., and Jeff Cox. 1992. *The Goal*: *A Process of Ongoing Improvement*. Great Barrington, MA: North River Press. (ISBN 0-88427-061-0)

Goodpasture, John C. 2002. *Managing Projects for Value*. Vienna, VA: Management Concepts. (ISBN 1-56726-138-8)

Harrington, H. James, et al. 2000. *Project Change Management*: *Applying Change Management to Improvement Projects*. New York: McGraw-Hill. (ISBN 0-07-027104-6)

Haugan, Gregory T. 2002. *Project Planning and Scheduling*. Vienna, VA: Management Concepts. (ISBN 1-56726-136-1)

———. 2002. *Effective Work Breakdown Structures*. Vienna, VA: Management Concepts. (ISBN 1-56726-135-3)

Hill, Peter R. 2001. *Practical Project Estimation*: *A Toolkit for Estimating Software Development Effort and Duration*. Warrandyte, Victoria, Australia: International Software Benchmarking Standards Group. (ISBN 0-9577201-1-4)

Jalote, Pankaj. 2000. *CMM in Practice*: *Processes for Executing Software Projects at Infosys*. Reading, MA: Addison-Wesley. (ISBN 0-201-61626-2)

Jensen, Bill. 2000. *Simplicity*: *The New Competitive Advantage in A World of More, Better, Faster*. Cambridge, MA: Perseus Books. (ISBN 0-7382-0210-X)

Kerzner, Harold. 1998. *In Search of Excellence in Project Management*. New York: John Wiley & Sons. (ISBN 0-442-02706-0)

———. 2001. *Project Management*: *A Systems Approach to Planning, Scheduling, and Controlling*. 7th ed. New York: John Wiley & Sons. (ISBN 0-471-39342-8)

Kloppenborg, Timothy J., and Joseph A. Petrick. 2002. *Managing Project Quality*. Vienna, VA: Management Concepts. (ISBN 1-56726-141-8)

Leach, Lawrence P. 1997. *The Critical Chain Project Managers' Fieldbook*. Idaho Falls, ID: Quality Systems.

———. 2000. *Critical Chain Project Management*. Boston: Artech House. (ISBN 1-58053-074-5)

———. 2005. *Critical Chain Project Management*. 2nd ed. Boston: Artech House. (ISBN 1-58053-903-3)

Levine, Harvey A. 2002. *Practical Project Management*: *Tips, Tactics, and Tools*. New York: John Wiley & Sons, Inc. (ISBN 0-471-20303-3)

Lewis, James P. 1995. *Project Planning, Scheduling, and Control*. Chicago: Probus Pub Co. (ISBN 1-55738-869-5)

———. 1998. *Mastering Project Management*. New York: McGraw-Hill. (ISBN 0-7863-1188-6)

————. 2000. *The Project Manager's Desk Reference*. 2nd ed. New York: McGraw-Hill. (ISBN 0-07-134750-X)

Martin, Paula. 1995. *Leading Project Management into the 21st Century: New Dimensions in Project Management and Accountability*. Cincinnati, OH: Martin Tate. (ISBN 0-943811-04-X)

McConnell, Steve. 1998. *Software Project Survival Guide*. Redmond, WA: Microsoft Press. (ISBN 1-57231-621-7)

————. 2004. *Professional Software Development: Shorter Schedules, Higher Quality Products, More Successful Projects, Enhanced Careers*. Boston: Addison-Wesley. (ISBN 0-321-19367-9)

Milosevic, Dragan Z. 2003. *Project Management ToolBox: Tools and Techniques for the Practicing Project Manager*. New York: John Wiley & Sons. (ISBN 0-471-20822-1)

Muther, Richard. 2000. *More Profitable Planning: Six Steps to Planning Anything*. Kansas City, MO: Management and Industrial Research Publications. (ISBN 0-933684-193)

Neuendorf, Steve. 2002. *Project Measurement*. Vienna, VA: Management Concepts. (ISBN 1-56726-140-X)

Nielsen, Jakob. 2000. *Designing Web Usability*. Indianapolis: New Riders Publishing. (ISBN 1-56205-810-X)

Phillips, Jack J. et al. 2002. *The Project Management Scorecard: Measuring the Success of Project Management Solutions*. Boston: Butterworth-Heinemann Ltd. (ISBN 0-7506-7449-0)

Pritchard, Carl L. 1998. *How to Build A Work Breakdown Structure: The Cornerstone of Project Management*. Arlington, VA: ESI International. (ISBN 1-890367-12-5)

————. 2001. *Risk Management: Concepts and Guidance*. Arlington, VA: ESI International. (ISBN 1-890367-30-3)

Pritchett, Price, and Brian Muirhead. 1998. *The Mars Pathfinder Approach to "Faster-Better-Cheaper"*. Dallas: Price Pritchett & Associates. (ISBN 0-944002-74-9)

Putnam, Lawrence H., and Ware Myers. 1992. *Measures for Excellence: Reliable Software On Time, Within Budget*. Englewood Cliffs, NJ: Prentice Hall PTR. (ISBN 0-135-67694-0)

Rad, Parviz F. 2002. *Project Estimating and Cost Management*. Vienna, PA: Management Concepts. (ISBN 1-56726-144-2)

Robertson, Suzanne, and James Robertson. 1999. *Mastering the Requirements Process*. Boston: Addison-Wesley. (ISBN 0-201-36046-2)

————. 2004. *Requirements-Led Project Management: Discovering David's Slingshot*. Boston: Addison-Wesley. (ISBN 0-321-18062-3)

Royer, Paul S. 2002. *Project Risk Management*: *A Proactive Approach*. Vienna, VA: Management Concepts. (ISBN 1-56726-139-6)

Schuyler, John. 2001. *Risk and Decision Analysis in Projects*. 2nd ed. Newtown Square, PA: Project Management Institute. (ISBN 1-880410-28-1)

Schwalbe, Kathy. 2000. *Information Technology Project Management*. Boston: Course Technology. (ISBN 0-7600-1180-X)

Stellman, Andrew, and Jennifer Greene. 2006. *Applied Software Project Management*. Sebastopol, CA: O'Reilly Media, Inc. (ISBN 0-596-00948-8)

Taylor, James. 2004. *Managing Information Technology Projects*. New York, NY: AMACOM. (ISBN 0-8144-0811-7)

TechRepublic. 2001. *IT Professional's Guide to Project Management*. Louisville, KY: TechRepublic. (ISBN 1-931490-16-3)

Verzuh, Eric. 1999. *The Fast Forward MBA in Project Management*. New York: John Wiley & Sons, Inc. (ISBN 0-471-32546-5)

Ward, J. LeRoy. 2000. *Project Management Terms*: *A Working Glossary*. Arlington, VA: ESI International. (ISBN 1-890367-25-7)

Whitten, Neal. 1995. *Managing Software Development Projects*. 2nd ed. New York: John Wiley & Sons, Inc. (ISBN 0-471-07683-X)

———. 2000. *The EnterPrize Organization*: *Organizing Software Projects for Accountability and Success*. Newtown Square, PA: Project Management Institute. (ISBN 1-880410-79-6)

———. 2005. *Neal Whitten's No-Nonsense Advice for Successful Projects*. Vienna, VA: Management Concepts. (ISBN 1-56726-155-8)

Wysocki, Robert K. 2006. *Effective Software Project Management*. New York: John Wiley & Sons. (ISBN 0-7645-9636-5)

Wysocki, Robert K., Robert Beck, Jr., and David B. Crane. 2000. *Effective Project Management*. 2nd ed. New York: John Wiley & Sons. (ISBN 0-471-36028-7)

Yourdon, Edward. 1999. *Death March*: *The Complete Software Developer's Guide to Surviving "Mission Impossible" Projects*. Upper Saddle River, NJ: Prentice Hall. (ISBN 0-13-014659-5)

Agile and Extreme Project Management

Aguanno, Kevin. 2004. *Managing Agile Projects*. Lakefield Ontario: Multi-Media Publications, Inc. (ISBN 1-895186-11-0)

Ajani, Shaun. 2002. *Extreme Project Management*: *Unique Methodologies, Resolute Principles, Astounding Results*. San Jose, CA: Writers Club Press. (ISBN 0-595-21335-9)

Ambler, Scott W. 2000. *The Unified Process Elaboration Phase*: *Best Practices in Implementing the UP*. Lawrence, KS: CMP Books. (ISBN 1-929629-05-2)

———. 2002. *Agile Modeling*: *Effective Practices for Extreme Programming and the Unified Process*. New York: John Wiley & Sons, Inc. (ISBN 0-471-20282-7)

———. 2004. *The Object Primer*: *Agile Model-Driven Development with UML 2.0*. 3rd ed. New York: Cambridge University Press. (ISBN 0-521-54018-6)

Ambler, Scott W., and Larry L. Constantine. 2000. *The Unified Process Inception Phase*: *Best Practices in Implementing the UP*. Lawrence, KS: CMP Books. (ISBN 1-929629-10-9)

———. 2000. *The Unified Process Construction Phase*: *Best Practices in Implementing the UP*. Lawrence, KS: CMP Books. (ISBN 1-929629-01-X)

Ambler, Scott W., and Pramod J. Sadalage. 2006. *Refactoring Databases*: *Evolutionary Database Design*. New Jersey: Addison-Wesley. (ISBN 0-321-293533)

Anderson, David J. 2004. *Agile Management for Software Engineering*: *Applying the Theory of Constraints for Business Results*. New Jersey: Prentice Hall PTR. (ISBN 0-13-142460-2)

Augustine, Sanjiv. 2005. *Managing Agile Projects*. Upper Saddle River, NJ: Prentice Hall PTR. (ISBN 0-13-124071-4)

Beck, Kent, and Martin Fowler. 2001. *Planning Extreme Programming*. Reading, MA: Addison-Wesley. (ISBN 0-201-71091-9)

Bentley, Colin. 2002. *Prince2*: *A Practical Handbook, Second Edition*. Boston, MA: Butterworth-Heinemann. (ISBN 0-7506-5330-2)

Boehm, Barry, and Richard Turner. 2004. *Balancing Agility and Discipline*: *A Guide for the Perplexed*. Boston: Addison-Wesley. (ISBN 0-321-18612-5)

Chin, Gary. 2004. *Agile Project Management*: *How to Succeed in the Face of Changing Project Requirements*. New York: AMACOM. (ISBN 0-8144-7176-5)

Cockburn, Alistair. 1998. *Surviving Object-Oriented Projects*. Boston: Addison-Wesley. (ISBN 0-201-49834-0)

———. 2001. *Writing Effective Use Cases*. Boston: Addison-Wesley. (ISBN 0-201-70225-8)

Cohn, Mike. 2004. *User Stories Applied for Agile Software Development*. Boston: Addison-Wesley. (ISBN 0-321-20568-5)

Derby, Esther, and Diana Larsen. 2006. *Agile Retrospectives*: *Making Good Teams Great*. NC: The Pragmatic Bookshelf. (ISBN 978-0-97761-664-0)

Eckstein, Jutta. 2004. *Agile Software Development in the Large*. New York: Dorsett House. (ISBN 0-932633-57-9)

Fowler, Martin. 2000. *Refactoring*: *Improving the Design of Existing Code*. Boston: Addison-Wesley. (ISBN 0-201-48567-2)

Goodpasture, John C. 2010. *Project Management the Agile Way*: *Making it Work in the Enterprise*. FL: J. Ross Publishing. (ISBN 978-1-60427-027-3)

Hass, Kathleen, B. (2009). *Managing Complex Projects*: *A New Model*. VA: Management Concepts. (ISBN 978-1-56726-233-9)

Highsmith, James A. III. 2000. *Adaptive Software Development*: *A Collaborative Approach to Managing Complex Systems*. New York: Dorset House. (ISBN 0-932633-40-4)

Highsmith, Jim. 2002. *Agile Software Development Ecosystems*. Boston: Addison-Wesley. (ISBN 0-201-76043-6)

———. 2004. *Agile Project Management*: *Creating Innovative Products*. Boston: Addison Wesley. (ISBN 0-321-21977-5)

Jeffries, Ron, Ann Henderson, and Chet Hendrickson. 2001. *Extreme Programming Installed*. Boston: Addison-Wesley. (ISBN 0-201-70842-6)

Kerth, Norman L. 2001. *Project Retrospectives*: *A Handbook for Team Reviews*. New York: Dorsett House. (ISBN 0-932633-44-7)

Koch, Alan S. 2005. *Agile Software Development*: *Evaluating the Methods for Your Organization*. Boston: Artech House. (ISBN 1-58053-842-8)

Kruchten, Philippe. 2000. *The Rational Unified Process*: *An Introduction*. 2nd ed. Boston: Addison-Wesley. (ISBN 0-201-70710-1)

Larman, Craig. 2004. *Agile and Iterative Development*: *A Manager's Guide*. Boston: Addison-Wesley. (ISBN 0-13-111155-8)

Leach, Lawrence P. 2006. *Lean Project Management*: *Eight Principles for Success*. Boise, ID: BookSurge Publishing. (ISBN 1-41964-406-8)

McConnell, Steve. 1996. *Rapid Development*: *Taming Wild Software Schedules*. Redmond, WA: Microsoft Press. (ISBN 1-55615-900-5)

Newkirk, James, and Robert C. Martin. 2001. *Extreme Programming in Practice*. Boston: Addison-Wesley. (ISBN 0-201-70937-6)

Poppendieck, Mary, and Tom Poppendieck. 2003. *Lean Software Development*: *An Agile Toolkit*. Boston: Addison Wesley. (ISBN 0-321-15078-3)

Schwaber, Ken. 2004. *Agile Project Management with Scrum*. Redmond, WA: Microsoft Press. (ISBN 0-7356-1993-X)

Stapleton, Jennifer. 1997. *DSDM*: *Dynamic Systems Development Method*. Harlow, England: Addison-Wesley. (ISBN 0-201-17889-3)

Succi, Giancarlo, and Michele Marchesi. 2001. *Extreme Programming Examined*. Boston: Addison-Wesley. (ISBN 0-201-71040-4)

Thomsett, Rob. 2002. *Radical Project Management*. Upper Saddle River, NJ: Prentice Hall. (ISBN 0-13-009486-2)

Wake, William C. 2002. *Extreme Programming Explored*. Boston: Addison-Wesley. (ISBN 0-201-73397-8)

Wysocki, Robert K. 2005. *Managing Complexity and Uncertainty in Software Projects*. MA: Cutter Consortium, Vol. 6, No. 7.

————. 2006. *How to be Successful in an Ever-Changing Project Landscape*. MA: EII Publications. (ISBN 1-933788-03-8)

————. 2010. *Adaptive Project Framework*: *Managing Complexity in the Face of Uncertainty*. MA: Addison-Wesley. (ISBN 978-0-321-52561-1)

Project Management Infrastructure

Block, Thomas R., and J. Davidson Frame. 1998. *The Project Office*. Menlo Park, CA: Crisp Publications. (ISBN 1-56052-443-X)

Cooper, Robert G., Scott J. Edgett, and Elko J. Kleinschmidt. 1998. *Portfolio Management for New Products*. Reading, MA: Perseus Books. (ISBN 0-201-32814-3)

Crawford, J. Kent. 2002. *Project Management Maturity Model*: *Providing a Proven Path to Project Management Excellence*. New York: Marcel Dekker, Inc. (ISBN 0-8247-0754-0)

————. 2002. *The Strategic Project Office*: *A Guide to Improving Organizational Performance*. New York: Marcel Dekker, Inc. (ISBN 0-8247-0750-8)

Dye, Lowell D., and James S. Pennypacker, editors. 1999. *Project Portfolio Management*: *Selecting and Prioritizing Projects for Competitive Advantage*. West Chester, PA: Center for Business Practices. (ISBN 1-929576-00-5)

Graham, Robert J., and Randall L. Englund. 1997. *Creating an Environment for Successful Projects*. San Francisco: Jossey-Bass. (ISBN 0-7879-0359-0)

Hallows, Jolyon. 2002. *The Project Management Office Toolkit*: *A Step-by-Step Guide to Setting Up a Project Management Office*. New York: AMACOM. (ISBN 0-8144-0663-7)

Hobbs, Brian, and Monique Aubry. 2010. *The Project Management Office* (PMO): *A Quest for Understanding*. PA: The Project Management Institute. (ISBN 978-1-933890-97-5)

Kerzner, Harold. 2001. *Strategic Planning for Project Management Using a Project Management Maturity Model*. New York: John Wiley & Sons. (ISBN 0-471-40039-4)

Kodama, Mitsuru. 2007. *Project-based Organization in the Knowledge-based Society*. London: Imperial College Press. (ISBN 978-186094-696-7)

Moore, Simon. 2010. *Strategic Project Portfolio Management: Enabling a Productive Organization*. NY: John Wiley & Sons. (ISBN 978-0-470-48195-0)

Paulk, Mark C., et al. 1994. *The Capability Maturity Model: Guidelines for Improving the Software Process*. Reading, MA: Addison-Wesley. (ISBN 0-201-54664-7)

Rad, Parviz F., and Ginger Levin. 2002. *The Advanced Project Management Office: A Comprehensive Look at Function and Implementation*. Boca Raton, FL: St. Lucie Press. (ISBN 1-57444-340-2)

Raynus, Joseph. 1999. *Software Process Improvement with CMM*. Boston: Artech House. (ISBN 0-89006-644-2)

Wysocki, Robert K. 2006. *How to Establish a Project Support Office: A Practical Guide to Its Establishment, Growth and Development*. MA: EII Publications. (ISBN 1-933788-19-4)

———. 2007. *"How to Establish a Project Support Office."* MA: Cutter Consortium, Vol. 8, No. 3.

———. 2011. *The Business Analyst / Project Manager: A New Partnership for Managing Complexity and Uncertainty*. NY: John Wiley & Sons. (ISBN 978-0-470-76744-3)

Managing the Realities of Projects

Smith, John M. 2001. *Troubled IT Projects: Prevention and Turnaround*. Herts, United Kingdom: The Institution of Electrical Engineers. (ISBN 0-85296-104-9)

Wysocki, Robert K. 2006. *"Distressed Projects: Prevention and Intervention Strategies."* MA: Cutter Consortium, Vol. 7, No. 8.

———. 2006. *"Managing a Multiple Team Project."* MA: Cutter Consortium Vol. 7, No. 4.

———. 2006. *Managing a Project That Involves Multiple Teams*. MA: EII Publications. (ISBN 1-933788-05-4)

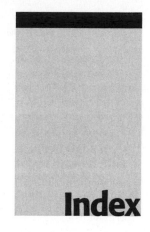

Index

A

A Team members, 228–229
AC (actual cost), 295–298, 638–639
accept, risk response, 84
acceptably leveled schedule, 267
acceptance test procedures (ATP), 312–314, 375. *See also* client acceptance
accommodators, 234–236, 238, 242, 244, 246–247
action to be taken, risk log, 85
active projects. *See* MANAGE active projects
activities. *See also* business processes; tasks
  bounded, 173
  business process, 119
  complex, 7
  defined, 6, 115
  tasks *v.*, 166
  unique, 6–7
  WBS completeness test, 172–175
activity duration estimates, 158, 163, 593

activity schedules
  design-build-test-implement approach, 179
  JPPS deliverable, 164
  launching, 21
actual cost (AC), 295–298, 638–639
ACWP (Actual Cost of Work Performed), 296, 639
ad hoc level, 589
Adams, Anthony, 279
adaptability
  APF, 435–437
  APM, 327–328, 445
  core project team members, 230
Adaptive Cycle Plan phase, 407–408
Adaptive PMLC models, 47, 49, 398–445. *See also* Adaptive Project Framework
  Agile models, 379
  APF, 379, 391, 406
  ASD, 379, 391, 406–407
    graphical depiction, 407
    phases, 406–408
  business value, 404–405
  cancellation, 399
  characteristics, 403

choosing, 408
client involvement, 405, 443–445
closing phase, 402–403
co-located teams, 383
defined, 398–400
DSDM, 57, 379, 391, 399–400,
    406, 438–440
  client involvement, 400, 405
  graphical depiction, 439–440
  software development projects,
    48, 406
graphical depiction, 49, 399
Iterative models *v.*, 378–379, 400
launching phase, 401
non-value-added work, 403–404, 409
planning phase, 400–401
PMLC models comparison, 55–56
process group-level diagram, 399
scope change requests, 404
scoping phase, 400
Scrum, 379, 391, 406, 439–443
  best-fit choice, 131
  client involvement, 439
  graphical depiction, 441–442
  process flow, 440–441
  Product Owner, 131, 405, 439–440,
    441–443
  rugby *v.*, 439
  Sprint, 441–443
software development projects, 46
solution clarity, 408
strengths, 403–405
types, 406
weaknesses, 405–406
when to use, 129, 443–445
*Adaptive Project Framework: Managing
  Complexity in the Face of Uncertainty*
  (Wysocki), 408
Adaptive Project Framework (APF),
  408–437. *See also* swim lanes
adapting, 435–437
Adaptive PMLC model, 379, 391, 406

APFists, 425, 427–428, 436
APM approach *v.*, 49
budget, 418
change, 411–412
Client Checkpoint, 429–433
  graphical depiction, 429
  PDQ case study, 433
  updated Scope Bank, 430–431
client involvement, 410–411
core values, 410–412
Cycle Build, 426–428
  functionality, 427
  graphical depiction, 427
  monitor/adjust, 428
Cycle Plan, 420–426
  graphical depiction, 421
  micro-level schedule, 423–426
  micro-level WBS, 421–426
  work packages, 426
defined, 409–410
graphical depiction, 413
implementing, 437
non-value-added work, 412, 423–424
observations on, 409–410
PDQ case study, 433, 464
phases, 412
PMLC models integration, 436–437
Post-Version Review, 433–435
  graphical depiction, 434
  questions, 433–435
  Version Scope *v.*, 433
software development projects,
  379–380, 408, 450
TPM *v.*, 410
value, 437
Version Scope, 412–420, 433
  COS, 413–414
  cycle timeboxes, 418–420
  cycles, 419–420
  deliverables, 413–414
  graphical depiction, 414
  POS, 414, 418–419

Post-Version Review *v.*, 433
prioritized scope triangle, 415–417
RBS, 414, 419
StageGates, 412–413, 419
WBS, 414, 419
Adaptive Software Development.
  See ASD
*Adaptive Software Development: A
  Collaborative Approach to Managing
  Complex Systems* (Highsmith), 406
adversarial relationship, 88
Agile Manifesto (Fowler &
  Highsmith), 35n1, 323, 379,
  379n1, 380
*Agile Project Management: Creating
  Innovative Products* (Highsmith), 324
Agile Project Management (APM),
  44–49, 377–451. *See also* Adaptive
  PMLC models; Iterative PMLC
  models
  adaptability, 327–328, 445
  Agile Manifesto, 35n1, 323, 379,
    379n1, 380
  APF *v.*, 49
  business value, 337
  change, 336
  client involvement, 331, 392
  client ownership, 332–333
  client's comfort zone, 332
  closing next iteration/cycle, 447
  closing project, 448
  co-located teams, 46–48, 59, 329,
    382–384, 388
  core team members, 228
  cycle timeboxes, 58
  discussion questions, 449–451
  Extreme PMLC models *v.*, 459–460
  flexibility, 327
  graphical depiction, 55
  history, 379–380
  implementing, 380–381
  INSPIRE *v.*, 457–458

launching next iteration/cycle,
    446–447
  models, 379
    non-value-added work, 384
    Q3/Q4 projects, 379
  monitoring/controlling next
    iteration/cycle, 447
  non-value-added work, 326, 400, 655
  planning next iteration/cycle, 446
  projects
    characteristics, 45–48
    client involvement, 46
    implementation, 380–381
    major issues, 380
    percentage of, 47, 154, 322, 377, 378
    risk level, 45
    untapped business opportunity, 45
    without known solution, 45
  risk, 328–329
  scoping next iteration/cycle, 445–446
  software development projects,
    323, 380
  team cohesiveness, 329
  teams, 388
  tools/templates/processes, 445
  TPM with, 47
  WBS, 48
  xPM *v.*, 52–53, 457
agile project portfolios
  closing projects, 580–581
  defined, 572
  HRMS, 383
  life cycle
    ESTABLISH portfolio strategy,
      573, 575
    EVALUATE project alignment,
      573, 575
    graphical depiction, 573–574
    MANAGE active projects, 573, 575,
      580–581
    phases, 573, 575
    PRIORITIZE phase, 573, 575

SELECT balanced portfolio, 573, 575, 577–580

project types, 581

risk, 576

Agile Project Portfolio Management (APPM), 572–581

challenges, 576–577

PMLC model integration, 574–576

Agile Software Development with Scrum (Schwaber & Beedle), 439

agreement, COS process, 108

aligned projects, 531

American Red Cross, 689

analyze current situation, distressed projects, 640–645, 654–655

Annotation flowchart symbol, 120–121

APF. *See* Adaptive Project Framework

APFists, 425, 427, 428, 436

APM. *See* Agile Project Management

appendices, project proposal, 220

APPM. *See* Agile Project Portfolio Management

approval process, POS, 144–147, 221

architectural-design tool, WBS, 167

As Is business process, 119, 604, 610, 623

ASD (Adaptive Software Development)

Adaptive PMLC model, 379, 391, 406

graphical depiction, 407

phases, 406–408

ashtrays, 132

Assessment and Analysis phase, CPIM, 600–602

assignable, S.M.A.R.T. characteristic, 137

assigning resources. *See* resource assignments

assignment sheets, work package, 275, 277

assimilators, 234, 242–243, 246–247

associate manager

multi-team projects, 665

PM/BA, 693, 698–699

assumptions, risks, obstacles section, POS, 140–141

ATP (acceptance test procedures), 312–314, 375. *See also* client acceptance

attachments, POS, 141–143

Aubry, Monique, 485, 485n1

autonomy, job design, 73

available slack, 268, 306

avoid, risk response, 84

avoidant, conflict resolution style, 248

B

B Team members, 228–229

BA (business analysis), 707–708, 710

background, project proposal, 219

balancing project teams, 233–235. *See also* conflict resolution; learning styles

BA/PM. *See* PM/BA

Barton, Clara, 689

BCG. *See* Boston Consulting Group

BCWP (Budgeted Cost of Work Performed), 296, 639

BCWS (Budgeted Cost of Work Scheduled), 296, 639

Beedle, Mike, 439

Bell Telephone Laboratories, 453

best-fit PMLC model

choosing, 57–60

complexity, 502

factors, 35

project characteristics, 36

solution clarity, 38

four-quadrant project landscape, 35, 324, 502

meaningful client involvement, 642

RBS, 31, 171

requirements completeness, 30, 130

requirements gathering, 634

best-fit project structure

multiple team projects, 686–687
  RUP, 131
  Scrum, 131
best-practices constraints, 206–207
Better Online Solutions, 372
bidder questions, 89
big-picture improvement, 609
Blanchard, Kenneth H., 225, 657
Boeing 777, 208
Bohr, Neils, 103
Boston Consulting Group (BCG)
    Products/Services Matrix, 533,
    535–536
bottom-up approach
  APF implementation, 437
  learning model, 1
  PSO implementation, 520
Boundaries flowchart symbol, 120–121
bounded activity, 173
BP⁴SO, 521–524. *See also* PSOs
BPM (business process management),
    689, 707–708, 710
BPMN (Business Process Management
    Notation), 125
brainstorming
  Assessment and Analysis Phase,
      CPIM, 601
  convention *v.*, 250
  divergers, 234
  Extreme PMLC model, 456
  INitiate, 459–460
  INSPIRE, 464, 469
  launching Process Group, 374
  problem-solving process, 243
  risk identification list, 79
  Root Cause Analysis results, 649
  SPeculate, 463
  team operating rules, 249–250
Breakdown Structure. *See* RBS;
    Resource Breakdown Structure;
    WBS
breakeven analysis, POS, 143

briefing tool, 133
Bruno, Giordano, 149
budget, APF, 418
budget estimate, 197–198
Budgeted Cost of Work Performed
    (BCWP), 296, 639
Budgeted Cost of Work Scheduled
    (BCWS), 296, 639
buffers, 368–372
  defined, 368–369
  management reserve *v.*, 258, 370
  managing, 370–372
  penetration, 370–372
  types, 369
Building Effective Project Teams
    (Wysocki), 235, 247
bureaucracy elimination, 607
burn charts, 290
Burns, Robert, 627
business analysis (BA), 707, 710
*Business Analysis Body of Knowledge
    Guide* (IIBA), 28
Business Analyst/Project Manager.
    See PM/BA
business climate, 58, 327, 336, 418,
    583, 647
business outcomes, COS, 109
business processes. *See also* processes
  BP4SO, 522
  building WBS, 180
  characteristics, 605–609
  CPIM, 119, 604–612, 623
    To Be, 119, 604, 610, 623
    characteristics, 605–609
    improvement opportunities, 609
    improvement project, 611–612
    indicators of needed improvement,
        609
    streamlining tools, 607–609
  defined, 119–120
  effectiveness, 606
  efficiency, 606

graphical depiction, 119
integrated into business processes
    (level 4), 590
non-value-added work, 609
process level, RBS, 115
streamlining tools, 607–609
business process diagramming, 117
    context diagrams, 122–123
    creating, 120–121
    flowcharts, 120–121, 124
    formats, 121–122
business process improvement project,
    611–612
business process management (BPM),
    689, 707–708, 710
Business Process Management
    Notation (BPMN), 125
business value
    Adaptive PMLC models,
        404–405
    APF, 437
    complexity/uncertainty domain *v.*,
        336–337
    Extreme PMLC models, 457
    incremental, 26–27, 29
    Incremental PMLC models, 356–357,
        359–360
    IRACIS, 26
    Linear PMLC models, 351
    MPx models, 53
    project classification, 19
    project management definition,
        27
    project's purpose, 8–9
    requirements and, 28–31
butcher paper, 162, 169
by-business-unit approach, installed
    deliverables, 315

C

Campbell Soup Co., 279
cancellation
    Adaptive PMLC models, 399

projects, Project Portfolio
    Management life cycle, 532
candidate risk driver template and
    assessment worksheet, 78, 80–81
Capability Maturity Model (CMM), 94,
    508, 525, 589
Capability Maturity Model Integrated
    (CMMI), 508, 589. *See also* maturity
capacity constrained buffers, 369
capital budget projects, 529
career planning, PM/BA landscape,
    706–707
CareerAgent model, 694, 706
Carlyle, Thomas, 689
cash cows, 535–536
cats, herd of, 215–216, 320
cause-and-effect diagrams. *See*
    fishbone diagrams
CCPM. *See* critical chain project
    management
celebrating success, 319–320
central limit theorem, 364
centralized EPSOs, 499–500
ceremonial acceptance, 313
certain events, 79. *See also* risks
CFs (critical factors), 591–594, 596–597,
    599–600, 603
    CHAOS report, 591, 596
    graphical depiction, 593
    project failure, 591
chair example, 185–186
challenge, 72
change
    Adaptive PMLC models, 403
    APF, 411–412
    APM, 336
    "Change or die," 35
    changing requirements and
        specification, 330, 501, 503, 707
    complexity/uncertainty domain *v.*,
        335–336
    every change is significant, 254
    Extreme PMLC models, 455–456

intolerance, 43, 152, 333, 390
  Linear PMLC models, 43, 348–349
  radical, milestone trend chart,
    291–292
change control process, 256–257
CHAOS Report, 591, 596, 707
chart of accounts (CoA), 178
Check Results phase, CPIM, 603
chefs/cooks analogy, 28, 33, 445, 449,
    475, 494, 502, 588, 684, 689
choice process, PMLC models, 56–60
  departments affected, 58–59
  organizational environment, 59
  team skills/competencies, 59–60
  total cost, 57
Churchill, Winston, 149
clarification, COS process, 108
clarity of purpose, 108–109
clients
  comfort zone, 332
  JPPS attendance, 161
  ownership, 332–333
  POS approval process, 146
  project notebook, 443
  Scoping Meeting, 111
  sign-off, 333
client acceptance, 313–314
  ATP, 312–314, 375
  ceremonial, 313
  formal, 313
Client Checkpoint, 429–433
  graphical depiction, 429
  PDQ case study, 433
  updated Scope Bank, 430–431
client expectations
  business process effectiveness, 605
  managing, 105–106
  wants v. needs, 37, 86, 106
client involvement
  Adaptive PMLC models, 405,
    443–445
  APF, 410–411
  APM, 46, 392

complexity/uncertainty domain v.,
    331–333
  Incremental PMLC models, 358, 360
  Iterative PMLC models, 386, 390–391,
    397
  lack of user input, 330, 502, 593, 707
  Scrum, 439
client teams, 227
  Agile projects, 378
  closing projects, 311
  development teams v., 46, 50, 52,
    237, 449
  qualified co-project manager,
    444–445
  selection criteria, 231
  xPM projects, 460
client-based escalation strategies, 307
client-facing, 116, 122, 351, 358
closing (Process Group), 311–320
  APM PMLC models, 447–448
  approval for, 308
  celebrating success, 319–320
  client acceptance, 313–314
  defined, 67
  deliverables installed, 314–315
  discussion questions, 320
  final project report, 319
  phase
    Adaptive PMLC models, 402–403
    Extreme PMLC models, 475
    Iterative PMLC models, 388–389
  post-implementation audit, 317–319
  processes, 67
  project documentation, 315–317
  steps, 312–313
  tools/templates/processes, 312
  TPM projects, 3, 311–320
closing projects, in agile portfolios,
    580–581
closing vendor contracts, 98–99
CMM. See Capability Maturity Model
CMMI. See Capability Maturity Model
    Integrated

CoA (chart of accounts), 178
Coad, Peter, 352
code reuse, 396
Collaborate phase, ASD, 406–407
collaboration
  Adaptive PMLC model, 405
  Agile manifesto, 379
  APF, 410
  APM approaches, 49, 331
  ASD, 406
  BA/PM professional, 709
  client and development team, 46
  co-located xPM team, 468
  conflict resolution style, 248–249
  DSDM, 438
  INSPIRE, 468–469
  JPPS, 164
  multiple team project, 658
  project kick-off meeting, 238
  prototyping PMLC model, 392
  PSO, 492, 495–496
  requirements management, 97
  scoping efforts, 105
  SPeculate stage, 467
co-located teams
  Adaptive PMLC models, 383
  APM, 46–48, 59, 329, 382–384, 388
  different time zones, 278
  INSPIRE, 469
  Iterative PMLC model, 383, 390–391
  Linear PMLC model, 347–348
  MPx, 329
  team war room, 253
  TPM, 59, 329, 388
  xPM, 329, 468
color-coded sticky notes, 155
combative, conflict resolution style,
  248
comfort zone, client, 332
common cause variation, 363–364
common sense, organized, 27, 65, 327,
  436, 689

communications management
  (Knowledge Area)
  complexity/uncertainty domain v.,
    330–331
  defined, 74–75
  listening skills, 107, 189, 236
  multiple team projects, 661
  project failures, 74, 105, 108, 259, 330
  questions, 74–75
  stakeholders, 74–75, 264
  team communications, 258–264
    effective channels, 260–262
    information content, 259–260
    information timing, 259
    with sponsor, 262–263
  upward communications filtering,
    263–264
completion
  date, 7–8
  projects, Project Portfolio
    Management life cycle, 532
  WBS, 172–176
complex activities, 7
complex projects, 707–709. *See also*
  professional development program
  disciplines needed
    BA, 707–708, 710
    BPM, 689, 707–708, 710
    IT, 689, 707–708, 710
    PM, 707–710
complexity/uncertainty domain,
  323–338. *See also* project
  management landscape
  adaptability, 328
  business value v., 336–337
  change v., 335–336
  client involvement v., 331–333
  communications v., 330–331
  discussion questions, 338
  Extreme PMLC models, 456
  flexibility, 327–328
  multiple team projects, 679–680, 686

RBS, 326–327
risk *v.*, 328–329
specification *v.*, 333–335
team cohesiveness *v.*, 329
TPM approach, 40
compressing schedules. *See* schedule
compression
concurrent component engineering,
408
concurrent swim lanes, 353, 387, 401,
408, 431, 602
Conditions of Satisfaction. *See* COS
"Conflict and Conflict Management"
(Thomas), 249
conflict resolution, 235–236, 241,
374, 675
avoidant, 248
collaborative, 248–249
combative, 248
Core Team, 675
resources, 249
team operating rules, 248–249
connected activities, 7
Connector flowchart symbol,
120, 121
consensus building, 249
constraints, 205–209
best-practices, 206–207
date, 209
dependencies *v.*, 205–209
design, 128
discretionary, 206
interproject, 208
logical, 207
management, 207–208
product, 128
project, 11, 128
technical, 206–207
TOC, 362–363, 382
unique requirements, 207
construction phase, RUP, 395
consultants, JPPS, 160

consultative decision-making model,
245
Consulting and Mentoring service
area, 485, 491–492
context diagrams, 122–123
contingency, CCPM, 364–365
contingency planning, risk response,
84
continuous improvement
defined, 611–612
level 5 maturity, 590–591
outsourcing *v.*, 119
Continuous Process Improvement
Model. *See* CPIM
contract management, 92–96
adversarial relationship, 88
final contract negotiation, 95–96
contract team members, 231–233, 266
contractors, project kick-off meeting,
238
contracts, 94–95
control charts, 615
controlling. *See* monitoring/
controlling
convention, 250
convergers, 234–235, 242–243, 246–247
Cooke, Ernest F., 279
cooks. *See* chefs/cooks analogy
coordinator, team meetings, 251
co-project managers, 27, 46, 131, 411,
429, 444–445, 449
core project teams, 227–230
JPPS attendance, 160–161
members, 227–230
characteristics, 229–230
selection criteria, 228–230
POS approval process, 145
Project Scoping Meeting, 110
Scoping Meeting, 111
Core Team (CT), 673–680. *See also*
multiple team projects
characteristics, 673–676

defined, 673
roles/responsibilities, 674–676
strengths, 676–678
structure, 674
weaknesses, 678–679
when to use, 679–680
core values, APF, 410–412
COS (Conditions of Satisfaction),
107–110
business outcomes, 109
clarity of purpose, 108–109
defined, 107
graphical depiction, 108
INSPIRE, 464
milestone reviews, 109–110
Root Cause Analysis, 336
steps, 108–109
Version Scope, 413–414
cost. *See also* earned value analysis;
scope triangle
AC, 295–298, 638–639
Cost Plus contracts, 94–95
earned value analysis, 98
estimating, 196–199
Linear PMLC models, 349
negative variances, 287–288
PMLC model choice process, 57
positive variances, 286–287
prioritizing, 15
reduced, success criteria, 139
resource leveling, 271
scope triangle variable, 12
time and cost summary page, 220
variance, 284
cost and benefit analyses, POS, 143
cost budgeting, 198
cost buffers, 369
cost control issues, 198–199
cost management (Knowledge Area),
68
cost performance index (CPI), 298–299,
557–562, 638–639

Couger, Daniel, 71, 71n1, 242–243, 246
CPI. *See* cost performance index
CPIM (Continuous Process
Improvement Model), 584, 591,
598–623
Assessment and Analysis phase,
600–602
benefits, 604
business processes, 119, 604–612, 623
To Be, 119, 604, 610, 623
characteristics, 605–609
improvement opportunities, 609
improvement project, 611–612
indicators of needed improvement,
609
streamlining tools, 607–609
Check Results phase, 603
discussion questions, 623
flowcharts, 615–617
Foundation phase, 599–600
graphical depiction, 598
Improvement Initiatives phase,
602–603
Iterative PMLC models, 397
overview, 480
PSO roles/responsibilities, 603
tools/templates/processes, 612–622
CPS (Creative Problem Solving)
model, 242–244
crashing the task, 185
crashpoint, 186
Crawford, J. Kent, 519
Crawford-Mason, Clare, 583
*Creative Problem Solving and
Opportunity Finding* (Couger), 242
Creative Problem Solving (CPS)
model, 242–244
creeps, 16–17. *See also* scope creep
effort, 17
feature, 17–18
hope, 17, 653
critical chain, 363

Critical Chain (Goldratt), 372
*Critical Chain Project Management,
    Second Edition* (Leach), 362–363,
    368–369, 372, 375, 556, 580
critical chain project management
    (CCPM), 362–373
  buffers, 368–372
    defined, 368–369
    management reserve *v.*, 258, 370
    managing, 370–372
    types, 369
  critical path *v.*, 363–367
  defined, 363
  planning steps, 366–368
  project network diagram, 366–367
  resource conflicts, 367–368
  scarce resources, 556, 580
  statistical validation, 364–366
  TOC, 362–363, 372
  TPM *v.*, 364, 366
  track record, 372–373
critical factors. *See* CFs
critical mission projects, 403, 445
critical path, 212–214
  APF, 423
  calculating, 213
  CCPM *v.*, 363–368
  defined, 210
  near-critical path, 214, 277
  negative time variances, 287
  non–critical path tasks, 229, 271, 287,
    306, 307, 308
  tasks, 210, 212, 214–216, 229, 271, 274,
    277
cross-project dependencies, 382
CT. *See* Core Team
cumulative reports, 282
Curly, 496–497
current period reports, 281
cut-over approach, installed
    deliverables, 314
Cycle Build, 426–428

functionality, 427
  graphical depiction, 427
  monitor/adjust, 428
Cycle Plan, 420–426
  graphical depiction, 421
  micro-level schedule, 423–426
  micro-level WBS, 421–426
  work packages, 426
cycle schedule, resource-loaded,
    424–425
cycle timeboxes
  Adaptive Cycle Plan, 407
  APM projects, 58, 401
  Version Scope, 418, 419–420
cycles
  Adaptive PMLC models, 55
  cycle-time reduction, 607
  Version Scope
    functions assigned, 420
    number of, 419–420
    objective statements for, 420

D

daily status meeting, 251–252, 302,
    305, 425
D'Angelo, Anthony J., 583
date constraints, 209
decentralized EPSOs, 499–500
decision action plan phase, 246–247
decision evaluation phase, 246–247
Decision flowchart symbol, 120–121
decision making. *See also* problem
    solving
  go/no-go, 12, 466, 469–470
  LSI, 233, 245–246
  model selection, 245
  phases, 246–247
  team operating rules, 244–247
defining part, Version Scope, 412
definitive cost estimate, 198
Delay flowchart symbol, 120–121
deliverables

completed activity, 173

installed, closing project, 314–315

JPPS, 163–164

Linear PMLC models, 349

Scoping Meeting, 112

Version Scope, 413–415

Delphi technique, 189–191

DeLuca, Jeff, 352

departmental approach, 180

departments affected, PMLC model
    choice process, 58–60

dependencies. *See also* constraints

constraints *v.*, 205–209

cross-project, 382

defined, 204

FF, 204–206, 268

FS, 204–208, 215–217, 223, 268, 270,
    290, 307

relationships, 204

SF, 204–205, 216

SS, 204–209, 215–217, 223,
    268, 307

types, 204–205

description reports, work package,
    275–276

design constraints, 128

design-build-test-implement
    approach, 177, 179

detailed plans, Linear PMLC models,
    349–350

detailed statement of work, 11, 94–95,
    220, 277

development, PSO, 495–497

development teams

Adaptive PMLC models, 405

Agile approaches, 378

APF, 383, 410

client teams *v.*, 46, 50, 52, 237, 449

closing projects, 311

distributed across several time
    zones, 348

Get Client Feedback, 393

Incremental PMLC models, 360

Iterative PMLC model, 49

launching phase, 643

Scrum, 439

well-understood technology
    infrastructure, 41

xPM projects, 460

deviations, standard, 290–293

diagramming conventions, project
    network, 204

Direction of Flow flowchart symbol,
    120–121

directive decision-making model, 244

Director, PM/BA, 693, 700–401

discretionary constraints, 206

discussion questions. *See also* PDQ
    case study

APM, 449–451

closing Process Group, 320

complexity/uncertainty domain, 338

CPIM, 623

distressed projects, 656

launching Process Group, 278

monitoring/controlling Process
    Group, 309

multiple team projects, 658, 663, 687

planning Process Group, 222–224

Process Groups, 101

professional development plan, 710

project management, 60–61

project portfolio management
    process, 581–582

PSOs, 525

scoping Process Group, 147

TPM, 376

xPM, 475–477

distressed projects, 627–656

characteristics, 628

defined, 628

discussion questions, 656

dynamic risk management process,
    635

EVA, 638–639
ignored in literature, 625
intervention management strategies, 639–651
  analyze current situation, 640–645, 654–655
  evaluate options, 640, 649–650, 655
  generate revised plan, 640, 650–651, 655
  revise desired goal, 640, 645–648, 655
intervention process template, 651–653
managing, 632–651
milestone trend charts, 637–638
overview, 626
prevention management strategies, 632–639
PSO roles/responsibilities, 653–655
reasons for failure, 629–632
requirements gathering, 633–634
scope change management process, 635–636
tools/templates/processes for prevention, 633–639
WBS construction, 634–635
divergers, 234–235, 242–243, 246–247
Dobens, Lloyd, 583
Document flowchart symbol, 120–121
documentation
  change control process, 256–257
  Incremental PMLC models, 358–359
  project, 315–317
  requirements, 18, 112, 125, 130, 340, 342, 629, 633
documented processes levels (levels 2-3), 589–590
Doran, George T., 137, 137n1
downsizing, 228
drum buffers, 369
DSDM: Dynamic Systems Development Method (Stapleton), 438

DSDM (Dynamic Systems Development Method), 438–440
  Adaptive PMLC model, 57, 379, 391, 399, 400, 406, 440
  client involvement, 400, 405
  graphical depiction, 439–440
  software development projects, 48, 406
duplication elimination, 607
DuPont, 149
dynamic planning, 152
dynamic RBS, 113
dynamic risk assessment, 82–84
dynamic risk management process, distressed projects, 635
Dynamic Systems Development Method. See DSDM
Dynamics of Conflict Resolution: A Practitioner's Guide (Mayer), 249

E
earliest start–latest finish (ES–LF) window, 266, 268–270, 306
early schedule, 210–213, 366–367
earned value (EV), 295–298, 638–639
earned value analysis (EVA), 293–301
  AC, 295–298, 638–639
  ACWP, 296, 639
  BCWP, 296, 639
  BCWS, 296, 639
  cost, 98
  defined, 293
  distressed projects, 638–639
  drawback, 293
  EV, 295–298, 638–639
  milestone trend charts integration with, 298–301, 639
  monitoring/controlling (Process Group), 68
  PV, 295–298, 638–639

S curve, 294
schedule, 98
simple metric, 173, 274
sponsors, 263
terminology, 296
variances, 287, 294–295
Effective Software Project Management (Wysocki), 118, 298
effectiveness, business process, 606
effort creep, 17
EII. *See* Enterprise Information Insights, Inc.
eiicorp.com, 513–514, 516, 709
elaboration phase, RUP, 395
Emertxe Project Management. *See* MPx
Englund, Randall L., 383n1. *See also* Graham-Englund Selection Model
Enterprise Information Insights, Inc. (EII), 23, 63, 279, 323, 339, 377, 514, 583
Enterprise PSOs (EPSOs), 499–500, 516
entrepreneurial risk, 76
EPSOs (Enterprise PSOs), 499–500, 516
equipment
  JPPS, 162
  project kick-off meeting, 238
  as resource, 193
error proofing, 607–608
escalation strategy. *See* problem escalation strategy
ES-LF (earliest start–latest finish) window, 266, 268–270, 306
ESTABLISH portfolio strategy
  Agile Project Portfolio life cycle, 573, 575
  BCG Products/Services Matrix, 533, 535–536
  Growth *versus* Survival Model, 533, 538
  Project Distribution Matrix, 533, 536–538

Project Investment Categories Model, 533, 538–539
Project Portfolio Management life cycle, 531, 532–539
Strategic Alignment Model, 533–535
estimating, 183–199. *See also* task duration
  budget, 197–198
  cost, 196–199
  cost budgeting *v.,* 198
  order of magnitude, 142, 197, 198, 223
  resource requirements, 192–195
  task duration, 184–185, 188–191
estimation life-cycles, 191–192
EV. *See* earned value
EVA. *See* earned value analysis
evaluate options, distressed projects, 640, 649–650, 655
EVALUATE project alignment
  Agile Project Portfolio life cycle, 573, 575
  Project Portfolio Management life cycle, 531, 539–540
evaluation of outcome/process, decision-making process, 246–247
every change is significant, 254
Evolutionary Development Waterfall, 48, 57, 131
exception reports, 282
executing process group, 64–65. *See also* launching
executive summary, project proposal, 219
Executive's Guide to Project Management: Organizational Process and Practices for Supporting Complex Projects (Wysocki), 521n2, 709
expectations gap, 105. *See also* client expectations
experience acquisition, 691, 702–703, 710. *See also* professional development program

expert advice, task duration estimation method, 189
external risks, 78
Extreme PMLC models, 38, 454–470, 502. *See also* MPx; xPM
  Agile projects *v.*, 459–460
  brainstorming, 456
  business value, 457
  change, 455–456
  characteristics, 455–456
  closing phase, 475
  closing project, 475
  defined, 454–455
  discussion questions, 475–477
  graphical depiction, 52, 55, 454
  INSPIRE, 457–470
    APM models *v.*, 457–458
    graphical depiction, 458
    Incubate, 467–469
    INitiate, 459–463
    REview, 469–470
    SPeculate, 463–467
  launching next phase, 474
  monitoring/controlling next phase, 474
  planning next phase, 473–474
  PMLC models comparison, 55–56
  scoping next phase, 472–473
  strengths, 456
  uncertainty, 456
  weaknesses, 457
  when to use, 129
Extreme Project Management. *See* xPM

F
facilitated group sessions, 117–118
facilitators
  JPPS attendance, 160
  RBS, 117, 131
  Scoping Meeting, 111
facilities

JPPS, 162
  project kick-off meeting, 238
  as resources, 193
failures. *See* project failures
FDD (feature-driven development)
  Linear PMLC models, 351, 352–355
feasibility studies, POS, 142–143
feature creep, 17–18
feature level, RBS, 115
feature-driven development (FDD)
  Linear PMLC models, 351–355
feedback, job design, 74
feedback loop, Linear PMLC model, 342
feeding buffers, 369
Felsing, John M., 352
FF (finish-to-finish) dependencies, 204, 205, 206, 268
FFP (Firm Fixed Price) contracts, 94
fiercely independent team cultures, 660
The Fifty Discipline (Senge), 362
final contract negotiation, 95–96
final project report, 319
financial analyses, POS, 142–143
finish-to-finish. *See* FF
finish-to-start. *See* FS
Firm Fixed Price (FFP) contracts, 94
fishbone diagrams, 612–615
5-Phase Project Management: A Practical Planning and Implementation Guide (Weiss & Wysocki), 172
fixed price contracts, 94
fixed resources, 8
flexibility, complexity/uncertainty domain, 327–328
flip charts, 155, 162, 169–170, 201, 238, 645
float (slack time), 209–210, 213–214, 287. *See also* slack
flowcharts

business process diagrams, 120–121, 124

CPIM, 615–617

symbols, 120–121

force field analysis, 620–622, 652

Forced Ranking model

PRIORITIZE projects, 541–542

Project Distribution Matrix and, 547, 550–552

scope triangle prioritization, 416

SELECT balanced portfolio, 550–552

SPeculate stage, 465

vendor selection, 90–91

formal acceptance, 313

format, project proposals, 221

Foundation phase, CPIM, 599–600

four quadrants, 34, 100, 321–322. *See also* Adaptive Project Framework; MPx; project management landscape; TPM; xPM

Fowler, Martin, 35n2, 323, 379, 379n1, 380

framing PSO objectives, 489–490

free slack, 150, 213–214, 268, 367

FS (finish-to-start) dependencies, 204–208, 215–217, 223, 268, 270, 290, 307

FTE (full-time equivalent), 579, 681

full-time equivalent (FTE), 579, 681

function level, RBS, 114

functional decomposition, noun-type approach, 178

functional managers

JPPS attendance, 161

POS approval process, 146

functional PSOs, 499

functional requirements, 128

functional specification, 11, 340, 434, 465, 707. *See also* requirements documentation; scope

future PSOs, 521–524

G

Gantt charts, 288–289

defined, 178

detailed statement of work, 220

project management, 35, 340

project network diagram *v.*, 200–201

gap, maturity, 600

generate revised plan, distressed projects, 640, 650–651, 655

geographic approach, 180

global requirements, 128

goals

POS project goal, 136–137

project management landscape, 34–39

projects, 7

The Goal (Goldratt), 362

Goldratt, Eliyahu M., 362, 372

go/no-go decision, 12, 466, 469–470

good news syndrome, 263–264

Graham, Robert J., 383n1

Graham-Englund Selection Model

agile version, 578–580

available staff capacity based on skills, 538

balanced portfolio selection, 547, 643

defined, 383

functional-level projects, 539

PSO, 505

SELECT balanced portfolio, 552–556

graphical reporting tools, 288–301. *See also* Gantt charts

grassroots approach. *See* bottom-up approach

Green, Estill I., 453, 469

"green field" approach, 610

Greenwalt, Crawford, 149

growth projects, 538

Growth *versus* Survival Model, 533, 538

Guide to Business Analysis Body of Knowledge (IIBA), 28
Guide to Project Management Body of Knowledge. See PMBOK Guide

H

Hammerskjöld, Dag, 311
happy path, 126
Hardaker, Maurice, 584
Harris Semiconductor, 372
Harvard Business Review, 530, 584
herd of cats, 215–216, 320
Hersey, Paul, 225, 657
Herzberg, Frederick, 71, 71n1
high change, xPM, 455–456
high speed, xPM, 455
Highsmith, Jim, 35n2, 323–324, 379, 379n1, 380, 406
histograms, 189–190, 617–619
historical data, task duration estimation method, 188–189
Hobbs, Brian, 485, 485n1
Honeywell Defense Avionics Systems, 372
hope creep, 17, 653
house, WBS for, 181–182
"How to Make a Team Work" (Hardaker & Ward), 584
How well did you do?, 25–27, 67, 444, 507, 690, 693
How will you do it?, 25–26, 65, 444, 690, 692
How will you know you did it?, 25–26, 64, 66, 104–105, 444, 690, 692
HRMS (Human Resource Management System)
  agile project portfolios, 383
  MPx, 54
  PSO staffing and development, 495, 497

hub-and-spoke
  BP⁴SO, 522–523
  PSOs, 499
human resource management (Knowledge Area), 69–74
  defined, 69–71
  hygiene factors, 70–71
  motivators, 70–74
Human Resource Management System. *See* HRMS
hygiene factors. *See also* motivators
  defined, 70
  list, 71

I

ID number, risk log, 85
ideal project team, 227
ideas to action, decision-making process, 246–247
IIBA (International Institute of Business Analysis). *See also* PMBOK
  Business Analysis Body of Knowledge Guide, 28
  PM/BA professional, 590
  requirements definition, 28–31, 113, 127
imbalanced project teams, 235
implementing
  APF, 437
  APM, 380–381
  PSOs, 483–484, 519–521
improved service, success criteria, 139
Improvement Initiatives phase, CPIM, 602–603
improvement programs. *See* CPIM
in trouble, project status, 556–557
inception phase, RUP, 394
incomplete requirements and specification, 330, 501, 503, 707
increased revenue, success criteria, 139
incremental business value, 26–27, 29

Incremental PMLC models
  business value, 356–357, 359–360
  characteristics, 356
  defined, 356
  graphical depiction, 44, 355
  Iterative approach v., 48
  Linear approach v., 43–44
  non-value-added work, 359, 404
  PMLC models comparison, 55–56
  strengths, 356–358
  tools/templates/processes, 361–362
  weaknesses, 358–361
  when to use, 129, 361
Incubate, 467–469
independent team cultures, 660
independent work assignments, 172,
    174, 269
informal level, 589
information technology (IT)
  BP⁴SO, 522
  CareerAgent model, 694, 706
  complex project managers, 689,
      707–708, 710
  investment plan, 527
  project failures, 629
  scarcity of professionals, 484
inherited projects, 133
inherited team members, 227
INitiate, 459–463
initiating, 64, 121, 483. See also scoping
Inspection flowchart symbol, 120–121
INSPIRE Extreme PMLC model,
    457–470
  APM models v., 457–458
  COS, 464
  graphical depiction, 458
  Incubate, 467–469
  INitiate, 459–463
  PDQ case study, 464
  POS, 460–462
  REview, 469–470
  scope triangle, 463
  SPeculate, 463–467
integrated into business processes
    (level 4), 590
integrated project plan/schedule,
    multi-team projects, 662–663
integration management (Knowledge
    Area)
  defined, 67
  Zone Map, 594–595
Integrative Swim Lanes
  defined, 431
  Probative Swim Lanes v., 431–432
International Benchmark Council, 151
International Institute of Business
    Analysis. See IIBA
interproject constraints, 208
intervention management strategies,
    distressed projects, 639–651
  analyze current situation, 640–645,
      654–655
  evaluate options, 640, 649–650, 655
  generate revised plan, 640, 650–651,
      655
  revise desired goal, 640, 645–648, 655
intervention process template,
    651–653
interviews, RBS method, 117
Inventory Management subsystem, 61,
    224, 376, 449, 570, 571
IRACIS, 26
Iron Triangle, 10–11, 13. See also scope
    triangle
Ishikawa diagrams. See fishbone
    diagrams
Israeli Aircraft Industry, 372
Issues Log, 302
IT. See information technology
iteration timeboxes, 398
iterations, Iterative PMLC models, 55,
    384, 385
iterative development, of WBS, 171
Iterative PMLC models, 46–49,
    384–398. See also prototyping PMLC
    model; RUP
  Adaptive PMLC models v., 378–379,
      400
  characteristics, 389
  client involvement, 386, 390–391, 397

closing phase, 388–389
co-located teams, 383, 390–391
CPIM, 397
defined, 384–389
graphical depiction, 48, 384
Incremental approach *v.*, 48
launching phase, 388
monitoring/controlling phase, 388
non-value-added work, 388
planning phase, 386–387
PMLC models comparison, 55–56
process group level view, 384
RUP, 379, 391, 396
scope change requests, 385–386
scoping phase, 386
software development projects, 48, 391
solution clarity, 389, 391, 397–398
strengths, 389–390
types, 391–397
weaknesses, 390–391
when to use, 129, 397–398

J

JAD (Joint Applications Design), 158, 707
Java Modeling in Color with UML (Coad, et al), 352
job design, 73–74
Joint Applications Design (JAD), 158, 707
Joint Project Planning Sessions. *See* JPPS
Joint Requirements Planning (JRP), 158
JPPS (Joint Project Planning Sessions)
agenda, 162–163
attendees, 159–162
conducting, 164
consultants, 160
core team, 228
defined, 157–158
deliverables, 163–164
facilities, 162

PDS, 240
planning, 158–164
POS, 159
purpose, 158
RSVPs, 162
WBS *v.*, 163, 168
JRP (Joint Requirements Planning), 158
just-in-time planning, 2, 51, 56, 338, 400, 403–404, 409, 412

K

Kepner, Charles H., 336
kick-off meetings. *See* project kick-off meetings
Knowledge Areas, 67–99. *See also* communications management; cost management; human resource management; integration management; procurement management; quality management; risk management; scope management; time management
PMBOK, 1
Process Groups-Knowledge Areas mapping, 99–101
process/practice maturity level plot, 595–596
Zone Map, 594–595
known resource, 196
Kolb, David, 233. *See also* Learning Styles Inventory

L

lack of executive support, 330, 501, 503, 707
lack of resources, 330, 501, 504, 593, 660, 708
lack of user input, 330, 502, 593, 707. *See also* client involvement
lag variables, 209–210
landscape. *See* PM/BA; project management landscape
Lao-Tzu, 225

large projects, WBS for, 171
Larry/Curly, 496–497
late schedules, 210, 212, 214, 367, 368
launching (Process Group), 225–278.
    See also development teams
  APM PMLC models, 446–447
  brainstorming, 374
  defined, 65–66
  development teams, 643
  discussion questions, 278
  executing, 64, 65
  phase
    Adaptive PMLC models, 401
    Extreme PMLC models, 474
    Iterative PMLC models, 388
  processes, 66
  project team recruitment, 227–236
  tools/templates/processes, 226
  TPM projects, 225–278
LCD projector, 162, 169, 238
Leach, Lawrence P., 362–363, 368–369,
    372, 375, 556, 580. *See also* critical
    chain project management
Learn phase, ASD, 406–407
learning styles, 233–235, 242–243,
    245, 247
  accommodators, 234–236, 238, 242,
    244, 246–247
  assimilators, 234, 242–243, 246–247
  convergers, 234–235, 242–243,
    246–247
  divergers, 234–235, 242–243, 246–247
Learning Styles Inventory (LSI),
    245–247
  decision making *v.*, 245–246
  Kolb, 233
  rational decision making model *v.*,
    246–247
Lefebvre, Eric, 352
left-to-right format, 122
lessons learned
  Linear PMLC models, 344

MANAGE active projects, 564
leveling resources. *See* resource
    leveling
levels. *See* maturity
Linear PMLC models. *See also*
    planning
  business value, 351
  change, 43, 348–349
  characteristics, 342–347
  co-located teams, 347–348
  cost, 349
  defined, 341–342
  detailed plans, 349–350
  feature-driven development, 351,
    352–355
  graphical depiction, 42, 341
  Incremental approach *v.*, 43–44
  non-value-added work, 341, 350, 404
  planning, 152
  PMLC models comparison, 55–56
  rapid, 351–355
  repetitive activities, 343–346
  risk history, 345–346
  scope change requests, 43–44, 342–
    343
  software development projects, 340
  strengths, 347–351
  task duration history, 344–345
  templates, 343–344, 346–347
  tools/templates/processes, 354–355
  variations, 351–354
  weakness, 42–43
  when to use, 129, 351
listening skills, 107, 189, 236
logic diagram, 200. *See also* project
    network diagram
logical constraints, 207
Logistics subsystem, 61, 224, 376
  complexity, 464
  INSPIRE, 476
  management reserve, 636, 656
  portfolio approach, 571

Longfellow, Henry Wadsworth, 311
LSI. *See* Learning Styles Inventory
Lucent Technologies, 372

M

Machiavelli, Niccolò, 481
"man on moon" statement, 34, 53, 459
MANAGE active projects
  Agile Project Portfolio life cycle, 573,
    580–581
  business value, 563
  CPI, 557–562
  lessons learned, 564
  Project Portfolio Management life
    cycle, 531, 556–564
  SPI, 557–563
management. *See also* Adaptive Project
  Framework; project management
  APF *v.*, 409
  micro-, 73, 174, 274, 421, 422,
    424, 662
management constraints, 207–208
management reserve
  buffers *v.*, 258, 370
  defined, 218, 257
  leveled resource schedule, 267
  Linear PLMC model, 44
  PDQ case study, 636, 656
  project network schedule,
    217–218
  Scope Bank *v.*, 258
  scope change requests, 343,
    357, 632
*Managing the Project Team: The Human
  Aspects of Project Management,
  Volume 3* (Verma), 241
market stability, 32, 58
marking pens, 155, 162
Markowitz, Henry, 531
masked behavior, 236
Mastering the Requirements Process
  (Robertson & Robertson), 116

materials
  materials and time contracts, 94
  as resource, 193
maturity. *See also* PQM; Zone Map
  Capability Maturity Model, 94, 508,
    525, 589
  Capability Maturity Model
    Integrated, 508, 589
  gap, 600
  Knowledge Areas process/practice
    maturity level plot, 595–596
  Level 1, 482, 494, 508, 516, 589, 686
  Level 2, 482, 508, 511, 519, 589, 686
  Level 3, 94, 450, 483, 508–509, 511,
    517–520, 589–590, 592, 612, 685–686
  Level 4, 483, 490, 508–509, 511, 517,
    519–520, 590, 612
  Level 5, 508–509, 511, 516–517, 519,
    590–591, 603–604, 693
  PMMA, 516, 592, 595, 597
  project management processes/
    practices
    levels, 589–591
    measuring, 591–598
  PSO, 508–509, 518–519
Mayer, Bernard S., 249
measurable
  S.M.A.R.T. characteristic, 137
  WBS completion, 172–173
Methods and Standards service area,
  485, 492–493
micro-level planning, 272–273, 409
micro-level schedule, 423–426
micro-level WBS, 272–273, 421–426
micro-management, 73, 174, 274,
  421–422, 424, 662
Miglione, R. Henry, 527
milestone trend charts, 290–293
  CPIM, 619
  distressed projects, 637–638
  EVA integration with, 298–301, 639
  run charts, 619

milestones
  COS milestone reviews, 109–110
  defined, 290
minutes
  status meeting, 304
  team meeting, 251
mission statements
  CPIM, 599
  PSO, 489, 516
mitigate, risk response, 85
Moe, 496–497
money, as resource, 193. *See also* scarce
    resources
monitoring/controlling (Process
    Group), 279–309
  APM PMLC models, 447
  defined, 66–67
  discussion questions, 309
  earned value analysis, 68
  phase
    Adaptive PMLC models, 401–402
    Extreme PMLC models, 474
    Iterative PMLC models, 388
  processes, 66
  progress reporting system,
      281–286
    frequency for reporting, 286
    what to report, 285–286
  project status reports, 281–286
    cumulative, 282
    current period reports, 281
    exception, 282
    stoplight, 282–283, 290
    variance, 283–284
    WBS as project-status-reporting
        tool, 168
  tools/templates/processes, 280–281
  TPM projects, 3, 279–309
Morris, William C., 246
MoSCoW, 417, 465, 543, 648
most-likely time, three-point
    technique, 191
motivators, 70–74
  defined, 70

hygiene factors *v.*, 70–71
  list, 72
mountain bike example, 178
Movement flowchart symbol, 120–121
MPx (Emertxe Project Management).
    See also xPM
  business value, 53
  characteristics, 54–55
  client's comfort zone, 332
  co-located teams, 329
  defined, 322, 471
  graphical depiction, 52, 55, 454
  nonsense category, 54, 322
  percent of projects, 47, 154
  R & D projects, 50–51, 53–54, 129, 322,
      329, 453, 455, 471, 536
  RFID technology, 54, 322
  risk, 328–329
  team cohesiveness, 329
  when to use, 471–472
  xPM *v.*, 55
Multiple Awards scenario, 93–94
multiple team (multi-team) projects,
    657–687
  associate manager, 665
  best-fit project structure, 686–687
  classifying, 665–667
  complexity/uncertainty, 679–680, 686
  criticality, 686
  CT approach, 673–680
    characteristics, 673–676
    defined, 673
    strengths, 676–678
    structure, 674
    weaknesses, 678–679
    when to use, 679–680
  defined, 657–658
  discussion questions, 658, 663, 687
  ignored in literature, 625, 686
  integrated project plan/schedule,
      662–663
  life cycle, 661–662
  management challenges, 659–665
    communication, 661

competing priorities, 661
different team processes, 661
fiercely independent team cultures, 660
teams from different companies, 660
multiple teams situation, 665–667
overview, 626
PDQ case study, 687
POs, 667–673
  characteristics, 668–670
  defined, 667
  PMOs v., 667
  PSOs v., 488
  strengths, 670–671
  structure, 668
  weaknesses, 671–672
  when to use, 672–673
project management structure, 661
reporting levels, 664
requirements gathering approach, 663
resource sharing, 664
scope change management process, 663
size, 686
ST approach, 680–686
  characteristics, 681–683
  defined, 680
  strengths, 684
  structure, 681
  weaknesses, 685
  when to use, 685–686
staffing, 665
team meeting structure, 663
team operating rules, 241
two-team situation, 665–666
types, 665
Must-do, Should-do, Postpone, 541, 543

N

naming PSOs, 484–485, 487–488
near-critical path, 214, 277
needs, wants v., 37, 86, 106

negative variances, 287–288
network diagrams. *See* project network diagram
network schedule. *See* project network schedule
new project proposal submission, project portfolio management process, 570–571
new technology, 330, 501, 504–505, 593, 644, 708
The New Rational Manager (Kepner & Tregoe), 336
nine Knowledge Areas. *See* Knowledge Areas
No Award scenario, 93
no earlier than, 209
no later than, 209
non–critical path tasks, 229, 271, 287, 306–308
non-functional requirements, 128
nonsense category, 54, 322. *See also* MPx
non-value-added work
  Adaptive PMLC model, 403–404, 409
  Agile projects, 384
  APF, 412, 423–424
  APM models, 326, 400, 655
  business processes, 609
  defined, 325
  Incremental PMLC model, 359, 404
  Iterative PMLC model, 388
  Linear PMLC model, 341, 350, 404
  organized common sense, 27
  PSO project support services, 491
  specification certainty, 334
  written communications, 331
  xPM, 655
norming, 277–278
notebook. *See* project notebook
noun-type approaches, to building WBS, 176–178

O

objectives
  approach, 179
  project proposal, 220
  unclear, 330, 501, 504, 593, 708
observation, RBS method, 117
obstacles section, POS, 140–141
off plan, project status, 556, 557
off-the-job training, 691, 702, 704, 710.
    See also professional development
    program
on plan, project status, 556–557
on this date, 209
"one size does not fit all," 33, 36
"one size fits all" approach, 18–19, 27,
    33, 36, 327, 409
one-page POS, 141
on-the-job training, 691, 702, 704, 710.
    See also professional development
    program
Operation flowchart symbol,
    120–121
opportunity/problem part, POS,
    134–135
optimistic time, three-point technique,
    190
Oral Roberts University, 527
Order Entry subsystem, 126–127
  business process, 120
  commercial off the shelf product, 570
  early-warning SPI tracking metric,
    656
  As Is/To Be business processes, 623
  PDQ, 61, 126–127
  PMLC model, 61, 376
  portfolio approach, 571
  Prototyping PMLC model, 394
  requirements, 636
  WBS, 224
order of magnitude estimate, 142, 197,
    198, 223
Order Submit, 61, 224, 376, 571

organizational approaches, to
    building WBS, 177, 179–180
*Organizational Behavior in Action: Skill
    Building Experiences* (Morris &
    Sashkin), 246
organizational environment, PMLC
    model choice process, 59
organizational placements, PSOs,
    499–501
organizational risks, 78
organizational structures, PSOs,
    497–499
organizational velocity, 356, 380
organized common sense, 27, 65, 327,
    436, 689
outcome, risk log, 85
outside consultants, 160, 433, 636, 644
outside contractors, 231, 233, 264, 644
outside the box, 242–243, 250, 451
outsourcing, 119, 227, 231, 348, 373, 605
over budget/ behind schedule project,
    300
overview of approach, project
    proposal, 220
ownership, by client, 332–333

P

pain curves, 151–152, 159, 634
Paired Comparisons model, 91, 465
  APF, 416–417
  PRIORITIZE projects, 541, 544–545
Palmer, Stephen R., 352
parallel approach, installed
    deliverables, 314
Pareto analysis, 617–619
Parkinson's Law, 218, 258
participative decision-making model,
    244–245
partitionable tasks, 187, 216
Paterno, Joe, 225
PDM (precedence diagramming
    method), 202–204

PDP. *See* professional development program

PDQ (Pizza Delivered Quickly) case study
 APF project, 433, 464
 To Be business process, 623
 Client Checkpoint problems, 433
 contract team members, 233
 daily status meetings, 264
 INSPIRE, 464
 Inventory Management, 61, 224, 376, 449, 570, 571
 As Is business process, 623
 Logistics, 61, 224, 376
  complexity, 464
  INSPIRE, 476
  management reserve, 636, 656
  portfolio approach, 571
 management reserve, 636, 656
 multiple team projects, 687
 Order Entry, 126–127
  commercial off the shelf product, 570
  early-warning SPI tracking metric, 656
  As Is/To Be business processes, 623
  PMLC model, 61, 376
  portfolio approach, 571
  Prototyping PMLC model, 394
  requirements, 636
  WBS, 224
 order entry, 61, 126–127
 Order Submit, 61, 224, 376, 571
 Pizza Factory Locator, 61, 224, 376, 571
 PMLC model choices, 61
 POS, 476
 project portfolio management process, 570–571
 prototyping, 394
 RBS, 449, 451
 reporting requirements, 309

Routing, 61, 224, 376, 570–571
SPI tracking metric, 656
subsystems
 Agile model, 449
 PMLC models, 61, 376
 WBS build, 224
use case, 126–127
PDS (Project Definition Statement)
 JPPS, 240
 POS v., 140, 159, 239–240
 project kick-off meeting working session agenda, 239–240
penetration, buffer, 370–372
people, as resources, 193–194. *See also* scarce resources
permanent program offices, 9, 484–485. *See also* PSOs
PERT (Project Evaluation and Review Technique), 154, 422
pessimistic time, three-point technique, 190
Phaedrus, 5
phased approach, installed deliverables, 314
phases
 Agile Project Portfolio life cycle, 573, 575
 APF, 412
 ASD, 406–408
 CPIM, 598
 decision-making process, 246–247
 Extreme models, 55
 5-Phase Project Management: A Practical Planning and Implementation Guide (Weiss & Wysocki), 172
 Project Portfolio Management life cycle, 530–531
 RUP, 394–395
physical decomposition, noun-type approach, 178

Pizza Delivered Quickly. *See* PDQ case study

Pizza Factory Locator subsystem, 61, 224, 376, 571

plan-driven TPM projects, 42, 325, 327, 330–331, 335

planned value (PV), 295–298, 638–639

planning (Process Group), 149–224. *See also* JPPS; WBS

  APM PMLC models, 446

  approaches, 2

  benefits, 153

  defined, 65

  discussion questions, 222–224

  dynamic, 152

  importance, 152–153

  just-in-time, 2, 51, 56, 338, 400, 403, 404, 409, 412

  phase

    Adaptive PMLC models, 400–401

    Extreme PMLC models, 473–474

    Iterative PMLC models, 386–387

  processes, 65

  PSOs, 509–519

  software packages, 153–154

  time, 156–157

  tools/templates/processes, 151–152, 154–156

  TPM projects, 149–224

  Version Scope, 412

Planning Meeting

  Project, 112, 113

  Sprint, 441

planning tool, WBS, 167–168

PM. *See* project management

PM/BA (Project Manager/Business Analyst). *See also* professional development program

  landscape, 694, 701–702

    career planning, 706–707

    graphical depiction, 694

    higher level position, 705–706

    for professional development, 701–702

    short-term professional goal, 703

    short-term professional goal, higher level, 705

  position family, 693–701

    Associate Manager, 693, 698–699

    Director, 693, 700–401

    graphical depiction, 695

    IIBA, 590

    Program Manager, 693, 700

    Senior Manager, 693, 699

    Task Manager, 693, 697–698

    Team Member, 693, 696–697

  work in progress, 709

PMBOK (*Project Management Book of Knowledge*) Guide, 24n1. *See also* Knowledge Areas; Process Groups

  Knowledge Areas, 1

  Process Groups, 2, 63–64

  team operating rules, 241

PMCA (Project Management Competency Assessment), 514–516

PMI (Project Management Institute), 2

  joining, 692

  project management definition, 24–25

PMLC (project management life cycle) models, 33–60. *See also* Adaptive PMLC models; Adaptive Project Framework; best-fit PMLC model; Extreme PMLC models; Incremental PMLC models; Iterative PMLC models; Linear PMLC models; prototyping PMLC model

  APF integration, 436–437

  APPM integration, 574–576

  choice process, 56–60

    WBS, 171

  comparison, 55–56

  defined, 33, 38

  differences, 56

Knowledge Areas, 67
PDQ case study, 61
Process Groups v., 2, 63, 321, 373–375
RBS, 129–132
recap, 55–56
similarities, 56
specification certainty, 333–335
types, 38, 502
PMMA (Project Management
    Maturity Assessment), 516, 592,
    595, 597
PMOs (Project Management Offices).
    See also project offices; PSOs
    POs v., 667
    PSOs v., 479, 483–484, 488
point estimate, 365
Polaris Missile Program, 202
portfolios. *See* agile project portfolios;
    project portfolios; project portfolio
    management process
portfolio managers, 533, 564–566
portfolio of services
    Consulting and Mentoring service
        area, 485, 491–492
    Methods and Standards service area,
        485, 492–493
    Project Managers service area, 486,
        487, 495–496
    Project Support service area, 485,
        490–491
    Software Tools service area, 486,
        493–494
    Training service area, 486, 494–495
POs. *See* project offices
POS (Project Overview Statement),
    132–147
    approval process, 144–147, 221
    assumptions, risks, obstacles section,
        140–141
    attachments, 141–143
    briefing tool, 133
    component parts, 133–134
    defined, 107–108
    financial analyses, 142–143

graphical depiction, 134
inherited projects, 133
INSPIRE, 460–462
JPPS, 159
one-page, 141
PDQ case study, 476
PDS v., 140, 159, 239–240
problem/opportunity part, 134–135
project goal, 136–137
project objectives, 137–138
project portfolio management
    process, 566–569
PSO, 510–512
purpose, 132–133
revised, 566–569
risk analysis, 142
Scoping Meeting, 110, 112
S.M.A.R.T. characteristics, 137
submitting, 144–147
success criteria, 138–140
Version Scope, 414, 418–419
positive variances, 286–287
post-implementation audit, 317–319
    agile portfolio, 580
    closing Process Group, 21, 27, 67
    improvement, 584, 591
    Post-Version Review v., 435
Post-It Note product, 51, 54, 123. *See
    also* sticky notes
postponed projects, 532
Post-Version Review, 433–435
    graphical depiction, 434
    questions, 433–435
    Version Scope v., 433
PQM (Process Quality Matrix), 591–
    593, 599–600
    completed, 593
    finalize, 597
    graphical depiction, 592–593
    initial, 596–597
    validate, 597
    Zone Map and, 592
*A Practical Guide to Feature-Driven
    Development* (Palmer & Felsing), 352

precedence diagramming method
    (PDM), 202–204
predecessor tasks, 203–204,
    210–212, 215
prevention management strategies,
    distressed projects, 632–639
primary actor, 126
prioritization approaches, scope
    triangle, 14–15, 415–417
  MoSCoW, 417, 465, 543, 648
PRIORITIZE projects
  Agile Project Portfolio life cycle,
    573, 575
  Forced Ranking, 541–542
  Must-do, Should-do, Postpone,
    541, 543
  Paired Comparisons Model, 541,
    544–545
  Project Portfolio Management life
    cycle, 531, 540–546
  Q-Sort model, 541, 542–543
  Risk/Benefit Matrix, 545–546
  weighted criteria, 541, 543–544
prioritized projects, 532
proactive PSOs, 498
Probative Swim Lanes
  defined, 48, 431
  Integrative Swim Lanes v., 431–432
problem escalation strategy, 306–308
  hierarchy, 307–308
  monitoring/controlling Process
    Group, 375
  scope triangle, 15–16
problem management meetings, 305
problem resolution
  CT member, 674–675
  meetings, 252
  scope triangle, 15–16
problem solving. See also decision
    making
  LSI, 233, 245–246
  team operating rules, 242–244
problem/opportunity part, POS,
    134–135

Process Control System, 340
processes. See also business processes;
    tools/templates/processes
  closing Process Group, 67
  launching Process Group, 66
  maturity
    levels, 589–591
    measuring, 591–598
  monitoring/controlling Process
    Group, 66
  planning Process Group, 65
  practice, 586–588
  process, 584–586
  scoping Process Group, 64
  six questions, 25, 27, 60, 64, 444, 690
Process Groups, 63–101. See also
    closing; launching; monitoring/
    controlling; planning; scoping
  discussion questions, 101
  Knowledge Areas-Process Groups
    mapping, 99–101
  misconceptions, 2, 63
  PMBOK Guide, 2, 63–64
  PMLC models v., 2, 63, 321, 373–375
  project management methodologies
    v., 2, 63, 100
process managers, POS approval
    process, 146
process owners, 161–162
process quality, 12
Process Quality Matrix. See PQM
process steps. See activities
procurement, 86
procurement management
    (Knowledge Area), 85–99
  defined, 85–86
  phases, 86
  vendor contracting, 92–96
  vendor evaluation, 89–92
  vendor management, 96–99
  vendor selection, 92
  vendor solicitation, 86–89
Product Backlog, 440–441
product constraints, 128

Product Owner, 131, 405, 439–443
product quality, 11
production prototyping, 47–48, 384–385, 391, 397, 409, 435, 634
professional activities, 692, 702, 704, 710
professional development program (PDP), 689–710. *See also* PM/BA
  complex projects, 707–709
    disciplines needed, 707–708
    project failure, 707–708
  components
    experience acquisition, 691, 702–703, 710
    off-the-job training, 691, 702, 704, 710
    on-the-job training, 691, 702, 704, 710
    professional activities, 692, 702, 704, 710
  discussion questions, 710
  overview, 625–626
  six questions, 690
  writing, 692–693, 710
Program Manager, PM/BA, 693, 700
program offices. *See also* project offices; PSOs
  permanent, 9, 484–485
  PSOs *v.*, 488
  temporary, 9, 46, 171, 484, 498
programs
  defined, 9, 498
  projects *v.*, 9, 498
progress reporting system
  frequency for reporting, 286
  project status reports, 281–286
    cumulative, 282
    current period reports, 281
    exception, 282
    stoplight, 282–283, 290
    variance, 283–284
    WBS as project-status-reporting tool, 168

what to report, 285–286
projects, 5–22. *See also* multiple team projects; project portfolios; software development projects; TPM; *specific projects*
  aligned, 531
  business-focused definition, 8–9
  classification, 18–22
    by project application, 21–22
    by project characteristics, 19–21
    rule, 19
  complex, 707–709
  definitions, 1–2, 6–9, 200, 528
  goals, 7
  prioritized, 532
  programs *v.*, 9, 498
  proposed, 531
  purpose, 8
  R & D, 50–51, 53–54, 129, 322, 329, 453, 455, 471, 536
  stages, Project Portfolio Management life cycle, 531–532
  subproject managers, 699
  subprojects, 7, 111, 171, 487, 500, 680, 684
  sub-subprojects, 684
  type A, 19–21
  type B, 20–21
  type C, 20–21
  type D, 20–21
project buffers, 369
project champion
  JPPS attendance, 159, 161
  status review meetings, 304
project change request, 254–255
project constraints, 11, 128
Project Definition Statement. *See* PDS
Project Distribution Matrix
  ESTABLISH portfolio strategy, 533, 536–538
  Forced Ranking model and, 547, 550–552
Project Evaluation and Review Technique (PERT), 154, 422

project failures. *See also* distressed projects
  CFs, 591
  changing requirements and specification, 330, 501, 503, 707
  executive level support, 59
  FDD Linear PMLC model, 354
  incomplete requirements and specification, 330, 501, 503, 707
  lack of executive support, 330, 501, 503, 707
  lack of resources, 330, 501, 504, 593, 660, 708
  lack of user input, 330, 502, 593, 707
  mid-1950s, 36–37
  new technology, 330, 501, 504–505, 593, 644, 708
  poor communications, 74, 105, 108, 259, 330
  poorly defined requirements, 130
  Rapid Linear PMLC model, 354
  risk assessment, 84–85, 221, 328
  Scoping Process Group, 104
  shared responsibility, 229
  Standish Group research, 59, 330, 479, 501–505, 520, 591, 596, 642, 707–708
  unclear objectives, 330, 501, 504, 593, 708
  unrealistic expectations, 80, 330, 501, 504, 593, 708
  unrealistic time frames, 330, 501, 504, 593, 708
  xPM, 50–51, 53, 329, 454
project finish date, shifting, 268–269
project goals, POS, 136–137
Project Impact Statement, 15–16, 40, 43, 255, 348, 663
project initiation, 11, 406–407, 486, 572
Project Initiation phase, ASD, 407
Project Investment Categories Model, 533, 538–539
project kick-off meetings, 407, 412, 630–631, 662. *See also* Version Scope

  attendees, 237–238
  defined, 236
  project manager-led part, 237
  purpose, 237
  sponsor-led part, 236
  working session agenda, 238–240
project management (PM), 23–61. *See also* critical chain project management; questions
  business value, 27
  complex projects, 707–710
  definitions
    PMI, 24–25
    working, 27–28
  discussion questions, 60–61
  fundamentals, 24–28
  Gantt charts, 35, 340
  infrastructure, 479–480
  old ways, 36–37
  "one size does not fit all," 33, 36
  "one size fits all" approach, 18–19, 27, 33, 36, 327, 409
  organized common sense, 27, 65, 327, 436, 689
  processes/practices
    levels, 589–591
    measuring, 591–598
  risks, 77–78
  significant changes, 2
  steady state, 24, 36
Project Management Book of Knowledge. *See* PMBOK
Project Management Competency Assessment (PMCA), 514–516
Project Management Institute. *See* PMI
project management landscape. *See also* Adaptive Project Framework; MPx; TPM; xPM
  complexity/uncertainty domain, 323–338
  definition uniqueness, 60, 321, 337–338
  four quadrants, 34, 100, 321–322
  goals, 34–39, 321

solution clarity, 34–39, 131, 156, 324, 389, 502

project management life cycle. *See* PMLC models

Project Management Maturity Assessment (PMMA), 516, 592, 595, 597

project management methodologies, 2, 63, 100

Project Management Offices (PMOs), 479, 483–485, 488. *See also* PSOs

project manager-based escalation strategies, 306

Project Manager/Business Analyst. *See* PM/BA

project manager-led part, 237

project managers
    co-project managers, 27, 46, 131, 411, 429, 444–445, 449
    cost control issues, 198–199
    JPPS attendance, 160
    POS approval process, 145
    Scoping Meeting, 111
    subteams, 9
    WBS architecture, 168

Project Managers service area, 486, 487, 495–496

The Project Management Office (PMO): A Quest for Understanding (Hobbs & Aubry), 485n1

project network diagram, 199–218
    CCPM, 366–367
    constraints, 205–209
    defined, 200
    dependency relationships, 204–205
    diagramming conventions, 204
    envisioning, 200
    Gantt chart *v.*, 200–201
    JPPS agenda, 163
    lag variables, 209–210
    PDM format, 202–204
    planning session, 157

project network schedule, 210–217

early schedule, 210–213, 366–367

finalizing, 271–273

initial
    analyzing, 214–215
    creating, 210–214

JPPS deliverable, 163–164

late schedules, 210, 212, 214, 367, 368

management reserve, 217–218

project notebook
    client experiences, 443
    closing (Process Group), 21
    electronic, 304, 317
    JPPS deliverable, 164
    outlines, as template, 343
    PSO and, 486, 490
    status review meetings, 304
    study historical data, 188

project objectives, POS, 137–138

project offices (POs), 667–673. *See also* multiple team projects; program offices
    characteristics, 668–670
    defined, 667
    PMOs *v.*, 667
    PSOs *v.*, 488
    roles/responsibilities, PO manager, 668–670
    strengths, 670–671
    structure, 668
    weaknesses, 671–672
    when to use, 672–673

Project Overview Statement. *See* POS

project portfolios. *See also* agile project portfolios
    defined, 10, 529–530
    specific, 487

Project Portfolio Management life cycle, 530–564
    Agile Project Portfolio life cycle *v.*, 573
    ESTABLISH portfolio strategy, 531–539

Agile Project Portfolio life cycle,
573, 575
BCG Products/Services Matrix, 533,
535–536
Growth *versus* Survival Model,
533, 538
Project Distribution Matrix, 533,
536–538
Project Investment Categories
Model, 533, 538–539
Project Portfolio Management life
cycle, 531, 532–539
Strategic Alignment Model,
533–535
EVALUATE project alignment, 531,
539–540
graphical depiction, 531
MANAGE active projects, 531,
556–564
business value, 563
CPI, 557–562
lessons learned, 564
Project Portfolio Management life
cycle, 531, 556–564
SPI, 557–563
phases, 530–531
PRIORITIZE projects, 531, 540–546
Forced Ranking, 541–542
Must-do, Should-do, Postpone,
541, 543
Paired Comparisons Model, 541,
544–545
Project Portfolio Management life
cycle, 531, 540–546
Q-Sort model, 541–543
Risk/Benefit Matrix, 545–546
weighted criteria, 541, 543–544
project stages, 531–532
SELECT balanced portfolio, 531,
546–556
Graham-Englund Selection Model,
552–556
Project Distribution Matrix/Forced
Ranking Model, 550–552

Project Portfolio Management life
cycle, 531, 546–556
Risk/Benefit Matrix, 552–556
Strategic Alignment Model, 548–
550
weighted criteria, 548–550
stages, 531–532
project portfolio management process,
527–582
defined, 530
discussion questions, 581–582
introduction, 528–530
overview, 480
PDQ case study, 570–571
project proposal submission, 566–571
new submission process, 570–571
revised POS, 566–569
two-step submission process,
569–570
PSO roles/responsibilities, 564–566
project proposals, 218–221
approval, 221
contents, 219–220
cost, 12
format, 221
JPPS deliverable, 218
writing, 218–221
project report. *See* reporting system
project review meetings, 252
project scope. *See* scope
project stakeholders
communications management,
74–75, 264
defined, 74, 264
project status meetings, 302–305
daily status meeting, 251–252, 302,
305, 425
format, 304
purpose, 303
when held, 303
who should attend, 302–303
project status reports, 281–286
cumulative, 282
current period reports, 281

exception, 282
stoplight, 282–283, 290
variance, 283–284
WBS as project-status-reporting
    tool, 168
project statuses
off plan, 556–557
on plan, 556–557
in trouble, 556–557
Project Support Offices. *See* PSOs
Project Support service area, 485,
    490–491
project support services, PSO, 490–491
project teams. *See* teams
proposals. *See* project proposals; RFPs
proposed projects, 531
prototyping PMLC model, 391–394
graphical depiction, 392–393
Iterative PMLC model *v.*, 393
production, 47–48, 384–385, 391, 397,
    409, 435, 634
RBS method, 118, 124
PSOs (Project Support Offices), 481–
    525. *See also* project offices
background, 482–484
BP⁴SO, 521–524
CPIM, 603
defined, 484–487
development, 495–497
discussion questions, 525
distressed projects, 653–655
enterprise, 499
EPSOs, 499–500, 516
establishing, 507–519
framing objectives, 489–490
functional, 499
future, 521–524
hub-and-spoke, 499
implementing, 483–484, 519–521
long-term goal, 517
maturity growth stages, 508–509,
    518–519
mission statements, 489, 516
naming, 484–485, 487–488

need
determining when needed, 501–505
spotting symptoms, 505–507
new technology, 504–505
non-value-added work, 491
organizational placements, 499–501
organizational structures, 497–499
overview, 479–480
permanent program offices, 9,
    484–485
planning, 509–519
PMOs *v.*, 479, 483, 484–485, 488
portfolio of services, 485–487
Consulting and Mentoring service
    area, 485, 491–492
Methods and Standards service
    area, 485, 492–493
Project Managers service area,
    486–487, 495–496
Project Support service area, 485,
    490–491
Software Tools service area, 486,
    493–494
Training service area, 486, 494–495
POS, 510–512
POs *v.*, 488
proactive, 498
project portfolio management,
    564–566
project portfolio management
    process, 564–566
project support services, 490–491
purposes, 486–487
questions, 507
reactive, 498
readiness assessment, 506–507
real, 497–498
reasons for implementing, 483–484
specific portfolio of projects, 487
staffing, 495–497
*The Strategic Project Office: A Guide
    to Improving Organizational
    Performance* (Crawford), 519
task force, 512–513

temporary program offices, 9, 46, 171, 484, 498

virtual, 497–498

PV (planned value), 295–298, 638–639

Q

Q3 projects, 379

Q4 projects, 379

Q-Sort model, 541–543

quality. *See also* process quality; product quality

prioritizing, 15

scope triangle variable, 11–12

quality assurance process, 69

quality control process, 69

quality management (Knowledge Area)

defined, 68–69

good investment, 12

quality planning process, 69

quality review, ASD, 408

questions. *See also* discussion questions

communications management, 74–75

distressed projects, intervention strategies, 639–651

How well did you do?, 25–27, 67, 444, 507, 690, 693

How will you do it?, 25–26, 65, 444, 690, 692

How will you know you did it?, 25–26, 64, 66, 104–105, 444, 690, 692

Post-Version Review, 433–435

project management practice, 586–588

project management process, 584–586

PSOs, 507

risk management, 76

six action areas, team operating rules, 241–242

What business situation is being addressed?, 25, 64, 444, 690

What do you need to do?, 25–26, 64, 104–105, 444, 690–692

What will you do?, 25–26, 65, 444, 690, 692

R

R & D (research and development) projects, 50–51, 53–54, 129, 322, 329, 453, 455, 471, 536. *See also* MPx; xPM

race example, 363–364

RAD (Rapid Applications Development), 707

radical change, milestone trend chart, 291–292

Radio Frequency Identification (RFID) technology, 54, 322

range estimate, 365

ranking matrix, scope triangle, 417–418

Rapid Applications Development (RAD), 707

Rapid Development Waterfall, 57, 502

rapid Linear PMLC models, 351–355

RASCI Matrix, 708

rational decision making model, 246–247

Rational Unified Process. *See* RUP

RBS (Requirements Breakdown Structure), 112–129

art, 115

assessing completeness, 129

best-fit PMLC model, 31

business process diagramming, 117

context diagrams, 122–123

creating, 120–121

flowcharts, 120–121, 124

formats, 121–122

completion, 33

complexity issues, 326–327

creating, 112–116

defined, 30–31

dynamic nature, 113

facilitated group sessions, 117, 118

feature level, 115

function level, 114
graphical depiction, 113–114, 165, 334
interviews method, 117
levels, 30, 113
methods, 116–118
observation method, 117
PDQ case study, 449, 451
Planning Meeting, 112
PMLC models, 129–132
process level, 115
prototyping, 118, 124
reasons for using, 116
requirements gathering
    approach, 131
science, 115
Scoping Meeting, 110, 112
software development projects, 326
sub-function level, 115
use cases, 118, 125–127
Version Scope, 414, 419
WBS v., 31, 116, 165–167, 169–171, 177
when to use, 112
reactive PSOs, 498
readiness assessment, PSO, 506–507
real PSOs, 497–498
realistic, S.M.A.R.T. characteristic,
    137
recognition, 72–73
reduced costs, success criteria, 139
repetitive activities, Linear PMLC
    model, 343–346
reporting system. See also progress
    reporting system
  final project report, 319
  graphical reporting tools, 288–301
  multiple team projects, 664
  PDQ, 309
Request for Information (RFI), 86–87,
    343, 570
requests, COS process, 108
Requests for Proposals. See RFPs
requirements
  business value and, 28–31
  categories, 127–128

changing requirements and
    specification, 330, 501, 503, 707
definitions
  author's, 29–31, 113, 127
  IIBA, 28–31, 113, 127
incomplete requirements and
    specification, 330, 501, 503, 707
product constraints, 128
project constraints, 128
project failures, 130
reuse, 117
unique, 207
Requirements Breakdown Structure.
  See RBS
requirements change request, 95,
  97, 708
requirements decomposition. See RBS
requirements documentation, 18, 112,
  125, 130, 340, 342, 629, 633
requirements gathering approach, 131.
  See also RBS
  distressed projects, 633–634
  multi-team projects, 663
requirements management, 97
research and development projects.
  See R & D projects
resources. See also HRMS; scarce
  resources
  known, 196
  lack, 330, 501, 504, 593, 660, 708
  multiple team projects, 664
  people, 193–194
  prioritizing, 15
  scheduling problem, 265–267
  scope triangle variable, 13
  types of, 192–193
resource assignments, 264–267
  JPPS deliverable, 164
  launching (Process Group), 21, 226
  organizational risks, 78
  substitute, 150, 271
Resource Breakdown Structure,
  194–195
resource buffers, 369

resource conflicts, CCPM, 367–368
resource leveling, 265–271
  acceptably leveled schedule, 267
  cost impact, 271
  resource-scheduling problem,
      265–267
  strategies, 268–271
resource limits, 8
resource loading
  graphs, smoothing, 269
  resource-loaded cycle schedule, 424
  task duration v., 185–187
resource manager-based escalation
    strategies, 306–307
resource managers
  JPPS attendance, 161
  POS approval process, 145–146
  problem escalation strategy, 15
resource planning, 195–196
resource requirements
  determining, 195
  estimating, 192–195
  JPPS deliverable, 163
  Linear PMLC models, 347
resource-loaded cycle schedule,
    424–425
response, COS process, 108
retainer contracts, 94
return on investment. *See* ROI
reuse
  code, 396
  requirements, 117
REview, 469–470
revise desired goal, distressed
    projects, 640, 645–648, 655
RFI (Request for Information), 86–87,
    343, 570
RFID (Radio Frequency Identification)
    technology, 54, 322
RFPs (Requests for Proposals)
  bidder questions, 89
  BP⁴SO, 524

contract team member, 233
defined, 86
final contract negotiation, 95–96
managing questions/responses, 88
participation in, 88
PDQ case study, 570
preparing/distributing, 87–88
recommended components, 88
templates library, 343
vender evaluation, 89–92
vendor contracting, 92–96
vendor evaluation, 89–92
vendor management, 96–99
vendor selection, 92
vendor solicitation, 86–89
risks
  analysis, POS, 142
  assessment, 79–84
    dynamic, 82–84
    static, 82
    worksheets, 78, 80–81, 83
  assumptions, risks, obstacles section
      (POS), 140–141
  certain events v., 79
  complexity/uncertainty domain v.,
      328–329
  defined, 75
  description, risk log, 85
  entrepreneurial, 76
  external, 78
  history, Linear PMLC models,
      345–346
  identification, 77–79
  level
    APM, 45
    PMLC model choice process, 57
    TPM, 41, 328–329
    xPM, 50–51, 328–329
  log, 85, 302, 346
  matrix, 82
  mitigation, 84–85
  monitoring, 85

organizational, 78
owner, risk log, 85
project management, 77–78
responses, 84–85
technical, 77
risk driver template and assessment
worksheet, 78, 80–81
risk management (Knowledge Area),
75–85
defined, 75–76
project failures, 84–85, 221, 328
questions, 76
skill variety, 73
Risk/Benefit Matrix, 545–546, 555
rkw@eiicorp.com, 513–514, 516, 709
Robertson, James C., 116
Robertson, Suzanne, 116
ROI (return on investment), 143, 396,
492, 501, 555, 604
Root Cause Analysis, 106, 336, 445
distressed projects, 640–641
fishbone diagrams, 612–615
template, 613
rotations, 492, 524
routine activities, Linear PMLC
model, 343–346
Routing subsystem, 61, 224, 376,
570–571
RSVPs, 162
rugby, 439
run charts, 619. See also milestone
trend charts
runner example, 363–364
RUP (Rational Unified Process),
394–397
best-fit choice, 131
construction phase, 395
elaboration, 395
graphical depiction, 395–396
inception, 394
Iterative PMLC model v., 379, 391, 396
phases, 394–395

transition, 395

S
S curve, 294
Sashkin, Marshall, 246
scarce resources. See also critical chain
project management
buffers, 368
CCPM, 556, 580
Incremental PMLC models, 356
JPPS, 159
Linear PMLC models, 357
non-value added work v., 325
requirements, higher order
definition, 31
Risk/Benefit Matrix, 555
substitute resources, 271
unique requirements constraints, 207
work packages, 240, 426
scatter diagrams, 619–620
schedule compression, 150, 152, 215–
217, 306–307, 354, 363, 373–374, 648
schedule performance index. See SPI
schedule shift, milestone trend chart,
292–293
schedules. See also project network
schedule
earned value analysis, 98
tasks, 268–271
Schwaber, Ken, 439
scientific wild a** guesses, 144
scope (project scope). See also scoping
defined, 11
prioritizing, 15
scope triangle variable, 11
Scope Bank
Adaptive PMLC model, 401–402, 404
APM project, 388, 447–448, 632
Cycle Build, 426
Cycle Plan, 420
daily status meeting, 305
management reserve v., 258

managing, 301–302
monitoring and control tool, 301–302
PMLC model choice process, 58
SWOT analysis, 650
timebox expires, 428
tracking, 402
updated contents, 430–431
scope change management process,
254–258
distressed projects, 635–636
multiple team projects, 663
project change request, 254–255
scope change requests
Adaptive PMLC models, 404
Incremental PMLC model, 44
Incremental PMLC models, 357
Iterative PMLC models, 385–386
Linear PMLC model, 43–44, 342–343
Super Team, 683
TPM, 40–41
scope creep, 16
scope management (Knowledge Area)
defined, 67–68
Zone Map, 595
scope triangle, 10–16. *See also* cost;
quality; resources; time
applying, 15–16
graphical depiction, 13, 415
INSPIRE, 463
Iron Triangle *v.*, 10–11, 13
prioritization approaches, 14–15,
415–417
problem escalation strategy, 15–16
ranking matrix, 417–418
risk identification template, 79
system in balance, 13–14
variables, 13
xPM, 53
scoping (Process Group), 103–147. *See
also* COS; POS
APM PMLC models, 445–446
defined, 64–65, 104
difficulty of, 2
discussion questions, 147

graphical depiction, 106–107
initiating, 64, 121, 483
phase
Adaptive PMLC models, 400
Extreme PMLC model, 472–473
Iterative PMLC models, 386
processes, 64
tools/templates/processes, 104–105
TPM projects, 103–147
Scoping Meeting. *See also* POS; RBS
agenda, 111–112
attendees, 110–111
defined, 110
deliverables, 112
POS, 110, 112
purpose, 110
RBS, 110, 112
Scrum, 439–443
Adaptive PMLC model, 379, 391,
406, 442
best-fit choice, 131
client involvement, 439
graphical depiction, 441–442
process flow, 440–441
Product Owner, 131, 405,
439–443
rugby *v.*, 439
Sprint, 441–443
Scrum Master, 405, 442
secondary actor, 126
SEI (Software Engineering Institute),
94, 409, 507–508, 589
SELECT balanced portfolio
Agile Project Portfolio life cycle, 573,
575, 577–580
Graham-Englund Selection Model,
552–556
Project Distribution Matrix/Forced
Ranking Model, 550–552
Project Portfolio Management life
cycle, 531, 546–556
Risk/Benefit Matrix, 552–556
Strategic Alignment Model, 548–550
weighted criteria, 548–550

selected projects, Project Portfolio
    Management life cycle, 532
selection criteria
    client teams, 231
    contract teams, 232–233
    core project team members, 228–230
    decision-making model, 245
Senge, Peter, 362
senior management
    PM/BA Senior Manager position,
        693, 699
    POS approval process, 145–147
separated group sessions, 118
SF (start-to-finish) dependencies, 204,
    205, 216
shifting project finish date, 268–269
sidebar meeting, 303
sign-off, client, 333
similarities to other activities, task
    duration estimation method, 188
simple language, 608
simplification, 607
Single Award scenario, 93
single group session, 118
situation decision generation, 246, 247
situation definition phase, decision-
    making process, 246–247
six action areas, team operating rules,
    241–242
six questions, 25, 27, 60, 64, 444, 690.
    See also questions
skill categories, 194
skill levels, 194
skill matrices, 193–194
slack
    available, 268, 306
    computing, 213–214
    defined, 268
    free, 150, 213–214, 268, 367
    total, 150, 213–214, 268, 367
    utilizing, 268, 306
    zero, 210, 214
slack time (float), 209–210, 213–214, 287
slippages, successive, 291

S.M.A.R.T. characteristics, 137, 137n1
SMEs. See subject matter experts
smoothing, 269
software development projects. See
    also ASD; RUP
    Adaptive PMLC models, 49
    APF, 379, 380, 408, 450
    APM, 323, 380
    distressed, 628
    interproject constraints, 208
    Iterative PMLC models, 48, 391
    Linear PMLC models, 340
    management constraints, 207
    RBS, 326
Software Engineering Institute (SEI),
    94, 409, 507–508, 589
software packages, planning and,
    153–154
Software Tools service area, 486,
    493–494
solution clarity, 34–39, 131, 156, 324,
    502. See also project management
    landscape
    Adaptive PMLC models, 408
    Extreme PMLC models, 457
    Iterative PMLC models, 389, 391,
        397–398
    TPM, 342
    xPM, 456–457
special cause variation, 364
specific, S.M.A.R.T. characteristic,
    137
specific portfolio of projects, 487
specifications
    changing requirements and
        specification, 330, 501, 503, 707
    complexity/uncertainty domain v.,
        333–335
    incomplete requirements and
        specification, 330, 501, 503, 707
    non-value added work, 334
SPeculate, 463–467
Speculate phase, ASD, 406–407
Spence Corporation, 103

SPI (schedule performance index),
    298–300, 557–563, 638–639,
    656
spider charts. *See* fishbone diagrams
sponsor-led part, 236
sponsors
    change in, 113, 141
    communication with, 262–263
    cost budgeting, 198
    project kick-off meeting, 238
    PSO portfolio management, 564
    xPM project completion, 53
Sprint, 441–443
SS (start-to-start) dependencies,
    204,–209, 215–217, 223,
    268, 307
ST. *See* Super Team
staffing
    BP⁴SO, 523–524
    multiple team projects, 665
    PSOs, 495–497
StageGates, 412–413, 419
stakeholders
    communications management,
        74–75, 264
    defined, 74, 264
standard deviations, 290–293
standardization, 608
Standish Group, 59, 330, 479, 501–505,
    520, 591, 596, 642, 707–708. *See also*
    project failures
Stapleton, Jennifer, 438
start-to-finish. *See* SF
start-to-start. *See* SS
statement of work, 11, 94, 95, 220, 277
static risk assessment, 82
statistical validation, CCPM, 365–366
status meetings. *See* project status
    meetings
steady state, 24, 36
sticky notes
    JPPS, 162
    planning (Process Group), 155
    Post-It Note product, 51, 54, 123

stoplight reports, 282–283, 290
Storage flowchart symbol, 120–121
Strategic Alignment Model, 533–535
The Strategic Project Office: A Guide
    to Improving Organizational
    Performance (Crawford), 519
streamlining tools, 607–609
stretching tasks, 270
sub-function level, RBS, 115
subject matter experts (SMEs), 92,
    145, 163, 197, 252, 331, 495, 524, 610,
    673–679
subproject managers, 699
subprojects, 7, 111, 171, 487, 500,
    680, 684
substitute resources, 150, 271
sub-subprojects, 684
subsystems (PDQ)
    Agile model, 449
    PMLC models, 61, 376
    WBS build, 224
subtasks, 272–273, 298
subteams
    Adaptive Cycle Plan, 407
    Assistant Project Manager, 682
    micro-level project planning, 272
    RBS to WBS conversion, 170
    swim lanes, 408, 473
    temporary program office, 9
success criteria, POS, 138–140
successive runs, 292
successive slippages, 291
successor tasks, 203–204, 210, 212–213,
    215–216, 268, 372
Super Team (ST), 680–686. *See also*
    multiple team projects
    characteristics, 681–683
    defined, 680
    strengths, 684
    structure, 681
    weaknesses, 685
    when to use, 685–686
supplier partnership, 609
support offices. *See* PSOs

SWAGs, 144
swim lanes
  business process diagrams, 122
  concurrent, 353, 387, 401, 408, 431, 602
  defined, 431
  FDD Linear PMLC model, 353–355
  Integrative, 431–432
  Probative, 431–432
  rapid Linear PMLC model, 351–355
SWOT analysis, 649, 650
systems design projects, 394, 671

T

tasks. *See also* work packages
  activities *v.*, 166
  crashing, 185
  crashpoint, 186
  critical path, 210, 212, 214–216, 229,
    271, 274, 277
  defined, 165
  non-critical path, 229, 271, 287,
    306–308
  partitionable, 187, 216
  predecessor, 203–204,
    210–212, 215
  stretching, 270
  subtasks, 272–273, 298
  successor, 203–204, 210, 212–213,
    215–216, 268, 372
  work packages, 181
task dependencies. *See* dependencies
task duration
  estimating, 184–185, 188–191
  Linear PMLC models, 344–345
  resource loading *v.*, 185–187
  variation in, 187–188, 363–364
  work effort *v.*, 184
task force, PSO, 512–513
task identity, job design, 73
Task Manager, PM/BA, 693,
  697–698
task scheduling, 268–271
task significance, job design, 73
task-on-the-arrow (TOA) method, 202

teams (project teams). *See also*
  co-located teams; core project
  teams; multiple team projects;
  professional development program
APM, 388
balancing, 233–235
Building Effective Project Teams
  (Wysocki), 235, 247
client teams, 227
  Agile projects, 378
  closing projects, 311
  development teams *v.*, 46, 50, 52,
    237, 449
  qualified co-project manager,
    444–445
  selection criteria, 231
  xPM projects, 460
components, 227
contract team members, 231–233, 266
from different companies, 660
ideal, 227
imbalanced, 235
norming stage, 277–278
POS approval process, 145
project kick-off meeting, 237
recruiting, 227–236
team deployment strategy, 235
team development plan, 235–236
TPM, 41, 388
team cohesiveness, 329
team communications, 258–264
  effective channels, 260–262
  information content, 259–260
  information timing, 259
  with sponsor, 262–263
  upward communications filtering,
    263–264
team meetings
  agenda preparation, 251
  coordinator, 251
  daily status meeting, 251–252, 302,
    305
  frequency, 250–251
  minutes, 251

multiple team projects, 663
problem resolution meetings, 252
project review meetings, 252
structure, 250–251
Team Member, PM/BA, 693,
    696–697
team operating rules, 241–252. *See also*
    brainstorming; conflict resolution;
    decision making; problem solving
brainstorming, 249–250
conflict resolution, 248–249
consensus building, 249
decision making, 244–247
multiple team projects, 241
PMBOK, 241
problem solving, 242–244
six action areas, 241–242
team meetings, 250–252
team skills/competencies, PMLC
    model choice process, 59–60
team war room, 252–254
contractors, 238
daily status meetings, 305, 425
operational uses, 253–254
physical layout, 253
risk monitoring, 85
whiteboards, 155–156
technical constraints, 206–207
technical risks, 77
technographers, 111, 160, 680
technology. *See also* information
    technology
incompetence, 330, 501, 503, 708
leveraging, 32, 37
market changes, 32
new, 330, 501, 504–505, 593, 644, 708
PMLC model choice process, 58
project classification by, 19–20
RFID, 54, 322
Type A projects, 20
well-understood technology
    infrastructure, 41
tech-temps, 231

templates. *See also* tools/templates/
    processes
candidate risk driver template and
    assessment worksheet, 78, 80–81
Linear PMLC models, 343–344,
    346–347
risk identification, 78–79
temporary program offices, 9, 46, 171,
    484, 498. *See also* PSOs
temporary project offices.
    See project offices
Texas Instruments, 132
Theory of Constraints (TOC),
    362–363, 382
thinking styles, 235
Thomas, Kenneth, 249
Thoreau, Henry David, 149
thought-process tool, WBS, 167
3M Post-It Note product, 51, 54, 123
three-point technique, 190–191
time. *See also* scarce resources
planning (Process Group), 156–157
prioritizing, 15
scope triangle variable, 12–13
S.M.A.R.T. characteristic, 137
three-point technique, 190–191
time and cost summary page, 220
time and materials contracts, 94
unrealistic time frames, 330, 501, 504,
    593, 708
time management (Knowledge Area),
    68
timeboxes. *See also* cycle timeboxes
iteration, 398
Version Scope, 418–420
To Be business process, 119, 604,
    610, 623
TOA (task-on-the-arrow) method, 202
TOC (Theory of Constraints),
    362–363, 382
Toledo, Ramon A. Mata, 71n1
tools/templates/processes
APM, 445

closing Process Group, 312
CPIM, 612–622
distressed projects, 633–639
Incremental PMLC models, 361–362
launching Process Group, 226
Linear PMLC models, 354–355
monitoring/controlling Process
    Group, 280–281
planning Process Group, 151–152,
    154–156
scoping Process Group, 104–105
xPM, 472–475
top-down approach, APF
    implementation, 437
top-down format, 122
total slack, 150, 213–214, 268, 367
TPM (traditional project
    management), 39–44, 339–376. *See
    also* closing; Incremental PMLC
    models; launching; Linear PMLC
    models; monitoring/controlling;
    planning; scoping
    APF *v.*, 410
    APM approaches with, 47
    buffers, 370
    business value, 336–337
    CCPM *v.*, 364, 366
    change intolerant, 43, 152, 333, 390
    characteristics, 40–42
    client involvement, 331
    co-located teams, 59, 329, 388
    complexity level, 40
    defined, 340
    discussion questions, 376
    flexibility, 327
    graphical depiction, 55
    percent of projects, 39, 42, 47, 322
    plan-driven, 42, 325, 327, 330–331, 335
    project teams, 41
    projects
        closing, 3, 311–320
        launching, 225–278
        monitoring/controlling, 3, 279–309

    planning, 2, 149–224
    scoping, 103–147
    risk level, 41, 328–329
    scope change requests, 40–41
    team cohesiveness, 329
    well-understood technology
        infrastructure, 41
    xPM *v.*, 53
traditional project management. *See*
    TPM
Training service area, 486, 494–495
transfer, risk response, 85
transition phase, RUP, 395
Transmission flowchart symbol,
    120–121
Tregoe, Benjamin B., 336
trigger values, 622, 628, 637,
    638, 656
trust, 230, 427, 677
two team situation, multi-team
    projects, 665–666
two-step submission process, project
    portfolio management, 569–570
type A projects, 19–21
type B projects, 20–21
type C projects, 20–21
type D projects, 20–21

U

UML (Unified Modeling Language),
    125, 352
uncertainty. *See also* complexity/
    uncertainty domain; solution
    clarity
    planning and, 153
    project classification, 18
unclear objectives, 330, 501, 504,
    593, 708
under budget/ahead schedule project,
    300
under budget/behind schedule
    project, 299
Unger, Elizabeth A., 71n1

Unified Modeling Language (UML), 125, 352
unique activities, 6–7
unique requirements, 207
unrealistic expectations, 80, 330, 501, 504, 593, 708
unrealistic time frames, 330, 501, 504, 593, 708
upgrading, 608
upward communications filtering, 263–264
use cases
  APF, 436
  diagrams, 126–127
  INSPIRE, 465
  PDQ case study, 623, 636
  RBS method, 118, 125–127
  RUP, 394, 397
user input. *See* client involvement
utilizing available slack, 268, 306

V

values. *See also* business value
  APF, 410–412
  value-added assessment, 607
Vargo, Ed, 583
variance reports, 283–284
variances, 286–288
  EVA, 287, 294, 295
  negative, 287–288
  positive, 286–287
variation, in task duration, 187–188, 363–364
velocity, organizational, 356, 380
vendors
  contracting, 92–96
  evaluation, 89–92
  evaluation criteria, 90
  management, 96–99
  monitoring progress/performance, 97–98
  selection, 92
  solicitation, 86–89

verb-type approaches, to building WBS, 177, 179
Verma, Vijay K., 241
Version Scope, 412–420. *See also* Adaptive Project Framework
  COS, 413–414
  cycle timeboxes, 418–420
  cycles
    functions assigned, 420
    number of, 419–420
    objective statements for, 420
  deliverables, 413–414
  graphical depiction, 414
  parts, 412
  POS, 414, 418–419
  Post-Version Review *v.*, 433
  prioritized scope triangle, 415–417
  RBS, 414, 419
  StageGates, 412–413, 419
  WBS, 414, 419
virtual PSOs, 497–498
vision statements. *See* mission statements

W

WAGs, 144
wall-mounted ashtrays, 132
Walmart, 322, 659–660, 673
wants, needs *v.*, 37, 86, 106
war room. *See* team war room
Ward, Bryan K., 584
waterfall approaches
  Evolutionary Development Waterfall, 48, 57, 131
  Rapid Development Waterfall, 57, 502
  for WBS, 183
WBS (Work Breakdown Structure), 164–183
  APM, 48
  building, 168–171
    approaches, 176–180
    RBS converted to WBS, 31, 116, 165–167, 169–171

CoA *v.*, 178
color-coded sticky notes, 155
completion criteria, 172–176
defined, 163–164
distressed projects, 634–635
FDD Linear PMLC models, 352
hierarchical visualization, 166
for house, 181–182
iterative development, 171
JPPS deliverable, 163, 168
for large projects, 171
micro-level, 272–273, 421, 422
noun-type approaches to building,
    176–178
organizational approaches to
    building, 177, 179–180
plan-driven TPM projects, 42
project replication, 22
project-status-reporting tool, 168
RBS *v.*, 31, 116, 165–167,
    169–171, 177
representing, 180–183
sub-functions *v.*, 115
uses for, 167–168
vendor contracting, 92, 99
verb-type approaches to building,
    177, 179
Version Scope, 414, 419
for waterfall systems development
    methodology, 183
whiteboard, 156
weighted criteria
  PRIORITIZE projects, 541, 543–544
  SELECT balanced portfolio, 548–550
weight-guessing example, 190
Weiss, Joseph, 172
What business situation is being
    addressed?, 25, 64, 444, 690
What do you need to do?, 25–26, 64,
    104, 105, 444, 690–692
What will you do?, 25–26, 65, 444,
    690, 692
whiteboards. *See also* team war room

planning (Process Group), 154,
    155–156
wide-band Delphi technique, 191
wild a** guesses, 144
Williams, John, 103
work assignments, independent, 172,
    174, 269
Work Breakdown Structure. *See* WBS
work effort, 184. *See also* task duration
work packages
  assignment sheets, 275, 277
  Cycle Plan, 426
  defined, 166, 181, 273–274
  description reports, 275–276
  format, 275–277
  project kick-off meeting working
      session agenda, 240
  purpose, 274
  scarce resources, 240, 426
  writing, 273–277
working session agenda, project kick-
    off meeting, 238–240
written communications, 331
Wysocki, Robert K.
  *Adaptive Project Framework: Managing
      Complexity in the Face of
      Uncertainty*, 408
  Building Effective Project Teams,
      235, 247
  Effective Software Project Management,
      118, 298
  Enterprise Information Insights, Inc.,
      23, 63, 279, 323, 339, 377, 514, 583
  *Executive's Guide to Project
      Management: Organizational
      Process and Practices for
      Supporting Complex Projects*,
      521n2, 709
  *5-Phase Project Management:
      A Practical Planning and
      Implementation Guide*, 172
  quotes, 23, 63, 279, 323, 339, 377, 583
  rkw@eiicorp.com, 513–514, 516, 709

X

xPM (Extreme Project Management),
  50–53, 453–477. *See also* MPx
  APM *v.*, 52–53, 457
  business value, 337
  change, 336
  characteristics, 455–456
  client involvement, 331–332
  client ownership, 332–333
  client's comfort zone, 332
  co-located teams, 329, 468
  core team members, 228
  defined, 454–455
  discussion questions, 475–477
  flexibility, 327
  graphical depiction, 52, 55, 454
  high change, 455–456
  high speed, 455
  INSPIRE, 457–470
    COS, 464
    graphical depiction, 458
    Incubate, 467–469
    INitiate, 459–463
    REview, 469–470
    SPeculate, 463–467
  life cycle, 454–470
  model, 51–53
  MPx *v.*, 55
  non-value-added work, 655
  percent of projects, 47, 154, 322
  project failures, 50–51, 53,
    329, 454
  R & D projects, 50–51, 53–54, 129, 322,
    329, 453, 455, 471, 536
  risk level, 50–51, 328–329
  scope triangle, 53
  solution clarity, 456–457
  strengths, 456
  team cohesiveness, 329
  tools/templates/processes, 472–475
  TPM *v.*, 53
  weaknesses, 457

Y-Z

zero slack, 210, 214
Zone Map, 591–595, 597–598, 600
  completed, 594
  graphical depiction, 592, 594
  PQM and, 592
  zones of interest, 593–594